Industry and Accumulation in Africa

WITHDRAWN

Industry and Accumulation in Africa

edited by

MARTIN FRANSMAN

Lecturer in Economics
University of Edinburgh

HEINEMANN
LONDON
IBADAN   NAIROBI

Heinemann Educational Books Ltd
22 Bedford Square, London WC1B 3HH
PMB 5205, Ibadan · PO Box 45314, Nairobi

EDINBURGH   MELBOURNE   AUCKLAND
HONG KONG   SINGAPORE   KUALA LAMPUR
NEW DELHI   KINGSTON   PORT OF SPAIN

Heinemann Educational Books Inc.
4 Front Street, Exeter, New Hampshire 03833, USA

British Library Cataloguing in Publication Data

Industry and accumulation in Africa. –
  (Studies in the economics of Africa; 11)
  1. Africa – Industries – Addresses, essays,
  lectures
  I. Fransman, Martin   II. Series
  338.096   HC502
ISBN 0 435 97139 5 cased
ISBN 0 435 97140 9 paperback

Set in 9 pt Times by Coats Dataprint Ltd.,
Inverness
Printed in Great Britain by
Biddles Ltd., Guildford, Surrey

Contents

89 - 663

List of Tables

List of Figures

Acknowledgements

The majority of the papers in this collection were first presented at a conference organized at the Centre of African Studies, University of Edinburgh. In this connection a major debt is owed to the Centre's staff and, in particular, to Grace Hunter without whose efforts this volume would not have been possible. As editor I must also acknowledge the patience and support given by my wife Tammy and the additional demands that were made on my daughter Judith. An acknowledgement is also due to all the contributors, who put up with the pressures and deadlines involved in getting this volume to the publishers on time.

The paper entitled 'Recent Industrial Development in Africa' is a statistical review for the period 1970–6 prepared by the Secretariat of the United Nations Industrial Development Organization. This was prepared for discussion at the Regional Symposium on Industrial Policies and Strategies for Internally Self-sustaining Development and Diversification and Collective Self-Reliance, 1978–2000, which was held in Nairobi from 11 to 18 September 1979 and was sponsored jointly by UNIDO, ECA and OAU. The document was not formally edited by the United Nations. The United Nations retains title to the text. Due acknowledgement is made to UNIDO for permission to reproduce this document, UNIDO/ICIS.117 dated 6 August 1979.

Introduction

MARTIN FRANSMAN

I Industry and Accumulation in Africa

In the first sentence of his book *Industry in Africa*, written over a decade ago, A. F. Ewing pointed out that his underlying thesis was that 'industry is the main lever of African development'. While this thesis is as true now (a point which will be elaborated upon in the following section) it is unfortunately clear that very little progress has been made since Ewing wrote his book. Thus the World Bank in its *World Development Report 1978* concluded in the case of sub-Saharan Africa that despite 'widespread attempts to force the pace of industrialization . . . the results . . . have generally been unsatisfactory' (p. 49). Several rough indications of the relatively poor performance of African countries as compared to other parts of the Third World can be given. While in 1960 developing countries as a whole contributed 6·9% to world manufacturing value added, this had increased to 8·6% by 1975. (The corresponding figures for developed market economies were 75·0% and 63·7% respectively and for centrally planned economies 18·1% and 27·7%.) However, the African share of world manufacturing value added increased only slightly during this period from 0·7% in 1960 to 0·8% in 1975, as shown in Table 1.

Another indication of the relatively poor performance of sub-Saharan African countries is provided by the product composition of non-fuel exports in 1975. As shown in Table 2, 52% of these exports from African countries were from the food and beverages sectors while only 9% consisted of manufactures as compared to 36% and 43% for all developing countries.

A further indication is the change in Africa's share in world exports of manufactures. While the average share was 1·12% in 1970–1 this fell to 0·60% in 1975–6. Africa was the only country group to record a fall over this time-period as is seen in Table 3.

A detailed breakdown of industrial development in individual African countries is given in the final chapter in this volume. It is worth repeating here the conclusion that is reached at the end of this chapter:

Table 1   *Share of developing regions in world manufacturing value added and annual increase of manufacturing output, 1960–75 (%)*

Year	Africa Share	Africa Increase over preceding year	Latin America Share	Latin America Increase over preceding year	South and East Asia Share	South and East Asia Increase over preceding year	West Asia Share	West Asia Increase over preceding year
1960	0·7	—	4·1	—	1·9	—	0·3	—
1961	0·7	6·2	4·2	8·6	1·9	8·8	0·3	11·6
1962	0·7	7·0	4·1	4·4	2·0	9·4	0·3	5·5
1963	0·7	8·0	3·9	2·3	2·0	8·8	0·3	10·1
1964	0·7	6·1	4·0	11·1	2·0	6·8	0·3	7·1
1965	0·7	8·6	3·9	5·4	1·9	5·1	0·3	9·0
1966	0·7	6·2	3·9	7·1	1·9	3·6	0·4	11·3
1967	0·7	1·9	3·9	3·9	1·9	6·2	0·4	9·6
1968	0·7	9·2	4·0	9·8	1·9	8·6	0·4	11·0
1969	0·7	9·4	4·0	8·5	2·0	11·4	0·4	11·9
1970	0·7	9·2	4·2	8·3	2·0	6·8	0·4	3·7
1971	0·7	5·6	4·4	8·4	2·1	6·9	0·4	9·5
1972	0·7	11·1	4·4	9·1	2·1	8·4	0·4	9·6
1973	0·8	15·3	4·5	9·2	2·2	11·8	0·5	10·8
1974	0·8	0·1	4·6	5·5	2·3	5·9	0·5	8·2
1975	0·8	0·1	4·8	1·1	2·5	6·6	0·5	8·0

Source: UNIDO, 1979, p. 37.

If Africa is to achieve its regional target of a 2% share in world industrial production by the year 2000 and thus meet its declared contribution to the Lima 25% target for the developing countries as a whole, it will need to maintain its share of Third World industrial production at a minimum of 8%. Table 20.11 indicates that from 1970 to 1976 Africa's share in Third World industrial production dropped from 9·4 to 8·2%. To halt this trend Africa will need to increase substantially its rate of industrial growth in the future. Roughly a doubling of the current rate to about 10% annually probably will be required.

The indication provided of Africa's relatively poor performance raises a large number of questions which include the following. How important is industrialization for the raising of productivity and living standards? How is the industrialization process in underdeveloped countries to be analysed and what internal forces help and hinder it? What are the major external constraints limiting industrialization? It is notable that these and other questions have not received the attention they deserve in the literature on Africa and, as is shown in the bibliography in this book, recent material on industrialization in African countries is seriously lacking. Indeed this is one of the major justifications for the present book.

However, while it is important to pose fundamental questions such as the above, the answers given will depend very much on the perspective of the author. There is no point in pretending that it is possible to establish a consensus on matters such as these. The aim of this introduction is precisely to point out some of the major differences which exist among the authors whose articles are contained in this book, and to compare their views with

Table 2 *Developing countries: product composition of non-fuel exports, 1975 (%)*

	Food and beverages	Non-Food agriculture	Metals and minerals	Manu-facturers	Total
Sub-Saharan Africa	52	13	26	9	100
Low-income Asia	32	17	9	42	100
All developing countries	36	9	12	43	100

Source: World Bank, 1978, p. 50.

those of other who have analysed industrialization in underdeveloped countries.

II Some Perspectives on Industry and Accumulation in Underdeveloped Countries

Ajit Singh in his chapter in this book and elsewhere has addressed the first question posed above, namely, the importance of industrialization for the raising of productivity and living standards. His answer is unequivocal: industrialization is a necessary condition for rising productivity and standards of living and this is true regardless of the 'political hue' of the state. Industrialization, and more specifically the development of the manufacturing sector, provides the 'dynamism' for increasing productivity and growth. It is this sector that 'has an "indefinite scope for technological progress through a continual increase in specialization, and the subdivision of productive processes"', and generates both static and dynamic economies. In this way manufacturing industry 'also imparts a technological dynamism to other sectors of the economy' (Singh, 1979). However, there are important qualitative divisions within the manufacturing sector itself. In this connection it has been empirically established that the growth of manufacturing output is generally associated with a relatively more rapid rate of growth in the capital and intermediate goods sector than in the consumer goods sector. Accordingly growth elasticities (measuring the responsiveness of change in manufacturing

Table 3 *Share in world exports of manufactures, by country group, 1970–1 and 1975–6 (%)*

Exporting area	Average share 1970–71	Average share 1975–76
Africa	1·12	0·60
Asian Middle East	0·25	0·46
Other Asia	3·07	4·90
Latin America	1·51	1·59
Centrally planned economies of Asia	0·57	0·62
OPEC countries	0·20	0·23

Source: UNIDO, 1979, p. 161.

value added for a given industrial branch to changes in per capita GDP) are greater in the former case. (See, for example, UNIDO, 1979, pp. 76–9.) Singh therefore concludes, for both theoretical and empirical reasons, that a successful process of industrialization requires the building of an economic 'structure' that is conducive to the raising of productivity throughout the economy. This requires, *inter alia*, that manufacturing value added constitutes a significant proportion (about 25%) of GDP, and that capital and intermediate goods production contribute substantially (Singh does not define this quantitatively) to manufacturing value added. This structure, together with the attendant human skills, will provide the dynamism for increasing productivity and capital accumulation.[1]

However, the problem still remains as to how this structure can be brought into existence. Here Singh's views differ substantially from those that suggest that a greater degree of influence should be given to world market prices in determining production and trade patterns in underdeveloped countries. One example of the latter view is the book by Little, Scitovsky and Scott which is discussed in the present volume in Nixson's contribution on import-substituting industrialization. Little, Scitovsky and Scott argue that policies of tariff and other protection aimed at encouraging the development of import-substituting industry have resulted in price distortions which have led to an inefficient allocation of resources. Although in some cases the 'promotion' of industry is desirable, it is suggested by these authors that, in general, substantial net benefits are to be achieved by reducing the barriers that insulate the domestic economy from world market forces, and giving a greater role to world market prices in determining comparative advantage and patterns of production and trade. On the contrary, Singh argues that in creating the necessary economic structures that are conducive to rising productivity, the state, far from planning according to the dictates of international market prices and comparative advantage, will often have to intervene precisely in order to insulate the economy from international market forces which in some instances may inhibit or even prevent the process of structural change. A specific example of such interventions might be the protection of 'learning processes' which form an inherent part of the development of a country's potential to produce technological changes.[2] From Singh's 'structuralist' point of view the neo-classical notion of 'inefficiency', referred to in connection with Little, Scitovsky and Scott, assumes a different meaning. Rather than yielding non-optimal patterns of resource allocation which can be improved through a 'correction' of price distortions, as the neo-classicals would have it, for Singh these 'inefficiencies' are an inherent part of the process of developing conducive structures which will yield optimal returns over the longer run.

But what about the politics of Singh's structural changes? In support of his argument Singh in his writings draws on the widely diverse examples of Japan, the Soviet Union, India, China, Tanzania and even Lesotho (the latter in one of his contributions to the present volume). How do the different political processes in these countries influence the industrialization 'strategies' of the state? Singh's answer to this is clear. His basic postulate is that for a country to increase productivity and raise living standards it is necessary for it to develop the manufacturing sector and the capital and intermediate goods sectors within it. Whether the state is 'reactionary' or 'progressive', the reality referred to in the postulate remains. In some cases the process of altering economic structures may be 'blocked', for example, by vested landed interests. But generally with the passage of time dominant groups come to realize and accept that the structural changes referred to are necessary. The 'success stories' in the world prove that government intervention and protection are necessary preconditions, and these cases include governments of widely divergent 'political hue'.

It is precisely in connection with the 'political' questions posed in the previous paragraph that the work of Singh is to be contrasted with that of Colin Leys whose articles are also included in the present volume. Leys is more exclusively concerned with the second question posed in the previous section: how is the industrialization process in underdeveloped countries to be analysed and what internal forces help and hinder it? He focuses on this question largely in the context of the debate on underdevelopment and dependency theory. Leys argues that capital accumulation in 'periphery countries' cannot be understood by an examination only of the operation of the world economy as dependency theorists suggest (e.g. the transfer of surplus from the 'periphery' to the 'centre'). In order to understand why a successful process of capital accumulation has occurred in some periphery countries and not in others, one dimension of the discussion must focus on the structure of social classes that has emerged in that particular country. In summarizing his argument Leys points out that 'what it says is that capitalist production relations may be considerably extended in a periphery social formation, and the productive forces may be considerably expanded within and through them, for reasons having primarily to do with the configuration of class forces preceding and during the colonial period'. In the case of Kenya, Leys, drawing partly on the work of Cowan, traces the emerging class power of the 'indigenous class of capital'. This class, for reasons that are discussed in the contributions by Leys and Cowan in the present volume, was extremely successful at accumulating during the colonial period despite 'massive competition from foreign capital of all kinds, and with very little support from the colonial state'. It was also heavily represented in the state apparatus due to its investment in education and accordingly it was 'exceptionally well placed to convert its natural dominance in the nationalist movement into a position of strategic control over the post-colonial political realignments.'

It is important to highlight the way in which Leys analyses the role of the state since the 'essential function of the state [in the post-colonial period] was to displace monopolies enjoyed by foreign capital and substitute monopolies for African capital, and also to supplement individual African capitals with state-finance capital and state-secured technology, to enable them to occupy the space created for them in the newly accessible economic sectors'. For Leys the state is not an independent force in the society rationally calculating ways of maximizing the benefits accruing to 'the people' and neither is it the instrument of foreign capital. Rather, in the Kenyan case, the state's 'initiatives reflected the existing class power of the indigenous bourgeoisie, based on the accumulation of capital they had already achieved'. These initiatives included facilitating the movement of African capital into the productive sectors of the economy (which Leys suggests has accelerated since 1977) and intervening in the area of technology and scale factors so as to 'push back' the limitations on the accumulation of the indigenous bourgeoisie. While

Leys concedes that much of the capital accumulated in this way in African hands will have been either unproductively invested or will have involved the acquisition of existing assets, he argues that 'the significance of these transactions for the long-run potential for accumulation by indigenous capital remains profound'.

In other words, for Leys the level and rate of capital accumulation in a periphery country is crucially determined by the emergence and current significance of class structures and class struggles. In this connection in the Kenyan case (and doubtless Leys would argue that this is generalizable to other periphery countries) it is the outcome of the struggle between foreign and indigenous capital that is critical. To the extent that indigenous capital emerges as the 'leading force' and the state accordingly reflects its dominant influence, capital accumulation in the periphery country (including industrialization) will be enhanced. However, the success of the indigenous bourgeoisie is never automatic and in some periphery countries foreign capital may remain the leading force.

Thus Leys's main concern is with internal class structures and struggles which may result in the state becoming the instrument for accelerating the process of capital accumulation and industrialization. While he does not consider the kinds of questions addressed by Singh (namely, the sorts of structures that would have to be fostered by the state if a successful process of accumulation were to take place) there is no logical reason inherent in his writings which would prevent him from accepting Singh's arguments. Conversely Singh's focus is on the appropriate structures rather than on the political processes required to bring them about, but again there seems to be no inherent reason why he should find the thrust of the Leys argument unacceptable.

However a sharp divergence of opinion exists between both Singh and Leys on the one hand and Murray on the other who addresses himself primarily to the third question asked in the previous section: what are the major external constraints limiting industrialization?[3]

Murray's point of departure in discussing industrialization in the Third World is an analysis of what Leys has referred to as 'the level of the "logic of capital"', that is, an analysis of 'the international logic of capital in general ... and its implications for the investment decisions of particular capitals in particular sectors in particular countries'. While Leys acknowledges that his study is concerned primarily with 'class relations and class struggles' in Kenya and with the 'process of domestic capital accumulation which has formed the basis for the constitution of one particular class' (i.e. the indigenous bourgeoisie), he argues that such a discussion must be complemented by an analysis of the international process of capital accumulation. However, the latter is not incorporated into his analysis apart from the few brief comments on economies of scale and technology referred to above.

Murray's prime concern is with the 'laws of location' in the international capitalist economy. These laws are derived from the 'economics of time' that underlie capitalist production and circulation: to reduce time is to reduce cost and the operation of the international market serves to facilitate the expanding accumulation of the least cost/time producers. The reduction of time requires increasing mechanization in both production and circulation and therefore changes in the labour process. The operation of the laws of time-economy produces on an international scale a geographically polarized location of industry. Conditions in the main centres of industrial activity are most conducive to further savings of time and hence reductions in cost as a result of what is more conventionally referred to as scale economies, external economies, economies of agglomeration, and so on. Industrial activity in the rest of the economy (viewed as a single international system rather than as a sum of nation-states) is confined to areas which for one reason or another – Murray discusses these reasons in detail – are immune to undermining competition from the major industrial centres, for example, because the cost of transport provides a measure of protection. Technological change and the attendant changes in the labour process tend to reinforce the centre's cost advantages while often undermining previously existing activities in the rest of the system. However, international production and circulation cost differentials do not by themselves determine the limits on accumulation in the 'periphery'. While it is in principle possible to bring about a process of autonomous accumulation in the periphery by insulating these areas from the competition of the world market, in practice the laws of time-economy will continue to cause negative effects. The reason is that 'when productivity differentials are high, when the immediate gains from trade and international factor movements appear considerable to holders of capital on both sides of the frontier, then the pressure both internal and external against an autarchic policy will also be large'. However, once protective measures are removed 'the peripheral area will be restricted to that production determined by the locational forces of the world market system'.

Thus Murray sees the process of capital accumulation in the Third World as severely constrained by the cost advantages of the industrial centres. His views are to be contrasted with those of Leys and Singh who emphasize (different) *internal* factors which facilitate successful industrialization in the Third World. For both these writers, although there are constraints on such industrialization imposed by international market pressures which bring the force of more productive external producers to bear on the local economy, the limitations on accumulation are not nearly as severe as is suggested by Murray. While Singh sees the creation of conducive economic structures as a necessary longer-run step in transcending the internationally determined limits, and Leys sees the successful struggle of indigenous accumulators as achieving the same result, they both assign to the 'periphery state' a far greater ability to manoeuvre and enhance accumulation than does Murray.

In passing, and in order to draw another contrast, a few comments on some of Chenery's writing on industrialization in underdeveloped countries may not be out of order. Many of Chenery's studies of industrialization have attempted, through cross-country analysis, to establish 'universal patterns of change'.[4] In the conclusion to his 1975 book with Syrquin it is pointed out that 'in describing the processes of development we have tried to replace the notion of a dichotomy between less developed and developed countries with the concept of a transition from one state to the other. This transition is defined by a set of structural changes that have almost always accompanied the growth of per capita income in recent decades.'[5] From the point of view of the present discussion it is unnecessary to explore either the evidence for the existence of such 'universal patterns' or the possible causes of these patterns. Furthermore it is accepted that it is important to ask whether there are cross-country and intertemporal uniformities and, if there are, to attempt to explain their existence. However, Chenery's work is to be distinguished from that of Leys and Murray. For Leys, as was shown, it is incorrect to attempt to separate structural change from the political processes which bring it about. If such an attempt is made, the illusion may be given, either that structural change occurs inevitably over time (as sometimes seems to be implied in Chenery's writings) or that structural change can be brought about by an 'enlightened' state which somehow circumvents the internal political process. However, whether or not a charge of this nature may legitimately be levelled against Chenery, it is clear that the absence of a political analysis does lead to problems. In another paper[6] Chenery and Hughes suggest that 'the observed intercountry uniformity in production patterns' has 'probably been accentuated by the widespread adoption of policies favouring import substitution over exports'. But as is shown in a number of studies in the present volume the imposition of import substituting policies is by no means automatic and is often opposed by competing interests and furthermore, as Nixson argues, the creation of a more appropriate industrialization policy requires fundamental political realignments. Equally problematical is Chenery's treatment of aspects of comparative advantage. In a discussion of the 'sources of comparative advantage' Chenery and Hughes point out that the 'leading exporters of the 1960s have been countries which have based their exports on low labour costs'. However, later they note that 'there is considerable variation of wage levels in manufacturing in countries at the same level of income, since wage levels are influenced by social and political as well as by economic factors'.[7] Yet the point is dropped and its possible implications remain unexamined. But it is clear in this case that the existence of trade patterns and corresponding structures of production which reflect a 'comparative advantage' in 'labour-intensive products' is at the same time the result of economic *and political* processes. These processes depend very much on the particular circumstances of each country and the attempts to establish 'universal patterns' gloss over and tend to obscure this important fact. It is noteworthy in this connection that most of the studies of the so-called 'success stories' such as South Korea, Brazil, Taiwan, and so on, fail to pay adequate attention to the political processes referred to.

The divergence between Chenery's perspective on the question of industrialization in underdeveloped countries and that of Murray brings out a different point. While Chenery focuses on the similarity between countries as per capita income increases, Murray pays attention to the constraints imposed by the simultaneous existence of lower-cost producers in other parts of the world economy. Whether or not Murray is correct about the severity of the limitations thus imposed, his analysis, unlike that of Chenery, admits the possibility of a conflict of interest. For Chenery the question does not arise.

To conclude this section we shall relate some of the points made by Nixson in this volume to the present discussion. Import substitution, the main topic of Nixson's chapter, has played an important part in industrialization in African countries. The World Bank, in its *World Development Report 1978*, points out in the case of sub-Saharan African countries that 'typically, three-quarters or more of industrial value added is in import substitutes, principally in relatively unsophisticated goods' (p. 49). It is Nixson's intention to point to some of the lessons that may be learned by African countries from the experience of other underdeveloped countries with import substituting industrialization.

Nixson's basic argument is that a market-based import substitution process is incapable of achieving the desired economic transformations. In summarizing part of his argument Nixson draws on the experience of other underdeveloped countries and contends that in the practice of these countries import substituting has not

> significantly alleviated the balance-of-payments constraint; it has led to a growing dependence on a largely imported, capital-intensive technology and has thus not created extensive employment opportunities or indigenous technological development; the process has been heavily dependent on foreign capital and has emphasized the establishment of consumer goods industries at the expense of investment and capital goods industries; it has led to what many would regard as an undesirable redistribution of income and in general it has failed to generate a sustained process of economic growth.

While this has been the experience of most underdeveloped countries following import substitution policies, Nixson stresses that this outcome should not be regarded as inevitable. However, he suggests that a significant degree of state intervention will be required in order to bring about the necessary economic changes which he specifies in some detail. Included in these changes, Nixson argues, together with Singh, is the necessity to facilitate the planned build-up of capital and intermediate goods industries. Nixson is also very aware of the political dimension of the strategy of industrialization which he suggests and he points out that this strategy 'would require, as a necessary precondition, radical political change within the LDCs themselves. Thus, while the development of import substituting industries may form a necessary first stage in the industrialization process, this process will require the meeting of numerous other conditions if it is to succeed.'

One of these 'other conditions' is an increase in agricultural productivity and growth and, in a book which emphasizes industrialization, it is particularly important to conclude the discussion in this section by highlighting the significance of agriculture. Most of the authors referred to in the present volume stress the complementary role of agriculture in the accumulation process. Singh (1979), in a discussion of China, points out that 'although modern industry has been the leading sector in economic growth, and has claimed the larger share of investment resources, since the late 1950s agriculture has been regarded as the "foundation" without which industrial development cannot be sustained'. In similar fashion Nixson stresses that

> in the majority of LDCs, industrial development cannot be separated from or pursued at the expense of agricultural development; in most LDCs land redistribution and agrarian reform are necessary prerequisites for the creation of larger markets for manufactured goods (both intermediate and final) in the rural areas ... in addition, agro-industrial development, spanning the two sectors and often with good export prospects ... needs to be given greater emphasis.

In the case of Kenya Leys also acknowledges the importance of agriculture in the general process of capital accumulation but points to the specific configuration of class forces which impede agricultural and therefore general accumulation. Referring to the 'multiple contradictions' in the process of the 'extension of capitalist production relations' in Kenya, Leys argues that

> a more immediate and severe contradiction lies, I think, in the powerful place of 'middle' peasant household production in agriculture, which may be approaching the limits of its expansion. Current policy thinking within the Kenyan state bureaucracy favours the extension of this form of production, based on high labour inputs per hectare, even though with apparently declining labour productivity (agricultural output per head of population seems to have declined steadily since 1970). While this would serve the interests of international capital which appropriates surplus value more or less directly from such production, it would hardly serve the interests of the indigenous bourgeoisie who, however, would confront a major political problem in any attempt to raise the productivity of labour and their own appropriation of surplus value by trying to extend capitalist relations of production in agriculture (e.g. by policies designed to polarize the smallholder areas towards kulak and capitalist farming on the one hand, and proletarianization on the other). Yet without an increase in agricultural productivity it seems doubtful if the momentum of capitalist production can be maintained in industry in the longer run.

In this regard the Kenyan case contrasts strongly with that in South Africa which is discussed in the chapter on that country in the present book. Many of the other country studies also refer to the role of agriculture in the industrialization process. It is to an analysis of the general arguments of these studies that we now turn.

III   The Country Studies

A   EAST AFRICA

Tanzania

Coulson begins his chapter with an historical examination of the development of manufacturing industry in Tanzania before independence. He then goes on to examine state intervention in the industrial sphere after independence and shows, amongst other things, the rapid growth in manufacturing parastatals. Tanzania's industrial performance in the post-independence period is then considered and Coulson suggests that although output and employment grew at a satisfactory rate between 1964 and 1977, the performance of the manufacturing sector was less good when assessed from the point of view of several indicators. These include the productivity of labour and capital, capacity utilization and import dependence. In assessing the industrial performance of Tanzania Coulson argues that in view of the difficult internal and external circumstances prevailing at the time of independence it is unlikely that rapid industrial investment would have occurred had it not been promoted by government. However, the scarcity of skilled management resources proved to be a serious constraint and some of the measures taken to improve matters may have presented further difficulties. Furthermore, attempts made to use workers' organizations to control the worst excesses of management were later abandoned and shopfloor initiative in almost all factories was eventually crushed. Coulson concludes that it is clear in retrospect that

> industrial investment should have been more selective; planned with a view to the integration of the economy, and to lessen import dependence; that much greater care should have been taken with machinery contracts; and that an opportunity was lost in which to make use of the expertise and awareness of the working class.

However, he suggests that even if these policies were followed

> industrialization would not have been easy in the world conditions of the 1970s. As an oil importer, and with few raw materials, Tanzania had little to offer world markets. There was no chance of industrialization in the hostile conditions of the capitalist world unless the state could avoid the unproductive investments which characterized its industrial strategy in the 1970s.

In his comments on Coulson's paper Hare draws on the Hungarian experience, suggesting that since both Hungary and Tanzania are pursuing socialist policies (and, it may be added, have encouraged the early development of heavy industry) there may be some lessons for the latter to draw from the former. Hare points to the Hungarian experience with import substitution in the 1950s which concentrated on steel and heavy engineering as the leading sectors and notes the difficulties posed by the problem of inefficiency. He then discusses the reorientation in policy that occurred in the late 1960s, paying particular attention to the central development programmes, which involved the implementation of several interrelated investment projects, and the increased emphasis given to exports. The latter followed from the small size of the domestic market and the importance of scale economies for many investment projects. In concluding Hare looks at the implications of the Hungarian experience for Tanzanian industrialization.

In his chapter Green divides Tanzanian industrialization policy into four phases and examines each of them: 'pre-independence; 1961–7 (pre-Arusha); 1967–73 (towards public sector dominance); post-1973 (towards an integrated strategy)'. The last phase is described in terms of an attempt to develop a coherent medium-term strategy which has been referred to in the Tanzanian context as the basic industry strategy. Having examined each of these phases in detail, Green goes on to consider three 'broad clusters of criticism' of Tanzanian industrialization policy: the surplus maximization critique, the dependence critique and the 'incompleteness' critique. The surplus maximization critique 'holds that Tanzanian industrialization strategy gives primacy to surplus maximization neither at project formulation level, in enterprise operations, nor in broader institutional and policy structures'. From the point of view of the dependence critique 'Tanzania should seek a much more rapid structural change to a neo-autarchic, integrated industrial sector. Capital goods production should receive pride of place at an early stage of industrialization.' Green associates this second critique with the views of Ajit Singh and raises a number of difficulties. In the first place Green questions whether, given existing levels of knowledge and skill in Tanzania, it is possible to start with capital goods as the primary focus in industrialization, or whether better long-term results would be achieved by concentrating on other subsectors for several years in order to create a base while the capital goods sector is being built up from an initially marginal and peripheral position. Second, Green questions whether there would be a sufficiently large spin-off from a domestic capital goods industry to offset the short-term surplus losses of having very expensive capital goods. Third, Green asks how precisely a capital goods industry is to be defined. 'Would a capital goods industry consisting basically of machine building without the supporting intermediate goods subsectors . . . be a useful type of industrial strategy?' Given limitations on available natural resources and the small size of the market, it 'would take a basic rejection, not merely qualification, of economies of scale and specialization to suppose that Tanzania should produce a complete range of machine tools'. The question of the appropriate role of international trade raised by Hare in connection with Hungary is clearly relevant here. The third criticism, the 'incompleteness critique', is intended to supplement rather than to surplant the existing Tanzanian strategy and contains three elements.

> First a perception that worker power is inadequate rather than too great. Second, an argument that therefore it would be desirable to have worker involvement which would be easier in smaller-scale, lower capital output industry requiring less cumbersome and authoritarian management structures and less foreigners. Finally, a parallel argument that, given the availability of resources in Tanzania, small-scale and labour-intensive . . . manufacturing would make more sense in terms of employment and of surplus generation.

In the concluding section Green spells out his own 'internal critique' which, while not constituting an alternative strategy, rests 'on an interpretation of the present Tanzanian industrialization strategy as consistent with the overall strategy of transition to socialism and self-reliance and as inherently possible' and views 'the process of Tanzanian industrialization over 1967–79 as predominantly positive'. At the same time Green's comments by implication 'constitute a case for incremental and tactical, rather than overall and strategic, changes in respect to Tanzanian industrialization'.

Bienefeld's chapter complements those of Coulson and Green although there are several divergences of analysis and opinion. In particular Bienefeld does not support Coulson's rather pessimistic assessment of the performance of the manufacturing sector. After a very detailed examination of both the adequacy of the available data and the accuracy of the empirical indicators of industrial performance, Bienefeld concludes that there is no evidence for the 'long term secular decline thesis' which some writers have suggested 'while the thesis that 1967 (the date of the Arusha Declaration) constituted a major turning point with respect to industrial performance receives scant support'. On the contrary, Bienefeld argues, in Tanzania 'a respectable macro-economic performance with respect to output and productivity has been sustained in industry', although this has been interrupted in 1975 and 1979 by major set-backs, due largely to adverse external circumstances. However this is not to suggest that past policy is beyond reproach. While criticisms 'must not be projected into the past without an appreciation of the political and administrative constraints under which such good intentions must always find expression', it is nonetheless true that some criticism of past decisions may validly be made. Some of these decisions may be criticized 'on grounds that they should have been more cautious in their use of foreign exchange and imported inputs; that they should have been more urgently concerned with the effective absorption of technology; that they should have been more aware of the need to co-ordinate agriculture and industry, and to ensure the growth of exports.' Accordingly Bienefeld suggests that, in coping with the current economic difficulties, the importance of factors such as these must be taken into account; he elaborates on this in the discussion in the last part of his chapter.

Bienefeld also takes issue with Green's characterization of the various 'clusters of criticism' of Tanzanian industrialization policy. For Bienefeld the main issue which distinguishes the various positions in this debate revolves around the question of the appropriate degree of state involvement in the economy. 'The Tanzanian strategy is based on the premise that the state should play a major and direct role in the country's economy, with a view to accelerating structural change, fostering the generation of externalities and mitigating the impact of growth on income differentials.' This is a position which Coulson, Green and Bienefeld all accept.

Kenya

The contribution made by Colin Leys has been discussed in the second section of this introduction where it was pointed out that Leys drew on the work of Cowan in formulating his own analysis of the indigenous bourgeoisie in Kenya. Cowan, in his chapter in the present volume, analyses in detail the colonial context which encouraged the accumulation and further development of this class whose roots he elsewhere traces to pre-colonial times. In the first part of his chapter Cowan examines the significant increase in British colonial 'development expenditure' which took place after the Second World War and explains this phenomenon both in terms of the postwar economic crisis in Britain and the struggle by the British state against the international hegemony of the United States. Expanded production of raw materials in the colonies was simultaneously seen as providing a boost to British accumulation (by making raw materials available and increasing the supply of food) and consequently as a means of resisting to some extent the growing domination of the United States. It is within this context that Cowan analyses the origins and operations of the Colonial (Commonwealth) Development Corporation. In the second part of his chapter Cowan, drawing on his own previous work, discusses the implications of colonial policy for the accumulation of the indigenous bourgeoisie, first in the case of wattle production and then in the case of tea. In the post-colonial period some of the members of this class were able to move into positions of managerial employment in the state, parastatal and private sectors from where they were able to engage in 'straddling', which Cowan defines as 'a specific historical form of accumulation in which the position of employment provides a base from which resources can be created

for the expanded reproduction of capital'. In this way the class may become
a genuine bourgeoisie based on expanded accumulation. An indication of this
is the fact that the 'most secure estimates show that there can be no more
serious questioning of the fact that estate agriculture is now predominantly
under the ownership of individuals of the indigenous class'. Although the
relationship between the indigenous class and foreign capital at the level of
economic control of enterprises is 'shot through with tension' it remains true
that in 'the case of manufacturing, it is becoming clear that the subsidiaries
of international firms, as much as those of the Commonwealth Development
Corporation and other public corporations, have provided a base from which
managing directors are able to create their own sources of local accumulation'.

It is the analysis of the relationship between the indigenous bourgeoisie and
foreign capital that forms the central theme of Kaplinsky's chapter, which in
turn has sparked off a debate to which both Colin Leys and John Henley
contribute in the present volume. Kaplinsky differs from Leys regarding the
extent to which the indigenous bourgeoisie in Kenya has managed to establish
its independence from foreign capital. This indigenous class is seen rather as
closely allied with foreign capital, and accordingly as incapable of forcing
indigenous accumulation at a rate above that determined by foreign capital.
Furthermore, Kaplinsky argues, the Kenyan economy exhibits a number of
structural weaknesses partly determined by its relative inefficiency with
respect to the rest of the world economy. These weaknesses serve to place
severe limitations on the possible extent of domestic accumulation. Accordingly, Kaplinsky concludes that his examination of the Kenyan case 'shows
that the possibilities for successful accumulation in an open economy of this
type are limited whatever the historical roots of the accumulating class (since)
the pattern of accumulation in such economies is significantly conditioned by
the nature of global accumulation and their interspersion in that global
process'. Although Kaplinsky does not expand on what he means by 'the
nature of global accumulation' it would seem that there are at least some
superficial similarities between his argument and that of Murray referred to
in the second part of this introduction. Both see the process of accumulation
in periphery economies as being severely constrained by the process of world
accumulation which tends to reproduce the economic dominance of producers
in the world's major economic centres. On the one hand, therefore, Kaplinsky
sees the indigenous bourgeoisie as too closely tied to foreign capital to serve
as a significant force for domestic accumulation, while on the other hand
further limitations on such accumulation are imposed by the accumulation and
increasing productivity of the most efficient producers in the world economy.
Kaplinsky accordingly concludes that 'the arguments of Leys do not disprove
the conclusions of the dependency school', although he adds that this 'does
not automatically lend credence to cruder formulations of dependency theory
which argue, or imply, that classes in peripheral economies are solely formed
through interaction with the global economy'.

Both Henley and Leys are extremely critical of Kaplinsky's evidence
purporting to reveal the relatively insignificant extent of accumulation by the
indigenous bourgeoisie. Henley uses some of Kaplinsky's evidence plus
additional information of his own to suggest that there has been an important
degree of accumulation undertaken by the (mainly Kikuyu) bourgeoisie, and

to argue that the extent of accumulation in the country as a whole over the past fifteen years has been far from unimpressive. Leys is particularly critical of Kaplinsky's defence of dependency theory and his conceptual approach which Leys argues is ahistorical. With regard to the relationship between the indigenous bourgeoisie and foreign capital and the role of the state, Leys reiterates that it is necessary to see the state 'as a register of the balance of class forces, including the strength of the indigenous bourgeoisie. Because this strength is relative, not absolute, the state's interventions in conflicts between indigenous and foreign capital also registers this relativity.' However, Leys stresses that 'the fundamental interests of capital coincide; that the general form of this coincidence in Kenya is the general need of all fractions and strata of the bourgeoisie for further investments of foreign capital'. But 'what are in conflict are the interests of different elements of the bourgeoisie differentially affected by the specific forms this takes. Among these are the interests of particular African capitalists *vis-à-vis* those of particular foreign capitals. The state's resolutions of these conflicts register a complex interaction of economic, political and ideological forces, which it would be difficult to say has not, over time, advanced and hence also expressed the *growing* strength of indigenous capital.'

B SOUTHERN AFRICA

South Africa

The South African case is of obvious importance in any discussion of industry and accumulation in Africa. Not only is South Africa a country that has achieved a relatively high level of industrialization, it also exerts a significant degree of influence over other African countries as is shown in the studies of Zimbabwe and Lesotho in this section.

In his chapter Fransman examines the views of Murray, Leys and Singh in the context of South Africa. In the first part of the chapter, which examines the growth of mining, agriculture and industry in the period prior to the Second World War, it is shown that a major factor facilitating the relatively rapid rate of industrialization was the successful steps taken to ensure a plentiful supply of African labour at profitable wage rates. A further factor which encouraged the industrialization process, particularly from the 1920s, was the protective measures imposed by the state in the interests of the emerging national bourgeoisie. Here there are obvious parallels to be drawn with the Kenyan indigenous bourgeoisie analysed by Leys although there are also many dissimilarities between the two cases. However, it is argued that although the struggles of the national bourgeoisie in South Africa did facilitate the industrialization process, there were a number of other unrelated factors which also provided a boost to industry. These were both external (including the rise in the price of gold such as occurred in 1932 when South Africa left the Gold Standard, and the effects of the Second World War) and internal (including the favourable conditions established in the African labour market to which reference has already been made).

In the second part of the chapter attention is focused on the manufacturing sector in the period after the Second World War. Here it is shown that firms based in South Africa have confronted the problems posed by the existence of lower-cost firms in the major industrial centres of the world as discussed by Murray. These problems have been reflected in the poor export performance of firms producing in South Africa and their dependence on imports of more sophisticated capital and intermediate goods and on the foreign exchange earnings of the mining and agricultural sectors. The growth of the South African economy has accordingly been limited. At the same time, however, it is shown that by the 1970s the structure of the South African economy closely approximated that which Singh argues is necessary for successful industrialization and growth: the manufacturing sector contributed about 25% to GDP and the capital and intermediate goods sector accounted for approximately 20% of manufacturing value added. However, while this structure might produce the dynamic effects suggested by Singh, the continued heavy reliance on foreign capital and technology inflows is stressed. Nevertheless, it is argued that despite the problematical features of the South African economy referred to, a continuation of the fairly rapid rate of growth within the present capitalist framework will depend on further favourable movements in the price of gold and on the ability of the state to contain the economic and political demands of the African working class.

Zimbabwe

The Zimbabwean case offers a study of many of the issues discussed in a general way in section II of this introduction. The Zimbabwean economy is of obvious a priori interest, not only because it is one of the most advanced in Africa, but also because, as a result of sanctions which were externally imposed, its economy has been relatively closed. Accordingly the Zimbabwean case may be expected to provide some indications of the economic changes that may be brought about as a result of a relatively autarchic economy. However, both Stoneman and Davies stress that this is a matter of degree since a significant amount of sanctions-busting occurred largely through South Africa.

Stoneman traces the early beginnings of industrialization in Southern Rhodesia and shows the effects on the manufacturing sector of the decision taken during the Second World War to stimulate the growth of secondary industry. A further stimulus to manufacturing industry was provided by the formation of the federation though this was at the expense of industry in the other two countries which received no protection from Southern Rhodesian industry. In the short run growth was further encouraged by the massive inflow of foreign capital though it is central to Stoneman's thesis that in the longer run this would have resulted in economic decline. However, fortuit- ously, sanctions were imposed in 1965 and the resulting closed economy meant that the decline that would otherwise have occurred was arrested since the outflows that would have accrued to foreign capital were prevented. Since the argument that large stocks of foreign capital lead to lower growth rates (and also a greater degree of inequality) plays a central role in Stoneman's chapter he goes to some length to provide the empirical econometric evidence in support of this contention. Stoneman refers in this connection to sixteen studies that have been carried out over the last decade and concludes that in the longer run, particularly in the manufacturing sector (though this may not be true of mining and oil extraction), the foreign stock of capital exerts an adverse effect on the economic structure of the recipient country which reduces the rate of economic growth below what it would have been with a lower stock. The significance of this in the Zimbabwean case is obvious since some two-thirds of the capital stock is foreign-owned and since in Stoneman's view great external pressures will be exerted post independence to open the economy and increase the inflow of foreign capital. In the final part of his chapter Stoneman makes a number of practical suggestions regarding 'the essential ingredients of a successful strategy designed to reduce drastically foreign capital's domination of the economy'. However, Stoneman is careful to point out that he does not propose a totally closed or autarchic strategy which denies any role to foreign capital or foreign technology.

After UDI structural changes were brought about in the manufacturing sector including a building-up of the intermediate goods sector (particularly basic metals and metal products) and increased efficiency in some consumer goods industries (e.g. textiles). Accumulation was also increased at the expense of black living standards with the state following urban-oriented policies and failing to undertake productive investment in the Tribal Trust Lands. Although the country's per capita income still places it firmly in the ranks of the poorer countries of the world, Stoneman suggests that Zimbabwe 'is nevertheless a great success story in African terms'. It is obviously important to attempt to understand the reasons for this success. In Stoneman's view there are two basic reasons. The first is the existence of excellent resources while the second is the 'simple chance that forced the adoption of planned self-reliant policies (i.e. as a result of sanctions) contrary to the ideology of the ruling Rhodesia Front Party'. As a result, while the country 'did not become autarchic, because of the close economic links with South Africa, it became much more self-reliant' and accordingly 'measures forced by sanctions prevented many of the harmful financial and structural effects of excessive dependence on foreign capital'. In his comment on Stoneman's paper Davies is more sceptical about the extent of Zimbabwean industrialization after 1965. While not necessarily disagreeing with Stoneman about the negative effects of foreign capital, Davies suggests that much of the post-1965 growth was due to pre-existing excess capacity and to state measures to foster growth at the expense of black consumption. Since these conditions were 'clearly the result of Rhodesia's historical development rather than of short-term policy measures' Davies concludes that the Zimbabwean experience cannot readily be generalized to other countries.

Lesotho

In the chapter on Lesotho Singh applies his views summarized earlier in this introduction to one of the most underdeveloped and least industrialized countries in Africa. Once again, however, protection is seen as providing the key, in this case the subsidization of agriculture in order to create the foundation for industrialization. In this way it is envisaged that the productivity of agriculture, presently extremely low as a result of over-population and the extensive system of migrant labour exports to the South African mines, will be significantly raised. In the longer run agricultural development together with the development of roads and electricity generation will provide the basis for an indigenous industrialization process. However, given the scarcity of indigenous resources, the financing of the proposed changes would have to come from external sources, through foreign

18   INTRODUCTION

aid and a re-negotiation of the Southern African Customs Union. Singh's
Lesotho study serves as an example of the extremely wide range of
applicability that he sees for his conceptual approach, since, as was pointed
out earlier, he suggests a similar strategy in the case of very different countries
such as India, China and Tanzania.

C WEST AFRICA

Nigeria

The picture that emerges in Forrest's chapter on Nigeria is one of fairly rapid
industrial growth as a result of the pursuance of import substituting policies
and, more recently, the impact of the oil industry. However, Forrest's chapter
suggests that the kinds of changes in industrial structure thought to be
important according to structuralist views such as those of Singh are not being
brought about in Nigeria. In particular the pattern of import substituting
industry has implied a rapid growth in consumer goods industries at the
expense of greater imports of intermediate and capital goods. The local capital
goods sector is extremely weak and little is currently being done to strengthen
it. However, with regard to intermediate goods such as steel the prospects are
brighter as a result of linkages with the oil industry. In general, according to
Forrest, the industrialization process in Nigeria has been accompanied by a
substantial degree of foreign involvement (in the form of foreign capital and
technology inflows) and there appears to be little of the 'independence' that
Leys claims to see in the Kenyan indigenous bourgeoisie. In this sense there
are obvious parallels to be drawn between Forrest on Nigeria and Kaplinsky
on Kenya. Thus Forrest concludes that

> the sphere of foreign capital accumulation has not been greatly affected
> by the growth of the Nigerian bourgeoisie, by indigenization, or by the
> extension of the state sector. The particular class structures of accumu-
> lation that have emerged in Nigeria provide little support for Leys's
> Kenyan view of an indigenous industrial bourgeoisie that is antagonistic
> to foreign capital. State intervention has generally favoured large-scale
> foreign enterprise, the indigenization exercise notwithstanding.

In the Nigerian case Forrest argues that a 'class alliance has formed between
foreign capital and bureaucratic and managerial elements of the bourgeoisie'
and while the state reflects this alliance it reflects particularly the dominant
influence of foreign capital:

> These class forces may be weakened and obscured by sectional and
> distributional conflicts, but it is they, in the absence of any independent
> industrial bourgeoisie, which largely determine the character, effective-
> ness and limits of state policy. Under these conditions the likelihood of
> long-term industrial strategies that involve the effective regulation and
> control of external economic relations or the independent internal
> development of state capitalist activity is remote.

According to Forrest the longer-run prospects for structural change and growth are not promising:

> If oil and the size of the Nigerian market overcome some of the constraints usually associated with import substituting industrialization, they also appear to entrench a system of accumulation that pre-empts any strategy which aims to accelerate industrial accumulation, create a diversified industrial base with vertical and horizontal linkages, and secure an indigenous technological capacity.

Ghana – The Volta River Project

The role of foreign capital is also at the centre of the case study by Dickinson of the Volta River project in Ghana. This study shows how Ghana, in pursuit of rapid industrialization through the provision of cheap electricity from the Volta Hydroelectric Dam, in fact became 'locked into' a structure that provided the aluminium smelter belonging to the Kaiser Corporation of the United States with extremely cheap electricity in terms of world prices while distributing very few benefits to the Ghanaian economy and its population. In fact local industries paid a price for their electricity substantially in excess of that charged to the smelter and they therefore, in effect, subsidised the Kaiser Corporation. Nor could the Ghanaian government unilaterally raise the price of electricity charged to the company since the latter retained the possibility of switching production to its other subsidiaries in other parts of the world.

Dickinson concludes that there were significant benefits that accrued to the Kaiser Corporation: 'As a large corporation with worldwide interests the cheap power from Akosombo has played a role in preserving its stake in world aluminium.' However, from the Ghanaian point of view

> the Volta River project has not been a success. It did not generate new industry, provide cheap electricity or give Ghana any stake or influence in the world aluminium industry. It continues to burden the Ghanaian economy and has tied up capital which might well have been better used in modest schemes more specifically directed to overcoming obstacles to industrialization.

Dickinson's ultimate assessment of the project stands in stark contrast to the hopes it originally generated: 'Cheap electricity for Ghanaians remains an illusion and even if it were provided there is no evidence to indicate that it would generate a leap forward in industrialization.'

D SMALL-SCALE INDUSTRY

Small-scale industry is of particular importance in the African context given the relatively low level and rate of industrialization that was mentioned in the first section of this introduction. For this reason it is given specific attention in this chapter.

Livingstone's chapter contains a very detailed examination of measures taken in Tanzania, Kenya and Botswana to promote small industry. The workshop-estates established in Tanzania are evaluated and contrasted with the 'extension' approach adopted in Kenya and the various institutions, including Brigades, that have been set up in Botswana. The discussion is in detail and a number of practical policy recommendations are made. For Livingstone the major problem confronting small industries (which he rigorously defines in the first part of his chapter) is one of undercapitalisation although they also face numbers of other difficulties which he examines. The conclusion arrived at after the assessment of the various programmes for the encouragement of small-scale industry emphasizes the advantage of a workshop-estate approach though it is pointed out that this approach 'would need to concentrate on appropriate standards and technologies and avoid the generally recognized disadvantages of ordinary industrial estates, but could be used to upgrade informal sector artisan enterprise in both rural and urban areas'.

It is the informal industrial sector in Lomé (Togo) which is the focus of the chapter by Demol, Nihan and Jondoh. The signifance of this sector is illustrated by the fact that the informal industrial sector in Lomé alone provides employment for an equivalent of 20% of formal sector employment in the entire country and does so at a considerably lower level of capital investment. If the large number of apprentices in this sector is added, the proportion rises to the equivalent of 50% of total formal sector employment. In summarizing their findings the authors point out that this sector

> provides opportunities for the absorption of a considerable number of unemployed young people; it gives productive employment to a sizeable body of workers ...; it stimulates the development not only of economic activity but also of skills and the use of labour-intensive technology; and it assists the redistribution of income.

In the final section of their chapter the authors put forward a number of policy suggestions. In essence they argue that the central feature of the informal industrial sector in Lomé, and its principal strength, lie in its internally generated dynamism. Accordingly they suggest that in intervening government must be very careful not to disrupt the dynamic processes that have contributed to the sector's success. They point out that 59% of the entrepreneurs interviewed were against any form of state intervention and 90% of them favoured the creation of mutual aid associations run by the entrepreneurs themselves. As opposed to Livingstone the authors therefore argue that 'a systematic recourse to the oft-recommended solution of capital injection and broadening of credit facilities, which are supposed to promote rapid business expansion, should be avoided'.

E   SURVEY OF INDUSTRIALIZATION IN AFRICA AND BIBLIOGRAPHY

In the final two parts a survey of industrialization in African countries is presented and a select bibliography is provided by Fincham for most of the country studies covered in this book and also for Zambia. The survey paints an Africa-wide picture and provides important new information, although no attempt will be made here to summarize the conclusions.

Notes

1   This point is also made by Ewing in his insightful book: 'The real issue remains the need, if serious development is contemplated, to launch a programme for the production of capital and intermediate goods ... with a view to changing the structure of the economy.' A.F. Ewing, 1968, p. 12.
2   A detailed and well-reasoned argument along these lines is presented in S. Lall, 1979 and 1980.
3   Although Murray's paper is not included in the present volume it is discussed here because it addresses the question of external constraints and it enables an important contrast to be drawn with the views of Singh and Leys (see Murray, 1973). The same applies to the work of Chenery referred to below.
4   Chenery and Syrquin, 1975, p. 135. See also Chenery, 1960, Chenery and Taylor, 1968, and Chenery and Hughes, 1973.
5   Chenery and Syrquin, 1975, p. 135.
6   Chenery and Hughes, 1973.
7   ibid.

References

Chenery, H. B. (1960) 'Patterns of industrial growth', *American Economic Review*, 50 (September), pp. 624–54.
Chenery, H. B. and Hughes, H. (1973) 'The international division of labour: the case of industry', in *Towards a New World Economy* (Rotterdam: Rotterdam University Press).
Chenery, H. B. and Syrquin, M. (1975) *Patterns of Development, 1950–1970* (London: Oxford University Press).
Chenery, H. B. and Taylor, L. (1968) 'Development patterns: among countries and over time', *Review of Economics and Statistics*, 50 (November), pp. 391–416.
Ewing, A. F. (1968) *Industry in Africa* (London: Oxford University Press).
Lall, S. (1979) 'Developing countries as exporters of technology and capital goods: the Indian experience', Oxford University Institute of Economics and Statistics (mimeo.).
Lall, S. (1980) 'Developing countries as exporters of industrial technology', *Research Policy*, 9, pp. 24–52.
Little, I., Scitovsky, T. and Scott, M. (1970) *Industry and Trade in Some Developing Countries* (London: Oxford University Press).
Murray, R. (1973) 'Underdevelopment, international firms and the international division of labour', in *Towards a New World Economy* (Rotterdam: Rotterdam University Press).
Singh, A. (1979) 'The "basic needs" approach to development vs the new international economic order: the significance of Third World industrialization', *World Development*, 7, pp. 585–606.
UNIDO (United Nations Industrial Development Organization) (1979) *World Industry since 1960: Progress and Prospects*, special issue of the Industrial Development Survey for the Third General Conference of UNIDO, New Delhi, 21 January – 8 February 1980 (New York: United Nations).
World Bank (1978) *World Development Report 1978* (Washington, DC: World Bank).

PART ONE
GENERAL OVERVIEWS

1 Industrialization in Africa: A Structuralist View

AJIT SINGH

Introduction

The editor of this book has invited me to write a short chapter presenting a general perspective on problems of economic development and industrialization in Africa. I am pleased to accept this invitation, particularly as it will make available a rather different approach to the subject from that of other authors whose contributions are included in this volume. The chapter is organized as follows. In section I, I outline a structuralist view of industrialization and comment on its main implications. The role of the state and the market in the process of industrialization are discussed in section II. Section III considers in broad terms constraints on industrialization in the present African context and comments on some policy issues.

I Industrialization and Economic Development: Structural Perspective[1]

There are good economic reasons why African and other Third World countries should regard rapid industrialization as essential for raising the standard of living of their peoples. A wide range of historical and cross-section studies indicate that manufacturing industry plays a leading role in economic development, in the specific sense that a 1% increase in gross domestic product is normally associated with a more than 1% increase in value added in manufacturing. (See, for example, Chenery, 1960; Kaldor, 1967; Chenery and Taylor, 1968; Paige, 1961; Kuznets, 1971; Cripps and Tarling, 1973; Chenery and Syrquin, 1975; UNCTAD, 1978.) Further, there is evidence that the growth elasticity of manufacturing is greater the lower the level of a country's per capita income. Table 1.1 reports the results of a recent comprehensive UNIDO (1979a) study based on data from nearly a hundred

Table 1.1 *Estimates[a] of the elasticities of manufacturing value added with respect to GDP for 98 countries in six groups (based on pooled times-series for 1960–75)*

Country[b] sample	Manufacturing elasticity			Per capita GDP (1970 dollars)		
	Maximum	Minimum	Mean	Minimum	Maximum	Mean
L_h	1·59	0·99	1·23	467	5,349	1,990
L_l	2·13	1·47	1·81	58	670	192
S_i	1·85	1·31	1·59	42	1,326	221
S_{2p}	1·42	1·02	1·16	102	3,460	952
S_{2i}	1·66	1·14	1·35	159	4,517	1,142
CP	1·62	1·08	1·30	227	2,099	841

Notes:
[a] The estimates are based on the following regression equation

$$\ln v_{it} = \alpha + \beta_1 \ln y_{it} + \beta_2 (\ln y_{it})^2 + U_{it}$$

where v is per capita manufacturing value added
  y is per capita GDP
  i is a country subscript
  t refers to the year
  U represents the disturbance term

[b] L_h: large high-income countries; L_l: large low-income;
  S_i: small low-income; S_{2p}: small with primary orientation;
  S_{2i}: small with industrial orientation; CP: centrally planned economies.
For further details see note 2, p. 34.
Source: UNIDO, 1979a.

developing and developed countries over the period 1960–75. The table gives pooled cross-section and time-series estimates of the growth elasticities of manufacturing for various groups of countries, distinguished by their size and certain other characteristics.[2] These estimates suggest that at the average levels of per capita incomes in the African countries, the value of this elasticity is about 1·6.[3]

There is a systematic body of economic reasoning which not only explains why manufacturing industry should expand at a faster rate than the economy as a whole during the course of economic development, but would also assign strategic causal significance to manufacturing in raising the overall rate of growth of productivity in the economy. Very briefly,[4] first, at the simplest level, as the income elasticity of demand for manufacturing is considerably greater than that for food and for agricultural products, manufacturing can be expected to grow at a relatively faster rate. Second, following the classic work of Allyn Young (1928) (and of course, before that, of Adam Smith and other classical economists), economists with a structural approach to economic growth argue that manufacturing is subject to increasing returns both in the static and, more important, in the dynamic sense of Kaldor. Because of these favourable demand elasticities and dynamic economies of scale, manufacturing industry not only grows more quickly than other sectors, but its growth is also normally associated with increased employment. In agriculture, on the other hand, where there is usually considerable disguised unemployment,

expansion of productivity and output is usually connected with a reduction in
the labour force employed. The expansion of manufacturing industry thus
helps raise the rate of growth of productivity in agriculture in two ways: (1)
by absorbing redundant labour, and (2) by providing modern industrial inputs,
which incidentally raise both land and labour productivity. Third, it is argued
that the expansion of manufacturing industry also increases the pace of
technical change and helps raise productivity growth in sectors other than
agriculture.[5]

The structural approach to the process of economic growth not only stresses
the key role of manufacturing but also suggests that within manufacturing
capital goods industries need to grow at a faster rate than consumer goods
industries. Again, both historical and cross-section studies of industrial
development confirm that the growth elasticity of producer goods industries
is usually considerably greater than 1, i.e. an $x\%$ increase in GDP is associated
with $Kx\%$ and $K^I x\%$ increases in the production of capital goods, and
consumer goods respectively, where K is greater than K^I; the value of K
normally tends to be above 1·5. Table 1.2 reports cross-section estimates of

Table 1.2 *Growth and size elasticities in selected individual manufacturing
industries for two country groups*[a]

Branch	Large countries		Small countries with modest resources	
	Growth	Size	Growth	Size
Food products	1·07	−0·11	0·54	−0·45
Beverages	1·15	−0·62	0·53	−0·25
Tobacco	0·65	−0·12	1·38	0·29
Textiles	1·02	−0·04	0·99	0·63
Clothing	1·55	−0·59	1·05	−0·20
Leather and fur products	1·15	−0·28	0·96	0·43
Footwear	1·14	−0·57	0·70	−0·29
Industrial chemicals	1·67	0·18	1·44	−0·01
Iron and steel	1·81	0·27	2·09	−0·04
Non-ferrous metals	1·44	0·09	1·23	−0·07
Metal products excl. machinery	1·48	−0·15	1·36	0·20
Non-electrical machinery	2·05	0·40	1·98	0·44
Electrical machinery	1·77	0·11	2·28	0·10
Transport equipment	1·86	0·25	1·60	−0·52
Professional and scientific equipment, photographic and optical goods	2·10	0·40	1·50	−0·26

Note:
[a] Elasticity estimates are based on the following regression equation fitted to data from
individual countries.

$$ln\ (v/N) = \beta_0 + \beta_1 \quad lny + \beta_2 lnN$$

where v is value added (in millions of 1970 US dollars),
      y is per capita GDP and
      N is population (in millions)
Cross-section data for 1970 for 25 large and 34 small countries were used in the
analysis.
Source: UNIDO, 1979a.

the elasticities for various branches of manufacturing industry, based separately on data from two groups of 'large' (population greater than 20 million) and small countries respectively. As in the case of Table 1.1, both developed and developing economies are included in the two samples; the underlying regression equations are based on statistics for the year 1970.

The table shows that in general growth elasticities have a much greater value than size elasticities. For large countries, the latter are in fact usually negative; for small countries, they are more often positive but still relatively quite small.[6] However, for both large and small economies the growth elasticity for consumer products – food, drink, tobacco – is usually around 1, whilst for machinery, transport equipment, iron and steel, it is substantially higher.[7] The reasons for this phenomenon again lie partly in demand conditions and partly in production conditions, but more importantly, in the interaction of the two. It is argued that in capital goods industries, such as engineering and machinery, there is greater scope for dynamic economies and technological change. Further, as Kaldor (1967, p. 30) has observed:

> The expansion of capacity in the investment goods sector feeds upon itself, by increasing the growth rate of demand for its own output, thereby providing both the incentives and the means for its own further expansion. The establishment of an investment goods sector thus provides for a built-in element of acceleration in the rate of growth of demand for manufactured goods.

The above analysis suggests that in order to achieve fast economic growth, the African countries should aim to change the structure of their economies by substantially increasing the share of manufacturing in national output and by corresponding changes within the structure of manufacturing industry itself. Many, but by no means all, economists would regard these aims as being unexceptionable. Three important objections to this emphasis on industrialization deserve examination however. First, in recent years it has been strongly urged by the ILO and other international development agencies that the primary focus of development in Third World countries should be to meet the minimum basic needs of the poorest sections of the population (food, clothing, shelter, etc.) as quickly as possible. It is suggested that rapid industrialization, at its best, makes little contribution to the achievement of such basic needs; more usually its pursuit may be at the expense of basic needs.

There is a complex relationship between 'basic needs' and industrialization which has been examined in detail in Singh (1979a). This analysis showed that not only is there no necessary contradiction between the two, but also fast expansion of industry is an *essential* condition for meeting the basic needs of the poor in the developing countries on a sustainable basis. The main reason for this is that, even allowing for considerable income redistribution, the achievement of basic needs in a typical LDC requires a very large increase in national income. For example, the ILO (1977) has estimated that if the minimum basic needs of the poorest 20% of the Third World population are to be satisfied by the end of the century, then notwithstanding feasible redistribution of income, national incomes in Third World countries must grow at a rate of 7–8% per annum. An exercise of this kind for the African countries alone is likely to yield a similar, if not somewhat higher, estimate of the required rate of economic growth. Thus, if the African countries were to set themselves the entirely reasonable target of removing absolute poverty (in the ILO sense) by the year 2000, this would entail, in view of the elasticity estimates in Table 1.1, an expansion of manufacturing industry in these countries at a rate of over 10% per annum. By past standards, the latter figure implies a very fast industrialization of these economies.

The second and related objection to the strategy of rapid industrialization is based on the belief that modern industry creates very little employment, whilst creation of employment opportunities is clearly a pressing concern in most Third World economies. Again, if one considers both the direct and indirect effects of industrialization on employment, and not only the immediate and temporary, but also the long-term and sustainable creation of employment opportunities, there is no ground for this criticism. As far as the *direct* effects are concerned, empirical data indicate that in the developing countries a 1% increase in manufacturing output is associated on average with about a 0·7% increase in employment.[8] During the period 1960–75 manufacturing employment in the Third World grew at a rate of about 5% per annum; the corresponding rate of growth of output was a little over 7%. In the second half of the period, 1968–75, both employment and output in Third World manufacturing grew at a faster rate – at 7% and 9% respectively. These employment growth rates[9] are much higher than the rate of growth of population in these countries and about the same as the rate of urbanization.

More important, industry creates employment indirectly by helping to increase production in other sectors of the economy, for example, agriculture and services. In agriculture, where as was noted earlier there is normally disguised unemployment, the elasticity of employment with respect to output tends to be very small, often near zero. The values of these elasticities are much higher in service industries; however, a sustainable growth of output and employment in many such industries, for example, domestic transport and distribution, depends crucially on the expansion of the primary and secondary sectors.[10]

Finally, it is sometimes suggested that the structural approach will lead to a neglect of agriculture in order to promote industry. This is, however, a misunderstanding of the argument. There is obviously an interrelationship between agricultural and industrial growth; what is therefore being suggested is that other things being equal, agricultural production should be stressed to the extent that it promotes industrial development and structural change. There are countries where agriculture has become a binding constraint on industrial development; in these countries, agriculture should clearly have priority. (See further Singh, 1979a; see also the chapter on Lesotho in this volume.)

II The State and the Market in Industrial Development

In a landmark paper published in the early 1950s the late Paul Baran (1952) argued that capitalist underdeveloped countries would not be able to bring about industrialization and sustained economic development because of certain important characteristics of their ruling classes. Basing his argument on the experience of Latin America and Asia, Baran suggested that the bourgeoisie in the developing countries, in view of its historical evolution, could not perform the same tasks of economic and social progress as it had done in the past in the West. In the circumstances prevailing in the post-independence period in the underdeveloped countries, the bourgeoisie was no longer the most progressive force, as it assimilated many of the cultural and social characteristics of the pre-capitalist ruling classes whom it was supposed to supplant. As Baran put it (1952):

> Afraid that a quarrel with the landed gentry might be exploited by the radical populist movement, the middle classes in these countries abandon all progressive attitudes in agrarian matters. Afraid that a conflict with church and the military might weaken the political authority of the government, the capitalist middle classes move away from liberal and pacifist currents. Afraid that hostility towards foreign interests might deprive them of military and other support in the case of a revolutionary emergency, the native capitalists have abandoned their previous anti-imperialist, nationalist platforms.

He therefore argued that only a fundamental change in the existing social order in the non-socialist developing countries could bring about long-term economic development.

Although Baran made major contributions to the understanding of the problems of economic development in many areas, this particular analysis has not been borne out by subsequent history. During the last three decades the Third World countries have made substantial achievements in industrialization and economic development. Although their share of world industrial production is still very small, it increased substantially between 1960 and 1977 – from about 6% to 9% (UNIDO, 1979a). Further, there is a group of Third World countries which have been especially successful in creating their own industrial capacities and capabilities. These countries are now providing actual and potential competition for the older industrial nations, not just in labour-intensive products but also in a range of capital-intensive industries like steel and shipbuilding. The crude steel output of developing countries increased from 2% of world production in 1950 to approximately 11% in 1977. Moreover, at a time of severe recession in the industry and despite EEC Industries Commissioner Davignon's warning to the developing countries 'to stop getting into manufacturing facilities, primarily steel, that provide competition for the rich world' they are planning to triple their steel production by 1985.[11]

However, the significant point with respect to Baran's traditional Marxist analysis is that the industrially successful Third World countries have included not only socialist countries like China, but many large and small non-socialist countries, e.g. Brazil, India, South Korea, Singapore, and Hong Kong. More important, the historical record indicates that among the non-socialist countries successful industrialization has been carried out under a variety of different economic regimes. A country like Brazil has relied on a relatively open trading regime and foreign investment by multinationals and achieved rapid industrial progress. On the other hand, India has followed the path of strict control on imports and foreign capital in building up its industrial base, which includes the most sophisticated capital goods industry in the Third World (Lall, 1980). To be sure, the specific economic policies followed by a country affect the pace and the content of industrial development; more important, they have a significant bearing on how the fruits of industrial progress are distributed. But the essential point in the present context is that Third World countries with widely varying economic and political regimes have been successful in creating an industrial base – 'successful' in the sense of having a large and diversified[12] manufacturing sector, possessing a trained labour force and the necessary skills for future industrial development to be self-sustaining.[13]

The next important observation is that in the industrially successful non-socialist Third World countries the state has normally played a major role in economic activity. This is even true of a country like Japan, which is usually regarded as the epitome of successful capitalist industrialization in the postwar period. At the end of the Second World War, the Japanese government concluded that the country's economic structure was inappropriate for its needs. The bulk of Japanese exports consisted of textiles and light manu-factured goods (i.e. labour-intensive products). In the view of the Ministry of International Trade and Industry, although such an economic structure may have conformed to the theory of comparative advantage (Japan being a labour-surplus economy at the time), it was not viable in the long run. The ministry, therefore, embarked on an industrial policy whose cornerstone is the so-called structural policy, aimed at adaptation and technological development of certain key industries thought to be vital to the economy. It is worth quoting in full Vice-Minister Ojimi's rationale for the ministry's policy (OECD, 1972; my italics):

> The MITI decided to establish in Japan industries which require intensive employment of capital and technology, *industries that in consideration of comparative cost of production should be the most inappropriate for Japan*, industries such as steel, oil-refining, petro-chemicals, automo-biles, aircraft, industrial machinery of all sorts, and electronics, including electronic computers. From a short-run, static viewpoint, encouragement of such industries would seem to conflict with economic rationalism. But from a long-range viewpoint, these are precisely the industries where income elasticity of demand is high, technological progress is rapid, and labour productivity rises fast. It was clear that without these industries it would be difficult to employ a population of 100 million and raise their standard of living to that of Europe and America with light industries alone; whether right or wrong, Japan had to have these heavy and chemical industries. According to Napoleon and Clausewitz, the secret of a successful strategy is the concentration of fighting power on the main battlegrounds; fortunately, owing to good luck and wisdom spawned by necessity, Japan has been able to concentrate its scant capital in strategic industries.

The role of the government in the structural transformation of Japan, and hence in bringing about its remarkable economic success, has been so crucial that, as Nino (1973) remarks, 'whereas [the] USA is said to be a country of [the] military industrial complex ... in this sense, Japan may be called a country of the government industrial complex'. The government has used a wide variety of instruments to develop key industries. The most important of these have been: bank finance, import controls and protection, control over foreign exchange and importation of foreign technology (Singh, 1979b). Such instruments, to a lesser or greater extent, have also been used in the economic transformation of countries like Brazil and South Korea, as well as India – that is, industrial development has not simply been left to private enterprise and the vagaries of the international marketplace.

One major conclusion to be drawn from the foregoing discussion and from the general experience of economic development in the postwar period is that diverse countries have been able to embark on industrialization despite their low initial levels of development and the forces of international competition, since the state was cohesive and purposive enough in its economic outlook. This is not, however, simply a matter of temporary protection for 'infant' industries until they can successfully compete in the international economy. Industrial development in the Third World countries, in view of its initial starting point, is likely to require prolonged protection from international competition for periods measured in several decades. Nevertheless, this need not be a cause for alarm. It is inadequate as well as misleading to judge the 'efficiency' of a country's industry entirely by the difference between domestic costs and prices and international prices. Apart from all the theoretical objections to such a procedure, it is worth reflecting that, on this basis, industrial development in the centrally planned economies of the Soviet Union and Eastern Europe would be regarded as being comprehensively inefficient (domestic prices and costs, at official exchange rates, are far higher than international prices). Yet these countries have achieved a remarkable degree of industrialization and economic development. Their share of world industrial production increased by 50% over a fifteen-year period – from 18% in 1960 to 27% in 1975 (UNIDO, 1979a). By comparative international standards, they have achieved high rates of growth of per capita industrial production and consumption, as well as high levels of employment and relatively stable prices. Any useful concept of economic efficiency requires a proper consideration of these broader issues; this is especially so for a developing country where such questions are necessarily paramount.[14]

In analysing the industrialization experience of the European countries during the last century, Alexander Gerschenkron (1952, 1963) noted that the more backward a country's economy, the greater the part played in its industrialization by special institutional factors. These (usually fostered by the government) were designed to increase the supply of capital to the nascent industry and, in addition, to provide it with less decentralized and better-informed enterpreneurial guidance. The more backward the country, the more pronounced, Gerschenkron observed, was the coerciveness and comprehensiveness of these factors. In view of the far greater degree of both absolute and relative backwardness of the African countries today (relative to late nineteenth-century Europe), the state, rather than the market, will necessarily have to play the central role in industrial development in these countries.

III   Constraints on African Industrial Growth

I shall now briefly examine some of the principal constraints on industrialization in the African countries today in the light of the previous discussion. As
the UNIDO chapter in this book amply demonstrates, the level of industrial
development in Africa is extremely low. Excluding South Africa, Africa
accounts for only 0·7% of world production of manufactures; in most African
countries, the share of manufacturing in national production is less than 10%.
Industry produces a limited range of relatively simple products. Africa's share
in world output of metal and engineering products remained unchanged at
0·2% in the fifteen years between 1955 and 1970; the share of metal and
engineering products in total industrial production during this period appears
to have declined. Of all developing regions, Africa has the lowest ratio of
engineering production to engineering imports (ECA, 1979).

As experience of industrialization in various parts of the world shows that
the key factor in industrial development is not natural resources but the skills
and capabilities of the people in the country concerned. An extremely
important and related factor is whether or not the society possesses the
appropriate social organization and institutions to harness science and
technology for industrial development. For example, a country like Japan has
very few natural resources. It has no ferrous metals, no non-ferrous metals,
and so on, and yet it is the second largest steel producer in the world; it is also
the world's most *efficient* steel producer, although it has to import most of the
raw materials for steel production. In general, Japan is an advanced industrial
country because of the skills of its people.

The African countries, because of their colonial history, started with a
particularly large handicap in this regard. At the time of independence the
labour force of most African countries was largely rural and unskilled. It was
predominantly illiterate. Even in the small modern sector, most of the African
labour force was without formal education. In Tanzania, for example, only
0·1% of the labour force around 1962 had higher education, compared with
3·8% in Japan and the USSR and 11·9% in the USA. Tanzania's first
manpower survey in 1962/3 showed that over 80% of all jobs that required a
university education were occupied by non-Africans. There were only twelve
African civil engineers; eight telecommunication engineers; nine
veterinarians; five chemists; and one forecaster. There were no geologists or
mechanical or electrical engineers. Of 600 graduate secondary school teachers
in the country only 38 were Africans. Similarly, in Zambia at the time of its
independence there were only 1,200 Africans with secondary school certifi-
cates and only 108 Zambian graduates (ECA, 1978). The initial position of
other African countries before independence from colonial rule was not very
different from that of Zambia and Tanzania.

Table 1.3, which speaks for itself, provides some indicators of the scientific
and technological capacity of African countries relative to the rest of the
world. Two observations are important with respect to this table. First, it is
necessary to emphasize that successful industrialization requires a change in
the attitudes and values of the society as a whole. It is, therefore, of major
importance rapidly to expand general education so as to inculcate a scientific
and experimental outlook in the population at large. This consideration points

to an acute dilemma between short and long-term requirements in the formulation of manpower development policies in the African countries. In the short term high-level skilled manpower (scientists, engineers, etc.) is urgently needed for immediate industrial tasks. The training of such manpower is extremely expensive, and could easily pre-empt resources from other parts of the educational budget. It would, however, be a shortsighted policy and would hamper industrialization if, as a consequence, adequate resources were not provided for primary education.

Second, African nations may find comfort in the fact that many of the Asian countries which now possess a sufficient educational, technological and scientific infrastructure for industrialization have essentially created it over the last two or three decades. The universities, technical and scientific establishments, research institutions, and so on, in these countries are now not only capable of self-sustained expansion, but have also played a crucial role in enabling them to compete with the advanced economies in several technologically sophisticated areas. As President Giscard d'Estaing remarked in commenting on the competition which Western Europe faces from the Third World: 'There have always been low wages in the world; what is new is that these countries have access to the same technologies as we have.'

Another significant constraint on African industrialization lies in the small size of many African countries. As Table A.1 in the UNIDO chapter shows, the median population of African nations in 1976 was less than 5 million. Fifteen countries had a population of less than 2 million. Empirical studies show that in general there is no correlation between size of population and the degree of industrialization, either in the developing countries or in the developed market economy countries (UNCTAD, 1978). Small and medium-sized countries can obviously achieve a high degree of industrialization through industrial specialization and trade. However, other things being equal, a larger population – generally speaking about 5 million or more – makes it easier for a developing country to embark on industrialization and to develop a diversified industrial structure.

In view of the small populations of African nations, they must necessarily rely more on trade. There have therefore been schemes for the establishment

Table 1.3 *Technological capacity – selected indicators*[a] *(averages expressed as medians for 1970 or latest year available)*

Science and technology	Developed market economy countries	Developing countries and territories		
		Africa	Asia	Latin America
Ratio of total stock of scientists and engineers per 10,000 pop.	112·00	5·80	22·00	69·00
Ratio of technicians per 10,000 pop.	142·30	8·30	23·40	72·20
Scientists and engineers engaged in R & D per 10,000 pop.	10·40	0·35	1·60	1·15
Technicians engaged in R & D per 10,000 pop.	8·20	0·40	0·60	1·40

Note: [a] The size of the sample countries varies by indicator.
Source: UNIDO, 1979b.

of common markets of contiguous African countries to promote specialization and trade. However, these have not been successful in Africa. The main reason is the large differences in the levels of development of the various countries; in a free trade situation, the more developed regions or countries have a tendency to develop even further without commensurate development in the less developed regions (Kaldor, 1970). For example, it is certainly arguable that industrial development in Tanzania was aided by that country's withdrawal from the East African common market and thus from competition with the more advanced Kenyan manufacturing industry. Nevertheless, industrialization in smaller African countries does require much more intra-African trade; the latter is more likely to increase and to aid the development of all the participating countries if it is *planned* rather than free trade. The international development agencies can play an important role by helping to create and implement such arrangements.

Finally, in the light of what was said in the last section about the fundamental importance of the government in fostering industrialization in conditions of economic backwardness, a major limitation on industrial development in Africa lies in the nature and the role of the state. There are two separate issues here: (1) whether the state is actively oriented towards promoting industry; and (2) whether it is capable of implementing such a programme. The first condition is more likely to be met, even in non-progressive African states, since most government leaders recognize that some form of industrial development is necessary for their survival (people nowadays expect it of them); they also find that, since it usually leads to foreign aid, etc., it is not contrary to their own immediate interests. Of course if the government is more enlightened in its attitudes, the country will benefit by possibly faster, but certainly more equitable, industrial and economic development (Singh, 1979a). However, the more important constraint in Africa is that in several countries, the state is not strong enough to implement a programme of industrialization. The lack of centralized state authority with the capability to carry out tasks of economic development remains a significant obstacle to industrialization.

Notes

1   The argument outlined below is different in important respects from that of the Latin-American structuralist school. In this section I have borrowed passages from an earlier paper, Singh (1981).

2   The number of countries in the six country groups identified in Table 1.1 was as follows: L_h 11; L_i 13; S_i 18; S_{2p} 19; S_{2i} 28; CP 9. The numbers of pooled time-series and cross-section observations for the period 1960–75 for the respective groups were 176, 208, 288, 304, 448 and 144. The regression equation given in Table 1.1 provided a very satisfactory fit in each of the country groups, as measured by R^2 and the standard error of the estimates.

3   A broadly similar estimate f the growth elasticity for manufacturing for a typical developing country was obtained by UNCTAD, 1978, in a cross-section study for 1970 of over fifty developing and developed market economy countries. The elasticities were estimated from the following regression equation: $\log v = \beta_0 + \beta_1 \log y + \beta_2 (\log y)^2 + \beta_3 \log N$. where v is value added per capita in manufacturing, y is per capita GDP and N is the size of the population. See further Singh, 1979a.

4   In the context of this chapter, this must necessarily be a brief outline of a vast

subject. Apart from the references given earlier in the text, see further Gomulka, 1971; Kaldor, 1975; Rowthorn, 1975a, b; Cornwall, 1976.

5　Arguments analogous to those above have been put forward by Kaldor and others in stressing the structural importance of the manufacturing sector in the growth of overall productivity in the *advanced* countries. More specifically, first, Cripps and Tarling, 1973, in their analysis of the growth process in advanced industrial countries during 1950–70, found confirmation for Kaldor's hypothesis that the 'faster the overall rate of growth, the greater is the *excess* of the rate of growth of manufacturing production over the rate of growth of the economy as a whole'. Secondly, even for advanced countries, where the scope for surplus labour in agriculture may be thought to be much less than in the developing countries, there was evidence that the faster the growth of industrial production and the faster the decline in non-industrial employment, the greater the increase in the growth of productivity in the economy as a whole. The following cross-section relationships were observed for these countries: for the periods 1950–65 and 1965–75 respectively.

1950–65

$$P_{GDP} = 1 \cdot 7 + 0 \cdot 53\, q_{ind} - 0 \cdot 81\, e_{ni} \quad R^2 = 0 \cdot 81$$
$$\qquad\qquad (\cdot 06) \qquad\quad (\cdot 202)$$

1965–75

$$P_{GDP} = 1 \cdot 15 + 0 \cdot 64\, q_{ind} - 0 \cdot 87\, e_{ni} \quad R^2 = 0 \cdot 96$$
$$\qquad\qquad (\cdot 06) \qquad\quad (0 \cdot 12)$$

where P_{GDP} is the productivity growth in the economy as a whole,

q_{ind} is the rate of growth of industrial production, and

e_{ni} is that of non-industrial employment.

See further Cripps and Tarling, 1973; Kaldor, 1975; Rowthorn, 1975a, 1975b.

6　The results for other types of small economies – i.e. those with abundant resources – are not reported in Table 1.2. Although the latter reveal somewhat different coefficients for the size elasticities, in general they also show substantially greater values of growth elasticities for producer goods than for the consumer goods industries. See further UNIDO, 1979a.

7　These elasticities reflect 'average' experience (being derived from a regression equation). They therefore do not mean that every country has to develop its own steel industry; however, this analysis does suggest the importance of developing capital goods industries for a country to achieve fast economic growth. A similar conclusion is reached by Leontieff *et al.*, 1977.

8　The value of this elasticity tends to be much lower in the developed industrial countries; further there is evidence that, unlike the experience of the developing countries, the elasticity of employment with respect to manufacturing output has fallen substantially in the industrial countries since the mid-1960s. (See Kaldor, 1975; Singh, 1977).

9　These employment growth rates exclude the contribution of small firms – normally firms employing 5 to 10 workers – because of the lack of availability of statistical data. Such firms in the so-called informal sector may account for a fairly large proportion of manufacturing employment in Third World economies, although not of manufacturing output. Expansion of manufacturing output and employment in the formal sector may sometimes be at the expense of the informal sector, but it need not necessarily be so. It could also help increase output and employment in small firms.

10　As Neild, 1979, rightly points out, many services are best viewed 'as a social charge on the production of goods rather than an alternative form of wealth creation. A nation cannot live by producing only health services, except to the extent that such services enhance the production of industrial and agricultural products or to the very limited extent that they can be exported'.

11　The figures for the Third World countries referred to in this paragraph do not include China. It is estimated that the inclusion of China would raise the Third World's share of world industrial production to about 13% in 1977.

12 Accounting for about 15–20% of total national production with a correspondingly large capital goods industry.
13 I do not here discuss the question of the 'efficiency' of the industrial sector which is a separate issue. See, however, below.
14 For a discussion of the concept of economic efficiency in the context of the issues raised above see Singh, 1977, 1979a. See also Singh and Bienefeld, 1977.

References

Baran, P.A. (1952) 'The political economy of backwardness', *Manchester School* (January).

Baran, P.A. (1957) *The Political Economy of Growth* (New York: Monthly Review Press).

Chenery, H.B. (1960) 'Patterns of industrial growth', *American Economic Review*, 50, 4 (September).

Chenery, H. B. and Syrquin, M. (1975) *Patterns of Development, 1950–70* (London: World Bank).

Chenery, H.B. and Taylor, L. (1968) 'Development patterns: among countries and over time', *Review of Economics and Statistics*, 50, 4 (November).

Cornwall, J. (1976) 'Diffusion, convergence and Kaldor's Laws', *Economic Journal* (June).

Cripps, T.F. and Tarling, R.J. (1973) *Growth in Advanced Capitalist Economies*, (Cambridge: Cambridge University Press).

ECA (1978) 'Manpower development and utilization policies and strategies with special reference to indigenisation of African economies', C/CN 14/CAP.7/10, Addis Ababa, 16 November.

ECA (1979) 'Recommendations, suggestions and comments on the provisional agenda for the general conference of UNIDO', ECA/CMI/ECIA.6/W-P/7/Rev.1, Addis Ababa, 8 October.

Gomulka, S. (1971) *Inventive Activity, Diffusion and Stages of Economic Growth* (Aarhus: Institute of Economics).

Gerschenkron, A. (1952) 'Economic backwardness in historical perspective', in B. Hoselitz (ed.), *The Progress of Underdeveloped Countries* (Chicago:

Gerschenkron, A. (1963) 'The early phases of industrialization in Russia and their relationship to the historical study of economic growth', in Barry E. Supple (ed.), *The Experience of Economic Growth* (New York: Random House).

ILO (1977) *Meeting Basic Needs: Strategies for Eradicating Mass Poverty and Unemployment* (Geneva: International Labour Office).

Kaldor, N. (1967) *Strategic Factors in Economic Development* (Ithaca, NY: Cornell University Press).

Kaldor, N. (1970) 'The case for regional policies', *Scottish Journal of Political Economy* (November).

Kaldor, N. (1975) 'Economic growth and the Verdoorn Law: a comment on R. Rowthorn's article', *Economic Journal* (December).

Kuznets, S. (1971) *Economic Growth of Nations* (Cambridge, Mass.: Harvard University Press).

Lall, S. (1980) 'Developing countries as exporters of technology: a first look at the Indian experience', (London: Macmillan, in press).

Leontieff, W. *et al.* (1977) *The Future of the World Economy* (New York: Oxford University Press).

Neild, R. R. (1979) 'Managed trade between industrial countries', in R. L. Major (ed.), *Britain's Trade and the Exchange Rate Policy* (London: Heinemann Educational Books).

OECD (1972) *The Industrial Policy of Japan* (Paris: Organization for Economic Co-operation and Development).

Nino, K. (1973) 'On efficiency and equity problems in industrial policy – with special reference to the Japanese experience', *Kobe University Economic Review*, 19.

Paige, D. (1961) 'Economic growth: the last hundred years', *National Institute Economic Review* (July).

Rowthorn, R. E. (1975a) 'What remains of Kaldor's Law', *Economic Journal* (March).

Rowthorn, R. E. (1975b) 'A reply to Lord Kaldor's comment', *Economic Journal* (December).

Singh, A. (1977) 'UK industry and the world economy: a case of de-industrialization?', *Cambridge Journal of Economics*, 1, 2 (June).

Singh, A. (1979a) 'The "basic needs" approach to development *versus* the new international economic order: the significance of Third World industrialization', *World Development* (June).

Singh, A. (1979b) 'North Sea Oil and the reconstruction of UK industry', in F. Blackaby (ed.), *De-industrialization* (London: Heinemann Educational Books).

Singh, A. (1981) 'Third World industrialization and the structure of the world economy', in D.Currie and W.Peters (eds) *Microeconomic Analysis: Essays in Microeconomic and Devlopment* (London: Croom Helm).

Singh, A. and Bienefeld, M. (1977) 'Industry and the urban economy in Tanzania' (mimeo.), background paper for the ILO/JASPA Employment Advisory Mission to Tanzania.

UNCTAD (1978) *Restructuring of World Industry: New Dimensions for Trade Co-operation* (New York: United Nations).

UNIDO (1979a) *World Industry since 1960: Progress and Prospects* (New York: United Nations).

UNIDO (1979b) *International Flows of Technology*, 3, UNIDO/IOD 326 19 December.

Young, Allyn (1928) 'Increasing returns and economic progress', *Economic Journal* (December).

2 Import-Substituting Industrialization

FRED NIXSON

Introduction

Import-substituting industrialization (ISI) has dominated the industrialization drives of the majority of the less developed countries (LDCs) in the post-World War Two period. Although the establishment of import-substituting industries can be traced back to earlier periods (the First World War and the economic depression of the late 1920s) for the larger Latin American economies such as Argentina, Brazil and Mexico,[1] the 1950s to early 1960s saw the large-scale implementation of conscious ISI policies in Latin America and in a number of important countries in South and South-East Asia (e.g. India, Pakistan, the Philippines). The early to mid-1960s saw the beginnings of large-scale ISI in several of the more important sub-Saharan African economies (Nigeria, Kenya, Ghana, Zambia) and in the smaller Latin American and South-East Asian economies. Although currently out of favour in orthodox development economics literature, ISI still tends to dominate the industrialization plans of most of the smaller, less industrialized LDCs.

It is the contention of this chapter that the ISI strategy, as implemented in a large number of countries, exhibits certain basic economic characteristics which allow us to draw broad conclusions about its relation to, and its impact on, the development process. Africa is the least industrialized of the less developed regions of the world[2] and given this relative industrial backwardness it can, in principle, 'learn' from the experience and mistakes of others. To say this is not to abstract from the sociopolitical environment within which economic policies/strategies are selected and implemented, nor does it imply that countries will choose the 'optimal' or 'correct' development strategy merely because it is pointed out to them. We must also avoid the confusion that arises in much of the development literature between analysis and policy prescription. This chapter concentrates on the former and only briefly draws a number of policy conclusions at the end.

A further point deserves mention. It is our belief that the ISI strategy cannot be properly understood without reference to a number of other key issues in development studies. These include:

the role of the transnational corporation (TNC) in the industrialization of the LDCs;
the problem of the choice of technique within the manufacturing sector and the role of the TNC within the technology transfer process;
issues arising from dependency theory and the role of the state in the development process;
issues relating to the distribution of income within the industrializing LDC.

These issues raise questions which cannot be covered within the confines of this chapter. Its scope is already ambitious, reflecting the fact that in the past ISI has been broadly viewed as a development strategy in its own right, rather than as merely an industrialization strategy. We must recognise, therefore, that we are only considering one aspect (albeit often the most important aspect) of a complex process of growth and change occurring in a large number of LDCs.

Although a number of good surveys of the ISI experience exist (Baer, 1972; Bruton, 1970; Helleiner, 1972; Hirschman, 1968; Little, Scitovsky and Scott, 1970; Winston, 1967; Sutcliffe, 1971) most of them relate to Latin America and South Asia, and very little comprehensive and systematic analysis of industrial development in Africa is available.

However, two general books on African industrialization may be given brief mention. Ewing (1968) discusses, *inter alia*, the Latin American record of industrialization and is critical of ISI, recognizing the limits of the ISI process, the rapid exhaustion of the 'easy' stage of ISI and the emphasis placed on consumer goods industries under the ISI strategy (these points will be discussed in greater detail below). Ewing stresses the need for the planned establishment of IS industries on a regional rather than a national basis within Africa and recognizes the need for the export of manufactured goods once the limits of IS are reached.

Pearson (1969, ch. 4) is critical of the dichotomy between import-substituting and export promoting industries and argues for 'Janus' industries serving both internal and external markets. However, he presents no general discussion of ISI.

In general, the better systematic critiques of the ISI process have centred on the experience of individual African economies. Mention should be made here of the ILO Report on Kenya (ILO, 1972); Seidman (1974) on Zambia; Killick (1978) and Steel (1972) on Ghana; Kilby (1969) on Nigeria; Rweyemamu (1973) on Tanzania and the World Bank Report on the Ivory Coast (World Bank 1978, Appendix B). Earlier work includes Van Arkadie (1964) and Maitra (1967) on East Africa.[3] The attempt has been made to integrate these studies into the main body of the text below, rather than discuss them individually and at length, given that they do not, in general, provide significant new insights into the ISI process. The main objective of this chapter is to assess the experience of ISI in Latin America, and to a lesser extent in Asia, and to see what broad conclusions can be drawn from that experience which may be of relevance to other, especially African, LDCs.

The Import Substitution 'Model' of Industrialization

Import substitution, in the context of this discussion, is taken to mean the domestic production of goods previously imported.[4] This appears, at first sight, to be a straightforward way of going about the creation of an indigenous industrial base and one that is likely to appeal to economic planners (see below). But within the overall ISI strategy, a number of options are in principle open to the industrializing LDC although such a statement implies the existence of an effectively planned economy. The following classification is based on Raj and Sen (1961):

(1)   the LDC can use its foreign exchange to import investment goods (e.g. looms), raw materials, fuels, etc., to manufacture consumer goods (cloth);
(2)   it can use its foreign exchange to import capital goods (machine tools) to make investment goods which in turn produce consumer goods, and to make intermediate goods (e.g. steel) and develop domestic raw material supplies;
(3)   it can use its foreign exchange to import capital goods to make capital goods which in turn make other capital goods, investment goods, etc.[5]

The ISI process was at one time characterized as 'industrialization by tightly separated stages' (Hirschman, 1968), that is, it was seen as a sequential process whereby countries would begin with the domestic production of consumer goods and then move to intermediate goods and finally to capital goods production. However, as we shall see below, such a sequence is extremely difficult to realize in practice. The majority of LDCs have pursued option 1 and have tended to 'get stuck' at that stage of industrialization.[6] The more advanced, semi-industrialized LDCs have moved on to option 2 and some of them (e.g. India and perhaps Brazil and Mexico) have established a growing domestic capital goods sector. Many attempts have been made to explain why LDCs find it difficult to make the transition from consumer to intermediate and capital goods. We refer to these analyses below but for the present we may note the obvious problems involved in such a sequence of development. Intermediate, investment and capital goods industries will place greater financial, technological and organizational demands on the LDCs and will probably require TNC co-operation for their establishment. It is not surprising, therefore, that we witness what Felix (1964) has referred to as the 'premature widening' of the productive structure (the production of increasingly sophisticated, high-income, durable consumer goods) rather than the smooth development of backward linkages into intermediate and capital goods industries (for the analysis of this problem in Nigeria, see the chapter by Forrest in this volume).

Origins, Concept and Measurement of ISI[7]

A variety of impulses have stimulated ISI. As noted above, ISI was initiated in many Latin American countries as a response to the disruption resulting from wars and international depression when there was either insufficient foreign exchange to pay for imports or when the imported goods themselves were not generally available. Since 1945 ISI has become more widespread, in many cases stimulated by balance-of-payments difficulties.[8] In general, the saving of foreign exchange through IS has been seen as an 'easier option' than the earning of additional foreign exchange through manufactured goods exports. The domestic market is easy to protect and the market for the particular product is a known and established one. Manufactured goods exports on the other hand require breaking into new markets and the devising and implementation of successful export promotion policies. The latter course of action is not impossible (witness the success of Hong Kong, South Korea, etc.) but is undoubtedly more difficult than ISI. The undeniably powerful and persistent appeal of the ISI strategy owes much to this consideration although there are other factors, economic, political and perhaps even psychological (the desire to demonstrate an ability to make something for oneself, rather than depend on imports), which must be given due weight in any explanation of the attraction of ISI.

In other cases, ISI has resulted from the deliberate imposition of protective tariffs by newly independent governments pursuing the objective of more rapid industrial development. In the latter case, the imposition of tariffs has usually forced transnational corporations (or local enterprises previously engaged in the import of manufactured goods) to establish domestic production facilities in order to protect their market position. Kilby's (1969) study of industrial development in Nigeria provides evidence for this 'market protection' hypothesis.[9]

In Latin America, the United Nations Economic Commission for Latin America (ECLA) gave intellectual respectability to the pressures from various social groups for accelerating the industrialization process (Felix, 1968). The move to an 'inward-looking' model of development, stimulated by the imposition of protective tariff barriers, was seen as a necessary condition for the creation of greater employment opportunities, the removal or alleviation of the balance-of-payments constraint and the securing and anchoring within the economy of the benefits of technical progress. ISI was thus seen as a conscious development strategy.[10] Such 'forced' ISI could be contrasted to what Hirschman (1968) has referred to as 'import swallowing', that is, the domestication of certain industries with locational characteristics that give them a high degree of natural protection against imports (industries producing heavy, bulky, costly-to-transport final products – building materials, brewing, etc.) and which can usually be established without massive government protection or intervention.

The distinction between ISI as a historical phenomenon (an *ex post* concept) and as a deliberately implemented development strategy (an *ex ante* concept) has not always been made clear in the literature. For Chenery (1960) ISI is a 'cause' of economic growth and from this it has been concluded that ISI can be used as a conscious development strategy.[11] Maizels (1963) has shown that the import content of supplies declines with the progress of industrialization, at least up to the point where a fairly mature level has been reached. It is clear, however, that ISI, thus defined, could be either a cause or a consequence of economic growth and conclusions drawn from studies based on the historical experience of other countries should not be uncritically used as the basis for the formulation of development policies for contemporary LDCs.[12]

The controversy surrounding the concept and measurement of ISI has generated a large literature which cannot be adequately covered here.[13] Sutcliffe (1971, p. 225) suggests that the term 'import substitution' should be used to cover 'only the direct substitution of domestic production for the import of the same product', a concept which, as he further argues, is 'more appropriately applied to immediate economic policy than to broad economic analysis' (loc. cit.). As already indicated above, this is the meaning given to import substitution in this chapter.

The significance of this point and the shortcomings of the ISI process become clear when we consider IS as a planning instrument. Under the ISI regime, the planner will usually consider a product suitable for domestic production if the domestic market, as given by the value or volume of imports of that product, is equal to, or greater than, the minimum economic output of a single manufacturing unit. Protection will be given to the domestic producer so that the price of the imported product, assuming that imports are permitted, will be equal to, or greater than, the price of the domestic product. Examples of this approach to the estimation of the ISI potential in East Africa can be found in the work of Maitra (1967) and Van Arkadie (1964). This approach raises a number of important issues.

(1) The market for imported goods is not likely to represent the demands of the population as a whole; ISI accepts the pattern of demand, and the underlying distribution of income, as given, whereas it may be both necessary and desirable to alter radically consumption patterns and distributional profiles, both aspects of the economic and sociopolitical structure which industrialization is intended to change; this is, of course, more than an attack on ISI *per se*, but that does not destroy the validity of the criticism. Seidman (1974, p. 605) emphasizes the income distribution factor when analysing what she refers to as the 'distorted growth' of IS industries in Zambia:

> the planners, by adopting an import-substitution policy, permitted inherited 'market forces' to shape decisions as to which manufacturing industries should be established, where, and how. This policy was re-inforced ... by the role of the inherited sets of institutions which, directly or indirectly, tended to ensure that existing 'market forces' did in fact govern the actual investment decisions made.[14]

(2) Trade data may not be sufficiently disaggregated to permit the identification of specific products, especially in the case of differentiated consumer goods; furthermore, if tariff protection is required, there will be a reduction in demand as a result of the higher price of the domestic product, unless the relevant price elasticity of demand is zero (Helleiner, 1972, ch. 6; Stoutjesdijk, 1967, ch. 1).

(3) At a more general level, it is not necessarily the case that products which do not enter the country (or only enter in small amounts) do not merit domestic production, nor does it mean that because certain products enter in large

amounts domestic production is desirable; industrialization may well require the domestic production of goods previously neither imported nor (of necessity) consumed.

(4) Under the ISI strategy, and resulting from the tariff structure, consumer goods are likely to take priority in the industrialization process, leading to what many would regard as a timid industrialization strategy which, although generating rapid growth in the short run, is unable to maintain this momentum in the medium and long run.

(5) Criteria based on import data say nothing about the suitability of the product for domestic production and there is a need for a further appraisal, taking into account, for example, the factor endowments (broadly defined) and the development objectives of the country concerned and the technological characteristics and demands of the project in question; once we admit to the importance of the other variables, however, we have moved beyond the ISI strategy as so far defined.

The general conclusion that emerges from points 3 to 5 above is that comprehensive industrial planning can be expected to give rise to an industrial sector which, in terms of both its composition and structure, will be very different from that emerging as a result of market-based ISI.

ISI: Alternative Critiques

Before looking in greater detail at the specific economic characteristics of the ISI process, it is useful to outline briefly two alternative critiques of the overall impact of ISI. For the sake of convenience and simplicity, we refer to these two schools of thought as the neo-classical and the structuralist/dependency schools, although strictly speaking only the former can be referred to as a 'school' of thought, presenting as it does a coherent and consistent (though not necessarily 'correct') critique of the ISI process.

In terms of their overall assessment of ISI, both schools exhibit certain similarities although their analyses of the causes of the problems identified of course differ. There would be broad agreement that most LDCs have relatively small, highly protected, inefficient, overdiversified industrial sectors, oligopolistic or monopolistic in structure, with substantial under-utilization of capacity, dependent upon capital-intensive technologies but with low levels of productivity and a low employment-creation potential.[15] Furthermore, many would accept the argument that government preoccupation with industrialization has led to the neglect of other sectors of the economy, especially agriculture, and that overall a significant bias against the export of both primary products and manufactured goods has been introduced into the economy. The balance-of-payments constraint has not been alleviated, a rigid, inelastic import structure has come into being and bottlenecks and distortions within the economy and aggravated by ISI have exacerbated already existing inflationary pressures.[16]

The ILO report on Kenya (ILO, 1972) presents a critique of the ISI process very much along these lines, and its proposals for reform are a mixture of both neo-classical and structuralist ideas, although most attention has been focused on the report's elaboration of a 'redistribution through growth' strategy.

Included in the report's recommendations are proposals for the revision of the system of protection, the placing of greater emphasis on export-led industrialization, the stricter control of foreign enterprises operating in Kenya, the implementation of fiscal reforms and the development of an indigenous technological base, as well as proposals for reform aimed at the agricultural, educational and informal sectors of the economy. The proposed reforms have not, in general, been politically acceptable to the Kenyan government and thus have not been adopted. There is little evidence which suggests that Kenya intends to reorientate its development effort along the lines envisaged in the report (see the chapters by Leys and Kaplinsky in this volume).

NEO-CLASSICAL CRITIQUE

This school attempts to explain the poor development performance of LDCs by the existence of distorted and inefficient factor and goods markets. The main cause of such 'imperfections' is to be found in government intervention in the economy, especially the promotion of domestic industries behind high tariff barriers. The key to economic development lies in the promotion of an efficient allocation of resources within the free market framework.

Little, Scitovsky and Scott's (1970) study is a classic example of this approach. They argue that excessive protection, permitting or encouraging the overdevelopment of ISI, violates the principle of comparative advantage and creates new, and aggravates existing, distortions in domestic factor and product markets. Labour is relatively overpriced, the domestic currency is overvalued in terms of foreign currencies and capital is relatively underpriced. Capital-intensive technologies are the result of such factor market imperfections and as a result unemployment is exacerbated. It is also argued that ISI has worsened existing inequalities in the distribution of income, redistributing income from agriculture to industry and, within the industrial sector itself, redistributing income from labour to capital.

The case is argued for the promotion of industrial development through policies which offset the disadvantages under which domestic industry suffers (for example, government provision of training facilities for the labour force). Protection should be lowered and rationalized, exchange rates devalued where necessary and the free play of market forces encouraged. The anticipated results of such reforms would include the elimination of inefficient domestic industries, the encouragement of exports and the removal of disincentives under which the other sectors of the economy labour. Killick's study of Ghanaian development (Killick, 1978) is firmly within the neo-classical framework and his advocacy of 'a reduced *degree* of intervention' and 'a greater willingness to let the market do what it is being prevented from doing' (Killick, 1978, p. 351) is consistent with neo-classical policy prescriptions.

STRUCTURALIST/DEPENDENCY CRITIQUE

The writers who can be included in this somewhat amorphous category focus attention, to varying degrees, on the distorted productive structure, largely a part of the colonial heritage, and the fragmented nature of markets within LDCs. Necessary structural change is unlikely, in their opinion, to result from the operation of market forces. They raise issues relating to the ownership and control of the means of production and the social relations arising from different ownership patterns, and they are concerned with such problems as: the contemporary foreign penetration of the economy manifested largely through the operations of transnational corporations; technological dependence; the distribution of income and the balance of social forces within the economy.

With respect to policy prescriptions, structuralists, as the name implies, place emphasis on the need for significant changes in the economic structure of the economy (land redistribution, agrarian reform, income redistribution, the promotion of 'national' interests) whereas those on the political left of this spectrum will stress the necessary political changes that must occur before any genuine economic restructuring becomes possible.

It is the present writer's opinion that the neo-classical critique grossly oversimplifies, and indeed misinterprets, the economic problems faced by LDCs. It provides some insights but these can be incorporated into a broadly based structuralist/dependency view of the industrialization process and the interpretation of ISI that follows is largely derived from that perspective.

The Impact of ISI on Imports and the Balance of Payments

Much attention has been focused on the behaviour of the import ratio (the ratio of total imports to national income) as ISI proceeds. In general, the import ratio can be expected to fall, but this, of course, does not imply a reduction in either the total value or volume of imports. In addition, it is likely that some minimum limit to the import ratio will exist (Robock, 1970).

Of greater analytical significance is the change in the composition of imports that occurs as ISI unfolds. Typically, as noted above, the process begins with the domestic manufacture of consumer goods (the highest tariffs are imposed on consumer goods imports and so we see the perverse result that the 'least' essential consumer goods industries are given the greatest degree of protection in the domestic market), and thus the commodity composition of imports changes. Consumer goods imports become relatively less important and imports of intermediate goods, fuels, machinery and equipment, and so on, become of greater significance. The ISI process thus increases the proportion of domestic value added dependent on imports and under these conditions, a decline in the availability of foreign exchange will lead to forced import curtailments and industrial recession. In general, the dependence of the economy on foreign trade, and its vulnerability to fluctuations in foreign exchange receipts is not significantly reduced. ISI, originally seen as a means of lessening the external dependence of the LDC, in fact appears merely to alter the character of that dependence.[17] This rigidity of the import structure is not total. There is always likely to be some margin of 'non-essential' or 'less essential' imports of finished goods which can be squeezed with little effect on domestic output or employment, but such a margin is likely to become narrower over time.

With respect to the wider impact of ISI on the balance of payments, there is no convincing evidence that ISI actually saves foreign exchange. Analytically, a number of different aspects of the relationship between ISI and the balance of payments can be singled out but in reality we must admit that such factors interact in a complex way and are not likely to be individually definable. Five aspects of the relationship are as follows.

(1) Imports stimulated by growing national income may create demands for foreign exchange greater than the amount saved by the domestic production of the goods previously imported. Leff and Netto (1966) constructed a sequential model to show the national income and balance-of-payments effects of an ISI programme. Applying the model to Brazil, they found that at the end of the sequence, despite massive ISI policies and foreign capital inflows, the balance-of-payments deficit was larger than at the beginning of the sequence.[18] In other words, the very success of ISI in creating additional income aggravates the foreign exchange constraint.

(2) The import intensity (or import content) of the ISI industries must be taken into account. Different domestically produced goods will have different import intensities.[19] This feature does not explain the worsening of the balance-of-payments deficit, except perhaps in the short run. In the longer run, once a given rate of growth is attained and maintained, the direct impact of current investment on demand for imports should be more than offset by the previous year's investment in ISI currently coming to fruition (Diaz-Alejandro, 1965). However, it is a factor that makes the actual savings on imports in reality less than would have been anticipated.

(3) The repatriation of profits, interest and dividends, royalty payments, and so on, resulting from TNC investment, must be taken into account. In the Leff and Netto model they have only a negligible effect on the balance of payments but in reality their impact is likely to be of some significance.

(4) The redistribution of income that occurs during the ISI process (see above) may favour those sectors or classes within the economy (the urban middle- and upper-income groups) which have a high marginal propensity to consume imported goods (or domestically produced import-intensive products), thus aggravating the balance-of-payments problem.

(5) Within the neo-classical methodological framework, certain cases of extreme inefficiency can be identified. The effective rate of protection (which shows the percentage by which value added at a given stage of fabrication in domestic industry can exceed what it would otherwise be in the absence of protection – see Little et al., 1970) may be so high that domestic value added, measured in world prices, is negative. That is, the value of the industry's inputs at world prices is higher than the value of its output at world prices, and thus the domestic activity actually costs the country foreign exchange.[20]

To conclude, therefore, the actual experience of ISI seems to suggest that if the sequence gets 'stuck' at the consumer goods stage, the LDC will not experience an alleviation of its balance-of-payments constraint. ISI may successfully create income and, to a lesser extent, employment, but its apparent inability to save foreign exchange will force the economy to become increasingly dependent on inflows of foreign capital (both private and public) to maintain the real capacity to import, assuming that export earnings cannot be significantly increased.[21]

ISI and Long-Run Growth and Development

A characteristic of the ISI process that has attracted a great deal of attention is the apparent inability of ISI to sustain a long-run rate of growth of national income in excess of the rate of growth of the capacity to import. After a brief period of growth, ISI appears to lose momentum, IS opportunities appear to become 'exhausted' and the foreign exchange constraint once again becomes dominant.

To refer to the 'exhaustion' of IS opportunities is not strictly correct. As we noted in our discussion of the ISI 'model' (above) the LDC can move from the substitution of consumer goods to intermediate and investment goods and ultimately to capital goods substitution. In practice, such a sequence is difficult to achieve, and in an illuminating analogy the ECLA report on Brazil (UN ELCA, 1964, pp. 6–7) likens the substitution process to the construction of a building 'of which every storey must be erected simultaneously', although the degree of concentration on each stage varies from one period to another.

Obviously it is not impossible to achieve this sequence, but what does seem likely is that it will not be achieved without massive and direct government intervention in the establishment of intermediate, investment and capital goods industries (as, for example, in India and Brazil). The free and spontaneous interplay of market forces (that is, what is referred to in this chapter as market-based ISI) is not sufficient and on their own, they are more likely to lead to the economic stagnation referred to above.

We can broadly distinguish between two sets of explanations as to why ISI has not succeeded in the longer run. The neo-classical school (e.g. Bruton, 1970) points to the distortion of the economy, the creation of activities 'alien' to the economic and social environment of the community and the lack of incentives for raising productivity resulting from government intervention in factor and product markets. The policy prescriptions arising from this analysis have already been referred to.

On the other hand, there are a number of explanations which we can include in our structuralist/dependency category. Such explanations, in their various ways, accept the premise that what is wrong is the ISI strategy itself, not merely its inefficient implementation (the neo-classical view). In other words, stagnationist tendencies are inherent within the ISI process itself. Such tendencies will effectively retard the further structural transformation of the LDC economy once a certain stage in the IS process has been reached and the underlying causes of these tendencies will have to be overcome before further structural change is possible. Each explanation, taken on its own, may illustrate only one aspect of a complex reality, but when they are taken together and analysed within a dynamic perspective we may begin to obtain a more complete understanding of the problem.

For the sake of clarity and brevity, we will list the major contributions:

(1) *The generation of structural imbalances.* The ECLA (1964) report on Brazil focused attention on the economic and social characteristics of the ISI process and noted the emergence or exacerbation of four sets of imbalances or disequilibria:

(a) sectoral imbalances between industry and agriculture,[22] and within the industrial sector itself between capital and consumer goods;

(b) regional imbalances;

(c) social imbalances (increasing inequality in the distribution of income);

(d) financial imbalances (the generation of inflationary pressures).

(2) *Inability of ISI to alleviate the balance-of-payments constraint.* We have already referred to this above, but in addition we must note the work of Felix (1968) on Argentina. He argues that in many Latin American countries ISI has lost the capacity to lower the import ratio and has become progressively more difficult to sustain with the move to intermediate and capital goods industries. Insufficient attention has been paid to the changing composition of final demand under ISI and only by postulating a persistent import bias to changes in the final demand mix can a levelling-off in the import ratio be adequately explained. Rising incomes shift demand towards products with high-income elasticities of demand and higher import intensities than products with slower growing demand, but such import-biased demand shifts also occur independently of income shifts as a result of the international demonstration effect. Testing the model with data from Argentina, Felix finds that the intermediate import requirements per composite unit of Argentine output were higher in 1960 than in 1953, although there had been considerable ISI in the intervening years.

(3) *Technological dependence.* Merhav (1969) has argued that the importation of technology developed in industrialized countries makes monopoly (used in a generic sense) inevitable at a low level of development in LDCs. In the industrialized countries monopolies grow via diversification, but in LDCs Merhav argues that such opportunities are restricted and shrink rapidly as a consequence of both the market restrictions engendered by monopoly and the dependence upon imports of capital goods. Monopolistic industries thus diversify into increasingly sub-optimal activities (sub-optimal relative to the size of the domestic market for the output of those activities) but this process cannot assure sustained growth because of the lack of a domestic capital goods sector. Furthermore, the very process itself creates a bias against the establishment of a domestic capital goods sector.

(4) *Insufficiency of domestic demand.* Baer and Maneschi (1971) build a short-run income determination model which shows that, in the absence of government counter-measures, stagnation is inevitable. They argue that ISI, pursued in the absence of structural change, results in the establishment of productive capacity within the industrial sector for which demand is inadequate. ISI is 'self-terminating' in that it neither generates sufficient income nor distributes it adequately to justify the full utilization and expansion of industrial capacity.[23]

Whatever the exact combination of factors, there seems to be clear evidence from a number of countries (for example, Brazil, Argentina, India, Pakistan) indicating the loss of momentum of the market-based ISI process and, *in extremis*, the collapse of the strategy amid growing social and political conflict. In some countries the collapse of ISI is marked by a change of government (often the result of a military coup) and the implementation of new economic policies. The slowing-down in the rate of growth of the Brazilian economy in the late 1950s to early 1960s, the military coup of 1964, the period of 'stabilization' that followed and the 'economic miracle' of 1968–73, associated as it was with the implementation of certain economic policies,[24] represents a classic example of the breakdown of the market-based ISI process and the need for this model of development to be transcended by a new economic and political order (see Baer, 1973; Bacha, 1977; Malan and Bonelli, 1977). We return to this point in our final section.

Conclusions: The Lessons for Africa

Although many LDCs have achieved significant rates of growth of manufacturing output during the postwar period, there has been widespread disillusion with the ISI experience. Certainly this form of industrialization is no longer seen as being synonymous with development and the expectations of its early advocates have not in general been realized. Industrial growth has been isolated from the overall growth of the economy and has led to the neglect of, or positive discrimination against, other sectors of the economy, especially agriculture.

To summarize the conclusions reached above: ISI has not, in practice, significantly alleviated the balance-of-payments constraint; it has led to a growing dependence on a largely imported, capital-intensive technology and has thus not created extensive employment opportunities or indigenous technological development; the process has been heavily dependent on foreign capital and has emphasized the establishment of consumer goods industries at the expense of investment and capital goods industries; it has led to what many would regard as an undesirable redistribution of income and in general it has failed to generate a sustained process of economic growth.

It must be emphasized that we are not arguing that these are the inevitable consequences of any attempt at industrialization in LDCs, nor should the argument be interpreted to mean that LDCs should not attempt to industrialize. Rather these are the conclusions drawn from a broad survey of the experiences of LDCs following a specific ISI strategy. Even so, however, we must guard against a too-mechanistic interpretation of the ISI experience. Much of the analysis appearing in the 1960s and early 1970s, both structuralist and Marxist, implied that stagnation and breakdown were inevitable, that structural constraints were rigid and unchanging and that sustained growth and structural change were not likely to be achieved. The continued industrial progress of some LDCs, however, in particular the increasing deepening of their industrial sectors through the establishment, often with direct state intervention, of intermediate and capital goods industries, forces us to reconsider these views and recognize that development is occurring (although it is development that is not necessarily desirable or beneficial to the interests of the vast mass of the population in these countries). The need for a continuous re-evaluation of the ISI experience, from which longer-term trends can be identified, cannot be over-emphasized.

The orthodox view of the 1970s, based on the above evidence, is that 'inward-looking' development strategies in general, and ISI in particular, have 'failed' and what is therefore needed is 'outward-looking', export-led industrialization.[25] This conclusion is largely derived from the view, commonly expressed, that industrial development is simply the consequence of the particular set of trade and commercial policies adopted, rather than being an objective pursued in its own right. In other words, because 'inward-looking' trade policies have allegedly failed, 'outward-looking' trade policies are the only alternative. Within Africa, the Ivory Coast is often cited as an example of successful export-led development, with particular emphasis placed on the export of agro-industrial exports (canned pineapples, plywood, palm oil, instant coffee, etc.) (World Bank, 1978, Appendix B).

It is difficult to see, however, in what sense ISI, as in practice implemented, can be regarded as a meaningful 'inward-looking' strategy of development. Apart from the fact that it involves the domestic production of goods previously imported, ISI does not in general result in greater self-reliance or self-sufficiency (which common sense would seem to imply should be the key constituents of any inward-looking policy). ISI as already pointed out, has been heavily dependent on foreign capital, technology and expertise, it has been based on the consumption patterns, tastes, marketing techniques, and so on, of the developed capitalist economies and the changes in the import structure and the failure to alleviate the balance-of-payments constraint have exacerbated the dependence of the IS economy on the external sector.

A meaningful inward-looking policy would involve the establishment of economic, social and political objectives consistent with the resources, aspirations and commitment to development of the LDCs themselves. Such a programme would not imply autarchic development but it would require that the presumed relationship between trade and development be reversed (ul Haq, 1973).[26] In addition, as Ajit Singh has recently argued (Singh, 1979), there is no necessary conflict between the meeting of the basic needs of the populations of the LDCs and the transformation of productive structures via industrialization. Indeed, industrialization, including the establishment of strategic capital goods industries, is essential to meet basic needs.

What, therefore, are the lessons that Africa can in principle 'learn' from the 'failure' of ISI elsewhere?[27] Seven major conclusions may be drawn from the above analysis.

(1)   In the majority of LDCs industrial development cannot be separated from, or pursued at the expense of, agricultural development; in most LDCs land redistribution and agrarian reform are necessary prerequisites for the creation of larger markets for manufactured goods (both intermediate and final) in the rural areas (this point is emphasized by both Aboyade and Islam in Streeten, 1973); in addition, agro-industrial development, spanning the two sectors and often with good export prospects (see the example of the Ivory Coast, cited above), needs to be given greater emphasis.

(2)   The reformulated inward-looking strategy still requires the full exploitation of existing, and the energetic development of new, export opportunities (see point 1 above); this is not to advocate, however, an orthodox export-led industrialization strategy.

(3)   A re-examination of the role and potential of regional economic integration is required; the majority of the sub-Saharan African economies are small, both in terms of total and per capita incomes and in terms of population size (more than two-thirds of the sub-Saharan economies have populations of

less than 10 million), and the prospects for development based solely on the home markets of these economies must inevitably be limited.

(4)   In addition, economic co-operation on a selective basis is required to ensure the rational and equitable establishment of heavy intermediate investment and capital goods industries, without which, as Stewart has emphasized (Stewart, 1976b; Stewart, 1977), indigenous technological development is not possible; we may also refer here to the need to establish repair and maintenance facilities and the need to train skilled labour in these areas, both of which might best be carried out on a regional basis.

(5)   Although not explicitly covered in this chapter, there is an obvious need for a radical reappraisal of the role of the transnational corporation in the industrialization process both in terms of the cost and the 'appropriateness' of the products and production technologies that it provides (see, for example, Langdon, 1975).

(6)   Government intervention in the industrialization process has in general been erratic and inconsistent; the need exists for a rational, planned allocation of resources in order to achieve development objectives as rapidly and efficiently as possible and this implies that greater emphasis must be placed on planning and plan implementation in the future than has actually been the case in the past.

(7)   ISI will, of course, continue to play a key role in the reformulated industrialization strategy but in association with the further processing and manufacture of primary products within the LDCs and the promotion of a wider range of exports.

The implementation of the strategy of industrialization outlined above would require, as a necessary precondition, radical political change within the LDCs themselves. This is not, of course, meant to imply that such political change is in itself a sufficient condition, nor that the direction and content of such change is without controversy. Even where radical political change has reconizably occurred, major problems remain and indeed are often aggravated by the changed economic and political circumstances. However, the basic objective of this chapter has been one of analysis rather than policy prescription and in this respect one final point needs to be made. Paraphrasing Stewart and Streeten (1976, p. 396), it is clear that too much effort has been put into the devising of industrialization strategies, whereas it is not the lack of such strategies, but rather the 'basic political contradiction between the schemes and the real as opposed to nominal objectives of decision makers, that is critical'.

Notes

Comments from Philip Leeson, Mo Yamin, Michael Tribe and Peter Lawrence are gratefully acknowledged. The usual disclaimer of course applies.
1   For an analysis of the social and political forces underlying industrialization in these countries, see Cardoso and Faletto, 1979, especially ch. 5.
2   According to UNIDO 1979, eighty-five LDCs for which data were available accounted for 8·6% of world manufacturing valued added in 1975. Of this total, Africa

accounted for 0·8%, Latin America accounted for 4·8% and South and East and West Asia accounted for 3·0%.

3   Clark, 1965, in the context of elaborating a planning model for East Africa, saw ISI as 'a prime potential source of structural change' (p. 63) and as 'the only way to restrain the growth of other imports and release foreign exchange for capital equipment' (p. 87).

4   The term 'import reproduction' is sometimes used to indicate that the domestic product is an exact replication of the good previously imported (see Stewart, 1976a).

5   Although problems of definition and measurement obviously exist, we assume, with Stewart (1976b, p. 121) that the capital/consumer goods distinction does not pose insuperable problems.

6   A few LDCs (Hong Kong, Taiwan, South Korea, Singapore) have adopted an export-led industrialization strategy and a number of the more industrialized of the LDCs occupy an intermediate position. For example, Brazil, Argentina, Mexico, India, Pakistan, Thailand and Malaysia are included by UNIDO, 1979, among the top ten LDC exporters of manufactured goods, but at least for the larger of these economies, the domestic market is still of importance and ISI, assuming more complex forms, remains significant. The relevance of the export-led industrialization 'model' to African economies is not explicitly considered in this chapter.

7   The following discussion draws heavily on Colman and Nixson, 1978, ch. 8.

8   Leff, 1967, distinguishes between the 'demand-diverting' and the 'supply-constraining' effects arising from import limitations. The former effect, by diverting demand from overseas to domestic supplies, stimulates domestic production. 'At the same time, however, lack of raw materials and other inputs from abroad may inhibit the ability of domestic producers to respond elastically to this additional demand for their products . . . for import stringency to generate growth based on import-substitution, the foreign exchange pinch must be limited to the range where demand diversion is present, but supply constraints do not inhibit the domestic production response' (Leff, 1967, pp. 499–500).

9   It is relevant to emphasize at this point that the industrialization process in LDCs has resulted from both the post-Second World War process of decolonization and the desire of the already politically independent states for industrial development *and* the increasingly oligopolistic structure of the developed capitalist economies, which together have resulted in the changed structure of capital exports to LDCs and the tentative emergence of a new international division of labour. On the significance of oligopolistic competition, see Yamin, 1979. For a discussion of the hypothesis that a new international division of labour is in fact emerging, see Szentes, 1971. A systematic discussion of the role of foreign capital in the industrialization process is outside the scope of this chapter. For a broad survey, see Colman and Nixson, 1978, chs 8–10.

10   Raul Prebisch, largely responsible for conceptualizing the ECLA view of development, became an early critic of the actual outcome of the ISI process. See his report to the first UNCTAD, 1964.

11   Chenery's analysis was based on a cross-section regression equation in which per capita value added in each industrial sector was regressed on per capita income and population. He found that, as income grew, the industrial sector grew more rapidly than the rest of the economy, and he distinguished a fairly uniform pattern of change in the production and import of industrial products. For each industry, the positive deviation from proportional (or 'normal') growth was calculated and Chenery concluded that for all sectors: 'The increased share of domestic production in total supply, defined here as import substitution . . . accounts for 50% of industrialization' (Chenery, 1960, p. 641).

12   For a criticism of the usefulness of the *ex post/ex ante* distinction, see Ahmad, 1968.

13   Important contributions have been made by: Steuer and Voivodas, 1965; Morley and Smith, 1970; Fane, 1973; Guillaumont, 1979.

14   It is not clear that the characterization of the growth process as 'distorted' serves any useful analytical purpose, given that it implies that there is some ideal pattern or model against which the actual experience can be compared. Rweyemamu, 1973,

ch. 3, refers to the 'perverse capitalist industrial development model' when discussing the Tanzanian experience. It is 'perverse' because, in its given institutional setting, it is unlikely to lead to self-generating and self-sustaining development, as was the case with classical industrial capitalism. At the same time, however, he admits to the impossibility of classical industrial growth repeating itself in contemporary LDCs (Rweyemamu, 1973, p. 90).

15 Inefficiency can manifest itself in many different forms and one is not necessarily subscribing to the neo-classical paradigm when this term is used.

16 For a discussion of the relationship between ISI and inflation, see Kirkpatrick and Nixson, 1976.

17 Baer, 1972, p. 106, notes that 'the net result of ISI has been to place Latin American countries in a new and more dangerous dependency relationship with the more advanced industrial countries than ever before'. See also Bruton, 1970, pp. 136–7. The economy also becomes extremely vulnerable to import price rises, witness the impact of rising oil prices on the LDCs.

18 Doherty, 1970, tentatively concludes that the balance-of-payments position may deteriorate as a result of ISI, depending on the sectoral composition of the ISI programme and various import propensities. See also Kim, 1974.

19 The ILO (1970) report on Colombia, for example, estimated that basic industrial consumer goods (clothing, furniture, footwear, etc.) had an import content of less than 5%, while other goods (electrical consumer durables) had an import content of about 30%.

20 In a study of 48 manufacturing industries in Pakistan, Soligo and Stern, 1965, found that in 23 industries, value added measured at world prices was negative. Fourteen of these industries were in the consumer goods sector. In a study of the Nigerian textile industry, Ekuerhare, 1978, found that 10 out of the 30 firms investigated had negative value added at world prices. The use of world prices in this type of calculation is not, of course, without controversy.

21 The neo-classical view emphasizes the overvalued exchange rate, the inward-looking nature of ISI, the neglect of the traditional exporting sectors and the consequent lack of incentives for export-led growth. There is undoubtedly some truth in these arguments. Much export pessimism results from the fact that little effort is put into export promotion, thus confirming the initial export pessimism.

22 The more general point is that the industrialization effort may be frustrated by the neglect of, or lack of progress in, other sectors of the economy. The importance of the close economic relationships between industrial and agricultural development in the majority of LDCs cannot be overemphasized.

23 Others (for example, Khan, 1963) have argued that ISI results in 'consumption liberalization', thus reducing savings and hence growth. Wells, 1973, dismisses the argument that the slowing-down in Brazilian growth in the early 1960s was due to the 'exhaustion' of ISI opportunities. Leff, 1967, argues that Brazil's stagnation resulted from constraints imposed by lagging import supplies.

24 These policies included the control of inflation; the elimination of price distortions; the modernization of capital markets; the introduction of incentives to direct resources to areas and sectors considered to be of high priority by the government; the attraction of foreign capital inflows and the use of public funds in infrastructure projects and certain government-owned heavy industries (Baer, 1973).

25 The export-led industrializers have been referred to above. For a discussion of the so-called post-ISI 'model' of development, see: De Pablo, 1977 (Argentina); Thorpe, 1977 (Peru); Berry and Thoumi, 1977 (Columbia); Aspra, 1977 (Mexico). The growing literature on Brazil's recent development experience referred to in the text is also relevant.

26 'Trade should not be regarded as a pace-setter in any relevant development strategy for the developing world but merely as a derivative. The developing countries should first define a viable strategy for attacking their problems of unemployment and mass poverty. Trade policies should be geared to meeting the objectives of such a strategy' (ul Haq, 1973, p. 101).

27 'Failure' is used in this respect to indicate that ISI has not achieved the objectives

of economic development, normatively defined. ISI has not failed if one can show that it has promoted or been consistent with the interests of certain groups or classes within the LDCs. The work of Kemal (1978) on Pakistan is of interest in this respect.

References

Aboyade, O. (1973) 'Advancing tropical african development: a defence of inward-looking strategy', in P. Streeten (ed.).

Ahmad, J. (1968) 'Import substitution and structural change in Indian manufacturing industry 1950–1966', *Journal of Development Studies* (April).

Ahmad, J. (1978) 'Import substitution – a survey of policy issues', *The Developing Economies*, XVI, 4 (December).

Aspra, L. A. (1977) 'Import substitution in Mexico past and present', *World Development*, 5, 1/2.

Bacha, E. E. (1977) 'Issues and evidence on recent Brazilian economic growth', *World Development*, 5, 1/2.

Baer, W. (1972) 'Import substitution and industrialization in Latin America: experiences and interpretations', *Latin American Research Review* (Spring).

Baer, W. (1973) 'The Brazilian boom 1968–72: an explanation and interpretation', *World Development*, 1, 8 (August).

Baer, W. and Maneschi, A. (1971) 'Import substitution, stagnation and structural change: an interpretation of the Brazilian case', *The Journal of Developing Areas* (January).

Berry, A. and Thoumi, F. (1977) 'Import substitution and beyond: Colombia', *World Development*, 5, 1/2.

Bruton, H. J. (1970) 'The import-substitution strategy of economic development: a survey', *Pakistan Development Review*, 10.

Cardoso, F. H. and Faletto, E. (1979) *Dependency and Development in Latin America* (California: University of California Press).

Chenery, H. B. (1960) 'Patterns of industrial growth', *American Economic Review* (September).

Clark, Paul G. (1965) *Development Planning in East Africa* (Nairobi: East African Publishing House).

Colman, D. and Nixson, F. I. (1978) *Economics of Change in Less Developed Countries* (Oxford: Philip Allan).

Desai, P. (1969) 'Alternative measures of import substitution', *Oxford Economic Papers*, n.s., 21, 3 (November).

Diaz-Alejandro, C. F. (1965) 'On the import intensity of import substitution', *Kyklos*, 18.

Doherty, N. (1970) 'Import substitution and the balance of payments', *Eastern African Economic Review*, 2, 2 (December).

Ekuerhare, B. (1978) 'The economic appraisal of import substituting industrialization with special reference to the Nigerian textile industry', University of Manchester, PhD thesis (mimeo.).

Ewing, A. F. (1968) *Industry in Africa* (London: Oxford University Press).

Fane, G. (1973) 'Consistent measures of import substitution', *Oxford Economic Papers*, 25, 2 (July).

Felix, D. (1964) 'Monetarists, structuralists and import-substituting industrialization: a critical appraisal', in W. Baer and I. Kerstenetzky (eds), *Inflation and Growth in Latin America* (Homewood, Ill.: Irwin, 1964).

Felix, D. (1968) 'The dilemma of import substitution – Argentina', in G. Papanek (ed.), *Development Policy – Theory and Practice* (Cambridge, Mass.: Harvard University Press, 1968).

Guillaumont, P. (1979) 'More on consistent measures of import substitution', *Oxford Economic Papers*, 31, 2 (July).

Helleiner, G. K. (1972) *International Trade and Economic Development* (Harmondsworth: Penguin).

Hirschman, A. O. (1968) 'The political economy of import-substituting industrialization in Latin America', *Quarterly Journal of Economics* (February).

ILO (1970) *Towards Full Employment: A Programme for Colombia* (Geneva: International Labour Office).

ILO (1972) *Employment, Incomes and Equality: A Strategy for Increasing Productive Employment in Kenya* (Geneva: International Labour Office).

Islam, N. (1973) 'National import substitution and inward-looking strategies: policies of less developed countries', in P. Streeten (ed.) (1973).

Kemal, A. R. (1978) 'An analysis of industrial efficiency in Pakistan, 1959–60 to 1969–70, University of Manchester, PhD thesis (mimeo).

Khan, A. R. (1963) 'Import substitution, export expansion and consumption liberalisation: a preliminary report', *Pakistan Development Review*, 3.

Kilby, P. (1969) *Industrialization in an Open Economy: Nigeria 1945–1966*, (Cambridge: Cambridge University Press).

Killick, T. (1978) *Development Economics in Action: A Study of Economic Policies in Ghana* (London: Heinemann Educational Books).

Kim, K. S. (1974) 'An interindustry comparison of the employment and balance of payments effects of import substitution in Kenya', *Eastern African Economic Review*, 6, 1 (June).

Kirkpatrick, C. H. and Nixson, F. I. (1976) 'The origins of inflation in less developed countries: a selective review', in M. Parkin and G. Zis (eds), *Inflation in Open Economies*, (Manchester: Manchester University Press, 1976).

Kirkpatrick, C. H. and Nixson, F. I. (eds), *The Industrialization of Less Developed Countries* (Manchester: Manchester University Press, forthcoming).

Langdon, S. (1975), 'Multinational corporations, taste transfer and underdevelopment: a case study from Kenya', *Review of African Political Economy*, 2.

Leff, N. H. (1967), 'Import constraints and development: causes of the recent decline of Brazilian economic growth', *Review of Economics and Statistics*, (November).

Leff, N. H. and Netto, A. D. (1966), 'Import substitution, foreign investment and international disequilibrium in Brazil', *Journal of Development Studies* (April).

Little, I., Scitovsky, T. and Scott, M. (1970), *Industry and Trade in Some*

Developing Countries: A Comparative Study, (London: Oxford University Press).

Maitra, P. (1967), *Import Substitution in East Africa* (Nairobi: Oxford University Press).

Maizels, A. (1963), *Industrial Growth and World Trade* (Cambridge: Cambridge University Press).

Malan, P. S. and Bonalli, R. (1977), 'The Brazilian economy in the seventies: old and new developments', *World Development*, 5, 1/2.

Merhav, M. (1969), *Technological Dependence, Monopoly and Growth* (Oxford: Pergamon).

Morawetz, D. (1974), *Employment implications of industrialization in developing countries: a survey*', *Economic Journal* (September).

Morley, S. A. and Smith, S. W. (1970), 'On the measurement of import substitution', *American Economic Review* (September).

Morley, S. A. and Smith, S. W. (1971), 'Import substitution and foreign investment in Brazil', *Oxford Economic Papers*, 23, 1 (March).

Pablo, J. C. de (1977), 'Beyond import substitution: the case of Argentina', *World Development*, 5, 1/2.

Pearson, D. S. (1969), *Industrial Development in East Africa* (Nairobi: Oxford University Press).

Raj, K. N. and Sen, A. K. (1961), 'Alternative patterns of growth under conditions of stagnant export earnings', *Oxford Economic Papers*, 13, 1 (February).

Robock, S. H. (1970), 'Industrialization through import-substitution or export industries: a false dichotomy', in J. W. Markham and G. F. Papanek (eds), *Industrial Organisation and Economic Growth* (New York: Houghton Mifflin, 1970).

Rweyemamu, J. (1973), *Underdevelopment and Industrialisation in Tanzania. A Study of Perverse Capitalist Industrial Development* (Nairobi: Oxford University Press).

Seidman, A. (1972), *Comparative Development Strategies in East Africa* (Nairobi: East African Publishing House).

Seidman, A. (1974), 'The distorted growth of import substitution industry: the Zambian case', *The Journal of Modern African Studies*, 12, 4.

Singh, A. (1979), 'The "basic needs" approach to development vs the new international economic order: the significance of Third World industrialization', *World Development*, 7, 6 (June).

Soligo, R. and Stern, J. J. (1965), 'Tariff protection, import substitution and investment efficiency', *Pakistan Development Review*, 5 (Summer).

Steel, W. F. (1972), 'Import substitution and excess capacity in Ghana', *Oxford Economic Papers*, n.s., 24, 2 (July).

Steuer, M. D. and Voivodas, C. (1965), 'Import substitution and Chenery's patterns of industrial growth – a further study',*Economica Internazionale*.

Stewart, F. (1976a), 'Kenya: strategies for development', in U. G. Damachi, G. Routh and A. R. E. Ali Taha (eds), *Development Paths in Africa and China* (London: Macmillan, 1976).

Stewart, F. (1976b), 'Capital goods in developing countries', in A. Cairncross and M. Puri (eds), *Employment, Income Distribution and Development Strategy: Problems of the Developing Countries* (London: Macmillan, 1976).

Stewart, F. (1977), *Technology and Underdevelopment* (London: Macmillan).

Stewart, F. and Streeten, P. (1976), 'New strategies for development: poverty, income distribution and growth', *Oxford Economic Papers*, 28, 3 (November).

Stoutjesdijk, E. J. (1967), *Uganda's Manufacturing Sector* (Nairobi: East African Publishing House).

Streeten, P. (ed.) (1973), *Trade Strategies for Development* (London: Macmillan).

Sutcliffe, R. B. (1971), *Industry and Underdevelopment* (Reading, Mass.: Addison-Wesley).

Szentes, T. (1971), *The Political Economy of Underdevelopment* (Budapest: Akademiai Kiado).

Thorp, R. (1977), 'The Post-Import-Substitution Era: The Case of Peru', *World Development*, 5, 1/2.

ul Haq, M. (1973), 'Industrialization and trade policies in the 1970s: developing country alternatives', in P. Streeten (ed.) (1973).

UNCTAD (1964), *Towards a New Trade Policy for Development* (Prebisch Report), (New York: United Nations).

UNECLA (1964), 'The growth and decline of import substitution in Brazil', *Economic Bulletin for Latin America*, 9, 1 (March).

UNIDO (United Nations Industrial Development Organization) (1979), *World Industry since 1960: Progress and Prospects* special issue of the Industrial Development Survey for the Third General Conference of UNIDO (New York: United Nations).

Van Arkadie, B. (1964), 'Import substitution and export promotion as aids to industrialisation in East Africa', *East African Economic Review*, n.s., 1.

Wells, J. (1973), 'Recent developments in Brazilian capitalism', *Bulletin of the Conference of Socialist Economists* (Winter).

Wells, J. (1974), 'Distribution of earnings, growth and the structure of demand in Brazil during the 1960s', *World Development*, 2, 1 (January).

Winston, G. C. (1967), 'Notes on the concept of import substitution', *Pakistan Development Review*, VII (Spring).

World Bank (1978), *Ivory Coast: The Challenge of Success* (Baltimore, Md: Johns Hopkins University Press).

Yamin, M. (1979), 'Direct foreign investment as an instrument of corporate rivalry – theory and evidence from LDCs', Department of Economics, University of Manchester (mimeo.); to be included in Kirkpatrick and Nixson (eds) *The Industrialisation of Less Developed Countries* (Manchester: Manchester University Press, forthcoming).

PART TWO
EAST AFRICA

3   The State and Industrialization in Tanzania

ANDREW COULSON

Introduction

This chapter is a study of the effectiveness of the Tanzanian state in increasing investment in manufacturing, considered in the light of the situation inherited at independence in 1961.

Five years earlier the manufacturing sector consisted of little more than the first-stage processing of crops for export. Between the world wars industrial interests in Britain had prevented nearly all investment in manufacturing for the local market; but meanwhile the settlers in neighbouring Kenya had sufficient autonomy to begin manufacturing in the 1920s, and the continuance of an East African common market enabled them to sell manufactured products to Tanganyika and Uganda as well as Kenya; the resulting imbalance in trade with Kenya worsened in the 1950s and 1960s.

The policy immediately after independence was to offer concessions to private (i.e. multinational) investment. Value added in manufacturing grew at around 10% per annum, but the government was dissatisfied with the amount of investment and with the resources that were leaving the country in the form of repatriated profits. From the mid-1960s it created institutions both to retain the surplus locally (nationalized banks and insurance companies) and to it invest it productively (manufacturing and agricultural parastatals). The process gathered momentum after the 1967 Arusha Declaration, when, with the assistance of capital inflows from abroad, capital formation soon exceeded 20% of GDP; 15% of this investment was in manufacturing.

The value added in manufacturing continued to rise, but at declining rates in the 1970s. There were several reasons for this. The country experienced balance-of-payments problems, particularly in 1974 and 1975, due to rises in the world price of oil, and internal disruption caused by the villagization programme; many of the new industries were import-dependent and had problems obtaining foreign exchange; there were shortages of water and electricity, caused by the rapid growth of demand both from industries and

Table 3.1 *Industrial establishments and manufacturers in Tanganyika, 1914–45*

	1914	1921	1931	1939	1945
Agricultural Processing for Export					
Cotton ginneries	n.a.	12	29	34	35 (3,937)
Sisal decortication	n.a.	n.a.	9	120	126 (n.a.)
Tea factories	—	—	1	4	6 (n.a.)
Coffee curing	—	—	—	10	11 (n.a.)
Rubber factories	—	—	—	—	12 (n.a.)
Meat products	—	—	1	—	—
Agricultural processing for internal use					
Flour mills	4	4	32	55	103 (1,314)
Rice mills	—	—	17	24	
Oil mills/soap factories	4	6	27	27	72 (590)
Copra drying	—	—	—	3	5 (100)
Sugar/jaggery	—	—	5	3	21 (n.a.)
Creameries/ghee factories	—	—	—	77	312 (1,721)
Tannery	—	—	—	—	1 (310)
Bacon curing	—	—	1	1	3 (69)
Manufacture for local market					
Salt	2	2	7	6	10 (1,084)
Cigarette and tobacco factories	1	1	1	4	4 (325)
Bakeries	—	—	—	38	44 (190)
Ice and soda water	3	3	46	46	30 (133)
Beer	—	—	—	1	1 (130)
Sawmills	—	—	18	22	29 (1,696)
Furniture makers	2	2	22	48	30 (210)
Fibreboard factory	—	—	—	—	1 (300)
Lime burning	1	2	13	11	14 (732)
Pottery	—	1	—	—	—
Jewellers	14	14	17	7	10 (20)
Printers	2	2	10	10	11 (75)
Miscellaneous					
Power stations	—	—	—	6	6 (201)
Others	—	—	12	26	8 (218)
TOTAL	33	49	269	583	905

Note: The figures in brackets show numbers of employees. For the factories with figures available, the average number of employees in 1945 was 18·4.
Source: Adapted from *Tanganyika Territory Blue Books*, 1921, 1931, 1939, 1945.

from a rising urban population; and last but not least, many plants were poorly conceived, wrongly sited, mechanically inefficient and so import-dependent that at world prices they contributed little value added. Some of the problems (such as inexperienced management) could be expected to improve over time; others were irreversible, and to that extent much of the investment was wasted.

Manufacturing Before Independence

In the nineteenth century those who lived in the land area of present-day Tanzania possessed craft skills in iron production, the making of iron implements, and in cotton cultivation, spinning and weaving.[1] But during the period of German rule, from about 1890 to 1914, local manufacture was largely replaced by imports. The Germans invested in agriculture and in the infrastructure needed to transport agricultural produce to the coast, but their commitment to manufacturing was minimal, as can be seen from the 1914 list of 'industries' shown in Table 3.1.

There was little significant change until the mid-1950s. It is apparent from Table 3.1 that the industrial establishments started between the two world wars were mainly associated with agricultural processing for export (34 cotton ginneries, 120 sisal factories, 4 tea factories, and 10 coffee curing factories), or were small-scale operations preparing food products or building materials for the local market. By 1945 there were six power stations, but the largest factories outside agricultural processing for export were a tannery, a fibreboard factory, and (inevitably, and depending on imported barley) the brewery.

Between the wars colonial policy in Tanganyika was to discourage industrial enterprises unless they were an essential aspect of agricultural production for export. Brett has shown how proposals by Japanese interests to start a match factory, and by British businessmen to process sisal forward into sisal rope, were prevented by British opposition, in contrast to the encouragement and government money given to 'Meat Rations Ltd', on the grounds that the latter would create a market for cattle in the Lake Province, and encourage destocking.[2]

Even the depression of the 1930s, which drastically lowered the world prices of agricultural exports and the income available to the government, was not allowed to stimulate industrialization in Tanganyika. Instead government expenditure was cut and government campaigns (including an element of coercion) succeeded in expanding agricultural production to such effect that the volume of imports of textiles and shoes hardly fell (Table 3.2).

In Kenya, on the other hand, settlers began processing agricultural products

Table 3.2 *Imports of (a) cotton piece goods and (b) boots and shoes, 1925–37.*

	Cotton piece goods		Boots and shoes	
	Value (£'000)	Volume ('000,000 yards)	Value (£'000)	Volume ('000 pairs)
1912	661			
1925	905	27	10	44
1931	443	28	14	203
1937	715	46	29	397

Source: Tanganyika Trade Reports: Die Deutschen Schutzgebiete 1912–1913 (following C. Leubuscher: *Tanganyika Territory: A Study of Economic Policy under Mandate* (London: Oxford University Press, 1944), p. 206, with 20 DM = £1.

Table 3.3 *Tanganyika's trade with Kenya and Uganda 1951 and 1958 (£ thousand)*

	1951	1958
Exports		
Tobacco, unmanufactured	123	440
Coconut oil	119	255
Wood, lumber and cork	142	(98)
Beans and peas, etc.	60	114
Hides, skins and fur skins	89	5
Electric energy	n.a.	70
Sugar and sugar preparations	—	4
Other	618	1,618
TOTAL	1,151	2,603
Imports		
Cigarettes	1,288	3,089
Beer	111	556
Wheat flour	349	565
Clothing and footwear	285	570
Manufacture of metals	n.a.	
Tea	144	371
Sugar and sugar preparations	216	457
Cement	—	565
Other	1,232	
TOTAL	3,625	9,038

Note: Exports are for use in Kenya and Uganda and imports for use in Tanganyika.
Source: *The Economic Development of Tanganyika* (Baltimore, Md: Johns Hopkins University Press for the IBRD, 1961) p. 474.

in the 1920s and ensured that East Africa remained a free trade area. Protective tariffs were imposed on a range of agricultural imports coming from outside East Africa as early as 1923, but there were no tariffs on the Kenya/ Tanganyika or Kenya/Uganda borders.[3] The main railway from the coast to Uganda passed through Nairobi, with branch lines to Moshi and Arusha in northern Tanganyika, and to Lake Victoria at Kisumu, linked by lake ferry to the Tanganikan ports of Mwanza, Bukoba and Musoma. Nairobi was thus an ideal centre from which to serve Kenya, Uganda and northern Tanganyika. Since the policy in Tanganyika was not to industrialize, the effect of the tariff policy was 'to deplete her revenue and impoverish her citizens by protecting the products of her neighbours'.[4] The imbalance was noted by the Permanent Mandates Commission in 1932,[5] and by Catherine Leubuscher writing in 1944.[6] By 1951 imports into Tanganyika from the rest of East Africa were more than three times as valuable as exports (Table 3.3).

The Korean War of 1949–53 created shortages of nearly all raw materials, which meant higher prices and increased earnings of foreign exchange for colonies such as Tanganyika. At the same time there were shortages of consumer goods in the capitalist centres, including Britain. Since consumer goods could not easily be supplied from Britain, the British authorities were prepared to encourage import substitution in their African colonies.

Tanganyika in particular experienced shortages of consumer goods in the years after the Second World War not least because of the heavy British government investment in the groundnuts scheme.[7] Despite this, import substitution did not get under way until the mid-1950s, and even then it was very slow. Comparing the list of industries in 1955[8] with that shown in Table 3.1 for 1945, the figures show a general expansion of activity without great change in structure. On the export side, the number of cotton ginneries remained the same (though they operated with only just over half as much labour as ten years earlier); the number of sisal decorticators had jumped from 126 to 232, employing 23,192 workers; there were eleven tea factories; rubber production had ceased, but tobacco processing had increased, and three cashew processing factories employed 307 workers.

As far as the local market was concerned, the number of flour and rice mills had more than tripled, the number of oil mills or soap factories had nearly doubled, and there had been spectacular expansion in woodworking. The first sugar factory had been built, but the fibreboard factory had closed and lime burning no longer appeared in the statistics. There were twenty power stations.

The most noticeable difference between the figures for 1945 and those for 1955 is the appearance of many workshops for maintenance and repair – of agricultural equipment, aircraft, bicycles, boats, electrical equipment, guns, typewriters, but above all motor vehicles (174 premises, employing 3,500 workers) and 'general engineering' (75 premises employing 2,012 workers). This was a consequence of the much-increased use of the petrol and diesel engine after the war.

The 1955 figures also show the beginnings of manufacturing, mainly for the local market. There were two aluminiumware factories, employing 22 workers between them: an 'iron and steel rolling mill', with 44 workers; a plant making tin cans with 218 workers (the main user of the cans, Tanganyika Packers, packing corn beef for export, was still under construction) and two small factories making industrial gases. There was one 'chemical products manufacturer' with 16 workers, a pharmaceutical 'factory' with 13 workers, and a paint mixing plant with 51 workers. There were twenty-six printers with 617 workers and twenty jewellers with 95 workers. The textile industry consisted of one tiny weaving mill with 28 workers, a dyeing and bleaching plant with 28 workers, and 795 tailors employing 1,812 workers – remarkable figures for a country one of whose main exports was cotton. These firms were owned either by Asians (the largest built with capital moved in from Kenya or Uganda), or by isolated foreign businessmen from a variety of non-African countries, or, in a few cases, by multinational corporations, mainly those who had already established factories in Kenya, or who had shares held by influential Kenyan settlers.[9]

By 1958 not much had changed, although there were now three chemical manufacturers, employing 91 workers, two breweries, two dyeing and bleaching works, and total employment in registered factories of 74,437, compared with 61,122 three years earlier. By 1963 there were six chemical plants (138 workers), four rubber factories, three plastics factories and three breweries.[10] The aluminium rolling mill employed 250 workers, and the textile industry had expanded to three weaving mills (687 workers), five dyeing works

(479 workers), a blanket factory employing 190 workers, a garment manufacturer employing 350 workers, and almost a thousand tailors and dress-
makers employing 2,500 workers between them. The manufacturing sector
remained incredibly weak, although the official figures credited it with
providing 3·5% of the GDP at factor cost.[11]

Independence and State Intervention

During the Second World War world economic power shifted decisively to the
United States, which was nearly self-sufficient in raw materials and did not
depend on colonies. It dominated its competitors through its multinational
corporations (which had the resources to buy or create subsidiaries in other
countries whenever the conditions of production made this profitable) and
through its influence over the international lending agencies (notably the IMF
and the World Bank). During the war chemical substitutes were produced,
mainly from oil, for cotton, sisal, rubber and other agricultural raw materials.
Oil and food grains became the strategic primary products, and neither was
exported, in the main, from colonies. Britain and France could see no
economic necessity to retain colonies, while the United States, itself a colony
that had successfully gained UDI, encouraged nationalist movements. India
gained independence in 1947, Ghana was promised it in 1951 and achieved it
in 1957, the Sudan became independent in 1956; Tanganyika, which was given
independence in 1961, was quickly followed by the rest of British and French
Africa.

The Korean War boom was the last occasion when the traditional raw
material exports were in genuine short supply. Thereafter given tonnages of
most of the traditional exports would purchase less and less manufactured
goods.[12] The newly independent states in Africa had little chance of competing
successfully in export markets for manufactured goods (other than their
processed agricultural products). Since they had no capital goods sectors they
were forced to import machinery, inputs for their newly created import
substitution industries and many consumer goods, and to seek capital from
overseas if they were to make many new investments.

The United Republic of Tanzania, created by the merger of Tanganyika and
Zanzibar in 1964, was in a particularly weak position. Its industrial sector was
tiny, and in the 1960s it became even more dependent on Kenya (Table 3.4).
There was, however, no shortage of industrial investments that could be made,
as the Arthur D. Little Report, based on orthodox ideas of input substitution
and export processing, had made clear.[13] Despite government willingness to
offer protection, and a Foreign Investment Protection Act which gave
guarantees of compensation if assets were nationalized, inflows of capital
from abroad were less than the profits being taken out (Table 3.5). The amount
of foreign investment remained small. Rweyemamu quotes figures showing
the book value of British investments in Tanzania rising from £8·0 million in
1960 to only £9·3 million in 1965, compared with £43·2 million in Kenya, £62
million in Rhodesia, and £391·7 million in South Africa.[14]

In order to speed up the rate of investment the government took three
actions. The first was to begin renegotiation of the customs union with Kenya.

Table 3.4 *Mainland Tanzania's trade with Kenya and Uganda, 1962, 1967, 1972, 1977 (million shs)*

Principal Commodities	1962	1967	1972	1977[a]
Exports				
Meat and meat preparations	1·6	2·3	1·3	—
Cereal and cereal preparations	5·0	2·8	3·3	—
Dairy products and margarine	3·4	0·6	1·0	—
Beans, peas and other legumes	5·7	6·4	8·5	—
Other food products	8·9	7·2	11·8	2·9
Tobacco, unmanufactured	1·3	5·7	15·8	2·7
Vegetable oils	8·1	8·4	1·3	—
Chemicals	0·8	2·6	3·6	1·6
Cotton piece goods	1·6	1·5	20·2	0·2
Clothing	0·2	1·3	2·7	2·3
Footwear	3·8	2·1	0·3	—
Aluminium circles	—	5·4	10·6	2·8
Other manufactured goods	11·8	11·9	23·8	12·9
Other commodities	12·6	24·8	28·8	5·1
TOTAL	64·8	83·0	133·1	30·5
Imports				
Meat and meat preparations	7·7	4·6	2·6	—
Cereal and cereal preparations	23·4	20·6	14·4	9·1
Dairy products[b]	7·3	15·7	39·5	2·4
Other food products	27·4	22·6	30·7	5·6
Beer	12·6	5·6	6·6	—
Petroleum products	0·2	35·1	31·1	6·2
Chemicals[c]	9·0	21·1	43·7	13·5
Cement	11·3	10·9	9·6	1·4
Cotton piece goods	18·4	16·9	0·5	—
Clothing	14·4	3·0	5·0	0·2
Footwear	10·3	6·5	7·6	—
Soap	11·7	5·8	12·2	0·1
Other manufactured goods	35·3	68·8	79·9	39·8
Other commodities	52·8	42·7	48·1	99·1
TOTAL	241·8	280·1	331·5	177·4

Notes:
[a] Provisional figures.
[b] Milk, eggs, margarine and shortening.
[c] Excluding soaps.
— Nil or insignificant.
Source: Bureau of Statistics, *Economic Survey 1977–8*, tables 11 and 12.

The 1964 Kampala Agreement identified certain industries to be established in Uganda or Tanzania to serve the whole East African market, and contained other provisions designed to promote industrial investment in Uganda and Tanzania.[15] Although the agreement was not ratified by Kenya, and investments were made in Kenya contrary to it, it did have some influence on the thinking of the multinationals, who established radio assembly, cigarette manufacture, cement production, a shoe factory and expanded aluminium

Table 3.5 *Gross profit outflows and net inflows of private capital, 1961–8 (million shs)*

Year	Profit outflows	Capital inflow
1961	−71·2	+50
1962	−73·0	+58
1963	−123·0	+155
1964	−93·0	+79
1965	−110·0	−6
1966	−114·0	+138
1967	−159·0	−66
1968	−114·0	+76
TOTAL	−857·2	+484

Source: J. Rweyemamu, 'The political economy of foreign investments in the underdeveloped countries', *The African Review*, 1, 1 (1971), p. 115.

products and sugar production in the 1960s, and a tyre factory in the early 1970s.

The second government action was to take control of the financial institutions that were essential intermediaries in taking surplus out of the country.[16] A central bank was created in 1966. Exchange control had been imposed on transfers outside East Africa in 1965, although it was not till 1971 that this was permanently extended to include transfers to Kenya and Uganda as well. In 1963 and 1965 the Tanganyika Insurance Company and the Tanzania Bank of Commerce were created, and then in 1967, following the Arusha Declaration, all insurance business in the country was confined by law to the National Insurance Corporation, and all the commercial banks were national-ized and merged into a single National Bank of Commerce. Despite initial management problems, these organizations were soon able to make large sums of money available for government or parastatal investment.

The government also created the Tanzania Rural Development Bank, which arranged credit for small-scale rural producers, and the Tanzania Investment Bank, which lent to medium-scale industrial and agricultural projects including many operated by parastatals. Both these banks were able to receive credits from multilateral and bilateral aid donors in the West, and to on-lend them to private producers or parastatals. Foreign grants and credits, nearly all on highly concessional terms, increased after the Arusha Declaration. The reasons for this are hard to untangle: donors were impressed with Tanzania's commitment to 'self-reliance', but also with its strategic position in Southern Africa, and the need to counter the propaganda value of China's agreement to build a railway from Dar es Salaam to the Zambian copperbelt. Local direct and indirect taxes were also increased, and the consequence of this, coupled with the new borrowing, was that capital formation rose to over 20% of GDP by 1970; by 1974 more than 60% of this capital formation was financed from abroad.[17]

This made possible the third government action, a greatly accelerated involvement in production through newly created 'parastatals'. In 1964 the Tanganyika Development Corporation was merged with the older Tanganyika

Agricultural Corporation to form the National Development Corporation, 'to facilitate and promote the economic development of Tanganyika'.[18] The new corporation also took over profitable government shareholdings in Williamson's Diamonds, Nyanza Salt Mines and Tanganyika (Meat) Packers, giving it an investment income of about 1 million pounds per year. In early 1966 the corporation received a cabinet instruction to use its position to acquire control of key areas of the economy.[19]

In 1967, also following the Arusha Declaration, NDC took majority shareholding in eight subsidiary companies of multinational corporations. This was the beginning of a wave of purchases, which included agricultural assets and property as well as manufacturing and commerce. Expansions of existing companies, and the creation of new ventures, meant that parastatal assets rose from shs 852 million at the end of 1966 to shs 1,542 million a year later, and then to shs 3,456 million by the end of 1971.[20] There was a proliferation of holding company parastatals (i.e. parastatals with shareholdings in other parastatals), as the National Development Corporation was split into four in 1969, and then into more as the newly formed agricultural and industrial parastatals themselves divided. Parastatal trading companies were established in each region, and 'development corporations' in each district. By 1974 there were 139 parastatals, and the number was still increasing.[21] Their role in the economy (and that of the public services which also expanded during the period) is captured by the figures in Table 3.6.

Table 3.6   *Regular wage employment by sector*

	1969	1974
Parastatal	42,522	90,220
Private	107,614	101,132
Public services	75,444	171,289

Source: P. Collier, 'Labour Market Allocation and Income Distribution'; *Tanzania – Basic Economic Report*, Annex III, IBRD, June 1977, table 3.

The manufacturing parastatals underwent a particularly rapid expansion, with assets rising from only shs 111 million in 1966 to shs 1,079 million in 1971, or 31% of total parastatal assets. Inevitably most of this (70%) went into the establishment of new firms, but several of these were extremely capital-consuming – 74% of the assets of the manufacturing parastatals in 1971 was owned by just nine firms (Table 3.7).[22]

Table 3.7   *Role of parastatals in manufacturing, 1960–75*

	1966	1969	1972	1975
Number of enterprises	13	31	43	47
Sales (shs million)	132	604	1,301	2,669
Value added	27	167	380	695
% of sector	9%	35%	47%	n.a.
Wages and salaries (shs million)	12	71	150	318
% of sector	10%	36%	49%	n.a.
Investment (shs million)	20	60	128	202
% of sector	13%	38%	39%	n.a.

Source: Bureau of Statistics.

Industrial Performance

It is not easy to interpret the macroeconomic data for the industrial sector. The figures for value added in the national accounts are often inconsistent with information from the (annual) survey of industrial production, and some of the published figures for employment are suspect because of difficulties in recording casual or daily paid labour, and doubt about the size of the informal sector. The most reliable figures are generally conceded to be those derived from the survey of industrial production, which covers firms employing ten workers or more, and for which data were collected (by the Labour Department, as part of its function of inspecting factories) even in colonial times.[23]

The data at constant prices are summarized in Table 3.8. At first sight the figures are impressive. They show value added in manufacturing and handicrafts rising two and a half times between 1964 and 1977, at a compound growth rate of 7·5% per annum, so that by 1977 the sector accounted for 9·5% of the GDP at factor cost. Wage employment in manufacturing rose even faster, from 23,583 in 1964 to 81,098 in 1977. Using the more reliable figures

Table 3.8 *Wage employment, value added and investment in manufacturing at constant (1966) prices*

Year	Wage employment in manufacturing[a]	Value added in manufacturing and handicrafts ('000,000 shs)[b]	Value added in manufacturing ('000,000 shs)[c]	Investment in manufacturing ('000,000 shs)[d]
1964	23,583	394	n.a.	n.a.
1965	25,729	446	227	n.a.
1966	29,890	525	295	153
1967	31,186	572	319	175
1968	35,359	611	357	204
1969	40,323	672	430	151
1970	43,417	716	485	281
1971	55,158	784	532	312
1972	55,389	850	599	240
1973	59,336	888	644	223
1974	64,921	903	705	n.a.
1975	74,135*	903	634	n.a.
1976*	73,907*	961	695	n.a.
1977*	81,098*	1013	n.a.	n.a.

Note:
* Estimated.
Sources:
[a] *Economic Surveys*, various years.
[b] *Economic Surveys*, various years, national accounts.
[c] Data for manufacturing industries employing ten or more workers, derived from the census of production, and found in *Economic Surveys* (1973–4, table 51, and 1977–8, table 48) deflated by the implicit deflator for manufacturing and handicrafts in the national accounts.
[d] Data from the Bureau of Statistics, deflated by the investment deflator for manufacturing in the national accounts, and given in the IBRD 1977 Report, table 3.

Figure 3.1   *Value added in manufacturing and handicrafts, 1960–1977*

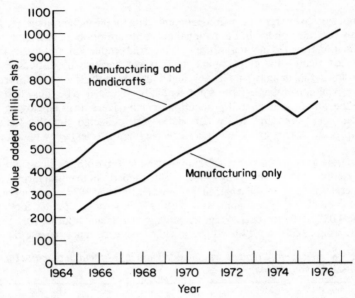

Source: Table 3.8

for industries employing ten or more workers, value added rose from shs 227 million in 1965 to 695 million in 1976, at a growth rate of 10·7% per annum.

But a closer examination of these figures suggests that not all was well, and that neither labour nor capital was being used productively. Value added per worker declined from shs 16,707 in 1964 to shs 12,491 in 1977 (at constant prices), while there was a rapid increase in capital investment in manufacturing in the early 1970s, which did not lead to an increased rate of growth of value added in the years which followed. Indeed if the value added figures are plotted on a graph against time (Figure 3.1), it can be seen that the residual (presumably) associated with handicrafts did not grow in the period, while both the figures for 'manufacturing and handicrafts' and for 'manufacturing industries employing ten workers or more' show approximately equal increases of around shs 50 million per year. In percentage terms this implies constantly declining growth rates over the period, e.g. from 13% between 1964 and 1965 down to 5% between 1976 and 1977 for manufacturing and handicrafts, and from 30% between 1965 and 1966 down to 10% between 1975 and 1976 for the industries employing ten workers or more.

In order to shed more light on these figures, a first step is to examine production figures for specific industries. Up-to-date data are published by the Bank of Tanzania for most of the important industries (regrettably excluding tyres, glass bottles and jars, cooking oil and shelled cashew nuts). These figures are reproduced in Table 3.9.

Many of the increases are striking. Textile production rose from 14 million square metres in 1966 to 83 million in 1978; beer production from 16 million litres in 1966 to 86 million in 1978; cement from 147,000 tonnes to 272,000;

Table 3.9 Production in selected industries

Commodity	Unit	1966	1967	1968	1969	1970	1971	1972	1973	1974	1975	1976	1977	1978
Textiles	sq.m	14,315	14,497	28,871	46,260	58,412	67,008	74,136	80,763	86,399	87,435	82,716	77,232	83,456
Beer	litres	15,816	23,275*	31,185*	33,140*	38,601*	53,915*	64,823*	62,234	63,659	64,264	69,511	75,129	85,764
Cigarettes	million	2,049	2,044	2,137	2,336	2,599	2,923	3,285	2,890	4,649	3,511	3,625	4,064	4,359
Cement	metric tonnes	—	146,910	156,338	167,632	176,826	179,313	236,956	314,000	296,000	266,000	244,339	246,500	272,000
Petroleum	metric tonnes	463,143	642,150	637,393	626,403	684,151	716,524	763,083	731,000	753,000	669,000	746,423	610,586	590,000
Iron sheets	metric tonnes	11,987	13,265	13,261	13,516	17,484	21,869	20,800	20,800	26,000	25,617	25,943	27,506	30,183
Enamelware	pieces	5,306	3,841	4,881	5,608	5,436	5,561	4,267	4,150	1,378	2,657	2,183	2,838	2,331
Blankets	sq.m	3,444	3,584	3,577	3,644	4,154	4,077	4,583	5,476	2,686	4,309	3,676	3,514	2,706
Fishnets	metric tonnes	109	108	127	148	303	286	229	524	463	210	248	528	n.a.
Aluminium	metric tonnes	2,666	1,524	2,073	2,323	2,701	3,427	3,602	3,332	3,660	3,247	3,446	4,005	4,048
Sisal ropes	metric tonnes	10,332	15,126	16,718	18,724	20,404	23,138	22,575	25,354	29,496	25,492	42,377	36,535	31,423
Pyrethrum extract	metric tonnes	203	291	190	177	110	177	204	156	148	189	138	128	62
Wheat flour	metric tonnes	40,351	41,820	42,916	42,075	43,119	50,002	47,459	51,979	34,194	35,485	72,690	80,975	87,940
Canned meat	metric tonnes	9,310	9,673	6,824	6,988	7,980	8,362	4,878	1,401	4,740	2,193	1,650	580	764
Batteries	pieces	—	—	5,543	11,278	15,026	24,012	36,552	45,049	48,001	50,301	57,870	64,664	70,914
Shoes	pairs	—	—	1,490	2,200	2,100	1,600	2,457	2,320	2,800	2,700	3,689	6,331	6,363
Rolled steel	metric tonnes	—	—	—	—	—	—	—	4,776	8,591	9,298	10,500	11,912	16,423
Chibuku	litres	—	—	—	—	—	—	—	7,092	6,203	9,612	10,365	13,560	15,226
Fertilizer	metric tonnes	—	—	—	—	—	—	—	32,594	58,778	59,327	42,146	36,886	44,443
Konyagi	cases	—	—	—	—	—	—	—	56,127	42,500	52,200	52,966	60,333	50,233

Note: * Beer and chibuku.
Source: Bank of Tanzania Economic Bulletin (March and December 1978), table 27.

shoes from 1·5 million pairs per annum to 6 million; rolled steel from 5,000 tonnes (in 1973) to 16,000. Yet the loss of dynamism in the 1970s is also clearly shown. Textile production reached its maximum in 1975; cigarettes in 1974; cement in 1973; refined petroleum in 1972; enamelware in 1969; blankets in 1973; and fertilizer production in 1975. Even beer production managed to stagnate between 1972 and 1975.

Parastatal performance was worse than that of the private sector. Although more capital-intensive than the private sector firms, the parastatals managed, in 1971, to add less value added per employee, and to pay higher wages.[24] Clark also found differences between the parastatal firms established before the Arusha Declaration and those established after the Declaration up till the end of 1971: the post-Arusha firms were more capital-intensive (both within each sector, and because of the sectors chosen), very much more intensive in their use of imports (74% of input was imported, compared with 30% for the older firms), and each unit of labour contributed less than half as much value added as in the older firms.[25]

Given this import dependence, it is not suprising that capacity utilization fell once foreign exchange was limited. Wangwe studied capacity utilization in thirty-nine manufacturing firms in 1974 and 1975, and his most significant conclusion was that 56% of the firms had problems securing foreign exchange, and that 60% of those imported 80% or more of their material inputs.[26]

Barker, Bhagavan, Collande and Wield studied twenty-eight factories in 1975, including a number of the largest parastatal firms. They too reported highly significant differences between firms started between 1961 and 1967 and firms started between 1967 and 1975. In 1973 the older firms generated domestic savings valued at 32% of their capital stock, while the newer firms saved less than 4%. Nearly 80% of the value added in the older firms was retained within the country, but only 50% of the value added in the more recent firms. 'The conclusion is that the post-Arusha period is characterized by industrial investments which are efficient vehicles only for transferring surplus outside the national economy.'[27] They also showed, by a careful allocation of production to three categories ('mass consumption', 'luxury consumption' and 'export production') that only 37% of production was directed to the production of the goods consumed by the mass of the population. Only 31% of the investment between 1966 and 1972 was for mass needs, and only 21% of the estimated expenditure between 1972 and 1975. Most of the factories were not expecting to change the balance of their production, but four were expecting to increase the proportion of exports, while three were expanding production of luxury goods – polyester textiles (based on imported raw materials), fashion shoes and strip matches; Philips Electronics was decreasing the proportion of the cheapest one-band radio sets. They concluded that 'there is little or no evidence that any redistribution of resources has taken place, either towards integrating the economy, or towards a rapid increase in production of goods to satisfy the basic needs of the workers and peasants'.[28]

Finally, in a number of important cases low productivity of capital and/or labour can be documented directly. Clark comments that the capital intensity of the automated bakery was greater than that of the oil refinery.[29] The fertilizer factory, the country's most expensive industrial investment, was dogged by a series of problems, and operated at less than half its designed capacity, with all its chemical inputs imported.[30] Cement production failed to rise despite large investments in the Dar es Salaam plant. Investment in a new system for evaporating brine to produce salt proved abortive and had to be largely abandoned, as did the cashew nut processing plant near Mtwara. Even though the labour-intensive Friendship Textile Mill was more profitable than the capital-intensive Mwatex, the government based its expansion plans on the latter.[31] In these cases capital was invested in such a way that almost certainly little return can be expected from it in future. The evidence of the foreign exchange dependence of the post-1967 investment, plus this evidence of the simple waste of resources, is sufficient to explain the figures of declining productivity in manufacturing.

An Assessment

It remains to attempt an assessment of what took place. Accepting the structuralist argument[32] that an industrial sector is essential in a country such as Tanzania, to achieve both growth and self-reliance, what could have been done? Given the almost non-existent starting point in (say) 1955, the relative strength of Nairobi and Mombasa, and the discouraging experiences of the first years of independence, it seems unlikely that there would have been rapid industrial investment if the government had not promoted it. This would have been even more the case in the 1970s, when world competition increased and Tanzania's balance-of-payments position worsened.

On the other hand, the managerial resources available to the National Development Corporation and the parastatals created subsequently were minimal. As a result they were forced to depend for management on foreigners or foreign companies, as well as being utterly dependent on imported technology.

Many poor contracts were signed. The early management agreements were particularly weak, and gave the foreign managements a great deal of freedom.[33] L. le Van Hall gives a list of no less than ten *parastatals* which were discovered taking money out of Tanzania through transfer pricing – one presumes that in most cases the Tanzanian board members or executives were ignorant of what was going on.[34] In wishing to create factories fast they were obviously vulnerable to the lures of turnkey projects (such as the bakery, the fertilizer factory and many others) and to suppliers' credits, with very little certainty that they were getting value for money. Even multinational investors with small shareholdings tended to maximize their short-term profits through profit on machinery sales, rather than their long-term profit through production over time.

The government recognized most of the problems, but was constantly late in dealing with them. The very large parastatals were split up to make them more accountable. Attempts were made to control credit to parastatals, but only after a massive increase in lending in 1970. Import controls were introduced (but then waived for firms that depended on imports for production). Price rises were only allowed once documentation was presented showing that costs had risen. The employment of high-level manpower, and the wages it could be paid, were limited. A 'standing committee on

74 THE STATE AND INDUSTRIALIZATION IN TANZANIA

management agreements', with strong legal representation, had to approve management agreements before they could be legally binding. The General Superintendance Company was employed to check the prices of goods about to be imported before they were shipped, in an attempt to limit transfer pricing. But in all these cases the problems were acute before the controls were instituted; and there was a danger that taken together the controls were so restrictive that they created very real problems for management, so that by the end of the 1970s there were pressures for them to be relaxed.[35]

Attempts were made to use workers' organizations to control the worst excesses of management; this philosophy appeared in a few much-quoted clauses of the 1971 *Mwongozo*, or TANU Guidelines.[36] The newly stabilized working class certainly showed itself articulate, in many cases more so than the Tanzanian managers who had much to fear from a cultural revolution in which workers exposed and discussed their failures.[37] The workers who in 1973 took over the Mount Carmel rubber factory threatened the continuation of any foreign investment; so these workers were arrested and dismissed and in the months which followed shopfloor initiative in almost all factories was crushed.[38]

Last, but not least, there was a commitment to industrialization but no mechanism for ensuring that individual industrial investments interlocked and made the best use of locally available resources. In neither the First Five-Year Development Plan (1964–9) nor the second (which began in 1969 and was extended to run till 1976) was there a coherent strategy. This meant that anyone who could make a persuasive case on paper for a particular factory could usually get it approved and financed. The Ministries of Finance and Planning disliked much of what was planned, but they were often without the means to stand up to the vested interests – local and foreign – who argued for particular projects.[39]

In retrospect, it is clear that industrial investment should have been more selective; planned with a view to the integration of the economy, and to lessen import dependence; that much greater care should have been taken with machinery contracts; and that an opportunity was lost in which to make use of the expertise and awareness of the working class. Even if these policies had been followed, industrialization would not have been easy in the world conditions of the 1970s. As an oil importer, and with few raw materials, Tanzania had little to offer world markets. There was no chance of industrialization in the hostile conditions of the capitalist world unless the state could avoid the unproductive investments[40] which characterized its industrial strategy in the 1970s.

Notes

I am grateful for comments by Steve Curry and Manfred Bienefield on earlier drafts of this chapter, even though I have not been able to accept all their suggestions.

1 H. Kjekshus, *Ecology Control and Economic Development in East African History* (London: Heinemann Educational Books, 1977), pp. 80–92, 105–110.
2 E. A. Brett, *Colonialism and Underdevelopment in East Africa* (London: Heinemann Educational Books, 1973), pp. 269–273; R. A. Austen *North-Western*

Tanzania under German and British Rule (New Haven, Conn.: Yale University Press 1968), pp. 195 and 242.

3   C. Leubuscher, *Tanganyika Territory: A Study of Economic Policy under Mandate* (London: Oxford University Press, 1944), pp. 103–5.

4   Sir S. Armitage-Smith, *Report on a Financial Mission to Tanganyika* Cmd 4182 (London: HMSO, 1933), p. 25.

5   See *Tanganyika Territory Blue Book*, 1932, Appendix VII.

6   Leubuscher, op. cit., p. 112 *et seq.*

7   See, for example, Alan Wood, *The Groundnut Affair* (London: Bodley Head, 1950).

8   *Annual Report for the Labour Department*, 1955, pp. 76–7, on which this and the subsequent paragraphs are based.

9   M. Honey 'Asian industrial activities in Tanganyika', Social Science Conference Paper, Dar es Salaam, 1973, pp. 11–16.

10   *Annual Report of the Labour Department*, 1958, pp. 75–7, and 1963, pp. 50–2.

11   *Background to the Budget: An Economic Survey, 1967–68* (Dar es Salaam: Government Printer, 1967), table 2.

12   The term of trade for Tanzania declined by 15% between 1964 and 1967, and by another 15% between 1967 and 1972, but recovered somewhat in the period 1973–7, despite the rises in the world price of oil.

13   Arthur D. Little Inc., *Tanganyika Industrial Development* (Dar es Salaam and Boston, 1961).

14   J. Rweyemamu, *Underdevelopment and Industrialization in Tanzania* (Nairobi: Oxford University Press, 1973), p. 41.

15   ibid., pp. 45–6, 118–19.

16   J. Loxley, 'Financial planning and control in Tanzania', in J. Rweyemamu, J. Loxley, J. Wicken and C. Nyirabu (eds), *Towards Socialist Planning*, (Dar es Salaam: Tanzania Publishing House, 1972), pp. 59–60. Also J. Loxley, 'Structural change in the monetary system of Tanzania', in L. Cliffe and J. Saul (eds), *Socialism in Tanzania*, Vol. 2 (Nairobi: East African Publishing House, 1973), pp. 102–111.

17   Based on figures in the IBRD *Tanzania – Basic Economic Report*, December 1977, tables 6 and 8.

18   K. E. Svendson, 'Decision making in the National Development Corporation,' in L. Cliffe and J. Saul (eds), *Socialism in Tanzania: An Interdisciplinary Reader*, Vol. 2 (Nairobi: East African Publishing House, 1973), p. 90.

19   R. C. Pratt, *The Critical Phase in Tanzania in 1945–1968* (Cambridge: Cambridge University Press, 1976), p. 230.

20   E. W. Clark, *Socialist Development and Public Investment in Tanzania 1964–73* (Toronto: University of Toronto Press, 1978), p. 103.

21   J. K. Nyerere, '*The Arusha Declaration Ten Years After*' (1977), reprinted in A. Coulson (ed.), *African Socialism in Practice: The Tanzanian Experience* (Nottingham: Spokesman Books, 1979), pp. 43–71.

22   Clark, op. cit., pp. 103, 119.

23   These statistical problems are discussed in the ILO report *Towards Self-Reliance: Development, Employment and Equity Issues in Tanzania* (Geneva: ILO Jobs and Skills Programme for Africa, 1978), pp. 81–6.

24   Clark, op. cit., p. 117.

25   ibid., pp. 135–6.

26   S. M. Wangwe, 'Factors influencing capacity utilization in Tanzanian manufacturing', *International Labour Review*, 115, 1 (1977), p. 69.

27   C. E. Barker, M. Bhagavan, P. von Mitschke-Collande and D. Wield, '*Industrial production and transfer of technology in Tanzania: the political economy of Tanzanian industrial enterprises*' (mimeo.), Institute of Development Studies, University of Dar es Salaam, 1976, ch, IV, p. 3.

28   ibid., ch. III.2, pp. 16–17.

29   Clark, op. cit., fn. 10, p. 143. The oil refinery cost shs 102 million and employed 317 workers, while the bakery cost shs 35 million and employed 86 workers, giving a capital cost of shs 407,000 per job created.

30   A. Coulson, 'Tanzania's fertilizer factory', *Journal of Modern African Studies*, 15, 1 (1977), pp. 119–125; reprinted in Coulson (ed.), op. cit., pp. 184–190.
31   The expansion was largely financed with an IBRD loan. But if the machinery specifications had included more labour-intensive machines, IBRD rules would have allowed textile machinery manufacturers in Brazil and India to tender for them.
32   For example, the arguments of R. Sutcliffe, *Industry and Underdevelopment* (Reading, Mass.: Addison Wesley, 1971), chs 2 and 3, and C. Y. Thomas, *Dependence and Transformation* (New York: Monthly Review Press, 1974), chs 5 and 6.
33   The difficulties inherent in management agreements are discussed in Ph. Packard, 'Corporate structure in agriculture and socialist development in Tanzania ...', in Coulson (ed.), op. cit., pp. 200–16.
34   L. le Van Hall, 'Transfer pricing – the issue for Tanzania', in Coulson (ed.), op. cit., pp. 191–9.
35   This was also the view of the 1977 IBRD report on the Tanzanian economy, but emphatically not that of the 1978 ILO/JASPA report (see especially pp. 123–36).
36   Reprinted in Coulson (ed.), op. cit., pp. 36–43. See especially Clauses 15 and 28.
37   Michaela von Freyhold, 'Notes on Tanzanian industrial workers', *Tanzania Notes and Records*, 81/82 (1977), pp. 15–22.
38   P. Mihyo, 'The struggle for workers' control in Tanzania', *Review of African Political Economy*, 4 (1975), pp. 72–85. See also H. Mapolu, 'The workers' movement in Tanzania', *Maji Maji*, 12 (September 1973), pp. 31–43. The reaction of foreign capital was expressed by the Tanganyika Development Finance Company Ltd, an investment bank which had lent money to the Mount Carmel Company and whose shareholders were NDC (Tanzanian), the Commonwealth Development Corporation (British), Deutsche Gesellschaft für Wirtschaftliche Zusammenarbeit (West German), and Nederlandse Overzeese Financierings-Maatschappij (of the Netherlands), whose directors made it clear that they would not continue investing if Mount Carmel was taken over by its workers.
39   The 'industrial programme' of the Second Five-Year Development Plan was based on a list of 385 projects 'in differing stages of preparation', (Vol. I, p. 65), but was not clear how this list related to the 40 projects included in the estimates of Volume II (p. 77). It also recognized that 'a central concern of the Second Plan period will be the fashioning of a longer term industrial strategy through the identification and preparation of projects in new industries meeting the more complex requirement of the new stage of industrialization' (Vol. I, p. 62). This task was entrusted to the Harvard Advisory Services. They in turn were influenced by Justinian Rweyemamu and by Clive Thomas's book *Dependence and Transformation* (New York: Monthly Review Press, 1973) which proposed a 'basic industry strategy'. The Third Five-Year Plan, published only in 1978, did include what purported to be such a strategy, but it could have little effect on investments during the plan period because the industrial investment budget was largely taken up with projects approved before the new policy was adopted. For a paper by the Harvard team which describes their methods of working, see M. Roemer, G. Tiddrick and D. Williams 'The range of strategic choice in Tanzanian industry', *Journal of Development Economics*, III, 1 (1976), pp. 257–76.
40   This is not to rule out investments in infrastructure and social services which can be *indirectly productive*, if they make possible production increases elsewhere. Social services are also valuable for their own sake, but no country can be unconcerned about production and productivity, as President Nyerere is well aware (e.g. see 'The Arusha Declaration ten years after', reprinted in Coulson (ed.), op. cit., especially pp. 60–3).

4 *Discussion Note on Chapter 3*

PAUL HARE

In these comments I shall be considering how far the Eastern European experience of industrialization, notably that of Hungary, may help to illuminate some of the problems currently being faced by Tanzania. The fact that Tanzania and Hungary are both, ostensibly, pursuing socialist development strategies suggests that the two countries may have sufficient in common for the former to learn some useful lessons from the latter. On the other hand, when the communist regime was established in Hungary in the late 1940s, the country already had a fair amount of industry and a moderately skilled and well-educated labour force. Tanzania enjoys no such advantages, and is faced instead with the tremendous task of industrializing from an extremely limited base, as Coulson's chapter makes quite clear.

Tanzania's early industrialization sought to achieve a measure of import substitution, though the results have been fairly mixed. For the more recent period there is evidence that in many branches of industry productivity is either falling or stagnant, and much of the established industrial capacity is under-utilized. These problems are hardly unique to Tanzania, but they do suggest that there is a need to rethink the approach to industrialization.

Study of the planned economies, and comparison with the Western industrialized countries, presents us with three basic approaches to economic development and industrialization. These are as follows:

(1) *Minimal government intervention* in economic affairs, with reliance on 'normal' market forces to stimulate investment. This approach is that followed by many of the Western economies; it relies on the existence of a large number of entrepreneurially minded people with the financial resources to back up their ideas and projects.

(2) *Central regulation of investment* with markets to allocate current production. This is a very loose way of describing the Hungarian approach since the reforms of 1968. It is a policy which makes sense in the context of a coherent development plan if the government has the power to enforce its policies: formulating investment plans if there is neither the power nor the ability to implement them is a waste of time and effort. Investment planning raises a number of important issues of relevance to Tanzania, particularly to

do with what may be called the 'industrial strategy', which are referred to below.

(3) *Central regulation of both investment and current production.* Rather imprecisely, this may be taken to characterize the Soviet approach to economic policy, and it leaves a very limited sphere of operation for market forces (notably the allocation of consumer goods to households and the allocation of labour to enterprises).

Of these three approaches, it seems most probable to the present author that (2) is of greatest interest for Tanzania. Accordingly the remainder of these comments will be concerned with the implications of (2), especially in relation to the choice of an appropriate industrial strategy. Now we have already referred to one such strategy, namely, that based on import substitution, which is discussed extensively by other contributors to this volume. Aside from questioning whether it is a viable strategy at all, much of the debate on import substitution concerns how the process should begin: either by substituting for imported consumer goods or by substituting for intermediate and capital goods. It is often tempting to go for the former, since the markets are already there and the relevant products are readily identified. But it is not necessarily desirable to base development on consumption patterns which may themselves be highly inequitable, and in any case, as many countries have discovered, developing consumer goods production itself induces substantial imports of intermediate and capital goods. Hence, initially at least, the net effect on the balance of payments could be unfavourable.

In common with much of the rest of Eastern Europe, Hungary's import substitution in the 1950s concentrated on developing a heavy industrial base with steel and heavy engineering as the leading sectors. With the benefit of hindsight, much of the development in those early years now appears to be fairly inefficient – either inappropriate for Hungary, given the country's poor resource base, or employing outdated technology – though one should not discount the value of learning by doing: experience in operating even inefficient machinery in the 1950s laid the foundation for impressive economic performance in the 1960s. Moreover, the trade restrictions which still prevailed in the 1950s may have left Hungary with few alternative development paths.

Now, however, world trade offers much wider opportunities than it did just after the Second World War. Hungary has pursued several policies in this connection, but some are only of peripheral concern in the present context, namely, Hungary's accession to GATT, her standard three-column tariff policy and licensing agreements to facilitate technology transfer. From the point of view of industrial strategy, two policies are of particular interest: central development programmes (CDPs) and a general export orientation.

The CDPs were initiated in the late 1960s to foster developments in a number of sectors, for example, vehicles, computers and petrochemicals. The intention was to concentrate investment resources into a few key areas judged to be important for the long-run development of the economy. Each CDP involved the implementation of several interrelated investment projects over about a decade (i.e. two five-year plan periods). Choice of sector was guided partly by Hungary's existing areas of expertise, partly by consideration of trade prospects: for all these CDPs were too large for the domestic market alone and would only be viable if export markets could be found.

This realization led on to the second policy: export orientation. Hungary is a small country (population 10 million) at a medium level of development; this means that many new investments, which are only economically viable if they are on a large enough scale to benefit from increasing returns to scale, have to make some use of export markets. Consequently, considerations of domestic development become closely intertwined with export prospects, and this has gradually resulted in investment policy being strongly influenced by export prospects. On the one hand this leads the central authorities to restrict development in fields where exports cannot be profitable; on the other hand, credits are now more readily available to support investments which lead to expansions in exports, especially in the Western markets. The result is a shift of emphasis in Hungary's development strategy, away from a policy which favours one or other sector (e.g. heavy industry rather than light industry, as in the 1950s), towards a new policy which is still selective, but where foreign trade opportunities provide the most important selection criterion. Since Hungary now exports almost half its national product, it is not altogether surprising that there has been such a shift.

What might Tanzania have to learn from this Hungarian experience? I would suggest that there are three points worth emphasizing here. First, it is important to build on and develop existing skills (*cf.* Hungary's CDPs). Some of Tanzania's more successful parastatals may well provide useful starting points for such developments. Second, emphasis on import substitution alone is a rather negative approach to development: many investment projects, especially in a small economy such as Tanzania's, cannot be very profitable without being too large for the domestic market. This points to some potential benefits from co-operation within East Africa, or might entail seeking export markets farther afield. Third, it needs to be emphasized that industrialization is an extremely complex social and economic process which is hardly likely to be achieved by adopting any single or simple policy orientation. This is just as true for Tanzania as it has been and continues to be in Hungary.

5 Industrialization in Tanzania

REGINALD HERBOLD GREEN

Our own reality – however fine and attractive the reality of others may be – can only be transformed by detailed knowledge of it, by our own effort, by our own sacrifices...

Amilcar Cabral

Tanzania is attempting to achieve change by deliberate policy and to maintain stability in both the direction and the process of change. We are under no illusions about the difficulties of the tasks we have undertaken. With few socialists we are trying to build socialism ... with few technicians we are trying to effect a fundamental transformation of our economy.

Julius K. Nyerere

Mistakes are mistakes.

Julius K. Nyerere

I Struggles, Processes and Snapshots

One of the disadvantages of trying to analyse and schematize Tanzania, including Tanzanian industrialization, is that almost any standard interpretation at first glance appears to fit and to offer insights but, on any attempt to apply it rigorously and in detail, appears to fit less and less well and to throw up obfuscations. In part this flows from the failure to consider the need for intermediate levels of theory and of contextual analysis between general theoretical/analytical political economic models and detailed operational analysis of particular political economies or sectors thereof. In part too it flows from very real struggles within and about Tanzanian industrialization. Struggles in at least three senses: class, intellectual and environmental.

Tanzania can be described as a state whose party and a majority of whose leadership are seriously attempting to achieve a transition to socialism.[1] The inherited colonial system was most certainly not socialist nor was 1961–7 evolution towards socialism. Moreover, the 1967 Arusha Declaration commitment to 'socialism and self-reliance' did not come after an armed revolution or even a change of government. Nor could it be asserted that levels of consciousness among workers and peasants were uniformly high or squarely focused on exploitation as inherent in capitalism.

This juxtaposition of commitments and strategies typically held and acted on by parties seizing control of the state other than by violence with a subsequent shift toward a socialist strategy but with continuity of party and government plus relatively low levels of consciousness has created its own possibilities and contradictions. There is a continual danger of loss of momentum – the transition was launched from a standing, not a running start. There are few overt manifestations of organized subclass resistance to change – or of 'premature' attempts to hasten it – but frequent manifestations of genuine confusion, inertia and passive non-co-operation.

The class and intellectual struggles overlap – especially with respect to industrialization – but do not coincide. Whether efficiency means maximum enterprise level surplus generation or whether that is only one aspect of efficiency is not an issue which finds socialists on one side and bourgeois economists on the other. Nor are questions of internal integration within the industrial sector, the role of manufactured exports, the nature of 'basic' in basic industries, questions on which Marxian and non-Marxian positions cluster about antipodean polar opposites.

Finally, there has been a struggle against a material context characterized by very low initial levels of productive forces (with a particularly low share in manufacturing) and a generally unfavourable external economic context. Over 1972–6 UN data showed Tanzania as losing 12% of the real purchasing power of GDP (not just of exports) by terms-of-trade shifts. The 1977 terms improvement from the coffee price boom was very short-lived, with the 1980 position worse than 1976. Combined with a stagnant or falling trend over 1965/7–1979 in physical volume of exports, the external environmental deterioration has created generalized inefficiencies because of extreme scarcity of foreign exchange. That loss of efficiency is particularly noticeable in the industrial sector and is beginning to be seen as raising very particular strategic issues in respect to sectoral integration, capital goods production and priorities to manufactured exports.

A struggle is by definition a process. A set of statistics and of analyses of outputs, institutions, or balances of power at any given time is by definition a snapshot of a point in that process. Therefore, a series of such snapshots is essential to understanding the continuities and contradictions, the ambiguities and achievements, the directions and the mistakes of any process. This poses peculiar problems with respect to Tanzania – the data are bad, the detailed empirical studies are few, the whole time since 1967 is short, the impact of the 1974 and 1978 external crises is hard to sort out from more basic trends. Any interpretation, let alone any projection, must be tentative and, especially with respect to the latter, hedged with the most endearing of the Duke of Wellington's standard comments: 'I may well be wrong.'

INDUSTRIALIZATION STRATEGY AND POLICY: A HISTORICAL NOTE

Industrialization strategy policy[2] can be divided into four phases: pre-independence; 1961–7 (pre-Arusha); 1967–73 (towards public sector dominance); 1973 (towards an integrated strategy). The colonial period strategy was *laissez-faire*, that is, the deliberate absence of any state strategy. The policy exceptions – e.g. Tanzania Packers (Liebig 50%/Tanganyika 50%) – were the result of private sector initiatives. What manufacturing there was, was concentrated on first-stage processing of commodity exports which was essential to export at all, namely, cotton ginning, coffee curing, sisal decortication, meat packing and tinning, tea drying. Domestic market consumer manufacturing was abnormally low, even for a very poor colony, because of the customs union with Kenya and Uganda which in effect made Tanganyika a captive market of Kenyan industry in return for Kenyan user subsidization of the losses incurred on Tanganyikan sectors of regional transport and communications enterprises.

With independence there was a change. The independent state pursued a strategy of industrialization by invitation centred on broad market final consumer goods plus three broad market intermediate plants – GCI (corrugated roofing) sheet, cement, petroleum refining. The means used included limited tax incentives, moderate protection against imports, joint ventures with foreign firms and – in a handful of cases – 100% public sector firms. The National Development Corporation was the focal entity for public sector participation but was not even peripherally involved in a majority of large-scale manufacturing enterprises.

Broad market is stressed deliberately. Very few luxury manufactures were – or are – produced if luxuries means either goods like Mercedes cars and brandy or, alternatively, products with very narrow markets. To 1967 the dominant reason was market logic – the Tanzanian upper-income consumer market was so narrow it made no sense to produce for it. To a degree even over 1961–7, and much more centrally thereafter, state commitments to more egalitarian income distribution[3] and to directing resources to the production of goods actually used by or potentially within the reach of most Tanzanians[4] pushed production choices in the same direction. True, wheat flour, GCI sheet, refined sugar, beer and cigarettes are not necessities. Maize meal, thatch, jaggery are substitutes for the first three and in general people presumably die later when deprived of the last two. But all five are broad market wage goods – indeed, among the most widely purchased items in rural as well as urban areas. It is important to stress this point because analyses of Tanzanian industrialization which find a high share of luxury goods[5] do so by including cigarettes, beer and similar items, for instance, leather shoes priced at one-third of the monthly minimum wage. Necessities they are not, broad market wage goods they are.[6]

The Arusha Declaration marked a sharp switch in strategy as to dominant mode of production. The public sector was made dominant in ownership by nationalization[7] and its dominance sustained by new investment while being extended by a build-up of citizen managerial and technical expertise.[8] Strategy on goods to be produced remained rather vague, but the shift to intermediate goods – e.g. tyres, fertilizer, metal sheet – combined with mopping up remaining mass market consumer goods – e.g. textiles – was systematic enough to be arguably an operational strategy if not one with a very coherent theoretical foundation.[9] Industrialization was one of the first sectors to which a decentralization strategy was applied with a limited number of secondary towns designated as preferred sites (as opposed to Dar es Salaam): a strategy which did radically alter the geographic pattern of new plants begun after 1971 as opposed to that of 1961–70.

The post-1973 phase can be described in terms of attempts to build, articulate and apply a coherent medium-term strategy. This strategy has been termed the basic industry strategy. How different it is in terms of the implications for future patterns of industrial sector production from the evolving but largely implicit 1967–72 strategy is not clear – the attempt at an articulated set of goals worked through to product or product group level within a medium-term, integrated sectoral framework is new. In part it had become necessary by 1973 because with the rapid growth of the public manufacturing sector NDC had been divested of several manufacturing subsectors and could no longer serve as an overall industrial programme formulation body.[10] Because the 1973–9 period has, with the exceptions of 1973 and 1977, been one of major economic crises, it is hard to separate secondary strategic and policy elements – whether taken in response to external events or for more endogenous reasons, from *ad hoc* adjustments to immediate constraints. For example, the Tanzania Textile Corporation's attempts to build up spares fabrication capacity in each of its mills owed something to a strategic concern for enhancing capital goods capacity beginning with spares, but rather more to specific import licensing constraints on maintaining adequate parts inventories.

The role of the private sector in manufacturing since 1967 has been the topic of rather diffuse and none too illuminating debate. Because decentralized public sector manufacturing – e.g. District Development Corporation, co-operative, village – has had very limited success, and efforts to support it – e.g. via SIDO (Small Industries Development Organization) – have had limited, if perhaps growing, success there has been increasingly broad agreement that for the medium-term small private manufacturing is not to be discouraged. Since 1973 the same stance has been taken fairly consistently in respect to domestic (in practice citizens of Asian ancestry) medium-scale private manufacturing especially in areas not seen as having broad sectoral implications or producing goods perceived as particularly vital. The policy considerations seem to have been reducing the number of claims on public sector analytical and personnel capacities, utilizing entrepreneurial talents otherwise idle, and in broadening the range of useful but secondary importance goods available, e.g. soft drinks, knitwear, leather shoes. Totally foreign-owned large manufacturing ventures, while not automatically banned – e.g. National in batteries and electrical goods – have been accepted only if the item did not figure on a short-term public plant establishment list and no parastatal sought to be a partner. For major new parastatal ventures minority equity and/or technical-managerial partners have been sought, more for knowledge than for finance. Since 1972 there has been a strategic view of such partners as temporary – to be phased out when Tanzania had acquired the knowledge to run the firm without them. While by no means uniformly applied, this strategy has been acted upon – in whole or in part – in a number of enterprises.

With few exceptions the partners chosen have been large foreign firms, including some from Asia and some which are by no means true TNCs. Two reasons underly that pattern. First, linking the public sector to domestic capitalists is viewed as contrary to a transition to socialism, likely to strengthen the presently very weak and fragmented citizen capitalist class and creating special difficulties for phasing out the private partner.[11] More positively, it has been believed that adequate knowledge was normally available only from large foreign firms and not from middle-size domestic capitalists.

From this historical sketch of overall strategy and policy it is possible to turn to a series of issues of particular concern to understanding or evaluating the Tanzanian industrialization process from 1967 to date:

(1) the basic industry strategy;
(2) ownership, surplus generation and control;
(3) technology, scale, capital/output ratios;
(4) productivity and efficiency;
(5) selected critiques.

II   The Basic Industry Strategy

What is meant, in Tanzania, by the term basic industry strategy? Any answer is to a degree misleading because there have been several intellectual influences and several key technocratic and political actors. What follows is an attempt to elucidate the origins and the content as perceived by a number of senior Tanzanian political, technocratic and managerial decision-takers.[12]

Four intellectual influences or strands appear to have been critical.

(1) *Balance* – in the sense of Ragnar Nurkse's Istanbul lectures arguing that the majority of the output of each sector of the economy should be utilized domestically and the majority of demand in each sector met from domestic production. This was a recurrent theme in policy formulation from 1967.[13]
(2) *Central* – as argued by Clive Thomas[14] in terms of a dozen key products (really product vectors or clusters) accounting for the bulk of global industrial production. The argument turns on developing integrated production centred on minimum efficient size units at intermediate good (e.g. steel) level which can then be built backward to raw material production (e.g. iron ore) and forward to final products (e.g. pails, machine tools).
(3) *Linkage* – not so much in the standard Hirschman forward and backward model as in that of Justinian Rweyemamu[15] which concentrated in principle on capital goods and in practice on intermediate goods, to supply materials for, and basic wage goods, to create adequate demand for, capital goods production.[16]
(4) *Vectoral* – indirectly from Hla Myint via a few Tanzanian and expatriate advisors and decision-takers arguing for proceeding with complete 'slices' (vectors) from raw material to finished products. A standard example was seed cotton – cotton lint, cotton seed – cottoncake, cottonseed oil, cotton yarn – textiles, margarine, animal feed – clothing, industrial textile products. Another led from iron ore to final capital and consumer products based on steel. The case as argued in Tanzania did not posit any theoretical starting point in the

vectoral sequence but did stress the importance of building up a series of linked stages rapidly, not remaining indefinitely at either the raw material or final product end of the vector.

These four influences clearly overlap and interlock. They can be seen as a subsequent stage to the mass market consumer goods and intermediate goods emphases and one aimed at integrating these with an enlarged raw material processing sector. Certainly they do not in the Tanzanian context, constitute a 'heavy industry'[17] strategy unless the heavy refers to number of linkages. There are no inherent prescriptions integral to the basic industry strategy as to scale, capital/output ratios, or technological sophistication. Each of these poses special problems in the Tanzania context which are examined in a later section.

The basic industry strategy has consistently been seen as oriented to self-reliance. It has rarely been explicitly perceived as autarchic – if only because several of the vectors cannot be completed in Tanzania either on the raw material or the final product end. Further, in the case of present raw material exports there has been fairly coherent strategic concern since 1972[18] with adding at least one or two stages of pre-export processing and manufacturing both to increase value added and to broaden the range of inputs available to domestic industry even if the bulk of output was exported in an intermediate stage (e.g. leather). However, in practice, the strategy continued the post-colonial pattern of low and unco-ordinated priority to exports[19] of manufactures either with respect to plants specifically oriented to external markets or, even more, to orienting plant sizes and output mixes to both domestic and external markets.[20] A shift in this respect took place only over 1980–1 and has yet to be fully articulated or operated.

The dominant technical figures were Justinian Rweyemamu (as Principal Secretary of Devplan and later as Economic Advisor to the President) and George Mbowe (of the Tanzania Investment Bank). The Harvard Development Advisory Service team was critical in data collection, organization and setting up a series of possible twenty-year scenarios[21] – the final official level co-ordination and formulation was dominantly by the Tanzanians.[22]

The key central decision-takers were President Julius Nyerere and Minister Amir Jamal (first at Commerce and Industries and subsequently at Finance and Planning). Each influenced the goals of the strategy and each paid close enough attention to successive formulations and proposals to understand what decisions they were taking in presenting the strategy to the cabinet and the party for endorsement as part of the Third Five-Year Plan.[23]

The broad case put for the strategy is threefold:

(1)   domestic economic integration;
(2)   national self-reliance;
(3)   surmounting the transformation problem either by producing key products domestically or by procuring them indirectly via production of exportables which can by trade be transformed into capital goods, fuel and raw materials not available domestically.

The first two strands are articulated and acted upon reasonably systematically. The third has not been equally stressed verbally and very much less in practice with the exceptions of certain processing activities, particularly cashew nut decortication (husking) and sisal twine spinning.

Attempts have been made to integrate the basic industry strategy with enhanced technological capacity. The point is that adaptation and designs in Tanzania are significantly hampered by the fact that they come up against the absence of machine building capacity. In the absence of that capacity it is not clear that Tanzania can gain much by adapting or designing machinery. The cost of having the adapted or redesigned machine custom-built abroad is likely to make its introduction, no matter how appropriate it may be, inappropriate once again on cost grounds. This, however, is an additional point within the basic industries strategy for a capital goods sector, rather than one of the premises from which it was constructed.

III   Ownership, Surplus Generation and Control

Since 1967 ownership has been viewed by Tanzanian decision-takers as a starting point. Socialism requires dominant public sector ownership. Second, Tanzania has not viewed it as practical to have African capitalism even if it wanted to. President Nyerere has consistently argued that it was doubtless practical to have capitalism in Africa but it was quite impractical to have African capitalism. The choice as perceived in Tanzania was between external capitalism or internal socialism; a choice one would be forced to take whether one were a socialist or a nationalist.

Ownership was also seen as critical to Tanzanianization of middle- and high-level posts or, alternatively, the level of national skills and ability to operate the productive process at all levels. The second formulation has probably been the more important – throughout the period 1967–79 there have been acute shortages of senior Tanzanian personnel. Granted some unnecessary positions have been created, but this has exacerbated a genuine shortage, not 'solved' an inconvenient surplus.

Tanzanianization has been perceived as essential to gaining experience – learning by doing – and to controlling from the inside rather than solely by external controls. Ownership without citizen personnel has been seen as having very distinct limits, especially in manufacturing, both as to gaining knowledge and experience at operational level and as to altering the balance between externally imposed controls and internal, operating control.[24] Scarcity of knowledge, personnel and institutions has led to four particular – perhaps transitory – policies:

(1)   extensive interim use of foreign partners to secure knowledge and personnel;
(2)   selection of key (or at least large) plants for public sector attention;
(3)   limited – and in any absolute sense inadequate – support for, or development of, decentralized public sector capacity to own and operate small or locally oriented enterprises;
(4)   fairly uniform tolerance of small-scale and a more ambiguous tolerance toward medium-scale domestic private enterprises so long as no major overt abuses in their operations came to party or government attention.[25]

While general to the public enterprise sector, these characteristics have been particularly prominent with respect to manufacturing.

Most Tanzanian central decision-takers and most public sector managers are in no doubt that ownership does not automatically bring control. The problem confronting them has been how best to deploy and to expand the limited, albeit fairly rapidly growing, numbers of citizen managers and technical personnel. In 1967 the then very limited capability for direct management was concentrated on banking – seen as crucial to overall economic control[26] – while management agreements and joint ventures were employed in manufacturing. Since then the typical pattern has been sequential – citizenization and degree of effective control is raised over time in most enterprises but starts at a low level in new enterprises.

Control over domestic private sector manufacturing has tended to take the form of encapsulation within a state-set framework. However, this is not directly from the public manufacturing sector but via means such as the Prices Commission and the Annual Credit Budget. The first controls, or at least influences, surplus generation in the sector, and the second controls access to working capital. The public sector has had remarkably little subcontracting to smaller units in the private sector and has made remarkably little specific use of its role as supplier to some of the smaller private sectors.

Controls in the sense of worker controls over production relations are a very complex and complicated area with patterns which vary from plant to plant. It also varies very much in the perception of the observer.[27] Workers' councils, while being very divergent in roles played, have considerable power over operations in many enterprises. Their ability to relate to structural and forward planning has tended to be quite low. The group most closely linked with them are plant-level branches of the party.[28] These in general interact fairly well with the workers' councils and the shopfloor workers. The party in most parastatals chooses a director of the corporation. This is supposed to be a shopfloor worker. Curiously the other worker director – from NUTA (the trade union federation) – is very rarely a shopfloor worker or indeed even an employee of the firm on whose board he is placed. NUTA has tended to put experts from its head office on boards. In fact workers' councils and NUTA often do not get on very well. NUTA seems to perceive the workers' councils – and plant party branches – to be much more meaningful to the workers than it is. Therefore it has had an unfortunate tendency to see them as a threat and be relatively unhelpful in worker education oriented to strengthening and increasing the effectiveness of worker participation.

One particular reason for this is that neither NUTA nor workers' councils are influential in respect of wages and salaries. Indeed, that is perhaps the area in which they have least influence. Decisions-takers have deliberately limited worker control in that direction:

(1)   to preserve surpluses for productive investment;
(2)   to limit differentials between high and low surplus generating enterprises and sectors.

There is evidence that differentials – at wage more than salary levels – between enterprises already tend to vary with capital intensity and value added per worker in ways not associated with worker effort or efficiency.[29] This pattern is not particularly consistent with either egalitarianism or socialist incentives as perceived by the President and Party Central Committee. It would probably be exacerbated by plant- or industry-level bargaining by workers councils.[30] Further it is not clear, if workers councils are to participate in management more broadly than as a sectional interest group, that levels of remuneration are a good starting point.

However, this interpretation only makes sense when viewed in the light of the worker influence on the party and the government which has resulted in nationally set – and reasonably well enforced – minimum wages which in real terms are the highest in Eastern Africa (£40 per month) while salary levels are by the same test the lowest (£135 a month after income tax for a middle and £185 for a top manager). Growing tensions existed between 1977–80 because the minimum wage – and in practice most other wages, albeit not salaries – is supposed to be adjusted for inflation at three- to four-year intervals but the minimum wage was not raised between 1975–9 while average wages rose at most by 25% despite perhaps 50% cost-of-living increases in 1975–9. Certainly salary-earners have, except for those promoted rapidly, fared even worse. Money salary scales in 1979 were 15% above 1967 levels (about equal to 1961 in fact) and since that 15% increase in mid-1974 their cost of living has more than doubled.[31] That sharing of austerity may limit discontent within firms and reduce hostility to the state, but it seems unlikely to prevent manufacturing sector wages becoming a more contentious issue than they have been in the past. In 1980 and 1981, minimum wage increases of 26% and 25% and general public sector increases of about 20% after tax did offset 1979/80 and 1980/1 inflation for minimum wage earners and limited its erosion at other levels, but did not remove the underlying problem.

Attempts to develop worker control have produced very unequal results. Each initiative has tended to rouse high hopes and fears, to have initial high visibility, to sink from the center of attention with some continued impact but neither what was hoped or expected or feared. Workers councils, party branches and worker directors have altered production relations but not transformed them. In many cases they remain abysmal[32] – a situation sharply criticized by some decision-takers, e.g. the President and Minister Jamal, and some senior public sector managers, e.g. TIB and subsequently TDFL chairman Mbowe – as a central element in efficiency and productivity problems. Open conflict has been rare. Its results have been ambiguous.[33] In those cases in which clear oppression by managers was demonstrated, the party usually backed the workers even if initial clashes bypassed proper procedures. That experience – over 1972/4 – combined with party branches at plants, may have led to reduced overt oppression and greater use of extant procedures; certainly such clashes are rarer in recent years. Clashes involving both oppression and opportunist tactics by individual workers have tended to lead to interminable negotiations, notably in two large public manufacturing enterprises, ending with some correction of abuses and some alteration of worker consciousness toward resisting individual worker proposals to start complaints by locking out managers.

Two other types of clash have been dealt with more harshly: wage claims by above-average wage groups disguised as worker control disputes[34] and random takeovers of private enterprises. The former were concentrated in transport over 1972–4 and while the state/party case was explained to workers, fairly clear job-security and penal threats were used to force return to port and bus posts. Private sector direct takeovers were initially vaguely encouraged; the first trio of firms were assisted with finance, personnel and contracts to become viable as *de facto* workers co-operatives. However, when this response threatened to give rise to wholesale takeovers of firms neither the workers nor the state could manage (the break point was a rubber manufacturing firm) and to create widespread panic in the private business sector leading to loss of production and services, the government reversed itself, holding that nationalization must be determined by the government on party authority, not by groups of workers acting on their own.[35]

SURPLUS

The debate on surplus in the Tanzanian public manufacturing sector is peculiar. Critics sometimes seem to imply that the sector is in overall deficit,[36] which is not (at least in 1980) and never has been the case sectorally albeit some firms have run up large deficits and/or taken extended periods to break through to profitability. Perhaps as a result, defenders often stress that sectoral surplus levels are substantial relative to assets[37] and on a rising trend. At that level, the defenders have the better of the debate – the Tanzania public enterprise manufacturing sector generates substantial operating surpluses, that is, it contributes to resources available for productive investment. However, that is not an entirely adequate answer. Manufacturing is a net user, not supplier, of investible funds – operating surpluses do not meet the total investment requirements of the sector. With a trend 1961–78 growth rate of 10% for large-scale manufacturing and a rising capital/output ratio largely because of structural shifts (55% food – drink – beverages in 1961, 33% in 1974; 11% petroleum, chemicals, rubber, glass, cement, metal products in 1961, 35% in 1974)[38] this is hardly surprising. But it does mean that the sector is a net user of resources (basically external borrowing), not a net provider.

Further, the enterprise profitability test is somewhat problematic. Tanzania has over 1969–79, and especially from 1973 onwards, built up a domestic price structure which has an internal logic, but is different both in average level and in relativities from global prices. It is to a high degree an administered market set of prices. Because investible surplus, especially in goods producing enterprises, is a stated government goal embodied in the 1973 Prices Act, the Price Commission has administered prices so that with reasonable effort – not necessarily best attainable efficiency of capacity or input use – a manufacturing enterprise can obtain 15–20% post-tax on net worth or 30% pre-tax on assets net of current liabilities. Surpluses in that context are not necessarily a true test of efficiency.

However, the range from highly negative to over 50 per cent suggests that there is no attempt to guarantee profits whatever a manufacturing parastatal does, nor to penalize excess profits resulting from better than anticipated cost control. Surplus is a requirement, taking one year with another for manufacturing ventures. Manufacturing ventures with consistent losses do have management fired and often have their structures rather radically shaken about. Such a venture is not likely to be closed, but large manufacturing ventures which after the first two or three years continue to have losses are viewed with great disapproval. That said, there is certainly perceived ambiguity in respect of levels and growth in surplus and even more in evaluating what kind of test of efficiency particular surplus levels are in the context of rigged market central planning. The 'obvious' answer quoted by the IMF and the World Bank is that if Tanzania used a system in which domestic prices were more closely linked to international prices and in which one had actual competition from imported goods, one would have a better test of efficiency. Of course one would also not have a socialist economy. Thus a 'slight' problem of this particular way of improving the functioning or evaluation of a socialist economy is that it would seem to improve one's ability to measuring its functioning by ending its socialism!

With respect to surpluses, there is no lack of perception on the part of the Tanzanian decision-makers – or a majority of public sector managers for that matter – that surpluses vanish or leak away (a) through still needing significant numbers of expatriate personnel, (b) from technology contracts, (c) through overpriced projects and (d) through transfer pricing. The answer to the first is assumed to be citizenization which seems to be sensible. The answer to the second and third has been to attempt to improve the evaluation and negotiating procedure.[39] The results are unequal. Certainly some recent contracts are a great deal better than others and many recent contracts are a great deal better than earlier ones. On the whole Tanzanian contracts are better than those from Kenya, or for that matter, those from Sri Lanka or the Philippines.[40] This might be argued to be shooting fish in a barrel, however, since some of the other contracts are so bad as to be virtually unbelievable. One of them oddly enough was a private sector to private sector contract.[41]

IV   Technology, Scale, Capital/Output Ratios

Here the important points are (1) trends and (2) reasons. Certainly there is a trend towards more sophisticated technology. This is paralleled by slightly better ability to choose on an informed basis. One reason that the slightly better ability to choose has not altered the shift towards higher technology is in many cases that about the time that one has created a better ability to choose, one can no longer buy the thing then seen to be appropriate. For example, there is an interesting debate on why instead of the elaborate programme for the 1974 plan for implementing doubling textile capacity by 1977, Tanzania did not simply build three more Friendship Textile Mills. Friendship had simpler technology, output nearer capacity, more worker control, more learning by doing, a better trading surplus record than any other mill (public or private). Unfortunately, this debate seems not to take into account that in 1973 and 1974 the Tanzanian government attempted to buy two more Friendship Textile Mills and was told by the Chinese that they had ceased production because they were obsolete.[42] Unfortunately from Tanzania's point of view, it is not now possible to replicate what is viewed at party and ministry, although less so at textile corporation, levels as the most successful of the textile mills. Some of the shifts to higher technology, like textiles, seem to result from a change in what is on offer.

The higher capital output ratio results largely from change in sectoral structure.[43] Cement and tyre plants have higher capital output ratios than aspirin tableting and packaging plants or than most first-stage export processing plant, e.g. coffee curing or sisal decorticating. The explosion of current price capital/labour ratios has two main causes: the structural shift and inflation. Over 1960–70 machinery and construction costs rose about 10% a year; since then annual escalation seems to have been in the 15–20% range.[44] Therefore a plant with a current price capital/labour ratio of, say, shs 10,000 in 1960 would if constructed in 1965 have had a K/N ratio of shs 17,250, in 1970 of shs 27,500 and in 1975 of about shs 65,000.[45]

The scale problem relates primarily to the fact that given actual manpower and knowledge constraints in Tanzania it has proved impossible to build up decentralized public enterprises. Regional development corporations have existed as have a variety of other regional or subregional public enterprises. A few of them are successful but no general pattern of success is yet to be achieved and a large number of disasters have resulted. Unfortunately these decentralized units are the types, or sizes, of parent body that would logically be associated with small-scale manufacturing. The attempt to run a large number of very small units in a national parastatal is not one that either experience or logic causes Tanzanians to be very enthusiastic about. Therefore there is a bias to a scale which probably is larger than optimal related to (1) wanting public sector not private sector development and (2) difficulties in developing decentralized public corporation control ownership management.

There has also been a significant rise in skill intensity and diversity. This has had the result that each time a new type of manufacturing is introduced it needs new expatriates. On the whole they are then run down again but over time this causes expatriate manufacturing personnel to rise slightly in absolute numbers even though there is a continuously declining percentage of expatriates in total high- and middle-level personnel. A large new plant, e.g. the fertilizer plant, may start with 150 expatriates which is a significant increase in the total number of expatriates in Tanzania, let alone in manufacturing. Ten years later the number is likely to be down to, say, fifteen. If soon after Tanzania brings the Songo Songo natural gas onshore through a pipeline to Kilwa and puts it into a petrochemical plant to produce feedstock for the fertilizer plant and for export,[46] this would require (for the well, the pipeline, the plant, the shipping of the petrochemicals) 100 plus expatriates. That jogs the expatriate numbers up again and starts a new ten-year run-down cycle. The point at which the training effort, the school of engineering, the technical colleges, and so on, will get ahead of the game so that one will have enough basically trained people in engineering and technology that one can send them on for specific training, possibly in a similar plant, during the erection of the plant and not have such startling increases in expatriates every time a major new plant is commissioned, is unclear. It is a goal but not one likely to be fulfilled until the late 1980s at best.

There have been attempts to grapple with the scale problem and with the technology problem. Interestingly, the tendency has been to attempt to grapple with them together. The assumption is basically (perhaps wrongly) that if one is going to build a petroleum refinery, or for that matter a natural gas conversion plant, it is unlikely to be either possible or practicable to develop a whole new technology for Tanzania and not very fruitful to try to work out minor adaptations. On the other hand in such manufactured goods as agricultural machinery it is likely that there are justifiable reasons for adapting and modifying the available machines, and that the new products would be suitable for small-scale, low-capital/output manufacture in Tanzania. Therefore the Tanzania Agricultural Mechanical Testing Unit is a research design and production unit for intermediate, agricultural equipment and probably the largest centre for applied work in manufacturing development. The promotional body linked with this effort is the Small Industries Development Organization. There are continuing efforts but no one could claim that a breakthrough has been achieved over a broad range of products or to a large number of viable small-scale units.

This analysis in no way suggests the absence of serious micro errors. Nor does it imply – the reverse would probably be the perception of most directly involved decision-takers, officials and technological personnel – that adequate priority has been given either to building up capacity for making informed technology choices, to creating systematic industry or skill-oriented training or to laying foundations for applied technological capacity articulated to manufacturing units capable of embodying it in machines. What it does suggest is that the record is not one of totally random choices, of a systematic pursuit of high technology or of an unawareness of the nature of underlying problems not readily resolveable during 1961–80. Further, criticism of the capital/output and skill intensity shifts emerges – however intended – as ultimately being criticism of the strategy of structural change toward an integrated industrial sector.

V Productivity and Efficiency

Productivity is highly unequal and on balance unsatisfactory as to levels and trends. Both a majority of Tanzanian and of expatriate (or of directly involved and academic) analysts, observers and participants agree on those points. There is little agreement on the causes, on the precise factual situation, on how serious the weaknesses are, or on what can be done to raise productivity.[48]

Until 1972 constant price output per worker in large-scale manufacturing enterprises rose and wages/salaries were a fairly constant proportion of value added. Capacity utilization was hard to measure meaningfully, in some (but not all) products quite low, and very uneven, with large public sector firms on average turning in better performances than large private ones.[49]

However, econometric analysis showed a decline in factor productivity for both capital and labour after 1965.[50] Similarly micro studies[51] have shown a number of specific productivity/efficiency problems, varying in degree and kind from firm to firm, and a number of contextual productivity/efficiency debilitating factors, notably scarcity of middle- and high-level personnel and the ramifications of the foreign exchange crisis plus the associated problems of electricity, water and transport availability. The interlocking nature of micro and exogenous causes makes enterprise or sectoral analysis after 1973 highly subjective and imprecise – an exogenous cause is also an ideal excuse[52] and an apparant enterprise-level failing may ultimately prove to be contextual.

The inequality of results and the data problems, let alone causal interpretations and allocations of results among causes, are illustrated by the eight (five public, three private) main mills in the textile subsector in 1976.[53] Two public sector mills were operating in the 80–95% range of 24 hours per day, 365 days a year rated capacity: one might suppose a level not sustainable in the long run. One was in the 50–60% range and two were at about 40%. Trends were quite divergent as well with two rising, one falling, two fluctuating. All three private sector mills seemed to be in the 30–40% range – one rising, one falling, one flat. Skills bottlenecks, while common to seven cases (the eighth is poaching), are different in degree and kind as are training programmes, degree of worker participation and of authoritarian management. Equally wide ranges appear in terms of problems of water and power supply, success at mastering technology at repair (parts fabrication), adaptation levels, citizenization of technical and managerial staff, cost and quality control. Comparability of even hard data is shaky, for instance, the plant with the largest fixed capital and capital/output ratio has lower absolute depreciation than a similar output plant with much lower fixed assets; the rated capacity data are very dubiously comparable as, in most cases, they come from very different suppliers who stood in very different relationships to the Tanzanian plants.

The productivity levels/trends issue has been the subject of political as well as technical debate. One pole is identified with the code words 'discipline' and 'incentive' – and with World Bank and IMF advice. Its leading Tanzanian spokesman has been the ex-Minister of Finance who in an October 1979 speech to managers asserted that productivity had fallen 50%[54] as a result of laziness and indiscipline by workers tolerated by managers. This rather strident call to arms for authoritarian, managerial discipline met with an immediate rejection by the President and probably played a part in Minister Mtei's resignation.

The alternative pole argues that one must analyse and tackle productivity on a case-by-case basis. Lazy workers and incompetent managers, like policy mistakes, are accepted as contributing factors, but lack of adequate education, training programmes, worker participation and experience are perceived as more significant. Its international study *locus classicus* is the JASPA/ILO 1977 Mission's report.[55] This position, interestingly, is reflected in the Tanzanian Investment Bank's study on productivity.[56] At the political level it has been enunciated by the President and the present Minister of Finance.

Turning to the linked topic of efficiency, it is useful to distinguish between micro efficiency and macro efficiency. Micro efficiency is particular, case-oriented, marginal and short term. At this level Tanzanian performance discloses vast inequalities and different observers take very different views of the level of micro efficiency or inefficiency. These are often hard to assess. For example, one of the textile mills cited at 90% of capacity output in 1976, in 1977 was at 70% of capacity. It lacked both water and power for periods adding up to about half of the year. It is not, therefore, self-evident what interpretation can be put on micro efficiency of the textile firm as such. More generally, what is the standard of comparison? Colonial Tanzania? Tanzania 1970? Private firms in Tanzania? 'Typical' industrial economy performance? Perfection? Further, if the demonstrated inefficiency in a given case is genuinely one of learning costs or if there are spin-offs, is micro efficiency a very good test? This leads to the question over what time-period to measure. If Tanzania is engaged in a process of structural change, it is probable that in the early portion of that process units necessary for its long-term success will look pretty micro inefficient. Furthermore, micro efficiency is usually used in such a way that at the end of the argument one realizes that the user thinks that efficiency is a noun, whereas efficiency presumably is an adjective which has to be related to what it is one is attempting to achieve, that is, efficiency in generating surplus, in reducing real resource cost, in learning, or relative to some package of goals.[57]

Macro efficiency can be defined as the contribution (or otherwise) of a sector strategy, or policy, or enterprise, or decision to the goals the central decision-taking group perceives as of overriding medium- and long-term importance. If an analyst rejects these goals, he can erect a different macro efficiency but good performance on his standards will be macro inefficiency in terms of the actual operative goals of the decision-takers. The Tanzanian manufacturing sector does have some claim to macro efficiency. It has continued to grow; it continues to generate surplus. It has had success in increasing the production of wage goods and agricultural inputs. Personnel citizenization does proceed. However, other aspects are less macro efficient by Tanzanian standards. In technology there is little progress. In getting capital goods production started there may or may not be a dynamic beginning with heavy metal rolling plus foundry and spare parts production. Contributions to overcoming the transformation problem are mixed – in import substitution manufacturing has done well; in generating exports its record is poor.[58]

The disastrous results of 1979 and 1981 with a fall in output of 25%, despite major additions to capacity (from 60–65%) relate lack of imported inputs and spares, and of transport. Attempts to cope with these problems have clearly overstretched managements and led to their increased micro inefficiency in other sectors. The macro efficiency question is one of inadequate attention to raising earned import capacity – including, albeit not necessarily primarily, from the industrial sector.

VI   A Paradox and a Cluster of Critiques

Manufacturing in Tanzania highlights the paradox of interaction between structural change and dependence in Tanzanian development more generally. If Tanzania still had the same economic and public service structure as it had at independence and had continued its pre-independence 2% a year real growth rate – instead of having significantly changed the structure of production and public services and grown between 4% and 5% a year – and still had the same numbers of high-level citizen personnel it has now (perhaps a 'slightly' unlikely combination), about 99% of the posts held by expatriates in 1979 would not exist or would be filled by citizens. Virtually every expatriate post that existed in Tanzania at the time of independence could now be filled by a citizen; it is a more rapid rate of growth and, in particular, structural change, which has meant that the number of expatriates, while declining from 90% of high-level manpower to 40% overall – and probably from 95% to 50% in manufacturing – has declined only marginally overall in absolute terms and may have risen in manufacturing. Similarly the fall in the ratio of imports to GDP was rather small to 1973 and very damaging thereafter. It was rather small although consumer manufactured goods have changed from 80% of total consumption imported at independence to perhaps 20% in 1973. Precisely because of the broader range of manufactured goods produced in Tanzania their absolute and relative import content has risen. The goods produced at independence were ones that had almost no import content. Similarly structural change altered the share of machinery in total fixed investment from 10% at independence to about 30% in the 1970s. The result of this has been that Tanzania has not been able to reduce the direct and indirect share of imports in investment which is still in the range of 60–70%. It has been reduced in construction materials and construction, but Tanzania has not reduced it in machinery where the share is still nearly 100%.

The general Tanzanian record, whether in material or political dynamic terms, is problematic, as are debates about the viability of Tanzanian transition and, assuming that it is viable, what it is a transition to. Industrialization is no exception. Three broad clusters of criticism – surplus maximization, dependence, incompleteness – are of special interest. The first two basically reject the strategy, the third is usually intended to alter or complement it within its existing goal framework.

The surplus maximization critique – both from the technocratic right (e.g. the World Bank) and from some radical critics (e.g. Andrew Coulson)[59] – holds that Tanzanian industrialization strategy neither gives primacy to surplus maximization at project formulation level, nor in enterprise operations nor in broader institutional and policy structures. Tanzanian decision-takers – especially those like the President and Minister of Finance who have repeatedly stressed the need for efficiency and public enterprise surpluses – would agree as to the lack of primacy, but retort that human beings, not surpluses or accumulation, were the sole subjects of, and primary means to, development. At that level the issue is ultimately one of values, not economics, albeit the Tanzanian performance in pure growth, modernization and domestic surplus generation terms is strong enough to prevent refutation of the argument that the party's values are quite consistent with economic advance in general and with industrialization in particular.

The surplus maximization analysis assumes that anything that is consumed, whether it is personal consumption or communal consumption, beyond some fairly minimal necessary level is a waste. Certainly Tanzania's minimum wage (by inspection of comparable countries' levels) is too high for purposes of surplus maximization. Left and right critics are at one in criticizing Tanzania on levels of mass consumption. This is an example at the most general level of applying surplus maximization to a political system in a way which assumes a virtually negative time-preference for output by decision-takers and abstracts from political viability. At a more specific level, all sorts of problems arise. Tanzania built an automatic bakery at Dar es Salaam, not to make a surplus, although with a rather desperate hope that it would avoid having a negative surplus.[60] The positive motive flowed from a perception that existing private bakeries were providing short-weighted, adulterated bread to wage-earners. This was viewed by a number of people – including the then Minister of Agriculture, an elected MP for one of the urban workers' constituencies – as a significant problem about which something should be done. Other decision-takers agreed with this perception. If such a concern to end exploitation can, in principle, be valid, then a system accepting its validity is quite inconsistent with evaluating the project undertaken for that reason solely on surplus maximization criteria.

At the level of project by project evaluation – *ex ante* and *ex post* – there can be no question that Tanzania has made serious mistakes.[61] For whatever reason, projections have been inaccurate and performance has often been inadequate and inadequately (or tardily) monitored. However, the operational questions are what can be done to improve procedures, data collection and analysis and broader managerial/bureaucratic concern for surplus generation as a critical goal. Related are the questions of what standards of comparison, benchmarks and rates of improvement can be identified to allow a less fragmented and subjective level of evaluation, control and correction.

Between the basic development values and project-by-project levels lies the question of economic systemic and structural change efficiency – including overall present and future surplus generation. In practice the surplus maximization approach overlooks or underemphasizes this level. Its central concerns are project level, and bricks and mortar (fixed capital) at that level. Working capital, investment in research and training (especially outside the firm), policy frameworks, extension services are all grossly underemphasized – or at best not integrated with project-level issues – because they do not appear in fixed capital formation. Tanzania has very real problems in achieving even minimally adequate sectoral and intersectoral (e.g. manufacturing – water/power) articulation. Both the project/enterprise and the broad target/overall allocation levels are distinctly better conceptualized and articulated. However, the surplus maximization critique, as usually posed, would divert attention from this priority problem and, probably, thereby reduce surplus generation.

The dependence critique is in one sense an inversion of the surplus maximization one. From this perspective Tanzania should seek a much more rapid structural change to a neo-autarchic, integrated industrial sector. Capital goods production should receive pride of place at an early stage of industrialization. Ajit Singh has formulated the argument as follows: basic needs cannot be met except through industrialization. Industrialization over time either stagnates or moves towards a predominance of intermediate and capital goods and final consumer goods. Therefore, sustained structural change requires priority attention to capital goods from an early stage. How severe a criticism of Tanzanian strategy Singh sees this as being is less clear – he is one of the authors of the JASPA study which does see sustained change as taking place.[62]

One difficulty of this line of criticism is that it raises questions of possibility. Is it a possible sequence in Tanzania – given existing levels of knowledge and skill – to start with capital goods as the primary focus in industrialization or would better long-term results be achieved by concentrating on other subsectors for several years while capital goods were being built up from initially 'marginal' (e.g. spares) and 'peripheral' (e.g. implements) areas to create a base? The second question is whether this would be a particularly efficient sequence with a spin-off from a domestic capital goods industry large enough to offset the short-term surplus losses of having very expensive capital goods.

These are not rhetorical questions, at least if they relate to degree of emphasis on capital goods rather than to a Cartesian either/or choice. Indeed, a valid criticism of the basic industry strategy is that while it sets a target of 40% of capital goods produced domestically for 1996 there does not seem to be any coherent mechanism – whether step by step incremental or once for all shift – for attaining it in the strategy's articulation.[63] A third question is precisely how a capital goods industry is to be defined. Would a capital goods industry consisting basically of machine building without the supporting intermediate goods subsectors – which in this case include an integrated iron and steel industry – be a useful type of industrial strategy? Further, Tanzania is a small country both in the sense that there are limits to the resources available (e.g. most metals are not known to be present in viable form) and in the sense that it is a small country in terms of levels of use. It would take a basic rejection, not merely qualification, of economies of scale and specialization to suppose that Tanzania should produce a complete range of machine tools.[64] However, the limited attention until 1979–80 on studying and forward planning for the light engineering/metal processing sector (since organized in MEDIA – Metal and Engineering Development Industries Association) does represent a lagged realization of one route towards significant expansion of capital goods production immediately feasible in the Tanzanian context.

The third group of critiques is somewhat different in that, by and large, it is intended to supplement rather than to supplant the existing strategy. As exemplified in the JASPA report[65] and the work of M.A. Bienefeld[66] it includes three elements.[67] First a perception that worker power is inadequate rather than too high. Second, an argument that therefore it would be desirable to have worker involvement which would be easier in smaller-scale, lower capital output industry requiring less cumbersome and authoritarian management structures and fewer foreigners. Finally a parallel argument that, given the availability of resources in Tanzania, small-scale and labour-intensive – as opposed to capital-intensive – manufacturing would make more sense in terms of employment and of surplus generation. There are certain problems about this line of argument. One is the difficulty of making it fit with public sector dominance. A second issue which has been debated, but not empirically tested, is whether the intermediate-scale enterprises are or are not very intensive in certain types of skilled and semi-skilled personpower so that the savings on capital are purchased at the price of greater use of resources which are even scarcer. And of course the objective question that if a way can be devised and used to operate this within the public sector, how will it in fact augment workers' power?

VII   An Internal Critique

It is also possible to build a critique of Tanzanian industrialization, from within the 'socialism and self-reliance' premises informing it, which is of more than a marginal or tidying-up nature.

First, the overall structural change goals are not adequately articulated. Vectoral and case-by-case selection of industries can be tools for implementing structural change. But in the absence of more coherent guidelines at sectoral level and more systematic iterative working from sector to subsector to product/enterprise and back, there is a real danger that the project will become the sole operational focus and the sectoral aims and interactions remain at the levels of theory and exhortation.

Second, certain tactical issues with respect to surplus generation and dependence require closer attention. Certain identifiable industrial complexes – e.g. ammonia/urea from natural gas – would be very capital-intensive, very large relative to the economy and the industrial sector, initially very heavily dependent on foreign knowledge, personnel, marketing arrangements and loan capital. Should they, therefore, be placed further down the time-sequence than a pure surplus generation (or a pure intrasectoral integration) criterion would suggest? Or are they justified as means to achieving a structural shift in the export/import imbalance and thus acting on the transformation problem? Are there not gaps in the production chains – e.g. spare parts for machinery, gypsum for cement, a range of dyes and chemicals for textiles – whose absence from domestic production radically reduces output and surplus of the enterprises using them, especially in the post-1973 foreign exchange crisis? If so, then the effect on sectoral output and surplus is relevant to evaluating both 'gap-filling' projects' true economic viability and their proper place in the industrialization time-sequence.

Third, despite a good deal of emphasis on small-scale decentralized public sector enterprise generation and on furthering worker control the results are inadequate in terms of Tanzanian goals. The problem does not appear to be lack of 'political will' or blocking power either of capitalists or a bureaucratic elite. Would a serious technico-institutional analysis of ways, means, constraints and sequences be appropriate?

Fourth, what is a workable substrategy for the capital goods subsector? Must it really wait on the definition and completion of an integrated steel industry – a probable event by 1996 but one not predictable much more definitely than that for genuinely technical reasons.[68] What can be done starting from major repair capacity, spare parts fabrication and building material production? From systematic allocation of financial, personnel and research/design resources to a series of sectors such as agricultural implements which do not embody 'high' technology and which are not appropriately or economically served by existing imports? How can present training, research, adaptation and design programmes be recast to provide a base for building up and supporting a capital goods sector?

Fifth, is the Tanzanian tactical approach of concentrating effort at any one time on a handful of critical problems, constraints or secondary contradictions which appear to be resolvable at that time adequate? It does avoid dispersion of scarce resources. It has yielded striking successes. But it also can allow avoidable mistakes to build up to crisis levels when earlier, lesser attention could have cut that process short. Further, it may switch attention too rapidly, in other words, before a new synthesis is embodied firmly enough in processes and institutions to be an ongoing dynamic which it is safe to handle routinely. The successive 1973–4 and 1978–80 crises of the National Milling Corporation may illustrate both points. Its 1973–4 failure to act on its own knowledge of impending grain shortages was overcome by other institutions and not treated as cause for any more systematic reform than sacking the general manager. The 1978–80 breakdown of data flows, and therefore of financial and stock control, suggests there were deeper structural causes which might more conveniently and inexpensively have been tackled in 1974. Even more seriously does the zigzag (unbalanced development) priority attention path systematically bias choice against policies which neither have high short-term payoff nor basic long-term structural justification but may be critical in the medium term? One reading of the 1974–7 response to external crisis as set out from within the system would support that doubt. Most targets were met, that for exports, while set, received no serious attention in 1974–6 (because it could not yield results until, say, 1977–8 and other approaches could) nor in 1977–8 (when the external balance problem appeared to have retreated).[69]

Sixth, the transformation problem has not been faced squarely with respect to industrialization or Tanzanian political economic policy more generally. Domestic surpluses can, except in a far more integrated economy than Tanzania will be even in 1996, be transformed into productive investment only through the use of imports. Indeed a high rate of growth of domestic output, even with structural change toward industrialization to integrate the economy, raises intermediate goods import requirements at least as fast as import substitution reduces consumer goods imports. Unless the transformation problem is resolved by exports, or by levels of external loans and grants so high relative to imports and investment as to be inconsistent with self-reliance, not only will fixed investment be constrained and particular plants produce below capacity, but generalized inefficiency will spread cancerously throughout the economy because of import starvation. What implications does this have for increased emphasis on net foreign exchange saving/earning in project selection and, more particularly, formulation? Can gap-filling substantially reduce imports? In 1981 the National Economic Survival Programme sought to tackle these questions and gave first priority to increasing exports as a means to allowing futher use of existing capacity in other sectors in the short term, and restoring investment in new capacity in the medium.

Is the combination of a domestic price system deliberately separated from the global consistent with adequate export levels given the somewhat fetishistic use of global prices as ceilings for the domestic producer returns on exports? Tanzania's general aversion to subsidizing enterprises is a sound guideline – surplus generation not surplus reduction is usually a necessary goal for a productive enterprise. However, since Tanzania is operating an autonomous price structure and foreign exchange budgeting, it appears sensible to argue that once it finds what foreign exchange is required, it should see what exports could produce that amount of foreign exchange at the lowest real resource cost. On that basis it is likely both that further processing from cotton and from hides and skins should have higher priority than it has had to date and that more systematic attention should be paid to building up exports in lines such as GCI (corrugated) sheet, metal pipes, cigarettes, processed foods, batteries, radios, which have shown signs in the past of being nearly or fully competitive in regional markets.

These criticisms do not constitute an alternative strategy. They rest on an interpretation of the present Tanzanian industrialization strategy as consistent with the overall strategy of transition to socialism and self-reliance and as inherently possible. While, by definition, stressing real or apparent inefficiencies and gaps within, as well as shortcomings in the implementation of, the strategy, they are likewise based on an interpretation of the process of Tanzanian industrialization over 1967–79 as predominantly positive. By implication at least, they also constitute a case for incremental and tactical, rather than overall and strategic, changes with respect to Tanzanian industrialization.

Whether Tanzania's industrialization strategy will in the event succeed is a rather different question. In the first place the critical transformation problem is much broader than manufacturing and cannot realistically be overcome primarily by action in the industrial sector. But unless it is overcome, the prognosis for all Tanzanian sectoral strategies must be gloomy. Second, the Tanzanian dynamic has been marked by struggle. It still is, and will continue to be. While both critics (whether conservative or radical) who gleefully, and supporters who sadly, projected the collapse of the Tanzanian transition to socialism have been proved wrong repeatedly over 1967–80, the outcome of both the domestic political economic and the external environmental struggles is problematic. This became even more true in 1981. Lack of imports eroded not only the ability to produce for (or transport goods to) the domestic market but also the effective export capacity. Given a lack of non-essential imports to cut radically worsening terms of trade and the vicious circle constraint on exports, other than some investment goods on project finance terms whose dropping would not free foreign exchange. Some new sources of external transfers in 1982 appear to be objectively necessary to avoid general – and especially industrial sector – collapse. Over the short term, industrialization is secondary to the outcome (unless remarkably and quite atypically badly mishandled); over the next decade it can play a significant role (positive or negative; only in a two-to three-decade perspective is it crucial.

Notes

Much of this chapter is based on participation in the process described as an adviser to or official of the Tanzanian government continuously over 1966–74 and 1979–81 since. None of the data used are viewed as secret by Tanzania but, unfortunately, the documents in which many are recorded are so perceived. The views and interpretations are those of the author and do not necessarily correspond to official Tanzanian positions.

1   See Mwansasu and Pratt, 1979, for a series of commentaries, interpretations and introductions to debates.

2   See A. Coulson's chapter in this volume for a more detailed presentation of other historical elements.

3   See Green in Mwansasu and Pratt, 1979, and JASPA, 1978, for more detailed presentations.

4   See Ake, 1972, for a lucid statement of this point.

5   For example, Barker et al., 1976, and to a lesser extent Rweyemamu, 1973.

6   Indeed even the cosmetic factory – rather to the author's surprise when he had dealings with it as an official – produced products directed primarily to the more affluent peasant and wage-earner market. The bulk of radio production was of models in the price range of one to two months' minimum wage. Only private saloon car repair stands out within manufacturing as a clearly upper-income consumer good dominated subsector.

7   See Green, 1978a.

8   See I. Parker in Mwansasu and Pratt, 1979.

9   Arguments in terms of self-reliance in basic consumer goods and internal economic integration (e.g. cotton to garments) were regularly advanced in official and political level discussions.

10   NDC, in fact, did not perform this role well nor systematically accept it as a duty. See Parker.

11   Certain citizen capitalists have served on parastatal boards and, in one case, as a general manager. However, the cases are few and care has been taken to avoid links between their private and public sector business roles.

12   The need to know what Tanzanians mean by the term is independent of whether the next stage is acceptance or criticism. The term's popular interpretation in Tanzania is goods produced in Tanzania by Tanzanians to meet Tanzanian needs and sold at fair prices.

13   Schubert's (1978) data suggest considerable progress in this respect when contrasted with other African economies.

14   Thomas in fact wrote his main exposition of this thesis while professor at the University of Dar es Salaam.

15   Rweyamamu, 1973.

16   In practice Rweyamamu retreated somewhat from the emphasis on machines and steel which is very prominent in his (1973) volume.

17   Another imprecise term as what is heavy varies from the product, to the plant size, to the technology, to the losses (or occasionally all at once).

18   The year in which it was pointedly underlined by a quotation from Dom Helder Camara on President Nyerere's official Christmas card.

19   See Clark's data.

20   This Cartesian division into export or domestic is not typical of most products or enterprises in economies with diversified industrial sectors.

21   See Roemer et al., 1976, for the DAS team's own interpretation of its work.

22   DAS's multiple strategies were oddly similar in actual product/project content and none is by any means identical to the actual Plan selection.

23   The identification of key figures does not imply that there were not other significant actors at official and decision-taker level. The author's self-exclusion is not mock modesty, he was not in Tanzania in 1975 and any influence was by comments to others early in the 1973–75 process or notes at later stages.

24   External controls are necessary even for public sector enterprises but the balance changes.

25   In 1977–79 there were some joint venture discussions with domestic capitalists but few or no actual results. While the state no longer saw such ventures as necessarily posing barriers to further steps in a transition to socialism it remained cautious, while the entrepreneurs were (correctly) worried that joint ventures would in most cases be an interim step to total public sector ownership within a decade.

26   Given the parallel concentration on control of external trade at enterprise and Bank of Tanzania level, the parallel to the Soviet new economic policy is rather striking. However, while the critical role of control over finance and foreign trade in a transition to socialism was stressed at official and decision-taker level, the NEP parallel or the debates surrounding it were rarely cited.

27   See Bienefeld, 1978, Mihyo, 1975, and Mapolu, 1973, for differing perceptions.

28   See Mwansasu in Mwansasu and Pratt, 1979.

29   Clark's (1978) data unfortunately do not separate out divergences caused by different skill intensities and training levels required.

30   NUTA does bargain at enterprise level but within fairly limited guidelines.

31   The only class who enjoyed higher average personal consumption power in 1977–78 than in 1973–4 was the peasants.

32   See the consultancy report to the TIB, especially section 35.

33   These paragraphs are based on semi-direct involvement with effects of several of these confrontations though not direct contact with the confrontations or negotiations proper.

34   In the bus case attitudes of passengers and very bad working conditions (overcrowded buses) were possibly as critical in causing the clash as wages per se but this was not how the then Vice-President perceived the dispute.

35   In the Mount Carmel Rubber case officials were quite startled at the reversal since on earlier precedents they had set to work to create a viable structure for a

worker-owned factory with a technical partner. Foreign investor reaction, if any, was not significant in this case. The key decision-taker in this case was a rural populist not generally seen as sympathetic to either capitalists – let alone Mt Carmel's owner – or managers but even less sympathetic to what he perceived (rightly or wrongly) as 'private' groups cloaking self-interest in party slogans while declining to use party channels or accept party discipline.

36   This line of criticism is common from World Bank and Fund functionaries but also has a radical (new left?) variant.

37   Twenty-seven per cent real rate of return on industrial capital in 1972–3 according to JASPA data (1978, p. 81). Total state investment in parastatals, excluding those of the East African Community, had a pre-tax rate of surplus of the order of 25–30% in the early 1970s.

38   JASPA, (1978, p. 76).

39   See Green, 1978a.

40   Contracts and papers presented at International Center for Law in Development – UP Law Center – Marga Institute conferences in Tagaytay (1977) and Colombo (1979) and at the 1979 conference organized by Y. Ghai at the University of Warwick.

41   From a rather non-random sample the author believes this to have been true in Tanzania as well. This is not very surprising – the domestic private firms had less data and less economic strength than the public sector.

42   Indeed for that reason serious problems are now arising in respect of spares and replacement machines; Mlawa, 1979–80.

43   See table cited on p. 76 of JASPA, 1978.

44   This is largely imported inflation although domestic construction sector bottlenecks have also been a contributing factor.

45   In addition to bedevilling comparisons, these trends have hampered project projections and evaluation of cost overruns especially in the post-1970 context of more rapid and more erratic price increases.

46   The natural gas/petrochemicals complex is likely to be the largest industrial (and export) project of 1981–5, albeit it is in fact a Ministry of Energy, not Industry, responsibility.

47   Mlawa, 1979–80.

48   For example, Jedrusek, 1977–80; Ellis, 1979–80; JASPA, 1978; Green et al., forthcoming; TIB, 1978.

49   JASPA, 1978.

50   Jedruszek, 1977–80.

51   Ellis, 1979–80; Jedruszek, 1977–80; TIB, 1978.

52   Mlawa, 1979–80.

53   Notably in the draft 1977 World Bank Report. Both Tanzanian official analysts and some external analysts consulted by them found it to be riddled with inaccuracies as well as so unacceptable to Tanzania in its proposals as to suggest either that its authors opposed socialism in principle whatever a state's own strategic choice was or that they could not relate to the internal logic of a socialist transition.

54   If 'accurate' this relates to incremental productivity of labour in public enterprises. Labour productivity per capita (in real terms) rose in 1978 and over 1974–8 as well as over 1967–78.   ·

55   See JASPA, 1978. The defence is perhaps overdone; the JASPA team was fairly evidently engaged in a polemic with the World Bank draft report.

56   TIB, 1978.

57   See Green, 1978b, for an example of a multiple goal case in which criticism based on different goals set by the critic is unlikely to be illuminating.

58   Imports to output ratios rose for the sector, almost certainly because of structural change. Maize meal (a typical pre-1961 manufacture) has a very low import content; textiles (typical of 1961–7 additions) a higher but still moderate one; vehicle tyres (a not atypical intermediate good of post-1967 establishment) a relatively high one but still with a significant import saving when contrasted to direct tyre imports.

59   See articles by A. Coulson reprinted in A. Coulson (ed.), *African Socialism in*

Practice: The Tanzanian Experience (London: Spokesman, 1979), especially the chapters on the automated bakery and fertilizer plant.
60 Green, 1978b.
61 Tanzania's officials are among the first to make this statement and it is a regular theme in the President's speeches. The difference is that the mistakes are viewed as a *de facto* price of learning by doing and cited as experience gained to use in the future.
62 But in his more rhetorical moments Singh has virtually defined the optimal capital good as a tank – not a tank for a reservoir or a brewery but a tank to shoot its way to Pretoria. This is not a ludicrous proposition intellectually or historically albeit it's present feasibility may be open to question. It certainly is, at least implicitly, a strong critique of Tanzanian (or Mozambican) industrial strategy. In this form the argument is the familiar sinews of industry/arsenals of war one which runs like a red thread through Tzarist and Soviet industrialization, most notably under Peter the Great and Stalin.
63 Rweyamamu, 1973, lays great stress on capital goods in his book but retreated – perhaps too far – in formulating actual initial industry targets.
64 cf. the Korean Democratic Republic. Export growth has exceeded that of GDP. Most exports have been transformed from raw to intermediate to final goods, e.g. iron ore, later steel, now machinery. Capital goods are a rising share of industrial production and exports but also of imports.
65 JASPA, 1978.
66 See Bienefeld, 1974 and 1978.
67 There are other criticisms as well but they are either specific to individual authors or appear to be marginal – tidying up in nature.
68 Steel is in any event today close to being a primary commodity with a buyer's market. As Tanzania has coal and iron ore of plausible quality and quantity there is little doubt – and has been little among senior Tanzanians for at least six years – that an integrated steel industry will be an appropriate part of the strategy. Serious unresolved technical issues affecting choice of ore deposit, fuel, smelting technology, location and by product recovery (vanadium) have made a final decision appear inappropriate.
69 Green *et al.*, forthcoming.

References

C. Ake, (1972) 'Tanzania: the progress of a decade', *African Review*, II, 1 (June).
C. Barker, M. Bhagavan, P. von Mitschke-Collande and D. Wield (1976), 'Industrial production and transfer of technology in Tanzania: the political economy of Tanzanian industrial enterprises' (Dar es Salaam: Institute of Development Studies).
M. A. Bienefeld (1974), *The Self-Employed of Urban Tanzania*, (Sussex: Institute of Development Studies, Discussion Paper 54).
M. A. Bienefeld (1977), *Trade Unions, and Peripheral Capitalism: The Case of Tanzania* (Sussex: Institute of Development Studies, Discussion Paper No. 122).
W. E. Clark (1978), *Socialist Development and Public Investment in Tanzania 1964–73* (Toronto: University of Toronto Press).
F. Ellis (1979–80), papers on agricultural pricing at Economic Research Bureau, University of Dar es Salaam.
R. H. Green (1978a), 'A guide to acquisition and initial operation', in J. Faundez and S. Picciotto (eds), *Nationalization of Multinationals in Peripheral Economies* (London: Macmillan).
R. H. Green (1978b), *The Automated Bakery: A Study of Decision-Taking*

Goals, Processes and Problems in Tanzania (Sussex: Institute of Development Studies, Discussion Paper No. 141).

R. H. Green, D. G. Rwegasira and B. Van Arkadie (forthcoming), *Crisis And Response: Balance Of Payments Management In Tanzania In The 1970s*, (The Hague: Institute of Social Studies).

JASPA (1978), *Towards Self Reliance: Development, Employment and Equity Issues in Tanzania* (Addis Ababa, International Labour Organization).

J. Jedruszek (1977–80), unpublished micro and macro industrial productivity studies at Economic Research Bureau, Dar es Salaam.

H. Mapolu (1973), 'The workers' movement in Tanzania', *Maji Maji*, 12 (September).

P. Mihyo (1975), 'The struggle for workers' control in Tanzania', *Review of African Political Economy*, 4.

H. Mlawa (1979–80), unpublished work in progress on Tanzania textile industry. Instute of Development Studies (Sussex) and Institute of Development Studies (Das es Salaam).

B. Mwansasu and C. Pratt (eds) (1979), *Towards Socialism in Tanzania*, (Dar es Salaam/Toronto: Tanzania Publishing House/University of Toronto).

M. Roemer, G. Tiddrick and D. Williams (1976), 'The range of strategic choices in Tanzanian industry', *Journal of Development Economics*, III, 1.

J. Rweyemamu (1973), *Underdevelopment and Industrialization in Tanzania* (London: Oxford University Press).

J. Schubert (1978), *DFG Project: Entwicklungstrategien in Afrika: Elfenbeinkuste, Malawi, Sambia, Tansania. Eine vergleichende Studie Zum Wehatnis von Entwicklung, Abhangigkeit und Aussenpolitik*, (Berlin: 'Kapital 4: Okonomishe Entwicklung und Abhangigkeit').

Tanzania (1962–79), *Economic Survey* (previously *Background to Budget*) (Government Printer: Dar es Salaam).

Tanzania (1978), Third Five-Year Development Plan (unofficial translation).

Tanzania (1961/2, 1979/80), *Budget Speeches* (Government Printer: Dar es Salaam).

TIB (Tanzania Investment Bank) (1978), *Productivity Management, Measurement And Improvement*, Consultancy report to TIB (Dar es Salaam)

C. Thomas (1973), *Dependence and Transformation*, (New York: Monthly Review Press).

6 *Evaluating Tanzanian Industrial Development*

MANFRED BIENEFELD

Tanzania's industrialization can only be assessed in the context of the wider debate concerned with Tanzania's development experience more generally. The fact that that wider debate has led to widespread disillusionment and repeated announcements of failure provides the particular context of the industrialization debate. Within that context the interpretation of industrial developments readily arrives at similarly negative conclusions.

In looking specifically at that industrialization debate, this chapter will suggest that such conclusions are currently based on highly problematic concepts and comparisons, and that any evaluation which is based on a wider and more defensible theoretical, historical and international perspective yields a rather different result.

In practice, even a description of Tanzania's industrialization is not an easy task because the statistical base is far from comprehensive and not always reliable. A critical assessment of that experience is inevitably more problematic, because apart from reliable empirical evidence, it requires: some specification of the superior alternative to which it is being compared; some analytic framework which suggests the means by which this superior alternative is thought to have been attainable; and some historical analysis which attempts to establish the plausibility of means. Unfortunately much of the existing critical discussion both of the overall strategy, and of industrialization as such, pays little attention to these requirements. All too often, the evidence is treated selectively and superficially, and the alternatives are neither spelled out nor shown to have been plausible options. The result is that the conclusions frequently amount either to little more than statements (of faith?) derived from a wider theoretical debate and applied with little connection to the particularities of the Tanzanian case, or to the implication of failure based on some more or less extensive list of particular problems.

In this chapter the explicit and implicit bases for these conclusions will first be briefly examined. This will be followed by an indication of how one might set about the task of arriving at a more meaningful and balanced evaluation.

What Is To Be Evaluated?

As Green has correctly observed in his chapter in this volume it is essential to begin by defining the objectives against which performance is to be judged. Furthermore, the relevant set of objectives cannot be dealt with separately and 'in turn', since their interdependence within the process of social and economic change demands that they be considered jointly. It goes without saying that such a process can only lead to imprecise conclusions, because the weight to be given to various objectives will and can never be precisely specified, and because the nature of the interdependence between variables is inevitably disputed and always subject to uncertainty in any particular instance. While it would thus be illusory to expect such a debate to be rigorously or unambiguously resolvable, it is important to recognize that this makes careful judgments about the likely impact of alternative courses of social and political action no less important. Of course, insofar as those judgments can and do themselves become the basis for action, they will themselves influence the course of events, thus increasing the uncertainty inherent in such analysis and emphasizing that any social scientific inquiry is necessarily part of the political and ideological process, protestations of objectivity notwithstanding.

The point of departure for this discussion must be to determine the relevant objectives of Tanzania's policies. The state's declared aims naturally appear at one level like those of most other states, indicating a desire to achieve growth, equity and political stability in a relatively liberal and democratic context. However, from 1967 onwards, the Tanzanian state's objectives were restated so as to give a greater than usual weight to equity, and to political stability, not based on overt repression. At the same time it was announced that the achievement of its objectives, thus restated, would require a significant shift away from the reliance on private capital acting on the basis of market signals, and towards a more direct social (state) control of resources in the context of socially/politically determined priorities. Since this latter strategy would necessarily inhibit the flow of private capital from abroad, and since it would reduce the *direct* economic influence of international investors and prices, it was said to be associated with the notion of 'self-reliance'.

This chapter will accept these objectives as a relevant and defensible norm against which to assess Tanzania's experience. This is not primarily, as in Green's case, because it happens to be the government's policy, but rather because it almost certainly approximated the priorities and social time preferences which the people of Tanzania did then, and would now, support. In short, even if all Tanzanians were fully convinced of some hypothetical negative correlation between a relatively greater short-term emphasis on equity and the longer run objectives of growth, equity and political stability, it is most unlikely that they would have opposed a relatively greater (relative in relation to the market induced pattern) weight being given to the consumption of the current, as against some future, generation.

Once the objectives are accepted it is of course possible to question the conclusion, that a greater degree of state involvement will assist in meeting these objectives. While it is neither possible nor appropriate to rehearse the theoretical disputes which address that issue in general, it is important to establish that a decisive and general answer to this question cannot be derived from purely theoretical propositions. As the chapter by Singh in this volume indicates, there is clearly a theoretical case to be made for the possibility that, especially in the context of technological backwardness, extensive state involvement in the economy can accelerate growth, *ceteris paribus*. At the same time it is obvious that such state involvement in the economy will not necessarily produce such desirable results. All will depend on the particular circumstances, including the relative strength of various class forces in the political and in the economic spheres; the skills and resources which are available, and the cultural and international context within which the process unfolds. The paper will return to this question, after considering the available evidence on industrialization.

The Industrialization Debate: The Evidence

An evaluation of the process of industrialization must consider the contribution which that process has made to the broader objectives earlier defined. What has been its contribution to growth? Its impact on income distribution?

Table 6.1   *Tanzania 1964–77: growth of monetary GDP (at 1966 prices) % per annum*

	Total monetary GDP %	Total monetary GDP (Finance Deleted) %	Total GDP %
1964–5	3·6	2·9	2·7
1965–6	14·4	17·1	12·8
1966–7	4·3	2·7	4·0
1967–8	6·6	7·1	5·2
1968–9	3·8	3·6	1·8
1969–70	7·4	8·3	5·8
1970–1	5·0	5·1	4·2
1971–2	6·2	6·6	6·7
1972–3	3·5	3·4	3·1
1973–4	3·7	3·2	2·5
1974–5	4·3	4·8	5·9
1975–6	3·0	3·1	6·4
1976–7	5·6	5·8	6·5
1977–8	—	—	5·6
1978–9	—	—	3·5*

Note:
* Provisional
Sources: Figures for Monetary GDP and Total GDP, for the period 1965 to 1977 were taken from *Hali ya Uchumi wa Taifa Katika Mwaka 1977-8*, Table 3. This was extended to 1979 by information obtained from the Ministry of Industry, and also contained in M.S.D. Bagachwa (Bagachwa 1980), p. 15.
The figures for Monetary GDP (finance deleted) are those used by Jedruszek in his paper on productivity change (Jedruszek, 1978, p. 76).

Figure 6.1   *Tanzania 1964–79: growth of GDP (1966 prices) % per annum.*

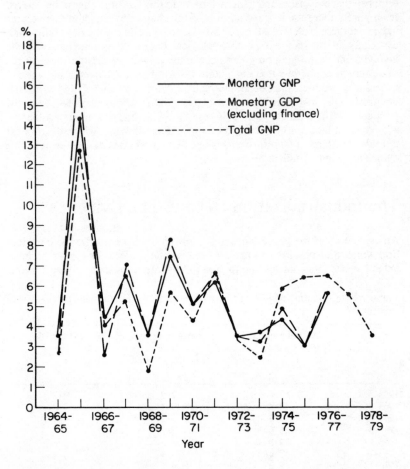

Source: *Hali ya Uchumi wa Taifa Katika Mwaka 1977/78*, except for the 1977–8 and 1978–9 figures which are provisional figures taken from Ministry of Industries. *Speech by the Hon. C.D. Msuya, MP, Minister for Industries to the Budget Session of the National Assembly for the 1979/80 Session*, p. 37.

Its role in the processes of social and political change? Finally, what has been the relationship between this sector and the rest of the economy?

Some of the evidence on these issues has been discussed by Coulson and Green in the preceding chapter. It is not intended to repeat that material here, but merely to indicate briefly the most significant results.

GDP: Growth of GDP (at constant prices) was 5.3% per annum between 1964 and 1977, and provisional figures to 1979 suggest that this rate has been more than maintained. Occasionally it is claimed (Jedruszek 1978, p. 12) that it 'is quite clear' that the rate of growth of total GDP in constant prices shows a declining tendency. This tendency is said to be revealed by dividing the

Year	Manufacturing VA Shs. mill (1)[a]	Manufacturing VA 1966=100	National accounts handicrafts VA Shs. mill (2)[a]	National accounts handicrafts VA Index 1966=100	Manufacturing & handicrafts value added (1)+(2) Shs. mill (3)[a]	Manufacturing & handicrafts value added Index 1966=100	Survey of industrial production manufacturing value added Shs. mill (4)[b]	Survey of industrial production Index 1966=100	Ratio of NA (Mnfrng)/SIP (mnfrng) (1)/4 (5)	Implicit estimate of handicrafts output using SIP estimate for manufacturing (3)-(4) (6)	(6) index	Index of industrial output: Silver and Kmietowicz (1966=100·0) (7)[c]	Implicit national accounts Deflator for mnfrng (8)[a]
1964	261	72	133	83	394	75							·94
1965	305	84	141	88	446	85	227	77	1·34	219	95	85	·96
1966	364	100	161	100	525	100	295	100	1·23	230	100	100	1·00
1967	403	111	169	105	572	109	319	108	1·26	253	110	104	1·00
1968	436	120	175	109	611	116	357	121	1·22	254	110	123	1·06
1969	496	136	176	109	672	128	431	146	1·15	241	105	134	1·10
1970	536	147	180	112	716	136	485	164	1·11	231	100	140	1·16
1971	593	163	186	116	784	149	529	179	1·12	255	111	167	1·21
1972	654	180	196	122	850	162	599	203	1·09	251	109	215	1·35
1973	684	188	204	127	888	169	645	219	1·06	243	106		1·42
1974	688	189	212	132	900	171	701	238	0·98	199	87		1·65
1975					903	172	634	215		269	117		1·96
1976					961	183	696	236		265	115		2·13
1977					1013	193							2·39
1978					1062*	202*							2·63*
1979					982*	187*							3·10*

Sources:

a *National Accounts of Tanzania 1966–1974*, was the basis for the figures between those two dates in columns (1), (2), (3) and (8). (From Tables 5, 7, 12 and 13). These were supplemented for 1964 and 1965 from *National Accounts of Tanzania 1964–1970* using Tables 5, 7, 12 and 13.
For reasons which are not explained the implicit deflators and the figures for manufacturing value added differ in these two series. This is presumably one reason why various secondary sources contain different figures. The statistics in columns 3 and 8 were further extended to 1977, using *Hali ya Uchumi wa Taifa Katika Mwaka 1977–78*. The Economic Survey 1977–78), Tables 1 and 3. Finally, columns 3 and 8 were extended to 1979 on the basis of information obtained from the Ministry of Industries, and also contained in (M.S.D. Bagachwa 1980, p. 15).

b The statistics for column 4 are taken from the *Surveys of Industrial Production* for 1966 (Table A3) and for 1969, 1972 and 1974 (Table A1). Current values have been expressed in 1966 prices by using the deflators provided in column 8. This series was extended to 1976 on the basis of *Haliya Uchumi wa Taifa Katika Mwaka 1977–78*, Table 48, p. 81.

c This series is based on a chained Laspeyres index built up from individual firm returns submitted for the Survey of Industrial Production. It is a superior measure to the others since it is better able to take account of changes in product mix, unevenly distributed price changes and the entry of new products and producers. The derivation of the index is explained in detail in M.S. Silver and Z.M. Kmietowicz (1977).

period into three sub-periods 1964–7, 1967–72 and 1972–6. However Table 6.1 and Figure 6.1 (including Jedruszek's figures) reveal the conclusion to be quite untenable. There is no long-term trend. There is merely a total aberration in 1966 and some slight decline during the crisis of the mid-1970s.

Manufacturing production: The experience with respect to manufacturing production can be summarised by saying that there was rapid long run expansion from the mid-1960s onwards, which was substantially depressed from the mid-1970s, in the context of the much intensified foreign exchange crisis that emerged in the wake of the 1973 'oil crisis'. Coulson presents somewhat sketchy data on the basis of which he asserts 'constantly declining growth rates' between 1964–5 and 1976–7 and stresses 'the loss of dynamism in the 1970s'. It is worth looking briefly at the evidence once more.

The difficulty with this discussion arises in part out of the differences between the various statistical series on which it is based. There are in fact three such series: the National Accounts estimates of manufacturing output (for firms with 5 or more employees); the National Accounts estimate of handicraft production ('all the residual establishments engaged in manufacturing and processing activities which are generally undertaken on a household or cottage industry basis');[1] and the Survey of Industrial Production (SIP) (establishments with 10 or more workers). Each of these series exhibits somewhat different trends and this has led to some confusion as different commentators stress the characteristics of one trend or another. However in reality the differences between the series need not be a problem, but can be

Table 6.2(b)　*Tanzania 1964–78: various estimates of annual rates of growth in manufacturing value added (1966 prices)*

	National accounts: manufacturing and handi- crafts %	National accounts: estimate of handicraft production %		Survey of industrial production: firms with 10 or more employees %	Silver and Kmietowicz's index of industrial production: %
		Implicit*	Actual		
1964–5	13·2		6·0		
1965–6	17·7	5·0	14·2	30·0	17·7
1966–7	9·0	10·0	5·0	8·1	4·0
1967–8	6·8	0·4	3·6	11·9	18·3
1968–9	10·0	−4·7	0·6	20·7	8·9
1969–70	6·6	−5·1	2·3	12·5	4·5
1970–1	9·5	10·4	3·3	9·1	19·3
1971–2	8·4	−1·6	5·4	13·2	28·7
1972–3	4·5	−3·2	4·1	7·7	—
1973–4	1·4	−18·1	3·9	8·9	—
1974–5	0·3	35·2	—	−9·6	—
1975–6	6·4	−1·5	—	9·8	—
1976–7	5·4	—	—	—	—
1977–8	4·8	—	—	—	—
1978–9	−7·5	—	—	—	—

Note:
* Using the National Accounts estimates of Manufacturing and Handicraft value added, and the SIP estimates of manufacturing output.

helpful in indicating changes taking place in the industrial sphere, so long as differences in coverage and reliability are borne clearly in mind.

The dominant features of these series (Tables 6.2(a) and (b), Figure 6.2) are the following: a substantial dynamism apparent in all the series (except handicraft production) until 1973; this is followed by a substantial slowing of growth in Manufacturing and Handicrafts (MH) where the consequent declining trend is marked by troughs in 1975 and 1979 and a fair recovery between 1975 and 1977, meanwhile the SIP index for larger scale industry shows a much greater resilience with its growth rates showing no significant trend over the entire period if the two extraordinary years of 1965–6 and 1974–5 are excluded.

Since the most reliable series is that based on the SIP, the declining trend of the National Accounts MH series requires explanation. The difference between the two series stems from the estimates which the National Accounts series makes for the output of units not included in the SIP.

These estimates are clearly problematic. The difference between the SIP estimate of manufacturing output (Table 6.2a column 4) and the National Accounts estimate of manufacturing only (Table 6.2a column 1) represents the implicit estimate of the output from all small scale production not covered by SIP. The relative importance (Table 6.2a column 5) and absolute size of this estimate decline steadily until in 1974 the implication is that these enterprises contribute a negative quantity to total output. This is clearly untenable.

The second set of activities for which the National Accounts estimate output are the largely domestic enterprises included under handicrafts. This series, which is relatively unreliable, exhibits a very slow growth trend until 1974, and is not separately provided after that date. However the implicit estimate for

Figure 6.2   *Growth rates of manufacturing value added (constant prices)*

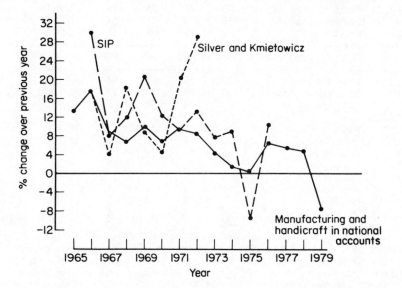

small scale and handicraft production (Table 6.2a column 6) still shows an estimate absolutely not much larger in 1976 than in 1971. This is most unlikely to be accurate, especially in view of SIDO's 1978 survey findings, which further corroborated with the widespread view that from the mid-1970s small scale manufacturing activity had enjoyed a significant and widespread revival.

In general these three series suggest a picture of substantial and sustained industrial expansion and an increasing centralization and concentration of industry. Together they suggest that large scale production has had the greater dynamism, and that overall growth has occurred in the face of a stagnant and relatively declining trend in small scale production. This is an important finding which can be corroborated elsewhere for certain periods but which appears to be at odds with developments through the mid-1970s.

The other feature of these series is the clarity with which the crisis of the mid-1970s appears to interrupt an otherwise almost level growth trend, starting from 1973 in the case of manufacturing and handicrafts, and appearing as a dramatic downturn in 1975 in the large-scale production series.

Fortunately some further light has been shed on this debate by the appearance of a sophisticated (chained Laspeyre's) index of manufacturing production for the period 1967 to 1972.[2] This index is calculated from individual firm returns, has the same coverage as the SIP index and was calculated in order to make it 'possible to decompose the overall change in the value of production into volume and price components' (Silver and

Table 6.3   *Tanzania 1961–78: contributions of various manufacturing sectors to total manufacturing value added and gross output*

ISIC	% of total gross output	1966	1969	1972	1974		
31/32/39	Consumer goods	70	65	65	56		
33-37	Intermediate goods	28	26	27	33		
38	Capital goods	2	9	8	11		
	% of total value added	1961	1966	1969	1972	1974	1978
31/32/39	Consumer goods	74	67	60	64	56	57
33-37	Intermediate goods	23	29	30	29	35	35
38	Capital goods	3	4	10	6	9	8
of which:							
311/2	Food	46	29	25	22	20	
313/4	Drink, tobacco	7	13	13	14	12	
32	Textiles, etc.	16	24	21	25	22	
33/4	Wood, paper	15	12	10	7	9	
35	Chemicals	4	8	12	12	20	
36	Non-metallic	2	3	4	5	3	
37	Metals	5	6	4	6	3	
38	Machinery		4	10	6	9	
39	Other	5	1	1	3	1	

Sources: The figures for 1966, 1969, 1972, 1974 are taken from the respective Surveys of Industrial Production (see Table 6.4). The figure for 1961 is based on the Census of Industries, as cited in (Phillips 1976, p. 50). The 1978 figures come from the Minister of Industry's Budget Speech 1979/80, pp. 38–9.

Kmietowicz, 1977, p. 1). This index focuses on 'work done' rather than on completed output, and is particularly suited to take account of the introduction of new products and industries. It clearly represents a significant contribution to this debate. Its effect is to reduce markedly the 1965–6 growth rate and to increase those between 1970 and 1972. Even though one may agree with the authors of this study that the figures for 1971–2 are overstated (Silver and Kmietowicz, 1977, pp. 15–16) due to possible shifts in value added as a proportion of gross output in some dynamic sectors (see Table 6.4), there is no doubt that these results undermine the sometimes politically motivated attempts to establish 1967 as a significant turning point, marking the beginning of some accelerating, secular decline. Indeed the authors of this particular study suggest 'that industrial production increased by 176.4 per cent during the period of seven years' (1965–72), and point out that 'the growth is particularly marked in the second half of the period covered and is closely related to the conscious expansion of the parastatals ... following the 1967 Arusha Declaration' (Silver and Kmietowicz, 1977, p. 10).

While this material has helped to clarify the pattern of industrial expansion up to 1972, it does not yet extend beyond that date. No doubt the difficulties of the mid-1970s will also be reflected in this series when it is extended, and that extension should be a high priority.

Table 6.4   *Tanzania 1966–74 (selected years): value added as a proportion of gross output*

ISIC Sector	Value added as proportion of gross output (%)							Change in % points 1966–74
	1966	1969	1971	1972	1973	1974	1976	
31 Food, drink, tobacco	0·24	0·27	0·31	0·30	0·29	0·29		+ 5
32 Textiles, clothing etc.	0·19	0·35	0·38	0·35	0·35	0·31		+12
TOTAL consumer goods	0·22	0·29		0·31		0·30		
33 Wood, furniture etc.	0·26	0·35	0·43	0·34	0·37	0·34		+ 8
34 Paper, printing etc.	0·34	0·47	0·39	0·36	0·38	0·43		+ 9
35 Chemicals, etc.	0·19	0·39	0·37	0·34	0·27	0·32		+11
36 Non-metallic etc.	0·30	0·45	0·39	0·60	0·46	0·39		+ 9
37 Metals etc.	0·22	0·24	0·17	0·23	0·24	0·17		− 5
TOTAL intermediate goods	0·24	0·36		0·35		0·32		
38 Machinery etc.	0·43	0·34	0·22	0·28	0·24	0·25		−18
TOTAL capital goods	0·43	0·34	0·22	0·28	0·24	0·25		−18
All manufacturing	0·23	0·31	0·32	0·32	0·30	0·30	0·28	+ 7

Sources: Survey of Industrial Production 1966 (Table 24a); 1969 (Summary Table IIA); 1974 (Table A4).
The figure for 1978 total manufacturing value added as a proportion of gross output is taken from *Hali ya Uchumi wa Taifa Katika Mwaka 1977/78*, Table 48.

STRUCTURAL CHANGE

Since independence there has been considerable structural change within the industrial sector (Tables 6.3 and 6.4). This, as Green rightly suggests, reflects the post Arusha shift towards the production of intermediate goods, and even a rudimentary beginning of capital goods production. At the same time the post 1969–72 decline in the proportion of value added in intermediate and capital goods production reflects both the rudimentary nature of many of the assembly operations to be found under this heading, and more generally the problems usually associated with import substitution strategies when these move to the production of producer goods. At that stage the problems of an intensified need for foreign technology/machinery can be expected to increase the costs of production and to intensify the sensitivity of the production structure to foreign exchange bottlenecks.

The statistics of Tables 3 and 4 are compatible with that interpretation, and this is further supported by the trends in Tanzania's balance of payments (Table 6.5) which emphasize: the degree to which the composition of imports has shifted away from consumer goods (except during the food crisis of 1974–5); the fact that the foreign exchange squeeze was developing endogenously prior to 1973–4; and the severity of the crisis which has been superimposed on that trend.

Finally, in view of the rapid growth of capital and intermediate goods imports it seems certain that the import intensity of manufacturing will have

Table 6.5 *Tanzania 1964–78: foreign merchandise trade trends and composition*

	Export Shs. million	Imports Shs. million	Balance of merchandise trade Shs. million	% of[a] exports which are manufactured %	Consumer goods as % of imports %
1962	1,193	1,127	+ 66	—	—
1963	1,417	1,153	+ 264	—	49
1964	1,597	1,259	+ 338	—	46
1965	1,465	1,405	+ 60	—	43
1966	1,878	1,691	+ 187	—	43
1967	1,761	1,625	+ 136	—	36
1968	1,717	1,834	− 117	—	40
1969	1,795	1,710	+ 83	—	38
1970	1,852	2,274	− 422	18·2	30
1971	1,989	2,725	− 736	21·9	25
1972	2,277	2,879	− 601	21·6	29
1973	2,581	3,479	− 898	17·0	30
1974	2,861	5,258	−2397	20·2	37
1975	2,765	5,694	−2929	19·4	31
1976	4,109	5,421	−1312	17·7	21
1977	4,536	6,199	−1663	13·2	19
1978[a]	3,553	8,118	−4565	14·7	20

Note:
[a] These figures are from Ministry of Industries (1979), pp. 40/41.
Source: The Annual Economic Survey 1968 for the years 1963–66, *Hali ya Uchumi wa Taifa Katika Mwaka 1977/78*, for 1962 and 1967–77.

increased. This supposition is corroborated by more detailed studies (Barker *et al.*, 1975). One of these suggests that imported inputs have risen from 10.2 to 14.6% of manufacturing gross output between 1961 and 1973 (Schubert, 1978, Section 4.3.2, p.54). This also completes the picture of a typical import substitution problem transformed into a crisis through an exogenous disturbance and the relative inflexibility of the internal manufacturing sector.

In this context it is to be expected that the internal interpretation of the Tanzanian economy has progressed only slowly. Nevertheless both backward and forward linkages have developed and in some respects the situation compares favourably with other African economies. Hence if one expresses the proportion of agricultural inputs derived from imports and that derived from backward linkages as a ratio *import propensity: backward linkages* the results are 1.2 (Malawi 1968), 0.74 (Zambia 1969) and 0.08 (Tanzania 1969), (Schubert 1978, Section 4.3.2, pp. 51/3).

The significance of these developments, and the question of appropriate policies to counter them, will be discussed in the last section of this chapter. In conclusion it is important once more to draw attention to the decline in the relative importance of small scale producers as one significant and problematic dimension of Tanzania's structural change in industry. It appears reasonably clear now that there has been a reversal in this trend, with a probable decline or stagnation until 1973–4 (Phillips, 1976, p. 50), and an apparent rapid expansion in such activities after that time.

EFFICIENCY

Not surprisingly the greatest uncertainty reigns with regard to the facts concerning the efficiency of resource use in manufacturing. Leaving for the moment the question of macro versus micro efficiency, the measures under discussion include labour productivity, capacity utilisation, profitability and the Incremental Capital Output Ratio (ICOR). Apart from the problems of interpretation, to which we shall turn later, these statistics are subject to particular uncertainty because in each case they are expressed through a more or less complex ratio, whose year on year changes are highly sensitive to the uncertainties in the underlying data series. When as in the ICOR discussions the further uncertainty of determining the appropriate lag is introduced, results become extremely sensitive to the assumptions made.

Labour productivity trends naturally depend upon which output and which employment measures are used. The four output series which are available have been discussed in a previous section. For employment the situation is unfortunately considerably worse. There are effectively two sources of information, the annual Survey of Employment and Earnings (covering firms with more than 5 employees) and the Survey of Industrial Production, which covers employment for the same sample from which it derives its output data (Table 6.6).

There are compelling reasons to reject the Employment and Earnings figures for purposes of 'productivity' calculations. In the first instance there are no output statistics with a similar coverage which means quite simply that the combination of these statistics with one of the manufacturing output series could not be used for purposes of determining points of inflection in any productivity series. This is reinforced by the fact that the figures represent a

Table 6.6   *Tanzania 1961–78: estimates of employment in manufacturing industry*

| | Employment and earnings | | | Survey of industrial production[b] | | | |
	Manufacturing employment[a]			A — 1974 issue: Hali ya Uchumi 77/78		B — 1972: Min. of Industry budget speech	
	('000's)	of whom casual %	Index 1970=100	('000's)	Index 1970=100	Index 1970=100	('000's)
1961	26·4	—	60	—	—	—	—
1962	23·4	—	54	—	—	—	—
1963	22·2	—	51	—	—	—	—
1964	23·6	—	54	—	—	—	—
1965	25·7	—	59	28·1	58	—	—
1966	29·9	18	68	32·6	67	—	—
1967	31·2	—	71	31·3	65	71	34·2
1968	35·4	—	81	38·1	79	88	42·4
1969	40·3	—	92	43·4		90	43·4
1970	43·7	—	100	48·3		100	48·3
1971	55·2	28	126	50·5	105	111	53·5
1972	55·4	23	127	54·7	113	129	62·1
1973	59·3	21	136	63·3		131	63·3
1974	64·9	17	149	70·0		145	70·0
1975	74·1	—	170	73·2		152	73·2
1976	76·0	—	174	74·2	154	155	75·0
1977	—	—	—	—		162	78·1
1978	—	—	—	—		168	81·2

Notes:
[a] These figures are taken from the Surveys of Employment and Earnings from 1962 through to 1974. The figures for 1975 and 76 are from the same source but cited from (T. Valentine 1980, p. 94). The figures refer to all workers, whether temporary or permanent, who worked for some days during June.
[b] The reason for presenting two series here lies in the fact that two different sets of figures have found currency, and both are from the 'same' official source. One series, based on the figures given in SIP 1974 and those of the *Hali ya Uchumi . . . 1977/78*, were also those used in the ILO/JASPA (1978) calculations. The second set is found in SIP 1972 and again in the Minister of Industry's Budget Speech 1979/80. These figures were used in the calculations of the IBRD's unpublished 1977 report. We will use series A, since these derive from the latest SIP report and are assumed to represent officially revised figures.

highly volatile measure in that they include all temporary labourers who have worked on 'some days during June'. When one notes that the proportion of casual workers (workers who have worked less than the full month) has fluctuated between, on one hand 17–18% in 1966 and in 1974, and 28% in 1971 this point should be clear enough.

Conversely the employment figures derived from the SIP have the same coverage as the output figures and refer to average employment calculated for four points in the year (at quarterly intervals). Even these figures are crude, since they make no allowance for hours worked, but they are the only ones which in conjunction with the SIP output figures can provide a reasonable indication of an aggregate trend in productivity. Unfortunately, though not surprisingly, all the various output and employment series have been used in

Figure 6.3(a)   *Tanzania 1964–77: annual change in value added per employee in monetary sector (1966 prices)*

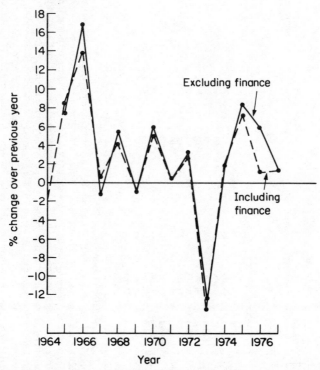

Figure 6.3(b)   *Tanzania 1963–77: indices of value added per monetary sector employee (1966 prices) 1966 = 100*

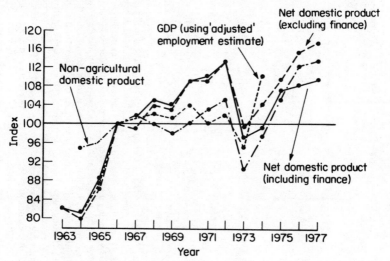

Table 6.7 Tanzania 1963–1977: real monetary sector net and gross domestic product per employee (1966 prices)

	Total[a] (1) Shs. million	Monetary GDP net of depreciation inc. finance (2) Shs. million	Monetary GDP excl. finance (3) Shs. million	'adjusted' estimate using national accounts (4) ('000s)	Monetary Employment and earnings Total excl. finance (5) ('000s)	Employment and earnings Total[d] finance (6) ('000s)	NDP per[b] employee inc. finance (2):(5) (7) Shs.	NDP per[b] employee excl. finance (3):(6) (8) Shs.	NDP per employee inc. finance based on (8) index	charge %	Output per Employee Index numbers NDP per employee excl. finance based on (8) index	charge %	GDP per employee using 'adjusted' estimate based on (1):(4) index	% charge
1963	3,765	3,402	2,924	507.4	340.3	340.3	9,997	8,323	82		80		81	
1964	3,901	3,449	2,987	497.2	351.3	351.3	9,818	8,948	81	-1.8	86	7.5	85	4.9
1965	4,463	3,562	3,516	485.0	333.8	333.8	10,671	10,449	88	8.7	100	16.8	100	17.7
1966	4,654	4,098	3,578	499.8	336.5	336.5	12,178	10,320	100	14.1	99	-1.3	101	1.0
1967	4,936	4,245	3,823	528.0	346.7	346.7	12,244	10,870	101	0.5	104	5.3	102	1.0
1968	5,122	4,487	3,958	548.6	351.7	351.7	12,758	10,758	105	4.2	103	-1.0	101	-1.0
1969	5,501	4,658	4,286	576.5	367.9	367.9	12,661	11,411	104	-0.8	109	6.0	104	3.0
1970	5,778	4,999	4,494	627.0	375.6	375.6	13,309	11,441	109	5.1	109	0.3	100	-3.8
1971	6,138	5,240	4,786	652.8	392.8	392.8	13,340	11,797	110	0.2	113	3.1	102	2.0
1972	6,355	5,559	4,812	723.8	405.7	405.7	13,702	10,326	113	2.7	99	-12.2	95	-6.9
1973	6,590	5,604	5,005	651.8	472.5	466.0	11,860	10,499	97	-13.4	100	1.7	110	15.8
1974	6,876	5,861	5,246		484.1	476.7	12,107	11,370	99	2.1	109	8.3		
1975	7,081	6,110	5,391		470.8	461.4	12,978	12,015	107	7.2	115	5.7		
1976	7,480	6,271	5,687		478.3	448.7	13,111	12,173	108	1.0	117	1.3		
1977		6,605			497.4	467.2	13,279		109	1.3				

Notes: a Source, Hali ya Uchumi . . . . 1977/78, Table 3, p. 8.   b As calculated in Jedruszek 1978.

c This is an estimate based on a procedure first adopted in the 'Second Turner Report' (ILO 1975, pp. 80–1). This procedure has been refined in several respects. The estimate is based on the National Accounts figures for 'Employee Compensation'. From this an estimate of total monetary sector employment is derived by dividing it by an average income figure derived from the 'Employment and Earnings' series. Previously, this was done by dividing the figure for Total Employee Compensation by the average income figure for all wage earners. In this case the incomes earned by those enumerated in Employment and Earnings were subtracted from total Employee Compensation leaving only the residual to be 'transformed' into an employment estimate. Since the major groups excluded from Employment and Earnings are non-estate agricultural workers and domestic servants, the residual was divided by average agricultural wages to obtain an estimate of labour input. As in the original procedure the figure thus obtained for 1967 was deflated to conform to the actual number of employees enumerated in the 1967 census which had not appeared in the 1967 Employment and Earnings. This means the original 1967 labour input indicator of 479,012 was deflated to the difference between census employment (499,792) and employment in Employment: Earnings (346,741)–i.e. 153,051. All labour input indicators were deflated in the same manner. The figure thus obtained as an estimate of 'unenumerated' employment was then added to the Employment and Earnings figure to obtain the adjusted estimate of column (7).

d It should be noted that in Jedruszek 1978 no deduction was made to the employment figures prior to 1973, when the employment and earnings series did not yet itemize financial sector employees separately.

most conceivable combinations with the result that there is considerable confusion, and a pretty general acceptance of a major declining trend. Coulson speaks of value added per worker declining by 25% between 1964 and 1977 and ends his discussion of various specific problems with the comment that 'this evidence ... is sufficient to explain the figures of declining productivity in manufacturing'. Green in his rather more nuanced discussion of trends and interpretations, nevertheless begins his discussion by accepting that 'econometric analysis showed a decline in factor productivity for both capital and labour after 1965'. The study to which Green refers (Jedruszek, 1978) was indeed a welcome effort to apply rigorous econometric techniques to the crucial problem of productivity, but unfortunately all of the main conclusions of the paper recall the old saying that the result of such efforts can never be stronger than the information which is used, and here the study has unfortunately merely introduced further complications, which make it even more difficult to discern the underlying trends. A brief exposition of these problems should assist in clarifying the available evidence.

Jedruszek begins with a brief consideration of efficiency across the economy as a whole. To this end he calculates a measure of Monetary sector GDP per employed person. He concludes 'that the average rates of growth of GDP and of productivity display a *decreasing tendency*' (emphasis in original) (Jedruszek, p.17). As in the earlier discussion of GDP as such, this illusion is created by averaging the data over each of three particular periods – 1964–7, 1967–72 and 1972–6. It can be readily observed (Figure 6.3(a) and 6.3(b), and Table 6.7) that the declining tendency which results is a product of this procedure. In fact Jedruszek's series shows a level trend, with two deviant results, 1966 and 1973. Were one to take these figures at face value the comment they should elicit would concern the rapidity and completeness of the recovery after the 1973 oil crisis. However at this point it is merely to be emphasized that strong (underlined) conclusions about decreasing tendencies cannot be drawn from this series.

Elsewhere (ILO Report 1975, pp. 50–1) the Employment and Earnings figures used in these calculations have been explicitly rejected as indicators of monetary sector employment – particularly because of their exclusion of non-estate agricultural labour. Hence an alternative estimate was calculated (see notes to Table 7) using National Accounts estimates of 'Compensation of Employees' and the average incomes of agricultural employees derived from the Employment and Earnings surveys. Unfortunately the construction of this index involves such heroic assumptions that it cannot be regarded with greater confidence, but merely represents another equally crude approximation. The resulting series (Figure 6.3b and Table 6.7) is once again dominated by the drastic change between 1965 and 1966. Apart from that one year the result does not deviate significantly from a level trend.

Somewhat ironically, if Jedruszek's or this series had been taken back to 1961–2 it would have superficially strengthened the case for a 'declining tendency' since those early years of independence saw a sharp reduction in wage employment, as a result of a general reorganization of labour which was most marked in sisal (Bienefeld, 1979). This problem is well known in that it led the 'Turner Report' (ILO, 1967) to posit a strong inverse correlation between wages and employment on the basis of aggregate data, when in fact the non-agricultural sector had combined substantial wage increases with rapid increases in employment.[3] This suggests at least that the above discussion should have concerned itself with non-agricultural trends. When this is done (Table 8, Figure 3b), albeit without considering depreciation, the pattern which emerges is significantly different. Here there is certainly no evidence of a pervasive declining tendency. Indeed, the noteworthy features of this series are three periods of increase 1964–7, 1969–72 and 1974–7 (with the latter being the strongest) interrupted by a period of consolidation 1967–9 (with a roughly level trend) and a sharp collapse in 1973.

One should not make too much of such statistics. The margins of error are high as has been repeatedly emphasized, but for what the statistics are worth, this is what they show. They do not show pervasive declining trends in aggregate production or in productivity when thus crudely defined.

Clearly there is a need to disaggregate these figures further. Jedruszek chooses to do this to an 'Industrial sector' which comprises manufacturing, mining, public utilities and construction. Furthermore for manufacturing he uses the National Accounts MH series. In addition he continues to group his data into the three previously indicated periods. Not altogether surprisingly then he discovers a picture which 'is much more dramatic than for the total monetary sector . . . there was nearly a steady decline in the *absolute level* of total factor productivity'. Indeed '*the deterioration in effectiveness of use of*

Table 6.8 *Tanzania 1965–72: monetary sector, non-agricultural GDP per employee (1966 prices)*

	Non-agricultural monetary GDP (Shs million)[a]	Monetary sector: Non-agric wage employees[b] ('000's)	GDP per employee Shs.	Index 1966= 100	% change over previous year
1964	2,583	187·7	13,761	95	
1965	2,707	194·6	13,911	96	1·1
1966	3,057	210·3	14,536	100	4·5
1967	3,304	222·9	14,823	102	2·0
1968	3,519	242·5	14,511	100	−2·1
1969	3,623	255·0	14,208	98	−2·1
1970	3,912	268·3	14,581	100	2·6
1971	4,256	283·9	15,005	103	2·9
1972	4,518	291·9	15,317	105	2·1
1973	4,730	363·5	13,012	90	−15·0
1974	5,074	360·1	14,091	97	8·3
1975	5,309	349·0	15,212	105	8·0
1976	5,467	335·9	16,276	112	7·0
1977	5,824	355·3	16,392	113	0·7

Notes:
[a] From *Hali Ya Uchumi Wa Taifa Katika Mwaka 1977–78*, Table 3, p. 11 and for 1964 from *The Economic Survey 1971–72*, Table 3, p. 7.
[b] *Survey of Employment and Earnings and Hali ya Uchumi . . .* 1977/78 Table 22, p. 45. The coverage of Employment and Earnings for non-agricultural employment is reasonably complete (the only exclusions being the military, foreign diplomatic employees and domestic servants) so that it can be used in conjunction with non agricultural GDP figures.

the labour factor is striking and implies very serious material losses in industrial production' (emphasis in original) (Jedruszek 1978, pp. 20–2).

Unfortunately this picture does not emerge as clearly as it might. The inclusion of mining is a major problem, since the rapid decline of the diamond deposits after 1967 produces a dramatic negative trend which lowers value added per employee by 50% between 1967 and 1976 (28% between 1967 and 1972). Given that mining made up almost 20 per cent of the composite sector in 1967, and given that in that year its absolute level of value added per employee was 223% of that of the weighted average of the other three sectors, its decline was bound to have a significant effect on the group as a whole. This effect would have been better eliminated from this particular discussion.

The second problem concerns the use of statistics covering manufacturing and handicrafts. Attention has already been drawn to the weakness of the handicrafts estimates and although these do serve a purpose in providing some approximation of that sector's fortunes they are quite unsuitable for detailed 'productivity' estimates. This difficulty is compounded by their use in conjunction with employment estimates taken directly from employment and earnings without adjustment for the inclusion of handicrafts. This produces two rather serious contradictions, which suggest the unsuitability of this combination.

The first is the paradoxical fact that although the national accounts 'adjustment' of SIP output/estimates implies a smaller and smaller volume of production outside of the activities covered in that survey (until in 1974 it implies a negative quantity – see p.13) the employment and earnings estimates of employment rise considerably more rapidly than the SIP employment figures between 1970 and 1976.

The second, even more untenable contradiction, concerns the fact that in five years between 1964 and 1976 the employment estimates taken from employment and earnings figures are absolutely smaller than those taken from the SIP. In general, therefore, either a negative or a very small number of employees are implicitly responsible for the Shs.200 to Shs.250 million of value added by which the national accounts manufacturing and handicrafts estimates exceed the SIP estimates of manufacturing value added. Since this difference represents between 20 and 50% of the total national accounts estimate the overall results derived from this comparison must be rejected. This naturally applies to all of the more sophisticated measures of 'pure' labour and 'pure' capital efficiency computed on the basis of such a series.

This conclusion means that the problem of periodization really fades into insignificance. The conclusion implies that the only viable estimates of manufacturing productivity are those derived from the SIP value added and employment statistics. It can be seen (Table 6.9, Figures 6.4a and 6.4b) that these produce trends which provide no basis for the 'long term secular decline thesis', while the thesis that 1967 constituted a major turning point with respect to industrial performance receives scant support. This thesis is knocked particularly hard by an index of output per unit of labour input for 1965–72 calculated in the basis of the Silver and Kmietowicz index of industrial output (Table 24, column 7) and a still rather crude, but relatively disaggregated measure of physical labour inputs (Silver, 1978). Partly by adjusting for the effect of new activities coming 'on stream', this series virtually eliminates the apparent explosive growth of output per individual worker between 1965 and

Table 6.9   *Tanzania 1964–78: indices of real value added per employee in industrial production (constant prices)*

	Survey of industrial production based indices (1966 = 100)		National accounts and employment and earning based indices (1966 = 100)	
	A[a]	B[b]	C[c]	D[d]
1964			95	86
1965	89	100	99	98
1966	100	100	100	100
1967	113 (103)	102	104	101
1968	104 (93)	98	98	90
1969	110	102	95	85
1970	111	94	93	83
1971	116 (109)	104	81	86
1972	121 (107)	126	87	90
1973	113		85	62
1974	111		79	75
1975	96		69	76
1976	104 (103)		72	86
1977			74	86
1978			75	

Note:

[a] Based on manufacturing value added (Table 6.2(a) col. 4) and average employment (Table 6 series A and B) from the *Surveys of Industrial Production, 1966 to 1974*. The figures for 1975 and 1976 are from *Hali ya Uchumi . . . . 1977/78*, Table 48. The figures in brackets are alternative estimates based on alternative employment figures which appear in various original sources (see Table 6).

[b] This is the index calculated by M. S. Silver (Silver, 1978) from SIP firm returns. It is based on an industrial production index (Table 6.2(a), col. 7) and employment estimates which are adjusted insofar as was possible for length of shifts.

[c] This is based on value added estimates for manufacturing and handicrafts in the national accounts (Table 6.2(a), col. 3), and manufacturing employment figures taken from Surveys of Employment and Earnings (Table 6).

[d] This is the 'Industry' index presented by Jedruszek (Jedruszek, 1976, p. 19) and based on national accounts and employment and earnings data for manufacturing, mining, construction and public utilities.

1967, but shows a very marked increase between 1970–2. The truth probably lies between the SIP based trends, Figure 4(a) and this series, Figure 6.4(b). The greatest flaw of the latter series being the failure of its index of industrial output to take full and adequate account of changes in the relationship between value added and gross output (Silver and Kmietowicz, 1977, pp. 13–15).

If these results go some way towards rectifying some of the more dramatic accounts of generalized productivity decline, they also confirm the severe difficulties which have beset Tanzania's industrial expansion since 1973, and hence reinforce the obvious point 'that increasing labour productivity is the key to economic development in Tanzania' (Silver, 1977, p.17), for the importance of achieving increased labour productivity rises when economic problems intensify, irrespective of whether these problems stem primarily from internal or external contradictions. However, if the evidence suggests a steady, though not a rapid, advance in output per manufacturing employee,

Figure 6.4(a), 6.4(b) and 6.4(c) *Tanzania 1964–78: indices of real value added per employee in industrial production, based on Table 6.9*

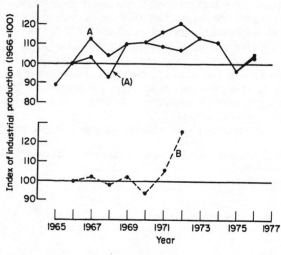

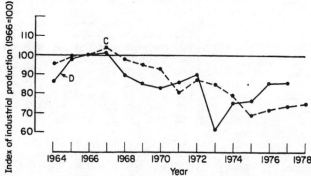

over the long term, it also shows this advance being significantly slowed down by the crisis of the 1970s and it tells us little or nothing about the cost at which this advance has been achieved. A discussion of efficiency requires a consideration of these costs and to these we shall now briefly turn.

Broadly speaking output per worker can be raised through structural change, through technical change or through 'human change' ('x-efficiency'). Each of these implies different potential costs.

The case for the importance of structural changes has been eloquently put by Ajit Singh in this volume. In Tanzania this was undoubtedly a significant source of overall productivity growth until the mid 1970s. Not only did the share of manufacturing output in total GDP rise steadily from less than 4% in 1960–2 to 10.1% in 1973, or from 10.3 to 14.0% of monetary GDP between 1964 and 1973, but also within manufacturing, the average increases in output per worker which have been noted, are the result of extremely diverse sectoral experiences. It is one major benefit of the productivity index constructed by Silver that it allows this diversity to be revealed through disaggregation to the (two digit) sectoral level. (Table 6.10. Figure 6.5). This reveals an astounding difference between the most and the least dynamic sectors, ranging from an increase in output per worker of 869%, to a decrease of 90% between 1965 and 1972. More significant is the fact that the seven sectors which showed significant increases in this measure accounted for 70% of total manufacturing value added in 1965 and included those with the highest levels of value added per worker at that time. Furthermore, the six sectors which recorded the largest increases in productivity, each also increased its share of total manufacturing value over this period. In short the average productivity of manufacturing production increased in part because growth was concentrated in the more productive sectors.

This does not mean that such structural change is an unambiguous benefit.

Table 6.10 *Tanzania 1965–72: sectoral indices of real value added (at 1965 prices) per employee*

ISIC	Sector	1965 value added per worker (Shs)	Rank	1965	1966	1967	1968	1969	1970	1971	1972	% change in value added per worker 1965–72
							Index (1965=1·00)					
				Significant increase								
36·7	Machinery	13,000	6	1·00	1·45	1·55	4·09	7·54	7·00	8·79	9·69	+869
34·5	Metal products	17,800	3	1·00	1·57	1·48	1·98	1·97	1·88	2·92	3·89	+289
23	Textiles	3,400	15	1·00	1·11	1·16	1·56	1·14	1·27	1·30	2·37	+137
21	Drinks	22,500	2	1·00	0·78	1·03	0·77	1·54	1·66	1·86	2·35	+135
31·2	Chemicals	24,400	1	1·00	0·77	0·59	0·56	0·90	1·21	1·27	1·39	+ 39
38	Vehicles**	3,700	14	1·00	0·74	1·02	0·72	0·93	1·17	1·12	1·35	+ 35
20	Food	8,100	10	1·00	1·03	1·52	1·15	1·52	1·22	1·34	1·06	+ 6
				Slight decline								
26	Furniture	8,400	9	1·00	1·01	0·82	0·70	0·99	0·88	1·19	0·96	− 4
22	Tobacco	12,200	7	1·00	0·92	0·79	1·05	0·59	0·68	0·71	0·89	− 11
28	Printing	8,700*	8	1·00	—	0·65	0·64	0·75	0·57	0·80	0·89	− 11
25	Wood	4,700	13	1·00	1·23	1138	1·39	1·32	1·20	1·28	0·87	− 13
				Significant decline								
29	Leather	15,500	4	1·00	1·03	0·79	1102	0·89	1·32	0·38	0·77	− 23
33	Non-metallic	7,900	11	1·00	0·87	0·71	0·80	0·58	0·55	0·35	0·38	− 62
24	Footwear	7,800	12	1·00	0·58	0·39	0·48	0·40	0·42	0·15	0·22	− 78
30	Rubber	14,400	5	1·00	1·15	1·12	0·77	0·70	0·62	0·61	0·19	− 81
27	Pulp, paper	8,700*	8	1·00	—	0·33	0·35	0·13	0·14	0·07	0·10	− 90
				Manufacturing industry								
	TOTAL	8,200		1·00	1·00	1·01	0·97	1·01	0·94	1·04	1·25	+ 25

Notes:
* Average of pulp, paper and printing publishing.
** Includes plastic.
Source: M.S. Silvery, 1978, pp. 9–11.

Figure 6.5 *Tanzania 1965–72. Sectoral indices of real (at 1966 prices) value added per employee (1965 = 1.00)*

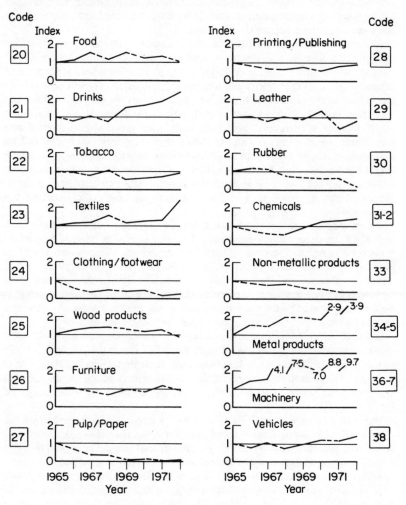

The fact that it occurred does not yet show that the externalities which one might anticipate were actually captured. Furthermore, the shift may have been produced by a process which generated foreign exchange liabilities that could not be supported in the medium term. Indeed we shall see later that this is just what seems to have occurred in Tanzania.

Attention must focus next on the use of capital. After all, even if average output per worker in manufacturing had been steadily falling this could well have represented a desirable development in a situation where absorption of labour must be a high priority and where capital is extremely scarce. In effect the achievement of a growth path which combines steady, and even rapid growth in output, with a higher growth rate of employment must under the circumstances be considered preferable to the same growth path achieved with less employment *unless* it can be shown that the former has involved an extremely wasteful use of capital, or has pushed up wage costs so as to reduce investible surplus and hence growth. Of course the latter situation would constitute a 'problem' only on the assumption of a particular pattern of social time preference. What then is the evidence for this critical part of the discussion?

Given the extreme weakness of estimates of capital stock which have to be imputed from depreciation allowances, the main empirical basis of discussion revolves around the Incremental Capital Output Ratio. This is well known to be a highly unstable measure whose instability derives from its sensitivity to structural change, and the fact that it is a ratio between marginal changes, observed in two very large aggregate quantities. The empirical 'evidence' is finally complicated by the uncertainty surrounding the appropriate lags which should be assumed to exist between investment and output.

While there has been some discussion of ICORs for the economy as a whole, it is not proposed to disentangle the problems of the evidence used in these cases. It can be safely said, however, that such figures have little, if any, meaning. They certainly have no significance for any productivity debate until and unless the major structural changes in the economy have been accounted for.

When one turns to the ICOR discussion for manufacturing production the results of such calculations depend essentially on the choice of the output series; the measure of investment used; the investment deflator; and the 'lag' which is assumed between investment and the consequent output.

When National Accounts estimates for output and investment are used, together with an investment deflator calculated on the basis of The Economic Surveys (IBRD, 1977, p.25) then an ICOR based on three year moving averages, with output lagged by one year, yields a steadily increasing ICOR between 1965–7 and 1972–4 (Table 6.11).

When a more detailed deflator for manufacturing investment was calculated from the National Accounts the same calculations yielded the same trend although the rise to 1972 was now much less. When this same deflator was used to relate investment in years t with average increments in output in year t and $t + 1$, the trend was considerably obscured although there was again a large increase in the ICOR in 1973.

Unfortunately, in this case, more reliable data cannot be drawn from the SIP, since its investment statistics do not include investments made in new projects prior to the year in which output is first produced. If, however, SIP

Table 6.11 *Tanzania 1965–75: estimates of incremental capital output ratios in manufacturing*

	Manufacturing investment[a] (shs. '000,000)		Weighted manufacturing investment deflator	ICOR				
	A	B		A[b]	B[c]	C[d]	D[e]	E[f]
1965	206		1·00					
1966	153	153	1·07			2·4	3·3	—
1967	175	174	1·02	3·2		4·0	5·6	—
1968	204	207	1·03	3·6	3·6	4·1	3·7	—
1969	151	155	1·07	3·7	3·7	3·0	2·4	·97
1970	281	298	1·14	3·7	3·8	5·4	6·1	D*
1971	312	280	1·45	4·3	4·1	4·3	4·9	2·4
1972	240	178	1·57	4·9	4·3	3·4	3·1	3·1
1973	223	196	1·75	6·6	5·7	7·4	3·5	2·8
1974		270					D*	3·3
1975								2·0

Notes:
* D means a decline in value added.
a These series are both taken from the National Accounts. The A series is that which appears in IBRD 1977 p. 25. The B series is based on the notion that 'average' deflators for fixed capital investment can be very misleading guides as deflators for manufacturing investment, since the former includes large items like domestic housing which do not appear in the latter. Because the National Accounts Parastatal Accounts were sufficiently detailed these were used to calculate deflators which reflect the differential rates of inflation experienced in different types of fixed capital, and the varying proportion in which these different types of assets appeared in the accounts of manufacturing parastatals.
b This is the IBRD series. It is based on current price manufacturing Investment figures from the National Accounts, deflated by the investment deflator in the Economic Surveys and divided by incremental value added for Manufacturing and Handicraft as in the National Accounts. Both investment and output figures are expressed as three year moving averages, with output lagged one year.
c This is the same as (b) except for the introduction of the weighted manufacturing investment deflator.
d This is the same as (c) except that investment in year *t* is related to the average increment in value added for years *t* and *t* + 1.
e This is the same as (d) except that value added figures are taken from the Surveys of Industrial Production.
f Figures for Manufacturing Parastatals taken from National Accounts and based on 3 year moving averages with value added lagged one year.

output figures are combined with the National Accounts investment figures (as a proxy for investment in large scale manufacturing), no consistent trend appears, and the big increase in the ICOR does not occur until 1974.

When one turns to the ICORs for the parastatals, the contrast is more striking, especially in view of the frequent assertion that parastatals are particularly inefficient producers. Here the same source which was happy to use National Accounts 'fixed capital formation' figures to approximate investment for manufacturing as a whole, unaccountably shifts to the use of 'changes in depreciation provisions' in the case of parastatals, even though the methodology section of the Accounts emphasizes the relative reliability of their estimates of parastatal investment, when compared to its other estimates of investment (*National Accounts 1966–74*, p. 6). When the National Accounts figures are used, along with National Accounts statistics on value added, the evidence for the manufacturing parastatals reveals a roughly constant ICOR between 1969–71 and 1973–5, with highly unstable results for 1967–8 (0.97) and 1968–70 (net decline in value added).

In short, until 1973–5 (depending on the series) the evidence we have on ICORs in manufacturing does not point clearly to a major deterioration in the relationship between capital and output. This means that the relatively rapid increases in employment were not combined with simultaneous modest increases in output per worker only at the cost of a large increase in less and less intensively utilized capital. If this is true then it should be reflected in the rates of profit, and this does indeed appear to be the case (Table 6.12). When operating surplus (value added, less labour costs and depreciation) is considered in relation to the highly inadequate but only available measure of capital stock, namely 'depreciation times ten' (assuming the effective life of capital as 10 years and historic cost) it emerges clearly that rates of profit in manufacturing have been consistently high, and have indeed risen somewhat since 1971. On an inflation accounting basis (expressing profit in terms of current purchasing power over investment goods) the years since 1972 when the investment deflator rises sharply, would undoubtedly show some decline in profitability as against the earlier period, but a substantial profit rate remains (Table 6.12, note c).

Green mentions this fact and cites ILO/JASPA's reference to it. Unfortunately, his subsequent elaboration of the fact that with administered prices the significance of such profitability is highly ambiguous, is written as if it constitutes a correction of the ILO/JASPA position. This is not the case since in that report this fact is discussed at length and accorded great significance. This is as it should be. However, two points are relevant to the further investigation of this question. The first concerns the fact that although cost-plus prices are too frequently used in setting Tanzania's prices, the basic objective of price controls was the protection of the consumer. Although this has a rather hollow ring after the inflation of the mid-1970s, it should be noted that a detailed study of the subject (R. Rice, 1976) concluded that 'price controls on imported products have been much less effective than on domestically manufactured products'. It further points out that 'the ex-factory prices of 83% of the uncontrolled items but only 33% of the controlled items in this sample are 5% or more higher than the landed cost of the imported substitute'.

The second comment which is relevant to the further consideration of this important issue, concerns the fact that when profitability exists together with output growth, employment expansion and increases in physical output per worker, its meaning may be questioned, not so much in relation to efficiency but rather from the point of view of social time preferences, or with respect to the relationship between the industrial sector and other parts of the economy like agriculture. These comments are *not* intended to deny the points Green and ILO/JASPA have made. Rather they are intended to draw attention to the issue in question and to suggest that it should not lead to the facile implication that therefore these 'profitability' figures constitute totally

Table 6.12 *Tanzania in 1965–76: profitability in manufacturing industry*

	Operating surplus in manufacturing[a] (shs. '000s) (1)	Capital stock[b] (shs. '000s) (2)	Return on capital[c] %
1965	78·3	323	24·2
1966	114·0	463	24·6
1967	109·5	563	19·4
1968	135·9	570	23·8
1969	172·1	886	19·4
1970	223·5	969	23·1
1971	282·2	998	28·3
1972	353·4	1,275	27·7
1973	348·4	1,644	21·2
1974	463·5	1,806	25·7
1975	475·0	1,800	26·4
1976	700·7	1,848	37·9

Notes:
[a] From the Surveys of Industrial Production, as reproduced in *The Economic Survey 1971–72*, (for 1965 to 1967) and *Hali ya Uchumi. . . . 1977–8* (for 1968 to 1976). Operating surplus is value added less labour cash and depreciation.
[b] From the same sources as (a). Capital stock is defined as 10 times depreciation.
[c] This is in current price accounting terms. If it is assumed that one tenth of the stock in 1976 was acquired in each of the preceding ten years, and if each tenth is valued in 1976 prices (using the investment deflator in Table 6.11) then the 1976 rate of return becomes 24·9%.

arbitrary quantities. The question requires a more detailed consideration of the pattern of prices and their changes over time.

Concerning the issue of capacity utilisation, the evidence is relatively unambiguous and the implications relatively straightforward. Low levels of utilisation are a major problem; they have been a problem for a long time, they fluctuate wildly over time and between different factories or sectors; and they are a standard feature of technologically undeveloped economies embarking upon industrialization, especially when these run into foreign exchange bottlenecks (Wangwe, 1976; ILO/JASPA, 1978). This is clearly an important problem which requires treatment, although its existence also serves to emphasize the positive significance of many of the trends described so far.

This leaves the question of productivity increases which can be derived directly from changes in the application of labour, without structural or technical change. Given the scarcity of foreign exchange, and hence of capital in the short and medium term, this source of productivity increase assumes vital importance. There can be no doubt that the resolution of Tanzania's current crisis will depend largely on its ability to achieve such increases in 'x-efficiency'.

This is not the case because past performance in this respect has been disastrous. Indeed the evidence provided here implies a modestly encouraging performance in that if one excepts the two crisis years of 1975 and 1979, a relatively rapid increase in employment has been combined with small increases in output per worker, with reasonably high levels of profit and with only a small, and uncertain, increase in manufacturing ICOR. At the same time the great variations in sectoral performances, and the significant impact of structural change on aggregate average figures, suggests that in many particular instances there has been a more discouraging trend. Furthermore, as both Coulson and Green show, there have been many individual instances of mismanagement and waste, although in many cases it is wise to accept that is not unusual for newly established projects to experience significant production difficulties. While certainly not all cases are explicable in this way, the generally poorer performance of the parastatals established after Arusha, noted in the late 1970s, probably owes a good deal to this factor. Indeed the IBRDs resident representative summed up his impressions after the completion of their extensive and highly critical 1977 report, by stating that the manufacturing parastatals were generally performing well, once their early 'teething problems' were resolved.[4] This does not negate the basic structural problems with many of these new projects, to which reference has been made, but it does suggest a more positive assessment with respect to past 'x-efficiency' is in order. The same is true if one takes into account the inevitable transitional costs of bringing Tanzanian management into controlling positions.

The cruel fact is, however, that none of these qualifications reduce the urgency of the need for greater advances on this front in future. The crisis in which the Tanzanian economy now finds itself will be resolvable only if such improvements are achieved. The only question is the proposed direction in which policy should move to allow this to be done.

Green's discussion of this issue is good and it is not proposed to repeat that here. Suffice it to say that the struggle is between one view, which considers it possible to improve performance only by bringing the market to bear much more directly on workers, so as to motivate and discipline through its particular combination of incentives, threats and uncertainties; and another which emphasizes the need to capture those benefits derivable from the greater commitment to be elicited from workers who have a secure position in a firm and who therefore can, at least hypothetically, be expected to make an investment in that firm's continued success, especially if management procedures are conducive to such behaviour.

Obviously neither of these positions exists in a pure form, and both must involve realistic compromises in practice. Both will require a degree of hierarchy. Both will require material incentives. Both will require mechanisms to deal with problem workers and problem managers. The difference is one of degree, but it is none the less important for that. And the results must be measured both in economic and in social and political terms.

Assessment and Analysis: The Strategic Choice

How does this summary of the evidence relate to the question of Tanzania's basic strategic choice? In this section that connection will be explored and it will be suggested that insofar as the acceptance of that choice is made dependent upon Tanzania's actual experience, that experience is neither so disastrous, nor are its problems so clearly related to that strategy, that it alone would justify the rejection of the strategy.

Unfortunately the two other Tanzania papers in this volume do not help to clarify the various issues involved in this debate. Coulson explicitly accepts the broad strategy as the only one effectively available, but then presents a discussion of Tanzania's experience which comes very near to being incompatible with that acceptance. Green, in his otherwise very interesting and helpful discussion, creates much confusion on this issue. He does this by suggesting that there are four basic critiques of Tanzania's industrialization strategy. Of these four, he argues, the two which basically reject the strategy are the 'surplus maximizing' arguments (ascribed to Coulson and the IBRD), and the dependency arguments (ascribed to Ajit Singh). In addition there are said to be two critiques 'from inside', one of which is thought to consider a heavy emphasis on small scale industry as an adequate industrial strategy (ascribed to myself), while the other is Green's own position as elaborated in his paper. The problem is that neither Coulson, nor Singh, criticize the strategy 'from outside' but explicitly accept its basic premises – Coulson as the least available evil, and Singh clearly as the only possible basis from which to capture the all-important nationally defined externalities which lie at the heart of the industrialization process.

In reality the various arguments are rather differently connected. The basic issue which divides people between those offering a critique from 'inside', and those offering it from 'outside' Tanzania's basic policy frame, concerns the question of state involvement in the economy. The Tanzanian strategy is based on the premise that the state should play a major and direct role in the country's economy, with a view to accelerating structural change, fostering the generation of externalities and mitigating the impact of growth on income differentials. To this end it is thought imperative that the state should play a major role in investment allocation, both through extensive ownership and through a price structure which is able clearly to reflect nationally defined priorities and long term objectives.

This position can be debated at the level of theory but a definitive generally applicable answer to the question cannot be established there, except where that theory is so ideologically orientated that its faith in the panacea of either competition, or planning, overrides all conceivable obstacles. Between these extreme and relatively uninteresting positions, the important debate concerns itself with the identification of those circumstances which are likely to justify more, or less, state intervention.

If one starts from traditional trade theory arguments one could say that the case for state intervention is weakest where technological capabilities are internationally equalized, where one is operating under equilibrium conditions and within the vicinity of full employment, where the distribution of productive assets and income and hence the pattern of demand is socially and politically justifiable, where factors of production (or at least capital) are internationally mobile, where external economies are of little importance, and where competition occurs within the context of many independent economic factors.

From this position it is possible to work backwards to establish the conditions which are most likely to increase the potential benefits to be derived from extensive state intervention. Hence if externalities are deemed import-ant, as Singh shows in this volume, there is a basic case to be made. This case is likely to become stronger if there is a substantial technological gap, and if the international economy exists under conditions of disequilibrium, especially if that involves high levels of unemployment. Under such conditions straight competition is likely to concentrate unemployment in the backward areas, as well as inhibiting the emergence of manufacturing activity and hence reducing the possibility of generating desirable external economies.

The case for intervention may be further strengthened if one adds: that many of the markets in which such economies deal are far from being competitive, but are frequently dominated by a few producers or buyers; that the existing patterns of wealth and income distribution cannot simply be accepted as a socially and politically uncontentious 'given datum'; and that all the major trading powers intervene in international trade and financial flows according to their perceived national interests.

These factors, when added to the historical circumstances of Tanzania at independence, its relative underdevelopment, even by comparison with Kenya, its resource poverty and its unfavourable location in relation to major markets, produce the basis for an argument that in Tanzania extensive state intervention could bring substantial potential benefits. While this conclusion is not thereby established as necessary, it is established as a possibility with both theoretical and historical plausibility.[5] It is also the position which Coulson explicitly accepts for Tanzania, and which Singh's arguments suggest for a wider range of economies.

However, to accept the argument, that under conditions such as those of Tanzania at independence there are hypothetical benefits to be derived from state intervention, does not imply that one should support Tanzania's strategic choice. For this one needs to establish the further condition that the nature of the state that would so intervene would have the capacity and the will to produce better results, either with respect to growth or distribution.

Here again the debate first arises at the level of theory. Certainly anyone must accept that state intervention may at times be a necessary, but can never be a sufficient condition for achieving more rapid, more equitable and/or more widely accepted socio-economic development. To give relatively greater scope to the unfolding of nationally based processes of social and political change could hypothetically foster the emergence of corrupt, stagnant and oppressive oligarchies. It is as well to remember from the outset that the market and its pervasive competitive principle has not only been a source of problems for some more backward economies. It has also been the means by which many corrupt and authoritarian regimes in history have been toppled, and stagnant economies mobilized.

In short, to espouse state intervention it is necessary to believe that the forces in control of the state represent the mass of the population, and that they have the capacity to serve those interests. Both of these propositions are fiercely disputed both in general and with respect to Tanzania. At the general level there are powerful arguments which posit oligarchic and repressive tendencies as the universal and inevitable result of extensive state control (Weber, 1947; Hegedus, 1976), while others make this case particularly strongly for technologically backward societies, as implied in Warren's phrase of 'premature socialism' (Warren, 1973; Bahro, 1978).

For those who do not accept such universalized arguments, the discussion shifts to a more detailed and concrete level. Broadly this involves an analysis of the class forces on which a state is based. More specifically in the development debate this has appeared as a dispute about the 'post-colonial' state, which has raised the possibility that in that context the broad, often populist nationalist liberation struggle may become the basis for a mass orientated state, particularly in view of the depth of material contradictions and the weakness of the bourgeois class forces often associated with that situation. The debate about the relative autonomy of the state (Alavi, 1972; Saul, 1974) raises these possibilities. Other protagonists in this debate have countered by arguing that whatever the original nature of class forces, the fact of state intervention will create its own oppressive 'bureaucratic class' and/or that the significant presence of foreign capital in the economy will ensure that its interests emerge dominant within such a relatively 'open' political context. Once more these questions cannot be resolved in the abstract, though they provide the background against which the analysis of the particular case proceeds. In effect this analysis must ultimately proceed on a largely inductive basis, for the state's potential ability to represent or to serve the interests of the mass of the population inevitably remains a matter for political struggle, and a matter which is revealed only in the course of that struggle.

This is where the specific analysis and critique of Tanzania's experience begins. The division between those viewing Tanzania's strategic choice from the outside or the inside, depends therefore on the position taken on these issues. It is clear that it is possible particularly on political grounds, to reject the possibility of effective and mass oriented state intervention out of hand, and from that position the details of Tanzania's experience become unnecessary for reaching a conclusion, and evidence is needed only insofar as it selectively reinforces this a priori conclusion. Naturally, the same problem arises at the other extreme, when the effectiveness of state intervention is deemed to be established beyond doubt at the theoretical level.

For the rest, the above debates establish a context in which both the possibility and the difficulty of state intervention are strongly emphasized. Politically this implies an engagement to support the strategic choice once it is made. Analytically it requires detailed and continuous monitoring of the results of that process in the particular case of Tanzania. This evidence then gradually determines whether the possibility of effective state intervention is transformed into a probability or a forlorn hope. The evidence which has been reviewed in the foregoing section, and the discussion contained in the following section are intended as a contribution to that debate.

While the general debate cannot be reviewed here, it is important to point out that a growing number of authors who began with a substantial sympathy for, and belief in, Tanzania's strategic choice have found the actual experience so contradictory and problematic as to lead them to the conclusion that the attempt has failed, and that it has achieved neither equity, nor efficiency. In general their argument concludes that a 'bureaucratic class' has in fact assumed power in Tanzania, and that it is wielding that power in its own interests. Hence the apparent failures of the state in achieving its objectives are seen not as the short-comings of a particularly difficult struggle, but as the logical consequence of this particular state's actual, as opposed to rhetorical, objectives (von Freyhold, 1979; Raikes, 1980). An earlier, and very much cruder version of this argument was put in terms which purported to show that all such problems were to be understood in relation to a state effectively dominated by foreign capital through the multinational subsidiaries (Shivji, 1975).

The more recent versions of this argument are powerful indictments which emphasize the real and serious problems which this strategy, and probably any similar, strategy must surmount. Their conclusions are not yet compelling because: they often take a partial rather than an overall view; they generally do not elaborate the alternative (the counter-factual case) against which the current strategy is thought to be a failure; and they do not, and cannot, reconcile their notion of the bureaucratic class with the income restraints which have been imposed on the members of that class, and which have intensified sharply in the latter half of the 1970s.

For these reasons the issue must continue to be a matter for debate. A sober assessment of the industrial performance of Tanzania does not support the most pessimistic conclusion, while the recent intensification of the squeeze on urban salaries, together with the encouragement of smaller scale production and the shift of relative prices towards agricultural products, suggests that even under current constraints a 'progressive' solution is being sought to contradictions (Bienefeld, 1979). In short it suggests that the struggle may be lost in the end, but it is by no means over.

Assessment and Analysis: Industrial Development

This discussion will attempt to identify the defining characteristics and the major contradictions of Tanzania's industrial development. It will not, and it cannot, attempt to provide specific policy advice, and it will not repeat Green's detailed exposition of many of the particular policy areas. It will, however, attempt to identify the broad directions in which particular solutions will have to be sought if the fundamental contradictions are to be resolved.

The detailed account of Tanzania's industrial experience can be summarized thus: a respectable macro-economic performance with respect to output and productivity has been sustained in industry, interrupted by major set-backs in 1975 and 1979. This aggregate performance has, however, obscured a number of significant and highly problematic features of this growth. Productivity performance has been extremely uneven, and in many specific areas of production there have been significant declines which obviously reflect major production problems. At the same time the inevitable foreign-exchange intensive early phase of industrialization had clearly been pushed ahead at a pace which was exceeding the economy's effective capacity (within this strategy) to earn foreign exchange, as well as straining its capacity to produce various essential domestic inputs for industry (cashews, pyrethreum, sisal, food). The resulting industrial vulnerability to the foreign exchange constraint and to the weather was cruelly exposed after 1973, when severe drought, the Uganda war and the oil price explosion turned a modest trade deficit into a disastrous foreign exchange gap.

The technical and organizational capacity of the country was already stretched to its limits by these policies, and had almost certainly already become one of the binding constraints to more rapid and certainly to more 'self-reliant' development. This capacity was gravely weakened and disorganized by the massive shortages and interruptions which emerged from 1973 onwards. Not surprisingly this structure proved very limited in its capacity to respond to the extraordinary demands of this new situation. It rapidly developed major discontinuities, a pervasive demoralization and, in the context of the ubiquitous shortages, a strong tendency towards corruption. The distribution systems suffered most severely, partly because they are inherently most difficult to control or supervise, and partly because the widespread disequilibria inevitably generated their greatest pressure at those points where buyer meets seller, irrespective of whether one or both of these actors is an official body.

In this context the political forces opposing the country's basic strategy have become stronger and more vocal. These include a significant section of the bureaucratic/managerial groups, whose opposition is based on the fact that under the existing policy their material position has been very sharply constrained. Indeed, contrary to some often repeated misconceptions, it is very clearly in this group's narrow and short-term material interest that the country's basic policy be abandoned. The current crisis has provided a context in which this demand can be expressed with more hope of popular support, since it feeds on the frustrations and doubts which have grown in response to the difficulties of the past six years.

With respect to industrial policy, the analysis presented above suggests that a number of major contradictions must be urgently resolved. It also suggests that past decisions can be criticized on grounds that they should have been more cautious in their use of foreign exchange and imported inputs; that they should have been more urgently concerned with the effective absorption of technology; that they should have been more aware of the need to co-ordinate agriculture and industry, and to ensure the growth of exports. Such criticisms are essentially justified, but they must not be projected into the past without an appreciation of the policial and administrative constraints under which such good intentions must always find expression. Furthermore, such advice must always be understood in relative, not in absolute, terms. Hence 'less' use of foreign technology cannot mean 'no' use of foreign technology. Pol Pot's Cambodia should be enough to convince anyone of that.

However once the relative nature of such advice is accepted, it becomes clear that 'wisdom with hindsight' must be treated with some caution. Events have shown that a lesser use of foreign technology would probably have been advisable, but that is based on what actually transpired after 1973. On the other hand it is not plausible to suggest that all planning prior to 1973 should have anticipated the events which have occurred since that date. This would not have been defensible at the time, nor can the world's multinational firms (supposedly highly efficient planners) claim to have made provision for these events. Nevertheless it is true that greater caution was urged at the time, and that every strategy must build in some safety margin against adverse external, or internal, developments. The fact is, that Tanzania was approaching a classic 'import substitution crisis' even without the changes which followed 1973. Those changes transformed a real and growing problem into a severe crisis. It constrained the economy's capacity to respond effectively to these problems, at the same time as it intensified the need for such a response. At this point, more important than recriminations of the past, is the vision of the future. Where does Tanzania's industrial policy go from here?

The answer should be derived from the evidence and the analysis presented above. Probably the most urgent matter is the restoration of the economy's external balance and this suggests two major policy directions: the first is an improvement of the relative position of agriculture, and the second is a more active concern with the structure of industry.

The shift of priority towards agriculture does not deny the basic arguments presented in Singh's paper in this volume. It represents rather recognition of a particular set of imbalances which have developed in Tanzania and which need to be rectified if the process of industrialization is to be once more accelerated and if it is to be compatible with the populist and egalitarian objectives of the current policy.

The shift towards agriculture is needed in order to improve the economy's export performance. It is needed in order to restore regular supplies to that range of industrial plants which were built specifically to process agricultural products. It is needed to cover the country's food requirements, to improve nutrition levels and to stabilize wage costs to industry. It is also needed to raise real incomes in the rural areas in order to deal with the equity issue and in order to orient industrial output more to the demands of the great mass of Tanzania's consumers. It is finally needed to consolidate the political base on which this policy must be built, since the urban political base has undoubtedly been weakened by recent events and larger and larger sections of it will be tempted to urge the abandonment of the strategy itself.

The second major direction for policy must be the intensification of efforts to reduce the import intensity of industrial production, in response to the current foreign exchange situation. In the long run this reinforces the need for the Basic Industries Strategy but in the short run it urges caution in the speed and in the manner with which one seeks to move towards that objective. Put bluntly, it is essential to recall that a move to capital goods industries is likely to be very foreign exchange intensive, and if pursued in a precipitous manner, this could completely destroy the viability of the existing strategy, as it did so clearly and dramatically in Peru in the mid-1970s (Weeks, 1976).

In general, a change in the import intensity of industrial production is necessarily a slow process. It can only be dealt with at the margins so to speak, since the physical structure of production has a considerable inflexibility once installed. The changes, at the margin, must therefore focus on the balance between small and large scale production, since there is no domestic technology capable of sustaining large scale industrial production. The crux of the matter becomes on one hand, a more careful selection of external technologies so as to reduce long term foreign exchange costs for machines, spares and production inputs. On the other hand, it implies a clearer and greater emphasis on the expansion of small scale industry, which is able to utilise otherwise virtually idle resources to satisfy the needs of domestic consumers. This emphasis is not espoused on principle, or without recognition of some potential political costs as Green seems to think (Green, p. 81), but because in the face of a severe shortage of foreign exchange, of a considerable narrowness of choice with respect to available large-scale technologies, and in the face of limited administrative capacities, this represents a direction in which expansion is possible and, under the circumstances, highly desirable.

Within these constraints and perspectives the move towards more basic industries must either be made with an initial emphasis on small scale engineering activities, or alternatively on the basis of large scale projects which are financed in such a way as to make only very limited demands on available foreign exchange.

Finally the current crisis demands that there should be the greatest emphasis placed on improving the productivity of existing industrial enterprises and on improving the distribution networks, both forward and backward from those enterprises. For the distribution problems there are no magical cures, least of all in my view, simply turning them over to the market. The discussion of distribution problems in Tanzania occasionally seems to move so far as to presume that hoarding and inefficiency in distribution are features unique to administered systems. It may be worth recalling that the problems of hoarding and of middlemen are central issues in the analysis of most rural systems, and that they are problems which are particularly acute in times of scarcity and market disequilibrium. It is not irrelevant that a senior AID official who had been involved in the 1974 emergency food relief was able to tell the ILO/JASPA group that in all his years of international relief work, the Tanzanian distribution system had been the most effective he had encountered in terms of getting the food to those who needed it. No doubt in Tanzania the attempt to control all aspects of distribution from the centre is ill advised. Indeed it is likely that this is an area where make-shift solutions will predominate for some time to come, and where some greater stability will be achieved only when shortages become less acute.

As for productivity there is little doubt that more 'open' management, more liberal use of incentives and more scope for worker and peasant pressure on management/bureaucracy/distribution networks continue to be the most important means of achieving this objective, especially if these are to be compatible with the Party's broader social and political objectives. This does not mean that all hierarchy can be dispensed with or that all social and other pressures to induce greater efforts are to be deplored. It does mean that a basic reliance on authoritarian irresponsible management obtaining discipline primarily through fear of the sack, and eliciting effort through completely individualized incentives is likely to be less effective in the long run and more problematic in the short run.

The current situation is thus one of both political and of economic crisis, whose outcome is essentially indeterminate. Many of the policy shifts indicated above have been instigated. Certainly there is in 1980 a much clearer emphasis on small scale production and according to SIDO officials a much clearer definition of areas of demand within which such forms of production are given precedence. Certainly there has been a shift of relative prices towards agriculture, although within that shift the emphasis on food crops has produced certain anomalies (Ellis 1980), which are currently receiving attention. Certainly there has been a recognition that medium scale engineering firms are to be encouraged, although the short run restraints required in the expansion of large scale import intensive manufacturing are not so clear at present. Certainly the line on urban income distribution has also been held, with upper income earners being most severely squeezed within the context of a general squeeze on the urban sector (Valentine, 1980). The resulting demand patterns, augur well for the consolidation of an industrial base along the lines which have been outlined here. No doubt the fact that the direct influence of private capital, over the direction and pace of investment flows, has been so extensively reduced over the past twelve years, can be regarded as at least one major reason why Tanzania's options in responding to these intense pressures continue to be wider than they are in most other developing countries.

Tanzania's importance for the development debate continues to be inordinately great. For rightists there is obviously much satisfaction in hearing the failure they always predicted announced so generally. For many utopian leftists the Tanzania reality seems so much at odds with their commendably high aspirations that it seems easiest to reject it altogether – together generally with all other existing socialisms. For some it seems a matter of finding ever new stars which may be imbued with the individual's dreams, only to be rejected when the real contradictions of that alternative social process emerge. Already the contradictions of Mozambique and Vietnam are leading to great restiveness in these ranks. Soon many would undoubtedly have fixed on Eritrea as the next 'pure' cause, except that it seems to have 'turned to dust' too early.

Meanwhile for Tanzania the struggle continues. The struggle for a modicum of human dignity, for a degree of control over its affairs and for the capacity to continue the development process with a degree of social justice. That struggle is immensely difficult and is always threatened with failure and degeneration into simple oligarchy. For the moment it seems to this observer that the Tanzanian case has not 'turned to dust' (Foster-Carter, 1980) and that the struggle continues. Indeed that struggle is very much in need of support, of constructive criticism and of serious analysis.

In the meantime it is as well to look as carefully as we can at the evidence we have. By comparison to virtually all other countries in sub-Saharan Africa, Tanzania's development has been more than respectable – whether in terms of growth, distribution, the extent of social polarization, political stability and the general political support enjoyed by its government and leadership. This may not be saying much but it is saying more than statements which compare it to South Korea or Brazil, and a great deal more than those which compare it to some unspecified implicit ideal.

Notes

1 For a detailed description of methods and coverage see *National Accounts of Tanzania 1966 to 1968: Sources and Methods*, issued by the Bureau of Statistics in 1971.
2 See Silver and Kmietowicz, 1977, for exposition of the methodology.
3 The second 'Turner Report' (ILO 1975 p. 24–5) acknowledges this earlier error and then seeks to show that while in the non-agricultural sector there was no absolute decline in employment, in the period of rapid real wage increase (1961–6) the growth of employment was very slow (1.6 per cent per annum) compared to the subsequent period (1967–1971), when it grew at 6.2 per cent per annum. Unfortunately this argument is no more convincing due to the fact that the annual growth rates clearly show that the 1961–6

average is a meaningless figure. Indeed, if the point is to identify turning points in employment growth the figures clearly indicate 1964 as that point.

Non-agricultural employment % change

1961–2	-1·9
1962–3	-9·5
1963–4	7·4
1964–5	3·7
1965–6	8·1
1966–7	6·0
1967–8	8·8
1968–9	5·2
1969–70	5·2
1970–1	5·8

4 Statement by Lyle Hansen to the ILO/JASPA mission August 1977. This view is also expressed in the report.

5 The contentiousness of this issue is such that no degree of qualification is likely to be adequate to avoid misinterpretation. In a recent article (Bienefeld, 1975) I repeatedly stressed the vital importance of trade and of the international division of labour, but argued that under certain specific circumstances, unrestricted trade could inhibit economic development. This, in order to indicate the circumstances under which bilateral trade arrangements might have a positive contribution to make. Alec Nove in a review in the EJ (March, 1979) is so stung by this argument that he actually states that in my paper 'the international division of labour is presented as little better than a conspiracy to exploit the poor' and then proceeds to ignore totally all other qualifications of the argument. In subsequent correspondence he has accepted that on this question the 'particular view which I ascribed to you is not held by you' (A. Nove to M. Bienefeld, August 17, 1979) but the review certainly highlights the fact that these issues are highly contentious and capable of eliciting incredible degrees of misinterpretation and over-reaction. In this context I should like to emphasize that the argument in this paper does not seek to assert the inevitable benefits of state intervention, but merely to set out systematically the issues which divide various protagonists in the debate about those benefits.

References

Alavi, H. (1972) 'The state in post-colonial societies', *New Left Review*, 74 (July/August).

Bagachwa, M.S.D. (1980) 'Industrialization in Tanzania: some issues', paper presented to ILO/University of Dar es Salaam, Tanzania: National Seminar on Development, Employment and Equity Issues, 21–25 July.

Bahro, R. (1978) *The Alternative in Eastern Europe* (London: New Left Books).

Barker, C.E., M.R. Bhagavan, P.M. von Mitschke-Collande, D.V. Wield (1975) 'Industrial production and transfer of technology in Tanzania: the political economy of Tanzanian industrial enterprises', Institute of Development Studies, University of Dar es Salaam, 1974–5 (mimeo.).

Bienefeld, M.A. (1979) 'Trade unions, the Labour process and the Tanzanian state', *Journal of Modern African Studies*, 17, 4 (December).

Bienefeld, M.A. (1975) 'Special gains from trade with socialist countries: the case of Tanzania', *World Development*, 3, 5 (May).

Clark, W.E. (1978) *Socialist Development and Public Investment in Tanzania 1964–1973* (Toronto: University of Toronto Press).

Ellis, F. (1980) 'Agricultural pricing policy in Tanzania 1970–1979: implications for agricultural output, rural incomes, and crop marketing costs', paper presented to the ILO/University of Dar es Salaam, Tanzania: National Seminar on Development, Employment and Equity Issues, 21–25 July.

Foster-Carter, A. (1980) 'The dogma of self-reliance', *The Guardian* (September 10).

Freyhold, von, M. (1979) *Ujamaa Villages in Tanzania. Analysis of a Social Experiment*, (London: Heinemann Educational Books).

Hegedus, A. (1976) *Socialism and Bureaucracy* (London: Allison & Busby).

IBRD Report (Unpublished) (1977) *Tanzania: Basic Economic Report, Annex V, Industry: Perspective and Strategic Choices*.

ILO (1967) 'Report to the Government of the United Republic of Tanzania on wages, incomes and prices policy' (The Turner Report), *Government Paper No. 3*, (Dar es Salaam).

ILO (1975) 'Report to the Government of Tanzania on the past, present and future of incomes policy in Tanzania' ('The Second Turner Report'), (Geneva ILO/OTA/Tanzania R. 10).

ILO/JASPA (1978) *Towards Self-Reliance* (Addis Ababa).

Jedruszek, J. (1978) 'Development in employment and productivity in Tanzania 1967–1977', *Economic Research Bureau Paper 78.5/6* (Dar es Salaam: University of Dar es Salaam).

Kim, K.S. (1978) 'Industrialization strategies in a developing socialist economy. An evaluation of the Tanzanian case', *The Developing Economies*, XVI, 3, (September) (Tokyo).

Kim, K.S., R.B. Mabele and M.J. Schultheis (eds) (1979) *Papers on the Political Economy of Tanzania*, (Nairobi/London: Heinemann Educational Books).

Ministry of Industries (1979) *Speech by the Hon. C.D. Msuya, M.P., Minister for Industries to the Budget Session of the National Assembly for the 1979/80 Session* (Dar es Salaam).

Phillips, D. (1976) 'Industrialization in Tanzania small scale production decentralization and a multi-technology program for industrial development', *ERB Paper 76.5* (Dar es Salaam: University of Dar es Salaam).

Raikes, P. (1980) *State and Agriculture in Tanzania*, (Brighton: Harvester Press).

Rice, R.C. (1976) 'The Tanzanian price control system: theory, practice and some possible improvements', *ERB Paper 76.4* University of Dar es Salaam (reprinted in K.S. Kim *et al.*, 1979).

Roemer, M., G.M. Tidrick and D. Williams (1973) 'The range of strategic choice in Tanzanian industry', paper presented to University of Toronto Conference on Development in Tanzania since 1967, April 22–24.

Rweyemamu, J. (1973) *Underdevelopment and Industrialization in Tanzania*, (Oxford: Oxford University Press).

Saul, J.S. (1974) 'The state in post-colonial societies – Tanzania', *Socialist Register for 1974* (London).

Schubert, J. (1978) *DFG Projekt: Entwicklungsstrategien in Afrika: Elfenbeinküste, Malawi, Sambia, Tansania, Kapitel 4: Okonomische Entwicklung und Abhängigkeit*, (Berlin.) (mimeo., draft).

Shivji, I.G. (1975) *Class Struggles in Tanzania*, (London: Heinemann Educational Books).

Silver, M.S. (1978) 'Labour productivity trends in Tanzania's manufacturing sector, 1965 to 1972', *University of Aston Management Centre Working Paper, No. 91* (April).

Silver, M.S. and Z.M. Kmietowicz, (1977) 'An index of industrial production for Tanzania. 1965 to 1972', *University of Aston Management Centre Working Paper, No. 83* (December).

United Republic of Tanzania (1972) *National Accounts of Tanzania 1966–1974*, (Dar es Salaam: Bureau of Statistics).

United Republic of Tanzania (1972) *National Accounts of Tanzania 1964 to 1970*, (Dar es Salaam: Bureau of Statistics).

United Republic of Tanzania (1971) *National Accounts of Tanzania 1966 to 1968: Sources and Methods*, (Dar es Salaam: Bureau of Statistics).

United Republic of Tanzania, *Survey of Industrial Production* (for each year from 1966 to 1974), (Dar es Salaam: Bureau of Statistics).

United Republic of Tanzania, *Employment and Earnings*, (for each year from 1963 to 1974), (Dar es Salaam: Bureau of Statistics).

United Republic of Tanzania, *Hali ya Uchumi wa Taifa Katika Mwaka 1977–78*, (The Economic Survey).

United Republic of Tanzania, *The Economic Survey 1971–72*.

United Republic of Tanzania, *The Economic Survey 1970–71*.

United Republic of Tanzania, *The Annual Economic Survey 1968 (A Background to the 1969/70 Budget)*.

Valentine, T. (1980) 'Wage policy in Tanzania since independence: trends and perceptions', paper presented to ILO/University of Dar es Salaam, Tanzania: National Seminar on Development, Employment and Equity Issues, 21–25 July.

Wangwe, S.M. (1976) 'Excess capacity in manufacturing industry: a case study of selected firms in Tanzania', *ERB Paper 76.2*, University of Dar es Salaam (reprinted in K.S. Kim *et al.*, 1979).

Warren, B. (1973) 'Imperialism and capitalist industrialization', *New Left Review*, 81 (September/October).

Weber, M. (1947) *The Theory of Social and Economic Organization*, (Oxford: Oxford University Press).

Weeks, J. (1976) 'Crisis and accumulation in the Peruvian economy 1967–1975', *The Review of Radical Political Economy*, 8, 4, (winter).

7   The British State and Agrarian Accumulation in Kenya

MICHAEL COWEN

This chapter has two parts. The first is an attempt to indicate how and why the postwar drive to increase colonial production arose out of a national response, by the leadership of the ruling Labour Party in Britain, to the hegemony which was possessed by the state of the United States over the British state. It was conflict with, as much as collaboration with, the United States which provided the zeal behind the last period of British colonialism. The second part of the chapter refers to the position of indigenous capital in Kenya. Here, the argument is that, in the drive to expand production in reserves of smallholding agriculture, the colonial state ran up against the antagonism which was expressed by the social force of indigenous capital, which was able to create and protect its own areas of, and sources for, accumulation after 1964. If this conflict did not become forcibly critical (in the way that the Mau Mau revolt was critical) then it was because a shift in the balance of class forces after 1964 made this indigenous class of capital the dominant political force until the demise of the Kenyatta regime in 1978.

I   The British Drive to Expand Colonial Production

Apparatuses of the British state were mobilized in 1947 to expand colonial production. This expansion was traumatic in the sense that a sheer quantitative leap in the scale of investment was accompanied by the intervention of state-controlled agencies in all spheres and phases of the circuit of capital. Evidence for the scale of state investment can be disposed of quickly, while the place of the state in the circuit of capital will be mentioned later. Between 1924 and 1944, I estimate that £18 million was actually expended, on parliamentary authority, by the British Treasury on all forms of colonial development. This expenditure, in twenty years, was less than four years' actual expenditure on Colonial Development and Welfare (CD and W)

Table 7.1   *Exchequer expenditure under Colonial Development Acts, 1875–1951 (£million)*

	Sanctioned	Actually advanced
1875–1915[a]	n.a.	4·4
1924–9[b]	13·5	7·0
1929–39[c]	10·0	6·5
1940–4[d]	20·0	4·5
1945–8[e]	30·8	14·0
1949–51[e]	60·2	44·0

Sources:
[a] Wicker, 1958, p. 173.
[b] Meredith, 1975, p. 486.
[c] ibid., p. 489.
[d] Creech Jones Memorandum (WP(44) 643), 'Future provision for CD and W', 15 November 1944, PREM 4/43 A/8.
[e] Wicker, 1955/6, p. 217, and Wicker, 1958, p. 176.

between 1945 and 1949 (£20 million). Even more graphically, actual expenditure on CD and W and the Colonial Development Corporation (CDC) was £44 million in the two years 1949–51 (see Table 7.1). A massive leap in the quantity of finance expended in this way cannot be ascribed simply to a general welfarist belief that 'something' had to be done about the welfare of 'colonial peoples'.[1]

The drive to expand production in the colonies followed directly from an ideological resolve of all representative factions of the postwar Labour government to counter what was generally thought to be the United States domination of the British national economy. This ideological resolve was not overdetermined but underpinned by a material necessity to overcome shortages, particularly of wage goods, in Britain. There was an absolute level of immediate shortage by 1947 which undercut the then current nutritional status of the population and the capacity to produce in Britain itself. Furthermore, there was the more general shortage of materials which frustrated the attempt to increase productivity, an attempt which also lay behind the current concern for why Britain, as a national entity, lagged so far behind the United States.

At the outset, the disinclination to regard United States power as an inexorable outcome, in a century-long historical sweep which shifted the centre of gravity away from Europe, was unmistakable. The point has been mentioned before, as by Gupta who quotes a Labour MP, Ernest Kinghorn, who urged in 1949 that 'Central Africa should be rapidly developed so as to make Britain independent of the USA'.[2] But this idea had been spelled out even more forcefully before, not by Stafford Cripps or John Strachey on the so-called left of the Labour cabinet, but on the right, by Ernest Bevin:

> What I am anxious to do, in order that we can develop an independent position with the United States instead of being supplicants, is to have a policy which, in addition to feeding our own industries adequately here, will give a priority to developments which will produce the raw materials in short supply . . .[3]

His policy was a colonial policy which was endorsed by Attlee and the whole cabinet, including Herbert Morrison (who was disposed to generally disagree with any proposition proffered by Bevin).[4]

The desire to reduce 'dependence'[5] upon and 'subservience'[6] to the United States, and to widen 'our freedom of action restricted by obligations of the kind imposed by the United States Loan Agreement [of 1945]',[7] was only made more urgent by the imperatives of the postwar dollar shortage. In short, whereas 42% of British imports came from dollar area countries in 1946 only 14% of exports went to these countries.[8] Ministerial belief was that the triangular system of exchange would be resurrected: raw materials would flow from the colonies to the United States; capital goods would go from the USA to Britain which would close the gap by exporting manufactures to the colonies. Commodities produced in the colonies would be dollar-earners (as exports to the USA) and dollar-savers (as substitute imports from the dollar area and thus exports to Britain). R. F. Harrod rightly described the belief as the 'new rage of mercantilism',[9] a national policy which supposed that exchange, between refurbished national economies, could be made separate from internal levels of production and consumption and the international location of capital, which was determined primarily by international firms.

We should note, for this British case of national economic development, that Gabriel Kolko (the foremost radical writer on the United States in the postwar world) did not quite hit the target when he wrote that the Labour government accepted the 1945 United States loan without much protest since it 'had neither a consistent theory of the relationship of the international economy to domestic socialism nor a clear vision of the larger exclusively power dimensions of the American loan campaign'.[10] Clearly, by 1947, the implication of the loan was pretty obvious and the theoretical inability to realize that relations of capital are not coterminous with the relations between nation states, was and is not exclusively limited to the pragmatism of 'anti-communist' British social democrats. Contemporary theories of dependency and state monopoly capitalism acutely register the conflation between the economic and the political.

Contrary to the arguments of Kolko and others, no neat dichotomy can be drawn between the internationalist doctrine of social democrats and the 'imperialist and bloc' strategy of British Conservatives, motivated by nationalist doctrine.[11] Certainly, this dichotomy was espoused by a wide range of active observers of Britain in 1947. The US ambassador in London, Lewis Douglas, had said in March 1947 that the British people would soon realize 'the enormity of their error' in electing a Labour government as a 'superficial' solution to the problems of 'war, devastation and hopelessness'. They would soon throw off 'the present yoke' and regain their freedom.[12] In early 1948, he changed his mind:

> On the ideological level, the election of a socialist-Labour government in Britain has strengthened that country's domestic position *vis-à-vis* Soviet propaganda. A government of this type is not so vulnerable with its own people as a Conservative regime might be to charges of reactionary prejudice against the Soviets.[13]

Or take the position of Dennis Healey, then secretary of the Labour Party's international department. He realized that the sharp distinction between 'democratic socialism' and communism was a necessary cornerstone of the wherewithal for American aid to flow to Europe. But this aid was a pre-emptory device to prevent economic collapse in Britain and Europe and the political outcome of economic collapse the demise of social democracy. Once economic collapse had been prevented, however, the 'internationalist' solution for Western European development was the incorporation of African colonies as the raw material hinterland for Europe, a solution which would make a social democratic Europe independent of the United States.[14]

The Truman administration could countenance no such solution. As late as August 1947, and during negotiations to establish the aborted International Trade Organization, Cripps (when President of the UK Board of Trade) was accused of going back on agreements, made from the Atlantic Charter onwards, to eradicate imperial preference in colonial territories.[15] The Labour government fought back strenuously, not only to maintain discrimination against US exports to the colonies, but also to ensure that any agreements which were made to extend multilateralism in trade were sufficiently cosmetic to satisfy the US Congress that the Truman administration was 'cracking Imperial Preference'.[16] Widely expressed American sentiments of anti-imperialism, which were directed against the European colonial powers, unearthed strongly felt national sentiments among British social democrats.

A good part of the Fabian-inspired energy which was expended after 1945 in the administration of colonial production was directed precisely at the New Deal contentions, of Roosevelt and others, that national independence was a precondition for the eradication of poverty and the other ill-effects of the earlier era of colonialism. However, in the era of late European colonialism, a significant Fabian tendency (as we shall observe below) expressed the belief that in Africa, at any rate, delayed national independence under a newly found managerial colonial state apparatus was the precondition for assistance to the impoverished. This political belief in the internationalization of welfare was promoted by a distinct British national insistence. To internationalize welfare was to transmit the rudiments of state-sponsored welfare schemes from Britain to the colonies. In Britain, and in contrast to most African colonial territories, welfare schemes had flowed from the political presence of organizations of labour within the state apparatus. And welfare could not easily be squared, as we shall see below, with the material necessity to expand colonial production for the restructuring of production in Britain itself.

In this connection, with the concern for colonial production for production in Britain, the extent of material shortages in Britain, in 1947, cannot be exaggerated. The draft of the *Economic Survey 1948* stresses that without foreign aid or the expansion of internal food production, food consumption would be reduced 'to levels that spell widespread malnutrition'. Raw material supplies would be reduced 'to a point that causes extensive unemployment. It is for this reason that measures to develop production in colonial territories are of cardinal importance.'[17] This was no mere speculation. Strachey (Minister of Food) declared, in confidence, that food supplies had deteriorated since the end of the war: 'the present diet of our people is generally considered inadequate'.[18] The Chief Medical Officer, in the Ministry of Health, reckoned that any further cut in rations (proposed as a result of projected import cuts to preserve the fast-dwindling 1945 US loan credits) would impose 'serious nutritional consequences for ... adolescents and heavy manual workers'.[19] Gorell Barnes (Attlee's Private Secretary and later a prime mover of colonial production schemes at the colonial office) advised the Prime Minister: 'Politics apart, I do not think it would be sound policy to reduce food supplies below the point where people can get sufficient food to maintain health and strength.'[20]

What were the politics of the 1947 crisis? Dalton (the then Chancellor of the Exchequer) summed up 'a most unpleasant dilemma': either the Labour government could refuse to ask for more US aid and thereby 'embark upon a major reversal of our economic policy' through obtaining supplies bilaterally (without the dollar as the medium of exchange) or it could accept further US aid and be 'under the strongest pressure not to alter our existing economic policy, even although this involves drawing upon our reserves'. And if the reserves were reduced, by refusing to cut food imports, 'we should be left defenceless against any conditions, no matter how intolerable, which the US government might wish to impose upon us'.[21] In the following I shall indicate what these conditions might have entailed. Here we should only note that in the event an extension of credits was provided in August 1947. The Truman administration agreed to the suspension of sterling convertibility and as one of three measures proposed by Attlee to counteract the immediate crisis, colonial production was to be expanded. (The other measures involved a reorganization of production in Britain itself to increase total output and direct resources to increase exports and reduce imports.)[22]

Why, it will be asked, should the colonies be the hinterland for the reorganization of British production? Simply to excuse the degree of political control which any British government could exert over a colonial government, which was greater than that which was exerted over non-colonial governments. Even if the margin of difference was not all that considerable, it was sufficient to make colonial production paramount. Thus, following the suspension of sterling convertibility in August 1947, bilateral negotiations were undertaken with a number of governments to settle the terms upon which raw material exports to Britain would be exchanged for British exports of coal, steel and other capital goods. The overriding impression which is gained from a perusal of these negotiations is summed up in the minuted words of a Treasury official: 'Suspension of convertibility had put the Treasury in a very weak position. It had broken a number of its agreements and it was, therefore, difficult for them to refuse discussion with governments concerned ...'[23] Thus, the Soviet Union government demanded guaranteed prices and delivery dates for industrial exports as part of any agreement to supply cereals, timber and other materials to Britain.[24] It was a condition that a Labour government could not easily meet, beset as it was with bouts of militancy by coal miners and other workers. But let us leave aside the more obvious cases such as Argentina and look at Britain's alleged small neo-colonies like Denmark and Eire. Danish negotiations reached such a pitch that British state officials demanded, but could not obtain, the removal of farmers (who had threatened to cut off butter supplies) from the Danish delegations.[25] British officials desperately prayed for the chance that in forthcoming elections 'socialists would take over the government'.[26] De Valera (the Irish Prime Minister) insisted that Ireland must be permitted to industrialize and, in lieu of a suspension of US imports to save dollars, demanded supplies of coal at British subsidized domestic prices.[27] British officials were implored by Attlee and other ministers to treat the Irish government 'gently' and not issue threats which 'might well be resented by the Irish as undue interference in their own affairs . . .'[28] Squeezed, therefore, between the United States and the populist forces which raged across Europe and the southern hemisphere in the immediate postwar period, the pursuit of a further colonial project in order to reorganize British production looked like the most likely outcome of the postwar conjunction.

Expanded colonial production would not merely secure material supplies to provide immediate physical relief; expanded production would also reduce the rate at which future prices of raw materials would increase. There was a collective appreciation that falling import prices for food would reduce the rate at which the value of wage goods would rise;[29] it was left to individuals like R. F. Harrod to point out (though not in his language and despite the fact he was opposed to the colonial project) that removing binding constraints on raw material shortages would increase the rate at which circulating capital turned over.[30] We can hardly fail to notice that these are the classic and most general weapons for the restructuring of productive capital. In the Britain of the immediate postwar period emphatic attention was paid to the question of productivity but the emphasis was as much on productivity for the nation as productivity for capital. Thus, we find the official cabinet Steering Committee on Economic Development (composed almost entirely of permanent secretaries) reporting that ministers were 'gravely concerned' about productivity.[31] Their proposed measures to counter falling absolute levels of productivity (in some sectors) were coupled with measures to attempt to narrow divergences, in average rates of productivity growth (for other sectors), between Britain and the United States. What is striking about the tone of these measures is their emphasis upon lengthening the working day as much as the desire to see labour redirected away from the construction of housing, and other services, and towards the production of capital goods.[32] A concern with the length of the working day is, of course, a focus upon the extraction of absolute surplus value and a focus which is normally attributed to the earliest periods of capitalism.

The point is that the declared and ideal aim of colonial production to compensate for the domination of the United States was quite consistent with the expressed aim of the Truman (and subsequent) administrations during the postwar period. It was not simply that colonial production would open sources of raw material supplies for the US economy. More fundamentally, as Maier has pointed out, the outcome, whether intended or not, was to 'transform political issues into problems of output'.[33] In the case of Britain, any distrust of nationalization measures was amply outweighed by the trust that a Labour government would increase production and productivity on a world scale. This was the way in which the opposition between labour and capital could be muted and the point was made clear in a report by Strachey to cabinet after an interview with Lewis Douglas (the US ambassador in London). The ambassador was opposed to any reduction in the current consumption of British workers since any reduction in the absolute level of real wages would lead to a fall in industrial output and:

[the workers] might react politically by moving away from the centre and towards the Left and the Right wings, thus producing an anti-Labour administration faced by a militant and unco-operative industrial labour movement which would be more or less under communist leadership.[34]

During 1947 the US administration informed the Labour government that 'American opinion' was against policies for cutting food and raw material imports into Britain but in favour of increased production, and particularly production in colonial territories. If American opinion was business opinion and if expanded production, in Britain and colonies, fuelled the demand for capital goods which were produced by US firms, then it met the desire, as expressed by officials of the British state, for American overseas investment in the colonies. This was a strange phenomenon and we should be clear how it was affected by the Cold War.

Cold War politics intervened very specifically in the British project for colonial production. British schemes for expanded production in the colonies were based exclusively on the economic premise that they would enhance production in Britain; schemes based on political premises, such as to fob off Russian influence in certain strategic areas, were relegated to the domain of the American state. The two sets of premises were kept quite separate and were consciously enunciated as such:

> [It is to] our joint advantage that the Arab countries, Persia and Afghanistan improve the economic conditions of their common people, so as to prevent the social unrest which provides fertile ground for communist propaganda and Soviet penetration. Our financial position does not however permit us to provide the capital which is essential to the long-term development schemes necessary to achieve this.[35]

The capital, it was implied, should come from the United States. Bevin once confused the two sets of premises and he received short shrift from the Colonial Office. In 1949 he proposed an international scheme for 'social and economic development' in the Nile valley (of Egypt, Sudan and Uganda) to bring 'large areas' of land under cultivation, remove Egyptian 'suspicions' of Britain and 'keep the Russians out of questions affecting the economic development of Africa'.[36] Andrew Cohen, of the Colonial Office, retorted that North Africa (the strategic area) should be kept separate from East Africa (the economic sphere for expanded production) and that an international scheme would intrude upon any established British exclusivity in colonial administration.[37]

In like manner, the withdrawal of British troops from Greece in 1947, and the threatened withdrawal from Germany, were employed by British ministers to compel the Truman administration, and the Republican-dominated Congress, to recognise the 'seriousness' of the British financial position and advance more financial aid.[38] Moreover, the withdrawal and threat of withdrawal would force United States capital to be invested in strategic areas. Diplomats called the ploy 'banging the anti-communist drum' and made much ironic play of the view that the Soviet Union was Britain's 'best ally' since Britain had become the first line of defence against the Russians.[35] 'As regards resistance to communism, the Secretary of State [Bevin] feels that no one –

and certainly no US statesman – has shown as firm and consistent a resistance to communism as he has himself.'[40] There should be little doubt, however, that the material burden of fighting communists had to be borne by the Americans. Any such aim for colonial production as a British project was entirely abstract and its impulses, from 1947, sprang entirely from the well-established set of material premises: to relieve production bottlenecks and assist in the productivity drive in Britain itself.

STATE CORPORATIONS AND PRIVATE ENTERPRISE

John Strachey, the popularizer of Marx in the 1930s and fellow traveller of the Communist Party, could hardly be accused of a lack of grasp of theory. His previous espousal of a kind of marxism put him in fine fettle when he came, as Minister of Food, to argue for expanded colonial production:

> The true end of production is consumption. More and more every year governments are compelled to look at the world's resources as one economic whole, in which different countries have different parts to play … Historically, nearly all the great forward movements of economic development that have added to the real wealth of the world have been started by individuals or groups motivated by an appreciation of the actual or potential consumer need for some new product, or source of supply.[41]

Note the adjectival *true* for the purpose of production: consumption is most certainly not a true end under capitalism but it should be the true end for the national entity of postwar Britain.

Capital, for Strachey, did not enter into the matter at all. The Colonial Office was to represent producers while the Ministry of Food would do the same for British consumers in 'this new field of public enterprise'[42] Herbert Morrison (as Lord President of the Council) was less inclined to evade the position of capital and his precepts for the organization of production and consumption obviously embraced his predilection for the managerial public corporation. But there was more to it than that. The task was to exclude firms, embodying the relation of commercial capital, from the circulation of commodities:

> We need first-hand information from experts on production – farmers, scientists and engineers, for example – as distinct from the expert buyers whose contracts are mainly with middle-men and governments.[43]

This exorcising of merchant capitalists was not confined to Labour ideologues. Oliver Stanley, Conservative Colonial Secretary in the war cabinet, had said during a Commons debate in 1943 that colonies had passed the stage for the '"get-rich-quick" type of entrepreneur' who looked for 'great profits' through bearing 'great risks'. Stanley hoped for 'a number of industrialists who will have a real desire, apart from the profit motive, to assist in this task of Imperial Development. Well, miracles do happen.' When the radical and anti-colonial leader of the minuscule Commonwealth Party, Sir Richard Acland, asked what would happen if this miracle did not come off, Stanley was adamant in his retort: 'No I never rely on miracles . . . I did try to make it plain that the whole resources of colonial governments and His Majesty's Government would already be committed to the full in various developments.'[44]

Therefore, it is not all that remarkable that the eschewing of private enterprise, and the promotion of state agencies to expand colonial production, provoked little or no antagonism from within the British state apparatuses. Sir Eric Plowden and H. Weeks, of the Central Economic Planning Staff,[45] did attack Morrison's proposals, while Treasury officials[46] who questioned the Stanley-Morrison line were informed by their superiors that 'on grounds of general policy' the Colonial Office felt that colonies 'ought not to be exploited by private enterprise'. Sidney Caine and others of the Colonial Office did not believe that they could rely on private enterprise to provide technical experts and money-capital for colonial development; in any case, private capital was not 'interested in the necessary degree of activity'.[47]

Now, as we shall have occasion to see for the Kenya case (in part II), the exact opposite actually occurred. Certainly state agencies entered into the administration of production and private forms of merchant capital were increasingly excluded from the circulation of commodities. Yet international firms, however much they may have desisted from entering into specific and necessary (necessary from the vantage point of the *true* end of production as consumption) forms of agrarian production, were well able to maintain their hold over international markets for commodities which were produced under the administration of public corporations.

Indeed, the impulse which spawned state management of schemes to expand agrarian production only made international competition as emphatic as the competition between capitals for the control over materials. Thus, in Tanganyika in late 1947, sisal estate owners set up a co-operative organization to market sisal freely on world markets. To market the commodity freely meant making the commodity available to US buyers and undermining British state-sponsored bulk buying schemes which guaranteed the forward purchase of the whole crop at lower than international prices for the commodity. A Colonial Office spokesman (Sir Gerald Clauson) pointed out: 'If we continued to buy the whole crop . . . we should be open to the charge of exploiting a trusteeship territory for our own advantage.'[48] The political fear that the United States administration might invoke the trusteeship agreement, which guaranteed open access to raw materials, was enough to make the Colonial Office make over a proportion of the 1948 crop to US buyers.

Exactly the same problem arose in connection with the allocation of capital goods to colonies for the express purpose of expanded production. A requisite measure of control over exports of steel and other equipment could not be achieved by committees of state officials. Firms continued to export to markets which were chosen at will, whether according to individual profitability or convenience and certainly not according to Strachey's specification of national need. Clauson again brought the problem to a head by calling for 'some major change in industrial organization . . . if we were to deal effectively with the competing demands for our products from desirable overseas markets'.[49] Morrison had appreciated the problem when he called for public corporations, coupled with a strong dose of central planning, to carry forward the national project for colonial production:

We are in a danger of making the worst of both planning and *laissez-faire* worlds if we leave the expansion of overseas supplies too much to the self-interest of producers who have little incentive [to produce] in present conditions and are up against heavy odds.[50]

Neither the sectional view of the colonial officials nor the general overview of Morrison was to prevail in the manner which they may have desired.

Rather, the resulting blend between the state control over individual schemes of production and company management of the circulation of commodities was culled, first, from the actual practices of state intervention in British industry[51] and, second, followed from a blindness which afflicted ministers and officials. For the second, if they could not control the international operations of firms, in all spheres of the circuit of capital, then it was far more opportune to remove capital from their field of vision. After all, they were dealing with the effects of investment incapacities in Britain and the colonies. It was this incapacity which rendered state intervention so necessary to raise the productivity of labour. These points cannot be overemphasized because institutions such as the Colonial (Commonwealth) Development Corporation are believed to have emerged from the welfarist principles which lay behind the Colonial Welfare and Development Acts of 1940 and 1945. If welfarism was one strand of colonial policy it was definitely distinct from the principles which established the Colonial Development Corporation.

THE COLONIAL DEVELOPMENT CORPORATION (CDC)

The model for the CDC was the Finance Corporation for Industry (FCI), which was sponsored by the Labour government in May 1945 to transfer temporary and longer-term money-capital to any 'industry [which] is not viewed favourably by investors in the prevailing economic or political climate'.[52] The purpose of the FCI was an attempt to overcome the then-current practices of banking capital in Britain. Financial institutions put a premium upon risk-free and redeemable securities for direct lending while paying inordinate attention to the return on the value of investments through the secondary market for shares and stock.[53] Industries which were (and are) not regarded favourably by the institutions of banking capital are those like steel, whose capacity for future capitalization outran, by far, their present capacity to generate internal funds for investment. Moreover, these industries have had to impose a relatively low gearing ratio to fend off the threat of takeover. Since the Labour government was also disposed to influence the location of industries in depressed regions, the FCI was heavily involved in the steel industry of Wales. It was financed by loans from commercial banks, not upon the security of any individual industry to which the FCI advanced finance, but on a £25 million share issue (of which 70% was subscribed by insurance companies and investment trusts as a pre-emptory gesture to fend off state intervention and 30% by the Bank of England).[54]

This was the background against which Viscount Portal (chairman of the Colonial Economic Development Council) proposed the formation of the CDC by privately writing to Attlee:

If this [Colonial Development *Finance* Corporation, emphasis added]
goes through and is approved, I feel certain that the amount at the disposal
of the Finance Corporation should be as large as our No. 1 Finance
Corporation [FCI] in this country . . .[55]

The Prime Minister, together with the Chancellor of the Exchequer, agreed.
The latter, Dalton, responded positively to a proposal that the CDC be
financed through a Treasury guarantee, up to a borrowing limit of £100 million:
'This is a Big Idea & we must back it.'[56] But, why £100 million? Well, this was
the authorized borrowing limit of the FCI, at four times its £25 million share
issue.[57] Also, it was a figure, as a Treasury official put it, 'which will capture
the public imagination'.[58] 'Capturing the public imagination' was no relation
expressing the accounting criteria for banking or any other sphere of capital.
It was an ideological relation of national economic development, expressed by
democratic socialists as much as by conservatives and individual capitalists.

It is of interest to note that such a corporation had been proposed by the
leading US representative, Taussig, of the Anglo-American Caribbean
Commission, as a vehicle designed to further US penetration in the West
Indies during the war. In 1942, Oliver Stanley (then Colonial Secretary)
reported to Anthony Eden (then Foreign Secretary) that he was opposed to
the 'rather dangerous idea of an Anglo-American Corporation to finance
development [in the Caribbean], which I did my best to discourage'.[59] The
proposal was rejected precisely because it had been proposed by the US
administration. As we mentioned earlier, in the postwar conjuncture no such
proposals were now rejected. Indeed, the World Bank, of the late 1940s, could
be construed as an Anglo-American finance corporation. From the Bank's
inception, the Colonial Office sought for its finance to back CDC projects with
money-capital, in dollars, and with American-produced capital equipment.

The CDC was akin neither to Colonial Development and Welfare funds, nor
to the public corporations which were set up after 1945 in Britain itself. For
the first, it is well known that the 1940 CD and W Acts represented a sharp
turn-about in colonial policy. Prior to 1940 a sharp distinction was made
between 'development' schemes and those of an 'ordinary administrative
character'; colonies had to finance the second out of internal revenues and
finance advanced under the 1929 Colonial Development Act could only be
employed for 'development' schemes.[60] Now, even the Treasury in 1940
wanted finance advanced for 'new or expanded social services which would
include almost any service of benefit to a colony' and 'would almost certainly
overlap to a considerable extent normal costs of administration'.[61] In 1944,
Oliver Stanley wrote, 'if we're unwilling to assume the burden [of colonial
assistance] are we justified in retaining a Colonial Empire?' and that to suggest
that finance could not be afforded was 'a confession of future national
impotence'.[62]

To be sure, there was a good deal of argument over both the 1940 and the
1945 Acts. The Treasury informed the Colonial Office, during 1940, that
'importance has been attached here [under war conditions] to the economic
side of the programme whereas . . . your memorandum tends to emphasize the
social side; no doubt you will continue to bear our point of view in mind'.[63]
And in 1944 the Chancellor of the Exchequer, Sir John Anderson, objected
to the size of Stanley's request for £150 million (over ten years) for CD and

W because of 'the financial exigencies of this country'.[64] The dispute went to cabinet, where Churchill (who had opposed the 1929 Act) pointed to the 'extreme gravity' of the expected postwar financial position and was 'very unwilling to see any rate of expenditure authorized in excess of that proposed by the Chancellor of the Exchequer'.[65] Stanley's request was scaled down to £120 million (with a maximum limit of £10 million for any year). The point is that whereas the cabinet was still alluding to colonial development as welfarist in 1944, it was clear that by 1947 finance for colonial development was now being advanced in inverse proportion to the well-being of the balance-of-payments position. In short, the scale of finance which was advanced to the CDC was raised precisely because of British 'financial exigencies' and not because finance for colonial development was in direct proportion to the ability of the state to pay for welfare assistance: colonial development was to compensate for a chronically bad balance-of-payments position.

In a brief exchange (in the *Review of Economic Studies*), Wicker and Hazelwood argued over Myint's interpretation for the apparent failure of CDC projects. Myint had suggested that:

> the root cause of failure lies not so much in the wrong choice of men and inefficient methods of administering the ventures but in the vagueness of the mandate itself which tries to compromise between the principle of obtaining economic returns and the principle of needs.[66]

However, this specification of a dual mandate – uniting economic return and social need – follows from the establishment of state corporations, institutions, or projects once the establishment has been thoroughly informed of and by political objectives. These objectives, to maintain national or regional production and employment, arise more often than not to counter the incapacities of investment 'unevenness' and 'permanent disequilibria' as it is normally termed) which are part of the unfettered expression of the international location of capital. National economic development is one such objective and it may be inspired by the action of labour upon, and in the class expression of, state power; equally it may be inspired to fend off the action of labour.

A dual mandate, therefore, was one combining British and colonial needs rather than one combining economic returns in general and social need in general. State-sponsored corporations in Britain could equally be forced to incur social costs (to maintain employment, to construct housing for workers, to construct roads and railways) which would not be covered by present or discounted revenues accruing to the projects of the corporation. This principle of need, contrary to Wicker's argument, was not a specific characteristic of CDC.[67] Nor, contrary to Hazelwood's argument, was the principle of inordinate risk (inordinate for capital, whether private or corporate), which was inherent in CDC projects, peculiar to the CDC.[68] The FCI accumulated losses for years and its losses were only temporarily offset by the sale of shares, to private corporations, in its steel-financing operations.[69] Now, what was specific about the CDC was that, first, the dual mandate was meant to be a balance of compromise between the fulfilment of a British national need and the fulfilment of a colonial need which was expressed as a territorial interest for each colony. Second, the institution was to be, in the characteristic British sense of such phenomena, a planning instrument which would permit the intervention of the state in all spheres of the circuit of capital. Let me expand on these two points.

(1) The conflict between a British need and a colonial need was inherent in the corporation right from its beginnings in 1947. When the CDC was first and formally proposed at a meeting of the Colonial Economic Development Council it was said that further finance for colonial development 'would only be provided for purposes likely to benefit the UK', and further that:

> This did not . . . mean that the colonies were to be exploited to their own detriment for the benefit of the UK . . . By encouraging the production of commodities and raw materials of which [Britain], and indeed the whole world, stood in need, the productivity and hence the standard of life of colonial peoples would be raised.[70]

The direction of purpose, as enunciated here in the mildest of tones, is unmistakable. No longer was the expansion of production to be the means for raising colonial welfare but rather an improved standard of living was a spin-off from, or a possible consequence of, production for consumption in Britain.

Yet, qualms were never removed, particularly from the long lineage of old-fashioned anti-imperialists who saw any such formulation of colonial production as contrary to the protection of colonial peoples against the thrust of European exploitation. On one occasion a protest was registered thus: 'The colonies are not British estates which can be exploited by the United Kingdom for her own advantage.'[71] The formulation even worried Bevin, whose Foreign Office was trying to fend off Soviet Union charges about 'inter-imperialist' rivalry between the United States and Britain.[72] However, there was more to it than qualms about exploitation. It was that CDC as an instrument of interterritorial centralized planning ran up against the barrier of decentralized, territorially located projects.

(2) To plan the direction of investment was tantamount to attempt to confront the anarchy of the spontaneous movement of capital, a movement which included the industrial capital of British origin and over which the state, whether in Britain or the colonies, had little hold. Planning, in this sense, was a commitment to establish projects upon the basis of international need and not upon the criterion of profitability. Equally, it was a commitment not to foresake a colonial territory when the need dried up, when the specific form of commodity production ceased having a use-value. This, apparently, was the often-expressed colonial need.[73] But, on what criterion could accounting losses by one or more projects in one territory be supported by accounting surpluses accruing to other projects in other territories? By what vestige of supremacy could the British state, through the CDC, allocate investment between colonies when the criterion of profitability was banished and replaced by that of international need?

This conflict could not be resolved easily. Any resolution would come only after the pretext of planning was abandoned and after the renunciation of the possibility that the corporation would incorporate all relations of all spheres in the circuit of capital. From 1951, this is exactly what happened. After accounting losses were accumulated (£10 million on financial advances of £38 million by 1954) and twenty-one projects were abandoned,[74] the CDC increasingly came to embody a relation of banking capital. The relations of industrial and commercial capital devolved increasingly upon the creation of subsidiary corporations, which were located for particular projects in each territory. Second, CDC projects typically became mixed-enterprise projects in which private and corporate capital came to participate.

Subsidiary corporations were subject to the surveillance of colonial (and then national) governments as much as to the accounting criteria of the interterritorial corporation. As we shall observe (in the case of tea production in Kenya), CDC certainly continued to provide a point of intersection between the different spheres of capital. Then, this point of intersection was little different from the classic conception of finance capital as the 'articulated combination of commercial, . . . industrial . . . and banking capital with banking capital being dominant but not determinant'.[75] As is well known, and as Thompson points out in this case, the difference between domination and determination is that the institutions of banking capital may determine where, and in what organizational form, production may take place. But the practices of these institutions cannot determine whether accumulation and the appropriation of production will eventuate.

In the case of tea in Kenya, a CDC subsidiary was created as a parastatal authority to bear the burden of administering production. It was administration in the most literal sense. Schemes for the expanded production of household-produced commodities were executed by personnel of the colonial (and then national) government's ministry of agriculture and provincial administration. One consequence, which will be spelt out later in more detail, was that the administration of production ran up against the propensities for, and practices of, accumulation by the indigenous class of capital. Another consequence was that technical operations, in production, were performed either by personnel, who were hired from tea companies or through management agreements which handed the management of tea factories over to the companies of corporate capital. Above all, any attempt to dominate the international circulation of commodities was relinquished. International marketing remained in the hands of international firms.

CDC was originally one non-capitalist institution, among many others, which contrived to centralize accumulation in Britain on the basis of decentralized productive activities in Africa and elsewhere. No single capitalist institution with a colonial past acted in this way. International firms, in cases of raw material production, decentralized accumulation away from Britain by augmenting productive capacity in colonial territories during the course of accumulation. In the case of Forestal for wattle production (which we briefly mention in part II), the firm engaged in the expansion of production in Kenya out of profits realized from accumulation in South Africa; accumulation in South Africa had been set in motion by profits realized out of productive activities in Argentina. The decisions to invest in South Africa and Kenya were made without reference to the national need for raw material consumption in Britain and the money-capital which set expanded production in motion in the southern hemisphere was not advanced from Britain. Probably the same applied to the case of Brooke Bond for tea production when the firm located capital in Kenya out of accumulation in India. And if this firm paid more obeisance to demands which issued out of the British state apparatus, it is largely because the international market for tea was centred upon London (and quite unlike the case of wattle where the comparative weight of the London market for tanning materials was minimal).

After 1954 CDC was unencumbered by a centralized planning function. The institution was then to be less a point of intersection between spheres of capital and to become more an agency of banking capital. Now the corporation could fulfil the original accounting criterion which, although formally drawn from the scheduled financial policy for nationalized corporations, was actually actively applied to the practices of the Finance Corporation for Industry: 'It shall be the duty of the Corporations [CDC] so to exercise and perform their functions as to secure that their revenues are not less than sufficient to meet all sums properly chargeable to their revenue account . . . taking one year with another.'[76] This criterion could be fulfilled reasonably well provided that financial surpluses (in the form of redeemed loan-capital) could be transferred to new projects in territories where the surpluses did not originate; and, provided that financial losses would be borne, during the early stages of projects, in part by colonial (and then national governments) and/or international firms and not by the corporation itself. What, then, would be the difference between the CDC as a public corporation and as a merchant bank? Why should the designation of a non-capitalist institution be retained when it becomes so embedded in an international circuit of capital?

I am not able to answer these questions satisfactorily. I can only suggest that the attempt to centralize accumulation in Britain was politically inspired and any action to this end demanded that a non-capitalist institution be established to fulfil the reconstruction of production in Britain itself. The specification of a national need, or a need which is not specific to competition between capitals, must be regarded as a political form of intervention. Political intervention is a deliberate means to protect investment and employment within the entity, territorial or otherwise, of the nation-state. If this is so, what is the order of difference between the 1929 Colonial Development Act and the ventures of 1947? After all, the 1929 Act was passed, again by a Labour government, to protect employment in Britain.[77]

The order of difference was that the 1947 ventures were no set of primitive instruments designed, crudely, to relieve a politically acute level of unemployment. On the contrary, colonial production was expanded to maintain and sustain a politically sanctioned level of full employment in Britain. Second, and it is in this way that the Kenya case enters the argument, the CDC and other such institutions could not avoid the task of holding a balance between a British need and a colonial need. Radicals have long argued that 'aid' extends 'elitism', that, in the words of David Lloyd George (the then Liberal Party leader), colonial development is nothing other than 'a consignment of push bicycles for enterprising niggers'[78] The fact of the matter was and is far from this conventional argument and it is to Kenya that we should now turn.

II   Kenya and the Indigenous Class of Capital

It can be argued that the colonial (and then national) need came to be expressed by the growing domination of an indigenous class of capital. This expression of a colonial need conveyed a good deal of generality for the spokesmen of colonial policy in Britain during the 1940s. Later, it was to inform and permeate the practices of the late colonial state in Kenya and elsewhere. One form of this expression was that of dependency. A second form was to emphasize the class character of national independence.

The first line of colonial policy was summed up by Oliver Stanley in 1943 when he was under acute pressure to conform to Roosevelt's insistence upon the principle of national independence. During a House of Commons debate he claimed that the object of colonial development was to make colonies financially self-supporting on the basis of a 'reasonable standard of life'. Otherwise any talk of self-government was 'humbug': 'There cannot be any real self-government if you are financially dependent. Political responsibility goes ill with financial dependence.'[79] The weight of irony hangs heavily when it is appreciated that this is the cornerstone of the charge *against* neo-colonialism, the cornerstone of any version of dependency theory.

More irony follows in the lengthy quotation below, also for 1943, which was taken from an anonymous paper in cabinet files:

> Socialists have tended to view colonial problems largely from the subjective point of view. They have seen imperialism as a projection into the colonial sphere of the capitalist exploitation which they experience at home ... In its revulsion from imperialism the socialist movement has often tended to ignore the exploitation of natives by natives which is often far worse than by the white capitalist and to assume that the necessary antidote to imperialism is self-government by the natives ...
>
> There is ... an antinomy between a government which rules in the interest of the governed and a wealthy class which seeks under cover or by use of government to get rich at the expense of the poorer sections of the community ... We should long ago in Africa have substituted state trading and state purchase and disposal of products for the individual trader method. In a word a socialist government ought to think more of introducing socialist methods into the administration of the colonial empire than of handing over government to a small number of educated natives with insufficient standards of honesty and civic duty.[80]

This piece, also probably framed as an antidote to pressure from the United States to make national independence the cardinal principle of the Atlantic Alliance, sums up particularly the Fabian position towards the capitalization of colonial production.

In general, the lines which can be drawn to separate right from left in these matters are blurred in a dimension through which socialism was taken to be the suppression of indigenous capital while conservatives sought to admonish the place of international firms in colonial production. Before turning to Kenya, we may note the remarks of a Tory MP, R.H. Turton, during the same debate in which Stanley urged state intervention to secure economic independence for the colonial territories. Turton asked why there was no 'native industry' in Nigeria and put the cause squarely on the Unilever subsidiary, United Africa Company (UAC):

> UAC is administered from London. There is no native capital in the whole of the enterprise, and yet that company has a secure and undisputed monopoly throughout the whole of West Africa ... There is widespread resentment throughout all the West African colonies at that virtual monopoly.[81]

The case of indigenous capital in Kenya will show that these remarks are not intended to represent a random and eccentric set of ideas but are rather the definitive expression of the active policies of colonial administrators during the expansion of household production.

Elsewhere, we have attempted to show how and why an indigenous class of capital in Kenya's Central Province was formed long before the agrarian reforms of the 1950s.[82] By the early 1920s an exclusive class had come to establish forms of commodity production which were based upon the direct employment of wage labour. Only the superficial appearance of a constricted scale of accumulation belied its character as expanded production to reproduce means of production rather than means of subsistence. At the end of the 1940s individuals of this class had entered into competition with Asian and European merchant capitalists, adopted aggressive strategies towards the acquisition of land and other instruments of production, and commanded forms of political organization (particularly the Kikuyu Central Association and Kenya African Union) which were directed towards removing the racial constraints over property-ownership. Now, when schemes for expanded colonial production were implemented (before the Mau Mau revolt of the early 1950s), the colonial administration found itself confronting an independent social force whose propensity for accumulation did not fit the object of expanded colonial production.

WATTLE AND TEA IN KENYA'S CENTRAL PROVINCE[83]

Whereas the indigenous class of capital had first planted wattle (from the early 1920s), by the early 1940s the middle peasantry had become the preponderant source of wattle production; the commodity was planted by virtually all households in Central Province and they survived as economic units of commodity production. As such, the ability of individuals of the indigenous class to accumulate was constricted on two counts: the effective supply of labour to producers of this class of capital was reduced and their further accumulation of land in the reserves of smallholding agriculture was prevented. This constriction aggravated the demand by the indigenous class for the acquisition of land in the white Highlands while it turned members of the class into stradders between the boundaries of trade and production. As much as producing wattle on the basis of employing wage labour, they turned to trade, purchasing bark from households and selling to a collusive duopsony of firms which extracted tannin from the bark. The extract was used as an agent for tanning leather.

During the interwar period one of the companies, Forestal, had relocated capital, first from Argentina (where it was the predominant producer of quebracho, the substitute for wattle) to South Africa and then from there to Kenya. Under the pressure of competition this second relocation to Kenya was a movement to protect the firm's command over international supplies of materials and markets for extract. It was the case that the spontaneous growth of production in Kenya, before the middle peasantry became the preponderant source of production, threatened to disturb the output and price decisions which were made by Forestal to equilibriate the international market for tanning extracts.

Officials of the colonial state in Kenya were invariably antagonistic towards this international firm. As long as they were loath to enter into the manufacture of extract and as long as they sought to maintain wattle production in Kenya, officials could not but accede to the demand by Forestal that they protect the establishment of a duopsony to purchase bark from household producers. Forestal fixed producer prices together with the quantities and qualities of bark which were to be purchased each buying season. The state's department of agriculture confirmed prices and administered the quantity and quality controls once they had been fixed by the firm.

This alignment of company and state was opposed most vociferously by individuals of the indigenous class of capital. Their association of producers and traders soon became indistinguishable from the Kenya African Union. They eroded quality and quantity controls and compaigned initially for their abolition while pressing for an increase in the producer price of bark. Ultimately, they campaigned for the deregulation of the duopsony to permit the association to establish its own factory for the processing of the bark. There is no doubt about the militancy of their agitation. When couched in terms reminiscent of the attack on the UAC in West Africa but amplified doubly by the racial tones which were made obvious by the presence of Asian and local European capitalists, the agitation was to make up one of the forces which led to the Mau Mau revolt. After the revolt, this agitation was to be resurrected around the terms upon which tea production was to be organized.

During the wattle period of the immediate postwar years the indigenous class met with the unrelenting consternation of state officials who sought to suppress both the private trade in bark and the political association of the larger traders and producers. The distrust of the 'middle class' (as the traders and producers were frequently called by officials) was to be equally emphatic during the tea period of the late 1950s and early 1960s. One difference now was that there was a widespread realization, by those manning the state apparatus, that state and capitalist company could not be associated as a single political entity in any project to counter the demands of producers. In another but exemplary context, Sir Edward Bridges (head of the British civil service and Permanent Secretary of the Treasury) urged, in 1947, that the Labour government adopt a wages policy but not through 'a "strong state" form of intervention' which would mean 'that all wage disputes would automatically become not conflicts with employers, but conflicts with the government'.[84] How prescient he was and in how haphazard a manner his kind of advice was taken up by governments in both Britain and Kenya.

In passing from wattle to tea we need only note that wattle rapidly ceased to have a use-value during the 1950s as the raw material boom fuelled the switch to synthetic tanning agents. More important for our purpose was that wattle bark soon lost its exchange value for household producers. Even as export prices rose rapidly during the boom, the producer price for bark failed to rise at a rate which could cover both an increase in consumer prices and an upward shift in the mass of households' necessary means of subsistence. In short, the revenue from wattle production covered the difference between wages from migratory labour and the value of labour power; but at relatively constant rates of productivity change, revenue from wattle and wages from migration failed to rise and so meet the quantum leap in the value of labour power, which had sprung from the enlarged postwar wants of producers. The decline in real wages was the other force making up the Mau Mau revolt.

Wattle had to be replaced by commodities whose value, in labour time, was increased through a change in labour productivity. It was this growth in productivity which featured so strongly in postwar colonial plans as sanctioned by the Colonial Economic Development Council (CEDC). Rarely did an occasion arise when Arthur Lewis (a member of CEDC) failed to issue a dissenting note of protest when any colonial plan did not contain an injunction to increase labour productivity in smallholding agriculture.[85] A lack of space prevents me from showing how the concern for productivity was to spell out conditions for the extraction of relative surplus value, particularly when producers were to reduce consumption out of direct production and consume commodities which were produced under conditions in which the average productivity of labour was rising. I think that this shift in the focus of appropriation, from absolute to relative surplus value extraction, was the most profound factor behind the schemes for expanded production in colonial territories. It was a factor which made it perfectly possible for the restructuring of productive capital to be achieved, after the war, through non-capitalist institutions.

The Department of Agriculture in Kenya started a pilot tea project in Nyeri District during 1948 after officials found that tea had been planted illegally in Central Province since 1948. Brooke Bond Ltd had no objection, in principle, to tea growing by Africans. What inflamed the firm was the state-sponsored project for what was called backyard production by households marketing sun-dried tea for local consumption. Brooke Bond described the 'government tea enterprise' as 'the "song of the shirt" [i.e.] sweated home labour competing with reasonable working conditions [of the tea estates]'.[86] In this strange complaint about exploitation, the material fear of the firm was that household production would compete with that part of the estate-produced tea output which was designated for local markets and which subsidized the higher-quality output which went on to international markets. Furthermore, it would be the state, as part of a conjunction incorporating merchant capital, through which profits out of expanded household production would be appropriated.

Now, in contrast the 1930s, officials were not unwilling to enter the processing of household-produced commodities. On the contrary, the Department of Agriculture rejected Brooke Bond's view that production should be developed through large-scale units and reckoned that any individual household in the province could start to produce. In 1951 it was suggested that the CDC produce a state-sponsored scheme for the planting and processing of tea. When the tea factory in Nyeri District was finally opened during 1957, more than £100,000 had been advanced from the CDC to the scheme although the original estimate (in 1951) had been no more than £20,000. Conversely, the

MICHAEL COWEN   161

actual producer price in 1962 (when the loan fund stood at £320,000) had
slumped to 40 cents per pound of greenleaf tea; the original estimate at current
prices (for a yield estimate of 500 pounds per acre) had put the expected price
at 200 cents per pound. This difference, between expected and actual prices,
arose precisely because interest charges on the loan fund were borne by
deductions from the producer price which was paid to tea growers.

Between the conception and implementation of the state-sponsored scheme,
international capital had intervened to ensure that household production
expanded in a form which ran counter to the propensity for accumulation by
the indigenous class of capital. First, state officials were in no political position
to control the rate of tea planting; they feared 'unpleasant political
repercussions' if they were to do so. Second, controversy raged within the
Department of Agriculture over the form, not only of manufacture, but of the
quality of tea which was to be produced.

We have mentioned the establishment (at a cost of £100,000) of a factory
to process high-quality greenleaf tea, and so realize the highest possible export
prices. At the other extreme, a proposal was made to process tea on tea
holdings using equipment which would cost no more than £180. This form of
manufacture would produce processed tea, on the holdings of the larger
producers, for local markets. There would be no central factory for processing
tea from all households, no control over the quality of greenleaf tea and no
systematic supervision of tea production. Revenue per holding and per acre
would be maximized at a producer price for processed tea which was lower
than the current price of estate-produced teas going to local markets.
However, revenues were higher than the expected and actual producer price
which was paid for greenleaf delivered to the state-sponsored factory. This
proposal was aligned to the production conditions facing the indigenous class
of capital and it was not implemented.

Nevertheless, during the early 1960s the marketing of sun-dried tea from the
holdings of Central Province reached the proportions of an avalanche which
threatened to swamp Brooke Bond's grip over local markets for manufactured
tea. For instance, in 1961 the estimated output of greenleaf tea which was
marketed as sun-dried tea in one division of Nyeri District was greater than
the output of greenleaf tea supplied from the area to the CDC subsidiary
corporation, the Special Crops Development Authority (later the Kenya Tea
Development Authority). Sun-dried tea was supplied to itinerant traders,
Asian- and African-owned trading companies and a tea manufacturer who
tried to eke out an export market in Rhodesia. Neither the costs of production,
which were expended in establishing the tea schemes, nor the amortization of
loan-capital advanced by the CDC, were recouped by the CDC subsidiary out
of the producer price for sun-dried tea. In yielding a higher revenue per acre
and per holding, sun-dried tea was a very attractive enterprise. It was dried
openly, without any manufacturing, from the plucking of up to five leaves per
stump whereas the higher-quality teas of the CDC subsidiary were manufactured from the plucking of only two leaves (plus a young bud) from each
stump. Sun-dried tea production not only threatened Brooke Bond's grip over
local markets but also subverted the form of control which had been designed
to expand colonial production.

We may note that as early as 1948 (and probably before decisions on the
allocation of money-capital and equipment for overseas investment were

formally approved in Britain by interdepartmental committees of officials. In the cases of proposed irrigation schemes for India and Iraq, the Sterling Area Development Working Party reckoned that the development of the schemes would be accompanied by an increase in population, a growth in local consumption and a reduction in the growth of commodity exports which would be produced under the aegis of the proposed schemes. It was concluded that Britain 'might not derive any direct benefit from the scheme' and that capital originating in the United States should be directed towards establishing the schemes.[87] So, in the case of tea in Kenya, it was not a simply matter of state–company collusion which was to eradicate the sale of sun-dried tea for local markets.

The sale of sun-dried tea was promoted by the indigenous class of capital through its Central Province Tea Growers Association. Between 1958 and 1963 the association waged a bitter campaign against the state apparatus and the CDC subsidiary. Like the wattle campaign of the 1940s, the indigenous class initially campaigned for a higher producer price for tea sold to, and a lower input price for stumps purchased from, the authority. Later, the association was to attempt to acquire a share in the ownership of factories, to change the terms of quality control and generally subvert the whole basis of control over the expanded household production of tea. The campaign was not successful but the possibility that the class could have destroyed the project for household production should not be discounted.

After March 1962 the administrative decree was enforced by legal action to rapidly eradicate the production and sale of sun-dried tea. The CDC, the World Bank, the West German government, together with international tea companies, proposed to advance £4·3 million to extend household production to other districts and provinces. All the loans were promised upon the condition that high-quality tea for international markets be produced and the production of sun-dried tea be eliminated. A series of political actions was executed (including the intervention of Jomo Kenyatta, then Minister of State for Constitutional Affairs and Economic Planning) to circumscribe the campaign of the Tea Growers' Association which had found a political base as a faction in the Kenya African National Union. The cadres of the association found a place of managerial employment in the successor to the CDC subsidiary, the Kenya Tea Development Authority.

From positions of managerial employment, individuals of the indigenous class were able to engage in straddling, a specific historical form of accumulation in which the position of employment provides a base from which sources can be created for the expanded reproduction of capital. The specific mechanisms of straddling do not concern us here and they have been exemplified elsewhere.[88] What should be indicated, however, is that the suppression of indigenous accumulation in areas of smallholding agriculture appears as both a series of historical moments (or conjunctures) and as a logical conjunction between two distinct and historically independent formations of capital. The formation of an indigenous class of capital was anterior to both the prewar penetration of colonial-type international firms and the postwar intervention of international capital, an intervention which was spearheaded by state corporations. Since these corporations have now become a part of the apparatus of the Kenya state, manned by individuals of the indigenous class of capital and subject to their control as a class, the whole plane and accompanying loci of accumulation have shifted to a new dimension.

In this new dimension of accumulation, the indigenous class is a bourgeoisie-in-formation. The most secure estimates show that there can be no more serious questioning of the fact that estate agriculture is now predominantly under the ownership of individuals of the indigenous class.[89] Any argument over the degree of ownership centres upon non-agricultural sectors and, even then, mainly upon the manufacturing sector. But argument over the degree to which economic control of enterprises, whether it be the management of production or of finance, is shared between the indigenous class and international institution of capital cannot be resolved through recourse to simple statistical indices. This whole question remains undertheorized and understudied. In the case of manufacturing, it is becoming clear that the subsidiaries of international firms, as much as those of the CDC and other public corporations, have provided a base from which managing directors are able to create their own sources of local accumulation.[90] My supposition is that the balance of advantage in the sharing of economic control of indigenously owned enterprises is shot through with tension and no single index of the balance of advantage can capture this tension. The conjunction of the late colonial period, which gave rise to the suppression, is still present and it is perfectly in order with this conjunction that a later generation of radicals and 'socialists' should be giving support to the belittling of indigenous accumulation.

Conclusions

(1)   It is difficult to establish criteria for evaluating the success of the postwar British project to expand colonial production. If the more obvious cases of the groundnuts scheme in Tanganyika and poultry production in the Gambia failed to deliver commodities, then there are other cases, such as tea in Kenya, where state-sponsored schemes have yielded, and unfailingly at that, expanded sources of commodity production for international markets. More generally, the fact that import prices of raw materials which were supplied to Britain rose so slowly (and for some not at all) between the mid-1950s and the late-1960s fulfilled the expectations of those at the British Treasury (and elsewhere) who argued for expanded production precisely on this basis. Any wider ambition to centralize accumulation in Britain could not be achieved within the aegis of the subjection of the British state to American hegemony and under conditions in which the import of capital (whether as American state-sponsored finance and equipment or as dollar investments made in Britain by international firms) was the counterpart to the export of capital for colonial production.

Current plans for a new international order, in which the needs of a northern and southern hemisphere are meant to be married, come over strongly as an attempt to replicate the plans (and including the Marshall Plan) of the late 1940s. In the British instance of the postwar conjunction, the colonial project was inspired by the nationalist response to reorganize a colonial hinterland which would compensate for, and eventually remove it was hoped, American domination. That the material premises for this project depended virtually upon the further internationalization of capital, as much as culminating in the reconstruction of productive capacity in Britain, did not dawn on the social democrat ministers and the peculiar kind of liberals who then manned the British state apparatus. One is struck by the confidence behind the nationalist sense of mission which propelled them to attempt to reorganize a colonial hinterland. Calls to resurrect this inspiration have a somewhat hollow and tired ring about them. I suspect that, for Britain at any rate, the same kind of inspiration has died along with the conjunction which made the inspiration possible. Furthermore, it is the need of the southern hemisphere which is expressed, now and most fervently, from nationalist positions. When classes of indigenous capital hold state power they espouse the call (such as that of Oliver Stanley) to match political with economic independence. They are also more able to accede the call (as for instance that of the Fabian socialists) from the international agencies of capital, and welfare, to 'assist' the 'rural poor' through schemes for household production and the like.

(2)   Household commodity production has been maintained and expanded by the most advanced layer of capital, an amalgam between state apparatuses and finance capital on an international scale of reckoning. The more archaic forms of capital, such as that of settler estate agriculture, and the indigenous development of capitalism with a focus on the extraction of absolute surplus value, have run on a trajectory which is counter to the expansion of household production. This expansion has provided a space in which individuals, even as wage workers, have been able to resist the direct proletarianization of their labour power. In the cases of Kenya, whether that of wattle or tea, there was no resistance by producers to the extension of commodity relations to household production. On the contrary, commodity production provides the means to reproduce subsistence without the compulsion to engage in direct wage labour processes. Household production is not competitive with capitalist enterprise through a separate set of social relations of production; it is distinguished from capitalist enterprise merely by the fact that work is organized on the basis of family labour. Equally, the compulsion to reproduce means of subsistence through family labour runs counter to capital's control over household production, however much it is this compulsion which gives capital its source of control over production.

We cannot designate this contemporary form of household production as that which belongs to either the most backward or most advanced form of capitalism. It used to be instinctively felt that the survival of artisans and peasants was part of a partially unfulfilled stage for the primitive accumulation of capital. Now, there is a current in advanced capitalism which runs towards self-management for the organization of work. Household production meets this current. Yet the particular political intervention of 1947 in Britain which spawned the schemes for expanded household production flowed from the double threat posed by the competitive pressure of capital elsewhere (and particularly in the United States) and the organized pressure of labour acting through and upon British state apparatuses. The national exhortations to increase production, and productivity, did not exactly register the index of an advanced capitalism in Britain itself. Also, that so much attention was paid to colonial schemes for production, to compensate for incapacities of productive organization in Britain, was indicative of the impasse which had come to pass

MICHAEL COWEN   165

in the development of capitalism in Britain. In this light, it is hardly surprising
that large-scale schemes for agrarian production failed to deliver commodities
while the schemes based on household production were very successful.

(3)   Maier has suggested that the intention of the United States 'to adjourn
class conflict for a consensus on growth'[91] was possible, not in mainland Asia,
but in Europe where 'the social basis for the politics of productivity was
present' and where 'war and Nazi occupation had shaken, but not uprooted,
a prevailingly bourgeois society with broad middle-class patterns of ownership
and culture'.[92] But what of sub-Saharan Africa and the particular case of
Kenya? Is the social basis of productivity to be rendered possible through the
stimulation of individual proprietorship in a culture where material fatalism is
hardly present?

First, the mere stimulation of individual proprietorship, which is what
household production has come to represent politically, is probably no
sufficient condition for the formation of a bourgeois society and certainly no
unequivocal necessary condition for the smothering of class conflict.[93] In the
Kenya of the 1970s antagonism to the concentration of property by the
indigenous class for the expanded reproduction of capital was expressed by
those who clamour incessantly for claims to individual proprietorship. They
are not only poor and marginalized peasants and the like; in the main they are
those who straddle from a base in employment to reproduce *their means of
subsistence* through small-scale enterprises. This is the crux of the matter.
There is an awareness in a society of early capitalism that the concentration
of property to reproduce the means of accumulation is antithetical to the
extension and entrenching of property rights to reproduce the means of
subsistence and, to boot, ideally outside the interstices of direct wage labour.
Second, the formation of a bourgeoisie usually, or in Europe at any rate,
precedes a state-sponsored drive to increase productivity because who else
other than the bourgeoisie, under capitalist conditions, will have the
willingness or the ability to do so? In cases such as Kenya, however, the
formation of the bourgeoisie has been coincidental with the long postwar drive
to increase production. The intervention of international capital has promoted
household commodity production without necessarily pauperizing producers
while the straddlers have not necessarily been marginalized. If it is on the
second ground that 'a consensus on growth' for material production obtains
in specific areas outside of Europe, then it is also the case that the first ground,
under conditions of early capitalism, is inherently unstable and is, whatever
the political regime, indeed part of the development of capitalism.

Notes

1   This was the gist of all Colonial office documents on colonial development between
1939 and 1944.
2   Gupta, 1975, p. 321.
3   Ernest Bevin (Foreign Secretary) to Attlee (Prime Minister), 7 July 1947, FO
371/62557.
4   Minutes, GEN 179 5th meeting, 28 July 1947, PREM 8/489; Attlee to Bevin, 8 July
1947, FO 371/62557.

5 Emmanuel Shinwell (Minister of Fuel and Power), CM(47) 74th conclusions, 25 August 1947, PREM 8/489.
6 Aneurin Bevan (Minister of Health), CM(47) 74th conclusions, 25 August 1947, PREM 8/489.
7 Ernest Bevin, GEN 179 10th meeting, 8 August 1947, PREM 8/490.
The American loan of 1945 was an emergency facility to replace the sudden suspension of lend-lease at the termination of war in Europe. American and Canadian credits were to be used to permit the continuation of imports into Britain from dollar area countries. See Gardner, 1956, and Kolko, 1972.
8 Lord Inverchapel (UK ambassador, Washington), speech script for Law Alumini Association, New York University, 10 March 1947, FO 371/60998.
9 Harrod, 1947, p. 62.
10 Kolko, 1972, p. 64.
11 ibid., p. 65.
12 British Consul General, Chicago, to North America Department, Foreign Office, 19 March 1947, FO 371/60999.
    Lewis Douglas had been a vice-president of American Cynamid Company, President of Mutual Life of New York, Principal and Vice-Chancellor of McGill University. He turned down a nomination to be the first president of the World Bank, although Henry Morgenthau, then Secretary of the Treasury, opposed the nomination because of Douglas's Wall Street connections. In any case, Douglas's brother-in-law, John McCloy, became the first President of the Bank. (Lord Inverchapel to Bevin, 11 March 1947, FO 371/60999.)
13 US Department of State (FRUS) 1948(3), p. 1092.
14 Healey to McNeil (Minister of State, Foreign Office), 'Draft statement on European Co-operation for the Marshall Plan', 2 February 1948, FO 371/68945.
15 The best studies for background are Gardner, 1956, Kolko, 1972, and Louis, 1977.
16 FO to UK delegation, ITO negotiations (Geneva), telegramme 1504 NEUTRAL, 20 August 1947; Cripps memorandum (CP(47)245), 'Trade Negotiations in Geneva. US requests on Tariffs and Preferences', 27 August 1947; CM(47) 77th Conclusions, 25 September 1947; Harold Wilson (Secretary for Overseas Trade) to Atlee, 15 December 1947, PREM 8/490.
17 ED(47) 53, para. 229, 12 December 1947, CAB 134/90.
18 Strachey memorandum (CP(47)170), 'Import Programme 1947–48', 31 May 1947, PREM 8/489.
19 Jameson to Perrot (Ministry of Food), 23 August 1947, PREM 8/489.
20 Gorell Barnes to Attlee, 17 May 1947, PREM 8/489.
21 Dalton memorandum (CP(47)221), 'Balance of Payments', 30 July 1947, PREM 8/489.
22 House of Commons, Debates, 5th series, Vol. 441, col. 1495, 6 August 1947.
23 Playfair, BP(ON)(47) 4th meeting, 24 September 1947, CAB 134/46.
24 Minutes, BP(ON)(47) 21st, 34th and 57th meetings, 21 October, 7 November and 11 December 1947 CAB 134/46.
25 Minutes, BP(ON)(47) 2nd meeting, 22 September 1947, CAB 134/46.
26 Minutes, BP(ON)(47) 9th meeting, 1 October 1947, CAB 134/46.
27 Minutes, BP(ON)(47) 7th meeting, 29 September 1947, CAB 134/46.
28 Minutes, BP(ON)(47) 14th meeting, 9 October 1947, CAB 134/46.
29 Treasury memorandum (BP WP(47)1) 25 May 1947, PREM 8/489.
30 Harrod, 1947, pp. 17–18, 41, 76–85, 151.
31 Minutes, ED(47) 1st meeting, 17 January 1947, CAB 134/90.
32 Minutes, ED(47) 5th and 6th meetings, 26 February and 3 March 1947, CAB 134/90.
33 Maier, 1977, p. 607.
34 Attlee's summary of Strachey's report, GEN 179, 19 May 1947, PREM 4/489.
35 Butler (Foreign Office) to Lord Inverchapel (UK ambassador, Washington), 28 January 1947, FO 371/60998.
36 Minutes, A(49) 1st meeting, 8 July 1949, CAB 134/1.

37 loc. cit.
38 Sargent (Foreign Office) to Inverchapel, telegramme 7907, 6 August 1947, FO 371/61003.
39 Edwards (British Embassy, Washington) to Kirkpatrick (Foreign Office), 5 November 1947, FO 371/61004.
40 Henniker (Foreign Office) to Sargent, 19 August 1947, FO 371/61003.
41 Strachey memorandum (FM 47/22) in Strachey to Atlee, 6 October 1947, PREM 8/456.
42 Strachey to Attlee, 6 October 1947, PREM 8/456.
43 Morrison memorandum (CP(47)169), 'Planning for Expansion', 2 June 1947, PREM 8/489.
44 House of Commons, *Debates*, 5th series, Vol. 391, cols 66–8, 13 July 1943.
45 Weeks (CEPS) to Plowden (CEPS), 23 May 1947, T229/101.
46 Rowe-Dutton (Treasury) to Playfair (Treasury), 15 May 1947, T 220/31.
47 Helsby (Treasury) to Crombie (Treasury) and Sillitoe (Treasury) to Compton (Treasury), 9 and 15 May 1947, T 220/31.
48 Minutes, BP(ON)(47) 50th meeting, 4 December 1947, CAB 134/46.
49 Minutes, BP(ON)(47) 39th meeting, 19 November 1947, CAB 134/46.
50 Morrison memorandum (CP(47)169), 2 June 1947, PREM 8/489.
51 I think that the classic study of the period is still that of Rogow, 1955.
52 Midgley and Burns, 1969, p. 77.
53 Frost, 1954, p. 190; Thompson, 1977, pp. 253 ff.
54 Grove, 1962, pp. 247–8; Page and Canaway, 1966, pp. 26–7.
55 Portal to Attlee, 10 April 1947, PREM 8/457.
Viscount Portal had been Minister of Works in the war cabinet and was a close crony of Churchill. In 1947, he was chairman of Great Western Railways. Before the war, he had built up Portals Limited, which then supplied bank notes to the Bank of England. He was an associate of Moseley in his 'pre-fascist phase', advised on depressed areas and was one-time chairman of the Special Areas Reconstruction Authority. (Addison, 1975, p. 177).
56 Minute in Fisher (Treasury) to Helsby (Treasury), 19 June 1947, T 220/31.
57 Creech Jones to Dalton, 28 April 1947, T 220/31.
58 Fisher to Helsby, 19 June 1947, T 220/31.
59 Stanley to Eden, 24 December 1942, FO 371/35310.
60 Abbott, 1971, p. 76.
61 Meeting, at Treasury, attended by Sir H. Wilson (Permanent Secretary, Treasury and Head of Civil Service) and others, 22 January 1940, T 220/17.
62 Stanley memorandum (WP(44)643), 'Future Provision for Colonial Development and Welfare', 15 November 1944, PREM 4/43 A/8.
63 Syers (Treasury) to Creasy (Colonial Office), 7 March 1940, T 220/17.
64 Stanley memorandum (WP(44)643), 15 November 1944, PREM 4/43 A/8.
65 WM(44) 152nd conclusions, 21 November 1944, PREM 4/43 8/8.
66 Myint, 1954, p. 139.
67 Wicker, 1955–6, pp. 213–16.
68 Hazelwood, 1955–6 p. 230.
69 Page and Canaway, 1966, p. 27.
70 CEDC (47) 13th minutes, 10 March 1947, CO 999/1.
71 CEDC (47), 13th minutes, 10 March 1947, CO 999/1; Colonial Primary Products Committee, Interim Report (CPP(474), December 1947, FO 371/62557.
72 Bevin to Attlee, 4 October 1947, PREM 8/456.
73 Cowen, 1979, ch. 4.
74 Wicker, 1955–6, pp. 220–1.
75 Thompson, 1977, p. 247.
76 Clause 15(1), Overseas Resources Development Bill (and also Act) 1947, T 220/31.
77 See Abbott, 1971; Meredith, 1975; Wicker, 1958.
78 Meredith, 1975, p. 486.
79 House of Commons, *Debates* 5th series, Vol. 391, col. 64, 13 July 1943.

80   Anon. memorandum, 'Imperialism and the Colonial Question', 18 June 1943, CAB 123/239.
81   House of Commons, *Debates* 5th series, Vol. 391, col. 109, 13 July 1943.
82   Cowen, 1972, 1976, 1979, chs 1 and 3; and for easy reference, Leys, 1978, pp. 246–9.
83   For the fuller details of this section, Cowen, 1979 and 1981a.
84   Bridges memorandum (ED(47)8), 'Wages and Prices Policy', 22 January 1947, CAB 134/90.
85   CEDC minutes, CEDC(46), (47), (48), November 1946 to November 1948, CO 999/1 and CO 999/2.
86   G. Brooke to Department of Agriculture, 2 January 1950; KNA: M of A, 4/116.
87   Minutes, SADWP(48), 3rd and 5th meetings, 23 March and 19 May 1948, T 236/1569.
88   See Cowen, 1977; Leys, 1978; Njonjo, 1977; Swainson, 1977.
89   Njonjo, 1977, pt 2.
90   Swainson, 1977, pt 3.
91   Maier, 1977, p. 607.
92   ibid., p. 630.
93   Cowen, 1981b.

References

Abbott, G. C. (1971), 'A re-examination of the 1929 Colonial Development Act', *Economic History Review*, 28, 3.

Addison, P. (1975), *The Road to 1945: British Politics and the Second World War* (London: Cape).

Cowen, M. P. (1972), 'Differentiation in a Kenya location', East Africa Universities Social Science Council Conference, Nairobi.

Cowen, M. P. (1976), 'Capital and peasant households' (mimeo.).

Cowen, M. P. (1979), 'Capital and household production: the case of wattle in Kenya's Central Province, 1903–1964', PhD thesis, University of Cambridge.

Cowen, M. P. (1981a), 'Commodity production in Kenya's Central Province', in J. Heyer, P. Roberts and G. Williams (eds), *Rural Development in Tropical Africa* (London: Macmillan).

Cowen, M. P. (1981b), 'Notes on the Nairobi discussion of the agrarian problem', *Review of African Political Economy*, 20.

Cowen, M. and Kinyanjui, K. (1977), *Some Problems of Class and Capital in Kenya* (Nairobi: Institute of Development Studies, Occasional Paper No. 26).

Frost, R. (1954), 'The Macmillan Gap 1931–53', *Oxford Economic Papers*, 6, 2.

Gardner, R. (1956), *Sterling Dollar Diplomacy* (London: Oxford University Press).

Grove, J. W. (1962), *Government and Industry in Britain* (London: Longmans).

Gupta, P. S. (1975), *Imperialism and the British Labour Movement* (London: Macmillan).

Harrod, R. F. (1947), *Are These Hardships Necessary?* (London: Hart-Davis).

Hazlewood, A. (1955–6), 'A note on the Colonial Development Corporation', *Review of Economic Studies*, 23, 3.

Kolko, J. and G. (1972), *The Limits of Power: The World and United States Foreign Policy, 1945–54* (New York: Harper & Row).

Leys, C. (1978), 'Capital accumulation, class formation and dependency – the significance of the Kenyan case', in R. Milliband and J. Saville (eds), *Socialist Register 1978* (London: Merlin).

Louis, W. R. (1977), *Imperialism at Bay 1941–1945: The United States and the Decolonization of the British Empire* (London: Oxford University Press).

Maier, C. S. (1977), 'The politics of productivity: foundations of American international economic policy after World War II', *International Organization*, 31, 4.

Meredith, D. (1975), 'The British government and colonial economic policy, 1919–39', *Economic History Review*, 28, 3.

Midgley, K. and Burns R. G. (1969), *Business Finance and the Capital Market* (London: Macmillan).

Myint, H. (1954), 'An interpretation of economic backwardness', *Oxford Economic Papers*, 6, 2.

Njonjo, A. (1977), 'The Africanization of the "white Highlands": a study on agrarian class struggle in Kenya, 1950–1974', PhD thesis, Princeton University.

Page, C. S. and Canaway, E. E. (1966), *Finance for Management* (London: Heinemann).

Rogow, A. A. (1955), *The Labour Government and British Industry, 1945–51* (Oxford: Blackwell).

Swainson, N. (1977), 'Foreign corporations and economic growth in Kenya', PhD thesis, London University (and now as *The Development of Corporate Capitalism Investment in Kenya 1918–77* (London: Heinemann Educational Books, 1980).

Thompson, G. (1977), 'The relationship between the financial and industrial sector in the United Kingdom economy', *Economy and Society*, 6, 3.

United States Department of State (1974), *Foreign Relations of the United States 1948*, Vol. 3 (Washington, DC: Government Printing Office).

Wicker, E. R. (1955–6), 'The Colonial Development Corporation (1948–54)', *Review of Economic Studies*, 23, 3.

Wicker, E. R. (1958), 'Colonial development and welfare, 1929–1957: the evolution of a policy', *Social and Economic Studies*, 7, 4.

8   Accumulation, Class Formation and Dependency: Kenya

COLIN LEYS

The aim of this chapter is to clarify some of the issues that have been posed in the theoretical debate about 'dependency' and to reconsider the evidence from Kenya in the light of this clarification – if possible, carrying the discussion a small step further in the process.[1]

I   Theoretical Questions

The most important question of all those which are at stake in the debate about 'dependency' is whether or not there are theoretical reasons for thinking that the ex-colonies cannot (as Marx put it) 'adopt the bourgeois mode of production' and develop their productive forces within it.[2] The underdevelopment or dependency school in general argues that the patterns of subordinate development established at the periphery of imperialism before and during the colonial phase are self-perpetuating. Frank, for instance, identified a historical sequence of mechanisms (the 'contradiction of continuity in change') through which metropolitan capital secured monopolies enabling it to appropriate the surplus generated at the periphery and largely transfer it to the metropoles, the latest and apparently most invulnerable mechanism being the monopoly of technology possessed by the leading multinational corporations.[3] Warren, in his well-known critique of the underdevelopment school, argued that the patterns of underdevelopment are self-eliminating because decolonization gives rise to regimes in the ex-colonies which need, and have some power to obtain, a measure of industrial development.[4] Admittedly this development is carried out by multinational industrial companies within the framework of imperialism but the multinationals as such, and the imperialist states, put no obstacles in the way of this development leading to further stages of industrialization and hence to a general process of capitalist development; and as a result, Warren argues, the industrialization of the Third World, and the spread of capitalist relations of production there, has in fact been going ahead rapidly.

Against Warren, Emmanuel argued that underdevelopment is indeed self-perpetuating, but not because it is the nature of multinational manufacturing capital to operate in the periphery precisely for the purpose of plundering the locally generated surpluses for the benefit of its owners in the metropoles, as the underdevelopment theorists proposed; but because its very presence at the periphery is always exceptional, all capital being drawn in general not to the periphery but to the areas of its greatest existing concentration, where demand is highest. And Emmanuel, supported by Petras and others, rather convincingly challenged Warren's general evidence for holding that industrialization and capitalist relations of production had actually spread rapidly at the periphery.[5] On the contrary, Emmanuel showed that much of the statistical evidence related to the growth of very small-scale craft production, with very low levels of productivity, and largely pre-capitalist or non-capitalist in character; that industrialization had not been accompanied by a rise of agricultural productivity, which is essential for sustaining any long-term development of capitalist industry; and that, in consequence, industrial output per head of population in the Third World had risen much more slowly than in the metropoles, so that the prospects of capital being drawn towards the periphery on an increasing scale, as Warren expected, were not increasing but diminishing.[6]

The bearing of this debate on the case of Kenya, and vice versa, can be approached in a preliminary way by looking at an aspect of the debate that was treated by the participants – mistakenly, I think – as a side-issue. Warren illustrated part of his case by citing data from twenty-two countries identified by Chenery as having the fastest-growing economies in the Third World. Petras and his colleagues criticized this on the grounds that all of these countries were in different ways *exceptional*.[7] Five had specially heavy inflows of foreign capital 'for reasons that are largely political' (Taiwan, Jordan, Puerto Rico, South Korea, Panama) and all of these except Taiwan were small. Nine others had enjoyed exceptionally rapid growth of primary exports and 'no Marxist scholar with whom we are familiar has ever argued that underdeveloped countries with rapidly developing primary export sectors cannot industrialize at least through the stage of light import substitution'.[8] The remaining eight also enjoyed unusually high levels of capital inflow and most of them also exhibited certain specially favourable features – Singapore and Costa Rica were 'tiny' countries and their industries, and those of the Philippines, were based on assembly operations so that their growth depended on low wages. Mexico had 'extraordinary' advantages derived from its tourist attractions and its proximity to the USA. Brazil's and Turkey's growth depended on a repressive redistribution of income from the poor to the rich.

The conclusion which Warren's critics drew from all this was that the manufacturing growth rates of these countries were not evidence of 'autonomous industrial growth' in the Third World, as Warren believed. But this is a case of too much zeal. Britain, too, was once an 'exceptional' case. This is an important part of the burden of the eighth section of Volume I of *Capital*. On the one hand, domestically.

The money capital formed by means of usury and commerce was prevented from turning into industrial capital by the feudal organization of the countryside and the guild associations of the towns. These fetters vanished with the dissolution of the feudal bands of retainers, and the expropriation and partial eviction of the rural population.

On the other, there was primitive accumulation abroad:

The discovery of gold and silver in America, the extirpation, enslavement and entombment in mines of the indigenous population of that continent, the beginnings of the conquest and plunder of India, and the conversion of Africa into a preserve for the commercial hunting of blackskins, are all things which characterize the dawn of the era of capitalist production. These idyllic proceedings are the chief moments of primitive accumulation. Hard on their heels follows the commercial war of the European nations, which has the globe as its battlefield ...

For the transition to the capitalist mode of production to occur, however, all these developments had to come together *somewhere*:

The different moments of primitive accumulation can be assigned in particular to Spain, Portugal, Holland, France and England, more or less in chronological order. These different moments are systematically combined together at the end of the seventeenth century in England; the combination embraces the colonies, the national debt, the modern tax system, and the system of protection. These methods depend in part on brute force, for instance the colonial system. But they all employ the power of the state.[9]

How else, but through such 'systematically combined moments' occurring in some particular place, could capitalist development – the progressive transformation of relations of production into capitalist ones through the expanded reproduction of industrial capital – ever occur? This is not to say that such 'combinations' can and eventually must occur everywhere, as Marx's earlier writings sometimes implied. But it does suggest the curiousness of the argument of Petras and his colleagues in this instance, which proceeds by 'removing' and 'subtracting' from Warren's list of rapidly industrializing countries in the Third World any which can be shown to have 'special' reasons for rapid industrialization. Behind this mode of reasoning one detects the straw man of a utopian conception of capitalist development, similar to the one which Warren rightly discerned as underlying much 'left' discussion of these questions: this time, a conception of capitalism developing evenly and universally throughout the Third World, without help from low wages based on repression, imperialist military expenditure, and so on.

Even Emmanuel dismisses the rather complex issues involved here with the remark that 'certain marginal movements of capital, concentrated for various reasons in some small country, such as Greece, Taiwan, or the Ivory Coast, may enable such a country to cross the threshold of development', adding – not altogether plausibly, it seems to me – that 'it is *because* the other countries do not follow this path of ultra-liberal opening to international capital, that the few countries that do follow it have a chance, however, slight, of succeeding with it'.[10] Apart from anything else, it is not obvious why *movements* of capital, even marginal ones, should be considered decisive, unless what is meant is that most of the capital formed at the periphery presently flows to the metropoles; on this assumption, capitalist production relations certainly cannot develop at the periphery, and what is needed is to *stop* the movements of capital that are generally occurring (though on Emmanuel's own data, the evidence actually suggests a modest net flow of capital to the periphery considered as a whole). But then, we cannot lightly dismiss the 'various reasons' why, in a significant number of cases, the flow of capital from the centre to the periphery has actually been sufficiently large to sustain capitalist development there.

To summarize: the debate about dependency and underdevelopment has not shown either that capitalist development cannot occur at the periphery (or 'in the Third World'), or that it is eventually bound to. What it demonstrates is, rather, the need to study and theorize the conditions under which some periphery countries have, and others have not, experienced significant measures of such growth. Broadly speaking, there seem to be three principal levels at which this work needs to be conducted: the level of the 'logic of capital', the level of capitalist geopolitics (imperialism) and the level of class relations and class struggles, in particular social formations, each level determining and being determined by the others. By the 'logic of capital' I am referring both to the international logic of capital in general – so-called 'capital-logic' – and to its implications for the investment decisions of particular capitals in particular sectors in particular countries. The level of 'capitalist geopolitics' refers to the forces which determine that, for instance, exceptionally large flows of 'official' capital (bilateral or multilateral) occur for certain countries, materially affecting the logic of 'private' capital flows, while comparable efforts of 'technical assistance', civil and military, and corresponding ideological and cultural efforts, equally determine the conditions for the reproduction of capital in those countries.

The rest of this chapter, however, will be concerned only with the last of the three levels, that of class relations and class struggles in a particular social formation, and furthermore, it will be largely concerned with the process of domestic capital accumulation which has formed the basis for the constitution of one particular class, rather than with classes and class struggles in general. This is doubly one-sided, and the result has at most the status of a working paper, subject to correction in the light of work at other levels, and on other aspects of the level of class relations and class struggles, which mostly remains to be done. Some justification for these limitations can be found, perhaps, in the fact that a focus on relations between classes constituted out of the pre-existing relations of production has been conspicuously missing from much of the previous discussion of the problem of development, and notably from the discussion of the idea of the 'articulation of modes of production' by means of which several influential writers have attempted to theorize the issues involved.[11]

This is a point forcibly made by Robert Brenner in his critique of Frank, Wallerstein and other 'neo-Smithian' theorists who–to oversimplify–have conceived of capitalist production relations developing in particular places, or not, according to the dictates of market forces, neglecting the particular presuppositions about the social structure which underlay the role assigned to the market by Smith in his account of the development of capitalism.[12] Brenner, correctly in my view, stresses instead the centrality of the class relations which Smith took as given. On this view, what is decisive for the development of capitalist production relations is the prior configuration and character of classes–for instance, the availability or otherwise of 'free' labour, the respective political power of non-landed and landed classes affecting the possibility of capital investment in land, and so on. The *dependentistas*

> failed to focus centrally on the productivity of labour as the essence and key to economic development. They did not see the degree to which the latter was, in turn, centrally bound up with historically specific class structures of production and surplus extraction, themselves the product of determinations beyond the market. Hence, they did not see the degree to which patterns of development or underdevelopment for an entire epoch might hinge upon the outcome of specific processes of class formation, of class struggle.[13]

What produces *under*development is not the 'transfer of surplus' appropriated by metropolitan capital from the periphery of the metropole, significant though this may be. Rather, such a transfer should be seen as an *effect* of structures at the periphery which militate against the productive investment of the surplus at the periphery. Speaking generally, these are class structures which permit absolute surplus labour to be appropriated, but prevent the realization of relative surplus value:

> in other words, the development of underdevelopment was rooted in the class structure of production based on the extension of absolute surplus labour, which determined a sharp *disjuncture* between the requirements for the development of the productive forces (productivity of labour) and the structure of profitability of the economy as a whole.[14]

Brenner's discussion may be open to the criticism that the class structures of the periphery tend to figure in it as determined by *past* struggles but appear relatively immune to determination by class struggles initiated by imperialism itself – thus tending to avoid the question which is central to theorists of the 'articulation of modes of production' (notably Rey), namely, what prevents capitalists, once capitalism has become dominant on a world scale, from removing such obstacles to its valorization as inhospitable or recalcitrant class structures in particular countries or regions? Brenner's answer would seem to be that nothing prevents this in general: it is a historical and conjunctural question whether the interests of the bourgeoisie require these obstacles to be overcome in a given case; and second, whether this is outweighed by the relative strength or weight of the class interests opposed to this.[15] While this seems to me correct, analysing the general nature of these relationships does seem to be an important task which needs to be undertaken, on the basis of a range of studies of which the Kenyan case reviewed here is at most a suggestive example.

II   Pre-colonial and Colonial Indigenous Accumulation in Kenya

The chief way in which the Kenyan experience is relevant to the theoretical questions discussed above may be simply stated. While several aspects of Kenya's development may at first sight seem to be illuminated by means of the concepts of underdevelopment and dependency, the process of domestic capital accumulation since the early 1940s does not lend itself so easily to analysis from this perspective.

This is particularly apparent in the period since independence. Once the uncertainties of the transition had been resolved, the high overall growth rate of the 1940s and 1950s was resumed (an absolute annual average rate of growth of 6·5%, or about 3% per annum per capita in real terms), with an all round increase in productivity, a steady decline in the non-monetary share of output (from 25% of GNP in 1964 to 19% in 1973), and some growth – its true extent is not known – in the share of wage and salary employment in total employment. In other words, the relatively high and sustained level of capital accumulation was accompanied by an extension of capitalist relations of production. A growing proportion of households came to depend on wage labour, and the reproduction of labour power was increasingly commercialized. By 1974–5 64% of the median small farm's household consumption was purchased for cash and 19% of its income was derived from wage labour (small farms accounted for approximately 75% of all Kenyan households, the remainder being more or less wholly dependent on wage employment or on income from capital).[16] In manufacturing, labour productivity rose (in large-scale firms the gross product per employee rose just under 20% between 1969 and 1973), and in relation to total labour costs, the gross product rose just under 23%, though in agriculture productivity appeared to stagnate in the 1970s, after rising in the 1960s.[17]

These developments attracted and were in turn reinforced by a net inflow of capital from abroad. Private capital inflows began to exceed profit outflows after 1970 and while the various measures taken after 1970 to curb hidden transfers of surplus (via overinvoicing, management and patent fee payments, etc.) could only be partially successful, covert outflows seem rather unlikely to have equalled, let alone exceeded the real rate of total net capital inflows, which ran at an annual average of K£42m. for the period 1968–75.[18] In any case, as Emmanuel has pointed out, the historic cost of the technology transferred to Kenya under management contracts and patent fees was far higher than the cost of these arrangements to Kenya.[19] Meanwhile the level of foreign indebtedness remained low, and was still further reduced in real terms by inflation.[20]

At this stage in the discussion, the general theoretical implications of all this for underdevelopment and dependency as explanatory concepts may be put to one side, permitting us to focus instead on the question: what is the explanation of the Kenyan growth process, and what significance does the explanation have for the prospects of capitalist development in Kenya in the future?

Kenya has not been in receipt of exceptionally large flows of official capital or technical assistance, nor has it had any exceptional growth of primary commodity exports or, in general, any major advantage in terms of endowment or location over neighbouring countries.[21] Nor, on the other hand, has its overall rate of growth been due to exceptional growth rates in one or two 'enclave' sectors unrelated to the rest of the economy. While some marked geographic and sectoral imbalances exist, growth has been more or less equally pronounced both in agriculture and outside it, in small- and large-scale farming, in manufacturing and in commerce, in the private and the public sectors, and so on.

A more plausible explanation of Kenyan economic growth since the 1940s lies, rather, in the specific social relations of production developed before, during and since the colonial period, and particularly – but in no sense exclusively, as will be seen – in the key role of the class formed out of the process of indigenous capital accumulation.

This process has been the subject of a highly original and complex analysis by M. P. Cowen, of which only a few central themes are essential here.[22] Cowen established that before the colonization of East Africa the relations of production existing in what is now Central Province – the most populous, productive and economically strategic area of Kenya – determined the formation of a class of accumulators of the principal means of production – land and livestock – through migration onto new land, raiding, and long-distance trade. The tendency of this accumulation, which was in large measure 'primitive', was to concentrate the means of production more and more in a few hands, excluding others from access to them, a tendency which those threatened with exclusion could overcome, by and large, only through migrating themselves (usually as labourers clearing land for others in return for stock and a share of the new land). Colonial settlement closed off further migration, by alienating land to white settlers. On the other hand the colonial state launched some, at least, of the pre-colonial accumulators on a fresh path of accumulation by appointing them 'chiefs' who were enabled to loot their new 'subjects' by means of unregulated taxes and fines, and to further accumulate land within the now restricted African land areas by engaging in costly litigation.

The transformation of this class into a class of agrarian capitalists (appropriating surplus value through wage labour proper) was, however, thwarted by (1) the settler farmers' monopoly, enforced by the colonial state, over most of the available African surplus labour; (2) parallel settler monopolies over the production of most of the agricultural commodities (notably coffee) or over markets (e.g. for maize), on which capitalist agriculture could be based; (3) the intervention of international capital – as opposed to small and medium settler capital – in commodity production either through plantation production (in the case of wattle), or through permitting the still-existing mass of smallholders to produce commodities under the supervision of large-scale foreign capital. This permitted the smallholdings to survive as units of production (a situation confirmed by the universal issue of freehold land titles from 1955 onwards) and deprived the indigenous class of capital of the opportunity to further enlarge their landholdings and exploit the labour of those who became proletarianized.

Meanwhile, the route of entry to the 'accumulator' class, and the basis of further accumulation for the individual agents within it, had necessarily shifted from the old forms of primitive accumulation to wage income, increasingly based on education; and to the sphere of commerce, the avenues for which were gradually widened by political pressure brought to bear on the colonial state by new organizations such as the Kikuyu Central Association and the Kavirondo Taxpayers Welfare Association – whose ascendancy also signified the displacement of the older, 'primitive' accumulating element within the indigenous class of capital, by the 'modern', educated element. Although these efforts preserved and even permitted some enlargement of the accumulated capital of this class, it was wholly confined to the sphere of circulation and hence to the limited share of surplus value to be obtained there, in face of unremitting pressure both from Asian merchant capital and from the growing weight of international productive capital.

By the end of the Second World War a direct challenge to this limitation was finally articulated by the militant wing of the Kenya African Union, leading in 1952 to the declaration of emergency. Meanwhile international capital had moved into Kenya on a much larger scale, and in the context of Britain's interest in expanding colonial commodity production as a contribution to the solution of the dollar shortage, the colonial state also began to dismantle the barriers to indigenous capital accumulation. African exclusion from the 'white Highlands', the ban on African-grown coffee, restriction on credit for Africans and opposition to the issue of individual land titles all disappeared. Finally, white settler capital was largely removed from the configuration of class forces by the independence settlement agreed in outline in 1961.

Cowen's object in tracing these developments is precisely to establish the specificity of the transition from pre-capitalist to capitalist relations of production, a transition seen as governed by the complex interaction of the forms and 'periods' of indigenous and foreign capital over the past hundred years – a question central to the theme of this chapter. For the moment, however, let us focus on the more limited question of the light which this perspective throws on the current role of indigenous capital accumulation in Kenya.

III Contemporary Indigenous Capital Accumulation

When negotiations for independence were begun in 1960, the economic and political weight of the indigenous owners of capital was already decisive.

The often-cited expansion of smallholder farm output that occurred in the decade 1955–64, for example – from K£5·2m. to K£14·0m. per annum – is remarkable not least for the capital investment it implies, especially when we consider that down to 1964 the cumulative total of government and bank lending to smallholders was only K£1·7m.[23] The size distribution of the output tells the same story. In Murang'a in 1970–1 14% of the members of one coffee co-operative studied by Lamb (i.e. all the growers of a given area in Kikuyu country) supplied 64% of the crop, and in the same season in two tea-growing locations of the neighbouring Nyeri District, studied by Cowen, 20% of the growers supplied 55% of the crop (in 1965 20% had supplied 64% of the total;[24]

in other words, the initial impetus came even more markedly from those with the capital to make the necessary investment and pay the necessary wages). Similar reflections are prompted by the fact that from 1959, when Africans became eligible to buy land in the former white Highlands, down to 1970, at least K£7m. and perhaps as much as K£10m. of privately owned capital, mostly from Central Province, was invested in large-farm purchase. Bearing in mind the degree of concentration involved in both the expansion of smallholder production, and the purchase of large farms from white settlers, these figures serve as useful if very rough indicators of the scale of accumulation which had been achieved during the colonial period by the indigenous class of capital, in spite of massive competition from foreign capital of all kinds, and with very little support from the colonial state.

Besides the scale of their capital, the indigenous class of capital – which after the reforms of the 1950s we can increasingly term an indigenous capitalist class – had a further highly significant asset. It was heavily concentrated in not only the largest ethnic group – composing with closely related neighbouring people about 25% of the total population – but also in the economic and political centre of the country. Combined with its strong representation in the state apparatus (due to its heavy investment in education) the indigenous bourgeoisie was exceptionally well placed to convert its natural dominance in the nationalist movement into a position of strategic control over the post-colonial political realignments needed for the next phase of accumulation. By mid-1966 – two and a half years after independence – these realignments had been completed and the framework of an effective 'power bloc' under the hegemony of the Kikuyu bourgeoisie was clearly established.

From this time onward the state apparatus superintended a series of measures which rapidly enlarged the sphere and the rate of indigenous capital accumulation. The principal measures used were trade licensing, state monopolies, state finance capital, state direction of private credit and state capitalist enterprise.

These measures have been discussed elsewhere and need not be recapitulated here.[25] Their effects may be seen in a broadly sequential pattern whereby in one sector after another, according to the relative difficulties posed for indigenous capital by varying technical and capital requirements, African capital became first significant, and then preponderant. The movement into the former 'white Highlands' began in 1959. By 1977 it was estimated that only 5% of the mixed farm area within the former 'white Highlands' remained in expatriate hands. The transfer to African owners of expatriate-owned ranches and coffee plantations was well advanced and the transfer of the much more concentrated tea estates was no longer impossible to envisage. By 1974 the Development Plan claimed that most 'small commercial firms have already been transferred to citizen ownership' and that 'larger and more intricate' firms still in foreign hands would be Kenyanized by 1978:[26] by 1977 the evidence suggested that this target would be substantially met. The transfer to African capital of urban real estate, already well advanced by 1976, received a fresh impetus from the sudden rise in liquidity due to the exceptional coffee sales of that year, and led to a rush to purchase the remaining foreign-owned large office blocks in central Nairobi, suggesting that the complete African occupation of this sector was no longer a distant prospect.

Information on the diverse range of activities comprised under 'services' is largely insufficient to disclose the rate of penetration by African capital. Passenger road transportation was largely in African hands by 1977 as were tour companies, laundries and dry cleaning, and a rapidly growing share of the hotel and restaurant sectors. Sectors still substantially in foreign or at least non-African hands were those still protected against African entry by a combination of technical and capital barriers, often reinforced by a degree of monopoly: e.g. construction, financial services, insurance, mining and manufacturing. But in each of these fields a significant degree of penetration had already begun, and in manufacturing, the most important of all, a new phase of African entry seemed to be beginning by 1977.

Except for 1975 and 1976, the rate of growth in each of the sectors progressively occupied by African capital remained high, and a conservative estimate suggests that the share of the total operating surplus accruing to African private capital by 1975 was of the order of a third, or about K£180m.,

Table 8.1 *Growth, operating surplus and share of African private capital by sector*

| Monetary economy | Percentage growth of GDP at constant prices | | | | Operating surplus 1975* K£m | Estimated share of African private capital % of col. 5 | K£m |
	Annual average 1964–72 (1)	1973–74 (2)	1974–75 (3)	1975–76 (4)	(5)	(6)	(7)
Agriculture	6·5	−0·6	−0·1	6·9	94·52	50	47·26
Forestry	6·3	12·4	0·2	4·3	1·80	25	0·45
Fishing	3·6	−5·1	—	4·5	1·27	50	0·64
Mining and quarrying	6·7	−9·9	2·8	10·1	1·62	0	0·00
Manufacturing and repairing	8·1	8·9	2·6	12·5	73·57	5	3·68
Building and construction	9·5	−9·7	−3·6	2·8	8·50	10	0·85
Electricity and water	7·8	9·4	10·9	11·8	9·08	0	0·00
Transport, storage and communication	7·6	−1·0	−3·0	6·0	24·34	50	12·17
Wholesale and retail trade	6·1	−3·1	−7·6	8·2	65·54	70	45·88
Banking, insurance and real estate	10·6	18·3	5·9	2·7	31·19	5	1·56
Ownership of dwellings	1·5	2·7	1·0	2·0	46·01	50	23·00
Other services	10·5	13·2	6·8	3·1	7·65	10	0·77
TOTAL enterprise	7·2	2·5	−0·1	7·2	365·09*	37	136·26

Note:
* Provisional figures (*Statistical Abstract*, 1976). The *Economic Survey*, 1977, shows a revised total of K£357·17m. The provisional total for 1976 was K£482·22m. Since a large part of this increase was coffee revenues, the effect would be to raise the African share of the total substantially for 1976.
Sources: *Development Plan 1974–78; Statistical Abstract 1976; Economic Survey 1977.*

sufficient to permit very substantial further movement into new sectors and subsectors (especially when one takes into consideration the limitations of the data, which tend to understate the output of African enterprise).[27] (See Table 8.1.). The essential function of the state was to displace monopolies enjoyed by foreign capital and substitute monopolies for African capital, and also to supplement individual African capitals with statefinance capital and state-secured technology, to enable them to occupy the space created for them in the newly accessible economic sectors.

In noting the important role of the state in facilitating this movement of African capital out of circulation and into production, we must avoid the mistake of attributing to it an independent role. Its initiatives reflected the existing class power of the indigenous bourgeoisie, based on the accumulation of capital they had already achieved.

This is not a merely academic point. Unless the exercise of state power after 1963 is grasped as a manifestation of the class power already achieved by the indigenous bourgeoisie, it can lead to serious mystification. The most common form of this is to see the state's economic role as expressing the 'modernizing' vision of the state bureaucracy (the 'elite'). On this view the whole process of the appropriation of surplus value by the exploiting classes disappears behind an ideological conception of 'development' in the interests of 'the people of Kenya'. Alternatively, one version of the dependency school sees the state as a more or less independent *mediator* between foreign capital and local capital according to some conception of a 'balance' which, since foreign capital is evidently much stronger, can only provide minor gains and compensations for local ('dependent') capital.[28]

Some such conception was at times implicit if not explicit in my own earlier work on Kenya. Instead of seeing the strength of the historical tendency lying behind the emergence of the African bourgeoisie I tended to see only the relatively small size and technical weakness of African capital in face of international capital, and to envisage the state as little more than a register of this general imbalance; rather than seeing the barriers of capital scale and technology as relative, and the state as the register of the leading edge of indigenous capital in its assault on those barriers.

The general theoretical error involved here needs no further emphasis, but it is worth while illustrating one of its many effects from another, related angle – the significance of contemporary forms of 'primitive' accumulation in countries like Kenya.

In Kenya the spectacular phase of accumulation through modern forms of plunder was probably the years from 1971 to 1975, commemorated in a celebrated series of pseudonymous articles in the *Sunday Times* in August 1975.[29] However, such practices as the commandeering of state-owned land and livestock or the semi-forcible takeover of expatriate farms or businesses, were not unknown earlier, and liberal observers were apt to be very preoccupied with these on moral grounds. But what needs to be considered about such practices, however, is not only their distributive effects, but their effects on production, in as much as they may contribute significantly to a concentration of capital in indigenous hands sufficient to overcome specific barriers of scale. The part played by primitive accumulation in the development of European capitalism is so well known that we should at least be ready to recognize its possible significance in a periphery country like Kenya today.[30]

Some forms of such accumulation have probably been pursued on quite a broad scale, moreover, such as the importation or export of goods whose import or export is supposed to be banned.[31] A spectacular special case which occurred in 1976–7 reinforces the general point. When the world price of coffee had risen to ten times the average price for 1975 it was estimated that between 10% and 30% of the entire Ugandan coffee crop, worth between K£20m. and K£60m., was being smuggled through Kenya rather than sold to the Ugandan Coffee Board. So valuable was coffee at this time that two 'robberies' of Ugandan coffee in transit on Kenya Railways in one week of August 1977 accounted for coffee worth K£400,000.[32]

Clearly, the scale of capital concentration which may be achieved through these forms of modern 'primitive' accumulation does not guarantee that such capital will be invested productively. Much of the capital accumulated in African hands in the last ten years will have been unproductively invested and much of what has been productively invested has involved the acquisition of existing assets, resulting in the transfer of capital into other sectors or out of the country. None the less the significance of these transactions for the long-run potential for further accumulation by indigenous capital remains profound. A striking example comes from the expatriate-owned coffee plantations. In 1974 the capital value of plantations, and also foreign-owned ranches was still considered a major barrier to their purchase by Africans.[33] But starting in 1973 and developing into a rush by 1975, about half of the total hectarage of foreign-owned coffee was bought by Africans; by the end of 1977, 57·3% of the total had changed hands, that is, nearly 18,000 hectares, worth about K£18m. at 1975 prices.[34] Most of this undoubtedly came from various sources of finance capital, but the funds in question were also largely the result of the previous phase of accumulation by Africans. And the process was already well advanced when the coffee boom began. By 1977 a high proportion of the new owners had paid off their loans and were actively searching for new investment opportunities. Speaking generally, and bearing in mind the concentration of coffee output in a few hands within the smallholder areas, rising from the earlier phases of capital accumulation, the effects of the coffee boom would be to put a large part of the K£200m. realized from coffee sales in 1976–7 alone (the equivalent figure for 1974–5 was K£33m.) into the hands of the indigenous capitalist class.[35] (It must be borne in mind that the coffee estates which changed hands in 1973–7 rarely afforded the new purchasers much land for household cultivation of other crops. They belonged to the realm of capitalist, not pre-capitalist relations of production.)

These reflections are relevant to the highly significant contemporary movement of African capital into manufacturing production. In commerce, returns are quick and the capital outlay is relatively small, but in the long run profits are liable to be forced down by competition from other commercial capitals and by industrial capital, in relation to a share of surplus value the total of which is determined at the point of production. In Kenya, this was experienced by the leading African capitalists as a rapidly narrowing scope for further displacement of foreign capital from the sphere of circulation, coupled with a growing awareness of the limitations of that sphere. These themes recurred in discussions with those concerned with industrial investment, such as the following.[36]

> In fifteen years, if the political climate of Kenya and the world economy
> stay stable, 90% of manufacturing will be Kenyan-owned. Where else is
> there for people to go? Agricultural land is finished – all the big farms are
> sold and divided up. Distribution is all taken up. Africans don't want to
> go into tourism, it is too risky – politically. And very tight [competitive].
> So they will go into manufacturing. As the market is narrow, this means
> they will buy into existing businesses. The public ones will go quietly by
> purchase. The price will rise till foreign owners, considering the risk, sell.
> Private ones will take longer but will gradually go. New ones will start with
> parastatal or local control.

This analysis (not all of it indisputable) reflected the viewpoint of a state
official. The (African) manager of a major multinational conglomerate,
himself also an active independent capitalist, said:

> In the early independence years, people lacked capital. Smallholdings
> under consolidation [the pooling of land fragments carried out in the 1950s
> when freehold titles were issued] generated a bit, then people moved into
> the Rift Valley schemes [in the former white Highlands] and most of them
> did quite well. Then the Africanization of trade generated more – if you
> had the breweries franchise at $3 \cdot 5\%$ it was a monopoly and people came
> to you [i.e. you didn't have to work to get customers]. In general, retail
> trade isn't hard and people learned to do it well. Now a point has been
> reached where people have some capital and want to know how to
> preserve it against inflation. Also they are starting to come into the income
> tax net and above a certain income, they realize income is not so
> important. What they want is to secure the future for their families and
> so on; and this means you must own productive assets – that is the only
> way you can make capital grow . . .

It was also interesting to note how the shift from the sphere of circulation to
that of production was reflected in a shift of class imagery, as evidenced in
several interviews:

> People think they must be a manufacturer to be someone. If you have a
> beer distributorship, that's nothing to be.
> The challenge of industrial investment is that you must wait for a return,
> but when it comes, it is higher.
> Local people don't want just to put their money in; they want control.

It would be misleading to say that by 1977 African capital was moving
primarily into manufacturing production. There was still considerable scope
for movement in the sphere of distribution and services. But the movement
into manufacturing was under way, with the following specific features:

(1) Capital was being *concentrated* in sufficient volume and in *appropriate
forms* for industrial investment. Five specific forms were in evidence. Most
common (especially in new investments), and perhaps in the long run most
significant, there were *syndicates*, usually of four or five individual capitalists,
formed to make one or sometimes several investments in manufacture, usually

taking 25–30% of the equity together with a state investment corporation and a foreign manufacturer, but sometimes with a controlling interest. Recent new projects involving such groups were plants to manufacture drugs, tea, shoes, soap, furfural, pipe fittings, plastic sacks for agriculture, etc. Second, *co-operatives* of various types had begun investing in manufacturing; usually these were agricultural (producer) co-operatives, moving into a project connected with farming (e.g. to produce fertilizer) but other types of co-operative were also increasingly moving along the now-familiar path from agricultural through commercial to manufacturing investment. This was particularly likely to happen to some land-purchase co-operatives which had invested in coffee plantations. Third, there were *mass investment companies*, of which the prototype was Gema Holdings Corporation, an offshoot of the Kikuyu, Embu and Meru Association, formed in 1971. Gema Holdings, formed in 1973, went public in 1976. It was controlled by a group of leading Kikuyu capitalists, with an original issued capital of K£1m. In August 1977 it offered Gema members K£2·5m. in new K£5 shares, an issue which was quickly taken up. Its non-agricultural investments already included a roofing tile factory and a new truck assembly plant, co-owned with Fiat. Other 'ethnic' investment companies were planning to follow this example. An earlier example, with different origins, was the ICDC Investment Company, an offshoot of the state-owned Industrial and Commercial Development Corporation. Set up in 1967 with initial funding and continuing management provided by the parent ICDC, its shares were sold to Africans. By 1970, its total capital value was K£100,000. By 1976 this had risen to K£700,000, with investments valued at K£1m. Fourth, a variety of *state economic institutions* had begun to act as industrial investment companies, in addition to the longer-established investment corporations (the ICDC and the Development Finance Company of Kenya, in which the state was a minority shareholder). This was particularly true of some of the large number of agricultural parastatals, which were beginning to invest in the processing of agricultural commodities: cashew nuts, vegetable dehydration, maize cob by-products, etc. The Agricultural Development Corporation (originally a state farm management organization) alone had invested in the manufacture of sugar, processed fruit, cattle feed, vegetable oils and the factory production of poultry, often in association with a private investor or syndicate. Finally, there had been a notable growth of *merchant and industrial banks*, some of them tapping new sources of foreign capital. This was true of the state-owned Industrial Development Bank, established in 1973, which by 1976 had increased its original capital by about 200% by drawing on World Bank funds.

(2) Skills and know-how had been accumulated. One of the most striking changes in Kenya since 1971 was the coming 'on stream' of a new generation of technically trained state economic functionaries. The Industrial Development Bank staff were a leading example of this, combining advanced technical (economic and accounting) qualifications with considerable specialized experience, but the pattern was being repeated in other organizations. Some of these new economic functionaries were themselves spearheading the entry of private African capital into manufacturing, under the freedom given to officials in 1971 to engage in private enterprise. The financial controller of one large parastatal had, thus, also established three manufacturing companies in

which he had a controlling interest, the largest of which had assets worth K£1·7m.

A very important skill is that of taking over an established company. In the late 1960s a land-purchase co-operative wishing to buy a farm from a white settler was almost wholly dependent on advice from political patrons. By the late 1970s such organizations generally knew most of what was needed in order to buy, manage, or subdivide a large farm, and some of them were learning how to buy and manage other kinds of asset. An extreme case of the acquisition of take-over skills was the takeover in 1975 of Mackenzie (Kenya) Ltd, a foreign trading conglomerate with assets of some K£2·7m., by a syndicate, one of whose two shareholders was the African chairman of the company, appointed three years previously. According to Swainson, this was only the first and so far most important of a number of similar takeovers which obviously depended largely on the inside knowledge of the leading figures involved.[37]

Swainson, the leading authority on corporate development in Kenya, considers that African advance into the manufacturing sector will be slow, and given the capital requirements of much manufacturing industry, this judgement seems reasonable. None the less the rate of return in this sector is relatively high (Langdon found that 20% on assets employed was the norm for foreign-owned subsidiaries) and there seems to be no obvious reason why the initial rate of African penetration achieved by 1977 should not gradually accelerate in the following decade.

IV   Formation of an Indigenous Bourgeoisie

To examine properly the process of class formation associated with indigenous capital accumulation – a process occurring at several levels (social, political and ideological as well as economic) and involving complex interactions between the events in the distinct 'historical times' of the different levels – would be a separate study in itself, far beyond the scope of this chapter. Here we can simply note certain rather obvious indicators of this process, which do little more than testify to its existence (even that little, however, has some bearing on the theoretical significance of the Kenyan case to which we must return in the final section).

(1) An increasingly evident differentiation during the decade in which the accumulators had spread out of their original base in circulation. Distinct fractions of African capital – primarily merchant, agricultural and industrial, but also financial (e.g. stockbroking) and rentier (e.g. real estate), all divisible also into large-scale/modern and small or medium-scale/archaic – had begun to crystallize around various recurrent issues: for instance, the scope and level of protection afforded to manufacturing (merchant capital favouring more limited protection), wage controls (more important for smaller, more archaic forms of capital, with lower levels of productivity), and so on.[38] Besides the formation of these class fractions the formation of certain significant strata (determined by political and ideological practices) could also be discerned: in particular, a small, older political stratum, heavily involved in the various

forms of modern primitive accumulation, increasingly giving way to a younger generation more equipped to dispense with primitive forms of accumulation and oriented strongly towards fully capitalist valorization of the inherited family capital: the higher-level 'straddlers', that is, holders of salaried positions, state, parastatal and corporate, using their salaries and their privileged access to credit to create independent basis of accumulation; and a stratum of low-profile entrepreneurs, in the classical mould, with sometimes surprisingly large capitals invested in relatively advanced fields of production, a stratum destined to assume greater importance through the long-run growth and deepening of its investments.

(2) A notable development of adjutant, auxiliary ranks immediately subordinate to and serving the African bourgeoisie: lawyers, accountants, stockbrokers, insurers, heart specialists and psychiatrists, as well as a layer of ideologists, including academics and journalists.

(3) A parallel development of bourgeois culture: increasing resort to private schooling, followed by university education at the family's expense in Britain or the USA (bourgeois parents increasingly regarded the University of Nairobi as intellectually and socially inferior, as well as unsafe, given its periodic encounters with the paramilitary police):[39] a distinctive bourgeois life-style in terms of housing, entertainment, and so on; a bourgeois marriage circuit with a manifestly dynastic aspect; the growth of a weekly and monthly magazine culture which reflected these tastes and interests, but also some of the more political concerns of its younger, more sophisticated elements for institutional reform and for the establishment of civil rights seen as essential in creating stable and reliable conditions for economic life.

(4) A progressive development of bourgeois class-consciousness through a series of struggles with other classes and fractions. The decisive years here were 1965–9, during which the political challenge of the petty-bourgeois/urban trade union/rural landless alliance led by Odinga and Kaggia was outmanoeuvred and finally destroyed in the banning of the Kenya People's Union in 1969. In the course of these struggles, the unionized working class was brought effectively under control of the state, first through a state-controlled union central organization, and subsequently by a ban on strike action and an effective system of wage controls. The petty-bourgeoisie was also decisively neutralized as an independent political force. The populist tendency maintained, after the break-up of the KPU, by a group of parliamentary backbenchers, was ultimately curbed through the murder of J. M. Kariuki and the subsequent detention (or exemplary jailing on conviction for offences) of his most effective successors; while the middle and poor peasants were as far as possible organized as clients under the patronage of the bourgeoisie through a comprehensive system of ethnic organizations with their associated 'self-help' movements, rival ethnic colleges of technology, ethnic investment holding companies, and so on.[40] These organizations and their offshoots, ostensibly trans-class, must be understood as class organizations of the bourgeoisie in its relations with the peasantry, just as the Federation of Kenyan Employers was the principal class organization of the bourgeoisie in relation to the organized working class; and as KANU – through its very lack of organization and effectiveness – was the class organization of the bourgeoisie in relation to all other classes, perpetuating their disorganization, their underdetermined condition, *vis-à-vis* the bourgeoisie which 'led' KANU

(superintending its endless factional struggles, and the repeated campaigns for party revitalization and reorganization, apparently preparing for an exercise in mass democracy which never came).[41]

V   Kenya and the Dependency Debate

The role of the indigenous bourgeoisie has been stressed virtually to the exclusion of that of any other class, partly to redress an obvious shortcoming in my own earlier work. The decolonization process in Kenya lasting roughly from the mid-1950s to the mid-1960s, was governed primarily by the neo-colonial 'class project' of international capital, but the subsequent period was determined primarily by the class project of the indigenous bourgeoisie, and the failure to grasp and interpret the nature of this dialectical shift was a serious one, due mainly to an inadequate historical analysis of the material bases of the different fractions of capital in Kenya.

But besides the need for historical reparation, it is equally important to put the indigenous bourgeoisie at the centre of any discussion of the bearing of the Kenyan case on the theoretical issues discussed at the beginning of this chapter. Put in its most general terms, the point seems to be that there were two distinctive (and indeed exceptional) circumstances affecting the development of the relations of production in Kenya. First, the existence of an indigenous process of capital accumulation in central Kenya which was sufficiently advanced at the moment of colonization for the accumulated capital, and the class places formed in the process of its accumulation, to be *transmitted* – albeit transformed in various ways – through the colonial period into the moment of decolonization: and second, the installation under colonialism of a foreign but *resident* bourgeoisie (the settler fraction) which, through the colonial state, appropriated a large part of the means of production (land and livestock) and secured the partial proletarianization of most of the population (and the complete proletarianization of a significant minority) while at the same time establishing (again largely by means of state intervention) the infrastructural and other conditions for the domestic accumulation of capital.

International capital played a part, too, intervening in particular to reduce the value of labour power by raising productivity in the staple food-producing sector, (i.e. reducing the exchange value of maize), advancing the large amounts of capital needed to extend commodity production (e.g. tea, tourism), and so on. But in a typical 'colonial trade economy' international capital (merchant, industrial, or state) appropriates surplus value partly through unequal exchange, and partly through direct controls over household commodity production, in ways which, broadly speaking, leave largely intact the forms and much of the substance of pre-capitalist relations of production (in particular the household ownership of the means of production and often limited dependence on commodity production for reproduction of the household as a productive unit); whereas in Kenya, this relationship between international capital and peasant households was established relatively late in the colonial period, and not before settler capital had made considerable inroads into the economic independence of the peasant household throughout large parts of the country. Moreover, the hegemony of settler capital created other conditions favourable to the *local* valorization of capital. The colonial state, in the era of settler hegemony, secured access to the whole East African market, which together with a common currency facilitated the realization of productive capital in Kenya and so opened the way to relatively early industrialization initiatives, simultaneously enabling merchant and finance capital located in Kenya to appropriate a significant share of the surplus value generated in Uganda and Tanganyika.

The dialectics of capital accumulation in Kenya thus involved (1) the subordination of indigenous capital to settler capital, but not its *destruction*. (2) the assertion by settler capital of claims on labour power and the means of production which greatly limited the scope for international capital to enter into direct relations of exploitation with peasant commodity producers, and undermined much more radically than in most African countries the pre-capitalist relations of production: and (3) the ability of the indigenous class of capital not only to substitute itself effectively for the settler fraction of capital at independence – that is, as an internal bourgeois, not a petty-bour-geois, class – but also to set about recovering from international capital a good part of the field of accumulation which it had succeeded in occupying. In effect, the indigenous capitalist class assumed the hegemonic place in a new 'power bloc' (i.e. alongside international capital and elements of non-indigen-ous local capital), in the context of an economy which was already capitalist in more than the usual sense: namely, not merely one in which the still preponderant pre-capitalist relations of production (peasant household com-modity production in particular) were subjected to the laws of the capitalist mode of production, in both direct and indirect ways; but also one in which for some important sectors, and to some extent for the 'economy as a whole', the 'structure of profitability' no longer depended simply on extending relations of exploitation based on absolute surplus labour (intensifying labour in various ways) but increasingly on raising labour productivity.

In less abstract terms, Kenya appears, from this analysis, as a modest example of a 'systematical combination of moments' conducive to the transition to the capitalist mode of production. This does *not* imply that no further obstacles remain in Kenya to the uninterrupted domestic accumulation of capital, that is, the uninterrupted development of the productive forces through the extension of capitalist production relations progressively throughout the entire economy. Nor does it imply that the indigenous bourgeoisie is 'progressive' in the anti-imperialist sense ascribed to it by the theorists of the Comintern, still less that it is preparing a bourgeois-democratic revolution for Kenya, in the nineteenth-century sense of *that* term. Nor, finally, does it imply a 'menshevik' political position of support for capitalism in Kenya as the necessary preliminary to communism. What it says is that capitalist production relations may be considerably extended in a periphery social formation, and the productive forces may be considerably expanded within and through them, for reasons having primarily to do with the configuration of class forces preceding and during the colonial period; and that the limits of such development cannot be determined from the sort of general considerations advanced by underdevelopment and dependency theory.

In the case of Kenya, while the extension of capitalist production relations has been extremely rapid since independence, the process is threatened by multiple contradictions. One is the well-known limitation of the internal market, which presses Kenyan industrial capital both towards the search for export markets – in which it has had some success, especially in 1977 after the loss of the Tanzanian market following the border closure – and towards foreign policies aimed at re-establishing a new *internal* market within the East African region.[42] These initiatives, which probably hold considerably more promise than the apparently more 'radical' alternative, proposed by the ILO, of internal income redistribution (in addition to being politically more acceptable to the bourgeoisie), should not be underestimated. However, the limitation remains a critical one for any economy not capable of producing, ultimately, for the *world* market: the question of how and in what terms a country such as Kenya may be enabled to transcend that limitation is all-important, even though it still lies somewhat in the future as far as Kenya is concerned, and certainly cannot be usefully speculated about here.

A more immediate and severe contradiction lies, I think, in the powerful place of 'middle' peasant household production in agriculture, which may be approaching the limits of its expansion.[43] Current policy thinking within the Kenyan state bureaucracy favours the extension of this form of production, based on high labour inputs per hectare, even though with apparently declining labour productivity (agricultural output per head of population seems to have declined steadily since 1970).[44] While this would serve the interests of international capital which appropriates surplus value more or less directly from such production, it would hardly serve the interests of the indigenous bourgeoisie who, however, would confront a major political problem in any attempt to raise the productivity of labour and their own appropriation of surplus value by trying to extend capitalist relations of production in agriculture (e.g. by policies designed to polarize the smallholder areas towards kulak and capitalist farming on the one hand, and proletarianization on the other). Yet without an increase in agricultural productivity, it seems doubtful if the momentum of capitalist production can be maintained in industry in the longer run. Here again, the limitations of the analysis of this chapter do not permit useful speculations about the development of this contradiction; though it too should not be attributed any absolute character.

As for the political character of the indigenous bourgeoisie, its interests are partly coincident with those of the international bourgeoisie, and partly in contradiction with them. If it is 'progressive', it is progressive in relation to the petty-bourgeoisie which seeks to defend, in general, relations of production – especially smallholding and petty trade – in which the exploitation of the workers does not expand the forces of production (however much that defence is couched in the rhetoric of populism and petty-bourgeois socialism). In relation to the workers, the indigenous bourgeoisie is exploitative and oppressive, and the bourgeois freedoms which a section of it increasingly desires – such as freedom from the disruption of production by unrestrained and unpredictable forms of primitive accumulation, freedom from political threats to the security of personal fortunes, freedom from low-quality and politically dependent judicial officials – are for itself, not for workers; furthermore this wish is in contradiction with the equally strong wish for a state capable of repressing both worker and petty-bourgeois attempts to organize industrial and political class struggle. To recognize the important role of the indigenous bourgeoisie in the combination of 'moments' giving rise to the development of capitalism in Kenya is, therefore, not to succumb to ideological illusions about its historic mission or its current political character.

In conclusion, the foregoing discussion can perhaps be linked to the broad theoretical issues raised at the beginning of this chapter, in the following way: the Kenya case seems to lend useful support to the general position adopted by Brenner, and may even help to put in somewhat clearer perspective the question which is at issue in the debate between Frank, Warren and Emmanuel. Frank, following Baran, located the primary mechanism of underdevelopment in processes of 'surplus transfer' ('loot', in Baran's paradigm case of India) from periphery to metropole by individual capitals. Warren, seeing no theoretical reason for attributing to individual capitals (at least after the decolonization process had ended in independence) any general motive to transfer surplus in this way, concluded that it would henceforward not do so, and so that capital formed at the periphery would be accumulated there too. Emmanuel, rejecting the alleged evidence that this was happening, proposed instead that capital is drawn towards the poles of its own existing accumulation.

The point of view suggested by this chapter is that all of these positions are mistaken in so far as they propose tendencies inherent in 'capitalism in general'; whereas that each of them may, on the other hand, be correct and illuminating considered as an explanation of the movement of capital, and its consequences for the development of capitalist production relations and capital accumulation, in particular historical circumstances. Thus Baran's paradigm case of India had two significant features. One was the nature of the pre-existing relations of production in India, let us call them quasi-feudal, which, as Marx eventually noted, proved highly resistant to displacement by capitalist ones. The other was the character of British capital at the period in question – still largely family capitals, still competitive, focused strongly on the necessity to expand constant capital within the existing production unit in order to maintain market shares. In these circumstances it was understandable that the original process of looting India in order to establish capitalist production in Britain should continue as a process of repatriation of profits earned from sales in India in order to expand capitalist production in Britain. The capitals which primarily figure in the work of Warren and Emmanuel, however, are corporate monopoly capitals, with the organizational capacity and political freedom to select their points of accumulation according to a global rationality. In this very different situation, the total combination of 'moments' at any given place in the 'periphery' (even this term must be increasingly questioned) becomes decisive, in relation to the corresponding combinations at the relevant places in the 'centre'. This of course is an excessively mechanical formulation. However, it is evident that – precisely in certain 'exceptional' instances – capital has flowed to, or simply been rapidly accumulated at, strategic points in the so-called periphery, where the relations of production and the balance of class forces have produced conditions permitting the realization of 'surplus profits';[45] while at the same time – precisely in certain similarly 'exceptional' countries in the so-called *centre* – there have been parallel processes of declining rates of accumulation, where the balance of class forces has given rise to conditions which have seemed hostile to the interests of capital, for example, Britain.

Notes

1 This chapter is based on a short visit to Kenya in the summer of 1977 financed by the Canada Council, and generously assisted by Dr David Court. Its intellectual debts, especially to Mike Cowen, should be obvious.

2 Cf. the contribution to the debate by Robert Brenner, who poses the same basic question ('The origins of capitalist development: a critique of neo-Smithian Marxism', *New Left Review*, 104, July–August 1977, pp. 25–92).

3 A. G. Frank, *Capitalism and Underdevelopment in Latin America* (New York: Monthly Review Press, 1969).

4 Bill Warren, 'Imperialism and capitalist industrialization', *New Left Review*, 81, September–October 1973.

5 Arghiri Emmanuel, 'Myths of development versus myths of underdevelopment', *New Left Review*, 85, May–June 1974, and P. McMichael, J. Petras and R. Rhodes, 'Imperialism and the contradictions of development', ibid.

6 The same general point is argued from different theoretical premises by Geoffrey Kay in *Development and Underdevelopment: A Marxist Analysis* (London: Macmillan, 1975).

7 McMichael *et al.*, op. cit., p. 96.

8 ibid.

9 *Capital*, Vol. I (Harmondsworth, Penguin, 1976), pp. 915–16.

10 op. cit., p. 78, italics in the original.

11 The same point was argued, very cursorily, in my 'Underdevelopment and dependency: critical notes', *Journal of Contemporary Asia*, 7, 1, 1977, p. 105. See also A. Foster-Carter, 'The modes of production controversy', *New Left Review*, 107, January–February 1978.

12 See note 3 above.

13 op. cit., p. 91.

14 op. cit., p. 85.

15 See Brenner, pp. 91–2, where he speculates on the possibility that industrial capital in the metropoles, eager for new markets and cheaper labour, may now lend new strength to the class interests behind industrialization at the periphery, enabling them to 'force the class structural shifts that would open the way to profitable investment'. By contrast Emmanuel, writing in 1974, considered the advanced countries 'nowadays too rich not to be able to absorb themselves, without difficulty, all the new capital that is formed in them' (Emmanuel, op. cit., p. 77).

16 Central Bureau of Statistics, *Integrated Rural Survey 1974–75* (Nairobi: Government Printer, 1977), tables 8.13 and 8.9.

17 Calculated from *Statistical Abstract 1976 Nairobi: Government Printer*, 1977, tables 109(a) and (b), 235 and 82(d). While these are very crude indicators, the tendencies seem large enough to be accepted as broadly valid for present purposes.

18 The real rate of net capital inflows is taken to be the inverse of the trade balance. Emmanuel (op. cit., pp. 75–7) argues convincingly that this is the best measure. The main measures taken against hidden transfers were a withholding tax on licence, patent and management fee payments, and a system of inspection of all imports in the country of origin.

19 op. cit., p. 63.

20 Debt service charges as a percentage of the value of exports, fell from 3·5% in 1971 to 2·5% in 1976. See *Economic Survey 1977*, (Nairobi: Government Printer, 1977), pp. 61–2.

21 Kenya's receipts of official capital aid per capita have been approximately equal to the average level for the continent as a whole. Moreover, a third of the largest single component of bilateral aid (the British) has been payments for land purchase from British nationals who repatriated about 60% of it to Britain again.

22 M. Cowen, 'Differentiation in a Kenya location', East African Universities Social Science Council, 8th Annual Conference, Nairobi 1972; 'Notes on agricultural wage labour in a Kenya location' (with F. Murage); 'Concentration of sales and assets; dairy

cattle and tea in Magutu, 1964–71; (Nairobi: Institute of Development Studies, Working Paper No. 146, 1974); 'Patterns of cattle ownership and dairy production: 1900–1965' (mimeo.) 1974; 'Wattle production in the Central Province: capital and household commodity production, 1903–1964'; 'Real wages in Central Kenya, 1924–1974' (mimeo.) 1976 (with P. Newman); 'Capital and peasant households' (mimeo.), July 1976; 'Notes on capital, class and household production' (mimeo.) n.d.; 'Some problems of income distribution in Kenya' (with K. Kinyanjui), (Nairobi: Institute for Development Studies, March 1977). The following section is almost wholly based on Cowen's work though it is in no way a summary or overview of it.

23 Leys, *Underdevelopment in Kenya*, (London: Heinemann Educational Books 1975), pp. 53 and 100.
24 The data from Lamb and Cowen are cited in J. Heyer *et al.*, *Agricultural Develpment in Kenya*, (Nairobi: Oxford University Press, 1976) pp. 195–7. Heyer notes (p. 18) that the controls applied to new growers of such crops in the 1950s were such that only the relatively rich could comply with them.
25 See Leys, *Underdevelopment in Kenya*, ch. 5, and N. Swainson, 'The rise of a national bourgeoisie in Kenya', *Review of African Political Economy*, 8, 1977, for fuller details.
26 *Development Plan 1974–78*, (Nairobi: Government Printer, 1974), p. 366. 'Citizens' includes non-Africans, mainly Asians. However the takeover by African capital of 'larger and more intricate firms' was well advanced by 1977, with 1,500 quit notices issued to Asian traders in 1973 alone (Economist Intelligence Unit report on Kenya, Uganda, Ethiopia and Somalia, No. 3, 1973). In 1974 sixty-nine large trading companies in Nairobi, including at least one major one owned by non-African Kenyan citizens, were accused of illegal importation and closed down until such time as, in practice, they agreed to sell the businesses to Africans (see Swainson, op. cit.).
27 In Table 8.1 the estimated African share of 'wholesale and retail trade' is set at 70% because this item in the national accounts includes hotels and restaurants where international and non-African domestic capital is still relatively strongly entrenched. 'Operating surplus' represents the value of total output less the cost of intermediate inputs and labour but includes consumption of fixed capital (i.e. depreciation) and is not equivalent to profits.
28 For example, S. Langdon, 'Multinational firms and the state in Kenya', *IDS Bulletin*, 9, 1, July 1977, pp. 36–41.
29 John Barry, 'Kenya on the brink', *Sunday Times*, 10, 17 and 24 August 1975.
30 E. Mandel concluded from the historical evidence for Britain that 'for the period 1760–1780 the profits from India and the West Indies alone (i.e. from plunder and slavery) *more than doubled* the accumulation of money available from rising industry alone' (*Marxist Economic Theory*, London: Merlin Press, 1968, p. 445).
31 Six licences for supposedly banned imports of basmati rice in 1971 were worth approximately K£3 million (see *Underdevelopment in Kenya*, p. 158). At the end of 1977 one of Kenya's biggest textile companies failed, apparently because of competition from illegal imports.
32 *Weekly Review*, 22 August 1977.
33 *Development Plan 1974–78*, pt 1, p. 216.
34 Annual report of the Coffee Board of Kenya of 1977, reported in *Weekly Review*, 5 May 1978.
35 For comparison, total GNP in current prices was K£1,253 million in 1976. In Nairobi in mid-1977 one heard many stories recounting the amazing windfalls of the new coffee estate owners, all of which had essentially the same features: an estate containing 100 acres of coffee trees was purchased for K£50,000 in 1974 with a down payment of K£10,000, the balance being borrowed from the Agricultural Finance Corporation. In 1976–7 the average price of a ton of coffee was about K£2,000, so the value of the crop at a ton per acre would be about K£220,000. Even if, as was common, the estate was fully managed for the owners after tax profits would still be at least K£100,000 for the season.
36 The following extracts are from interviews with state, parastatal and private company officials in Nairobi in 1977.

37 N. Swainson, 'Foreign corporations and economic growth in Kenya', PhD thesis, London University, 1977, p. 249. This pathbreaking study was published by Heinemann Educational Books in 1980 as *The Development of Corporate Capitalism in Kenya, 1918–77.*

38 In identifying these fractions and their mutual relations, it is more than ever necessary to distinguish between 'places' in the relations of production, which are determined by the historical processes of development, and the agents who occupy the places, some of them occupying more places than one.

39 I owe this point to M. P. Cowen. It was strikingly borne out in interviews.

40 The middle and poor peasantry thus constituted a typical 'supporting' class for the bloc of classes in power, a class kept 'underdetermined' through the ideology of tribalism, in particular.

41 The real significance of the often intense factional struggles within local branches of the party, a party without a real function, would seem to be to serve as partly ritual periodic indicators of the relative strengths of bourgeois and petty-bourgeois class fractions. It should perhaps be added that the state apparatus also served as the class organization of the indigenous bourgeoisie in relation to the international bourgeoisie, and the presidency, with its surrounding apparatus, also served as the class organization of the indigenous bourgeoisie in relation to the non-indigenous domestic bourgeoisie.

42 In 1976 Kenyan exports to Tanzania were worth K£33m. or roughly 13% of all Kenyan exports, offset by imports from Tanzania worth K£12m. The loss of this market through Tanzania's closure of the border in February 1977 was serious but was offset by the domestic market expansion resulting from the coffee boom, and to a lesser but significant extent by expanding exports to other regional markets. Kenya's handling of relations with Tanzania, which contributed to the border closure, is difficult to explain in terms of the interests of Kenyan capital, and an explanation should perhaps be sought in the excessively confident pursuit of those interests by the Kenyan state apparatus.

43 'Now, within the contemporary period of expanded household production, the reproduction of households out of produced commodities is reaching the limits of existing commodity forms of production' (Cowen, 'Some problems of income distribution in Kenya', op. cit., section 3, p. 36).

44 The quantity index of monetary sector agriculture rose from 100 in 1972 to 101·8 in 1975, and monetary agricultural GDP rose from K£94·3m. to K£95·2m. in the same period. This was before the impact of the better weather and prices of 1976–7, but suggests that per capita agricultural output is tending to decline in the medium run.

45 In the sense proposed by Ernest Mandel in *Late Capitalism* (London: New Left Books, 1976), ch. 3.

9 Capitalist Accumulation in the Periphery: Kenya

RAPHIE KAPLINSKY

I

Colin Leys, author of one of the most interesting studies of underdevelopment in recent years (Leys, 1975), has caused considerable surprise in the literature by his reassessment of his pioneering study (Leys, 1978); Chapter 8 in this volume. The particular point of contention has been the characterization of the indigenous industrial bourgeoisie. In the earlier study (which was given significant support by Langdon, 1976) Leys argued that the indigenous bourgeoisie – which he termed an 'auxiliary bourgeoisie' – was largely defined by its relationship to foreign capital and that it saw its future in alliance with that of foreign capital. Langdon supported this, characterizing the 'insider bourgeoisie' as bargaining with foreign capital for a greater proportion of the surplus generated by foreign capital to be distributed to the Kenyan elite. But he, too, saw the interests between the indigenous bourgeoisie and foreign capital as being basically harmonious, rather than antagonistic.

Leys's recent assessment of the earlier analysis seems to have been influenced by two factors. The first is the research of Cowen[1] which traces the roots of the indigenous bourgeoisie back to pre-colonial times[2]. This, Leys argues, gives the lie to the characterization of the indigenous bourgeoisie solely in relation to foreign capital. The second factor underlying Leys's reassessment is the difference in the aspirations of the indigenous bourgeoisie between his earlier fieldwork (1971–3) and his visit to Kenya in 1977. In this latter period Leys encountered a very strong desire by the indigenous bourgeoisie to supplant foreign capital.

Leys (1978) points out that the significance of the characterization of the Kenyan bourgeoisie stretches beyond an analysis of the Kenyan economy *per se* since it has significant implications for underdevelopment theory in general. Moreover, it poses perhaps the most basic question of all: is successful capitalist accumulation at the periphery of the global economy possible?

There is general agreement that the debate on Kenya has far-reaching implications for the literature and it is in this context that this chapter is written. Specifically I shall attempt to add to the literature various sets of data accumulated during a protracted stay in Kenya. One subset of this data arises from a project undertaken for the National Christian Council of Kenya (Kaplinsky, forthcoming) in an attempt to update the earlier study entitled *Who Controls Industry in Kenya* (NCCK, 1968). This monograph includes detailed information on the ownership of all large-scale (i.e. over fifty employees) manufacturing firms and all tourist firms operating in Kenya in 1976. However, before proceeding to outline the results of this research (section III) it is desirable to set out Leys's basic argument and this is done in section II below. Finally I conclude with an assessment of the implications of our data for Leys's and, therefore, move to a position on the debate concerning accumulation in peripheral capitalist economies.

II

Noting the divergence in opinions between Frank (1969), Warren (1973) and Emmanuel (1974), Leys states the context of his re-evaluation.

> The most important question of all those which are at stake in the debate about 'dependency' is whether or not there are theoretical reasons for thinking that the ex-colonies cannot (as Marx put it) 'adopt the bourgeois mode of production' and develop their productive forces within it. (p. 170)

> .. the debate about dependency and underdevelopment has not shown either that capitalist development cannot occur at the periphery (or 'in the Third World'), or that it is eventually bound to. What it demonstrates, rather, is the need to study and theorize the conditions under which other periphery countries have, and others have not, experienced significant measures of growth. (p. 173)

In this context Leys is concerned with

> class relations and class struggles in a particular social formation ... and furthermore it will largely be concerned with the process of domestic capital accumulation which has formed the basis for the constitution of one particular class. [For] what produces *under*development is not the 'transfer of surplus' appropriated by metropolitan capital from the periphery of the metropole, significant as this may be. Rather, such a transfer should be seen as an *effect* of structures at the periphery which militate against the productive investment of the surplus at the periphery. (p 173)

Leys then traces the historical growth of the Kenyan economy, a subject I shall consider further in section III below, and concludes that a

> plausible explanation of Kenyan economic growth since the 1940s lies rather in the specific social relations of production developed before,

> during and since the colonial period, and particularly – but in no sense
> exclusively ... in the key role of the class formed out of the process of
> indigenous capital accumulation. (p. 176)

The control of this class over the state, Leys argues, originally largely through
ethnic links, led to the accumulation of surplus through state-protected
merchant, distribution and service activities. Increasingly this allowed the
indigenous bourgeoisie to buy out foreign capital in farming, service and
manufacturing sectors, helped in recent years by capital accumulated through
the ivory, charcoal and coffee trades.

The move into the manufacturing sector has been aided by the development
of appropriate skills and institutional forms, notably syndicates of individual
investors, co-operatives, mass investment companies and parastatals. Moreover the state assists indigenous Kenyans in moving from the sphere of
circulation to that of production. But, and this leads Leys to state the major
error in his 1975 study, this does not imply a relatively autonomous state.

> Some such conception was at times implicit if not explicit in my own
> earlier work on Kenya. Instead of seeing the strength of the historical
> tendency lying behind the emergence of the African bourgeoisie I tended
> to see only the relatively small size and technical weakness of African
> capital in the face of international capital, and to envisage the state as little
> more than a register of this general imbalance; rather than seeing the
> barriers of capital scale and technology as relative, and the state as the
> register of the leading edge of indigenous capital in its assault on those
> barriers. (p. 180)

Leys concludes that

> Kenya appears, from this analysis, as a modest example of a 'systematical
> combination of moments' conducive to the transition to the capitalist
> mode of production. This does *not* imply that no further obstacles remain
> in Kenya to the uninterrupted domestic accumulation of capital ... [But]
> ... What it says is that capitalist production relations may be considerably
> extended in a periphery social formation, and the productive forces may
> be considerably expanded within and through them, for reasons having
> primarily to do with the configuration of class forces preceding and during
> the colonial period: and that the limits of such development cannot be
> determined from the sort of general considerations advanced by
> underdevelopment and dependency theory. (p. 187)

Leys is aware of the empirical gaps in Kenyan studies and notes that:

> (Chapter 8) has at most the status of a working paper, subject to correction
> in the light of work at other levels, and on other aspects of the level of
> class relations and class struggles, which mostly remains to be done.

In my view I am able to marshal new empirical data which can be brought
to bear on five hypotheses which can be drawn out of Leys and the subsidiary

analyses of Swainson (1977 and 1980). After stating these five hypotheses I proceed to examine them in greater detail. The five hypotheses are:

(1)   The Kenyan economy has seen a successful period of economic growth since independence.
(2)   An independent[3] indigenous industrial bourgeoisie now exists.
(3)   There has been a significant increase in ownership and control of industry by this indigenous bourgeoisie which has moved to supplant foreign capital holdings.
(4)   The state has moved from a mediating position to an instrument for increased indigenous control over foreign capital.
(5)   The Kenyan economy will see continued successful capitalist accumulation.

It may be thought that these five hypotheses are straw men in that detailed chapter and verse cannot necessarily be cited from the various works of Leys and Swainson. Yet I believe that they provide a fair representation of their views. The dependency school which they challenge argues that industrial development in small peripheral economies is conditioned, and moreover limited, by their relation to the global economy. The Cowen–Leys–Swainson school, as I understand it, challenges the 'dependentistas' by

(a)   pointing to the indigenous roots of the capitalist class;
(b)   noting that they, in part by manipulating the state, have moved to supplant foreign capital;
(c)   believing that such a momentum is sustainable.

For these three phenomena, especially the last two, to hold, I believe that the five hypotheses which I have drawn out must be sustainable. The testing of these hypotheses against observable reality is the task of this section.

(a) ECONOMIC TRANSFORMATION IN KENYA[4]

It is often believed that the Kenyan economy has been a 'success story', witnessing high and sustained economic growth since independence. Indeed this appears to be the view of Leys who argues that not only has there been a significant increase in the penetration of the monetary economy (associated with an extension of capitalist relations of production), but that this has been accompanied by significant economic growth and structural change. Labour productivity is said to have grown, transfer pricing by MNCs been brought under control and new markets found, following the loss of markets in Tanzania and Uganda. In sum, economic growth is said to have resulted from structural transformation and both have occurred with the spread of capitalist production relations. Let us examine each of these assertions in turn.

(i) Extension of capitalist relations of production

There is no doubt that capitalist relations of production have extended significantly over the years. The prime indicator available to illustrate this change is that of the percentage of GDP contributed by the monetary and non-monetary sectors respectively (the criterion used by Leys), which

Table 9.1 *Percentage of GDP (at constant prices) of monetary, semi-monetary, private economy and government services*

	1964	1969	1973	1974	1976
Semi-monetary economy	27·0	24·0	21·0	20·8	19·6
Monetary economy	73·0	76·0	79·0	79·2	80·4
of which:					
Enterprises and non-profit institutions	59·3	60·2	62·1	61·1	61·6
Private householders	0·9	0·8	0·8	0·9	1·1
Government services	12·8	15·0	16·1	17·2	17·8

Sources: *Statistical Abstract*, 1977, table 45(b); *Statistical Abstract*, 1975, table 45.

suggests a growth in production for exchange. As is shown in Table 9.1 the share of GDP contributed by the non-monetary sector fell steadily, from 27% in 1964 to 19·6% in 1976. But a close look at Table 9.1 suggests that the extent of this transformation may be misleading since a proportion of this decline is accounted for by significant increases in government expenditure (and therefore revenue), particularly on education, health and (especially over the last two years) in defence. Not all of this increase in government expenditure is reflected in the growth of monetized production since a significant proportion of this state expenditure has been financed by budgetary deficits, aid and foreign loans. Thus while it is my *judgement* that Leys is correct in interpreting a significant extension in capitalist relations of production, the evidence used to support this contention is subject to qualification.

Table 9.2 *Sectoral composition of imports (%) (excluding imports from Tanzania and Uganda)*

	1964	1969	1973	1974	1975
Capital formation	12·8	17·7	20·6	13·3	18·1
Intermediates	61·4	59·5	61·9	72·2	66·7
Final consumption	25·8	22·8	17·6	14·5	15·2
Petroleum, gas, coal	11·0	10·7	16·9	23·2	28·2

Source: *Statistical Abstract*, 1977, tables 78(a)–(e).

Table 9.3 *Share of manufacturers in GDP and exports, selected years (excluding exports to Tanzania and Uganda)*

Share of manufacturers in	1964	1965	1969	1973	1974	1975	1976	1977
GDP	10·4		11·9	12·8	13·3	12·4	12·1	12·7
Exports		11·5	11·8	12·6	13·1	13·2	11·8	

Source: *Statistical Abstract*, 1977, tables 45(a) and 59(a); *Statistical Abstract*, 1975, tables 44(a) and 55(a); *Economic Survey*, 1978, table 2.1.

(ii) Changes in economic structure

Changes in the structure of the Kenyan economy have in fact been rather limited. Despite significant changes in the composition of imports (see Table 9.2) which has occurred as a result of the policy of import substitution, the share of the manufacturing sector in GDP[5] grew slowly in the first thirteen years of independence (Table 9.3). This is reflected in the share of manufacturers in exports where, despite repeated trumpeting of improved performance, their share remained essentially static over the time-period (Table 9.3).

In the same period there has been a steady worsening in the balance of payments and trade as shown in Table 9.4. While these problems were alleviated by the boom in coffee prices in 1977–8, they returned very quickly as coffee prices moderated and by the end of 1978 the balance of trade was back in the red. It is an inescapable conclusion that there is an underlying and growing deficit on trade. The more positive picture on invisibles is largely accounted for by the contribution of the tourist industry. But, even taking this into account, the deficit on the current account is large and is growing despite the temporary benefits of the coffee boom in 1976 and 1977.

Leys also suggests that

> Private capital inflows began to exceed profit outflows after 1970 and while the various measures taken after 1970 to curb hidden transfers of surplus (via overinvoicing, management and patent fees, etc.) could only be partially successful, covert outflows seem rather unlikely to have equalled, let alone exceeded the real rate of total net capital inflows ...
>
> The main measures taken against hidden transfers were withholding tax on licence, patent and management fee payments, and a system of inspection of all imports in the country of origin.

However, my own research undertaken for the Kenyan government (and unfortunately therefore not available for publication) suggests that there has been little or no curbing of such transfer pricing. A preliminary investigation of five traded items showed transfer pricing on an annual basis of over K£6m., with overinvoicing of two sets of equipment purchases of over K£1·5m. and substantial overinvoicing of service charges.[6] Moreover the large stock of foreign investment has led to *declared* surplus transfer which exceeds equity inflows, thereby exacerbating balance-of-payments difficulties. This trend can be seen from Table 9.5 which lists surplus outflows (dividends, plus a large proportion of rentals, royalties, technical/management/consultancy/professional fees, directors/head office expenses, commission/commitment/agency fees and intercompany accounts) and inflows for the period May 1977 to April 1978. It is interesting to note that outgoing technical/management/consultancy/professional fees alone exceeded new capital inflows, while the outflow of dividends on past investments exceeded the inflow of new investments by 67%. A significant proportion of the surplus generated therefore seeps abroad.

In summary, therefore, there is little evidence of any profound change in economic structure. Kenya remains a predominately agricultural economy exporting primary products and importing manufactures. Although import

Table 9.4   *Kenya's balance of payments, 1966–78 (£ million)*

	1966	1967	1968	1969	1970	1971	1972	1973	1974	1975	1976	1977	1978
Trade of Physical Goods													
Imports	111·8	106·6	114·8	117·0	142·0	184·1	184·0	215·2	369·4	352·2	389·4	535·1	723·3
Exports	86·8	59·6	62·9	68·5	77·5	78·3	95·5	128·9	170·1	176·5	312·1	470·9	366·5
Balance	−25·0	−47·0	−51·8	−48·4	−64·6	−105·8	−88·5	−86·2	−199·3	−175·7	−77·3	−64·2	−356·8
Trade in Services													
Imports	53·0	55·0	61·9	65·5	71·4	69·4	75·5	80·5	124·2	137·3	178·3	150·1	170·9
Exports	71·5	71·0	84·2	93·7	105·0	120·9	116·7	108·8	384·8	182·0	203·7	234·8	275·2
Balance	18·5	16·0	22·3	28·2	33·6	51·5	41·2	20·3	46·7	47·7	54·7	88·3	104·3
Overall Balance of Payments (goods and services)	−6·6	21·5	−14·1	−2·9	−16·6	−39·9	−24·3	−46·8	−122	−83·9	−51·9	24·1	−252·5

Sources: Economic Survey, 1979, table 4.9; Economic Survey, 1978, table 4.9; Economic Survey, 1977, table 3.1; Economic Survey, 1974, table 1.13; Statistical Abstract, 1977, table 56; Economic Survey, 1972, table 1.13; Economic Survey, 1970, table 1.12.

Table 9.5   *Invisible transactions, including surplus outflows and inflows, 1977–8 (K£)*

Transport	9,079,418
Dividends	17,664,413
Interest	13,696,019
Rentals	13,634
Royalties	1,003,593
Technical/management/consultancy/professional fees	12,129,746
Directors'/head office expenses	3,027,229
Commission/commitment agents' fees	3,575,879
Intercompany accounts	24,394,192
Loan repayments and capital repatriation	32,157,992
Inflow of new equity capital	10,579,671

substitution has seen some change in the composition of imports the underlying pattern is one of increasing balance-of-payments problems. Heavy net outflows of surpluses, largely arising from foreign investment, further exacerbate these balance-of-payments difficulties.

(iii) Economic growth

The growth of the Kenyan economy has not in fact been as rapid as has been believed. As is shown in Table 9.6 there was a period of substantial growth in per capita incomes between 1964 and 1973, but this subsequently tailed off. The rise in per capita incomes in 1977 (and that in 1978 which is not yet recorded in published documents) is almost entirely due to the dramatic rise in coffee prices and it is unlikely that real per capita incomes in 1979 (which are not available at the time of writing) will have exceeded those in 1973. If coffee and tea earnings had remained at their 1975 levels, then real per capita incomes (in 1972 prices) would have been only £51·4 in 1977.

Leys points to a further indicator of economic growth, that of increases in labour productivity. However, the conclusions which are drawn are open to question for two reasons. First Leys takes no account of inflation in calculating the 'just under 20%' increase in the productivity of labour between 1969 and 1973.[7] But second (and much more important), such an increase in the productivity of labour in a particular sector alone is a poor indicator of generalized growth, since it might have occurred at a high cost in terms of fixed capital and imports.

Table 9.6   *Real per capita income (£ value for 1972) and population growth, 1964–76*

	1964	1968	1969	1970	1971	1972
GDP per capita (£)	43·2	49·8	49·5	51·4	52·2	54·6

	1973	1974	1975	1976	1977	1978
GDP per capita (£)	55·3	55·7	54·3	55·2	57·9	59·1

Sources: For GDP: *Statistical Abstract*, 1975, table 44(b); *Statistical Abstract*, 1977, table 45(b); *Economic Survey*, 1978; *Economic Survey*, 1979. For population growth: *Kenya Statistical Digest*, XV, 4, and XI, 2.

In fact this is precisely what has occurred in Kenya over the years. Accumulation in the industrial sector has taken place in plants which are of low productivity when compared to global productivity levels and which have required heavy protection. Hence even the heavy effective protection offered to the textile industry has had to be supplemented by import controls on so-called 'second-hand clothing',[8] at a significant cost to the consumer.[9] Similarly the decision to assemble commercial vehicles has not necessarily had the desired effect. In one case, that of Volkswagen microbuses, the foreign exchange costs of the kits even exceeded that of fully built-up vehicles.[10]

Industrialization in Kenya has therefore been of a heavily protected nature and has been paid for by consumers of non-food products, particularly in the rural areas, who for most of the period have suffered adverse terms of trade with the industrial sector (see Table 9.7), compared to those prevailing at independence in 1964. Taking into account the drain of surplus via the terms of trade, the channelling of savings through the banking network and state development expenditure in rural areas, Sharply (cited in Maitha, 1976) estimated a transfer of surplus from rural to urban areas of £49·6m. in 1964, rising to £123·4m. in 1974 and totalling £681·2m. in the period 1964–74.

Such industrialization was thus financed by modest gains in agricultural productivity, particularly in the 1960s. However, as Leys points out, increases in agricultural productivity have begun to tail off and it appears that whatever direction class formation in the countryside will take[11] two factors will limit

Table 9.7 *Price index for agricultural and non-agricultural products and domestic terms of trade between the two sectors, 1964–76*

Year	Weighted index of prices received by the agricultural sector for crops livestock and dairy products	Weighted index of non-agricultural prices paid by the agricultural sector for inputs and consumer items	Domestic terms of trade
	(1)	(2)	(3)
1964	100·0	100·0	100·0
1965	96·8	105·5	91·8
1966	99·0	108·7	91·0
1967	96·5	109·6	88·0
1968	95·4	110·1	86·7
1969	96·0	109·3	87·8
1970	103·0	110·7	93·1
1971	102·8	119·5	86·0
1972	117·6	126·1	93·2
1973	151·6	145·4	104·8
1974	151·9	179·2	84·8
1975	171·6	208·5	82·3
1976	254·0	224·5	113·1

Note:
The terms of trade in the third column are obtained by placing column 1 over column 2. If the terms of trade are less than 100 then the prices received by the agricultural sector have fallen more than those it buys; if the terms of trade are more than 100, then agricultural prices have risen *more* than the prices of inputs and manufactured goods.
Source: J. Sharpley, 'Terms of trade tables' (mimeo.), Nairobi, 1978.

further growth in the sector.[12] The first concerns the non-availability of good agricultural land with all suitable land now under cultivation. And second, perhaps more important, Kenya which until now has largely been self-suffi-cient in food production faces the future with the probability of ongoing and increasing deficits in food supply and demand. The trend growth in agricultural productivity has been lower than that of population growth with little likelihood that this relationship will be changed in the future.

The consequence of this discussion, therefore, is to place doubts upon the much-vaunted past economic performance of the Kenyan economy. Some limited structural transformation occurred between independence and the early 1970s, and was accompanied by a significant increase in per capita incomes. Since then real per capita incomes have stagnated and accumulation in industry has been financed by limited growth in agricultural productivity, balance-of-payments deficits and the temporary boom in coffee prices. However, now that coffee prices have fallen nearer to the long-run trend price and agricultural growth has begun to peter out, serious doubts must be placed on the long-run growth potential of the economy and the sustainable nature of protected industrialization and the consequent mode of accumulation. An indication of this has been the decreasing inflow of foreign investment with most new projects being joint ventures between machinery and service suppliers (who extract their surpluses in forms other than dividends) in joint ventures with parastatal agencies and development banks.

(b) THE INDIGENOUS INDUSTRIAL BOURGEOISIE IN KENYA

Leys points to the failure of his earlier analysis to foresee the emergence of an indigenous industrial bourgeoisie. This failure was said to arise from an analysis preoccupied with what was currently in existence. But the works of Swainson and the impressions gained in a recent visit to Kenya seem to have led Leys to accept that even if the indigenous industrial bourgeoisie is not yet fully formed, its emergence – in contradistinction to an 'auxiliary bourgeoisie' in alliance with foreign capital – is only a matter of time.

There are two important origins of such an indigenous industrial bour-geoisie. The first is from the pool of small, petty accumulators amongst whom may emerge the large-scale independent industrialists of the future. Of this group we have little to say, but merely remark that studies of such industrialists point to their very small-scale nature and their investment in technologies which show little scope for intensified accumulation, but expand extensively through replication (see Kaplinsky, 1975). The second source of future industrialists is from the group which is currently engaged in large-scale accumulation, assisted through links with the state and/or foreign capital. My comments on the existence of an indigenous industrial bourgeoisie are based on an analysis of this latter group of industrialists. (We address ourselves briefly to co-operative companies such as Gema at a later stage.)

Noting the dangers of linear extrapolation in a dynamic situation of class formation, we can proceed to an analysis of the characteristics of existing industrialists in large-scale enterprises. As pointed out earlier, the empirical information is drawn from a detailed study of ownership patterns in all large-scale manufacturing activities and all tourist firms operating in 1976. The source material was drawn from annual returns of such companies to the Companies Registrar in Sheria House, Nairobi. As part of these annual returns, each company is required to name all current directors, and to list all other companies of which they are directors.

In my study of these firms (of which, including information collected to determine ultimate ownership, I have detailed records of around 2,000 firms) the names of some individuals recurred. Basically these people can be divided into three different groups, namely:

(1) those of settler origin (e.g. the Block family, Madhavani, Chandaria, Sir Ernest Vasey, the Bellhouse family, M. W. Harley, etc.);

(2) indigenous Kenyans holding directorships purely on an *ex officio* basis (e.g. L. Kibinge, Permanent Secretary of the Ministry of Commerce and Industry);

(3) indigenous Kenyans holding directorships in firms in which they have an active interest, as well as in firms in which they act on an *ex officio* basis.

The undergoing analysis is based upon the third group of individuals. The information was obtained by chasing up the detailed ownership patterns of all firms in which they were listed as directors. From this information their activities are divided into firms in which they were directors without holding shares, and firms in which they also had a personal interest.[13]

Twelve accumulators of this sort (i.e. in category 3 above) emerged during the course of this study, and the details of their *ex officio* directorships and their directorships in firms in which they have personal holdings are shown in Tables 9.8(a), 9.8(b) and 9.9. In reviewing this list it is noticeable that:

(1) Most indigenous accumulators have links with foreign capital, even if we only consider the firms in which they have a direct stake. But even some of the accumulators who are not in joint ventures with foreign capital are linked through licensing agreements. For example, one of these produces a wide range of plastic articles under licence from various foreign firms.[14]

(2) As yet, with the exception of Ngengi Muigai and Udi Gecaga, the scale of these investments is modest.

(3) Only five of these accumulators have investments in more than one manufacturing firm. In Karume's case, this comprises holdings in two sawmills and shares in Tiger Shoe Co. (a company often characterized as being in conflict with foreign capital).[15] Matiba's manufacturing activities comprise two flower nurseries and a share in a construction company run by two ex-settlers. Wanjigi (a former head of the ICDC, the government's major parastal in manufacturing) has investments in three manufacturing firms – in two cases he has a very small shareholding (in Bata, a foreign firm, and in Carbacid, owned by ex-settlers) and in the third case is engaged in a joint venture with two other Kenyans, making concrete pipes. Once again only Gecaga and and Muigai stand out as having holdings in numerous industrial enterprises.

(4) Gecaga and Muigai are in a group apart. Both used close family relationships with Kenyatta to build their empires and amongst Kenyan industrialists Muigai is known as the political heavyweight and Gecaga as the shrewd businessman. Of the two, Muigai has distanced himself further from

Table 9.8(a) *Directorships without personal shareholding in firms predominately owned by indigenous and non-indigenous Kenyans, parastatals, foreign capital and public companies*

Directors	Total no. of firms	Indigenous Kenyans		Non-indigenous Kenyans		Parastatals		Foreign capital		Public companies	
		No.	Total equity K£	No.	Total equity K£	No.	Total equity K£	No.	Total equity K£	No.	Total equity K£
Justus K. Kalinga	2	1	2,500	1	10,000						
James Njenga Karume	3							1	30,000	3	655,000
Peter Muiga Kenyatta	4	2	105			1	66,000				
J. Matere Keriri	25			2	230,000	18	12,949,933	2	1,616,000		
Kenneth Stanley Njindo Matiba	12			5	467,000	4	520,000			7	13,000,000
Ngengi Muigai	4							4	n.a.		
Charles Njonjo	2			2	1,300			1	253,000	1	200,000
Dunstan Omari	29			7	484,477			19	9,819,362	1	12,342,983 about
Charles Wanyoike Rubia	8	3	2,717,000	1	2,000 about			2	850,000	3	15,000,000
James Maina Wanjigi	7			2	1,000,000			3	809,693	2	1,600,000
Francis Mwangi Thuo	5	2	n.a.			2	5,000	1	7,600		
Eliud Matu Wamae	57					57	32,274,341				
Udi Gecaga	24	2	189					22	14,282,101		

Note: For Tables 9.8(a), 9.8(b) and 9.9 total number of firms is lower than summation of individual column numbers due to fact that some firms are joint ventures between different categories of investors.

Table 9.8. (b) *Directorships with personal shareholding in firms predominantly owned by indigenous and non-indigenous Kenyans parastatals, foreign capital and public companies*

Directors	Total no. of firms	Nuclear Family			Indigenous Kenyans (non-family)			Non-indigenous Kenyans			Parastatals			Foreign Capital		
		No.	Total equity K£	Personal equity K£	No.	Total equity K£	Personal equity K£	No.	Total equity K£	Personal equity K£	No.	Total equity K£	Personal equity K£	No.	Total equity K£	Personal equity K£
Justus K. Kalinga	4	2	28	25	2	608	13,900				1	6,154	13,292			
James Njenga Karume	14	2	46,800	62,000	11	38,569	224,878									
Peter Muiga Kenyatta	15				6	30,822	460,899	6	2,416	9,435				2	2,575	52,500
J. Matere Keriri	0															
Kenneth Stanley Njindo Matiba	4	1	99	100	1	100	1,600	2	500	101,000						
Ngengi Muigai	18	1	99	100	9	768,500	7,279,029	2	913	5,493	4	115,480	1,064,000	4	905,882	3,800,362
Charles Njonjo	10							7	25,000	744,600				1	n.a.	53,500
Dunstan Omari	5				2	203	7,500	3	242	1,004						
Charles Wanyoike Rubia	4	1	4,000	5,000	2	3,350	16,000	1	1,000	25,000						
James Maina Wanjigi	12	4	1,003	1,007	4	16,651	52,624	2	11,008	1,008,002				1	2,240	5,600,000
Francis Mwangi Thuo	6				3	2,040	9,000	3	1,598	7,600						
Eliud Matu Wamae	8	3	8,002	8,004	2	1,110	25,020	1	6,750	15,000	1	3,480	60,000			
Udi Gecaga	11	5		520,100	2	6,000	35,000							4	1,650,000	5,063,671

Table 9.9 *Sectoral distribution of firms with personal shareholding.*

				SECTORS (Nos.)			
	Industry	Commerce	Services	Holding companies*	Transport	Farming	Unknown
Justus K. Kalinga	1	1	1	1			1
James Njenga Karume	3	2		2	6		2
Peter Muiga Kenyatta	1	3	4	2	2	2	1
J. Matere Keriri							
Kenneth Stanley Njindo Matiba	3	3		2	1		1
Ngengi Muigai	7			5		3	
Charles Njonjo	1	1		3	1	4	
Dunstan Omari			1	3			
Charles Wanyoike Rubia	1	1	2				1
James Maina Wanjigi	3	3	2			1	2
Francis Mwangi Thuo		2	2	2			
Eliud Matu Wamae	1	1	3	1	1		1
Udi Gecaga	4			7			

Note: *Holding companies are used to control investments in the other sectors included in this table.

foreign capital, and since his takeover of Mackenzie Kenya (from which he has subsequently been excluded) he has begun to expand his manufacturing interests. Gecaga, despite what is often believed, remains closely allied to Lonrho, as can be seen in his operation of an exclusive Lonrho technology to make a modern substitute for traditional beers (chibuku). Perhaps the best example of the alliance and close identity between these two accumulators and foreign capital is their joint investments in the new vehicle assembly plant in Mombasa (AVA). The state (through the Treasury and the Industrial Development Bank) holds a nominal majority equity (51%) in AVA, the remaining shares being held equally by Lonrho and a joint Gecaga–Muigai company. Real control over AVA is however held by the minority parties and is exercised through a technical services agreement with a Kenyan-registered firm representing Gecaga, Muigai, Inchcape and Lonrho. The function of this agreement (which provides comprehensive control over a complete range of decisions), was to take all decisions away from the board of directors.[16] Although it is too early to offer proof, it appears as if this control will be used to shift the realization of surplus away from the point of production (where profits have to be shared with the state) to distribution (where Lonrho, Gecaga and Muigai control all of the outlets) and possibly even in the purchasing of knocked-down kits where these three minority parties may act as intermediaries.

The point of discussing this example at great length is to illustrate that even the two most prominent indigenous accumulators are in very close alliance with foreign capital in a joint venture contracted in very recent years (1976–8).

Although the argument for the pre-eminence of a 'national bourgeoisie' does not necessarily preclude any links with foreign capital, the extensive links which these twelve industrialists have with foreign capital as well as their almost total reliance on foreign technology and market power makes it difficult to see them in such a pre-eminent position.

One further point needs to be made and this is that it is by no means certain that indigenous ownership will lead to local reinvestment, since there is an observed tendency for even local capitalists to repatriate surplus abroad. As the accountant of a large multinational accounting firm remarked of his clientele (comprising both foreign capital and indigenous capitalists), the indigenous capitalists were more guilty of 'transfer pricing' than the foreign subsidiaries. Furthermore, the evidence suggests (see Kaplinsky, 1980a) that the types of investments made by local capitalists are often indistinguishable from those made by foreign capital.

However, there is no doubt, as any discussions with aspirant indigenous industrialists will rapidly show, that there exists a very strong *desire* to supplant foreign capital. Moreover there are pockets in the state (e.g. the Central Bank and parts of the Ministry of Commerce and Industry) which offer clear support for these aspirations. What remains dubious is the extent to which such aspirations can be met. Although these are yet early days to reach a definitive viewpoint, the discussion which follows below on ownership, control and the role of the state will provide the reader with further insights.

(c) THE TRANSFER OF OWNERSHIP AND CONTROL FROM FOREIGN TO LOCAL CAPITAL

In discussing the extent to which ownership has been transferred from foreign to local capital over the years, I shall be drawing upon the study which I have undertaken for the NCCK and which was mentioned earlier. Readers who want to pursue the subject further can refer to the monograph itself – here I shall confine myself to the major conclusions of relevance. Before presenting the data – in which I shall, where feasible, distinguish between ownership and control – it is necessary to make a number of points. First, the data only refer to large-scale manufacturing (i.e. firms employing more than fifty workers) and all (small and large) tourist and hotel firms. As Leys points out, ownership of agriculture (except for some of the large estates) is now almost entirely indigenous,[17] as is much of small-scale industry and services. Second, in the data which are presented below 'Kenyan ownership' refers only to the place of residence of the ultimate owners and does not distinguish between citizens and non-citizens, nor between indigenous and non-indigenous citizens.[18] In calculating the place of residence of the owners I have worked my way through the various holding companies to determine the place of residence of the ultimate owners.[19] And third, in analysing the data on the 421 firms[20] operating in 1976, I have divided them into three groups, distinguishing between different sectors, size-groups and foreign-ownership groups.

(i) Ownership

The basic data on ownership, considered by sector and size group, are shown in Table 9.10. At first glance the overall conclusions seem to validate the assertion that there has been a transfer of ownership from foreign to local capital. The share of total issued capital owned by foreign residents plummeted dramatically between 1966 and 1976 from 59·3% to 42% and although there were some exceptions (e.g. in the wood, furniture, paper, printing and large tourist sectors), this pattern seemed to be common to most sectors and size-groups of firms.

In view of this decline in overall ownership held by foreign residents we might be tempted to conclude that because Kenyan residents owned more of the economy in 1976 than in 1966, they therefore had greater control over it. However, a more detailed look at the data on ownership points to a different conclusion. In Table 9.11 we break down the extent of foreign ownership into those firms where foreign residents controlled various proportions of the total issued capital. From this table we can note that one of the main reasons why the overall share of foreign ownership declined was because there was a very marked tendency of the wholly owned foreign subsidiaries to sell off a minority of their shares to local residents. Thus, whereas over three-quarters of foreign capital was in wholly owned subsidiaries in 1966, this proportion fell to less than half by 1976. However these firms seldom sold off more than 50% of their shares so that they have been able to keep control over their subsidiaries despite the respectability gained by selling off shares to local residents. Whereas 7·5% of foreign investment in 1966 was in firms controlled more than 50% by Kenyan residents, this actually fell slightly to 6·4% by 1976.

A more striking confirmation of this pattern emerges from Table 9.12. The

Table 9.10 Foreign ownership of a large-scale manufacturing and of all tourist firms, 1966–76.

Type of firm	1966			1976			Growth of total issued capital 1966–1976 %	Growth of foreign owned issued capital 1966–1976 %
	Total issued capital K£	Total foreign owned issued capital K£	% of issued capital foreign owned	Total issued capital K£	Total foreign owned issued capital K£	% of issued capital foreign owned		
(a) By industry								
Food, beverages	14,876,072	7,250,526	48·7	45,863,454	13,253,442	28·9	308	183
Textiles, leather	2,150,727	1,223,597	56·9	14,849,560	8,393,968	56·5	690	686
Wood, furniture	435,660	5,000	1·2	1,264,697	189,546	15·0	290	3,791
Paper, printing	528,486	5,291	1·0	8,104,734	3,279,144	40·5	1,534	61,976
Chemicals, rubber	8,628,955	7,698,132	89·2	19,121,916	13,607,520	71·2	222	177
Pottery, glass	2,241,450	1,126,352	50·3	2,337,000	1,036,980	44·4	104	92
Basic metals	300,004	100,003	33·3	2,100,000	571,725	27·2	700	572
Fabricated metal products	1,814,776	1,154,340	63·6	8,713,301	4,438,560	50·9	480	385
Other manufacturing	103,770	73,614	70·9	443,008	143,459	32·4	427	195
Total manufacturing	31,079,540	18,636,831	60·0	44,914,116	19,627,468	43·7	331	241
Large tourist	785,190	13,181	1·7	7,709,327	2,017,287	26·2	982	15,305
Small tourist	51,015	n.a.	n.a.	1,366,281	2	0·0	2,678	n.a.
(b) By size of issued capital (K£)								
1–99	66	6	9·1	115	6	5·2	174	100
100–999	3,762	987	26·2	4,760	539	11·3	127	55
1,000–9,999	240,460	30,325	12·6	307,650	27,980	9·1	128	92
10,000–49,999	1,690,013	481,869	28·5	2,258,508	387,032	17·1	134	80
50,000–199,999	5,000,130	2,629,740	52·6	12,331,231	4,246,753	34·4	247	162
200,000–999,900	10,330,875	5,574,177	5·4	33,407,599	15,409,875	46·1	323	277
Over 1,000,000	14,173,740	9,932,896	70·1	63,562,890	26,859,127	42·3	449	270
TOTAL	31,439,046	18,650,000	59·3	111,872,750	46,931,312	42	355·8	251·6

Table 9.11 *Breakdown of foreign ownership by its share in each firm, 1966–76.*

Foreign ownership group	Foreign owned issued capital (£K)	% share of total	Foreign owned issued capital	% share of total
1–10	35,439	0·2	225,002	0·5
11–25	96,847	0·5	550,104	1·0
26–50	1,260,140	6·8	2,186,028	4·9
51–95	3,012,504	16·2	21,584,140	48·0
96–100	14,192,912	76·3	20,419,036	45·4
TOTAL	18,597,842	100·0	44,964,310	100·0

information in this table concerns all these firms (of which there were 263) which operated in both 1966 and 1976. The table shows that whereas 59·3% of all these firms were wholly Kenyan-owned in 1966, this percentage fell to 50% in 1976, and while 68·8% were majority Kenyan-owned in 1966, this figure fell to 64·6% in 1976. In fact more firms changed from majority Kenyan to majority foreign ownership (that is, twenty) than from majority foreign to majority Kenyan ownership (that is, nine between 1966 and 1976)!

Given the fact that the bulk of foreign investment (by value) moved from wholly foreign-owned to majority foreign-owned (see Table 9.11), the results in Table 9.12 suggest that at the same time some of the smaller foreign firms increased their holdings from majority to wholly foreign ownership in the same period.

Thus it appears as if the increased share of the large-scale industrial and the tourist economy owned by Kenyan residents seems to arise because of the establishment of new (small) firms by Kenyan residents, because many of the larger wholly foreign-owned firms sold off a small proportion of their shares to local residents and because of advances in ownership by parastatals. In those cases where firms existed in both 1966 and 1976 the share held by foreign firms (especially if we consider only the controlling interest) actually seemed to *increase* between 1968 and 1976. Moreover, if we were to open up the 'Kenyan resident' category we would undoubtedly find that a great number

Table 9.12 *Cumulative number and percentage of firms operating in both 1966 and 1976 in different foreign-ownership groups (number of such firms is 263)*

Share of equity held by foreign residents	1966		1976	
	No.	%	No.	%
0	156	59·3	132	50·0
0–10	163	62·0	142	54·0
0–25	166	63·1	152	57·8
0–50	181	68·8	170	64·6
0–95	200	76·0	197	74·9
100	63	24·0	66	25·1

of these were non-citizens and that many of the citizens were of non-indigenous origin. An indication of this is that whereas only 13·7% of total issued capital in 1976 was British-based, 31·9% of the total number of directors were British citizens. And, further, a very large (although unspecified) share of Kenyan-based investment was accounted for by state and parastatal institutions (see Leys and Borges, 1979), thereby further reducing the ultimate share of ownership accounted for by the indigenous industrial bourgeoisie. While it is difficult to conclude that the share of foreign ownership has increased over the decade, it is equally difficult to concur with Leys and Swainson that there has been a significant transfer of ownership from foreign capital to the indigenous bourgeoisie in large-scale manufacturing and tourism. At best one can conclude that little overall change occurred in the time-period.

(ii) Control

Of course ownership is not identical to control. In fact there are many reasons to believe that control is of greater relevance than ownership, since it determines the rate and nature of accumulation and the distribution of surplus. I have already given an example (footnote 19) to illustrate this point – and could give more, if necessary. But here I wish to make the generalization that foreign capital tends to command a greater degree of control over large-scale manufacturing and tourism than its share of ownership.[21] Table 9.13 offers further support for this generalization and from it we can see that if we consider the citizenship of the majority of directors as a proxy for control, almost a third of all large-scale manufacturing and service firms were majority-controlled by foreign citizens despite being majority-owned by Kenyan residents. Although some of this is accounted for by the fact that many Kenyan residents are foreign citizens, undoubtedly some cases include firms which are of the type being discussed. There was a limited advance in the proportion of firms owned and 'controlled' by Kenyan nationals, but the great majority of these firms were smaller, locally owned enterprises.[22]

In summary, then, the evidence available does not appear to support the hypothesis that there has been a significant shift of ownership (let alone

Table 9.13   *Ownership and 'control', 1966–76**

	Number		Percentage	
	1966	1976	1966	1976
Kenya-owned, Kenya-controlled	67	187	30·9	43·1
Kenya-owned, foreign-controlled	72	125	33·2	28·8
Foreign-owned, Kenya-controlled	13	21	6·0	4·8
Foreign-owned, foreign-controlled	65	101	30·0	23·3
TOTAL	217	434	100·0	100·0

Note: * 'Control' is defined in terms of nationality of majority of directions.

control) from foreign capital to an indigenous industrial bourgeoisie, although there seems to be a trend towards the establishment of new Kenyan-owned and controlled enterprises and an advance in parastatal participation.

(d) THE STATE AS AN INSTRUMENT OF THE INDIGENOUS INDUSTRIAL BOURGEOISIE

The fourth hypothesis which can be drawn out of the re-evaluation of the Kenyan case by Leys and others concerns the role of the state. While Leys (1975) and Langdon (1976) had characterized the state as harmonizing the alliance between foreign capital and the 'auxiliary bourgeoisie',[23] the re-evaluation characterizes the state as being an instrument used by the indigenous bourgeoisie to squeeze out foreign capital.[24]

The state, of course, is not an homogeneous entity. In my experience, the 'national' interest is most clearly articulated by the Central Bank and by middle-level officers in most ministries and parastatals (a subject to which we shall return later). But the important point is to note which faction prevails when conflicts arise in actions to be taken by the state. I wish to give four examples to support my contention that the state shows little evidence of taking an antagonistic stance to foreign capital, all of which have occurred in the recent post-1975 period, when it is argued that the capital acquired through primitive accumulation via charcoal and ivory, and latterly through coffee, removed the capital constraint faced by the indigenous bourgeoisie in supplanting foreign capital (see, Leys, Chapter 8).

(i) The Gema–Fiat joint venture

Leys identifies mass investment companies such as Gema Holdings as being one instrument enabling the extension of the indigenous industrial bourgeoisie, and he points to a joint venture with Fiat as an example of this. In actual fact this example supports an entirely different conclusion. In the post-1973 period the state decided to encourage the local assembly of commercial vehicles and after considering a number of proposals, three projects were agreed. One was a joint venture between Leyland (45%), the Treasury (35%) and a local public company distributing these vehicles (20%); the second was between General Motors (49%) and the ICDC (51%); and the third between the Treasury (26%), the IDB (25%) and Lonrho/Inchcape/Gecaga/Muigai, the latter group representing the distributors. Finding itself excluded from a market in which it had a significant share (and which showed the potential for future growth), Fiat selected what it thought to be a very powerful local partner (Gema Holdings)[25] in an attempt to press its right to assemble vehicles. However, despite the undoubtedly powerful support of Gema Holdings, the three existing MNCs in alliance with equally powerful local interests allied to foreign capital (i.e. Gecaga and Muigai) eventually managed to crush the bid by Fiat–Gema Holdings. In this case the alliance between foreign capital and the 'auxiliary bourgeoisie' managed to halt the bid by local capital, in so far as it was represented by Gema Holdings, a group hitherto not in alliance with any foreign capital.

(ii) ICDC-Firm X

There existed a widespread (and almost certainly correct) view in the early 1970s that profits were being transfer-priced out of Kenya through the use of management, technical service and other contracts. As a consequence a 20% withholding tax was placed upon all such fees on the assumption that half of these service fees were bogus (corporate tax being about 40%).

When X negotiated its joint venture with ICDC, it requested that this provision be removed, since it claimed that the service fees covered real costs and it was illegitimate to tax these. The Central Bank refused this request. X then approached ICDC, its joint venture partners, and ICDC intervened on its behalf. After a long tussle between the ICDC and the Central Bank[26] the issue was ultimately decided in X's favour and no taxes were levied on its service payments.

(iii) ICDC loans

The ICDC is the largest parastatal in the industrial and service sectors and is constituted under the Ministry of Commerce and Industry. Broadly speaking the ICDC is subdivided into two different operations, its small loan schemes offering loans for small-scale industry, commerce and property, and the large-scale ventures, where ICDC is in partnership with foreign capital and (in a few isolated cases) with local public companies.

In 1975 the state faced an acute budgetary crisis and expenditure in all ministries was limited severely. Faced with the decision to cut expenditure, the ICDC stopped all loans to small-scale enterprises (almost all of whom were of indigenous origin) and continued its investments in joint ventures with foreign capital unabated.

(iv) Loans to foreign capital

As mentioned earlier, the Central Bank repeatedly took a more 'national' line than other parts of the state system. In an attempt to increase the net foreign exchange inflow from foreign investment the Central Bank has over the past decade consistently attempted to limit the ability of foreign firms to borrow locally, although the precise percentages allowed have varied over the years.

Two factors have diminished the effectiveness of this policy. The first is that the Central Bank has only had the ability to restrict borrowing from local commercial banks. In response many foreign firms have borrowed from the parastatal banks such as the IDB, the DFCK and the EADB. A glance at the annual reports of these institutions (as well as that of the ICDC) will show extensive loans to foreign subsidiaries. The second factor limiting the success of this policy has been the tendency for exceptions to be made, particularly when parastatals and ministries have intervened in support of foreign capital.

Evidence that the policy to limit loans to foreign capital has failed can be seen from Table 9.14 which provides information on the debt/equity ratios of different foreign-ownership groups in large-scale manufacturing and all tourist firms. As can be seen there is no evidence of decreased gearing as the share of foreign ownership increased, and indeed regression analysis confirmed that

Table 9.14 Debt equity ratios of large-scale manufacturing and all tourist firms 1966–76*

Type of firm	Total debt		Average debt		Debt equity	
	1966	1976	1966	1976	1966	1976
(a) By industry						
Food, beverages	1,406,619	7,856,908	25,118	100,730	3·1	0·8
Textiles, leather	1,005,093	6,896,895	38,657	153,264	10·0	3·3
Wood, furniture	101,070	1,321,318	7,219	34,772	0·1	1·1
Paper, printing	114,235	4,154,497	9,520	188,841	21·9	409·7
Chemicals, rubber	734,882	4,085,467	19,862	64,849	0·3	20·3
Pottery, glass	309,987	8,432,501	20,666	281,083	0·2	2·6
Basic metals	0	1,533,853	0	306,771	0·0	0·6
Fabricated metal products	515,113	4,856,810	14,718	78,336	0·3	2·02
Other manufacturing	3,338	174,252	556	19,361	5·6	1·0
Large tourist	n.a.	n.a.	n.a.	n.a.	770·0	67·2
Small tourist	n.a.	n.a.	n.a.	n.a.	1,029·0	1·2
(b) By size of issued capital (£)						
1–99	0	4,850	0	970	0·0	1,513·0
100–999	36,626	1,027,419	2,442	85,618	19·3	2,113·0
1,000–9,999	744,627	1,021,468	15,197	17,313	7·7	6·8
10,000–49,999	726,599	3,825,398	12,315	43,470	1·2	3·3
50,000–199,999	1,597,584	6,131,238	42,042	63,867	0·4	1·4
200,000–999,999	508,120	18,431,156	17,521	259,594	0·1	1·4
Over 1,000,000	576,782	8,870,973	82,397	422,427	0·1	0·3
(c) By share of foreign ownership (£)						
0	1,341,834	14,651,144	13,977	73,996	142·2	2·6
1–10	183,329	2,600,009	30,555	236,365	1·7	2·1
11–25	20,000	2,710,758	6,667	301,195	0·03	3·3
26–50	961,097	2,900,065	87,373	170,592	0·3	146·5
51–95	393,956	12,297,619	17,129	351,361	1·7	1·2
96–100	987,837	3,686,236	17,331	50,496	6·9	123·0
TOTAL	4,190,338	39,312,502	19,673	111,683	74·6	34·0

Note: *Debt equity ratios for each group are the average of these ratios for each firm and not a group's total debt divided by its total equity.

the gearing ratios of wholly foreign-owned firms (i.e. over 95%) were *significantly higher* than average.

No doubt these four examples do not provide conclusive evidence that the state is closely allied with foreign capital. However, they do each illustrate that there is evidence that despite the representation of the 'national' position in some parts of the state apparatus, there are many cases of significance where the position of foreign capital has won out over that of local capital. Even if this segment of the state were to predominate, it is not clear whether this would reflect a tendency to supplant foreign capital (as Leys and Swainson argue) or to squeeze out a larger share of the surplus, perhaps for an 'insider faction' as Langdon argued. And, moreover, these examples are drawn from the most recent time-period during which the state is supposed to have become more closely allied to the position of the indigenous bourgeoisie. Thus the state remains a 'soft touch' as a joint venture partner. Whereas the declared past tax rate of return for local public companies was around 14% between 1966 and 1976, and that for foreign companies was over 30%, the Treasury currently has a rate of return of only 5% on its investments in joint ventures in large-scale industry.

(e) SUCCESSFUL CAPITALIST ACCUMULATION WILL CONTINUE

In (a) above I argued that the evidence suggests that the significant economic growth of the 1960s began to taper off in the 1970s. The accumulation which had occurred in large-scale industry had been 'inefficient' when compared to global standards and required a very high protection. It had been financed by growth in agricultural productivity in the 1960s (through the terms of trade), foreign loans, balance-of-payments deficits and (temporarily) the boom in coffee prices.

But, as was pointed out, accumulation of this type faces severe, if not overwhelming, difficulties. The pattern of import substituting industrialization makes very inefficient use of foreign exchange and the underlying deepening deficit in the balance of payments is drawing the process to a halt. Moreover there are strong grounds to believe (as Leys acknowledges) that the scope for further growth in agricultural productivity is limited so that continued accumulation will almost certainly require reductions in rural consumption and in that of urban labour. As it is, real wages in large-scale industry fell between 1966 and 1977 (Kaplinsky, forthcoming), and it is an open question how much further they can decline without disturbing Kenya's political 'tranquillity'.

Although it is notoriously difficult to predict future rates of growth, barring windfalls such as the discovery of oil or a sustained boom in coffee or tea prices, it is only possible to envisage continued accumulation of this type in Kenya if there is rapid growth in manufactured exports. This will not only ease the balance-of-payments problems, but by enabling fuller capacity utilization and through the discipline of the international market, will allow for greater efficiency in production. Leys asserts that a successful breakthrough has been made. But the evidence certainly does not bear this out (see Tables 9.3 and 9.4) and conversations I have had with Keta (Kenya External Trade Authority) confirm a rather pessimistic view on this front. Although a new export processing zone is being established and although some success has been made in enticing an Italian textile firm to this estate, future prospects for manufactured exports look bleak. It is significant therefore that the new five-year plan recognizes the limitations to this type of economic growth and places great emphasis on the development of small-scale industry, involving different fractions of capital than that hitherto involved and discussed in the above sections.

III

Let us return to the basic issue under discussion. Palma (1979) points to at least two major and divergent viewpoints in Marxist-inspired theories of under-development. The first argues that the spread of the capitalist mode of production to the periphery is inevitable and that sustainable industrial accumulation will occur in much of the periphery as a consequence. The second and opposing view is that it is in the nature of capitalist accumulation at the world level that sustainable industrial accumulation in the periphery is most unlikely, if not impossible.

Leys responds to these generalized positions by asserting that there is no *a priori* evidence that such accumulation at the periphery is impossible. If the subject is to be discussed sensibly, he argues, it is important to consider the particularities of individual countries, paying attention to the indigenous origins of capitalist classes. He, and others, point to the Kenyan case as an illustration that sustained accumulation has occurred in at least one peripheral economy and that this is only explicable if one considers the indigenous roots of the accumulating class. Moreover, despite caveats,[27] both Leys and Swainson imply that this pattern of accumulation will continue, at least in the short and medium term.

I have tried to respond to Leys's very stimulating reassessment of an earlier position (which I believe is the correct one) by examining the Kenyan case in great detail. The extension of capitalist relations of production is not challenged. But I am more sceptical as to the past performance and sustainable nature of accumulation and in the extent to which indigenous capitalists have been able to squeeze out foreign ones. In particular, I have tried to identify five hypotheses to this latter argument and, after examining the evidence, I am drawn to the conclusion that this reassessment is not supportable. More specifically, I believe that the evidence does not support the contentions that:

(1)   there has been sustained economic growth in Kenya;
(2)   an independent indigenous industrial bourgeoisie exists;
(3)   this bourgeoisie has squeezed out foreign capital in manufacturing and tourism;
(4)   the state has assumed an antagonistic position towards foreign capital;[28]
(5)   sustainable accumulation in large-scale industry will continue in the future at historic rates.

But what does all this have to say about the general possibilities for successful industrial accumulation at the periphery? In my view one must distinguish between three types of peripheral economies,[29] namely:

(1) large ones with sizeable internal markets (e.g. India);
(2) labour processing economies (e.g. Taiwan, Singapore);
(3) small, non-oil producing economies (e.g. Kenya).

In so far as the Kenyan case can be generalized, I believe it shows that the possibilities for successful accumulation in an open economy of this type are limited whatever the historical roots of the accumulating class. While the subject obviously bears further extended discussion, it is my view that the pattern of accumulation in such economies is significantly conditioned by the nature of global accumulation and their interspersion in that global process. Economies of the first type may yet exhibit sustainable accumulation as they are able to insulate themselves from the global market. Moreover, because of the large size of their internal markets, the scale of production may be large enough to support the growth of an indigenous technological capability and even for the export of capital goods to other peripheral economies (Lall, 1979).

More debatable, however, are the prospects of these peripheral economies which have seen rapid rates of industrial and manufactured export growth over the past two decades. It is these newly industrializing economies (such as South Korea, Taiwan, Singapore and Hong Kong) which have largely led Warren [1973], Leys and others to argue that peripheral economies are capable of extended economic growth through the development of their manufacturing sectors. But before their 'success' is generalized to other peripheral economies, it is necessary to query if the industrialization of these economies was not the consequence of a particular phase in the development of latter-day capitalism. Clearly this is in itself an important debate and deserves fuller treatment – here we shall only sketch out one possible line of argument (see also Kaplinsky 1980b).

The first two decades after the Second World War were a period of reconstruction. In all major industrial economies effective demand exceeded available supply. Then towards the mid-1960s the increasing economies of scale in production, allied with a growing ability of 'national' firms to meet home demand, led to the interpenetration of 'national' capitals and the expansion of MNCs. Not only did trade grow rapidly, but so too did foreign investment which grew from $256 million in 1951 to $180 billion in 1976.

Global competition became increasingly severe, particularly in the case of the rapid penetration of the US market by the more efficient Japanese and European firms. Faced with this competition US capital (initially, and then followed by competitors) began to locate parts of its production in low-wage economies. However, this was always only a temporary expedient and such defensive foreign investments were rapidly met and overcome by competitors, many of whom also located parts of the production process in labour processing zones in peripheral economies.

Partly for these reasons the 1970s ended on a note of increasing structural unemployment. Of the major industrial economies, only the US economy had more workers in manufacturing in 1979 than in 1971. The result has been, and undoubtedly will increasingly be, that there will be pressures towards import controls in these industrial economies and for various reasons (see Kaplinsky, 1979) it is likely that these import controls will fall unevenly against peripheral economies and against indigenously owned firms in these economies.

For these reasons it is possible that the phenomenon of manufactured export led growth, which underlies much of the Warren and latter-Leys position, will be a phenomenon of the past two decades. Peripheral accumulation will therefore have to depend largely upon internal markets and in so far as productivity continues to be closely associated with scale, then accumulation in small import substituting industrializing economies can only occur at the expense of income transfers within these economies. I have argued in earlier sections that increasingly there will be limits to such income transfers in Kenya. It is not equally likely that this will be true of other small peripheral economies?

Finally, to observe, as I believe I have, that the arguments of Leys and Swainson do not disprove the conclusions of the dependency school does not automatically lend credence to cruder formulations of dependency theory which argue, or imply, that classes in peripheral economies are solely formed through interaction with the global economy. Clearly this is incorrect. But, I believe, there is strong evidence to argue that whatever the roots of such classes, their future development is circumscribed by the relation of the particular economy to the global economy. More specifically in relation to Kenya, I believe that the evidence shows that although an indigenous capitalist class has managed to carve out a slice of the benefits arising from accumulation in large-scale industry, this has arisen from an alliance between this class and foreign capital. Not only does little prospect emerge for indigenous capital to squeeze out foreign capital but the inbuilt contradictions of economies of this type make it difficult to foresee that such a pattern of accumulation – with or without foreign capital – can proceed in a viable form.

In conclusion, a note of caution is perhaps most relevant. Although the evidence for Kenya seems to me to be relatively unambiguous, capitalism is an ever-changing phenomenon. It may well be that despite this period of stagnation in the 1970s and despite the evident failure of the indigenous bourgeoisie to supplant foreign capital in the fifteen years since independence, we will yet see sustainable accumulation of a similar type in Kenya, dominated by an indigenous industrial bourgeoisie. But, I believe, the evidence points the other way.

Notes

I am grateful to Manfred Bienefeld, David Evans, Martin Godfrey, Reg Green and Robin Murray for their comments upon an earlier draft. Since this chapter was written a number of events have occurred which reinforce its conclusions. Notably these have been a dramatic crisis in the balance of payments and a consequent reduction in the squeezing of foreign investment, the exclusion of Muigai from the control of Mackenzie Kenya, and Gecaga from the chairmanship of Lonrho Kenya, and in the importation of a significant proportion of Kenya's food needs. Although this importation of food reflects two bad climatic seasons, there has been a secular decline in agricultural productivity growth over the past decade and food self-sufficiency in the 1980s seems unlikely.

1   See the list of these works in note 22 of Chapter 8 in this volume.

2   Although it is not clear from Ley's characterization whether the point Cowen makes is that there always has been differentiation in Kenyan society or whether the roots of specific members of the new indigenous bourgeoisie can be traced back to pre-colonial times.

3   The word 'independent' should not be taken to mean that this indigenous bourgeoisie has no dependent links with foreign capital and technology, for such absolute independence is unlikely, even in economies with a vigorous, accumulating indigenous bourgeoisie such as Japan. It should rather be seen in its relativist sense, implying an ability to maintain accumulation independently from foreign capital and with some significant measure of indigenous technological capability.

4   For a discussion of the changes in the Kenyan economy see ch. 2 in R. Kaplinsky (forthcoming). Information is given in that study for most years between 1964 and 1977, some of which has been excluded in the following analysis for ease of presentation. Readers are referred to the above study for the fuller details.

5   Of course accumulation need not necessarily be limited to the industrial sector. But I draw these trends out since the analyses of Leys and Swainson lean heavily upon the emergence of an indigenous bourgeoisie in this sector, particularly in large scale manufacturing.

6   Which frequently exceeded declared profits, particularly in joint ventures with parastatal organizations. An evaluation of the private firm monitoring transfer pricing suggested that, if anything, the cost of its services substantially exceeded the resultant savings in foreign exchange.

7   Over these two time-periods the middle-income price index increased by 10%.

8   Which were, in fact, brand new clothes imported from Hong Kong.

9   For example, according to the Integrated Rural Survey, rural consumers spend about 17% of their total incomes on clothing. The ban on the import of 'second-hand clothing' more than doubled the cost to the consumer. Hence this act of protection alone reduced total rural incomes by more than 8%!

10 Although this may have been due, in part, to pricing policies by Volkswagen.

11 Leys sees the powerful place of 'middle peasant household production in agriculture' as an obstacle to growth in agriculture.

12 I am grateful to David Feldman for pointing out these two factors.

13 I do not pretend that this is a complete set of all their personal holdings. But, since they arise from an investigation of the ownership of all tourist and large-scale manufacturing firms in 1976, I believe that it includes their major industrial holdings and a large proportion of their significant non-industrial and non-agricultural holdings.

14 In one case this comprises a licence to produce toothbrushes with a European firm. The royalties (at 10% of net sales with a minimum fee) are more onerous than almost all royalty agreements between foreign firms and their Kenyan subsidiaries (usually less than 5% of net sales). Moreover the agreement specifies minimum expenditures on marketing (of which 25% goes to the Norwegian firm as a 'marketing service fee') and provides for comprehensive control over production, machine inputs and marketing by the foreign firm. Hardly a sign of an 'independent accumulator'!

15 In reality, however, as Langdon points out, the state has played a very careful role in mediating between Tiger Shoes and Bata, allowing each to corner a different segment of the large market.

16 Partly because the minority parties were concerned that firm-specific information would be passed on to competitors through government representatives who sat on the boards of all three vehicle assembling firms.

17 Although Njonjo, (1978), provides evidence that significant landholdings remain in non-indigenous hands, much of that resident abroad.

18 A constraint imposed upon us by the nature of the information filed in a company's annual returns.

19 For example the *Standard* newspaper is wholly owned by a Kenyan public firm, Consolidated Holdings. However 50·3% of Consolidated Holdings was owned by Lonrho (and the remainder by local residents). The 'foreign' share of the *Standard* is thus calculated as 50·3%. In other cases it was necessary to go through numerous

holding companies – thus we have information for over 2,000 firms, although only 421 fit into the category of 'large-scale manufacturing and tourism'.

20 The totals in the various categories, however, do not always add up to 421 since the data for all firms were not complete.

21 For example, as we saw in the case of the *Standard* newspaper above, although 49% of equity is locally owned, foreign control is absolute. Moreover, even where foreign control is in a minority, but in a public firm owned by a large number of small-scale investors, the interests of foreign capital may yet prevail over local capital.

22 Thus although wholly Kenyan-owned firms accounted for 60% of the total number of firms in the sample, they represented only 37% of total issued capital.

23 Langdon, in particular, extended the argument to illustrate how this included an appropriation of part of the surplus by members of the state apparatus as well.

24 Thereby, in the view of Leys, not falling into the trap of characterizing the state as being relatively autonomous.

25 Gema Holdings (the Gikuyu, Embu and Meru Association) is often cited as the prime expression of the interests of the indigenous bourgeoisie.

26 During which X offered estimates of future service payments which were subsequently exceeded by a significant factor in each of the first two years of operation!

27 Particularly in Ley's recent paper to the Canadian Political Science Association.

28 In fact I believe that Leys, Swainson and others are reacting to an identifiable hostility to foreign capital (and some aspects of its 'culture') which is prevalent in Kenya. In my experience these views are predominantly held by middle-level civil servants and small-scale industrialists in competition with foreign subsidiaries. In both cases these two groups have not gained directly from the prominent position held by foreign capital in the Kenyan economy.

29 These are merely types, of course, and individual economies may have particular differences such as those conditioned by geographical and strategic factors.

References

A. Emmanuel (1974) 'Myths of development versus myths of underdevelopment', *New Left Review* 85.

A. G. Frank (1969) *Capitalism and Underdevelopment in Latin America* (New York: Monthly Review Press).

R. Kaplinsky (1975) *An Analysis of ICDC Small Industrial Loan Commitments* (Nairobi: Institute of Development Studies, Working Paper No. 251).

R. Kaplinsky (1979) 'The impact of microelectronics technology on LDC exports of manufactures to DCs' (mimeo.), Brighton.

R. Kaplinsky (1980a) 'Inappropriate products and techniques: the case of breakfast cereals in Kenya', *Review of African Political Economy*, 14.

R. Kaplinsky (1980b) 'Microelectronics and the Third World' (mimeo.), Brighton.

R. Kaplinsky (forthcoming) *Ownership and Equity in Kenya, 1966–1976* (Nairobi: NCCK).

S. Lall (1979) 'Developing countries as exporters of technology and capital goods' (mimeo.), Oxford.

S. Langdon (1976) 'Multinational corporations in the political economy of Kenya', D.Phil. thesis, University of Sussex (published by Macmillan in 1980).

C. Leys (1975) *Underdevelopment in Kenya: The Political Economy of Neo-Colonialism* (London: Heinemann Educational Books).

C. Leys with J. Borges (1979) 'State capitalism in Kenya', paper prepared for the annual meeting of the Canadian Political Science Association, Saskatoon, 30 May – 1 June.

J. K. Maitha (1976) 'The Kenyan economy', in J. Heyer *et al.*, *Agricultural Development in Kenya: An Economic Assessment*, (Nairobi: Oxford University Press).

NCCK (1968) *Who Controls Industry in Kenya?* (Nairobi: East African Publishing House).

A. Njonjo (1978) 'The Africanization of the "white Highlands': a study in agrarian class struggles in Kenya, 1950–1974', PhD thesis, Princeton University.

G. Palma (1979) 'Underdevelopment and Marxism: from Marx to the theories of imperialism and dependency', *Thames Papers in Political Economy* (NE London Polytechnic).

N. Swainson (1977) 'The rise of a national bourgeoisie in Kenya', *Review of African Political Economy*, 8.

N. Swainson (1980) *The Development of Corporate Capitalism in Kenya 1918–77* (London: Heinemann Educational Books).

B. Warren (1973) 'Imperialism and capitalist industrialization', *New Left Review*, 81.

10 Discussion Note on Chapter 9

JOHN S. HENLEY

Kaplinsky's chapter 'Capitalist accumulation in the periphery: Kenya' attempts to correct Colin Leys's deviation from his previous commitment to dependency theory expounded in his book *Underdevelopment in Kenya*. While Leys's book undoubtedly remains the outstanding account of the development of the post-colonial political economy of Kenya, it is not without its faults. In particular, Leys's formulation of the development process in Kenya in that book would seem excessively externally determined. His recent retreat (see Chapter 8) from a position of denying any autonomy to local Kenyan interests to one of recognizing the potential of the indigenous bourgeoisie for independent capital accumulation might appear an unexceptional adjustment to his original model. However, while Leys's book upset many of Kenya's admirers with its portrayal of Kenya as an economy run by a clique of self-seeking and parasitic compradors, his new line seems to have offended at least one Kenya watcher with a longstanding interest in its industrialization policies.

Certainly I share Kaplinsky's concern that Leys may have been over-reacting to the specific and unusual set of economic conditions prevailing in Kenya during 1977 when he returned to Kenya to review his earlier work. At that time, Kenyans were making huge fortunes out of smuggling large quantities of coffee from Uganda where the marketing system had collapsed, and reselling on the booming international market. It was said that 'red monkey disease' caught from counting large quantities of the maroon one hundred Kenya shilling denomination banknotes was endemic amongst certain groups. A vast informal market grew up over night at Chebkube on the Kenya border to sell Uganda coffee traders commodities available for Kenyan currency but unavailable in a Uganda starved of even the barest necessities. During a few short months primitive accumulation occurred at a truly prodigious rate though eventually world coffee prices fell back. Kenyan coffee was adulterated with inferior Ugandan varieties by the unscrupulous, and price inflation, the result of the enormous expansion of the money supply, forced the government to react to curb the 'boom'. While no doubt the heady atmosphere of the summer of 1977 brought on by the removal of Kenya's perennial foreign exchange constraint stimulated much loose talk of indigenous entrepeneurial activity, I am not sure that Kaplinsky's evidence refutes Leys's change of position. Leys is a good deal more cautious about the 'systematical combination of moments' than Kaplinsky gives him credit for.

First, his representation of Leys's argument seriously oversimplifies its logical structure. In particular, he completely excludes Cowen's work from his critique, despite Leys's acknowledgement of this work as the starting point of his own new line. The central argument Cowen advances is that present-day modes of capital accumulation amongst the Kikuyu bourgeoisie have their roots firmly located in pre-colonial Kenya. They have developed from those roots by adjusting and reacting to obstacles to accumulation through political action. While Cowen admits that one of the functions of the post-colonial state has been to mediate between foreign capital and local interests, he argues this is not its sole function for its political base is founded on the interests of local accumulators. As Leys observes:

'In noting the important role of the state in facilitating this movement of African capital out of circulation and into production we must avoid the mistake of attributing to it an independent role. Its initiatives reflected the existing class power of the indigenous bourgeoisie, based on the accumulation of capital they had already achieved.(p. 180)

To refute the proposition that an industrial bourgeoisie now exists in Kenya, it is necessary to demonstrate the lack of indigenous accumulation through industrial production. Kaplinsky claims to show no profound change in the economic structure even though Leys only suggests a trend in terms of concentration 'in sufficient volume and in appropriate form for industrial investment'. Nevertheless, Kaplinsky's Table 9.8(b) reveals that two of his chosen twelve accumulators have amassed £K1·8m. and £K1·6m. respectively – hardly a poor performance given that they were both still at university when Kenya attained independence! Even so, Kaplinsky only looks at equity shares in industry and tourism; he ignores asset values, turnover and profits attributable to shareholders – surely more reliable indicators of accumulation of wealth?

His indicators of structural change are so aggregated as to be insensitive to the kinds of changes Leys is suggesting. For example, he argues that an increase in government expenditure does not represent an extension of capitalist relations of production. Perhaps this is correct but with respect to an avowedly capitalist economy the onus of proof must lie with Kaplinsky to demonstrate that schooling and health expenditure does not improve productive forces and strengthen capitalist accumulation. His Table 9.4 seems to be constructed to present Kenya's balance of payments in the worst possible light, since both 1965 and 1977 were exceptional, for in these years Kenya registered a positive balance of payments on its current account, while 1971 and 1974 were the worst two years for deficits before 1978. More misleading is his assertion that Kenya has experienced a decrease in foreign investment, yet between 1975 and 1977 private long-term capital inflow doubled from £K14·7m. to £K30m. Of course, there are serious foreign exchange constraints to further industrialization through import substitution. A more sympathetic observer might infer that this is likely to provide further incentives to indigenous industrial accumulators to innovate with local materials and resources. He might also have noted that two of the largest and most recent industrial projects are specifically geared to local resources, namely, furfural from maize cobs and industrial alcohol from molasses.

He uses the establishment of vehicle assembly plants in Kenya both to argue that they are inefficient and give rise to excessive repartriation of profits and that there ought to be a fourth plant to build Fiat trucks. Quite why the group of businessmen involved in Gema should be more virtuous and economically efficient in their dealings with Fiat than the other villains of his piece is not clear. Is it conceivable that the economists in the Treasury at least were able to block a fourth vehicle assembly plant? His evidence on low productivity is based on hearsay and anecdote. His analysis of economic growth fails to mention that Kenya has one of the highest birth rates in the world, at around 4·2%. Hence maintaining per capita real income and agricultural production is no mean feat, for instance, between 1969 and 1977, in absolute terms production increased by 20%. His note suggesting a decline of 13% in per capita output fails to observe that his time-period ended with a severe drought year, 1974–5.

The second part of Kaplinsky's chapter is potentially the most critical to his argument but again his evidence is ambiguous and his interpretation rather sweeping. First of all he states explicitly that he is not concerned with members of the industrial bourgeoisie who emerge from the 'pool of small petty accumulators' while these are precisely the group of central interest to Cowen. However it is impossible from his chapter to judge from whence his chosen twelve accumulators come. I would guess at least Njenga Karume would claim to have started his business career as a very small-scale accumulator. Three are relatives of the late President Kenyatta but is it adequate to build a theory on the behaviour of two of them? Others on the list do not seem to have very large shareholdings but are nevertheless very wealthy men. How have they accumulated? If the issued share capital of a private company is only £K100 does that mean the value of the enterprise is necessarily the same amount? The Leys's argument, in my view, stands or falls on the evidence of concentration of wealth, whatever its sources, coupled with active investment in industrial production. Information on shareholdings is very imperfect evidence, one way or the other.

The second part of Kaplinsky's chapter is interesting in that it does not suggest any slackening of the grip of foreign interests on Kenya's manufacturing industry. Even so, his Table 9.12 indicates a threefold increase in the number of Kenyan-owned and controlled firms. He notes that their issued capital was not very large but as we have already pointed out private companies do not usually attempt to maintain any relationship between issued capital and asset values. While he is probably right to argue they are mostly small companies this is not necessarily so. It is tempting to ask how big an increase in numbers Kaplinsky would require before accepting that there is an industrial bourgeoisie emerging in Kenya? Quite why a decline in real wages has any necessary bearing on the formation of this class is unclear. A better indicator might be the 'wabenzi ratio' – the proportion of Mercedes Benz cars to other makes on the roads of Kenya given that per capita income is more or less stable!

Kaplinsky does make some good general points about the immensity of the problems confronting autonomous industrial accumulators in peripheral economies and he is quite right for taking Leys to task for avoiding the crucial issue of the quantitative significance of the local industrial bourgeoisie. On the other hand it is nonsense to imply all Kenyan businessmen are in hock to foreign capital. The resilience of Kikuyu entrepreneurs in adversity has been demonstrated time and time again. Since the death of Kenyatta, the assumption of power by a non-Kikuyu president, and the general election of November 1979, Rubia has become a cabinet minister; Karume and Ngengi Muigai are now assistant ministers; and Matiba is an MP. Of course, if we accept Kaplinsky's view that these people have no independent resources but are merely agents of foreign capital, then this indicates a closing of ranks at the highest political level against the nascent indigenous industrial bourgeoisie. On the other hand, if we at least partly accept Cowen's thesis, this may be interpreted as the Kikuyu bourgeoisie pursuing its traditional strategy of political action to protect and enlarge its sphere of accumulation. In short, the struggle continues at the periphery as it has always done. Conditions change and Kaplinsky is probably right that they are getting more difficult in Kenya but it is ethnocentric to suggest the natives can never be expected to do anything on their own. We may deplore their choices and political methods but that is a different issue.

11 Kenya: What Does 'Dependency' Explain?

COLIN LEYS

Kaplinsky's (Chapter 9) argument brings out unusually clearly the empiricist and a-historical character of dependency theory. After fairly summarizing the main elements of the argument which I put forward, he criticizes not this, but five 'hypotheses' which, he thinks, may be drawn from what I and others have said; and what is most significant is that, in the end, much of what he says might be true, without affecting the validity of the argument which I put forward. The reason for this is that Kaplinsky, like all dependency theorists, has not grasped conceptually the historical process of capital accumulation and class formation. His view of Kenya starts and finishes with *appearances*, as they present themselves at a more or less fixed point in time; and the most palpable and pervasive of these, in the context of his own recent work (a follow-up to *Who Controls Industry in Kenya*), is the preponderance of foreign capital in manufacturing and large-scale tourism, its manifestly superior financial and organizational resources, its technological and market monopolies, and so on. The obverse of this appearance is the relative weakness of indigenous capital; hence it is conceived of as 'dependent', auxiliary, 'petty', and so forth, and as such incapable of playing a significant role in expanding the forces of production.

Yet the history of the sixteen years since independence in Kenya shows one thing unambiguously: a massive retreat by non-indigenous capital *out of* one sphere of accumulation after another *into* – in particular – manufacturing and large-scale tourism. How this could have occurred without a *decline* of real per capita incomes – let alone the roughly 25% *increase* which Kaplinsky's own Table 9.6 records – when population growth, as Henley points out, was over 3% per annum, is entirely incomprehensible from the standpoint of 'dependency'. Perhaps Kaplinsky does not consider the indigenous farmers, wholesale and retail traders, transporters, hotel and tour operators, office block owners, and so forth, who have moved into these spheres, as capitalists; perhaps for him it is enough that many of them were 'small' (i.e. 'petty'?) so that the question of how they were able to occupy these sectors, and how they have sustained capital accumulation within them subsequently, is of no interest. The fact is that this happened, not only supporting the growth of real incomes referred to, but generating some large further accumulations of capital in African hands.

That these events, momentous as they have been in human terms as well as historically, should still not seem significant even after a 'protracted stay' in Kenya, is interesting in itself; and it means that Kaplinsky is unable to account for the recent appearance, even in the manufacturing sector (which occupies his almost exclusive attention), of African capitalists. For him, they must apparently *either* graduate from the ranks of the 'apprentice' small workshop owners so beloved of the technocrats of the 'industrial estate' school, which he quite reasonably thinks an unpromising line of advance (as if the whole industrial revolution had to be replayed in miniature in every industrializing country!); *or* they are a mystery, explicable only in terms of marriages of convenience between foreign capital and a few, historically non-significant, African individuals. How even they came to be capable of playing this role is not explained. That they had capital of their own to invest is not remarked on (perhaps foreigners gave it to them?). Their political strength is emphasized, as if the power of the state, 'the concentrated and organized force of society', as Marx said, had not *always* played a decisive role in the 'genesis of the industrial capitalist'. And their links with foreign capital are stressed, including even the fact that one manufacturer produced under licence from a foreign firm, as if such connections were not part and parcel of modern industrial capitalism everywhere. The possibility that these individuals are only the most prominent of a growing number who, having accumulated capital in other sectors, now have the necessary skills, confidence and political strength to push their way into manufacturing, apparently cannot be accepted by Kaplinsky because he cannot really envisage the historical process which has produced them.

Having said this – somewhat forcefully, because the most useful result of this exchange, to my mind, would be to do something to help finally rid ourselves of the ideological handicap of dependency theory – some of the related weaknesses of Kaplinsky's chapter should also be pointed out.

First of all, what the evidence suggests is the *fact of African entry* into manufacturing industry, not the 'existence' of an indigenous industrial bourgeoisie (hypothesis 2), and not even that the emergence of an indigenous industrial bourgeoisie is 'only a matter of time'. Kaplinsky reformulates the argument in this way, not to make it easier to refute, but – again – because he does not conceive of the phenomenon historically. For him, either there is an African industrial bourgeoisie or there is not; either its present scale makes it likely to get bigger, or it does not. The argument actually advanced by myself and others, however, is that what is significant is the process of formation, through political struggle and ideological and cultural struggle, as well as through accumulation and reinvestment, of an indigenous capitalist class. This class has recently established a place for itself, however modest, in manufacturing (my actual words were: 'in manufacturing . . . a new phase of African entry seemed to be beginning by 1977'). What its future in that sector will be is not a matter of *time*, but of the course of its struggles, at least some of which it has so far won. Kaplinsky's figures on ownership and control are, from this point of view, irrelevant. He has gone to some trouble to distinguish Kenyan residents from foreign residents among the shareholders, but this means that his figures for 'Kenyan' ownership and control (which include non-African residents) in no way indicate the share of African capital in this process. A relevant figure, for a very specific sector, and one particularly favourable to indigenous capital, is the companies in which the Kenyan parastatals have invested. In this sector the proportion of state capital invested in companies in which Africans had a majority shareholding rose from 0·1% to 2·6% between 1966 and 1976, and the proportion invested in companies in which Africans were minority shareholders rose from 0·1% to 18·2%. The current position of Africans in the equity of manufacturing generally is unquestionably small. What is, or should be, of interest, however, is the rate, scope and conditions of the growth that has occurred in their share, on which Kaplinsky puts forward no evidence at all.

With regard to the role of the state, the 'hypothesis' which Kaplinsky attributes to me reveals a further misunderstanding. According to him, it follows from my argument that 'the state has moved from a mediating position to an instrument for increased indigenous control over foreign capital' (which later becomes 'the state has assumed an antagonistic position to foreign capital'). But my point was not that the *state* has 'moved', but that it is necessary for *us* to move, from the 'dependency' conception of the state as a somehow independent mediator, to understanding the state as a register of the balance of class forces, including the strength of the indigenous bourgeoisie. Because this strength is relative, not absolute, the state's interventions in conflicts between indigenous and foreign capital also registers this relativity; the inspection of individual cases, out of context, *naturally* reveals this, and the *only* way to grasp the significance of what is going on is to study the whole process historically, to identify and explain the trends in the relationship between the processes of capital accumulation, class formation and class struggles, and the evolution and activity of the state.

What Kaplinsky, I suspect, thinks is that the state must either be *neutral*, or it must be the *instrument* of one or the other of these contending fractions of capital. But what has to be grasped is that the fundamental interests of capital coincide; that the general form of this coincidence in Kenya is the general need of all fractions and strata of the bourgeoisie for further investments of foreign capital; and that what are in conflict are the interests of different elements of the bourgeoisie differentially affected by the specific forms this takes. Among these are the interests of particular African capitalists *vis-à-vis* those of particular foreign capitals. The state's resolutions of these conflicts register a complex interaction of economic, political and ideological forces, which it would be difficult to say has not, over time, advanced and hence also expressed the *growing* strength of indigenous capital.[1]

As for Kaplinsky's effort to downplay the growth of the Kenyan economy, it is not at first clear why he should want to do this, as it involves some distinctly strained arguments, some of which have been sufficiently criticized by Henley. Kaplinsky goes to some lengths to prove that there has been little structural change in the Kenyan economy, and in particular that the share of manufacturing in GDP has not risen much. I have never argued otherwise, though given the fact that real GDP roughly *doubled* between 1964 and 1976, the fact that the share of manufacturing *rose* at all is possibly equally significant. The question is one of *growth within capitalist production relations*, not – at this stage – one of the relative share of manufacturing. I agree that the extent of the development of capitalist production relations is an urgent matter for research, yet it would be hard to argue that the growth that has occurred has been accompanied by a *decline* in such relations. Another curious argument advanced by Kaplinsky is that Kenya has not 'seen a successful period of economic growth since independence' (which later becomes 'there has not been *sustained* economic growth in Kenya') the grounds being that growth in volume terms fell off markedly after 1973. It is difficult to know what to make of this. There are several advanced capitalist countries, including Britain, which would have been happy to have the absolute rate of growth actually achieved by Kenya since 1973, even though it is true that for popular well-being (as if capitalist growth had anything to do with *that*) Kenya, with a population growing at 3·2% per annum, needs to do even better. In order to argue that capitalist growth has occurred, Kaplinsky implies that one would have to show that it occurred evenly, uninterruptedly, regardless of the international recession, oil price increases, and so on. As Bill Warren pointed out almost a decade ago, what underlies dependency theory is a tacit idealized model of 'capitalist development', without inequalities, unevennesses, cycles, and so forth, such that the performance of no actual Third World economy could ever be described as 'successful' development (to use Kaplinsky's own word) in terms of it. It is not hard to see that this is what underlies Kaplinsky's discussion of the extent of Kenya's recent growth; and it also underlies his view of the character of the development that has occurred, and of its future prospects.

The capitalist growth that has occurred, he thinks, may have increased productivity, but only through a form of primitive accumulation from rural consumers via heavy tariff protection. It is also structurally dependent on the continual polarization of the economy into a protected, capital-intensive modern sector, permitting high rates of return which allow the payment of high wages which in turn permit the further introduction of more manufacturing technology from high-income economies: a structural vicious circle leaving a steadily larger proportion of the population in the position of impoverished subsidizers of the high-income minority.

These are serious issues. Capitalist growth has historically always been grounded on primitive accumulation and given rise to acute inequalities. The important questions are (1) whether the growth that has occurred in Kenya represents a real expansion of the productive forces; and (2) whether an alternative pattern is historically possible which would expand them faster, with lesser or greater costs in terms of the current living standards of the masses.

The former is debatable on various grounds but it seems to me difficult not to conclude that in every sector of the capitalist economy, including manufacturing, production has increased absolutely and per unit of labour, while real output per head has also risen for the economy as a whole. As to the question of alternatives, the difficulty with Kaplinsky's view is precisely that it implicitly contrasts the performance of actually existing peripheral capitalism in Kenya with some putative alternative strategy of development without any specified class character or location in historical possibilities. Frances Stewart has confronted this problem much more frankly than most dependency writers, reviewing three possible alternatives: factor price reforms; 'redistribution with growth' as advocated by the ILO mission to

Kenya in 1972; and what she calls 'disciplined socialism'. The first she rejects as politically impracticable, given the interests vested in the existing price structures, and in any case impotent to effect structural changes. The second is also judged politically unlikely; in addition, Stewart considers it probably internally inconsistent as a strategy of *capitalist* growth. The third alternative, socialism, is judged historically even more improbable.

The most likely alternative, however, not discussed by Stewart, seems to be a strategy *labelled* 'socialist', put forward by the petty-bourgeoisie, involving 'state socialism' in industry and trade along lines already broadly chartered in Ghana, Uganda and Tanzania. It is very difficult to believe that this alternative holds out the possibility of more rapid expansion of production at lower social cost than the historical path so far actually pursued in Kenya.

Because the dependency school sees the periphery as 'locked into under-development', it tends to minimize the development which actually occurs there; when the fact of such development cannot be denied, it is decried as inegalitarian, unbalanced, anti-popular; and, when this is admitted, it is, finally, dismissed as being at most short-lived and illusory. Kaplinsky's argument also follows this pattern, concluding by seeing further capital accumulation in Kenya as 'doomed' because of its inefficiency, which gives rise to a growing and ultimately fatal balance-of-payments problem, and because of declining agricultural productivity.

These considerations also have force, but none the less appear relative. For example, Kenya's balance-of-payments problem is still comparatively modest, however much more serious it is than prior to 1971. Agricultural production has tended to grow more slowly but the apparent constraints appear more social and political than technical and are certainly not absolute. As for manufactured exports, the opportunities presented by the overthrow of Amin in both Uganda and, on a slightly longer-term view, in Tanzania, are considerable, and it seems to me premature, to say the least, to consider that Kenya's internal market represents the impermeable limits of manufacturing production. In general, Kaplinsky's attempt to classify all peripheral economies into three types, only one of which – those with 'sizeable internal markets' – may be able to sustain 'successful accumulation', seems implausible (Hong Kong? Taiwan?) and indefensibly schematic.

As I took care to point out in Chapter 8, to say this is not to argue, let alone demonstrate, that Kenya is destined to undergo twenty or fifty years of *sustained* capitalist growth. But the class forces which have sustained its growth so far, with the state apparatus developed for this purpose, have surely not yet exhausted their potentialities.

Note

1   One of Kaplinsky's 'cases' actually reveals a misconception of the class forces involved which stems from the same empiricist root as the other misconceptions already discussed. According to him, in the 1975 budgetary crisis, the ICDC stopped all loans under its small loans scheme, but not its large-scale investments. He sees this as

evidence of the relative strength of foreign capital, which was involved in the projects receiving large-scale funds, and the relative weakness of the indigenous bourgeoisie. But the recipients of small-scale ICDC loans were broadly petty-bourgeois – i.e. not completely dependent on, or committed to, 'self-expanding' capital, capital laid out for the purpose of enlarging it; if this programme was halted, what was sacrificed was their interests, not those of the indigenous bourgeoisie proper, who were by this time no longer interested in ICDC small industrial loans (average value in 1976: K3,002) or small commercial loans (average value in 1976: K921).

Bibliographic Notes

For the reference to Warren see the references for Chapter 9.

The data on companies in which parastatals have invested is in C. Leys and Jane Borges, 'State capital in Kenya', *Canadian Journal of African Studies*, 14,2 (1980) pp.307–17. The reference to Frances Stewart is to 'Kenya: strategies for development', in U. Damachi *et al.* (eds), *Development Paths in Africa and China* (New York: Macmillan 1976, pp. 80–111'.

PART THREE
SOUTHERN AFRICA

12 *Capital Accumulation in South Africa*

MARTIN FRANSMAN

I Introduction

This chapter is divided into two broad parts. In section II the process of capital accumulation in South Africa from the 1880s to the Second World War is examined. In section III the major structural features of the economy in the postwar period are analysed and the implications of these features for future accumulation are considered.

In section II it is shown that mining and agriculture facilitated a process of fairly rapid industrialization. Accordingly in the first two parts of this section the factors contributing to the growth of the mining and agricultural sectors are discussed. In the third part the growth of manufacturing industry is considered up to the Second World War.

In section III the criteria for successful industrialization suggested by Singh are analysed and it is shown that South Africa has probably met these criteria. Some other structural features of the economy are then discussed. These include the pattern of imports of capital goods and the local capacity to generate technological change. However, it is argued that although these features do limit the extent of capital accumulation in South Africa they do not preclude the continued expansion of the manufacturing sector. One of the factors encouraging the growth of this sector is the access that South African-based firms have to the markets of other African countries and this is considered next. Finally the state's labour policies since the Second World War are briefly discussed.

II Capital Accumulation in South Africa pre-Second World War

(a) THE GOLD MINING INDUSTRY

The gold mining industry (and to a lesser extent the diamond mining industry which began in 1870) provided the basis for rapid accumulation after 1886. Capital accumulation in the gold mining industry resulted in a substantial increase, over a very short period of time, in the internal market for both agricultural and manufactured goods – both consumer goods and intermediate goods such as engineering products and explosives in the earlier stages. The establishment of the gold mining industry also led to a massive inflow of capital, technology and skills and to an increase in government tax revenue. Foreign exchange holdings were increased by the export of gold and over time this facilitated the further growth of the manufacturing and agricultural sectors. It is clear for these and other reasons that the gold mining industry played a central role in accelerating the process of capital accumulation during the late nineteenth and early twentieth centuries and it is accordingly important to understand the major factors that influenced the growth of this industry.

In this connection perhaps the single most significant factor related to the determination of the price of gold. Since gold served as the international medium of exchange and store of value and as such played a crucial role in facilitating international trade and capital flows, greater attempts were made by the major Western governments than in the case of other commodities to stabilize the price of gold. The advantage from the point of view of the mining houses was that prices fluctuated less frequently in a downward direction than with other commodities and to this extent risk was reduced. However the disadvantage was that with the price of gold *externally* determined and held constant for frequently long periods of time, mining profits were extremely sensitive to rising costs.[1] In Table 12.1 the major components of the working costs of the gold mines are given for the years 1911–31.

Since profits were so sensitive to increases in costs, close attention was paid by the mining industry to ways of holding these costs constant or even reducing them. In this connection it was black wages that were most amenable to control by the gold mining industry and a number of steps were taken to reduce black wages. The most important of these on the demand side was the formation of

Table 12.1 *Selected components of working costs of goldmining industry as proportion of total revenue, 1911–51*

	1911	1916	1921	1926	1931
White cash earnings as proportion of revenue	24·2	20·4	24·5	18·1	18·8
Black cash earnings as proportion of revenue	16·4	15·7	13·6	15·2	15·8
Stores consumed as proportion of revenue	33·2	31·0	33·1	33·0	34·3

Source: Wilson, 1972, p. 160.

monopsonistic hiring practices by the Chamber of Mines which acted on behalf of the mining companies. As early as 1893 the Chamber of Mines established a Native Labour Department which was charged with ensuring an adequate supply of labour and reducing the level of African wages. Worried by the fact that 'a great deal of trouble and money were being thrown away by the competition for natives',[2] the Chamber in 1896 established its own recruiting organization, the Witwatersrand Native Labour Association (WNLA). By 1899 the Association had succeeded in raising a labour force of 100,000 at a wage rate 'considerably lower' than it had been ten years earlier.[3] In 1912 the Chamber established the Native Recruiting Corporation (NRC) to recruit African labour from within South Africa and neighbouring Bechuanaland, Basutoland and Swaziland. In this way the mine-owners were able to eliminate competition between themselves and successfully establish a monopsonistic position in the African labour market, a 'market' that included Mozambique and soon extended as far as Tanzania, Malawi, Zambia and Angola.

After the Anglo-Boer War ended in 1902 the Chamber had succeeded in lowering the unskilled wage rate to R3·00 from the average R5·00 before the war. One writer has suggested that apart from farm employment 'this was probably the lowest cash wage for black labour in the whole of Southern Africa'[4] and this, together with extremely dangerous working conditions (in 1903 the death rate was 80 per 1,000 workers),[5] meant that the mines faced a critical labour shortage.

Some idea of the demand for African labour by the mines is given by the employment figures. African employment on the mines increased rapidly from 1886 when gold mining began. By 1894 42,500 Africans were employed, 100,000 in 1899, 183,793 in 1910 and 210,238 in 1931. However, given the low wages and also the relatively healthy state of production in many African areas in the earlier years, the supply of African labour was often inadequate. Accordingly a number of measures were taken by both the Chamber of Mines and the state to increase the supply of labour available at the prevailing wage rate. These measures included the imposition of taxes on Africans which had to be paid in cash and which in most cases required the seeking of employment since the sale of sufficient agricultural produce was usually not possible.[6] In addition the recruiting system was extended beyond the offices and recruiting posts of WNLA and the NRC and many traders in African areas were offered a 'capitation fee' for recruited labour.[7] Another measure was to pay traditional African rulers a commission on contracted labour.[8] Attempts were even made to recruit labour from north China. However as a result of mounting criticism recruiting from China was stopped in 1906 and many of the Chinese labourers were repatriated. Labour costs were also held down by the compound system which provided cheap dormitory accommodation for male miners. Since their families remained in the African areas in South Africa and in neighbouring countries and continued to provide for family needs by local production the mines were accordingly able to pay lower wages than would have been necessary if the wage were the sole source of maintenance for the entire family. In this sense, as Wolpe (1972) has pointed out, the African areas in effect subsidized the employers of migrant labour.[9]   ·

The attempts by the mines to hold down African labour costs were extremely successful and Francis Wilson has calculated that African cash earnings on the mines in 1969 were no higher in real terms than they had been in 1911. During the same period the real cash earnings of white employees, employed mainly in more supervisory roles, increased by 70%.[10] However, the system of labour coercion that has been described did not go unopposed by African miners and before the Second World War there were at least two major strikes, in 1920 and 1946.[11]

With an adequate supply of cheap unskilled labour the gold mining industry was able to survive within the severe limitations imposed by the international price of gold.[12] However the rate of return in gold mining until the late 1960s was not particularly high though sudden price increases, such as in 1932 when South Africa left the Gold Standard, led to huge increases in revenue. Thus S. H. Frankel estimated that from 1887 to 1932 the rate of return to capital invested in the gold mining industry was around 4–5%.[13] From 1935 to 1963 he calculated that the rate of return was 4·3% which compared with 7% for UK equities.[14] However, these figures are apt to be misleading and the ease with which the gold mines were able to raise their capital requirements on both international and local markets shows that other factors were also important, not least of which must have been the small degree of risk resulting from the relative absence of downward price movements.

Nevertheless it was the growth of the mining industry which provided the foundation for a more generalized process of accumulation and industrialization in South Africa. In the following part the role of agriculture will be briefly examined.

(b) THE ROLE OF AGRICULTURE

It is widely acknowledged that the growth of productivity in agriculture is a necessary condition for successful industrialization. Agriculture's contribution includes markets for manufactured goods, food for the growing urban/industrial population, raw materials for the agricultural-processing industries and also foreign exchange. In the South African case it was the early transition from semi-feudal to capitalist farming by the 1920s which laid the basis for large increases in agricultural output and productivity. In this respect the South African case was significantly different from many other under-developed countries where the power of feudal land-owning classes remained unbroken for far longer.[15]

As Morris has shown,[16] the South African case was one where (white) semi-feudal land-owners were transformed, with the aid of state intervention, into capitalist farmers. These 'semi-feudal' relations took a number of different forms ranging from sharecropping arrangements or 'farming-on-the-half', whereby the tenant, using his own implements, cultivated the land and paid the owner half of the output as rent, to labour-tenancy agreements whereby the tenant was given possession of some arable and grazing land, from which he and his family received the bulk of their income, in return for labour services. From the (white) land-owner's point of view these arrangements, under the prevailing circumstances, often provided the most suitable way of utilizing their land while the tenant obtained access to arable and grazing land on which his prized cattle could be kept and was relatively free of the control imposed on full-time farm labourers. However one implication of this system was that labour remained tied to the land on individual farms thus exacerbating labour shortages on other farms, particularly expanding commercial farms employing wage labour in one form or another. Pressure from the latter farmers led to the state introduction of a number of measures which attempted to regulate the number of squatters allowed on farms. Several measures were introduced before the Union of South Africa was formed in 1910 but the first significant step taken after 1910 was the Land Act of 1913 which provided for the elimination of rent squatting. However, with the exception of the Orange Free State this Act was not widely enforced and the practice continued in many parts of the country. Further measures were later taken by the state. But there were also economic pressures that resulted in the transformation of semi-feudal relations. One of the more important of these was rising land values which resulted from the increased commercialization of agriculture as internal markets expanded and which made it more difficult for farmers to have large parts of their land utilized unproductively by tenants.

Morris has subtly examined the various pressures that acted to transform semi-feudal agricultural relations and has shown that by the 1920s most labour-tenancy agreements had changed qualitatively so that the value of land made available to labour tenants decreased sharply relative to wages paid in cash and kind. Thus 'labour tenants' came increasingly to resemble wage labourers with diminishing plots of land. Accordingly Morris concludes that 'there can no longer be any doubt about the capitalist nature of commercial agriculture in South Africa by at least the second decade of the twentieth century'.

However labour supply problems did not only stem from labour being 'tied' on semi-feudal farms. In the later part of the nineteenth century labour supply difficulties were also partly attributable to the option that many potential African workers had of living on 'reserves' where agricultural conditions were still reasonably favourable. But in the twentieth century, and particularly from its third decade, the problem stemmed more from the relatively unattractive conditions offered to African agricultural labourers as compared to conditions in other sectors. It has already been mentioned that agricultural wages were substantially below those in mining while even the latter were far lower than wages prevailing in the urban manufacturing and services sectors. Accordingly other measures were taken by the state to ensure an adequate supply of African labour to agriculture at prevailing wage rates. These included laws preventing Africans from owning land in 'white South Africa'. The 1913 Land Act unified pre-existing laws and it and the 1936 Land Act prohibited African land ownership in some 87% of the country. Pass laws were used to prevent eflux of labour in an attempt to insulate the agricultural labour market and African labour was also recruited from neighbouring countries. However the labour shortage problem in agriculture persisted until after the Second World War.

State intervention was by no means limited to attempts to improve labour cost and supply conditions for capitalist farmers and efforts were also made, particularly after 1924, with the advent of a government that gave greater weight to the interests of these farmers, to influence agricultural prices directly. In general the state aimed not only to reduce the sharp fluctuations in agricultural prices and revenues but also to stop the worsening change in the sectoral terms of trade. Numerous measures were taken from 1926 which affected sugar, dairy products, wheat, maize and wool.[17] However, the major

Table 12.2 *Index of physical volume of farm output, 1911–59 (1936/9=100)*

Year	Livestock and arable	Livestock	Arable
1911	47	53	43
1921	60	68	55
1931	83	97	71
1941	106	110	102
1951	140	133	146
1959	181	162	197

*Source:*Houghton, 1969, p. 47.

intervention occurred in 1937 with agriculture, unlike mining or even manufacturing, still feeling the severe effects of the depression. In this year the Marketing Act was passed which made provision for the establishment of producer-controlled marketing boards and single-channel marketing. The passing of this Act, together with the granting of subsidies, tariff protection and quantitative import controls, which had the effect of raising domestic prices above international levels, bears testimony to the significant degree of influence exerted by agricultural interests at the level of the state. In large part the costs, including the costs of infrastructural improvement and the railway's tariff rating policies which favoured agriculture, were borne by the gold mining industry which contributed significantly to state revenues, particularly after the rise in the gold price in 1932 and the consequent imposition on the mines of the heavy excess profits tax.[18]

To conclude this part, we have seen that state intervention was crucial in creating the conditions for increasing agricultural productivity and output and in this way facilitating a more general process of capital accumulation and industrialization. The state played an important role in hastening the erosion of semi-feudal relations in agriculture and through this and other measures, such as those aimed at improving the labour supply and the sectoral terms of trade, it accelerated agricultural growth. One measure of this growth is the change in physical volume of farm output and the figures for the years 1911–59 are provided in Table 12.2.

Another indicator of agricultural growth is the number of motor tractors used on farms in the non-reserve areas. From 1,302 in 1926 these increased to 6,019 in 1937, 20,292 in 1946, 48,422 in 1950 and 119,196 in 1960 although the figures fail to take into account the improving levels of technology embodied in the tractors.[19]

(c) THE GROWTH OF MANUFACTURING INDUSTRY

In 1915, as is shown in Table 12.3, the contribution of manufacturing to GDP was relatively insignificant amounting to 5·7% as compared to agriculture, forestry and fishing (18·6%) and mining and quarrying (22·0%). The 1915/16 industrial census revealed that existing manufacturing industry fell into three major categories: firms producing inputs for the mining industry, producing final consumer goods and processing agricultural commodities. First in importance in terms of value added were engineering, foundry and blacksmithing shops. Only three other industries had an average value added per

Table 12.3 *Percentage distribution of gross domestic product at factor cost by kind of economic activity, 1911–77 (at current prices)*

Year	Agriculture, forestry and fishing	Mining and quarrying	Manufacturing
1911	21·1	27·6	3·8
1915	18·6	22·0	5·7
1920	22·2	18·3	7·3
1925	20·1	16·1	7·7
1930	14·2	15·6	9·3
1935	14·1	19·6	10·7
1940	12·7	18·8	12·4
1945	12·4	13·0	15·3
1950	17·7	13·5	16·4
1955	15·5	12·6	18·3
1960	12·3	14·2	18·7
1965	9·9	13·1	21·9
1970	8·2	10·2	23·6
1975	8·3	12·3	22·6
1976	7·8	11·9	23·3
1977	8·0	12·7	22·4

Source: *Union Statistics for Fifty Years*, 1960; South African Reserve Bank, *Quarterly Bulletin*, March 1976; *South African Statistics*, 1978.

establishment in excess of £10,000 and these were explosives and match works (£152,000), breweries (£40,000) and sugar mills (£33,000).[20] By 1925 the manufacturing sector had increased its contribution to GDP to 7·7% and from this year the growth of this sector accelerated significantly. This is shown in Table 12.4 which reveals the substantial rate of growth that took place from 1925 to 1955 (with the exception of 1929–33, the depression years and before South Africa left the Gold Standard in 1932). By 1955 manufacturing contributed 18·3% to GDP.

However, it is far more difficult to be precise about the relative importance to be attached to the different factors causing the growth of manufacturing industry. On the one hand it is clear that the protective tariffs imposed after 1925 had some effect, but on the other hand there were other changes that also stimulated the manufacturing sector. These included the large rise in the price of gold in 1932 and the growth in the internal market that this together with the growth in agricultural output led to.[21] In addition, both the mining and agricultural sectors provided necessary foreign exchange. There were also the

Table 12.4 *Average annual rate of growth in each period, 1925–55*

	1925–9	1929–33	1933–9	1939–45	1945–55
Number of establishments	1·0	0·3	5·3	1·3	4·7
All workers	5·5	−2·0	12·8	8·8	8·1
White workers	8·0	1·3	10·5	3·3	6·4
Black workers	4·5	−4·0	14·7	12·3	8·8
Value of gross output	9·8	−4·6	18·0	19·3	26·6
Value of net output	9·3	−3·3	15·0	19·3	24·9

Source: Houghton, 1969, p. 120.

positive effects of the Second World War which stimulated demand and provided *de facto* protection.

But although it is difficult to weight the various factors influencing the manufacturing sector it is clear that 1925 marked a watershed in the development of this sector if only because very little was done by the state before this date to promote manufacturing industry. In an important contribution Kaplan (1977) has explained this in terms of the primacy of mining interests in the determination of state intervention until 1924. Whether or not mining took precedence over agriculture and manufacturing to the extent that Kaplan suggests, it is clear that very little was done before 1924 to encourage manufacturing. Although Smuts's South African Party established the Board of Trade and Industries it did nothing in effect to further secondary industry. The membership of the Board served on a part-time basis and no one engaged in manufacturing was appointed to serve on it. Its lack of intervention 'bitterly disappointed industrial interests, hoping for a definitely protectionist policy'.[22] Kaplan explains this in terms of the conflicting interests of the mining industry which opposed the protection of secondary industry on the grounds that it would substantially raise mining costs. In contrast to Smuts's party, Hertzog's Nationalist Party, primarily representing agricultural interests, in its manifesto for the 1924 election, promised 'a definite policy of protection for industry'.[23] Kaplan argues that for a number of complex reasons[24] 'national' interests, primarily agriculture and manufacturing, after 1924 came to be the determining force influencing state policy.[25] In the event the Board of Trade and Industries was reconstituted after the 1924 election and its interventions resulted in the Customs Tariff Act of 1925 which was the first state measure designed to protect industry rather than raise revenue.[26] A statement by the first chairman of the reconstituted Board summarized the divergence of interest existing:

> the government of the time (i.e. pre-1924) had no policy of protecting South African manufacturing industry and was largely guided by the propaganda of the gold mining industry and by the 'hi falutin' views on free trade incessantly enunciated by the Chambers of Commerce which regarded themselves exclusively and inexorably as a Chamber of Importers. The measures of Smuts' government were aimed at regulating rather than protecting and developing manufacturing industry.[27]

The Customs Tariff Act of 1925 gave protection primarily to consumer goods industry. Provision was made for a rebate system whereby capital goods and other necessary imports bore either no, or a low, duty and this limited the negative effects on agriculture and the mining industry. However, the gold mining industry protested on the ground that many of the protected items constituted 'necessities of life' and the effect would be an increase in the level of wages with adverse effects for profitability. This view was put forward strongly in a letter to the Board of Trade and Industries by the Chamber of Mines in 1925:

> the attitude of the Chamber is that the interests of the mining industry . . . are best served by free trade, and the only recommendation they could make is that all the necessaries of such production [in the mining industry] should be placed upon a free list.[28]

Similar opposition stemmed from the gold mining industry which opposed Act No. 11 of 1928 which authorized the establishment of the state-controlled South African Iron and Steel Industrial Corporation Ltd (ISCOR). However Kaplan has shown that, contrary to mining, agricultural interests supported moves towards import substituting industrialization. Such moves, it was felt, could lead to a more rapidly growing market though they might at the same time result in higher costs for manufactured inputs.

From the above it is therefore clear that the promotion of domestic manufacturing industry did not suit all interests and protection and the ensuing growth in the manufacturing sector were the result of intense struggles and were by no means an 'automatic' part of the accumulation process.

(d) CONCLUSION

In this section the process of accumulation in South Africa has been examined from the late 1880s to the Second World War. It was shown that the growth of the gold mining industry from this date laid the foundation for a more generalized pattern of accumulation and industrialization. However, agriculture also played a central role in the accumulation process and it was seen in this connection that state intervention was crucial in assisting the emergence of capitalist farming. Thus by the 1920s agriculture outside the reserves was predominantly capitalist and this provided the basis for increasing productivity and more rapid accumulation. However, it was also shown that attempts made by the Chamber of Mines and by farmers, both assisted by the state, to obtain an adequate supply of labour at profitable rates were an inherent part of the accumulation process. These attempts involved the introduction of repressive institutions of labour control that undoubtedly had the effect of lowering labour costs.

While the manufacturing sector benefited from the growth of the mining and agricultural sectors its own growth was stimulated by the introduction of protective measures after 1925. In this connection it was shown that these measures were the result of a successful struggle waged by 'national' elements with an interest in enhancing domestic accumulation. However, other external factors also played an important role in accelerating the growth of the manufacturing sector, for example the rise in the price of gold after 1932 and the Second World War.

It remains now to relate the discussion in this section to some of the views on industrialization referred to in the introduction to this book. To begin with it is clear from the South African case that the process of capital accumulation was at the same time a process of political struggle involving the intervention of the state. This emerged most clearly in the various measures documented aimed at procuring satisfactory labour supplies at profitable rates. It also emerged in the struggle of 'national' interests to secure protection from competition abroad. The problem with Chenery's cross-sectional and time-series regression analyses is that they do lend themselves to conclusions about 'normal patterns of production and trade'.[29] While it certainly is relevant that there appears to be a considerable degree of cross-country similarity regarding the pattern of production and trade at different levels of income, it is this that must be *explained*. Yet any explanation which fails to place at the centre the kinds of political struggles referred to cannot but be unsatisfactory. For these reasons Leys is certainly correct to emphasize the importance of class struggle and the role of the state as he does in his Kenyan study in this book.

III Capital Accumulation in South Africa Post-Second World War

In this section the growth of the manufacturing sector since the war is examined and some comments are made on future growth prospects. In part III(b) it is shown that while policies of import substitution gave protection primarily to consumer goods, the capital goods and intermediate goods sectors contributed significantly to manufacturing value added. It is accordingly suggested that the 'Singh criteria' for industrialization (discussed elsewhere in this book) have been fulfilled. In part III(c) some other structural features of the economy are discussed and the implications of these features for future accumulation are examined. In part III(d) the importance of other African countries for accumulation in South Africa is analysed while aspects of labour policy since the war are looked at in part III(e).

(a) INTRODUCTION

As was shown in Table 12.3, by 1945 the contributions of the manufacturing sector to GDP exceeded that of both the mining and quarrying sector and the agricultural, forestry and fishing sector. By 1977 the manufacturing sector contributed 23·1% of GDP, while the percentages for the other two sectors were 12·7 and 8·0 respectively. During the 1960s, after the militant opposition to the state was temporarily defeated in the post-Sharpeville period, the overall growth rate in South Africa was significantly higher than in most other Western industrialized countries.

In the next part the role played by protection will be considered and the changed structure of manufacturing industry will be examined.

(b) PROTECTION AND THE STRUCTURE OF MANUFACTURING INDUSTRY

In the introduction to this book and in his own contribution the views of Ajit Singh on industrialization in Third World countries are presented. Singh argues that government intervention and protection are necessary in order to create economic structures that are conducive to rising productivity and growth. In particular he suggests that manufacturing value added must be a significant proportion of GDP (about 25%) and that the capital goods and intermediate goods sectors must contribute substantially (the desirable proportion is unspecified) to manufacturing value added since it is these sectors that exhibit the highest growth elasticities (see Singh, 1979). This economic structure will enable the country to reap the benefits of dynamic externalities and learning effects which are greatest in the manufacturing part of the economy in general and specifically in the capital and intermediate goods sectors. A successful industrialization process therefore requires

Table 12.5   *Weighted average rates of effective tariff protection*

	Ei 1956/7	Ei 1963/4
Domestic consumption	10·98	14·6
Intermediate goods	3·07	5·5
Capital equipment and investment goods	−1·4	1·87
Exports	0·11	2·2
Imports	−3·15	1·13

Source: Zarenda, 1977.

government intervention in order to bring about this kind of economic structure.

It has been shown above that in the South African case the protection of manufacturing industry was a significant feature since 1925 and that currently manufacturing value added is almost 25% of GDP (which is 'significant' given the large contribution made by gold mining to GDP). In Table 12.5 rates of effective protection (Ei) are presented for five sectors of the economy for the

Table 12.6   *Value added and employment in the manufacturing sector, 1972* (R thousand)

		Value added R '000	%	Total employment No.	%
1	Total manufacturing	3,758,949	100·0	1,131,061	100·0
2	Food	399,896	10·6	136,224	12·0
3	Beverages	127,305	3·4	24,327	2·2
4	Tobacco products	25,398	0·7	3,728	0·3
5	Textiles	234,276	6·2	101,781	9·0
6	Wearing apparel, except footwear	151,018	4·0	92,261	8·2
7	Leather and leather products	18,437	0·5	8,429	0·7
8	Footwear	46,472	1·2	24,524	2·2
9	Wood and wood and cork products	66,852	1·8	46,529	4·1
10	Furniture and fixtures, except primarily of metal	63,628	1·7	25,322	2·2
11	Paper and paper products	140,656	3·7	32,305	2·9
12	Printing, publishing and allied industries	171,661	4·6	33,675	3·0
13	Chemicals and chemical products	466,996	12·4	70,878	6·3
14	Rubber products	66,434	1·8	16,233	1·4
15	Plastic products not elsewhere specified	54,982	1·5	15,913	1·4
16	Pottery, china and earthenware	8,663	0·2	4,083	0·4
17	Glass and glass products	35,258	0·9	9,120	0·8
18	Other non-metallic mineral products	183,391	4·9	67,591	6·0
19	Iron and steel basic industries	313,900	8·4	72,183	6·4
20	Non-ferrous metal basic industries	62,910	1·7	14,553	1·3
21	Fabricated metal products, except machinery and equipment	344,796	9·2	113,033	10·0
22	Machinery, except electrical machinery	249,096	6·6	66,641	5·9
23	Electrical machinery	188,291	5·0	49,986	4·4
24	Motor vehicles, parts and accessories	109,590	5·1	57,637	5·0
25	Transport equipment, except motor vehicles	83,772	2·2	23,612	2·1
26	Miscellaneous industries	64,270	1·7	20,493	1·8

Source: *South African Statistics*, 1978.

years 1956/7 and 1963/4, the latest dates for which figures on effective protection are available. (The 'import' and 'export' sectors were defined as those with imports and exports of at least 20% of the value of domestic production.)

From Table 12.5 it is clear that the highest rates of protection were given to consumer goods followed by intermediate goods and capital goods. The protection of the capital goods sector was either very low or (in 1956/7) even negative.[30] Clearly the South African case involved the substitution primarily of consumer goods imports. However, despite the fact that the capital goods sector received relatively little protection, its contribution to manufacturing value added was not insignificant. If we define the capital goods sector as including subsectors 22 to 25 in Table 12.6 (although there are many problems with this definition of 'capital goods' particularly since these subsectors also include goods that are not capital goods) then it appears that this sector contributes about 19% to total manufacturing value added: machinery, except electrical machinery, comprising 6·6% of manufacturing value added (and ranking fifth in terms of contributions to manufacturing value added); motor

Table 12.7   *The manufacturing and capital goods sectors in some countries*

	S Korea	S Africa	Brazil	India	Iran	Hungary	UK	Germany
1a Manufacturing as % of GDP 1960	12	23	26	14	11	—	32	40
1b Manufacturing as % of GDP 1977	25	22*	—	16	13	—	25	38
2 Machinery and transport equipment as % of value added in manufacturing 1975	23	17	30	12	26	32	32	33
3a Machinery and transport equipment as % of merchandise exports, 1960	—	4	—	1	0	38	44	44
3b Machinery and transport equipment as % of merchandise exports, 1976	17	5·1*	10	6	0	34	40	48
4a Machinery and transport equipment as % of merchandise imports, 1960	12	37	36	30	23	28	8	10
4b Machinery and transport equipment as % of merchandise imports, 1976	27	54·9*	29	19	45	31	21	18
5a Percentage of labour force in industry, 1960	9	30	15	11	23	35	48	48
5b Percentage of labour force in industry, 1977	33	30	20	11	32	58	43	48

Note: * *South African Statistics*, 1978 (merchandise imports and exports measured f.o.b.).
Source: *World Development Report*, 1979.

vehicles, parts and accessories, 5·1% (ranking seventh); electrical machinery, 5·0% (ranking eighth); and transport equipment, except motor vehicles, 2·2% (ranking fourteenth).[31]

In Table 12.7 the machinery and transport equipment component of the manufacturing sector in South Africa is compared with that in a number of other countries for the year 1975 (row 2). Although the circumstances of these countries differ widely, also with respect to government policy relating to the capital goods sector, it can be seen that South Africa compares reasonably favourably with South Korea and India if not so well with Iran and Brazil. (We shall return later to other aspects of this table. In Tables 12A.1 and 12A.2 of the appendix a more detailed breakdown is provided of the machinery and electrical machinery sectors.)

With regard to intermediate goods it can be seen from Table 12.6 that these goods were (with the exception of manufactured food) the most important contributors to manufacturing value added. The four most important subsectors in terms of value added were: chemicals and chemical products (12·4% of total manufacturing value added); food (10·6%); fabricated metal products, except machinery and equipment (9·2%); and iron and steel basic industries (8·4%). Significantly these subsectors, again with the exception of food, showed amongst the highest growth elasticities (measuring the responsiveness of manufacturing value added in the subsector to a change in per capita GDP) in a recent UNIDO study of large countries (with populations above 20 million) and small countries with ample resources and an industrial orientation (UNIDO, 1979, p. 78). In Tables 12A.3 and 12A.4 of the appendix a further breakdown is given of the chemicals and chemical products sector and the fabricated metal products sector.

Furthermore it can be shown that the agricultural sector made an important contribution to the manufacturing sector, particularly, of course, to food products. In this connection some quantitative idea of the importance of agriculture is given in Tables 12A.5 and 12A.6 in the appendix. In Table 12A.5 it is shown that agricultural direct intermediate inputs into the manufacturing sector, mainly processing industries, amounted to some 53% of the total output of the agricultural, forestry and fishing sector. Furthermore about 20% of the latter sector's output was exported thus contributing to foreign exchange earnings which in effect are largely used by the manufacturing sector, a point to which we shall later return. Table 12A.6 shows the most important manufactured direct intermediate inputs into agriculture. These tables serve to reiterate the importance of agriculture in any discussion of manufacturing and highlight the significance of the transition from 'semi-feudal' to more productive capitalist production relations mentioned earlier.

However, policies of protection from 1925 certainly had the effect of substantially reducing imports as a percentage of total supply. This was particularly true in the period 1926–7 to 1963–4 although from the latter date to 1975, while it was also true of the consumer goods sector, it was less so in the cases of the intermediate goods and capital goods sectors. This is shown in Table 12.8.

Nevertheless it is quite clear from the evidence presented thus far that substantial changes occurred in the economic structure of South Africa from 1925 and it may be reasonably concluded that these changes brought about the kind of conditions which Singh regards as necessary for increasing

Table 12.8 *Imports per sector as a percentage of total supply, 1926–7 and 1963–4 (at 1956–7 prices) and 1975*

Sector	1926–7	1963–4	1975
	%	%	%
Agriculture, forestry and fishing	8	6	4·4
Gold mines	—	—	0·0
Coal mines	1	—	0·6
Other mines	2	18	50·5
Foodstuffs, beverages and tobacco	15	5	5·0
Textiles	89	43	21·2
Clothing	76	8	6·1
Footwear	40	3	11·3
Wood	74	27	17·0
Furniture	15	1	6·8
Paper and paper products	91	23	16·9
Printing and publishing	17	9	11·7
Leather and leather products	37	30	19·1
Rubber products	88	9	14·4
Basic chemicals	40	34	
Miscellaneous chemicals	43	23	
Petroleum and coal	87	32	12·2
Non-metallic minerals	42	11	
Basic metals	92	22	
Metal products	67	12	
Machinery	96	62	61·5
Electrical machinery	90	37	40·7
Transport equipment	73	37	34·2
Motor vehicles and repairs	83	36	35·3
Miscellaneous manufacturing	74	40	54·1

Sources: Calculated from Reynders Commission (see South Africa, 1972) and South African Department of Statistics, Report No. 09-16-03, Input-Output tables, 1975.

productivity and growth. In part III(c) a number of other structural features of the economy will be examined and the implications of these features for future industrialization and growth assessed.

(c) SOME OTHER CHARACTERISTICS OF THE SOUTH AFRICAN ECONOMY

This part is divided into three subsections. In the first some aspects of South Africa's trading patterns are examined with a view to throwing further light on several important structural features of the economy. Here particular attention is paid to the current account of the balance of payments and to the change in composition of imports and exports since the Second World War. The growing proportional significance of machinery and transport equipment in merchandise imports is examined and a rough measure of the relative 'competitiveness' of various sectors of the economy is discussed. Two related features of the structure of the South African manufacturing sector are highlighted: (1) the use within this sector of a high proportion of imported capital goods (i.e. imported embodied technology) and (2) the fact that this sector was not a major earner of foreign exchange but utilized the foreign exchange earned in other sectors to purchase imported inputs.

Table 12.9   Current account of the South African balance of payments at current prices, 1946–77 (R million)

Year	Merchandise exports (f.o.b.)	Net gold output	Service receipts	Merchandise imports (f.o.b.)	Service payments	Total goods and services (net receipts +)	Transfers (net receipts)	Balance on current account	GDP	Merchandise exports as a % of GDP	Merchandise imports as % of GPD
1946	161	203	80	-435	-170	-161	-6	-167	1,751	9.2	24.8
1947	215	195	82	-608	-196	-312	-42	-354	1,932	11.1	31.5
1948	286	200	100	-713	-226	-353	16	-337	2,136	13.4	33.4
1949	289	227	108	-635	-234	-245	3	-242	2,290	12.6	27.7
1950	429	294	115	-614	-269	-45	6	-39	2,662	16.1	23.1
1951	575	300	130	-938	-336	-269	10	-259	2,909	19.8	32.2
1952	575	304	146	-839	-362	-176	17	-159	3,116	18.5	26.9
1953	592	306	146	-862	-365	-183	16	-167	3,537	16.7	24.4
1954	660	329	162	-887	-386	-122	17	-105	3,808	17.3	23.3
1955	737	366	178	-972	-423	-114	21	-93	4,025	18.3	24.2
1956	819	395	199	-997	-449	-33	22	-11	4,339	18.9	23.0
1957	888	429	215	-1,109	-458	-35	19	-16	4,583	19.4	24.2
1958	776	440	205	-1,126	-457	-162	20	-142	4,711	16.5	23.9
1959	879	503	217	-995	-454	44	18	168	4,993	17.6	19.9
1960	881	530	229	-1,124	-472	44	-7	37	5,274	16.7	21.3
1961	923	576	236	-1,017	-490	228	-13	215	5,546	16.6	18.3
1962	948	632	253	-1,041	-484	308	9	317	5,912	16.0	17.6
1963	1,024	688	262	-1,283	-538	153	13	166	6,555	15.6	19.6
1964	1,074	736	305	-1,578	-603	-66	18	-48	7,209	14.9	21.9
1965	1,067	775	319	-1,799	-681	-319	23	-296	7,879	13.5	22.8
1966	1,216	769	350	-1,645	-723	-33	32	-1	8,555	14.0	19.2
1967	1,323	775	433	-1,942	-811	-222	41	-181	9,459	14.0	20.5
1968	1,513	769	480	-1,885	-905	-26	72	47	9,757	15.5	19.3
1969	1,486	847	517	-2,148	-1,045	-344	61	-283	10,854	13.7	19.8
1970	1,453	837	581	-2,582	-1,206	-917	49	-868	11,839	12.3	21.8
1971	1,551	922	677	-2,923	-1,325	-1,098	41	-1,057	13,078	11.9	22.4
1972	2,216	1,161	762	-2,840	-1,436	-137	47	-90	14,681	15.1	19.3
1973	2,517	1,770	962	-3,550	-1,765	-66	14	-52	17,978	14.0	19.8
1974	3,164	2,565	1,114	-5,768	-2,157	-1,082	84	-998	21,987	14.4	26.2
1975*	3,653	2,540	1,400	-6,742	-2,802	-1,951	138	-1,813	24,688	14.8	27.3
1976*	4,889	2,346	1,505	-7,443	-3,023	-1,726	96	-1,630	27,710	17.6	26.9
1977*	6,332	2,795	1,615	-6,893	-3,145	-704	47	751	31,450	20.1	21.9

Note: *Preliminary figures. Source: South African Government Statistics.

In the second subsection some information is provided on the importance of foreign capital inflows and on domestic research capacity. An indication is also given of transfers of external technology to the manufacturing sector. Finally in the last subsection comments are made on some implications of the structural features of the economy for future accumulation.

(i) Trade and some features of the manufacturing sector

As is shown in Table 12.9 there has not been a decline in the ratio of merchandise imports to GDP since the end of the Second World War. In the case of the merchandise export ratio (excluding gold) there has, if anything (and if 1976 and 1977 are excluded), been a slight decline since the war. This indicates that as far as visible items are concerned there has been no relaxation of the foreign exchange constraint.

However, Table 12.9 also reveals the significant contribution made by the gold mining industry. In 1968 net gold output was 41% of merchandise imports and the same proportion was recorded in 1977. Nevertheless, as can be seen from the same table, the balance on current account was negative for most years since 1946.

Since the Second World War there has been a significant shift in the composition of imports as is depicted in Table 12.10. Most significant has been the increase in the machinery and transport equipment components which increased from 20% to 53% of total imports. On the other hand food and manufactured goods decreased from 12% to 4% and from 35% to 19% respectively. In the case of exports crude materials fell from 44% to 21% while

Table 12.10 *Proportions of total imports and exports by various categories, 1946–70 (figures are in percentages and refer to SITC)*

	1946	1950	1955	1960	1965	1970	1975
Imports							
Food	12·3	7·0	4·4	4·4	3·6	4·0	3·6
Beverages	1·1	0·4	0·9	0·7	0·7	1·0	0·9
Crude materials	6·8	9·4	7·3	6·7	7·5	4·7	5·1
Mineral fuels	3·6	8·8	7·6	6·8	5·3	5·0	0·2
Animal and vegetable products	8·8	1·3	0·9	0·8	0·6	0·4	0·4
Chemicals	4·6	4·4	6·8	7·0	7·1	7·8	9·3
Manufactured goods	35·1	36·4	31·0	28·6	24·3	19·5	18·7
Machinery and transport equipment	19·7	25·5	31·8	36·9	42·1	46·7	53·1
Miscellaneous	15·5	5·9	7·8	7·4	7·0	8·9	7·7
Exports							
Food	10·1	11·6	21·2	21·4	21·3	19·7	31·7
Beverages	2·5	1·1	0·7	0·7	1·1	0·9	0·6
Crude materials	43·8	37·8	43·2	41·9	34·8	23·2	20·6
Mineral fuels	5·6	2·5	1·6	1·7	2·9	5·2	1·5
Animal and vegetable products	0·5	1·3	0·8	0·1	0·9	0·6	0·7
Chemicals	4·7	4·7	4·4	4·4	3·4	4·5	4·1
Manufactured goods	23·2	19·8	20·0	22·8	26·7	28·1	26·0
Machinery and transport equipment	1·6	2·9	4·3	4·5	4·5	1·4	5·8
Miscellaneous	6·1	2·8	3·5	2·6	8·6	1·3	1·3

Sources: Union Statistics for Fifty Years, 1960; South African Statistics, 1974, 1978.

Table 12.11   *Breakdown of imports and exports of capital goods according to Brussels Trade Nomenclature*

	Imports (f.o.b.)		Exports (f.o.b.)	
	1971	1972	1971	1972
1 Total (excluding gold)	2,887,036,692	2,819,379,685	1,568,834,167	2,046,644,967
2 Section XVI	785,136,512	772,939,305	97,536,430	96,601,406
3 Of which:				
a Chapter 84: Boilers, Machinery and Mechanical Appliances: Parts Thereof	572,485,785	543,530,909	75,199,888	76,391,710
b Chapter 85: Electrical Machinery and Equipment: Parts thereof	212,650,727	229,408,396	22,336,542	20,209,696
4a Section XVII	579,731,780	569,736,855	35,134,717	36,373,436
4b (2)+(4a)	1,364,868,292	1,342,676,160	132,671,147	132,974,842
5 Of which:				
a Chapter 86: Railway and Tramway Locomotives, Rolling Stock and Parts thereof; Railway and Tramway Track Fixtures and Fittings; Traffic Signalling Equipment of All Kinds (not electrically powered)	29,030,692	33,174,386	2,911,194	2,899,756
b Chapter 87: Vehicles (excl. Railway or Tramway Rolling Stock) and Parts thereof	471,558,771	443,381,601	23,772,525	26,224,945
c Chapter 88: Aircraft and Parts thereof; Parachutes; Catapults and similar Aircraft Launching Gear; Ground Flying Trainers	70,131,459	80,618,101	4,350,689	3,289,421
d Chapter 89: Ships, Boats and Floating Structures	9,010,858	12,562,767	4,100,309	3,959,314
6 (2)+(4a) as percentage of (1)	47·3%	47·6%	8·5%	6·5%
7 3a as % of 1 (as % of Sections XVI and XVII)	19·8(41·9)	19·3(40·5)	4·8(56·7)	3·7(57·5)
8 3b as % of 1 (as % of Sections XVI and XVII)	7·4(15·6)	8·1(17·1)	1·4(16·8)	1·0(15·2)
9 5a as % of 1 (as % of Sections XVI and XVII)	1·0(2·1)	1·2(2·5)	0·2(2·2)	0·1(2·2)
10 5b as % of 1 (as % of Sections XVI and XVII)	16·3(34·6)	15·7(33·0)	1·5(17·9)	1·3(19·7)
11 5c as % of 1 (as % of Sections XVI and XVII)	2·4(5·1)	2·9(6·0)	0·3(3·3)	0·2(2·5)
12 5d as % of 1 (as % of Sections XVI and XVII)	0·3(0·7)	0·5(0·9)	0·3(3·1)	0·2(3·0)

Source: Republic of South Africa, Department of Customs and Excise, *Foreign Trade Statistics*, Vols I and II, 1972.

food increased from 10% to 32% and manufactured goods increased only slightly from 23% to 26%.

The most significant feature of the change in the composition of imports from the point of view of the present discussion is the increasing importance of capital goods imports (i.e. the import of embodied technology). In this connection it is of interest to compare the South African case with that of some other more industrialized underdeveloped countries (although the reasons for the discrepancies cannot be explored here). In Table 12.7 it was shown that in South Africa imports of machinery and transport equipment as a percentage of total merchandise imports increased from 37% in 1960 to 55% in 1976. In Brazil and India, countries which have for a long period actively encouraged the development of a local capital goods industry, the proportion declined from 36% to 29% and from 30% to 19% respectively over the same period. However in South Korea, where until recently not so much emphasis was given to building up the capital goods sector, the proportion increased from 12% to 27%.

In Table 12.11 a more detailed breakdown is provided of imports and exports of capital goods for the years 1971 and 1972 (the latest years for which detailed data exist). Here it is shown that the most important categories of capital goods imported were those recorded under Chapter 84 according to the Brussels Trade Nomenclature (i.e. boilers, machinery and mechanical appliances: parts thereof) and Chapter 87 (vehicles – including railway or tramway rolling stock – and parts thereof). These items constituted 19% and 16% respectively of total merchandise imports and 41% and 33% of total imports of 'capital goods' (i.e. Chapters 86 to 89). However it was items under the same chapters that contributed most to exports of capital goods: Chapter 84 contributed 5% to total merchandise exports (excluding gold) and 57% to total 'capital goods' exports, while Chapter 87 accounted for 2% and 18% respectively.

A rough indication of the international competitiveness of sectors of the South African economy is provided by an examination of export/import ratios. The higher the ratio of exports to imports, the more 'competitive' is the sector. (This indicator must be treated with great caution since it also measures the effect of government intervention, exchange rates, other barriers to trade, etc.) Nevertheless as can be seen from Table 12.12 (and as seems intuitively very reasonable) South African 'competitiveness' is greatest in raw materials. For the other 'sectors' (categorized in terms of use and stage of processing) imports greatly exceed exports and this is particularly so in the case of capital equipment.[32]

Further information on select parts of the 'capital goods' sector is provided

Table 12.12   *Export/import ratios, by use and stage of processing, 1972–6*

	1972	1973	1974	1975	1976
Raw materials	4·80	4·30	3·30	4·70	4·60
Total processed or manufactured materials	0·54	0·54	0·48	0·42	0·49
Total capital equipment	0·11	0·10	0·09	0·07	0·08
Total articles ready for retail sale or consumers' use	0·10	0·07	0·19	0·18	0·10

Source: South African Statistics, 1978.

in Table 12.13. Here it is shown that the import of agricultural machinery and
equipment was 2·6 times the domestic output of the same items. In the case
of other machinery, except electrical machinery, the figure was 1·5 and in
electrical machinery, apparatus and supplies 0·6. (However a good proportion
of the latter goods were consumer goods and in 1973 some 45% of the sales
of this sector consisted of electrical appliances and housewares.) On the other
hand, as can be seen from the table, exports were a small proportion of total
output and the export/import ratio was low. The implication of these figures
is that the 'capital goods' sector is the least 'competitive' in the economy.

The analysis thus far has pointed to two related features of the structure of
the South African manufacturing sector: (1) the use within this sector of a high
proportion of imported capital goods and (2) the fact that this sector was not
a major earner of foreign exchange but utilized the foreign exchange earned
in other sectors to purchase imported inputs. In 1972 the Reynders
Commission of Inquiry into Export Trade drew attention to both these
features. The commission reported that 'imported capital equipment in the
manufacturing industry represented approximately 70% of fixed investment
in that sector during the period 1956–64 . . . '.[33] The commission also noted that
'at present manufacturing industry exports about 10% of its gross volume of
production . . . [p.10] . . . the rapid growth of the manufacturing sector in the
past has been facilitated by . . . the exports of the gold mining industry (p.17)'.[34]
In 1975 about 9·4% of the total output of the manufacturing sector was
exported.[35] As is shown in Table 12.9 above net gold output in 1970 and 1971
was about 32% of merchandise imports; in 1977 the figure was 41%. From
Table 12.10 above it is seen that food and crude materials constituted just over
50% of total exports in 1975, while food and beverages alone constituted about
21%.

Attention has so far been confined to the current account of the balance of

Table 12.13 *The capital goods sector, total output, imports and exports,*
1975

	Q (total output)	M (total imports)	X (total exports)	$\frac{M}{Q}$	$\frac{X}{Q}$	$\frac{X}{M}$
1 Agricultural machinery and equipment	107·96	280·92	6·50	2·60	0·06	0·02
2 Other machinery except electrical machinery	830·14	1,215·97	69·43	1·47	0·08	0·08
3 Electrical machinery, apparatus and supplies	536·33	292·41	20·15	0·55	0·04	0·04
4 TOTAL A	1,474·43	1,789·30	96·08	1·21	0·07	0·05
5 TOTAL B*	1,179·45	1,628·50	85·00	1·38	0·07	0·05

Note: *Total B = Total A minus electrical appliances and housewares (the latter
assumed to constitute, as in 1973 figures for sales, 45% of electrical machinery,
apparatus and supplies). Since figures do not exist it is also assumed, though this may
be inaccurate, that 45% of imports and exports are made up of electrical appliances and
housewares.
Source: South African Department of Statistics, Report No. 09-16-01, Input-Output
Tables, 1975.

Table 12.14 *Financing of gross domestic investment, 1946–77* (R million)

	Gross domestic saving (1)	Net capital inflow from rest of world (2)	Change in gold for exchange reserves (3)	Gross domestic investment (4)	% (2)÷(4)
1946	218	80	87	385	22
1947	178	352	2	532	66
1948	236	165	172	573	29
1949	311	105	137	553	19
1950	516	182	−143	555	33
1951	501	187	72	760	25
1952	592	144	15	751	19
1953	681	113	54	848	13
1954	803	193	−88	908	21
1955	869	51	42	962	5
1956	973	35	−24	984	4
1957	1,059	−47	63	1,075	—
1958	1,012	134	8	1,154	12
1959	1,177	−61	−107	1,009	—
1960	1,187	−180	143	1,150	—
1961	1,362	−129	−86	1,147	—
1962	1,435	−88	−229	1,118	—
1963	1,679	−80	−86	1,513	—
1964	1,710	−41	89	1,758	—
1965	1,902	255	41	2,198	12
1966	2,103	141	−140	2,104	7
1967	2,510	162	19	2,691	6
1968	2,561	456	−534	2,483	18
1969	2,760	218	65	3,043	7
1970	2,845	582	286	3,713	16
1971	3,172	818	239	4,229	19
1972	3,946	449	−359	4,036	11
1973	4,985	−46	98	5,037	—
1974	6,030	899	99	7,028	13
1975	6,669	1,926	−113	8,482	23
1976	6,978	1,110	520	8,608	13
1977	9,054	−1,096	345	8,303	—

Sources: South African Reserve Bank, *Quarterly Bulletin*, various issues; *South African Statistics*, 1978.

payments. Since inflows of foreign capital and technology played an important role this aspect of the South African economy will now be briefly examined.

(ii) Foreign capital and technology

The importance of the import of embodied foreign technology (mainly in the form of imported capital goods) has already been discussed. Attention is now turned to foreign capital inflows and some evidence is also provided on the use by the manufacturing sector of externally derived technology and on domestic capacity to produce technological change.

After the Second World War foreign capital flowed into South Africa in substantial quantities. Table 12.14 shows that in 1946, 1947 and 1948 net foreign capital inflow constituted 22%, 66% and 29% respectively of gross domestic investment. Although the figure declined somewhat to 19% in 1949, the year after the National Party government came to power, it rose in the following year to 33%. From 1959 to 1964 the net foreign capital inflow was negative as a result of the negative effects of the world recession on the South African economy in 1959, the Sharpeville massacre in 1960 and the wave of black opposition and state oppression that followed. The net outflow of foreign capital during this period revealed the extent to which such flows responded to political instability and risk, a feature that was to become important again in the post-Soweto period after 1976.

Average rates of return on investments in South Africa appear to be significantly higher than other parts of the world. Evidence for this is presented in Table 12.15 for direct UK investment in South Africa from 1966 to 1974, although it should be kept in mind that this period represents a time of relative political calm and furthermore that the figures might not be reliable due to practices of transfer pricing, and so on. Most foreign direct investment went into the manufacturing sector which received on average 57% of such UK investment and 65% of US investment (from 1965 to 1971).[36] Very little information exists on the transfer of technology to South Africa. However, the picture that does emerge from the information available is one of a manufacturing sector that undertakes little research and development expenditure and imports foreign technology through licensing and other know-how agreements.

Some information on local research and development is provided by the 1972 Reynders Commission. Several points appear from this information. First a relatively large proportion of R and D expenditure is undertaken by the state as compared to some other industrialized countries. In 1968/9 61% of total R and D expenditure was undertaken by the state, compared to 25% in the UK (in 1967/8) and 14% in the USA (1969). The private sector accounted for 27% of the total, compared to 60% in the UK and 69% in the USA. Second, the bulk of R and D expenditure was allocated to agriculture rather than manufacturing, again reflecting the relatively high level of dependence of the latter sector on external technology. Of total R and D expenditure 31% related to agriculture followed by manufacturing (23·4%), services (22·8%) and mining (22·7%). Government devoted the bulk of its R and D expenditure to agriculture (44%) followed by services (30%), manufacturing (15%) and mining (10%). The breakdown of R and D expenditure in the private sector shows the dominance of mining (52%) followed by manufacturing (42%), services (3%) and agriculture (3%). Quite clearly, therefore, the extent of R and D activities by the mining sector is significantly greater than its contribution to GDP. The figures also indicate the state's subsidizing role *vis-à-vis* the agricultural sector. However, locally generated technology remains insignificant in international terms as is shown by figures reflecting the export of such technology. 'Overseas marketing of South African technological services

Table 12.15   *Average rate of return on direct UK investments, 1966–74*

| | Rate of return (%) | | | | |
	1966	1968	1970	1972	1974
Investments in South Africa	12·8	11·7	11·8	11·0	20·9
Investments in all foreign countries	8·4	9·0	9·3	10·9	14·2

Source: UK Department of Trade and Industry, *Business Monitor*, M4.

under royalty, licensing, copyright and patent agreements is still extremely limited and earnings from this source amounted to only R1 million during the period 1966 to 1970.'[37] (At that time R1 was approximately equal to $US 1·40.)

Further light on the technological dependence of the manufacturing sector is provided by statistics on royalties paid and received by subsector and these are given in Table 12.16.

The important information is contained in the last two columns. Column E, showing the ratio of royalty payments to value added, provides an indication of the dependence of the subsector on external sources of technology, that is, strictly speaking, external to the firm. The six subsectors that exhibit the highest ratios are (in descending order): rubber products, electrical machinery, machinery (except electrical machinery), other non-metallic mineral products, motor vehicles, parts, accessories, and chemicals/chemical products (the latter was also the largest contributor to total manufacturing value added). Column F shows the ratio of royalties paid to royalties received. If it is assumed that when a firm in a subsector makes a royalty payment to another South African-based firm the latter firm is in the same subsector, then column F gives some idea of the extent of payments *abroad* for technology received. This of course is not the same as dependence on *foreign* technology since some of the firms receiving royalty payments will be directly or indirectly owned or controlled by foreign firms.) Since all the figures in column F substantially exceed unity (where royalty payments and receipts are equal) an indication is given of the substantial reliance on transfers of technology from abroad.

(iii) *Structural features of the South African economy and future accumulation*

In this chapter the following structural features of the South African economy have been identified: (1) the foreign exchange constraint has not been significantly relieved since the Second World War (at least until the most recent – mid-1979/80 – extraordinary rise in the price of gold): for most years during this period the current account has been in deficit, the ratio of both merchandise exports and imports to GDP has not changed substantially, and the inflow of foreign capital (which has been shown to be highly sensitive to political risk) has been important for the maintenance of gold and foreign exchange holdings and for the financing of gross domestic investment; (2) the manufacturing sector exports only about 10% of its output and is therefore a net user of foreign exchange contributed by the mining and agricultural sectors; (3) the composition of imports has changed significantly since the war so that over 50% of imports are in the machinery and transport equipment category; (4) the 'Singh criteria' for successful industrialization (regarding the contributions of manufacturing value added to GDP and the capital and intermediate goods sectors to manufacturing – see Chapter 1 and the introduction to this book) have probably been satisfied as was shown in section III(*b*) above; (5) although a number of important technological advances have been made in some areas (with particular prominence probably in the gold mining and military-related industries) the technology generating capacity of the economy is limited in most areas and particularly in manufacturing. In the rest of this section some tentative thoughts will be offered on several implications of these features for future accumulation.

Table 12.16 Royalties paid and received by the manufacturing sector, 1972

	A Net output (R '000)	B Royalties paid (R '000)	C Royalties received (R '000)	D Subsidies received (R '000)	E Royalty paid: net output %	F Royalty paid royalty received
1 Total manufacturing	3,758,949	30,215	1,142	43,726	0·80	26·5
2 Food	399,896	592	144	31,974	0·15	4·1
3 Beverages	127,305	846	0	0	0·71	–
4 Tobacco products	25,398	1	0	0	0·004	–
5 Textiles	234,276	922	37	0	0·38	24·9
6 Wearing apparel, except footwear	151,018	771	121	0	0·51	6·37
7 Leather and leather products	18,437	52	18	0	0·27	2·9
8 Footwear	46,472	84	5	0	0·18	14·8
9 Wood and wood and cork products	66,852	156	11	0	0·24	14·2
10 Furniture and fixtures, except primarily of metal	63,628	224	5	0	0·35	44·8
11 Paper and paper products	140,656	958	0	0	0·68	–
12 Printing, publishing and allied industries	171,661	1,528	32	0	0·89	47·8
13 Chemicals and chemical products	466,996	5,684	56	11,738*	1·22	101·5
14 Rubber products	66,434	1,403	2	0	2·11	701·5
15 Plastic products not elsewhere specified	54,982	501	7	0	0·91	71·6
16 Pottery, china and earthenware	8,663	55	0	0	0·64	–
17 Glass and glass products	35,258	110	29	0	0·31	3·8
18 Other non-metallic mineral products	183,391	2,754	6	0	1·50	459·0
19 Iron and steel basic industries	313,900	1,181	0	0	0·38	–
20 Non-ferrous metal basic industries	62,910	2	1	0	0·003	2·0
21 Fabricated metal products, exc. machinery, equip.	344,796	1,133	78	0	0·34	14·5
22 Machinery, except electrical machinery	249,096	4,094	287	0	1·64	14·3
23 Electrical machinery	188,291	3,781	198	0	2·01	19·1
24 Motor vehicles, parts and accessories	109,590	2,557	13	0	1·34	196·7
25 Transport equipment, except motor vehicles	83,772	399	15	15	0·48	26·6
26 Miscellaneous industries	64,270	347	77	0	0·54	4·5

Note: * All from fertilizer subsidies. Source: South African Department of Statistics, Census of Manufacturing, 1972.

A major feature of the South African economy is that the manufacturing sector, which is the most important in terms of contribution to GDP, requires foreign exchange earned by the mining and agricultural sectors and a continued inflow of foreign capital for its expansion. However, while this is the situation at present, future changes depend very much on the perspective brought to bear on the question. In this connection we shall briefly take up the opposing views of Murray and Singh presented in the introduction to this book.

Murray argues that producers in underdeveloped countries, including the more industrialized of these countries, will tend to increase their productivity at rates slower than for producers in the world's major industrial centres. This differential rate of change in productivity will constitute a limitation on capital accumulation in underdeveloped countries. In the South African case it has been shown that there is ample evidence to suggest that at the present point in time there is a wide productivity differential between domestic manufacturers and producers in the major industrial centres of the world. This is reflected in the imports of capital goods and the poor export performance of this sector. To the extent that this persists over time it will imply a continued and ever-increasing reliance by the manufacturing sector on foreign exchange earned by mining and agriculture. If the domestic replacement of imported capital and intermediate goods and technology is not increased this will mean that the growth of manufacturing industry will be limited by foreign exchange availabilities.

On the other hand Singh argues that competition from the major industrial centres does not constitute a severe constraint on capital accumulation and industrialization in underdeveloped countries. Competition from lower-cost producers in these centres need not prevent increasing levels of industrialization in underdeveloped countries if government provides protection and intervenes in order to create appropriate economic structures. Under these conditions the industrialization process will continue despite the existence of lower-cost producers elsewhere in the world economy (given the minimum foreign exchange earning capacity necessary). In the longer run, as a result of the appropriate structures, the less industrialized country might (not will, i.e. the possibility exists) become, at least in some areas of activity, the most productive centre. In this connection Singh often quotes the Japanese case which he argues is a 'path' that is open to at least some of the underdeveloped countries. Relating these arguments to the South African case, it may well be, contrary to Murray, that South Africa will be able to establish an international competitiveness in certain areas of manufacturing activity. To the extent that this occurs the constraints of the size of the local market will be lessened as export markets become available and the manufacturing sector will increase its exports thus contributing to a further relaxation of the foreign exchange constraint. In this connection it should be recalled that South Africa has probably fulfilled the 'Singh criteria'.

Several observations may be made, in the context of the opposing views of Murray and Singh, about future accumulation in South Africa. To begin with it is important to realize that the reliance by the manufacturing sector on foreign exchange earned by the mining and agricultural sectors is not necessarily a factor that will prevent the expansion of the manufacturing sector and therefore limit the accumulation of capital generally. Particularly important in this connection is the favourable long-term movement in the price of gold. Gold will continue to be the international money material for the simple reason that there is no substitute. As Samuel Brittan has recently pointed out, even prior to the international economic crisis of the last few years, gold has, for most of recorded history, more or less retained its real value against goods and services.[38] The same has not been true of the major Western currencies, particularly the dollar, which are the main alternatives to gold in the international sphere. 'The markets', Brittan pointed out, remain 'sceptical of either the ability or the will of governments to limit the supply of paper currency when the going gets rough. And who, in the face of the historical evidence, is to say that they are wrong?'[39] A higher price of gold increases the amount of 'payable' gold-bearing ore thus extending the life of the mines. Similarly, although there are different determining factors, there is no reason why agriculture should not continue to be a significant foreign exchange earner. Accordingly, even if the manufacturing sector does *not* become 'internationally competitive' it is possible for this sector to continue to grow and enable increasing productivity to take place in all sectors of the economy. (However, as discussed below, there are not necessarily the same grounds for 'optimism' with regard to increasing employment.) This holds even if there were *declining* competitiveness in the manufacturing sector although it now seems clear that some earlier official reports which argued that South African manufacturers faced declining competitiveness as a result of (unspecified) 'structural' factors were unduly pessimistic. Commenting on the widening gap during the 1960s between merchandise imports and exports (excluding gold), the Reynders Commission on exports related this phenomenon to:

> reduced import replacement opportunities on the one hand, and the declining competitive position of exporters of specially *[sic]* semi-pro-cessed and processed goods on the other. Although the disparity was accelerated by inflationary conditions in the domestic economy particu-larly since 1968, its structural character should be noted . . .[40]

However, as can be calculated from Table 12.9, the ratio of merchandise exports (excluding gold) to merchandise imports which was 0·74 and 0·80 in 1966 and 1968 respectively was 0·78 in 1972, 0·55 in 1974, 0·66 in 1976 and 0·92 in 1977. Furthermore processed or manufactured goods remained a more or less constant proportion of total exports (around 55%) as did raw materials (around 42%) during the 1970s until 1977. For these reasons a conclusion about declining competitiveness would appear to be unwarranted.

A further consideration is that too static a view should not be taken of the 'technology constraint' in examining the factors likely to limit capital accumulation. As is clear from the work of Sanjaya Lall in India[41] and Jorge Katz in Argentina,[42] increases in productivity are also possible from activities of imitation, modification and adaptation of imported technologies and in some cases these have enabled firms in the country concerned to establish export markets. However it is also probably unwise to make the opposite error of overemphasizing the importance of this form of 'technological change'; in most cases the advantages which Murray sees accruing to firms in the world's major industrial centres *do* place them in a relatively strong position. But of course this does not deny the possibility of major technological breakthroughs

in particular areas by specific underdeveloped countries (and neither is the
possibility denied of a relative decline in the position of former major industrial
centres as is happening in the case of Britain). In addition it is worth bearing
in mind the point made by Colin Leys in Chapter 8 in this book regarding the
ability of the state to intervene on behalf of indigenous classes in order to 'push
back' the limitations confronting their accumulation.

Regarding the state's role in facilitating accumulation there is some evidence
to suggest that despite the existence of lower-cost competitors in the major
industrial centres of the world, the South African state has not performed as
well as it might have. In this connection one indicator is the South African
performance in the area of imports and exports of machinery and transport
equipment as compared to that of South Korea and Brazil (with more 'open'
economies) and India (with a more 'closed' economy). The data are presented
in Table 12.7. In 1976 South African exports of machinery and transport
equipment were 5·1% of merchandise exports (excluding gold) while the
corresponding figure for Brazil was 10%, 17% for South Korea and 6% for
India (the latter having a manufacturing sector that in 1977 contributed 16%
to GDP compared to 22% in South Africa). South African imports of the same
items were 55% of total merchandise imports while the proportion was 29%
for Brazil, 27% for South Korea and 19% for India. Since these countries also
faced competition from the same major industrial centres in the world as did
South Africa (i.e. the 'Murray constraint') there is some evidence to suggest
that South African state policy has not been as successful as it might have
been. In this connection it might well be that the foreign exchange contribution
particularly of the gold mining industry but also of the agriculture sector has
been such as to prevent pressure being placed on the manufacturing sector to
export and earn foreign exchange.

Lastly it is necessary to say something about an important factor
encouraging the industrialization process in South Africa, namely, the
competitive position which South African-based producers have enjoyed in
neighbouring African countries. This is discussed in the following section.

(d) THE IMPORTANCE OF OTHER AFRICAN COUNTRIES FOR ACCUMULATION IN SOUTH AFRICA

As is shown in Table 12.17 some 16% of total exports (excluding services and
gold) went to other African countries in 1963–70. During the same period about
6% of imports came from such countries. In 1976 the figures for exports to
and imports from Africa were 11% and 5% respectively.[43] However, these
figures disguise the significance of such trade since they fail to take into
account the composition of trade flows with other African countries. In 1973
an official regional study of South Africa's balance of payments pointed to the
importance of trade with other African countries (van der Merwe and du
Plessis, 1973):

> South Africa provides more sophisticated manufactured goods to African
> countries. On the other hand, imports from African countries are
> relatively low, because most of the agricultural and mining products
> exported by African countries, and in particular by the countries in
> Southern Africa, are produced locally in South Africa.[44]

This contrasted strongly with South Africa's trade with the industrialized countries as noted by the same authors:

> As a developing economy with large mineral resources, South Africa supplies mainly raw materials to the more industrial countries of the world and imports intermediate and capital goods from them. These countries also provide capital, technical know-how, financial services and shipping facilities, which are essential for the development of the South African economy.[45]

South Africa's main advantage, as the Reynders Commission clearly saw, derives from its proximity to African markets thus decreasing transport costs and enabling knowledge of these markets to be acquired by firms based in

Table 12.17   *Geographical distribution of exports and imports (%)**

	1947–54	1955–62	1963–70
Exports			
Africa	20·9	20·7	16·2
Europe	63·2	59·5	58·2
UK	(30·5)	(35·3)	(33·7)
France	(10·7)	(3·8)	(3·1)
West Germany	(4·4)	(4·8)	(6·5)
Italy	(4·6)	(4·3)	(3·6)
Netherlands	(3·6)	(2·6)	(2·1)
Belgium	(3·2)	(4·6)	(4·1)
America	10·4	10·7	11·3
USA	(8·6)	(9·1)	(10·6)
Asia	4·0	7·6	13·1
Japan	(1·0)	(3·9)	(10·6)
Oceania	1·5	1·5	1·2
TOTAL	100·0	100·0	100·0
Imports			
Africa	7·1	7·1	6·3
Europe	50·4	55·2	55·2
UK	(35·0)	(31·7)	(25·9)
France	(1·3)	(2·0)	(3·0)
West Germany	(3·0)	(9·2)	(12·5)
Italy	(2·1)	(2·3)	(3·7)
Netherlands	(1·3)	(2·3)	(2·4)
Belgium	(2·1)	(1·8)	(1·2)
America	30·7	23·4	21·6
USA	(24·3)	(18·9)	(17·8)
Asia	10·9	13·3	15·1
Japan	(1·8)	(3·2)	(6·8)
Oceania	0·9	1·0	1·8
TOTAL	100·0	100·0	100·0

Note: * Exports and imports exclude services.
Source: South African Reserve Bank, *Quarterly Bulletin*, September 1971.

South Africa. In addition infrastructural factors, particularly the road and railway system in southern and central Africa, tend to give firms based in South Africa a transport cost advantage over competitors in the more industrialized countries. For these reasons South African-based firms have in many cases been able successfully to export to African countries while remaining unable to break into other international markets. These exports allow the producers to overcome, to some extent, the limitations of the domestic market and, to the extent that economies of scale operate, to achieve lower costs.

An example of the extent to which accumulation in South Africa benefits from trade with other African countries is the case of the capital goods sector which, as was noted earlier, is one of the most dynamic sectors in any economy. With regard to the machinery sector (excluding electrical machinery) the Reynders Commission concluded that this sector 'can hardly be expected to develop without reasonable protection' since it 'cannot satisfactorily compete (against imports) in the local market'.[46] However, the commission also pointed out that the forecast rate of growth in this sector 'will be detrimentally affected by a change in the political situation in adjacent territories which have been a major outlet for South African producers during the past seven years during which exports have been increasing at a rate of 12·8%'.[47] Similarly with regard to the electrical machinery and equipment sector the commission, while pointing out that this sector 'would seem to be very sensitive to foreign competition', concluded that 'exports to African countries adjacent to South Africa appear to promise some hope of growth should the political climate improve'.[48] Recent figures for Swaziland give some indication of this. In 1973 while total imports into Swaziland amounted to R68·2 million, R62·9 million of this came from South Africa. The largest single import item totalling R16·3 million (or about 26% of total imports) was machinery and transport equipment. Of this R15·3 million came from South Africa.

The services part of the current account provides an indication of the significance of receipts from investments in other African countries and of migrant labour flows from these countries. From 1957 to 1972 between 41% (1972) and 63% (1957 to 1961) of total service receipts came from Africa. These receipts 'can mainly be attributed to dividends received on investments, expenditure by tourists from neighbouring countries and domestic [i.e. in South Africa] expenditure of migrant workers from their earnings in South Africa'. From 1957 to 1972 25% of total service payments were 'payments to African countries, consisting mainly of the remuneration of (foreign) migrant workers'.[49]

Statistics on capital flows between South Africa and individual African countries do not exist. However Table 12.18 gives an idea of the average annual capital movements on capital account for Africa as a whole and a comparison with other geographical areas.

Between 1957 and 1964 there was an average annual net outflow of capital to Africa of R9 million. During this period there was a total average annual outflow of capital from South Africa amounting to R60 million, largely as a result of the post-Sharpeville crisis. Although a breakdown of this figure is not available it reflects in large part direct and non-direct investment by South African companies in other African countries. From 1965 to 1972 there was

Table 12.18   *Average annual net identified capital movements by area (inflow + or outflow −) (R million)*

	1956–64	1965–72	1957–72
Total Europe	−38	254	108
EEC	(−37)	(247)	(105)
Other Europe	(−1)	(7)	(3)
America	−12	54	21
Asia	− 2	15	6
Africa	− 9	3	−3
Oceania	− 1	1	1
Unallocated	—	2	1
TOTAL	−60	329	134

Source: South African Reserve Bank, *Quarterly Bulletin*, September 1973, table 5, p. 20.

an average annual net inflow of capital from other African countries amounting to R3 million. While here too a breakdown is unavailable, it seems likely that the net inflow, despite continuing direct and non-direct investment by South African-based companies in Africa as well as loans by the South African government, is largely attributable to capital movements from Rhodesia after UDI in 1965.

Furthermore there are indications that not only do South African-based producers gain from proximity to other southern and central African countries and from South Africa's relative degree of industrialization, but they also benefit in the longer run from the 'backwash' effects that hinder the development of industry in these other countries. This is shown most clearly in the case of Botswana, Lesotho and Swaziland (the three economically weaker countries in the Southern African Customs Union) although similar effects are likely to operate, though to a lesser extent, in other southern and central African countries. Selwyn (1975) has shown that production costs in these three countries tend to be significantly higher than in the South African industrial centres. Even the supposed major source of 'comparative advantage' in these countries, namely, cheap unskilled and semi-skilled labour, turns out on closer examination to be illusory. Thus Selwyn concludes that the 'efficiency wage', the money wage corrected for the efficiency of labour (due to experience and training), is no lower than in the industrial centres in South Africa. These centres also gain from economies of agglomeration, lower infrastructure costs, better communications, access to knowledge, and so on. The end result is that lower-cost producers based in South Africa effectively dominate the markets of these countries which are in most instances unable to establish industry to produce for the large South African markets. Only where special circumstances prevail, such as access to local resources, has large-scale manufacturing industry successfully been established. However some types of small-scale industry have also been affected by the backwash effects. Thus the ILO–JASPA report on Swaziland in 1976 gives as a major reason for the surprising absence of an 'informal sector' the competition from lower-cost producers in South Africa. Although the Customs Union agreement does make provision for the protection of 'infant industries', in very few cases have protective measures been used to establish industry in the three countries.

Thus other African countries, and particularly those in southern Africa, have with good economic reason come to be seen as South Africa's 'natural market'. This is acknowledged in licensing and other know-how agreements made in South Africa with foreign firms which restrict exports to African countries. The Reynders Commission drew a 10% sample from a register of such agreements kept by the South African Department of Industries. This sample revealed that 'none of the agreements provided for export outside African territories'. In only 30% of the cases was the 'sales territory' restricted to South Africa while in 56% of the cases it was limited to South Africa, Botswana, Lesotho, Swaziland, Malawi, Rhodesia, Angola and Mozambique.[50]

(e) SOME ASPECTS OF LABOUR POLICY SINCE THE SECOND WORLD WAR

The Second World War had a significant positive effect on manufacturing output as a result of the increased demand for manufactured goods including military equipment and the *de facto* protection enjoyed by South African-based manufacturers. With the conscription of large numbers of white workers this implied a large increase in the demand for African labour and there followed a huge influx of Africans from white-owned farms and the 'reserves'. The wages of African workers rose substantially increasing to about 10% per annum in real terms between 1940 and 1945.[51] The sharp increase in demand for labour during this period was accompanied by labour shortages particularly in agriculture and manufacturing and a rising level of African industrial organization. During the war and immediately after it there was a good deal of disagreement at the level of white political parties and the state over the future of the migrant labour system, influx control, the pass laws and the question of African 'rights' in the urban areas, including the right to form trade unions. The 'line' that ultimately prevailed was that associated with the apartheid policies of the National Party which won the 1948 general election. These policies essentially implied far stricter measures of control over African labour (and to a lesser extent Indian and Coloured labour): the migrant labour system, whereby African workers retained ties in the rural areas where their families remained, was perpetuated for manufacturing[52] as well as mining and this was accompanied by a tightening of the influx control and pass legislation. Two important implications of these policies were that they provided a partial solution to the labour supply problems of agriculture and they enabled the confining of unemployed and underemployed Africans to the 'homelands' (officially called 'bantustans') thus establishing a greater degree of 'political stability' in the urban areas. In the latter areas a policy of racially segregated housing was accompanied by a thicket of legislation controlling all aspects of the lives of urban Africans. The pass laws were rigidly enforced in the attempt to stem the drift of Africans to the towns and convictions under the pass legislation increased from 264,300 in 1952 to over 600,000 in 1971 which amounted to 1,685 prosecutions a day. The official rationale behind these measures was made clear: 'Racial and class differences will make a homogeneous Native proletariat which will eventually lose all contact with its former rural relations ... No government can view with equanimity the de-tribalization of large numbers of Natives congregated in amorphous masses in large industrial centres.'[53] However, if the market was to be given a restricted role in the allocation of labour as a result of political dangers, it was necessary to find alternative bureaucratic means of allocating African labour to the available jobs. The 'labour bureaux system' provided the answer. This system, which was originally established in 1949, required every African male to register at the local labour bureau and prevented the employment of African labour without the permission of the local labour bureaux. In 1969 the system was extended to the reserves and later, in order to counter the problems of low productivity and high labour turnover that accompanied the contract labour system, a 'call-in card' system was established which enabled an African worker to be placed with the same employer after his contract had ended and he had returned to the rural areas. At the same time within the so-called homelands political jurisdiction was extended over a limited number of local matters to newly created political institutions.

However, the control of African labour also extended to the jobs that African workers were permitted by law and, more important, by de facto practice to perform. In effect this meant that Africans were largely confined to unskilled and semi-skilled operative positions while whites occupied more skilled and supervisory positions. With the dissolution of artisanal skills as capital intensity increased after the war these operative positions became more important and further changes in capital intensity and/or changes in demand for labour of different skills were accompanied by a complex process of bargaining between employers, state representatives and white unions (African unions were, until very recently, in effect prohibited). The end result of this process frequently meant that Africans were allowed to perform tasks previously denied them (through a process of 'job reclassification' and 'job dilution') and white workers were paid for having agreed to African 'advancement'. While the system undoubtedly implied inefficiencies in labour allocation and reallocation, it meant at the same time that the wage costs, particularly of unskilled and semi-skilled workers, were kept relatively low.

More recently, however, there have been indications of some change which seems to be related to two sets of connected factors. First and foremost there has been the rising level of structural unemployment in South Africa. Simkins has distinguished two periods: 1961–9 and 1970–9. During the first period the unemployment rate rose from 10% to 12% and the unemployment level from 700,000 to 1,000,000 while during the second period the unemployment rate was projected to rise from 12% to 19% and the unemployment level from 1,000,000 to 2,000,000.[54] Although Simkins saw his figures as tentative there was support from a wide spectrum of writers suggesting that in the mid-1970s the level of unemployment ranged from a 'low' estimate of about 1 million (10·2% of the labour force) to a 'high' estimate of about 1·85 million (18·6%).[55] Second, and related to rising unemployment and inflationary pressures, there were indications of growing unrest dating from the Durban strikes in 1973[56] and the greatly increased number of strikes by African workers in the following years. The Soweto events of June 1976 served to highlight the seriousness of the situation.

The response of the state to this situation would appear to be threefold. First the state is attempting to confine the unemployed and underemployed to the 'homelands' where they will remain the responsibility of the local authorities. Thus on the one hand the entire African population has so far been given *de jure* membership of one of the 'homelands', including permanently urbanized Africans, and on the other the unemployed have been moved from urban areas and white-owned farms to the 'homelands'. Second attempts are being made to bring the so-called unregistered African trade unions under stricter state control by legalizing African unions while imposing severe restrictions. The Wiehahn Commission and state implementation of some of its recommendations are the main examples in this connection.[57] Third numerous efforts are being made both by the state and by private industry, to extend previously non-existing privileges particularly to the urban African 'middle classes'. As Oppenheimer put it: 'What is required is greater confidence, internally and externally, in the economic and particularly the political future of South Africa'.[58] Although the currently high gold price provides additional room for manoeuvre the underlying problems remain and it seems inconceivable that it will be possible to provide the bulk of the black population with rising living standards and employment.[59]

IV Conclusion

In the first section of this chapter the process of capital accumulation in South Africa from the 1880s to the Second World War was examined. Specific attention was paid to the gold mining industry and to agriculture and the part that they played in facilitating industrialization.

In the second part the postwar period was discussed and the major structural features of the economy were analysed. Here it was shown that while the 'Singh criteria' have been satisfied, imported capital goods remained more than 50% of total merchandise imports and local technological capacity was limited. Nevertheless it was argued that these structural conditions are consistent with a continued growth of the manufacturing sector. Finally the state's labour policy since the war was briefly described.

Appendices

TABLES

Table 12A.1 *Value added and employment in the machinery (except electrical machinery) sector, 1972 (R thousand)*

	Value added		Total employment	
	R '000	%	No.	%
Total machinery (except electrical machinery)	249,096	100·0	66,641	100·0
Agricultural machinery except tractors	15,798	6·3	5,600	8·4
Industrial machinery and equipment	153,441	61·6	39,849	59·9
Refrigerators, washing machines, stoves and ovens	25,464	10·2	8,351	12·6
Air conditioning and ventilation machinery	13,416	5·4	3,695	5·6
All other machinery	40,975	16·5	9,146	13·8

Source: South African Statistics, 1978.

Table 12A.2 *Value added and employment in the electrical machinery, apparatus, appliances and supplies sector, 1972 (R thousand)*

	Value added		Total employment	
	R '000	%	No.	%
Total electrical machinery, apparatus, appliances and supplies	188,291	100·0	49,986	100·0
Electrical industrial machinery and apparatus	62,521	33·2	17,398	34·8
Radio, TV and other electronic and communication equipment and apparatus	58,108	30·9	15,644	31·2
Electrical appliances and housewares	10,790	5·7	3,606	7·2
Insulated wires and cables	26,134	13·9	5,131	10·2
Dry and wet cell batteries	17,425	9·2	3,944	7·8
All other electrical products	13,314	7·1	4,263	8·6

Source: *South African Statistics, 1978.*

Table 12A.3 *Value added and employment in the chemicals and chemical products sector, 1972 (R thousand)*

| | Value added | | Total employment | |
	R '000	%	No.	%
Total chemicals and chemical products	466,996	100·0	70,878	100·0
Basic industrial chemicals except fertilizers	78,890	16·9	13,506	19·0
Fertilizers	37,999	8·1	5,812	8·1
Pesticides, insecticides, fungicides and herbicides	11,071	2·4	2,212	3·1
Paints, varnishes and lacquers	24,777	5·3	5,868	8·3
Soap, other cleaning compounds and candles	38,809	8·3	4,584	6·5
Other chemicals and chemical products	275,451	59·0	38,896	54·9

Source: South African Statistics, 1978.

Table 12A.4 *Value added and employment in the fabricated metal products (except machinery and equipment) sector, 1972 (R thousand)*

| | Value added | | Total employment | |
	R '000	%	No.	%
Total fabricated metal products	344,796	100·0	113,033	100·0
Cutlery, hand tools and general hardware	9,251	2·7	3,773	3·4
Furniture primarily of metal	20,331	5·9	6,797	6·0
Building hardware	38,491	11·2	11,337	10·0
Structural steel work, prefabricated steel buildings	87,751	25·5	28,296	25·0
Ornamental and architectural metal work	4,922	1·4	1,990	1·8
Boiler manufacture and installation	12,872	3·7	3,413	3·0
Sheet metal products	13,288	3·9	5,031	4·4
Tinware	33,316	9·7	11,217	9·9
Cables, wire products and gates	27,377	8·0	9,581	8·5
Springs	4,073	1·2	1,496	1·3
Headed and threaded items	11,696	3·4	3,998	3·5
Engineering workshops, welding, fitting and turning	17,437	5·1	4,829	4·2
Electroplating, anodizing, tinning, etc.	10,657	3·1	4,264	3·8
All other metal products	53,335	15·1	17,111	15·0

Source: South African Statistics, 1978.

Table 12A.5 *Destination of output of agriculture, forestry and fishing sector, 1975 (R million)*

1 Total agriculture, forestry and fishing output	3,072·02
2 Total exports	597·76
3 2 as percentage of 1	19·50%
4 Agricultural direct intermediate inputs into:	
meat, dairy products, fish processing	661·00
grain, sugar and animal foods processing	672·00
other food processing	176·00
beverage industries	74·86
tobacco products	37·00
wool scouring, cotton ginning and dyeing of wool and cotton	18·31
5 Total of 4	1,639·17
6 5 as percentage of 1	53·40%

Source: South African Department of Statistics, Report No. 09-16-03, Input-Output Tables, 1975.

Table 12A.6 *Manufactured direct intermediate inputs into agriculture, 1975 (R million)*

Manufactured direct intermediate inputs into:	
1 Grain, sugar and animal feeds processing	221·43
2 As proportion of total output of 1	18%
3 Fertilizers and pesticides	228·64
4 As proportion of total output of 3	78%
5 Other basic chemicals and petroleum and coal products	48·48
6 As proportion of total output of 5	4%
7 Agricultural machinery and equipment	36·77
8 As proportion of total output of 7	34%

Note: Part of the output of the manufacturing sector, especially the capital goods sector, goes into agriculture in the form of final demand by the latter (e.g. gross domestic fixed investment) rather than as an intermediate demand. Accordingly these figures substantially understate the importance of the agricultural for the manufacturing sector. Furthermore, it is only direct effects which are shown here while indirect effects are also significant, so that these figures do not give a good idea of the effects on output of a change in final demand.
Source: South African Department of Statistics, Report No. 09-16-03, Input-Output Tables, 1975.

Table 12A.7 *Capacity utilization and gross fixed capital investment in manufacturing 1970–78*

Year	Capacity utilization	Gross fixed investment in manufacturing				Private investment as percentages of total %
		Total		Private		
		Current prices Rm	1970 prices Rm	Current prices Rm	1970* prices Rm	
1970	n.a.	594	594	448	448	75·4
1971	86·0	675	638	547	517	81·0
1972	87·0	809	687	629	534	77·8
1973	89·2	1,043	808	633	490	60·7
1974	89·5	1,217	832	800	547	65·7
1975	88·0	1,471	840	1,029	588	70·0
1976	86·6	1,518	738	1,148	558	75·6
1977	83·7	1,677	746	1,104	491	65·8
1978	84·8	1,980	793	1,084	434	54·7

Note: *Computed assuming same price indexes as total manufacturing.
Source: *Ratcliffe*, 1979.

B   Commodity Production and Migrant Labour in Lesotho

It has been decided for two reasons to include a brief discussion on Lesotho. In the first place a discussion of African agriculture complements the earlier section on 'white' agriculture and the Basutho example is one of a period of extremely successful agricultural commodity production. Second, the Basutho case is also one where for a number of reasons agricultural production was undermined and the bulk of the male population turned into a migrant proletariat. In section II above the gold mining industry was considered and the importance of labour recruitment at relatively low wages was stressed. The example of the Basutho provides an idea of some of the factors which in this case influenced the supply of labour to the mines.

An important study of the origins of migrant labour in Lesotho has recently been completed by Judy Kimble and this section draws heavily on her work.[60] Kimble points out that by as early as 1850 'Lesotho was acknowledged as the 'granary' of the Orange River Sovereignty, and by the end of the 1860s, their cereals were being sent into the towns of the northeastern Cape Colony'.[61] The white farmers living in the Sovereignty were engaged mainly in wool farming and could not compete against Basutho cereals. However, it is central to Kimble's thesis that although during the years 1830–70 'non-chiefly homesteads began to participate in exchange to some degree'[62] it was primarily the demand by the ruling Basutho lineage 'for certain commodities central to the continued reproduction of its position of supremacy [within Basutho society] – cattle, guns and horses – which gave rise to commodity production on a significant scale'.[63] But whatever the reason for the trade it is clear that

Basutho producers were efficient and were able successfully to supply local markets. From the early 1870s Basutho commodity production was considerably intensified by the opening of the Kimberley diamond mines and the consequent sharp rise in prices, particularly of wheat but also of maize and sorghum, between the years 1870 and 1876. Missionary accounts refer to this period as one of remarkable prosperity in Lesotho and reference was made to the rapidly increasing number of trading stores operating in the country and the growing purchase of manufactured consumer and producer goods.

However by the mid-1880s the prosperity had ended and most Basutho were impoverished and thereafter became increasingly dependent on the sale of their labour. The reasons for this rapid transition are numerous and while it is not yet possible to give a precise account of the relative importance of each of the causes, it is possible to make some meaningful observations. One early cause was the protective measures passed by the Free State Volksraad from at least 1874, which took the form of a wagon tax intended to encourage local white cereal producers.[64] Second, there were the disruptive effects of the Gun War of 1880–1 and the inter-chief disturbances that followed. Third, and perhaps most important, there was the intrusion of 'modernizing influences' in the form of the extension of the railway line. Thus in '1886 . . . the railways from the coastal ports finally reached Kimberley, and the markets of the subcontinent were flooded with quantities of Australian and colonial wheat'. Accordingly 'the exceptionally abundant harvests of 1886 and 1887 found no outlet'.[65] After this period the Basutho were never again successful agricultural exporters and they came to depend increasingly on the sale of their labour. In 1906 2·6% of the labour employed by the Chamber of Mines came from Lesotho. By 1936 this had increased to 14·5% and 17·5% by 1969.[66] In addition many Basutho were employed on white farms and in towns.

In this way successful agricultural commodity producers were turned into migrant labourers and Lesotho became a labour exporting country.

Notes

I wish to thank Chris Allen, John Markakis, John Sender and Ajit Singh for helpful comments on part or all of this chapter. Obviously none of them is responsible for the present contents.

1   This point is also made by Johnstone, 1976.

2   Transvaal Chamber of Mines, Tenth Annual Report (1898), p 455A, quoted in Wilson, 1972, p 3.

3   ibid., p. 4. See also Johnstone, 1976, ch. 1.

4   ibid., p. 4.

5   loc. cit.

6   That the imposers of such taxes intended not only to raise revenue but also to obtain a supply of labour is revealed in the following quotation by Cecil Rhodes. Rhodes, who was the largest of the mining magnates, was also the Prime Minister of the Cape Colony and in introducing the Glen Grey Act in 1894 in the Cape Parliament which proposed a tax of 10 shillings on selected individuals he pointed out that by imposing this tax 'you will remove (the natives) from that life of sloth and laziness, you will teach them the dignity of labour and make them contribute to the prosperity of the State . . . (Cape of Good Hope, Hansard, 1894 in South Africa, London: OUP, p. 362; cited in van der Horst, Native Labour 1964, pp. 148–52.

7 These traders often extended credit to potential migrant labourers and as indebtedness increased migrants were forced to sign labour contracts with the mines (Johnstone, 1976, ch. 1).

8 Evidence given to the Transvaal Labour Commission of 1904 by a recruiter in Swaziland made it clear that one of the Swazi Queens was in effect also a labour recruiter in the pay of the Chamber of Mines (Transvaal Labour Commission, 1904, p. 103–106). Since the traditional rulers exerted a good deal of influence over their subjects they were able significantly to increase the recruiting rate.

9 There were many different factors affecting the supply of labour to the mines from the various parts of the mines' 'catchment area'. In the appendix the case of the Basutho is briefly examined.

10 Wilson, 1972, p. 46. The most illuminating work on the role of white labour in South Africa is contained in Davies, 1979. In the 1970s, however, for a number of reasons that cannot be considered here, real black wages rose substantially.

11 For the latter see D. O'Meara, 1975. However, it should not be inferred from what has been said above that the mines' revenue constraint resulting from the external determination of the price of gold meant that African wages and conditions could not be improved. Trapido, 1971, has commented that 'even if we accept the imperative of the Chamber of Mines' cost structure . . . it would have been possible to raise African wages significantly some time between 1932 [when the gold price rose significantly] and 1950 . . . In practice the opposite occurred. In 1934 the Chamber of Mines rejected the Mine Native Wages Commission's recommendation that wages be raised by 3d per shift, and in 1946 the African mine-workers' strike resulted in the uninhibited use of state coercive machinery' (p. 315).

12 It is perhaps necessary to point out that the *minimum* price of gold was in fact determined in South Africa, i.e. the price below which the mining of gold, given the cost of labour, and other costs, would have been unprofitable and hence not undertaken by private capital.

13 Frankel, 1935.

14 Frankel, 1967, calculated in current terms.

15 This point has been stressed by M. Morris and D. Kaplan in particular.

16 Morris, 1975.

17 See Wilson, 1971, p. 138–40.

18 See Kaplan, 1977, for a more detailed discussion of this tax.

19 The aim of this section has been primarily to examine the emergence of capitalist agriculture in the non-reserve areas of South Africa. A brief account of African agriculture in the Basutho case and the origins of labour migration from this area to South African farms, mines and factories is given in the appendix.

20 Kooy and Robertson, 1966, p. 209.

21 Clearly in the absence of protection part of this growing market would have been captured by foreign producers, but presumably not all of it. The point being made here is that it was not protection *per se* that encouraged the growth of manufacturing but protection together with the other factors referred to.

22 Kooy and Robertson, 1966, p. 211.

23 Kaplan, 1977, p. 183.

24 See his dissertation for an elaboration.

25 Legassick tends to support this although he gives far more weight to agricultural interests (1975 and 1977a).

26 See also Botha, 1973.

27 Kaplan, 1977, p. 184.

28 ibid., p. 187

29 For an application of the Chenery and Syrquin analysis (see the introduction to this book) to South Africa, see Simkins, 1979.

30 However in the 1970s increasing incentives were given to the machine tool industry (Ratcliffe, 1979, p. 408).

31 In Brazil in 1971 'capital goods' contributed $19 \cdot 1\%$ to the value of manufacturing output: machinery $4 \cdot 6\%$, electrical and communications equipment $5 \cdot 3\%$ and transport equipment $9 \cdot 2\%$. See Tyler, 1976, p. 865.

32   An indication of capacity utilization is given in Table 12A.7 in the appendix.
33   South Africa, 1972, p. 41.
34   ibid.
35   Calculated from South African Government, Input-Output Tables, 1975.
36   Suckling, 1974, tables 9 and 10. See also McHenry, 1975, and Seidman, 1977.
37   South Africa, 1972, Vol. 1, p. 244.
38   *Financial Times*, 4 January 1980, p. 12.
39   ibid.
40   South Africa, 1972, pp. 55–7.
41   Lall, 1979.
42   See references to Katz in ibid.
43   These figures exclude labour, one of the most important imports from other African countries. Because of the sensitive nature of South African trade with other African countries an official breakdown of trade by country is not available.
44   van der Merwe and du Plessis, 1973, pp. 16–17.
45   ibid., p. 19.
46   South Africa, 1972, Vol. I, p. 231.
47   ibid.
48   ibid.
49   van der Merwe and du Plessis, 1973, p. 19.
50   South Africa, 1972, Vol.II, p. 609.
51   Davies, 1979, pp. 332–3.
52   However, a proportion of the African labour force in manufacturing was permanently urbanized, those classified under section 10 of the Group Areas Act.
53   Union Government, Board of Trade and Industry, Report 282, Pretoria, 1945, para. 35.
54   Simkins, 1976, 1977.
55   Legassick and Innes, 1977, p. 452.
56   Institute for Industrial Education, 1974.
57   *South African Labour Bulletin*, 1979; Davies, 1979.
58   Oppenheimer, 1979. However, Oppenheimer's suggestions are contradictory. On the one hand he argues that 'In South Africa as a whole ... the trend towards capital-intensive industry is natural at this stage in our development and cannot be reversed' and indeed that it must be enhanced, partly financed by foreign capital inflows. However, on the other hand he notes that African unemployment 'is now estimated to be not less than 800,000 and may be substantially higher' and suggests that it is politically necessary to reduce unemployment levels. It is by no means obvious that a faster rate of growth assisted by foreign capital inflows will lead to a significant fall in unemployment. The outcome in all probability will be that the 'homelands' will be allocated a greater role in maintaining the unemployed often under conditions of low productivity agriculture.
59   While Kaplan has provided a detailed analysis of this period (Kaplan, 1977), Davies has written the most comprehensive account of the position of white workers in South African society (Davies, 1979). See also Legassick, 1974, 1975, 1977a and 1977b.
60   Kimble, 1978.
61   ibid., p. 295.
62   ibid., p. 153.
63   ibid., p. 298.
64   ibid., pp. 210 *et seq.*
65   ibid., p. 235 and Germond, *Chronicles of Basutoland*, p. 469.
66   Wilson, 1972, p. 70. For a comparison with the Swaziland case where there was little production of agricultural products for sale but substantial dependence on wage labour; see Fransman, 1978.

References

Anglo-American Corporation of South Africa Limited (1979) *Chairman's Statement*.

Botha, D. J. J. (1973) 'On tariff policy – the formative years', *South African Journal of Economics*, 41, 4, pp. 321–55.

Christian Concern for Southern Africa (1979) *Britain's Economic Links with South Africa; A Study of Lasting Ties and a Preliminary Assessment of the Impact of Disengagement* (London: Christian Concern for Southern Africa).

Clarke, D. G. (1977) 'Foreign African labour inflows to South Africa and "unemployment" in Southern Africa', paper presented at the Workshop on Unemployment and Labour Reallocation, University of Natal, Pieter-maritzburg.

Davies, R. H. (1979a) *Capital, State and White Labour in South Africa 1900–1960* (Brighton: Harvester Press).

Davies, R. H. (1979b) 'Capital restructuring and the modification of the racial division of labour in South Africa', *Journal of Southern African Studies*, 5, 2.

Du Plessis, S. P. J. (1976) 'Effective tariff protection in South Africa', *South African Journal of Economics*, 44, 2, pp. 158–70.

First, R., Steele, J. and Gurney, C. (1972) *The South African Connection* (London: Temple Smith).

Frankel, S. H. (1935) 'Return to capital investment in the Witwatersrand gold mining industry 1887–1932', *Economic Journal*, XLV.

Frankel, S. H. (1967) *Investment and the Return to Equity Capital in the South African Gold Mining Industry, 1887–1965* (Oxford: Blackwell).

Fransman, M. J. (1978) 'The state and development in Swaziland', D.Phil. dissertation, University of Sussex.

Germond, R. C. (1967) *Chronicles of Basutoland*, Morija-Lesotho: Morija Sesuto Book Depot.

Holden, M. G. and P. (1975) 'An intertemporal calculation of effective rates of protection for South Africa', *South African Journal of Economics*, 43, 3, pp. 370–9.

Houghton, D. H. (1969) *The South African Economy* (Cape Town: Oxford University Press).

Institute For Industrial Education (1974) *The Durban Strikes, 1973* (Durban: Institute for Industrial Education in association with Ravan Press).

Johnstone, F. A. (1976) *Class, Race and Gold: A Study of Class Relations and Racial Discrimination in South Africa* (London: Routledge & Kegan Paul).

Kaplan, D. E. (1976) 'The politics of industrial protection in South Africa, 1910–39', *Journal of Southern African Studies*, 3, 1, pp. 70–91.

Kaplan, D. E. (1977) 'Class conflict, capital accumulation and the state: an historical analysis of the state in twentieth century South Africa', D.Phil. dissertation submitted to the University of Sussex.

Kimble, J. (1978) 'Towards an understanding of the political economy of Lesotho: the origins of commodity production and migrant labour, 1830– c. 1885', MA dissertation, National University of Lesotho.

Kooy, M. and Robertson, H. M. (1966) 'The South African Board of Trade and Industries; the South African customs tariff and the development of South African industries', *South African Journal of Economics*, 34, 3, pp. 205–24.

Lachmann, D. (1974) 'Import restrictions and exchange rates', *South African Journal of Economics*, 42, 1, pp. 25–42.

Lall, S. (1979) 'Developing countries as exporters of technology and capital goods: the Indian experience' (mimeo.), Oxford University Institute of Economics and Statistics.

Legassick, M. (1974) 'Ideology, legislation and economy in post-1948 South Africa', *Journal of Southern African Studies*, 1, 1.

Legassick, M. (1975) 'South Africa: capital accumulation and violence', *Economy and Society*, 3, 3.

Legassick, M. (1977a) 'Gold, agriculture and secondary industry in South Africa, 1885–1970', in Palmer, R. and Parsons, N. (eds) *The Roots of Rural Poverty in Central and Southern Africa* (London: Heinemann Educational Books).

Legassick, M. and Innes, D. (1977b) 'Capital restructuring and apartheid: a critique of constructive engagement', *African Affairs*, 76, 305, pp. 437–82.

Lumby, A. B. (1976) 'Tariffs and gold in South Africa', *South African Journal of Economics*, 44, 2, pp. 139–57

McHenry, D. (1975) *United States Firms in South Africa* (Africa Publications Trust/Study Project on External Investment in South Africa and Namibia).

Morris, M. (1976) 'The development of capitalism in South African agriculture', *Economy and Society*, 5, 3.

Murray, R. (1973) 'Underdevelopment, international firms, and the international division of labour', in *Towards a New World Economy* (Rotterdam: Rotterdam University Press).

O'Meara, D. (1975) 'The 1946 African mineworkers' strike and the political economy of South Africa', *Journal of Commonwealth and Comparative Politics*, 13, 2.

Ratcliffe, A. E. (1979) 'Industrial development policy: changes during the 1970s', *South African Journal of Economics*, 47, 4, pp. 397–421.

Seidman, A. and N. (1977) *US Multinationals in Southern Africa* (Dar es Salaam: Tanzanian Publishing House).

Selwyn, P. (1975) *Industries in the Southern African Periphery. A Study of Industrial Development in Botswana, Lesotho and Swaziland* (London: Croom Helm in association with the Institute of Development Studies, Sussex).

Simkins, C. (1976) 'Employment, unemployment and growth in South Africa, 1961–1979', Saldry Working Paper No. 4.

Simkins, C. (1977) 'Measuring and predicting unemployment in South Africa, 1960–77', paper presented at the Workshop on Unemployment and Labour Reallocation, University of Natal, Pietermaritzburg.

Singh, A. (1979) 'The "Basic Needs" approach to development vs the new international economic order: the significance of third world industrialization', *World Development*, 7, pp. 585–606.

South Africa Board of Trade and Industries Report No. 282 (1945) *Investiga-*

tion into *Manufacturing Industries in the Union of South Africa*, First Interim Report (Pretoria: Government Printer).

South Africa (1958) *Report on Commission of Enquiry into the Policy Relating to the Protection of Industries in South Africa* (Viljoen Commission), UG 36/1958. (Pretoria: Government Printer).

South Africa (1972) *Report of the Commission of Inquiry into the Export Trade of the Republic of South Africa* (Reynders Commission), RP 69/72. (Pretoria: Government Printer).

South Africa Departments of Labour and of Mines (1979) *Report of the Commission of Inquiry into Labour Legislation: Part 1* (Wiehahn Commission) (Pretoria: Government Printer).

South African Labour Bulletin (1979) 'Focus on Wiehahn', 5, 2.

Suckling, J., Weiss, R. and Innes D. (1975) *The Economic Factor* (London: Africa Publications Trust/Study Project on External Investment in South Africa).

Trapido, S. (1970–1) 'South Africa in a comparative study of industrialization', *Journal of Development Studies* 8, 3, pp. 309-20.

Tyler, W. G. (1976) 'Brazilian industrialization and industrial policies: a survey, *World Development*, 4, 10/11, pp. 863–82.

UNIDO (United Nations Industrial Development Organization) (1979) *World Industry since 1960: Progress and Prospects*, special issue of the Industrial Development Survey for the Third General Conference of UNIDO, New Delhi, 2 January – 8 February 1980 (New York: United Nations).

Van Der Merwe, E. J. and Du Plessis, D. P. (1973) 'A regional classification of South Africa's balance of payments, 1957 to 1972', *South African Reserve Bank Quarterly Bulletin* (September).

Wilson, F. (1971) 'Farming 1866–1966' in Wilson, M. and Thompson, L. (eds), *The Oxford History of South Africa* (London: Oxford University Press).

Wilson, F. (1972) *Labour in the South African Gold Mines, 1911–1969* (Cambridge: Cambridge University Press).

Wolpe, H. (1972) 'Capitalism and cheap labour power in South Africa', *Economy and Society*, 1, 4.

Zarenda, H. (1977) 'The policy of state intervention in the establishment and development of manufacturing industry in South Africa', MA thesis submitted to the Faculty of Arts, University of the Witwatersrand, Johannesburg.

13 *Industrialization and Self-Reliance in Zimbabwe**

COLIN STONEMAN

I Introduction

This chapter is to a large extent complementary to my recent paper 'Zimbabwe's prospects as an economic power' given as the second Noel Buxton Lecture[1] in the Institute of Commonwealth Studies, University of London. It aims to give a brief history of the development of industry in Southern Rhodesia, concentrating on its diversification and integration under conditions of war and sanctions; and to establish the conditions under which Zimbabwe's potential as an industrial power may begin to be realized.

The main thesis is that the relative success observed to date is due only in part to the richness of natural resources, and owes more to a series of fortuitous circumstances than to orthodox economic policies which have been honoured for long periods in the breach rather than the application. Accordingly I shall maintain that a return to legality under open economic policies, far from releasing energies that have been suppressed under sanctions and partial isolation, will release inhibiting forces which have hitherto been controlled on the pretext of fighting sanctions. For different reasons, associated with the proximity of the Republic of South Africa, and the power of foreign capital, I shall also maintain that (orthodox) radical approaches are likely to fail.

Section II is historical and descriptive of the present economy. Section III lists the particular problems which will be faced on opening the economy, whilst section IV describes some recent general evidence taken from the experience of other developing countries as to the likely consequences of

*This chapter was written in November 1979 before Zimbabwe's independence was achieved. It should be noted in particular that although the name 'Patriotic Front' was used to describe the tactical alliance between Robert Mugabe's ZANU and Joshua Nkomo's ZAPU, since the independence election campaign, ZAPU has called itself 'Patriotic Front', while ZANU is usually referred to as ZANU (PF) to distinguish itself from the small ZANU (Sithole).

allowing the continuation of foreign ownership of most productive capital. Finally, in section V, I attempt to establish the requirements for an alternative strategy which is consistent with the published aims of the Patriotic Front to create a genuinely independent, self-reliant, democratic economy.

II The Path of Rhodesian Industrialization

The early years of the economic history of Southern Rhodesia and an analysis of the class interests which influenced it have been well described by Arrighi[2] and summarized elsewhere by myself.[3,4] Accordingly I shall refer to only the main features of the pre-UDI period here.

(a) 1890–1945

Industrialization began in Rhodesia with the entry of the Pioneer Column of Cecil Rhodes and his British South Africa Company. This is not to say that pre-colonial African societies were exclusively peasant (mining for copper and gold had been carried on from at least four centuries earlier), but during the nineteenth century war and invasion had disrupted earlier organization, and the invasion of 1890 and the suppression of later liberation struggles cut off any connection with these earlier traditions. The 'pioneers' came to the country not to trade or farm or merely to extend the British Empire, but to establish a mining industry, knowing that the area was rich in gold. To this end settlers were allocated land and mining claims and before the turn of the century a railway line from Vryburg in South Africa had reached Salisbury through Bechuanaland (now Botswana) and went on to the Mozambique port of Beira. Before long it was extended north to Northern Rhodesia. The development of 'European' commercial agriculture was a later process, following on the realization by the BSA Co. that the mineral wealth was much less than in South Africa, though, together with the exploitation of the large area of excellent arable land, it still justified maintaining the large infrastructural investments already made. But in the early stages the market provided by the new mining community and associated white settlers was met largely by African farmers; early white farmers were unsuccessful, or even where relatively successful, still easily undercut by the Africans. So the point to be emphasized is that a common view of Southern Rhodesia as a settler farming community with some development of mining and manufacturing industry is the reverse of the actual early experience: white farming only became a commercial success in the 1920s and 1930s (mainly, that is, after the BSA Co. relinquished government to the settlers in 1923) and through a series of restrictions on blacks to prevent their successful competition, and progressive alienation of the best farmland into 'white' areas.

   The early mining industry was divided between small settler miners (mainly in gold) and a number of foreign companies, either established mining companies like Turner & Newall in asbestos and the US Union Carbide, and Foote Minerals in chrome, or mining-ranching companies like Lonrho (founded as the London and Rhodesia Mining and Land Company in 1909). During the slump of the 1930s the colony was thrown very much on its own resources, and the settler-dominated government introduced a number of measures which, if not directly opposed to the interests of foreign capital, would not have originated in a more foreign-dominated polity. These included further infrastructural developments, including road building, the establishment of the Electricity Supply Commission and the Roasting Plant. The latter processed low-grade gold ores, and greatly benefited mainly small-scale, domestic gold miners. But these state initiatives were merely the prelude to the far more significant decision during the Second World War to directly stimulate the growth of secondary industry. Thus profits from the wartime boom were partially diverted by the state into enterprises which because of the tiny size of the economy would never have been considered viable by foreign investors. The major examples are the production of iron and steel ('Risco' at Que Que) and cotton spinning (at Gatooma). These state enterprises were denationalized once they became commercially viable in the 1950s, and bought up largely by foreign capital. However, later stages in the production of clothing and metal products were left to private capital which during the war was necessarily mainly domestic, and this provided the initial stimulus to settler-owned secondary industry.

(b) 1945–65

After the war a number of causes produced a boom which involved a massive influx of both capital and settlers (massive, that is, for so small an economy), and development proceeded rapidly from the base established during the relative isolation of slump and war. The growth rate of national income in money terms (constant price estimates are not available) never fell below 10% over the years 1946 to 1957, and the average rate was over 15% (and certainly over 10% in real terms). Over the period 1946–53 the value of gross output in manufacturing industries increased from £17·3m. to £61·9m. (a 20% average growth rate); including construction and infrastructural sectors, the value of gross output rose from £22·8m. in 1946 to £86·3m. in 1952 (24·8% average growth rate). Data are available[5] for a breakdown of the manufacturing industry into major groups as shown in Table 13.1.

An increasing proportion of the output of manufacturing industry was exported. Over the period 1945–53 visible exports nearly quadrupled, rising to over half of GDP in value, and showing a slight swing away from the typical colonial pattern of heavy bias towards primary products. Minerals declined in relative importance, but due to the rapid rise of tobacco growing, agriculture increased its share. Manufactured exports increased fifteen-fold in value to £15·2m. rising to a quarter of the total. In 1953 about two-thirds of manufactured exports was accounted for by food, beverages, tobacco, textiles, footwear, apparel, and made-up textiles. However, exports approaching £1m. in value each were made by the chemical, non-metallic mineral, and metal industries, whilst electrical machinery and transport equipment exports were also growing rapidly. Very nearly all the manufactured exports went to neighbouring countries, however, in contrast to the primary exports which went almost entirely overseas (and mainly to Britain).

The boom continued into the federal period up to 1957; thereafter low copper prices and political uncertainties had a depressing effect on the economies of all three countries in the federation. Growth rates in the manufacturing industry in Southern Rhodesia fell to about half their earlier levels. Nevertheless by 1965 gross output in the manufacturing sector totalled £215·4m., as compared with £34·8m. in mining and £72·1m. in European agriculture. From 1945 to 1965 the share of manufacturing in GDP had increased from 12·5% to 19·7% (and it is now about 24%), whilst mining had fallen from 12·9% to 7·1% (about the present level, although the low point was 5·1% in 1963) and European agriculture had fallen from around 20% to 12·2% (about 11% now).

Although the consolidation of many statistics into Federal accounts during the years 1954–63 prevents detailed statistical evidence on a number of developments, certain trends are clear. There can be no doubt that federation greatly strengthened the economy of Southern Rhodesia, and that it did this in part at the expense of Northern Rhodesia and Nyasaland. Thus the growth of manufacturing industry in Southern Rhodesia was significantly above the Federal average, and above the rate of growth of the consumer market, whereas in the other two territories it was considerably below.[6] Rhodesia received supplies of cheap labour from Nyasaland, and the large copper revenues of Northern Rhodesia financed a high proportion of the Federation's (in fact Southern Rhodesia's) investment. Both territories provided captive markets for Rhodesia's new manufactured exports, many of which would not have been able to compete either in terms of price or quality on the world market. On the other hand, although these new industries may not yet have been able to stand up to world market competition without protection (including a greater degree of competition from South Africa after 1955), the even more backward industries in the other two territories received no protection from their relatively more advanced southern neighbour. Finally, generally accepted that the political and economic promise of the

Table 13.1 *Gross output and average growth rate of Rhodesian industry 1946–53*

Sector	Gross output (£m.) 1946	1953	Average growth rate
Food manufacturing	5·6	18·8	19·0
Beverages	1·2	3·4	16·5
Tobacco manufacturing	1·3	4·0	17·5
Textiles and clothes	2·4	8·8	20·8
Wood manufactures (except furniture)	0·6	1·9	18·3
Furniture and fixtures	0·3	1·3	22·3
Paper, printing, publishing	0·6	2·4	21·6
Rubber	0·1	0·2	15·3
Chemicals	1·0	3·9	21·9
Non-metallic minerals	0·8	3·8	24·4
Metal manufacturing	1·9	6·8	20·3
Transport (manufacture and repair)	1·1	4·8	24·1
Miscellaneous	0·5	1·7	17·7
TOTAL manufacturing	17·3	61·9	20·0

Source: *Monthly Digest of Statistics*, June 1955.

Federation ensured a continuation of the very high capital inflows of the immediate postwar period, at any rate up to 1958.

The conclusion I wish to draw from this experience is that, first, relatively closed conditions coupled with a measure of domestic political control during the slump and war years allowed the establishment of a small industrial base; second, the postwar boom brought very open conditions involving massive foreign investment at a time when most other countries were in no position to undercut Rhodesia in its home or neighbouring markets; third, that in the Federal period Rhodesia benefited from both artificial and natural protection of its new industries whilst losing none of the initial benefits of large foreign capital inflows into new industry and infrastructure. (Infrastructural investment, including the Kariba hydroelectric scheme, probably, and most unusually, ran ahead of the industrial needs of Southern Rhodesia in the Federal period, providing a stock that was to be drawn on after UDI). Finally, although the two years between the end of the Federation and UDI were bad (as Federal protection and privileged markets began to disappear, investment income outflows reached record levels, and net capital outflows began to occur), the advent of sanctions and the need to combat the effects resulted in a closing of the economy which could never have been justified ideologically, but which prevented a serious haemorrhaging of the industrial base. The new protection, at a time when recent investment from abroad had largely obviated the need for further inflows (which in any event had ceased), provided the conditions for a further deepening and diversification of industry.

Because of Federation and UDI, there are only two years in the last twenty-five for which detailed (or even any) trade statistics are available, 1964 and 1965. In 1965 (the following data are taken from the *Annual Statement of External Trade, 1965*), exports were valued at £149·2m., of which unmanufactured tobacco accounted for £47·0m., minerals £32·4m. and other agricultural exports £5·5m., the balance of £64·4m. being almost entirely manufactured goods. The latter thus accounted for over 43% of exports (despite the dramatic rise in tobacco exports) as compared with about 25% in 1953. Furthermore only 37·5% of the manufactured exports (as compared with about two-thirds in 1953) were accounted for by the food, beverage, textile, tobacco, footwear and apparel industries. Aside from these, other industries exported the following amounts: pig iron, £2·5m.; radios, £2·1m.; ferrochrome £1·7m.; passenger cars £1·6m.; iron or steel bars, rounds, angles, etc., £1·2m.; rubber tyres and tubes, £1·1m.; motor trucks and vans, £1·1m.; fertilizers, £1·0m.; soaps and detergents, £0·9m.; furniture and fixtures, £0·8m.; paper and cardboard containers, £0·7m.; coke, £0·7m.; insulated electric cable and wire, £0·7m.; structural steel and finished structural parts, £0·7m.; asbestos cement products, £0·6m.; iron and steel ingots, billets, etc., £0·6m.; non-electrical machinery, not elsewhere specified, £0·6m.; medicinal and pharmaceutical products, £0·5m.; paints, varnishes, distempers, £0·5m.; enamelware and holloware, £0·5m.; copper bar and rod, £0·4m.; mining machinery, £0·4m. In all some eighty-seven commodities are listed as having earned over £100,000 in foreign exchange, with a further thirty-seven earning between £20,000 and £100,000. Classified by broad commodity groups, meat exports earned £7·9m., other foods (manufactured) £2·9m.; beverages and manufactured tobacco, £2·8m.; textiles, £3·4m.; clothing and footwear, £7·1m.; chemicals and non-metallic mineral products, £6·4m.; basic metal industries, £6·6m.; metal manufactures, £3·4m.; machinery and transport equipment, £8·9m.; and miscellaneous manufactures, £14·1m. Information about the *current* level and constitution of exports is of course speculative. It is thought that visible exports may now be earning about $600m. (or £400m. at the current exchange rate, representing a reduction in value in real terms, and a reduction from about 44% to 26% of GDP; *total* exports, that is including re-exports and 'invisibles' came to £188·5m. or 55·2% of GDP in 1965). Of these, it seems likely that nearly all the mining output of $250m. (say 90% or $225m.) is exported, and agricultural exports are generally thought to be between $250m. and $300m., mainly tobacco, sugar, beef and maize; this would suggest that manufactured exports have fallen back to between 12% and 20% of the total.

(c) 1965–75

After UDI under the impact of sanctions, a number of events occurred which changed the direction of the development of the economy. One group of changes will be seen to have been clearly unfavourable for the future Zimbabwe: the slow shift away from a bias towards white needs in particular and urban needs in general instigated by the Federal mythology of 'partnership', was reversed by the Rhodesian Front when it came to power in 1962, and after UDI the new course was dramatically reinforced by the political need to safeguard white living standards in the initially more stringent circumstances (real GDP fell by about 4% in 1966). This could only be done at the expense of black living standards, and in particular of those in rural areas. Investment was concentrated on the industrial sector, and the already overcrowded 'Tribal Trust Lands' were starved of investment and expected to carry ever-heavier burdens of disguised social security support for urban workers who became unemployed or who received inadequate wages. Black employment had reached 600,000 in 1956, but stagnated at a little above this level until 1968, only rising to above 700,000 for the first time in 1969. Accordingly, although black wages rose (but slower than white wages), they went to a steadily declining proportion of the population, and average consumption fell. The market thus became more distorted in the direction of luxury consumption, a tendency reinforced by sanctions against imports. A number of manufacturing industries (in particular in food processing and clothing) had developed to supply black needs both domestically and in the Federation, and their attention was redirected to the white market: reports after UDI refer to locally made cornflakes, fashion goods and many other items previously imported. Luxury consumption subsectors have increased their share of gross output, for instance soft drinks and chocolate and confectionery. Much of the new industry has therefore been at the expense of far more urgently needed rural investment and is furthermore geared to supplying luxury products on a very small scale, rather than the basic requirements of the population as a whole.

Another group of changes,[7] however, has probably strengthened and improved the structure of the economy. This concerns in particular the very high proportion of investment devoted to the basic metals and metal products sectors, and the considerable increase in efficiency achieved by the textile sector. Pulp and paper, basic industrial chemicals, plastic products, clay products, glass and cement and electrical machinery, are subsectors which have also increased their share of total gross output. All these developments are likely to prove beneficial to the needs of the future state; whilst accepting that their scale was determined by a biased income distribution and therefore highly restricted market, they represent bases (which might not have easily been established under more open economic conditions) from which advances can be made. As a whole, the contribution of the manufacturing sector to GDP increased from 19·7% in 1965 to 25·2% in 1974 (at roughly which level it has remained since); mining has shown less steady progress from a minimum of 5·1% in 1963 to 7·1% in 1965, then, after declining, reaching 7·2% in 1974.

We may begin a closer look at industrial development by examining the mining industry. It now employs some 60,000 workers (4,000 of whom are white) and has a gross output of about $250m. Six minerals are of comparable importance: asbestos, gold, nickel, copper, chromium and coal (copper and nickel having risen in relative importance since UDI – indeed the nickel industry hardly existed then). Some dozens of other minerals are mined on a smaller scale, of which phosphates, iron ore, limestone, tin, tungsten, lithium and emeralds deserve mention. The industry is highly concentrated: in 1974 fourteen mines each employing more than a thousand workers produced 73·6% of gross output, and sixty-eight produced about 95%. The remaining 5% is produced by some 200–400 'small-worker' mines (production in many is highly dependent on price levels), mostly in gold (with a few in tungsten). A few of these small mines are owned by blacks. It is likely that about 90% of the output is exported as it is much beyond any conceivable needs of Zimbabwean industry. This applies particularly to gold, chromium, (exported now entirely as ferrochrome), nickel, asbestos and copper; about half the coal used to be exported to Zambia, and may now be exported to South Africa. Phosphates, iron ore and limestone on the other hand are largely consumed locally. It is not possible from the available statistics to determine whether a trend towards greater utilization of local inputs has occurred. Total purchases and changes in stocks rose from 31·6% of gross output in 1965 to 36·7% in 1975, with 'materials' constituting about 62% of each total (these would include both local and imported goods), electricity falling from 17% to 12%, coal and coke rising from 1% to 2%, but with work given out (almost certainly local) rising from 11% to 19% of the total. Meanwhile payments for services dropped slightly from 8·5% to 8·3% of gross output, but charges made by head offices abroad and royalties, which are included in service payments, fell from 27·7% to 13·0%.

Gross output in the manufacturing sector increased from $404m. in 1965 to $1,318m. in 1975, with employment rising from 79,379 to 152,055. Table 13.2 shows sectoral changes.

The considerable increases in importance of textiles (that is, cotton ginning, spinning, weaving and finishing of textiles and carpets) and the metal industries represent the most structurally useful changes, and are the result of state intervention. In the case of textiles there was substantial investment, and clothing manufacturers were required to buy a yard of local cloth for every yard imported. Furthermore productivity has increased considerably (in contrast to most other sectors). As for the metals sectors, the state has recognized their crucial importance, in particular by its support for the expansion of Risco through the purchase of the latest technology in a major sanctions-busting deal which doubled capacity to about 1 million tonnes per

Table 13.2 *Manufacturing industry*

Sector	1965	1975
Food manufacturing	25·9	20·2
Beverages	4·9	4·7
Tobacco manufacturing	4·7	2·1
Textiles	7·5	10·4
Clothing and shoes	7·1	6·7
Wood manufactures (except furniture)	1·9	1·3
Furniture and fixtures	1·5	1·5
Pulp, paper, and products	2·5	2·7
Printing, publishing, etc.	2·9	2·6
Rubber	1·9	1·6
Chemicals	11·9	10·7
Non-metallic minerals	2·4	3·7
Basic metal industries	6·7	11·6
Metal products	7·0	10·5
Electrical machinery	2·8	3·0
Transport equipment	7·6	4·3
Miscellaneous	0·8	2·4
TOTAL	100.0	100.0

Source: *Census of Production, 1974–5.*

year. Financial problems associated with this deal and the failure to find export markets following its exposure have resulted in the state's share in ownership rising to about a half. The industry as a whole contains a number of large companies, both local (Morewear), South African (Anglo-American, Stewarts & Lloyds), and British (John Brown, British Steel and many others). Integration with the mining industry must have increased, for the smelting of ores has increased (whereas most chromium used to be exported as chrome ore, it is now all exported as ferrochrome, of much higher unit value), and the list of products includes many mining implements and machines and vehicles.

The most obvious weakness of manufacturing industry is in the chemical sector. Although basic industrial chemicals have increased slightly as a proportion of total gross output, they still only contribute 1%, and largely because of problems in the fertilizer subsector, the sector as a whole has decreased in importance. Thanks to developments in phosphates and sulphuric acid production by AECI, Zimbabwe is now self-sufficient in phosphatic fertilizers but investments in nitrogenous fertilizer plant, originally using the surplus electricity from Kariba, now use 13% of a deficient supply so that both ammonia and urea have to be imported in addition. Perhaps most significant is the absence of a petrochemical industry. Only just before UDI, Lonrho's pipeline from Beira to the Feruka refinery came on stream, but both have been inactive since. As a result a whole central sector of a modern chemical industry is absent, although plastics have risen in importance but entirely on the basis of pellets imported from South Africa. Indeed, much of the activity in the chemical and pharmaceutical industries is more a matter of mixing and pelleting than undertaking more substantial productive activities.

Manufacturing industry as a whole increased its number of products from

1059 to 3837 between 1966 and 1970, with the number of productive units employing more than ten workers rising from 665 to 1036 (since when there has been relative stability). It should, however, be reiterated that a high proportion of these new products were for the luxury market. About 2,500 products were produced by monopolies or near-monopolies, a situation that is no doubt not unreasonable in so small an economy, and will have been promoted by state licensing (in particular through control of foreign exchange for imports of materials and equipment). This situation is one in which more open conditions could easily result in either the destruction of local industries if protection is withdrawn, or wasteful duplication. But the latter appears to exist already in a number of areas: the ARnI register of manufacturers for 1978 lists fifteen varieties of hair shampoo, ten hand creams, five lipsticks, seven types of swimming pool paint, ten varieties of pet food, and so forth. Clearly these products offer the luxury of choice in a range of luxury products. More serious from the point of view of future needs is that there are fourteen companies making pharmaceutical products, thirteen household paints, eleven toiletries, ten refrigerators, nine wet batteries and four radios. Many of these involve association with international companies and their brand names; since UDI most licensing, trade mark and similar constraints on technology transfer have been waived, so that local firms and subsidiaries could proliferate at low cost. On independence, control will again be exerted, almost certainly resulting in the rationalization of many non-viable lines. This is clearly a field in which state action and guidance is needed to ensure that standardization leads to products for which local inputs (instead of contractually obligatory imports) can be used, and which can be adapted to production for a mass rather than a luxury market. A point that will be taken up in section V is that while the process of rationalization will result in the writing off of a proportion of assets, the state must not be deceived into nationalizing or paying high compensation for assets which it could obtain at knock-down prices.

(d) Some Comparisons

Little detailed information is available on other industrial sectors. Overall data for the construction industry, electricity and water are shown in Table 13.3. Finally Table 13.4 gives some international comparisons.

Table 13.3   *Gross output by industry*

	1965		1975*	
	$'000	%	$'000	%
Construction	51,934	9·1	242,083	13·0
Electricity	39,858	7·0	86,626	4·6
Water	5,798	1·0	9,308	0·5
Mining	71,051	12·4	210,454	11·3
Manufacturing	404,007	70·6	1,318,414	70·6
TOTAL	572,645	100·0	1,866,885	100·0

Note: *In the slump following 1975, the construction sector was most severely affected (employment fell from a peak of 59,000 to 36,000); about a quarter of output and employment in construction is in the public sector.
Source: *Census of Production*, 1974–75.

Table 13.4   *Value of industrial output, 1976 (£ million)*

	Population ('000,000)	Mining	Manu-facturing	Electricity and water	Construction
South Africa	26·0	1,889	3,699	450	773
Algeria	16·0	2,146	1,141	110	1,160
Nigeria	80·0	3,636	920	55	678
Zimbabwe	6·5	115	315*	39	54
Kenya	13·0	5	201	32	96
Zaire	24·3	60	62	3	32
Botswana	0·7	8	9	4	12
Zambia	5·0	204	187	23	109

Note: *This figure is less than that given in Rhodesian statistical publications.
Source: United Nations, *Statistics of Production*, 1977.

III   Immediate Problems

An end to the war and international recognition will naturally bring a number of economic benefits to Zimbabwe. Unless deliberate contrary decisions are taken, the economy will again be made extremely open, and questions will therefore arise on matters of protection of some industries, exchange control, profit remittance, payment out of blocked accounts, rationalization of overdiversified or unviable enterprises, foreign takeover of such profitable enterprises as are not yet in foreign hands, finance of the foreign debt, finance of infrastructural deficiencies, and so forth. In addition the ending of the war and white domination will require immediate attention to be paid to repair of war damage, resettlement of people displaced by the war, land redistribution and consequent resettlement of blacks on land at present owned by whites, and training of more blacks to take over positions vacated by departing whites. As if this range of problems were not enough, geopolitical factors are also likely to be critical: under any government conceivable after the ending of the war, even the most moderate would require at least the beginning of fundamental changes in the relationship with South Africa. As that country owns about half the stock of foreign capital (and therefore about a third of all productive investment) in the country, and is the major export partner, a whole range of economic problems would follow policies of economic realignment. Beyond that it is clear that radical policies might attract reprisals from South Africa, whether of an economic or military character. And all but the most conservative government would eventually, if not immediately, make Zimbabwe into a new 'front-line' state. This last point would on its own call into question the ability of the country to attract the benefits of an open policy (such as the immediate balance-of-payments advantages of large inflows of private capital) whilst leaving most of the disadvantages unchanged. There is insufficient space here to discuss all these points in detail (some have been discussed in the paper referred to in note 1), so it will merely be observed at this point that two diametrically opposed views are often defended. First, the need for extreme caution: repairing war damage first, dismantling controls next, then land redistribution followed by other structural changes, the weakening of economic links with South Africa, reintegration into the central and Eastern African economic area, and last of all confrontation with South Africa. Because of the very high likelihood that such a cautious approach would never get beyond the second or third stages, and even then would meet severe problems consequent on the clash between the foreign ownership of the economy and the people's expectations, it is on the other hand argued, as it is here, that the occasion for structural changes is precisely when other changes will have to be made anyway. However, as will be argued in section V, this does not necessarily mean that all problems must find instant solutions (were this conceivable). Rather the argument put forward there is that the intention to effect such changes must not only be embodied in political pronouncements but that the more immediate problems (such as resettlement of refugees, exchange control and protection) must be dealt with so that they contribute towards, rather than help to avoid, the desired structural changes.

IV   Foreign Capital and the Economy

Many volumes have been published in the last few years on the benefits and disadvantages of reliance on private foreign investment for developing countries. This section has a more modest aim than attempting to resolve the controversy. I have already contributed to the debate in general elsewhere,[8] and with reference to Zimbabwe in particular.[9] What I wish to do here is to draw attention to some recent highly significant empirical work. First, however, it should be made quite clear that advocacy of a policy involving a considerable reduction in foreign ownership of, and influence over, an economy, is some way short of arguing for autarchy. Totally unindustrialized or devastated areas may simply have no option but to seek foreign aid in whatever form it is offered: thus we may cite on the one hand a small almost totally neglected colony such as Botswana, which on independence probably had no possibility of 'hauling itself up by its bootstraps'; on the other hand, both the Soviet Union and China sought foreign investment in certain crucial sectors of industry, whilst taking some care not to surrender their ability to determine overall policy.

If it can be agreed that a strategy of dependence on foreign capital may well produce *growth*, but not necessarily *development* (since structural weaknesses either persist or are strengthened, so that poverty deepens amidst growing wealth and a balanced economy rarely results), then *self-reliance* is required as a central ingredient of a development policy. This may be quite consistent with using (and paying for) private foreign investment in certain sectors. It cannot be consistent with tolerating foreign ownership of some two-thirds of productive investment as in present-day Zimbabwe.

However some recent work by and large takes a different approach: instead of implicitly accepting that foreign capital does increase the growth rate, and then attempting to draw up a balance sheet of the structural costs and benefits, This work questions whether foreign capital *in fact* increases the economic growth rate. If it does, then the discussion as to whether it helps or hinders *development* remains central. But if it does *not* in fact increase the growth rate, but rather lowers it, then the host country is losing on both counts.

Over the last decade some sixteen significant independent studies have been carried out in this field, investigating the cross-national evidence of the effects of foreign investment and aid on economic growth and inequality. The first were by Griffin and Enos[10,11] and prompted an orthodox response from Papanek[12] who claimed that both aid and foreign investment raised growth rates; this was rebutted in the case of foreign investment by Stoneman.[13] More recently several new studies have contributed further evidence, and all sixteen studies have been surveyed by Bornschier *et al.*[14] After explaining apparent inconsistencies and carrying out further analyses so as to test hypotheses about the causes of such inconsistencies, they come to conclusions which are highly significant statistically and will be surprising to many.

In particular it is clear that large stocks of foreign investment *lower* the economic growth rates of developing countries and *increase* the level of inequality. The authors point out that the findings are consistent with dependency theory (although they alone are not capable of *proving* such a complex theoretical framework), and require explanation by those wishing to maintain more orthodox theories which defend open policies towards foreign capital and trade. On the other hand they explicitly deny that the studies prove the dominance of external factors over internal processes of class formation and political organization: the external and internal processes cannot be separated so as to claim that one or other is dominant. As foreign capital increases inequality so it is likely to be promoted or protected by dominant minority classes, whether they are characterized as a rising bourgeoisie or a state bureaucracy just as it is likely to be opposed by movements seeking a reduction in inequality.

It is worth quoting the conclusion of this survey at some length because of the great relevance of its findings to the situation that Zimbabwe will find itself in after independence:

> Our review of the evidence has produced the following assessment of the empirical relationships with which we are concerned: (1) The effect of direct foreign investment and foreign aid has been to increase economic inequality within countries. This effect holds for income inequality, land inequality, and sectoral income inequality. (2) *Flows* of direct foreign investment and foreign aid have had a *short-term* effect of increasing the relative rate of economic growth of countries. (3) *Stocks* of direct foreign investment and foreign aid have had the cumulative effect of decreasing the relative rate of economic growth of countries. This effect is small in the short-run (1–5 years) and gets larger in the long run (5–20 years). (4) This relationship, however, has been conditional on the level of development of countries. Foreign investment and aid have had negative effects in both richer and poorer developing countries, but the effect is stronger in the richer than in the poorer countries. (5) These relationships hold independent of geographical area. (Note 14, p. 677; italics in original.)

The authors also draw attention to some of their own recent studies which have attempted to trace the structural mechanisms causing the above effects. They find that:

> foreign investment tends to produce uneven growth across economic sectors. Such uneven development may be one mechanism by which foreign investment leads to a lowered rate of growth .... foreign investment leads to increasing income inequality, early monopolisation, and structural underemployment, thus favouring early saturation of effective demand and lowering the rate of capital formation in a country. And since capital formation is a major cause of increasing growth, this reduction in capital formation is another mechanism by which foreign investment reduces growth. Finally .... one of the ways in which foreign investment reduces growth is by reducing state power, and hence the ability of the state to undertake a policy of growth, independent of the class interests created by foreign capital. (ibid., p. 678)

These conclusions must now be related to the more general question of industrialization. Can they be explained, not as above in terms of a causal relationship (i.e. stocks of foreign capital *cause* a reduction in the economic growth rate), but rather through both phenomena being the *effects* of a third factor? One possibility in this connection is that countries embarking on import substituting industrialization naturally attract foreign investment during the initial growth stage. However, once 'easy' import substitution is exhausted there is both a larger foreign capital stock and a lower growth rate, so giving the illusion of there having been a causal relationship.

This may indeed be a part, but it is unlikely to be the whole, of the explanation. To test such a hypothesis conclusively it would be necessary to re-run the regressions using a quantitative control for degree of import substitution already achieved; plainly there would be a number of conceptual and statistical difficulties to be overcome, but these need not be insuperable. However, most of the studies did use a number of controls, some of which may be considered reasonable proxies for import substitution; and some studies also lagged the stock measure and found that as the lag period is lengthened the negative effects on growth increase, a finding easier to explain in terms of the causation of harmful structural effects by the stock. Controls used may be grouped under seven headings. First, given that relative wealth or level of development may attract foreign investment (i.e. there is a measure of positive causation in the opposite direction to that under discussion), in the absence of a control a bias to finding a *positive* correlation would be expected (but is not always found). When the prior level of economic development *is* included as a control variable, negative effects become more apparent. (This control is probably the best single proxy for a 'degree of import substitution achieved' control.) Second are other dependence measures, such as trade, investment, aid, number of subsidiaries of multinational corporations; third, the percentage of GDP in mining and oil production; fourth, population growth; fifth, income inequality; sixth, total capital formation; and seventh, degree of state power.

Therefore the most likely conclusion, given the present state of knowledge, is that the initial effects of foreign investment on growth rates may be positive (if only because of the balance-of-payments effect), and may remain so in the case of mining and oil extraction; but that in other sectors in the medium and long run and in manufacturing industry in particular, adverse effects on the economic structure (which may *include* overconcentration on import substitution of consumer goods on the part of foreign companies) reduce the rate of economic growth below what it would have been with a lower stock.

The relevance of these findings to the particular situation of Zimbabwe should be clear. Zimbabwe has an economy which has reached, in some sectors, a relatively high level of development. Some two-thirds of the productive investment is owned by foreign capital, which has, however, for long periods been effectively controlled locally (thus possibly reducing some of its negative effects – certainly since UDI foreign investment income payments have been greatly reduced as part of the fight against sanctions). Independent Zimbabwe will be under intense pressure from one of the most powerful blocks of foreign economic power in Africa, and this pressure will not only seek to open the economy to make up for past closure, to 'rationalize' diversification and maintain the share of national investment in the urban sector, but also more generally to determine the general lines of economic policy and the 'climate for investment'. Piecemeal or pragmatic state action (seeking accomodations, guidelines, joint ventures, minority holdings, some nationalization with generous compensation and management contracts, and so forth), that is the type of policy often erroneously described as 'socialist' or 'African socialist', will in the face of such an economic power block be no more successful in reducing inequality, tackling rural poverty, establishing economic independence or producing rapid economic growth than in many other African states. In fact both because of the dominance of the foreign sector and the fact that Zimbabwe counts as one of the relatively richer of the poor countries (see conclusion 4 in the above quotation), it seems highly likely that the negative effects of foreign capital will operate at higher than average levels.

Although I have concentrated in this chapter on the role played by foreign capital in Rhodesian industrialization, and return in section V to measures that will be necessary to cope with it, it should be clear that the scope allowed to foreign capital is only one dimension of an overall development strategy. In general foreign capital is rightly associated with 'open' strategies, although it would be mistaken to regard alternative strategies as totally closed or autarchic, or to deny any role to foreign capital or technological aid in them. Similarly it would be mistaken to regard import substituting industrialization (ISI) as a form of 'closed' strategy. Rather it is a short-term tactic (in an 'open' strategy) designed to reduce balance-of-payments pressures and create local employment; it can hardly be dignified with the label 'strategy' because its development into full-scale industrialization (including intermediate and capital goods industries) is not planned but merely hoped for through the supposed operation of market forces (and as Fred Nixson shows in Chapter 2 of the present volume, rarely achieved). ISI can hardly be said to be 'closed' (beyond the trivial level of selective infant-industry protection) for common results are an *increase* in the activity of subsidiaries of multinational corporations wishing to get behind the tariff barriers, and an *increase* in imports of non-consumer goods.

I would support the 'Singh view' discussed in Chapter 1 of the present book that protection is essential in any process of bringing about the structural changes necessary to allow self-sustaining industrialization. But I would wish to emphasize that ISI is not sufficient. As Singh makes clear[15] attention to both agriculture and the capital goods industries are the necessary components of a viable industrialization strategy. And this in turn demands planning, and consequently a degree of isolation from world market forces which would otherwise impose a logic relating to the *existing* situation (division of labour, comparative advantage, market size, income distribution, and so forth) rather than to the situation which it was desired to create. This is not to call for an impossible autarchy, but for more self-reliance. As the main bearers of market forces, foreign-controlled companies must be the main concern of planners wishing to escape from underdevelopment; however, I would not claim that their control, although *necessary*, would be sufficient in itself.

The relevance of Zimbabwe's partial success in industrializing deserves further comment in this context. It should first be remarked that although it is indeed only partial (Zimbabwe's per capita income still leaves it firmly in the ranks of poor countries, although not the poorest), and although it may also become stalled because of the poverty of the majority and the small market size, it is nevertheless a great success story in African terms. But it seems quite clear to me that it is not a success either of ISI or of foreign capital, or of *any* orthodox economic policy. The main factors would appear to be the existence of excellent resources – climatic and mineral in particular – and simple chance, that forced the adoption of planned self-reliant policies contrary to the ideology of the ruling group. Thus while Rhodesian Front politicians continued to pay lip service to the ideals of an open economy, competition and the free market, they were obliged to institute stringent exchange and trade control, to license monopolies, to direct the behaviour of companies and to take on a progressively larger share of investment through the state. Measures forced by sanctions prevented many of the harmful financial and structural effects of excessive dependence on foreign capital, which was in effect 'Rhodesian-ized'. The country did not become autarchic, because of the close economic links with South Africa, but it became much more self-reliant. At this stage it would be risky to predict the outcome of a re-opening of the economy, because two opposing tendencies will be released. On the one hand there will be the benefit of immediately available finance for a number of prospects which have been held back by sanctions: tobacco growing and the export of chrome are examples. On the other there is a risk of an immediate outflow of blocked funds, and capital following rationalization of many lines that at present depend on continuing protection. I would expect the unfavourable tendencies to predominate, particularly in the uncertain political climate that is likely to obtain. Even if the re-opening of the economy is gradual, the longer-term structural effects of foreign capital dominance would soon make their presence felt, the pursuit of shorter-term profitability bringing about an end to processes deepening industrialization.

V   Planned Co-operative Divestment

In this section I attempt to set out the requirements for a policy towards foreign capital which avoids both the ineffectiveness of *laissez-faire* or reformist approaches, and the military and economic perils of wholesale expropriation. Impossible though this may seem at first sight, a listing of the requirements of a successful policy does suggest at least one way in which the aims of the Patriotic Front could be attained. These aims, as set out in their rejection of the 'Anglo-American' proposals in 1977 are:[16]

– the destruction of colonialism and its institutions
– the attainment of genuine independence
– the democratisation not only of the vote but of *all institutions* and the way of life in Zimbabwe.
It is this total objective of democracy that the colonialist fears most, hence his resort to 'controlled democracy' to produce neo-colonialist puppets. (original italics)

And more recently[17] they have stated:

Experience in many African countries that have attained independence during the past two decades shows that, unless the directions of economic and social policy are clearly established before independence, and policy decisions are taken soon after independence, new vested interests get stronger and become more powerful in defending existing structures ... Genuine independence connotes genuine control of the resources, reduction of over-dependence on external forces, determination of the purposes for which the resources of the country are used and the creation of institutions of a decision-making process in which the masses fully participate and in which their interests are fully reflected.

They recognize that 'the magnitude of the problems and the tasks involved in achieving the long-term objectives rule out partial or reformist solutions and policies'.
    An attempt to list the essential ingredients of a successful strategy designed to drastically reduce foreign capital's domination of the economy must now be made. There must be:

(1) The political will and popular support, especially in rural areas, to carry through a radical restructuring. This will entail acquiescence on the part of the aspiring African bourgeoisie who expect at present to take over inflated white income levels.
(2) A strong bargaining position which restricts options available to foreign capital.
(3) The means to require foreign capital to co-operate in its eventual demise, by both maintaining output and investment in the interim, and training workers and managers to take over.
(4) Sufficient skilled workers or availability of expatriates to fill any vacancies left by departing white settlers.

(5) The co-operation of the workforce in monitoring the activities of managers and owners so as to detect at an early stage any decisions on the part of the latter to sabotage or abandon enterprises or to oppose the wider strategy.
(6) Finance to compensate owners for enterprises taken into public ownership in a viable condition.
(7) Acquiescence of parent countries of the foreign capital involved in control and takeover.
(8) Acquiescence (at least) or co-operation from neighbouring states in the restructuring, and eventual willingness to enter into regional co-operation agreements concerning siting of large investments, trade and transportation.

This list may of course be extended, but at this stage it is more important to establish the viability of the overall strategy through asking to what extent these requirements can be met. Probably the first prerequisite, arising out of (1), would be a 'Harare Declaration', that the medium-term aim of economic policy was to meet basic needs of the entire population through co-operative action to transform the economy from a competitive, capitalist, foreign-dominated one to a co-operative, socialist, locally owned one. Foreign and settler-owned enterprises would be left in no doubt that their ownership and control is to pass into local, preferably co-operative hands after a transition period appropriate to the particular social, economic and technical problems involved.

As regards (2), Zimbabwe is almost certainly in a stronger bargaining position than most countries because of the diversity of its natural and industrial resources. To take the example of mining: whereas Zambia could not drive a hard bargain with just two colluding copper companies in an industry which was responsible for some 40% of GDP and 95% of exports, Zimbabwe's economy is much more balanced as between mining, manufacturing industry, agriculture and service sectors. With mining, accounting for only 7% of GDP and about a third of exports (only about a fifth in pre-UDI times), the whole industry is, if important, not absolutely vital. But given its division over six major minerals, with several large companies in each (except coal), but hardly any duplication of these companies (Anglo-American Corporation is the major exception), an intransigent company could hardly shut down (or deny markets to) even one-sixth of the industry. In manufacturing, the same would apply in general: Zimbabwe might not like to put, say, the plastics or rubber subsectors at risk, but then many African countries lack these in any case. More critical, of course, because of the highly integrated nature of modern industry, would be certain keysectors in which one foreign firm had a monopoly. For example, British Oxygen holds a near-monopoly of industrial gases, and the supply of welding equipment and materials; Metal Box has a monopoly of tin can production for the large food canning industry. Nevertheless, the occasional poor bargain or even defeat need not jeopardize the whole strategy. Intransigent firms in crucial sectors might have to be made exceptions until other problems are solved and new alternatives found.

The third requirement, apparently the major stumbling block, might be surprisingly easily solved. Companies could be obliged to co-operate by being told that they would be paid compensation for their assets on eventual takeover, *if* (a) they maintained output in the interim, (b) they invested appropriately so as to begin to fit the enterprise into a national economic plan,

(c) they resisted the temptation to 'bleed' the enterprise, either by material or financial exports whether through excessive profits, 'head office charges', or transfer pricing and (d) they trained their workforce so that the enterprise could continue in operation without the need for an expensive management contract. Clearly the success of achievement of these requirements would have to be independently assessed (possibly by an international organization), as would an appropriate level of compensation. The latter need not be considered to be a right, rather a payment for services rendered as under (a) to (d) above; in the case of oil firms and others judged centrally complicit in sanctions busting, immediate expropriation might be undertaken, subject to (7) below.

Availability of skilled workers is a whole topic in its own right; see the recent manpower study performed for the Patriotic Front by the IUEF.[18] A general point of relevance may be mentioned here: lack of formal skills amongst blacks in Zimbabwean industry is to a considerable extent an artefact of the existing racist society; large numbers of blacks are *in fact* if not in name highly skilled through job experience; in addition large numbers of school and college graduates have been denied appropriate opportunities hitherto.

Point (5) derives in part from the Mozambiquan experience: often the workers themselves are the only ones in a position to diagnose when certain activities by the owners or managers amount to sabotage (and in the case of small firms, closure might go unnoticed for a period). Thus an immediate move towards a co-operative or worker-controlled organization of industry becomes not a democratic luxury, but a necessity.

Clearly the eventual transfer of ownership of industry, whose capital value is estimated at £1,000 to £1,400 million, from foreign to local ownership, represents a problem of similar magnitude to the resettlement of the white farms (for which a similar sum would be required if compensation at present market values were to be paid). Such sums are beyond the immediate means of larger and richer states than Zimbabwe, and this explains why the Anglo-American plan included a 'Zimbabwe Development Fund' one of whose purposes was connected with the land question. The lack of precise guarantees in the Lancaster House Settlement proposals is of course one of the least satisfactory features. Nevertheless it is clear that such funds might in themselves be used to constrain the economic independence of Zimbabwe, as for example British loans to Kenya to compensate white farmers not only bound the country to a neo-colonial status, worsened the income distribution, and so on, but also starved the resettled farms of adequate investment because of the indebtedness of the purchasers. If the problem can be solved in Zimbabwe's case, the ingredients must involve, first international aid in recognition of the historical record of land alienation and exploitation, plus the burdens and devastation of the war of liberation; such aid might be sought from a range of sympathetic states outside the OECD orbit. Second, the policy must be timed carefully: some expropriation may be recognized to be appropriate as under (3); some industries or farms could be paid for quite early, and start a flow of funds for later acquisitions; some firms may be caught in sabotage, forfeiting their right to compensation or international sympathy and support; others may quite simply have to be given a ten or even fifteen-year transition period. In the meantime, with the lifting of sanctions, the export potential of the country must be considerable, both in the revival of earlier successful commodities like tobacco, and also more recent ones like sugar and nickel. Manufacturing exports may also recover. The policy, that is, will have to be relatively gradual, but need be no less radical for that.

Point (7), acquiescence of parent countries,[7] in particular South Africa, should be achieved if the companies themselves acquiesce, or if particular companies' past behaviour or future sabotage speaks for itself. Clearly an imponderable is the extent to which Zimbabwe will become a front-line state in the continent's continuing confrontation with racist South Africa: not only this economic strategy could be threatened by military invasion. However, there is one advantage to this strategy not shared by some others in the extent to which some individual South African-owned companies could be potential hostages and their compensation at risk.

Regarding point (8) neighbouring states apart from South Africa are unlikely to oppose, and in some case will support such a strategy.[18] Zimbabwe's economic weight will in any case have to be used with discretion, and care for the pride of neighbours: Zimbabwe must not become a sub-imperial power in the area, but should seek co-operation on as equal terms as possible, recognizing the sacrifices that Mozambique and Zambia in particular have made in the liberation struggle.

Concluding Remarks

The prospects for Zimbabwe remain hazardous, militarily, politically and economically. The Lancaster House Conference has concentrated on forcing a political solution for a situation that is unresolved militarily, so that there can be no confidence that the war will not be renewed once Britain's formal responsibilities are at an end. The economic issues have been largely ignored, or rather the hidden assumption has been that shifts away from structures which have been determined on colonial and racial lines are to be minimized.

When eventually the political and military situation is resolved, a wide range of economic problems will have to be faced. Should Zimbabwe then have a Patriotic Front government with a majority sufficient to allow it to move towards economic independence, it is submitted that solutions can be found meeting the need for radical change, possibly along the lines set out above, which will avoid the perils or debilitating compromises of orthodox solutions. Then Africa's second centre of industrial power could provide a service and an inspiration to the continent.

Notes

1   C. Stoneman, 'Zimbabwe's prospects as an industrial power', *Journal of Commonwealth and Comparative Politics*, 18 (1980) xviii, pp. 14-27.
2   G. Arrighi, *The Political Economy of Rhodesia*. (The Hague: Mouton, 1967).
3   C. Stoneman, 'Foreign capital and the prospects for Zimbabwe', *World Development*, 4 (1976), pp. 25–58.

4 C. Stoneman, 'Foreign capital and the reconstruction of Zimbabwe', *Review of African Political Economy*, 11 (1978), pp. 62–83.

5 Most numerical data are taken from official statistics, published by the Central Statistical Office, Salisbury. Only the title, e.g. *Monthly Digest of Statistics* is given in the text.

6 D.S. Pearson and W.S. Taylor, *Break-up* (Salisbury: Phoenix Group, 1963).

7 In this section I have drawn on material in notes 3 and 4, and in addition two reports prepared for the UNCTAD *Economic and Social Survey of Zimbabwe*: D. Wield, 'Technology and Zimbabwean industry', and C. Stoneman, 'Foreign capital in Zimbabwe' in *Zimbabwe: Towards a New Order: An Economic and Social Survey*, Working Papers, Volume I (Geneva: United Nations, 1981), pp. 101–68 and 413–539.

8 C. Stoneman, 'Foreign capital and economic growth', *World Development*, 3 (1975), pp. 11–26.

9 See note 3.

10 K.B. Griffin and J.L. Enos, 'Foreign assistance: objectives and consequences', *Economic Development and Cultural Change*, 18 (1970), pp. 313–27.

11 K.B. Griffin, 'Foreign capital, domestic savings and economic development', *Bulletin of the Oxford University Institute of Economics And Statistics*, 32 (1970), pp. 99–112.

12 G.F. Papanek, 'Aid, foreign private investment, savings and growth in less developed countries', *Journal of Political Economy*, 81 (1973), pp. 120–30.

13 See note 8.

14 V. Bornschier, C. Chase-Dunn, and R. Rubinson, 'Cross-national evidence of the effects of foreign investment and aid on economic growth and inequality: a survey of findings and a reanalysis', *American Journal of Sociology*, 84 (1978), pp. 651–83.

15 A. Singh, 'The "basic needs" approach to development vs the new international economic order: the significance of third world industrialization', *World Development*, 7 (1979), pp. 585 – 606.

16 J. Nkomo and R. Mugabe, *Statement* of 12 September 1977 (mimeo.).

17 Draft Work Programme for the *Economic and Social Survey of Zimbabwe*, UNCTAD, 1978 (mimeo.).

18 *Zimbabwe Manpower Survey*, 3 vols (Geneva: International University Exchange Fund, 1979).

Additional Reading.

A number of papers on various aspects of the Rhodesian economy can be found in two series of publications: *Mambo Occasional Papers* (Socio-Economic Series), Mambo Press, Gwelo; and *From Rhodesia to Zimbabwe*, Catholic Institute for International Relations, London. A useful short economic summary is John Sprack, *Rhodesia: South Africa's Sixth Province*, International Defence and Aid Fund, London, 1974. On the question of the adverse effects of foreign capital on growth see note 14, but also a number of references in note 8.

14 *Discussion Note on Chapter 13*

ROB DAVIES

Dr Stoneman's chapter addresses itself to two related questions. First, what has been the nature and pattern of Rhodesian industrialization, particularly in the post-UDI period? Second, what problems and policy options does such industrialization present for a future Zimbabwe? He identifies two important trends in the post-UDI economy. On the one hand, investment was biased towards the urban, industrial sector, as the economy became increasingly geared to meeting white consumer demands. On the other hand, a very high proportion of investment was devoted to the basic metals and metal products sectors, while a number of other manufacturing subsectors improved their share of total gross output. The former trend creates problems for Zimbabwe, in that it has increased the problem of rural poverty; the latter trend has probably strengthened the industrial structure of the economy. In my comments I wish to concentrate mainly upon the question of post-UDI industrialization.

Accepting for the moment Dr Stoneman's approach, I am not sure that the statistical picture he paints is entirely accurate. First, I would question the use of gross output as an indicator of industrialization. I shall return to this point, but one can see from Table 14.1 that in terms of net output, expansion of the sectors he points to is not quite so marked. Second, even if one does use gross output figures, it is necessary to examine them in constant price terms, particularly since price changes differ between sectors. Table 14.1 again gives some adjusted figures. On the basis of these figures I would argue that the unadjusted figures Dr Stoneman uses exaggerate the shift to intermediate industries. Third, and most important, by ending in 1975 I think that Dr Stoneman misses significant changes that occurred after that date. As Table 14.2 shows, there was a substantial downturn in the economy from 1975 onwards. Table 14.1 indicates that this was accompanied by a change in the structure of the manufacturing sector. Dr Stoneman deliberately ends in 1975, since, in his view, the downturn was due primarily to the war, and therefore, in a sense, abnormal. This is a major area of disagreement between us, to which I shall return.

One can quarrel over these statistical issues, but to do so is not particularly fruitful. I would rather take a different line, and – unfairly to Dr Stoneman –

say that I would have approached the issue from a different angle to his. Perhaps if I outline my approach it may illustrate some general criticisms.

The post-UDI period can be broken into two phases. As Table 14.2 shows, there was general growth by most indicators until 1974, while since 1975 growth rates have generally been negative. (Furthermore, manufacturing output as a proportion of GDP rose until 1974, whereafter it declined.) This raises two questions:

(1) Was the initial growth primarily a result of the enforced (relative) autarchy, or of the particular nature of the Rhodesian political economy and the accumulation process within it?
(2) Was the post-1975 recession primarily the result of the war (which intensified from 1973) or of other more fundamental forces operating in the economy?

The answers to these questions are obviously relevant for future Zimbabwean policy. But they are also of more general interest. Post-UDI Rhodesia seems to offer a case study of an autarchic economy. The answer to the first question will give some idea of the extent to which one can generalize from the Rhodesian experience. And, if the recession was not primarily due to the war, there may be implications for the longer-term viability of autarchic strategies.

Obviously it is impossible to answer these questions fully in a discussion of this length. I would therefore confine myself to some brief observations.

(1) One can question whether industrialization actually took place. Although it is conventional to use manufacturing value added figures as an indicator of industrialization, I would argue that one really needs a measure of the expansion of the industrial base, or of expansion of industrial productive capacity. Those who use value added imply that there is relatively full capacity utilization of industrial stock, so that a rise in the relative share of manufacturing value added can be taken as a surrogate measure of the changing productive structure of the economy. Ramsay (1974) has estimated that in Rhodesia in 1962 utilization of capital stock was less than 60% of capacity. Thus the observed growth in manufacturing output may have been primarily on the basis of existing excess capacity. Net investment in manufacturing between 1955 and 1964 averaged 11·7% of capital stock, while between 1965 and 1972 it averaged 4·4% which *seems* to support the hypothesis.

Of course, measuring industrialization by reference solely to capital stock and investment is inadequate, since it does not allow for technological change and input substitution.

(2) If we accept that there *was* in fact industrialization after UDI, one can ask what the basis of that industrialization was. This is not a question of simply the funding of investment, but rather of the sources of surplus. Dr Stoneman's references to biased investment and the distorted market might be taken as an indication that surplus was appropriated from increasing underdevelopment of the rural economy. Clarke's work also points to the importance of primitive accumulation in Rhodesian development (e.g. Clarke, 1974, 1977). Table 14.3, which shows that the share of profits in GDP rose until 1974 and subsequently

Table 14.1 Structure of manufacturing sector

	Shares in gross output (%)											Shares in net output (%)		
	Current prices					Constant 1964 prices						Current prices		1975 at 1965 prices
	1965	1970	1975	1976	1977	1965	1970	1975	1976	1977	1978	1965	1975	1975
Foodstuffs (incl. stockfeeds)	24·0	22·4	19·7	21·9	23·9	25·2	25·6	24·9	27·6	30·7	30·1	15·7	9·4	14·9
Drink and tobacco	8·3	8·0	7·0	7·6	7·7	8·8	7·2	7·7	8·3	8·0	8·2	15·9	9·5	13·4
Textiles incl. ginning	6·9	9·3	10·4	11·2	11·1	7·1	9·0	9·0	8·6	8·9	9·1	6·6	8·6	8·1
Clothes and footwear	6·4	7·5	6·7	6·3	5·8	7·0	6·2	5·1	5·1	5·1	5·2	8·3	8·3	5·8
Wood and furniture	3·6	3·6	2·8	2·8	2·4	3·5	3·6	3·0	2·9	2·6	2·4	4·0	3·4	3·3
Paper, printing and publishing	5·1	5·5	5·6	4·8	4·8	5·7	5·1	4·6	4·4	4·2	4·6	7·9	6·7	6·2
Chemical and petrol products	16·6	13·4	14·0	13·4	14·1	14·6	13·7	13·7	12·8	13·0	13·0	11·1	13·2	10·1
Non-metallic mineral products	2·3	3·8	3·7	3·3	3·0	2·2	3·0	3·0	2·7	2·3	1·7	4·0	4·7	5·3
Metals and metal products	15·4	21·9	25·1	24·2	22·6	16·0	19·6	22·8	22·1	19·7	20·3	21·3	30·8	29·4
Transport equipment	9·9	3·3	3·9	3·3	3·4	8·8	6·0	5·1	4·2	4·1	3·7	4·2	4·0	2·4
Other manufactures	1·4	1·1	1·0	1·0	1·1	1·0	1·0	1·1	1·2	1·2	1·4	1·0	1·4	1·1

Sources: Rhodesia, Census of Industrial Production, 1974/5, CSO, Salisbury; Rhodesia, Monthly Digest of Statistics, CSO, Salisbury.

Table 14.2 *Some relevant rates of growth (% change on previous year)*

		1965	1966	1967	1968	1969	1970	1971	1972	1973	1974	1975	1976	1977	1978
GNP 1965 prices		–	-2·5	8·8	2·5	15·2	3·4	11·3	9·0	3·5	10·1	-1·4	-2·4	-6·5	3·1
Gross output of manufacturing sector	Value current price	9·5	-4·7	4·9	10·7	17·3	17·6	17·4	14·8	16·7	23·9	10·0	2·4	1·2	–
	Volume	8·9	-9·2	8·9	9·4	12·8	11·9	7·8	15·0	8·1	7·0	-0·9	-5·8	-6·0	-0·3
Employment in manufacturing		5·2	-0·3	7·2	11·0	8·9	10·4	6·2	7·4	6·7	8·5	3·1	-1·5	-5·5	-3·9
Gross fixed capital formation in manufacturing		–	–	14·4	97·1	-1·8	-6·9	22·5	7·6	76·1	162·2	8·7	-31·2	8·6	–

Source: Rhodesia, *Monthly Digest of Statistics*, CSO, Salisbury.

Table 14.3 *Functional shares (% of GDP at factor cost)*

	1965	1966	1967	1968	1969	1970	1971	1972	1973	1974	1975	1976	1977	1978
Wages and salaries	57·9	59·4	56·6	59·2	54·6	56·1	54·3	53·0	54·0	51·3	55·2	56·9	61·7	62·4
Gross operating profit	39·8	38·2	41·0	38·3	43·0	41·3	43·2	44·6	43·6	46·5	42·6	41·0	36·1	33·4
Of which non-financial companies	22·4	18·7	20·2	20·7	21·9	24·3	24·8	26·2	29·0	30·4	28·1	26·6	23·8	23·2

Source: Rhodesia, *Monthly Digest of Statistics*, CSO, Salisbury

fell, could perhaps be taken as providing some evidence of accumulation from surpluses derived from the industrial sector.

(3) Whichever of these two points one accepts, it tends to suggest that the Rhodesian experience may not readily be generalized. Obviously sanctions provided a protected market which could potentially be used for rapid expansion of industrial output. But that potential could only be realized either because of the existing excess capacity, or because of the ability of the political economic system to enforce rapid accumulation, an ability which was clearly the result of Rhodesia's historical development rather than some short-term policy measures. Without either of these preconditions it is unlikely that relative autarchy will lead to rapid industrialization.

(4) This reduces somewhat the second question as to why the post-1975 recession occurred. Nevertheless, I would like to make some observations.

(a) Dr Stoneman disregards the post-1975 experience largely on the grounds that the escalation of the war was primarily responsible for the recession. While I agree that the war had a disruptive effect on the economy, and that it played a critical role in leading to current changes, I would argue that it has played this role largely by increasing the discomfit of the whites. Because of the substitution of black for white workers that has taken place, I would argue that the effects of the war on output have not been great, and that one has therefore to look elsewhere for the primary reasons for the recession.

(b) There are reasons why autarchic *capitalist* accumulation is not sustainable in the long term. Certainly, variants of Marxist analysis would suggest that this is the case for capitalist economies which do not have access to external markets.

(c) I *feel* that it is not coincidental that Rhodesia's recession coincides with the general world recession. Examining whether there is a causal relationship might raise interesting questions about the ability of an economy to insulate itself from the capitalist world economy, and about the way in which cycles are transmitted internationally.

References

Clarke D.G. (1974) *Contract Workers and Underdevelopment in Rhodesia* (Gwelo: Mambo Press).

Clarke D.G. (1977) *Agricultural and Plantation Workers in Rhodesia* (Gwelo: Mambo Press).

Ramsay D. (1974) 'Productivity and capital in Rhodesian manufacturing, 1955 – 72', *Rhodesian Journal of Economics*, 8,2 (June).

15 *Foreign Aid for Structural Change: Lesotho*

AJIT SINGH

I Introduction

Lesotho is a small mountainous country with a population of a little over one million which became independent from British rule in 1966. The country is entirely land-locked within the Republic of South Africa (RSA). A large part of Lesotho's labour force works in the South African mines; the country's economy has the unenviable distinction of being more dependent on migrant labour force than that of almost any other country in the world. Lesotho's GDP per capita is also among the world's lowest. Gross national income per head of population is relatively much higher because of mine workers' remittances. In 1976, GNI per capita was estimated to be $170, which would still place Lesotho among the world's 25 poorest countries (World Bank, 1978).

In order to place the issues of industrial development policy in their proper perspective, it is essential first to outline the main parameters, as well as the institutional constraints within which the Lesotho economy operates. This will be done in section II. Section III will examine changes in the structure of the economy, and of the industrial sector, over the last decade. Industrial performance in recent years will be considered in section IV. Section V will report on the results of a survey of large industrial enterprises undertaken in September 1978, and examine factor limiting industrial expansion at the microeconomic level. The extremely important issue of the Customs Union will be analysed in section VI. Finally section VII will sum up the policy conclusions.

II   The Main Parameters of the Lesotho Economy and the Institutional Constraints

THE ECONOMIC PARAMETERS

The economy of Lesotho is dominated by two important characteristics: (a) the export of workers to South Africa and (b) subsistence agriculture. On the basis of the 1976 census, and allowing for the known sources of bias in it,[1] the country's potential labour force in that year has been estimated to be 588,400. Of that number, as Table 15.1 shows, more than 120,000 were employed in South African mines, which amounts to over 20% of the labour force, and over 40% of the male labour force. Relative to mining and total migrant employment, wage employment in the formal sector in the domestic economy is quite small – constituting only 6.8% of the labour force. A mere 1.3 per cent of the economically active population was employed in manufacturing in 1976. The bulk of the labour force (over 65%) is engaged in agriculture or in the informal urban sector, but mostly the former.

The importance of the earnings of Basotho working abroad to the Lesotho economy cannot be exaggerated. In 1976–7 migrant earnings exceeded the country's gross domestic product at factor cost by 30%. Remittances[2] (which are about two thirds of the earnings) constituted nearly half of the gross national income. They are vital to the balance of payments, being nearly ten

Table 15.1   *Labour force and employment in Lesotho, 1976*

	Numbers	% of total labour force
Labour force[a]	588,400	
Males	282,300	48·0
Females	306,100	52·0
Migrant employment	160,400[b]	27·3
of which employment in S. African mines	121,716[b]	20·7
Employment in the formal sector in Lesotho	40,000	6·8
Mining and quarrying	1,500	0·2
Manufacturing	7,500	1·3
Utilities	850	0·1
Construction	9,000	1·5
Wholesale and retail	75,000	1·3
Transport	3,000	0·5
Government	10,000	1·7
Other	1,150	0·2
Residual employment in agriculture and informal sector	388,000	65·9

Notes:
[a] Estimated at 90 per cent of the 15–64 age group after deductions for invalids, pregnant women and people in full-time education.
[b] The figures for total migrant employment are for the financial year 1976, whilst those for mining employment are for the calendar year.
Source: Data supplied by the Lesotho authorities based on the population census conducted in April, 1976.

times as large as the exports.[3] Indirectly, migrant remittances also have a major bearing on the government revenue. (See further below.)

The importance of migrant earnings and employment for the Lesotho economy has increased significantly over time, particularly over the period 1973–7. The average numbers employed in South African gold mines and collieries rose from about 60,000 during the years 1963–4, to 85,000 during 1969–70, to about 105,000 during 1973–4 and to 129,000 in 1977 (Hill, 1978). At the same time owing to an increase in gold prices and the sharp rise in mining wages, average cash earnings of a Basotho mine worker in South Africa have increased from R 242 in 1973, to R 748 in 1975 and to R 1,128 in 1977 – a phenomenal annual rate of increase of 53% over the period 1973–7.[4] Consequently, whereas in 1972–1973 the migrant mining earnings were 40.5% of Lesotho GDP, by 1976–7, they were 106% of GDP.[5]

However, there are indications that mining employment peaked in 1977. Between 1977 and 1978, Basotho employment in South African mines fell by approximately 5,000, i.e. by 3·9%. More significantly, this decrease occurred despite an overall rise of 3·4% in total employment in the South African mining sector. Analysis of the future employment trends by Lesotho government economists suggests that there is unlikely to be any increase, and most probably a further reduction in Basotho employed as mineworkers in South Africa. The main reason for this is the South African policy of progressively using more labour from the homelands and thus internalizing labour supplies, which also accords with the attempts by the mining companies, for strategic economic considerations, to diversify their labour sources.

Nevertheless, in contrast to the observed buoyancy of migrant workers' earnings and employment over the last two decades, Lesotho's agriculture and live-stock rearing sector – the main source of domestic output and employment – is characterized by low productivity and long term stagnation. Although adequate agricultural statistics are not available over a longer run of years, there is general agreement that there has been no long run increase in agricultural production or land productivity over the last quarter century (See Jones, 1977; JASPA, 1979). The country is not currently self-sufficient in the main food crops and has to import substantial amounts of grain and other agricultural products from South Africa.

The export of workers to South Africa reacts on the agricultural sector in several ways. First the departure of able-bodied men means that measures of long-term investment in land which involve heavy manual work (e.g. soil conservation and improvement, terracing etc., which are essential in a mountainous country such as Lesotho) are neglected. One consequence of this is that soil erosion, caused also partly by overgrazing, is a major current and prospective threat to Lesotho's agriculture. Secondly and much more importantly, because of mining earnings, agriculture has increasingly become a marginal activity for the average farming family. The Rural Household Consumption and Expenditure Surveys show that in 1967–9, income arising from agricultural sources accounted for over 60% of the average household income; by 1973–4, this proportion had fallen to a little over 40%; and in 1977, it was less than 30% (of which agriculture income by itself constituted only 17% and domestic off-farm activities the remaining 12%).[6] It is significant that with the sharp increase in mine earnings, there has been a large decline in the cultivated area in recent years. For the four principal crops (maize, sorghum, wheat and beans), the area under cultivation fell by a third between 1973–4 and 1976–7.

As the industrial sector is very small, the normal functioning of the Lesotho economy reveals that the country is trapped in the grip of a particularly vicious circle of cumulative causation. Basotho miners earn money in South Africa which is either spent there, or is remitted to Lesotho where it is mostly used to purchase industrial and agricultural products from South Africa. Basotho have a relatively high saving propensity, but their savings, through the banking system, are largely invested in South Africa rather than in Lesotho.[7] The domestic economy of Lesotho benefits very little from migration and is harmed in the classic pattern in which a backward region in a country may become even more backward through normal market processes as a consequence of being associated with the more advanced regions.[8] In view of the seriously harmful human and social effects of migrant mining employment, and the quite understandable desire of the Government and the people of Lesotho to develop their own economy, it is essential to attempt to change these economic parameters, however difficult the task. This is made even more urgent by the political situation in Southern Africa, as well as by the probable long-term decline in the demand for Basotho mining labour.

INSTITUTIONAL CONSTRAINTS

There are two main institutional constraints on the Lesotho economy. First, along with Swaziland, Botswana and South Africa, Lesotho is a member of a free trade area, the South African Customs Union (SACU). Although there are some differences of opinion with respect to the *de facto* provisions of the 1969 renegotiation of the customs union treaty (see Mosley, 1978; Robson, 1978; Landell-Mills, 1971), it restricts Lesotho's ability to provide infant industry-type protection to its industrial or agricultural products. However, under the Lomé Convention, Lesotho (as well as Botswana and Swaziland) has concessional access to the EEC markets which is not available to South Africa.

There are no duties imposed on imports from South Africa (the main source of imports), but the country receives revenue from SACU according to the following formula:[9]

$$R = (i+p) / (I+P) (C+E+S) (1 \cdot 42)$$

Where R = revenue received by Lesotho

i, I = total value of imports into Lesotho and Customs Union respectively

p, P = total value of dutiable goods produced and consumed in Lesotho and Customs Union respectively

$C+E+S$ = total collection of customs, excise and sales duties within the Customs Union.

The full implication of this formula will be discussed later; it is sufficient to note here that the receipts from SACU constituted over 60% of the total government revenue in 1977–8.

Secondly, Lesotho belongs to the Rand Monetary Area and uses the South African rand as its currency. The country, therefore, has no control over its money supply or the exchange rate. One consequence of this, as well as the other economic ties with the South African economy, is that changes in the price level in Lesotho usually mirror those in South Africa. It is proposed to shortly introduce Lesotho's own national currency, but the new currency unit (Maloti) will be on a par with the rand, freely convertible into rand and fully backed by the rand.

FOREIGN AID AND ECONOMIC POLICY

In view of the degree of Lesotho's economic underdevelopment, it would require an extraordinary effort to reduce her dependence on migrant employment and earnings and to generate sustainable expansion of the domestic economy. However, recently the country has had the good fortune of receiving, and being promised, relatively very large amounts of foreign aid. This has been especially so since the Transkei-related difficulties with the South African Government in 1977 and the UN Assistant Secretary-General Farah's visit to Lesotho. According to the UNDP estimates (UNDP, 1978), Lesotho received and spent in 1977, development assistance amounting to $48·6 million, which included $18·5 million of technical assistance, $21·6 million of capital loans and grants, and $8·5 million of food aid. More significantly, however, as compared with the capital assistance expenditure in 1977 of $21·6 million, there were aid commitments of $231·9 million in the pipeline for the years after 1977. In other words, the country had used in 1977 less than ten per cent of the aid promised for capital development projects.

Without minimizing the difficulties of absorptive capacity and recurrent costs associated with foreign aid, it surely provides by virtue of its sheer size, a major opportunity for Lesotho to break out of the circle of economic backwardness. A fundamental issue of economic policy is therefore how best to use this aid to reduce dependence on migrant labour and to generate long-term, self-sustaining growth in the domestic economy. For unless external assistance is used in a purposive manner, given the economic parameters outlined above, it could simply mean aid for South African industry, rather than for Lesotho (since most goods have to be imported from South Africa). It is in this overall context that the problems and prospects of the industrial economy will be examined in the following sections.

III   Structural Change in the Lesotho Economy 1967-77

STRUCTURE OF GROSS DOMESTIC PRODUCT

Table 15.2 shows Lesotho's GDP by industrial origin for the years (April-March) 1970–1 to 1977–8. The last two columns indicate changes in the structure of domestic output over a ten year period – 1967–8 to 1977–8.

Since 1970, Lesotho's GDP has more or less tripled at current prices. However, since the economy experienced an average rate of inflation of 12–13% per year during this period the volume of domestic production has increased at the average rate of 5–6% per annum.[10] There has also been

Table 15.2 Lesotho: Gross Domestic Product at factor cost, by industrial origin, 1973–4 to 1977–8 (in R million, at current prices 1970–1; sectoral shares in GDP, 1967–8 and 1977–8)

	1970–1	1973–4	1974–5	1975–6	1976–7	1977–8	1967–8	1977–8
							Share in total GDP[a]	
Agriculture	17·3	35·5	35·2	37·7	43·6	38·1	41·9	30·1
Crops		(19·3)	(17·1)	(18·8)	(24·5)	(18·0)	(25·1)	(14·2)
Livestock		(16·2)	(18·1)	(18·8)	(19·1)	(20·1)	(16·8)	(15·9)
Mining and quarrying	0·7	0·2	1·1	1·7	2·7	3·0	2·5	2·4
Manufacturing	1·2	1·8	3·2	3·6	3·8	2·6	2·1	2·1
Building and construction	1·1	1·7	1·0	2·6	5·3	13·1	2·2	10·4
Wholesale and retail		6·5	10·8	12·0	14·9	17·0	12·8	13·4
Catering	6·0	2·0	2·4	4·3	6·1	8·7	0·3	6·9
Transport and communication	0·6	1·7	2·1	2·1	2·9	3·6	1·4	2·8
Ownership of dwellings		7·6	8·6	8·8	10·9	15·0	15·3	11·8
Central Government	15·6	6·6	6·3	9·3	11·5	18·7	16·3	14·8
Other[b]		5·3	5·0	5·2	4·6	6·7	5·2	5·3
TOTAL	42·5	68·9	75·7	87·3	106·3	126·5	100·0	100·0

Notes: a In per cent.
b Includes electricity and water, finance, insurance and business and other services.
Sources: Kingdom of Lesotho, Bureau of Statistics, National Accounts 1974–5; data provided by the Lesotho authorities, and IMF staff estimates and Hill, 1978.

considerable structural change over the last decade. The share of crop agriculture has sharply declined from 25% of total output in 1967–8 to about 14% in 1977–8, reflecting the poor performance of this sector. However livestock rearing, mining and manufacturing more or less maintained their relative shares, i.e. these sectors grew at the same rate as the average for the economy.

The largest increases in relative shares have been recorded by building and construction, and by catering. The increase in the share of the former, from 2·2% in 1967–8 to over 10% of the GDP in 1977–8, indicates the high level of investment in the building of the basic infrastructure (particularly roads) of the economy. Rise in the share of catering reflects the growth of the hotel industry and tourism. The number of tourists has increased from 10,000 in 1970 to 175,000 in 1977; most tourists, however, came from South Africa.

INDUSTRIAL OUTPUT AND EMPLOYMENT

At the time of independence, Lesotho's industrial sector was what may charitably be described as rudimentary. Table 15.3 below shows the size distribution of enterprises in manufacturing and construction in the urban formal sector in 1969. In manufacturing alone there were only 16 establishments, employing 714 workers. Further, as one would expect, the manufacturing sector was unintegrated and the ratio of the net output to total output was low:[11]

Gross output in manufacturing (1969)	R 2·083 m
Net output (value added)	R 0·585 m
Net output/gross output	R 0·281 m

Although Lesotho has few natural resources, this is not the primary reason for the lack of industrial development in the country. For Lesotho's neighbours, Botswana and Swaziland, who are better endowed with such resources, have not experienced a dramatically greater degree of industrialization. Besides, in more general terms, countries such as Singapore and Hong Kong, let alone Japan, have managed to industrialize without many natural endowments. Lesotho's industrial backwardness at the time of independence had more to do with its colonial status and its 'subordinate' relationship to the South African economy (see Selwyn, 1975).

Over the last decade, the government has made vigorous efforts (see section IV) to increase the tempo of industrial activity and to create more

Table 15.3 *Size of manufacturing and construction enterprises, Lesotho, 1969*

Number of employees	Number of establishments	Numbers employed
0–20	5	53
21–100	11	444
Over 100	7	879
	23	1,375

Source: Selwyn, 1975.

manufacturing employment. It is estimated that by 1974–5 registered manufacturing industry employed about 3,000 workers and accounted for 12% of total wage employment in Lesotho. Manufacturing also provided about 20% of merchandise exports in that year. During the First Five Year Plan, 1969–70 to 1974–5, a number of new manufacturing units were established to produce a variety of consumer products: pottery, umbrellas, sheepskin products, electric lamps, furniture, and so on (Jones, 1977). The progress of manufacturing industry during the Second Five Year Plan will be reviewed in sections IV and V, which will also examine the nature of constraints on industrial growth at the present stage of Lesotho's development.

IV Recent Performance of Manufacturing Industry and Factors Limiting Industrial Expansion

SECOND FIVE YEAR PLAN (1975-80): TARGETS FOR MANUFACTURING INDUSTRY

The Second Plan estimated that Lesotho's male labour force will grow by 37,500 over the period of 1975–80. It was therefore necessary to create 7,500 male jobs per year even before any of the present migrants could be absorbed. It was planned that most of the additional jobs would be created in construction and agriculture. The target set for what may be called the organized modern sector – industry, mines, commerce and tourism – was about 7,000 new jobs; of this the target for manufacturing industry alone was 4,500.

The revised[12] Second Five Year Plan envisaged a total investment expenditure of R407 million over the period 1975–80. The larger part of this was intended for agriculture and rural development (about 25%) and economic infrastructure (a little over 20%). Approximately ten per cent of the investment resources (R42 million) was earmarked for industry, commerce and tourism.

MEASURES TO PROMOTE INDUSTRIAL DEVELOPMENT

The Government of Lesotho has used a variety of measures to encourage industrial development. The Second Plan document stated: 'It is the Government's policy to leave the development of manufacturing primarily to the private sector. Its incentive policies and its aid in providing finance, suitable sites and where appropriate industrial buildings ... are all aimed at assisting the private entrepreneur' (Chapter 9). The chief agencies for implementing this industrial policy are two state owned organizations, Lesotho National Development Corporation (LNDC) and Basotho Enterprise Development Corporation (BEDCO). LNDC provides long-term finance (including equity participation) as well as a host of other services to large and medium scale enterprises in the urban formal sector. BEDCO's task is to assist in the establishment and growth of small Basotho enterprises by providing loans, training, facilities for businessmen, and so on.

As there is an acute shortage of Basotho entrepreneurs, managers and of higher level skilled and technical personnel, LNDC has had to acquire a majority shareholding in a large number of enterprises it has assisted. In June 1978, LNDC had 38 subsidiary companies (i.e. where it owned more than 50% of equity) operating in manufacturing, tourism, real estate and service industries. In addition the Corporation was associated with 15 other companies through minority shareholdings or long-term loans. Table 15.4 provides a summary of LNDC activities in the modern sector. It is estimated that 80 – 90% of Lesotho's industrial output is produced by LNDC assisted enterprises.[13]

The Government has made vigorous efforts to attract foreign investment, including South African investment. Under the Pioneer Industries Encouragement Act, approved industrial firms are given a six year tax holiday, or alternatively they can have accelerated depreciation allowances and other special concessions. There are no restrictions on repatriation of profits or capital by foreign firms.[14]

In September, 1978, LNDC and the Anglo-American Corporation jointly organized a special seminar in Maseru with foreign businessmen which was addressed both by the Prime Minister and by the Minister of Industries.

INDUSTRIAL PROGRESS: 1975–8

The Central Planning and Development Office's 1977–8 review of employment and investment in industry, mines and tourism provides useful information on the progress of the modern sector in the first three years of the Second Five Year Plan. The detailed employment and investment targets (revalued at 1978 prices) for this sector for the Second Plan were as reported in Table 15.5.

These data implied an investment of R11,700 per job. This figure was largely due to capital intensive investments in Hilton Hotel and in the Letseng Diamond mines.

Between 1975 and 1978, the actual achievement in terms of employment was only the creation of 1697 new jobs, which was 26% of the 1975–80 target. The sectoral break-down was as follows:

Industry	609 jobs	14% of the target
Commerce	279 jobs	28% ,,
Tourism	127 jobs	25% ,,
Mines	682 jobs	62% ,,

The corresponding achievements up to March, 1978 for public and private investment expenditures are reported below:

	Public	*Private*
Industry	31%	17%
Commerce	47%	30%
Tourism	87% (others)	
	45% (Hilton)	
Mining		103%

Table 15.4   *Size distribution and employment in LNDC assisted enterprises and subsidiaries, June 1978*

	Enterprises		Employment					Enterprise size distribution					
	Number	Average size	Basotho No.	%	Expatriates No.	%	Overall	1–10	11–25	25–50	51–100	101–200	Over 200
Summary													
LNDC Group	38	74	2,679	66	128	56	3·0	3	7	11	8	6	3
Associated enterprises	15	82	1,364	34	99	44	2·3	0	5	6	1	2	1
TOTAL	53	76	4,043	100	227	100	5·3	3	12	17	9	8	4
Sector analysis													
Resource-based	5	181	829	21	79	35	—	0	0	4	0	0	1
Other manufacturing	21	61	1,406	35	38	17	—	0	4	6	6	5	0
Service industries	14	34	501	12	22	10	—	2	3	5	3	1	0
Real estate	3	195	586	14	12	5	—	0	0	1	0	1	1
Tourism	10	79	721	18	76	33	—	1	5	1	0	1	2
TOTAL	53	76	4,043	100	227	100	5·3	3	12	17	9	8	4
LNDC Group													
Agric, food and distribution	5	60	301	11	12	10	—	0	1	2	1	1	0
Automotive	2	44	86	3	2	2	—	0	0	2	0	0	0
Basotho Enterprises	5	49	246	9	0	0	—	2	0	2	0	1	0
Building material, construction	4	140	564	22	12	10	—	0	0	2	0	0	1
Consumer products	5	67	329	13	7	6	—	0	0	1	4	0	0
Handicrafts	5	65	273	10	3	2	—	0	2	0	0	2	0
Real estate	1	23	27	1	1	1	—	0	0	1	0	0	0
Tourism, hotels and travel	9	94	702	27	76	60	—	1	4	1	1	0	2
Development corporation	2	53	93	4	12	10	—	0	0	0	2	0	0
TOTAL	38	74	2,261	100	125	100	4·5	3	7	11	8	5	3

Source: NDC Employment Survey.

Notes to Table 15.4: The survey does not cover the whole of the modern sector in Lesotho *but* only LNDC generated enterprises and LNDC associated enterprises.
The survey *excludes* new projects coming on stream after June 1978.
LNDC Group: Companies and units in which LNDC has an equity stake or management contract. These will also include the Head Office staff of the functional Corporations BEDCO, LHC and LNDC.
Associated enterprises: Companies and units established through LNDC assistance, e.g. loan, rented building etc., but excluding those enterprises for which only an industrial site was provided by LNDC.
Resource-based: Enterprises relying on Lesotho natural resources for over half of their input of raw material (e.g. diamonds, wood, mohair, clay etc).
Other manufacturing: Includes processing, assembly and handicrafts.
Service industries: Includes commerce, distribution, garages, development corporation.
Real estate: Includes construction etc.
Tourism: Includes hotels, restaurants, etc.

These data indicate the following costs per job for the period 1975–1978:

Industry	8,878 R
Commerce	10,980 R
Tourism	24,450 R
TOTAL	31,420 R
TOTAL	11,603 R
(less Hilton & Letseng)	

Thus in the first three years of the Plan, there was substantial under-achievement in all sectors except mining. The extremely high investment costs per job were partly due to the relatively better investment 'performance' of the capital intensive sectors, and partly due to the fact that in the other sectors progress

Table 15.5   *Employment and investment targets in the modern sector: Second Plan* (1975–80)

Employment		Investment (R'000)	
Manufacturing	4,500	Manufacturing	
		Private	13,650
		Public	10,740
Commerce	500	Commerce	
		Private	4,550
		Public	3,580
Tourism	1,000	Tourism	
		Public	3,580
		Hilton	12,000
Mines	1,100	Mines	
		Private	
		(Letseng)	35,000
TOTAL	7,100		83,100

Source: JASPA (1979).

in meeting planned employment targets was even slower than that for planned investment. Progress in industry with respect to both employment and investment was particularly poor, and it is unlikely that even half the Second Plan targets for the manufacturing sector for 1980 will be met.

V   Survey of Large Enterprises

In order to discover the reasons for poor industrial performance, the ILO/JASPA mission, in 1978, conducted a small microeconomic survey of large enterprises. The survey involved interviews with company managements and covered the following enterprises: Lesotho Milling Company, Lesotho Sheepskin Products, Lesotho Tractor and Construction Machinery, Maloti Furniture, Royal Lesotho Tapestry Works, Ta Hsing and Tobenno Enterprises Manufacturing and Tranalquip (Lesotho). These enterprises were a reasonable cross section of the 21 LNDC associated or subsidiary manufacturing companies; they employed about 50% of the total manufacturing labour force of the LNDC enterprises.

Surprisingly, at the level of the individual firm, the survey revealed good grounds for optimism about Lesotho's industrial prospects. It may be useful to consider briefly the case of what seemed to be the most impressive of these enterprises, Maloti Furniture. This company employed 235 workers (including 5 expatriates) and had an annual turnover of R1·2 m. It produced furniture from timber imported from Swaziland; about half its market was in Europe and half in South Africa. The company's products were highly competitive; its rate of profit on turnover was 14.7% and on capital invested 45%. The company was in the process of expanding its operations and diversifying into other fields such as cane furniture. With a small additional capital investment of R100,000, the company was expecting to employ well over 100 extra workers, which gave an extremely favourable cost of investment per job as compared with the average manufacturing figures reported above. The main reason for the company's success appeared to be excellent management.

In general the survey revealed the fundamental importance of the management factor in Lesotho's present circumstances. The country does not as yet have its own top managers, nor does it possess foremen and middle managers in sufficient quantity. LNDC has to bring in foreign investors or expatriate management teams on contract and it therefore must be extremely careful in the choice it makes. After experience with enterprises made unviable by inappropriate managements, but which normally efficient management teams would have had no difficulty in running profitably, the Corporation has tightened its internal control mechanisms and accounting procedures.

The survey uniformly showed that the quality of Basotho labour force was very good. The relative cost of labour was not so important (in most of these enterprises this was only a small portion of the total cost of production) as the fact that the labour force was used to industrial discipline. There was very little absenteeism and the workers readily adapted themselves to industrial tasks and were easily trainable. The acting Industries Minister told the investment promotion seminar at Maseru in 1978: 'You will find here one of the hardest

Table 15.6   *Gains and losses to Lesotho with a separate market (estimates for 1973 in R thousand)*

Source of gain or loss	Gain (+)/Loss (−)
1. Enlarged domestic market (impact on GDP)	11,328
2. Reduced exports to South Africa[a]	−520
3. Change in revenue	−5,992
4. Change in the cost of living[a]	−7,686

Note: [a]Alternative high and low estimates have been omitted and only medium estimates are presented in this summary table.
Source: Mosley, 1978.

working people in the world, indeed people whose resourcefulness has contributed to a marked degree to the industrial development of our neighbours. You will find a trained and disciplined labour force whose previous exposure to an industrialized society will mean high levels of productivity and profitability comparable to those of South Africa itself.' This assessment was confirmed by the actual experience of the top managers (all expatriates) interviewed in the survey.

The size of the market and competition with South African industry was an important constraint for some firms. In these cases, the domestic market in Lesotho itself was much larger than the minimum efficient level of production, but the market was being supplied from RSA and these companies were finding it very difficult to obtain a sufficient share of it. There was also some evidence that foreign companies had decided to locate in Lesotho because of its access to the European market. One company was faced with quota restrictions on its export to the EEC from its home country because of the Multiple Fibre Agreement. For another company, the decision to establish a small subsidiary in Lesotho was simply an insurance policy in view of the uncertain situation in Southern Africa and the possibility of economic sanctions against RSA.

VI   The South African Customs Union

A major policy question for industrial development in an underdeveloped economy like that of Lesotho is whether or not it should continue to be a part of a free trade area with a far more developed and diversified economy like that of South Africa. This is a complex issue which requires detailed empirical investigation. Fortunately, some useful work has been done on this subject both by outside scholars and by economists within the government. This research will be reviewed and commented upon here with a view to clarifying the nature of the policy options.

Mosley (1978) has tried to estimate the costs and benefits of the customs union for the economically weaker countries Botswana, Lesotho and Swaziland. Under varying assumptions, he has provided quantitative estimates of the effects of Lesotho's (as well as Botswana and Swaziland's) withdrawal from SACU. The following effects are considered:

(1) industrial development in Lesotho due to import substitution and protection against South African goods;
(2) the loss of South African markets by existing Lesotho industries;
(3) the impact on the government revenue;
(4) and the impact on the cost of living.

Estimated gains and losses to Lesotho under the above headings, on the basis of the 1973 data, are reported in Table 15.6.

The main economic assumptions of this exercise are: (1) all industrial products in which Lesotho's imports from South Africa were greater than the output of the average plant in South Africa are shifted to Lesotho; (2) that the South African response to Lesotho's withdrawal from SACU is simply to impose tariffs on Lesotho's goods at the same rate as it does on goods imported from the rest of the world; (3) that price elasticity of Lesotho's existing industrial exports to South Africa is unity; (4) that the government of Lesotho loses the SACU revenue receipts as calculated by the formula given in section II, and instead has to collect its own customs revenue; and (5) the additional administrative costs of customs collection are 5% of tax yields.

Although each of these and other assumptions can be questioned, they provide a useful starting point for analysing the effects of the customs union. Mosley concluded that on the reasonable 'intermediate' assumptions, there would be a net loss to Lesotho if she were to withdraw from the SACU. This conclusion, however, even in its own terms was rightly questioned by Robson (1978) in a comment on Mosley's paper. He pointed out that Mosley had been in error in aggregating together (1), (2), (3) and (4) in Table 15.6, since it is only (1) and (2) which represent gains and losses to Lesotho's national income. The revenue loss to the government and the increase in the cost of living (item (3) and (4)), as measured, do not constitute a loss to the nation as a whole, but to the government or to some category of citizens which would in part be compensated for by gains to other categories. Robson, therefore recalculated (3) and (4) in terms of the impact on Lesotho's national income. Robson's revised calculations are presented in Table 15.7.

Table 15.7 shows that on 'intermediate' assumptions, there would be a small net gain (2.4% of GNP) to Lesotho if it were not a member of the common

Table 15.7 *Revised estimates of gains and losses to Lesotho with a separate market (R thousand)*

Source of gain or less	Gain (+)/Loss (−)
1. Enlarged domestic market	11,328
2. Reduced exports to South Africa	−520
3. Revenue loss	
i. Loss of compensation	−4,400
ii. Cost of tax administration	−732
4. Efficiency cost of import substitution	−2,738
Overall balance	+2,938
	(= 2.4% of GNP)

Note: As in table 15.6, estimated gains or losses only on the basis of intermediate assumptions are reported.
Source: Robson, 1978.

market. However, Robson thought that the underlying assumptions were somewhat optimistic, and the hypothesized gains were too small to warrant Lesotho's withdrawal from SACU.

In assessing the validity of the above analysis, the following points deserve consideration. First, the size of the possible gain from import substitution industrialization – of more than R11 million – is enormous. It is 8 times the value added by manufacturing industry in Lesotho in 1973.[15] There are of course well known difficulties with the concept of 'shiftable' industry (which is the basis of the calculation), but the measurement biases can go either way, and there are good grounds for believing that Mosley's method does not overestimate the realizable gain from this source.

Secondly Robson's estimates in Table 15.7 show a very large figure for 'revenue loss'. This figure is, however, based on the assumption that the factor of 1·42 in the SACU revenue formula given in section II represents a net transfer of resources from South Africa to Lesotho as compensation for the disadvantages of belonging to the market. Recent work carried out at the Lesotho Ministry of Finance suggests that this assumption is incorrect. A detailed analysis of Lesotho's import structure indicates that there is *no* compensation element at all in the revenue formula, and there is, therefore, no net transfer from South Africa to Lesotho.[16] If the Ministry's estimates, which are based on later data for 1977 are accepted at all, this would raise the net gain figure in Table 15.7 several fold.[17]

Thirdly, and most importantly, Mosley and Robson have not taken into account the effects on Lesotho's agriculture. As seen in section II, a major reason for Lesotho's agricultural malaise is that the rate of return is very low, especially as compared with what could be earned by migrant mine workers in South Africa. As there is evidence that agricultural production in Lesotho is likely to be price elastic (see JASPA, 1979), protection should lead to increased domestic output. In fact there may be an even better case for protection for Lesotho's agriculture against South African products than for her industry.

The foregoing analysis suggests the following policy conclusions. First, the Mosley–Robson type of exercise on the effects of the free trade area on Lesotho's economy should be carried out on the latest data. It should be extended to include agriculture and other sectors. Secondly, the question of withdrawal from SACU is not simply an economic matter, but clearly must depend upon political considerations (for instance, whether or not South Africa would retaliate in other spheres). Thirdly, it is important to emphasize that from the point of view of economic policy, the question is not simply of withdrawal *versus* non-withdrawal. Lesotho could attempt to renegotiate the terms of the customs union agreement, as indeed has been done more than once in the last decade. In such renegotiation, Lesotho could seek protection for particular agricultural and industrial products (see section VII below). She could also attempt to obtain adequate compensation for the disadvantages of being associated with a very much larger and more prosperous partner (as is being currently demanded by Ireland, Italy and the UK in the EEC). More information and research on the gains and losses of belonging to SACU would greatly strenghten Lesotho's hand in such negotiations.

VII Policy Conclusions

A major policy objective of the Government of Lesotho is to reduce the country's dependence on the export of its workers to South Africa. Given the relative size of the migrant labour force, this would be a painful process (in the sense of involving economic sacrifices in the interim period) for any country. It is even more so for Lesotho in view of her economic backwardness. However, Lesotho's options have been increased and the task of readjustment of the economy made relatively easier by the foreign aid which is being provided by the international community.

Lesotho should clearly use foreign aid to create long-term national economic assets which will yield income and employment on a sustainable basis. It is, however, also necessary for the donor countries to soften the terms of the aid if Lesotho is to achieve the desired structural changes in the economy over a reasonable time-span. In particular, the donors should reduce the requirements of counterpart contributions to enable the country to substantially increase the proportion of aid which it currently uses relative to that which is committed. (See section on 'Foreign aid and economic policy'). As Lesotho has an extremely underdeveloped basic economic infrastructure, the first priority at this stage must be accorded to the development of roads, electricity and other elements of the infrastructure. This is recognized by the Government and there is already a major roads programme underway to bring about the economic integration of the mountainous country. The development and subsequent maintenance of the road network would be a useful source of employment. The Government should similarly give priority attention to the generation of electricity and to its availability in the various parts of the country.

In the same way, there is a rather different kind of long-term infrastructural project which the government should urgently consider. This would be a large programme of afforestation on the higher mountain slopes, to be carried out over a 10 – 15 year period. It would undoubtedly be an expensive project but one which seems to promise several important advantages to the country. First, by checking soil erosion – and the seriousness of this problem cannot be exaggerated – this would lead to increased agricultural production. Secondly, it would provide raw materials for a variety of wood-based industries. Thirdly, being labour intensive, it would also create considerable employment during the process of development. The project is briefly described in the accompanying appendix; it certainly merits a detailed feasibility study.

Along with roads, electricity and afforestation, an equal priority should be given to rural development. Lesotho must attempt to be self-sufficient in the main staples and reduce agricultural imports. However, in addition to the government's current efforts through rural development projects, agricultural expansion also requires other major policy steps. First, the Government should consider limiting the numbers going to work in the South African mines – initially, at the current level. The limit should be progressively reduced according to economic circumstances (perhaps at the rate of 2 to 3% a year), by agreement with the mine companies and the government of RSA.[18] This is necessary to increase the supply of able-bodied male labour needed for

terracing and other long term agricultural improvements, and more importantly to induce the realization in rural families that they should not continue
to rely mainly on mine earnings, but instead attempt to improve their own
farms. Secondly, since the current rate of return on agriculture is very low,
the Government should raise the purchase price of agricultural produce so as
to provide an adequate incentive for increasing production. This involves
according protection to agricultural products, and therefore an agreement with
the partners in the Customs Union.[19] In Lesotho's present circumstances, it
is necessary to give greater priority to the building of the infrastructure and
to agriculture than to industry. This is due both to the degree of the country's
underdevelopment, and to the fact that in the short and medium term,
infrastructure and agriculture will be the main sources of increased employment for the Basotho. The industrial sector, being small, can absorb only small
amounts of labour. However, industrial expansion is required to raise the
overall level of productivity in the economy, for technical progress, for
reducing the industrial import bill, and at a *later* stage to absorb labour which
will be released with the expansion of productivity and production in
agriculture.

Lesotho's main industrial advantage is that despite its economic backwardness, because of historical circumstances, it possesses a labour force which
is used to industrial discipline and is adaptable to industrial tasks. By African
standards, the labour force is also relatively more educated (Jones, 1977).
However, the government needs to be much more purposeful in the creation
of industries than it has been up until now. There are few benefits in attracting
foreign investors at any terms and letting them establish any kinds of
manufacturing enterprises which they choose. A multinational company may
set up a small subsidiary in Lesotho to take advantage of some particular tax,
or other, concessions and then leave after a few years, as indeed has happened
in certain cases. The government should attempt to establish industries, either
itself or through foreign investment, where current and potential linkages with
the rest of the economy are the greatest.

It was noted earlier that a major constraint on Lesotho's industrial
development at present is the acute dearth of management skills. It is,
however, necessary not only to provide formal management training to the
Basotho, but it is also essential to recognize that such skills are best acquired
by 'learning by doing' (see Singh and Bienefeld, 1977). This imposes a
short-term cost which a developing country has inevitably to bear in the
interest of long-term development of management capabilities. This factor
needs to be given proper weight in the government and LNDC monitoring of
the existing industrial enterprises and in the establishment of new ones.

There is also considerable scope for *selective* and planned import-substituting industrial development in Lesotho, since it imports almost all its
industrial requirements. This potential has been tapped very little. The
government should seek to provide infant industry protection to a limited
range of products, for which Lesotho's import demand is large relative to the
efficient plant size ('efficient' in terms of Lesotho's costs and prices) and for
which there exists maximum potential for linkages with the rest of the
economy. It has been argued that the SACU agreement does provide for infant
industry protection but that Lesotho has never sought to make use of the
provision (Robson, 1978). Clearly this should be done as a matter of priority;

with a protected and assured market, the government would also find it much easier to attract the right kind of foreign investment. Similarly, in the government's own purchases – and public expenditure is a considerable proportion of the total expenditure – the Ministries should be instructed to give clear preference to Lesotho enterprises, a policy which they do not appear to have systematically adopted so far.

Appendix

PROPOSED LONG-TERM PROGRAMME FOR AFFORESTATION IN LESOTHO[20]

Lesotho suffers from heavy soil erosion resulting from fast running rain water from the steep and absolutely barren mountain slopes. This leads to continuing decline in arable land and in both quantity and quality of grazing land.

Checking of soil erosion on a massive scale should therefore be one of the foremost efforts in agricultural development. Afforestation of mountain slopes will not only check soil erosion but will change the whole ecology, improve and enrich the soils, reduce climatic hazards, including frequent drought conditions, and improve the pastures. Planting, cultivation and protection of trees will offer employment on a large scale. The forest wealth that will be created, should lead to development of forest based industries like logging, wood and timber processing, making of poles, boxes and hooks, match sticks, pulp, veneer, etc. which would generate further wealth and employment in the country.

The importance of afforestation in the country has been long recognized primarily as a soil conservation measure and for meeting the basic needs for fuel and agricultural timber in the rural areas. Over the past three decades, the Soil Conservation Unit of the Ministry of Agriculture has been planting pines and eucalyptus at high altitudes of seven to eight thousand feet, willows and poplars along and around the river streams and dongas. These plantations indicate the species which can thrive in Lesotho, the altitudes up to which they can be grown and the manner in which the different species can be dispersed in the various areas. In recent years, the plantation efforts have been, and are being, made under the woodlot project, but these efforts are mostly confined to the lowlands and foothills and have, at least in some cases, resulted in encroachment on arable land.

The plantations are needed more on the higher mountain slopes which are absolutely barren and where most of the soil erosion originates. The cost of plantation, protection and management is, of course, very high at the higher altitudes, but balanced land-use planning would generally suggest crop husbandry in the lowlands, on the foothills and in the valleys; development of grazing lands on the lower slopes, and afforestation on the higher slopes.

The cold climate, high altitudes and extensive rock formations can be advanced as arguments against any programme of extensive afforestation in Lesotho. But the fact that cold climate and high altitudes are not an insurmountable hindrance is well demonstrated by whatever little plantations of pine, eucalyptus, willow and poplar one sees all over the country, except at the very high altitudes of 9,000 feet and above. It is also well known that given a place to stand, the trees find and create their own soil. So wherever some soils are available in between the rocks, the trees can be planted. Lesotho can learn a lot from her sister country, Swaziland, where the mountain slopes up to 7,000 feet are extensively covered with man-made forests of pine, eucalyptus and wattle trees.

Afforestation, however, needs a very heavy investment; the cost of protection and raising the trees is also heavy, and management difficult. The gestation period, varying from 10–15 years for the species recommended for Lesotho, is however, not so long as it is in the case of tropical forests; but is also not short compared to other investment efforts which are productive in much shorter periods. Any planning for afforestation and forest development has further to envisage the setting up of industries for exploitation of wood and timber and forest products. A feasibility study is necessary for examining the various aspects of afforestation and the development of forest industries in the country.

Notes

This is a revised version of a paper which was earlier written as a background report for the JASPA/ILO Employment Advisory Mission to the Government of Lesotho. The Mission, of which I was a member, visited the country in September 1978. I am grateful to Dr S.B.L. Nigam, Chief of the Mission and Director of ILO's Jobs and Skill Programme for Africa in Addis Ababa, for permission to publish the paper. I should also like to thank Dr Nigam and other members of the mission, as well as officials of the Government of Lesotho and those of international agencies at Maseru, for valuable discussions; I am particularly indebted to Mr. Neil Robertson for his helpful comments on an earlier draft. The usual caveat is especially important in this case; none of the above mentioned individuals or organizations are in anyway responsible for the views expressed or the errors which may remain.

1 See JASPA (1979). Because of these biases and other inconsistencies, Table 15.1 is best regarded as providing only rough orders of magnitude.

2 'Remittances' consist of cash brought back into Lesotho, deferred pay and remittances, and the value of goods purchased in South Africa which are then imported into Lesotho.

3 In 1977–8, while the recorded value of Lesotho's exports was R12·0 million, migrant remittances during that year amounted to R118·3 million.

4 However, despite this impressive wage increase, mining wages are among the lowest industrial wages in South Africa. Allowing for the income in kind which the miners receive (food, accommodation, etc.), the average wage is just above the urban PDL.

5 Total migrant earnings, as opposed to mining earnings abroad, were, as noted earlier, 130% of GDP at factor cost in 1976–1977.

6 Hill, 1978; Robertson, 1978.

7 In a recent survey of 37 African countries and Lesotho, Lesotho had the second lowest ratio of total domestic lending to total commercial bank financial assets. In December 1977, Lesotho's ratio was 0·49; this compared with an average of 0·83, and a range of 0·48 to 0·97 for the 37 African countries. Excluding Burundi, the range for the 36 remaining countries was 0·63 to 0·97. Similarly private sector lending to private sector deposit ratio (defined as claims on private sector to deposits of business and households) in Lesotho was 0·35; the average ratio for the 37 African countries was 1·14

and the range was 0·35 to 3·53. I am indebted to Mr. Neil Robertson for providing this information.
8   See Hicks, 1969; Kaldor, 1974; Bagchi, 1976a,b; Singh, 1977.
9   See further Mosley, 1978.
10 For a discussion of the limitations of the statistical data about the Lesotho economy, see JASPA, 1979.
11 See further Selwyn, 1975.
12 As a result of the border problems connected with the establishment of Transkei, the Second Plan was revised and enlarged in 1977.
13 The following discussion is mainly concerned with 'large' scale industry which produces most of Lesotho's industrial output. For an account of the small scale and informal sector industry, as well as the activities of BEDCO, see Ngwenya, 1978.
14 See the Acting Industries Minister, the Honourable K.T.J. Rakhetla's speech at the LNDC-AAC investment promotion seminar at Maseru in September 1978.
15 As Table 15.2 shows, total value added by manufacturing industry in Lesotho in 1973–74 amounted only to R1.8 million.
16 The preliminary conclusion of the Ministry's officials was as follows: 'There is, therefore, no charity in the formula, and no compensation for those protective costs of the tariff not measured here, the polarization of development, the loss of fiscal discretion or any of the other disadvantages of membership.' Cf. JASPA, 1979.
17 It should also be noted that the negative figure of R2.7 million in Table 15.7, indicating the 'efficiency cost of import substitution', is based implicitly on the assumption that Lesotho has a fully employed economy; that is clearly not the case.
18 It has been suggested that since there is likely to be a reduction in the South African demand for Lesotho's labour in any case, this step is not necessary. However from the point of view of the Lesotho Government, a planned and purposeful decline in the mining labour force is surely to be preferred to that arising from uncontrolled market forces, or the vagaries of the South African Government's policies towards the homelands and the peripheral countries.
19 It has been argued by some, but by no means all, agricultural economists that a sustained increase in agricultural production in Lesotho can only come about if there is a major reform of the system of land-tenure. Even if this were true, such major institutional changes usually take place over a long period of time (unless, of course, there is a violent revolution). A policy of protection for Lesotho's agriculture, on the other hand, has an immediate effect; it also does not preclude in any way, feasible measures of land reform.
20 This appendix is based on information supplied by officials of the Ministry of Agriculture.

References

Bagchi, A. K. (1976a) 'De-industrialization in Gangetic Bihar 1809–1901 and its implications', in Barun De *et al.*, *Essays in Honour of S. C. Sarkar* (New Delhi: People's Publishing House).

Bagchi, A. K. (1976b) 'De-industrialization in India in the 19th century: some theoretical implications', *Journal of Development Studies* (January).

Hicks, J. R. (1969) *A Theory of Economic History* (Oxford: Clarendon Press).

Hill, D. W. (1978) 'Migration to the Republic of South Africa', background paper for the JASPA/ILO Mission (Maseru).

JASPA (1979) *Options for a Dependent Economy* (ILO: Addis Ababa).

Jones, D. (1977) *Aid and Development in Southern Africa* (London: Overseas Development Institute).

Kaldor, N. K. (1970) 'The case for regional policies', *Scottish Journal of Political Economy* (November).

Landell-Mills, P. M. (1971) 'The 1969 Southern African Customs Agreement', *Journal of Modern African Studies*, 9, 2 (August).

Mosley, Paul (1978) 'The Southern African Customs Union, a reappraisal', *World Development*, 6, 1.

Ngwenya, M. A. R. (1978) 'The nature of Basotho owned, managed and operated enterprises: a survey of their problems and of possible remedial measures' (Maseru).

Robson, Peter (1978) 'Reappraising the Southern African Customs Union: a comment', *World Development*, 6, 2.

Selwyn, Percy (1975) *Industries in the Southern African Periphery* (London: Croom Helm).

Singh, A. (1977) 'UK industry and the world economy: a case of de-industrialization'; *Cambridge Journal of Economics* (June).

Singh, A. and Bienefeld, F. M. (1977) 'Industry and urban economy in Tanzania', background paper for the JASPA/ILO Employment Advisory Mission to Tanzania, 1977 (mimeo.).

World Bank (1977) 'Appraisal of the Lesotho National Development Corporation (LNDC) and its subsidiary Basotho Enterprises Development Corporation (BEDCO)', report number 1332a–LSO (Washington, DC, March).

World Bank (1978) *World Development Report* (Washington, DC)

UNDP (1978) '*Development Assistance, Lesotho, 1977*' (Maseru, Lesotho, July).

PART FOUR
WEST AFRICA

16 Recent Developments in Nigerian Industrialization

TOM FORREST

In this chapter we begin with an outline of early import-substituting industrialization in Nigeria and the underlying social structure that supported and conditioned it. Evidence is then presented on the growth and structure of manufacturing industry. Next, the conditions surrounding Nigeria's industrialization when oil revenues and state expenditures increased in the 1970s are explored by reference to four areas of state policy: trade, state investment, indigenization and technology. In the concluding section, we examine the relations between import substituting industrialization, the class conditions of accumulation, and the existence of a rentier oil state.

I Early Industrialization

The incorporation of Nigeria into the world economy was achieved through the expansion of peasant commodity production. There was little plantation agriculture in Nigeria and a large land-owning class was absent. Commodity production provided the economic foundation for the operations of foreign merchant capitalists and the regional pattern of power and wealth that was consolidated in the 1950s. Industrialization came late relative to other African countries. It had been discouraged by the colonial regime, by the merchant, banking and shipping monopolies, and later by the operation of the marketing board system which excluded African merchants and appropriated surplus funds to London. In the 1950s shifts in power away from the metropolitan centre and increased competition led to local market protection and the establishment of large-scale industry dominated by foreign capital and supplemented by state capital. This was heavily concentrated in the federal territory of Lagos with secondary concentrations in the Kano/Kaduna and Port Harcourt/Aba zones and minor pockets in Ibadan, Benin and Enugu. These forms and patterns of incorporation meant that the Nigerian bourgeoisie was weak, small scale, largely commercial in orientation, fragmented and regional in outlook. Indigenous private capital did not play any significant role in the development of medium and large-scale industry. It could provide no challenge to foreign capital which made its alliance with the political class and the bureaucracy. The educated elite joined the bureaucracy and the professions and, from the security of these privileged occupations, pursued other sources of income in property, contracting and commerce. Nationalist opposition to the dominance of foreign interests in the economy was limited. State policies which aimed to exclude foreign enterprise were directed first at the produce buying, transport and distributive sectors, and then, after the public service had been Nigerianized, at expatriate employment in industry. In the distributive sector, the measures were generally vague and ineffectual.[1]

With the approach of independence, the state provided finance, tax incentives and protection in the early stages of industrialization. Agriculture provided the financial resources for this support.[2] Considerations of market protection, various types of state subsidy, and tariff escalation due to balance-of-payments difficulties in the early 1960s, all encouraged the expansion of foreign capital from its commercial base into manufacture and prompted the flow of new investment from abroad. The extent to which the merchant monopolies actually dropped their commercial activities for manufacture is easily exaggerated.[3] Shifts in the structure of imports towards intermediate and capital goods have favoured these companies. Light consumer goods with limited domestic linkages, assembly plants and a few intermediate plants like cement, rubber tyres and glass replaced imports. Import substitution, which involved the establishment of capitalist relations and the internationalization of production and consumption and the use of capital intensive technology, was not part of any planned coherent strategy of industrialization. The First Plan (1962–8), which was a collection of regional plans, was essentially a list of public expenditures. It maintained the open door policy and reliance upon foreign capital. Federal authority was weak. The classic instance of federal impotence in the face of struggles for regional advantages was the failure to locate the iron and steel project which had first been proposed in 1958.[4] Regional competition and public corruption led to considerable waste. As the First Republic ended, industry suffered from duplication of plants, uneconomic location and a wave of contractor-financed turnkey projects.

The state provided an essential support role for private capital accumulation. This support was heavily biased towards large foreign-controlled enterprises despite a number of attempts to encourage Nigerian enterprise through loan schemes and industrial development centres. The state provided

Table 16.1 *Structure of equity in large-scale manufacturing (%)*

	1963	1975
Private Nigerian	10%	20%
Private non-Nigerian	68%	42%
Federal Government	3%	24%
State governments	19%	14%

Source: Federal Office of Statistics, Industrial Survey.

Table 16.2 *Nigeria: stock of direct private investment, end-1967 ($ million)*

	Canada	Denmark	France	Germany	Italy	Japan	Netherlands	Sweden	Switzerland	United Kingdom	United States	DAC Total
Petroleum, of which:	–	–	75·0	–	40·0	–	147·0	–	–	343·0	55·0	760·0
Production	–	–	72·0	–	38·0	–	140·0	–	–	326·0	150·0	726·0
Refining	–	–	–	–	–	–	4·0	–	–	10·0	–	14·0
Marketing	–	–	3·0	–	(2·0)	–	(3·0)	–	–	7·0	5·0	20·0
Transport	–	–	–	–	–	–	–	–	–	–	–	–
Mining and smelting	–	–	–	–	–	–	–	–	–	14·9	1·0	15·9
Agriculture	–	1·0	–	–	–	–	–	–	–	5·0	–	5·0
Manufacturing	8·0	0·4	15·0	6·0	3·0	3·0	11·0	1·0	3·0	96·8	16·0	163·8
Trade	–	–	10·0	1·4	1·0	–	3·0	–	2·0	84·2	8·0	110·0
Public utilities	–	–	–	–	–	–	–	–	–	–	–	–
Transport	–	–	–	–	–	–	–	–	8	–	–	–
Banking	–	–	–	–	–	–	–	–	–	25·0	2·0	27·0
Tourism	–	–	–	–	–	–	–	–	–	–	–	–
Other	–	–	–	–	–	–	–	–	–	27·1	–	27·1
TOTAL	8·0	1·4	100·0	7·4	44·0	3·0	161·0	1·0	5·0	596·0	182·0	1,108·8

Source: Stock of Private Direct Investments by DAC Countries in Developing Countries, End 1967, OECD, Paris, 1972.

Table 16.3   *Foreign direct investment in Nigeria by type*

	1965	%	1970	%	1976	%
Agriculture, forestry and fishing	11·0	1·6	11·2	1·1	21·9	0·9
Mining	293·0	41·4	515·4	51·4	918·6	39·4
Manufacturing and processing	135·6	19·2	224·8	22·4	550·7	23·6
Transport and communications	11·4	1·6	13·8	1·4	11·0	0·5
Trading and business services	181·2	25·6	206·6	20·6	624·8	26·8
Building and construction	39·2	5·5	13·8	1·4	122·8	5·3
Others	36·0	5·1	17·6	1·7	84·0	3·6
TOTAL	707·4	100	1,003·2	100	2,333·8	100·1

Source: *Economic and Financial Review*, 11, 1, June 1973; *Nigeria's Principal Economic and Financial Indicators 1970–1978*, Central Bank.

Table 16.4   *Foreign direct investment in Nigeria by origin (₦ million)*

	1965	%	1970	%	1976	%
UK	371·0	52·4	444·4	44·3	942·0	40·4
USA	116·4	16·5	230·0	22·9	376·2	16·1
W. Europe	158·8	22·4	224·8	22·4	653·1	28·0
Others	61·2	8·7	104·0	10·4	362·5	15·5
TOTAL	707·4	100	1,003·2	100	2,333·8	100

Source: As Table 16.3.

Table 16.5   *Selected non-oil items on balance-of-payments account (£ million)*

	1960/5	Av. 1970	1971	1972	1973
Net direct private investment	56·0	93·6	128·8	102·0	70·8
Profits and dividends	−33·0	−100·0	−109·8	−148·8	−161·1
Other services[b]	−14·6[c]	−26·3	−51·6	−58·0	−245·8

	1974	1975	1976	1977	1978[a]
Net direct private investment	−4·6	42·6	54·7	136·3	26·1
Profits and dividends	−153·7	−147·0	−136·5	−156·5	−104·6
Other services[b]	−322·9	−439·9	−360·1	−165·6	−136·0

Notes: [a] 1978 is provisional.
[b] Other services include management, technical and consultancy fees, commission and brokerage, royalties, education and other minor items.
[c] 1963/5 average obtained by subtracting oil services in Pearson from Central Bank figures.
Sources: IBRD, 1974; Central Bank of Nigeria, *Annual Reports*; Pearson, 1970.

infrastructure, public utilities, fiscal incentives, equity and loan capital and industrial estates. The first textile and cement plants were initiated by state capital. A major vehicle for this support was the regional development corporations which were funded by surpluses from the marketing boards. Investment by these boards was regarded as a pump-priming exercise to be relinquished once industry had been established and a class of private investors had emerged. In 1963, for example, the premier of the Eastern Region, invited 383 distinguished personalities to Enugu to discuss the sale and distribution of state assests in twenty-three companies.[5] Wholly-owned state enterprises were generally unsuccessful. After an exhaustive survey of the Western Region Development Corporation, Teriba concluded by stressing the superiority of an industrial development strategy, relying on minority investment in private industry, over that relying on exclusive investment and management by public development institutions.[6] An inquiry into the Northern Nigeria Development Corporation found only one out of twelve wholly financed projects worth encouraging.[7]

In 1963 the pattern of equity in large-scale industry was foreign 68%, private Nigerian 10%, federal government 3% and regional governments 19% (Table 16.1).[8] The breakdown of foreign capital by activity and source is shown in Tables 16.2, 16.3 and 16.4. In 1967 $760m. or 68% of total foreign investment was accounted for by the oil industry. British investment was dominant in banking, trade and manufacture. Since then the British share has fallen (see Table 16.4). The distribution of foreign investment activity shows little change (see Table 16.3).

On the balance-of-payments account the net inflow of non-oil direct investment, which averaged N56m. over 1960–65, slowed down over the civil war period. Immediately after the war it picked up, but it then fell following the indigenization decree (see Table 16.5). Since the mid-1960s net inflows of direct investment on both oil and non-oil accounts have been much smaller than declared outflows of profit and dividends. Whereas, in the first half of the 1960s non-oil net investment more than covered outflows of profit and dividends and other services, the 1970s show a strong reversal of that position as investment matured and local sources of finance-capital increased. Payments for services have increased relative to profits, due in part to the indigenization programme which reduced foreign equity and heightened the importance of foreign control through imported technology.

II   Growth and Structure

The index of manufacturing output has grown rapidly since 1963. The average annual growth over the periods 1963–7, 1967–72 and 1972–8 was 13·6%, 10·2% and 13·3% respectively (Table 16.6). (The middle period includes the period of the civil war and production in the war-affected Eastern States is not included in the index.) Much industry was destroyed during the war. The war interrupted high growth rates especially in the Port Harcourt area, and industrial recovery over the whole area of the former Eastern Region was slow. Outside the East, wartime import and foreign exchange controls brought high capacity utilization and erratic growth. Gross fixed capital formation fell

Table 16.6   *Nigeria: index of manufacturing output (1972=100)*

		% Change
1963	40·7	
1964	40·3	21·1
1965	53·2	7·9
1966	59·4	11·7
1967	60·7	2·2
1968	60·6	−0·2
1969	79·8	31·7
1970	88·9	11·4
1971	94·0	5·7
1972	100·0	6·3
1973	123·0	23·0
1974	119·5	−3·3
1975	147·7	23·6
1976	182·2	23·4
1977	193·5	6·2
1978	220·2	13·8

Notes:
1 This index has been linked to an older index with base 1965.
2 From mid-1967 to second quarter 1971 production from Eastern States is excluded.
3 1978 is estimate.
Source: Annual Reports, Central Bank of Nigeria.

for two years (1967/8–1968/9) and investment in plant and machinery was severely affected. Immediately following the war industrial output grew slowly. Federal spending on infrastructure and basic utilities lagged well behind planned expenditure for several years. In the last period (1972–8) very large oil revenues were monetized by government spending. This led to a commercial and construction boom, and inflation. For industry, the large profits from vastly enlarged markets were only marginally offset by power shortages or port congestion, or by competition from imports which were encouraged by the erosion of tariffs and appreciation of the naira. The optimism of the third plan (1975–80) which saw 'no savings and foreign exchange constraints during the plan period and beyond', proved shortlived as the balance of payments went into deficit in 1976. Oil revenues faltered in

Table 16.7   *Trends in import composition, 1960–78 (% shares)*

	1960	1965	1972	1978
Consumer goods	61	45	36	28
Durable			(10)	(8)
Non-durable			(26)	(20)
Capital goods	22	31	37	49
Raw materials	17	24	26	24

Note: 1978 is provisional.
Sources: P. Kilby, *Industrialisation in an Open Economy, Nigeria 1945–66 (Cambridge, 1969).*
Central Bank, Annual Reports.

Table 16.8 *Number of establishments, employment, gross output and value added in Manufacturing 1964 and 1975 (gross output) and value added (₦ million).*

Industry Group	Number of establishments 1964	1975	Employment 1964	1975	Gross output 1964	1975	Value added 1964	1975
Food and beverages	147	277	10,985	46,485	89·15	461·84	37·02	200·09
Tobacco, beer, spirit	20	17	3,997	10,476	29·12	221·42	19·22	128·82
Textile	46	132	9,381	60,673	18·12	458·71	7·70	197·06
Leather	22	41	1,969	6,231	6·77	69·33	2·50	40·46
Wooden products	104	276	11,838	21,517	18·02	92·26	10·68	44·08
Paper, printing	80	123	6,340	17,510	7·79	151·39	4·35	71·26
Chemical products	37	56	3,887	12,855	26·03	370·93	12·15	189·91
Rubber products	35	33	6,875	11,312	21·58	66·72	9·40	39·81
Plastic	0	33	0	5,201	0·00	54·90	0·00	19·72
Pottery and glass	6	16	489	1,907	0·37	12·55	0·11	5·83
Other non-metallic	20	95	3,732	12,947	6·54	74·33	8·34	41·15
Basic metal	36	122	5,622	27,684	44·44	315·42	8·53	124·92
Machinery	4	7	95	469	0·81	3·18	0·16	2·08
Electrical equipment	8	25	400	3,427	1·28	48·44	0·45	20·66
Transport	13	14	2,082	4,284	16·64	191·79	2·49	54·30
Miscellaneous	12	23	866	1,265	2·56	17·87	1·23	5·29
TOTAL	590	1,290	68,558	244,243	298·31	2,611·09	124·33	1,185·33

Source: Industrial Survey 1964 and 1975. Federal Office of Statistics.

1977/8 and government spending and bank credit were cut back to send the economy into recession. Industrial growth slowed down temporarily.

The rapid growth of Nigerian manufacturing has not been associated with any marked shifts in industrial structure, though it is possible to isolate certain trends for discussion. The share of manufacturing in GDP rose from 5% in 1960 to 9% in 1977.[9] Much of the growth has been concentrated in the consumer goods sector. The weakness of the intermediate and capital goods sectors remains. The structure of imports indicates a sustained shift towards capital goods (Table 16.7). Tables 16.8 and 16.9 show that the share of light consumer goods in value added has fallen slightly over the period 1963–75, despite the rapid growth in the textile industry (especially synthetic fibres). The rising share of the textile industry is to be expected with a protected market in an essentially agrarian economy. The garment industry is mainly small scale and so falls outside the enumerated sector. In 1978 a long overdue ban was placed on imported clothing to encourage domestic industry. The relative decline of the food sector is due in part to a drastic fall in the output of the vegetable oil milling sector (groundnut and palm oil). Unlike the Ivory Coast, where agricultural growth has provided the basis for a vigorous expansion of processing industries, Nigeria's industries have, with the exception of flour

Table 16.9 *Structural change in Nigerian manufacturing, 1964–75*

	Share of value added 1964	1975	Share of employment 1964	1975
Food and beverages	29·8	16·9	16·0	19·0
Tobacco, beer and spirit	15·5	10·9	5·8	4·3
Textile	6·2	16·2	13·7	24·8
Leather	2·0	3·4	2·9	2·6
Wooden product	8·6	3·7	17·3	8·8
Paper, printing, etc.	3·5	6·0	9·3	7·2
Chemical product	9·8	16·0	5·7	5·3
Rubber	7·6	3·3	10·0	4·6
Plastic	0·0	1·7	0·0	2·1
Pottery and glass	0·1	0·5	0·7	0·8
Other non-metallic	6·7	3·5	5·4	5·3
Basic metal	6·9	10·5	8·2	11·3
Machinery	0·1	0·2	0·1	0·2
Electrical equipment	0·4	1·7	0·6	1·4
Transport	2·0	4·6	3·0	1·8
Miscellaneous	1·0	0·5	1·3	0·5
TOTAL	100·2	99·6	100·0	100·0

Source: Industrial Survey 1964 and 1975.

and livestock feed milling based on imported wheat and maize, stagnated or declined as a result of discrimination against agriculture. The groundnut crushing industry has a capacity of over 1 million tons, far in excess of past or likely future supplies. Apart from the adverse effect of the Sahel drought, the industry has also suffered from the low prices which the Commodity Board, its sole supplier, pays to the farmer, and from competition with imported oils. The mills have resorted to milling cottonseed and importing foreign oils for processing. Sugar processing has grown slowly leaving a large gap for imports. Rubber processing has also declined in significance.

Apart from textiles, other products experiencing fast growth in the 1970s were vehicle assembly, soaps and detergents, soft drinks, pharmaceuticals, beer, paints and roofing sheets. Six highly protected and subsidized vehicle assembly plants were set up in quick succession. Car assembly plants include Volkswagen (Lagos) and Peugeot (Kaduna); in truck assembly, Leyland (Ibadan), Steyr (Bauchi), Fiat (Kano) and Daimler-Benz (Enugu) have followed the older Bedford plant. Given the size of the Nigerian market, economies of scale will be realized. How quickly the industry builds up backward linkages depends on how strictly the state enforces its objective of full local content. For Nigeria backward linkages imply new industries and a few foreign component companies have followed the assembly plants.

The high ranking of the chemicals sector is explained not by the presence of basic industrial chemicals but by the growth of pharmaceuticals, soaps and detergents, and cosmetics. Nigeria has been slow to realize the potential for downstream petroleum-related activities. With two new refineries at Warri and Kaduna virtually completed, this sector will expand. A polyproplene plant is planned for Warri and a petrochemicals plant for Port Harcourt. In 1978, some twenty years after the start of the oil industry, only 5% of associated gases were used in industry.[10] A large liquified natural gas project at Bonny has been held up by uncertainties over the US energy market.

Given high demand, and locational advantages provided by high transport costs, the performance of the cement industry is poor. In 1977 the proportion of domestic production to total supply was 15%. The industry, which is largely state-owned, has suffered from management and infrastructural problems and difficulties with technical partners. Local fertilizer production is limited to a single superphosphate plant at Kaduna, which is a turnkey project relying on imported rock from Togo. This is to be followed by a nitrogenous plant at Port Harcourt.

The machinery and electrical equipment sector is very limited in size and scope. With few exceptions, demand for agricultural machinery has not given rise to fabricating plants. State ventures with foreign partners are to be the basis of a machine tools industry at Oshogbo and Aba, and transformer and meter industries at Abeokuta and Zaria.

In the basic metals sector there has been some expansion of small plants. These include cast iron plants, the processing of imported aluminum, the fabrication of containers, storage tanks and truck frames, and tin smelting at Jos. Plans for a steel industry in its present form were put forward in 1970. After a search for iron ore and coal deposits, the location for a blast furnace plant at Ajaokuta was decided in 1975.[11] The plant is due to start production in 1985. A turnkey direct reduction plant is being constructed at Warri to use power from the Sapele natural gas plant, and production of steel is expected to begin in 1981. Ore will be shipped from Guinea where Nigeria has an equity interest in the Mefergui-Nimba mines. Three steel rolling mills are to be constructed at Oshogbo, Katsina and Jos.

III   Industrial Policy

The main objectives of industrial policy pursued through an import substituting strategy have been rapid growth and a diversified industrial structure. In the early 1970s heavy industry was reserved for the public sector and federal direct investment in industry has since increased. An indigenization programme, which aimed to increase domestic control of large-scale industry and promote local enterprise, was also launched. In general, industrial policy has been directed at the large-scale sector. Little attention has been given to the small and medium-scale sectors which have been discriminated against.[12] Industrial employment and the spatial distribution of industrial activity (with the exception of federal projects) have also been of little concern.

(a)   TRADE POLICIES

Trade policies in the form of tariffs, quantitative restrictions and exchange rate management have been more important than other forms of tax and control in determining industrial structure in Nigeria. At independence trade and payments controls were moderate. In the early 1960s tariffs rose for revenue and protection purposes. During the civil war foreign exchange controls and import licensing were imposed. They were gradually relaxed after the war, but as state expenditures increased, inflation accelerated. Anti-inflation policy was directed at an increased flow of imports achieved through tariff cuts and appreciation of the naira. Commercial lobbies were active in pressing for the tariff cuts which were not restricted to essential items and included consumer durables, soap, footwear and beer. These measures reflect a recurring dilemma between tariff protection for industry and cost-of-living considerations. The expansion of imports could not be sustained and by the time of the 1977–8 budget trade policy had become more restrictive and discriminating.[13] Imported capital goods are cheapened by use of the Approved User scheme. In 1978 a new decree prohibited banned items for a minimum of eight years in an attempt to avoid frequent reversals of policy and encourage manufacture.

A study of net effective protection arising from trade policy across fifty-four industrial groups in 1977 indicates disincentives to export-oriented industries and import substituting intermediate industry based on local raw materials.[14] It also shows moderate incentives to consumer goods industries processing domestic raw materials, and substantial incentives for low value added, import substituting consumer industries and assembly plants that are based on imported raw materials. It is estimated that 45% of industry by value added at world prices would be better off under free trade conditions, 36% probably or possibly viable, and the remainder in varying degrees unviable. The total subsidy to industry arising from trade policies is estimated at ₦326m. (23% of value added at domestic prices or 30% of value added at world prices).

Industrial protection discriminated against agriculture through a terms of trade that was worsened up to the early 1970s by the pricing policies of the marketing boards. Agricultural exports were then discouraged by the appreciation of the naira following the arrival of large oil revenues. The heavy reliance on oil exports and the practical absence of any manufactured exports has brought a new initiative to promote exports[15] (Table 16.10). The pressure for this policy at this particular stage of Nigeria's industrialization appears to come from the bureaucracy, academics and the conspicuous success of Brazilian trade drives in Nigeria. It does not originate within industry which has experienced few constraints from the domestic market. It seems unlikely that Nigeria will achieve significant export of manufactured goods in the near future even if the state is prepared to give large export subsidies to offset the disincentives of an overvalued exchange rate and high infrastructure and

Table 16.10   *Nigeria's export structure (₦ million)*

	1972	1978
Agricultural products	172·0	412·8
Mineral products	1,177·3	5,402·5
Manufactured and semi-manufactured	37·3	42.8
Agricultural	(18·1)	(31·4)
Other	(19·2)	(11·4)
Other exports	35·2	193·7
TOTAL	1,421·8	6,051·8

Note: 1978 is Provisional.
Source: Central Bank Annual Reports.

labour costs. Potential export industries include oil refining, pulp and paper, and furniture. A strong export drive would further externalize the economy, making it more dependent on foreign technology and management at a time when strategic basic industries have not been established, let alone a technological base secured within them.

Nigerian diplomacy backed by oil wealth was largely responsible for the creation of the Economic Community of West African States (ECOWAS) in 1975. The ECOWAS Treaty provides for the creation of a customs union and harmonization of economic policies over a period of fifteen years. While it is early to assess the practical outcome of this initiative, it is very unlikely to herald any break with prevailing patterns of neo-colonial incorporation by way of a reorientation of existing trade patterns, control over foreign investment, or shifts in the location of industrial activity within the West African subregion. The recorded volume of intra-West African trade is presently extremely small. Trade with ECOWAS partners was provisionally estimated to account for only 1·6% of Nigeria's trade by value in 1978.[16] Trade and investment flows with EEC countries have not weakened since independence, though oil exports have allowed Nigeria to diversify her export markets. Through the Lomé Convention these financial, technological and trade ties will be maintained. Trade preferences under the convention are important. For the Ivory Coast further substantial investment in the textile industry is dependent on access to European markets. Nigeria is to receive a high proportion of various forms of EEC aid for industrial development,[17] and will be preoccupied with producing for the internal market for some time to come. Trade with other centres of capital accumulation has grown. Notably, Nigeria's trade with Brazil has increased rapidly and Brazilian management and technology has begun to penetrate the Nigerian economy encouraged by a series of state agreements and ventures. The economies of the West African subregion will continue to be subordinate to the requirements of international capital. This is not to argue that Nigeria will not exercise considerable economic leverage in the area. Nigeria has interests in iron ore, sugar and cement projects in West African countries and access to the Nigerian market could be important for neighbouring countries in the future.

(b) STATE INVESTMENT

From a weak position relative to the regions in the 1950s and early 1960s, the federal centre became stronger under military rule. Backed by the army, the power of the federal bureaucracy increased. Following the creation of new states and changes in the system of federal revenue allocation, the distributable pool at the centre was enlarged. The increased importance of oil as a source of revenue ensured the absolute dominance of federal expenditures. The share of federal expenditure (including transfers to the states) in GDP rose from 12% in 1966 to 36% in 1977. It was against this background of increased federal financial and political strength that the Second (1970–4) and Third Plans (1975–80) launched an expanded role for the public sector. Public expenditure was financed initially from oil surpluses but free spending brought budget deficits which began in 1975–6 and later threatened state investment activity in the oil and steel sectors. The momentum was only maintained by external borrowing in the Eurodollar market. The limits to this form of borrowing in the shape of two jumbo loans worth $1,700m. were quickly reached. With the rapid fall in foreign exchange reserves, the willingness of international bankers to lend was probably dependent on the prior announcement of a package of incentives to encourage further exploration and drilling by oil companies. In spite of this, the $1,000m. target for the second loan was not met. German banks, already committed to German projects in Nigeria, declined to switch their credits to the general jumbo loan. The whole episode revealed a serious loss of domestic control over oil policy and state expenditures. Recently, numerous smaller project-related loans and export credits have been raised. Nigeria, by virtue of its oil reserves and size, has also had relatively easy access to funds from the IBRD, the European Industrial Bank and the European Development Fund.

Priority has been given to infrastructure which received 31% of federal capital expenditures over 1970–7/8 (roads ₦3036m., communications ₦1,130m., water transport ₦513m. and air transport ₦385m.). An active policy of direct participation in industry has been pursued through state corporations and companies (oil production, exploration, refining and marketing; iron and steel mining; car and truck assembly; cement; building materials; pulp and paper; fertilizer; salt; machine tools; distilling; agro-industry; furniture – see Table 16.11). In a number of these sectors the state has a monopoly. There has been a consolidation and extension of state ownership in other institutions (commercial and merchant banks, development banks, insurance companies). Taken in conjunction with indirect forms of investment through industrial development banks (Nigerian Industrial Development Bank, Nigerian Bank for Commerce and Industry) and state level investment corporations, there is no doubt that public investment in industry has been growing faster than private investment. Since its inception in 1963 the NIDB has sanctioned ₦294m. of loans and equity in 343 projects (December 1978). At June 1978 the NIDB and NBCI had projects worth over ₦400m. in the

Table 16.11   *Federal capital expenditure on industry, 1970–77/8 (₦ million)*

Oil	1,321·1
Joint ventures	(514·6)
Refineries	(506·0)
Other	(308·5)
Industrial development banks	282·2
Iron and steel	161·4
Cement	169·5
Pulp and paper	96·6
Sugar	97·5
Mining	38·6
Car assembly	26·9
Salt	8·3
Fertilizer	17·8
Small scale industries	10·9
Industrial development centres	3·7
Other	44·3
TOTAL	2,286·8

Sources: Federal Capital and Current Estimates, and Accountant General Reports.

pipeline.[18] Below the federal level, I estimate conservatively that state investment corporations held investments worth ₦120m. by the end of 1978.[19] With the exception of three older regional institutions, all these corporations were formed in the last decade. These corporations provide a platform for collaboration between foreign technical partners, indigenous private capital and state capital. Some of them actively promote ventures by seeking and concentrating local private capital, securing foreign technical partners and providing management services.

Finally, the impact of federal expenditures on industrial location should be noted. Industrial development has been very uneven with a strong concentration in Lagos. This imbalance has grown. In 1964 Lagos State accounted for 37% of value added and 35% of employment in large-scale industry.[20] By 1975 these figures had risen to 69% and 43% respectively, implying that productivity was growing much faster in Lagos than elsewhere. Among the reasons for this imbalance is the attraction of a port location given the incentive structure and emphasis on industries using imported raw materials and the fact that Port Harcourt, the other comparable location, suffered severe war damage. It was also the policy of the former Western regional government to attract industry to the Ikeja industrial estate near Lagos. The creation of states leading to state competition for industry and the wider spread of federal expenditure should promote industrial dispersion. Federal investment in manufacturing, much of it still to materialize, will also contribute to a wider geographical spread of industry.

(c) INDIGENIZATION

Increased federal power, dissatisfaction with the results of the foreign investment strategy,[21] the continued weakness of indigenous enterprise,[22] and the bitter experience of the civil war provided the context for the indigenization decrees. Indigenization of ownership by decree took place in two phases over the period 1974–8. This was a period in which greatly enlarged state expenditure and wage and salary awards created excessive liquidity in the economy and made the financing of indigenization possible. The first phase required under schedule one exclusive Nigerian control of categories of retail trade, service and small-scale enterprises many of which were owned by Lebanese families.[23] This reserved for Nigerians entertainment and media activities, brick and bread making, garment and candle manufacture, some local processing and assembly (rice milling, tyre retreading, and blending and bottling of alcoholic drinks), retail trading, and in the service sector, hairdressing, road haulage, and dry cleaning. Three enterprises originally included in schedule one were subsequently transferred to schedule two (electronics assembly, clearing and forwarding agencies and haulage of petroleum products by road). These were all enterprises that Nigerians had already begun to enter. The decree did not affect the discrimination against low-technology enterprises in favour of the state-protected, state-subsidized, foreign-controlled sector. Under schedule two, certain enterprises with capital in excess of ₦400,000 or a turnover of at least ₦1 million were required to secure at least 40% local participation through the issue of equity capital. The total value of transactions was estimated at ₦100 million, including ₦30 million for public issues and ₦70 million for private issues and enterprise sales.[24] Public issues were heavily oversubscribed at the low share prices set by the Capital Issues Commission in order to extend Nigerian participation. The sale of shares marked a significant step in the accumulation and concentration of wealth amongst the bureaucratic, professional and intermediary classes. Lagos and the Western states benefited disproportionately from these issues. In Kano the group of large merchant/industrialists acquired a few enterprises and diversified their activities. Foreign enterprises took advantage of the opportunity to institutionalize their networks of clientage by selling shares to, and appointing their distributors as, directors.[25]

The second phase of indigenization stemmed directly from dissatisfaction with the results of the first phase in terms of administration, compliance and equity, and from the fall of the Gowon regime. It gave rise to anxiety amongst foreign investors that a creeping nationalization was under way. These fears were extinguished once the comprehensive terms of the new decree were announced. Under the decree, all enterprises were covered by three schedules covering full, majority and minority Nigerian ownership. In general, higher-technology areas were reserved for foreign ownership, though there were significant exceptions. For example, the commercial activities of the old mercantile monopolies were specifically exempted from full Nigerian ownership and simply extended Nigerian participation from 40% to 60%. Certain older established enterprises like tobacco, textiles and pharmaceuticals remain with a majority foreign interest. Eighty-one companies went public with shares valued at ₦214m., while another ₦117m. worth of equity was transferred privately.[26] State agencies and institutions took up a small though significant share of the equity aided by preference under the allocation rules.[27] Only at the tail end of the exercise were issues undersubscribed. The terms of the decree ensured a wide distribution of share-ownership. This has left foreign control intact even if the number of senior Nigerian executives and directors has increased. It has also reduced the threat to large companies of state takeover on occasions of mass nationalism.[28] In effect, it is capitalism that has been indigenized, not through the takeover or withdrawal of foreign capital, but through higher forms of collaboration, accommodation and institutionalization. Although no firm judgement can be made, I would argue that the decree only marginally lowered the rate of investment in the manufacturing sector through its effect on new foreign investment decisions. In financial terms, while it is clear that the decree facilitated foreign disinvestment and the net flow of foreign capital diminished (see Table 16.5), over 40% of share transactions were for offers of subscription rather than sale, thereby generating additional funds. Some part of the funds from share sales may not be repatriated. Many companies took advantage of very high profits to expand their capital base through script issues. In addition, as we have seen, public sector investment in manufacturing has been substantial.

(d) TECHNOLOGY

A constant theme in official pronouncements on development policy in the 1970s has been the need for a more self-reliant economy. As regards technology, the achievement of this objective was usually seen in terms of the transfer of technology, the training of skilled manpower and research. It gave rise to the National Science and Technology Development Agency and, more recently, a Ministry of Science and Technology and a National Office of Industrial Property.[29] In spite of this concern, Nigeria's technological capacity, its ability to absorb and use technology, and to innovate, remains very limited. The basic problem remains untouched by the training of manpower, by a management boom dictated by the needs of international capital, or by research in isolated institutes that is not commercialized. The weakness of Nigeria's technological position has its roots in the neo-colonial economy. There is a massive disarticulation between the consumption of foreign technology and the indigenous control and generation of technology. This gap has been accentuated in Nigeria by the importance of administrative and managerial classes who superintend foreign technology and by the oil boom which strengthened the forces against planned technological evolution. These conditions surrounding the acquisition and organization of technology result in the wastage of trained manpower and in the truncation, disorientation and fragmentation of learning processes. At the other extreme, under conditions of autarchy with no MNC presence in secessionist Biafra, adaptive innovation in the oil and weapons industry flourished. The power of the bureaucracy declined sharply and scientists and engineers enjoyed unprecedented status and freedom.

In a number of ways the state has attempted to promote the forces of production. State ventures in the manufacturing sector usually aim at accelerating the transfer of technology. Yet, as Dr Adeboye has argued, there are a number of reasons why state participation may actually block or hinder the transfer of technology.[30, 31] First, there is a thorough misconception of technology by state officials who see it simply as the operation of productive facilities. Design, fabrication, erection, commissioning and maintenance are ignored. Second, it is suggested that government participation legitimizes the non-transfer of technology. Adeboye writes:

> government projects have much easier access to expatriate quotas which makes nonsense of the hard bargaining which precedes government investment. These projects tend to have a much higher import content of human and material inputs because the normal constraints that face the private investor are easily by-passed by the so-called technical partners. Not a single application for expatriate quota, import licence or special concession by these facilities has been rejected in our experience.[32]

Third, most state officials are thoroughly sceptical about the ability of Nigerians especially as regards entrusting them with crucial roles in manufacturing enterprises. All of the chief executives of twelve of the thirteen major public sector manufacturing facilities that have begun production in the last six years are expatriates. Finally, there is a false sense of urgency once the government has decided to implement the projects. Turnkey projects are preferred since they provide maximum insulation for state officials. Projects tend to be implemented simultaneously rather than sequentially which means that the opportunity for learning from one project and carrying over those lessons to future projects hardly takes place (pulp and paper, salt, cement). Turner examined the transfer of technology in the oil industry.[33] She found that there was no significant state-led transfer of technology in exploration and production, service companies, downstream activities and the Nigerianization of personnel. This followed from the comprador nature of the state and its officials.

One way in which state concerns could play a more positive role in the development in local technology is for public companies to develop research and production facilities. Public companies could also redirect demand to local industries like metal fabrication.[34] So far product innovation in the metal fabrication industry has been limited mainly to static structures for buildings, automative body work and furniture. As major process industries and manufacturing units grow up there is the opportunity to encourage a more sophisticated and diversified fabrication industry. Adaptive innovation does not have to wait for an iron and steel or capital goods industry. An essential ingredient in any effective strategy to create an indigenous technological capacity is a measure of protection from foreign technology. To that extent, the notion of a beneficial 'transfer of technology' from the industrialized countries to Nigeria is very misleading.

IV   Concluding Remarks

In what ways has the pattern of capital accumulation, and the social structure that conditions it, changed from the picture presented earlier in this chapter? Our interpretation, admittedly over a short time-span and on slender evidence, suggests that the sphere of foreign capital accumulation has not been greatly affected by the growth of the Nigerian bourgeoisie, by indigenization, or by the extension of the state sector. The particular class structures of accumulation that have emerged in Nigeria provide little support for Leys's Kenyan view of an indigenous industrial bourgeoisie that is antagonistic to foreign capital.[35] State intervention has generally favoured large-scale foreign enterprise, the indigenization exercise notwithstanding. The bourgeoisie has acquired considerable wealth from commerce, urban property and the exercise of managerial, administrative and professional skills. In the import and distributive trades businessmen have increased their scale of operation. They captured the cement trade by tapping relatively low-cost sources of supply.[36] They took over the trade in agricultural produce. They moved into the assembly of items previously imported, and into shipping where a number of joint ventures have been formed. The big commercial bourgeoisie (Henry Stephens, Ibru, Folawiyo, Fanz) has extended its intermediary and property interests with little movement into manufacture. In the case of Kano there is some evidence of a shift from commerce to manufacture (Dantata, Gashash, Rabiu). Although one can detect, since the 1960s, a group of Nigerian entrepreneurs who have established larger-scale industries usually in association with foreign technical partners and state capital (textiles, paints, plastics, pharmaceuticals, soft drinks, beer, ceramics, bricks and tiles, pipes, agro-industry), they themselves have not provided a challenge to foreign capital, and they are scarcely represented in the leading business organs of the Lagos Chamber of Commerce and the Nigerian Institute of Management.

Many new state ventures have been formed in the 1970s. Downstream oil linkages and a steel industry are about to materialize. There is little indication that state industrial activity is yet creating a state capitalism with any degree of financial and technological autonomy, or planning. Where joint ventures have been formed, it is usually indicative of support for foreign capital from a passive rentier state. As our discussion of technology showed, state participation, far from reducing dependency, may increase it. The bureaucratic and managerial classes are committed to an open economy and strong links with international capital. They gain as participants in a salary-and-fringe-benefit regime that is led by the high productivity multinational sector. Partly as a consequence of the high level of rewards in the private sector, there was a steady movement of senior civil servants and technocrats from the public sector in the 1970s. This weakened the state sector and provided foreign enterprise with information, contacts and advice. This form of public support for private accumulation is masked by the pervasive rhetoric of the mixed economy to which the actors subscribe.

The basic process of import substituting industrialization has not altered since it was initiated twenty-five years ago. Market protection and import controls are applied, but not vigorously, or consistently, and the structure of incentives tends to favour low value added, assembly-type activities. Discrimination in the use and control over imported technology is minimal. The high quantitative performance of the manufacturing sector persists with a range of industry that slowly widens to include more consumer durable and intermediate enterprises. In the absence of oil, this process of import substitution would have been stifled by severe external imbalances and by inflationary pressures from the agricultural sector. In principle, oil provides the finance to offset high-cost industrialization, to import food and to initiate the structural transformation of the economy. It also gives the potential for additional leverage in external economic relations in terms of bargaining abroad and controlling access to the lucrative Nigerian market. In practice, oil is a double-edged weapon which is difficult to wield effectively under the class conditions of accumulation that have emerged in Nigeria. A build-up of oil revenues, caused by exogenous factors, increases the pressure to open the economy and heightens distributive struggles over state expenditures. Oil reinforces the intermediary strata, strengthens the external value of the naira and finances bureaucratic expansion. With civil rule and a greater diffusion of political power, these pressures will be difficult to resist. Under present conditions, the long-term strategic choice between further externalization of the economy, or a degree of closure and domestic control, is not effectively posed, much less answered.

Capitalist production in industry has expanded through a process of import substitution that is regulated and subsidized by the state. Initially, this industry was financed by revenue from exports of agricultural produce and by inflows of foreign capital. Recently it has been financed by oil revenues. To a large extent these industries are dependent on imported machinery, raw materials and management. Local enterprises have operated on a much smaller scale with simple technology. The few local businessmen who have entered industry on a large scale have depended heavily on foreign management and technology. Local investment has taken a rising share in the profitable state-protected monopolistic sector. This investment does not generally occur independently of, or in competition with foreign capital; the competition is between foreign capitals for a larger share of the Nigerian market through imports, assembly, and local production. As a form of collaboration, this participation has been institutionalized and legitimized by the 'indigenization' decrees. Other highly profitable, low-risk intermediary activities, which depend on imported goods and technology and on access to state and foreign corporate decisions, have expanded in harness with the rentier oil state. A class alliance has formed between foreign capital and bureaucratic and managerial elements of the bourgeoisie. These class forces may be weakened and obscured by sectional and distributional conflicts, but it is they, in the absence of any independent industrial bourgeoisie, which largely determine the character, effectiveness and limits of state policy. Under these conditions the likelihood of long-term industrial strategies that involve the effective regulation and control of external economic relations or the independent internal development of state capitalist activity is remote. Regulation is made more difficult by the erratic windfall nature of state revenues and the unimpeded pressures to increase state expenditures. If oil and the size of the Nigerian market overcome some of the constraints usually associated with import substituting industrialization, they also appear to entrench a system of accumulation that pre-empts any strategy which aims to accelerate industrial accumulation, create a diversified industrial base with vertical and horizontal linkages and secure an indigenous technological capacity.

Notes

I would like to thank Tony Berret, Frances Stewart, Shamsuddeen Usman and Gavin Williams for their comments on versions of this chapter.

1 The various policy statements and committees are discussed in Olakanpo, 1968.
2 For an account of agricultural policy in Nigeria, see Forrest, 1980.
3 A ranking by turnover (1976) of the top ten publicly quoted companies reveals, with two exceptions, a remarkable roll call of old mercantile interests: (1) UAC ₦576m., (2) John Holts ₦289m., (3) J. Berger ₦235m., (4) SCOA ₦195m., (5) CFAO ₦155m., (6) UTC ₦138m., (7) Leventis Motors ₦131m., (8) PZ ₦125m., (9) Mobil Oil ₦115m., (10) R. T. Briscoe N95m. Large companies were exempted from the provisions of schedule one of the second indigenization decree which would have curtailed their trading activities, provided they had a turnover of at least ₦25 million and operated in at least ten states of the federation.
4 Aboyade, 1968.
5 Eastern Nigeria, 1963.
6 Teriba, 1966.
7 Northern Nigeria, 1966.
8 Large-scale refers to industry with ten employees or more. There is evidence of serious underestimation in the Federal Office of Statistics survey. A UNDP–ILO survey of the East Central State in 1974 counted 553 manufacturing enterprises with ten or more employees (UNDP–ILO, 1975). The FOS survey of that date included only 151 firms.
9 IBRD, 1979.
10 *Financial Times*, 20 August 1978.
11 *Daily Times*, 13 March 1976.
12 Among the biases against small-scale enterprises are the preferential access to resources which the large-scale, state-protected sector enjoys, the operation of bureaucratic controls (e.g. import licences), the criteria for government assistance and bank credit which require them to meet bureaucratic regulations and associated costs that are far beyond their means or not within their narrow profit margins (see Williams 1974 and references cited therein). There is also the pervasive influence of the Lagos

advertising industry which pre-empts product competition and the use of alternative technologies.

13   For discussion of budget policy see Forrest and Odama, forthcoming.

14   IBRD, 1978.

15   The Nigerian Export Promotion Council was set up 1977.

16   Central Bank of Nigeria, *Annual Report*, 1978.

17   Carlsen, 1978.

18   ibid.

19   This does not include investments held by state ministries.

20   Carlsen, 1978.

21   Akeredolu-Ale, 1976.

22   Other official measures commonly cited as helping indigenous enterprise in the 1970s include the small-scale industries credit scheme, guidelines for commercial bank credit, the raising of minimum thresholds for expatriate tenders for building and engineering contracts, and the break up of sole distributorships.

23   For a full account and analysis of the first phase of indigenization, see Collins, 1977, and references cited therein.

24   ibid.

25   ibid.; Hoogvelt, 1980.

26   Sanusi, 1979.

27   A preliminary calculation, based on eleven major issues, shows that public agencies secured 16% of the shares.

28   This argument is not affected by selective action against companies that are heavily involved in South Africa. Nigeria's policy on southern Africa has occasionally led it into an anti-imperialist position as, for example, in the recognition of Angola. In 1978, public agency accounts with Barclays Bank were banned (for eighteen months) and the bank was forced to reduce its expatriate personnel. This subsequently precipitated a reduction in Barclays International equity from 40% to 20% through public sale. In 1979, the federal military government took over British Petroleum's remaining interests in Shell/BP and a oil marketing company. There was also a three-month ban on tenders by British companies for federal projects.

29   The National Science and Technology Development Agency replaced the Nigerian Council for Science and Technology in 1976. It was responsible for the supervision and funding of twenty-two research institutes. In 1977/8 expenditure was N73m.

30   Adeboye, 1979. This section relies heavily on Dr Adeboye's work.

31   The dependency of public sector enterprises on foreign management, consultancy and technology is borne out by foreign exchange payments for contract and services. In 1977, public sector payments were N217m. compared with N79m. for the private sector; see Falegan, 1978. In 1978 the management of Nigerian Railways and Nigerian Airways was given over to Rail India and KLM respectively.

32   This point was also made by Mr Olu Akinkugbe at the Nigerian Economic Society symposium, 1974.

33   Turner, 1976.

34   Iteke, 1978.

35   Leys, 1977.

36   Turner, 1977; Fajemirokun, 1978.

References

Aboyade, O. (1968) 'The relations between central and local institutions in the development process', *Nigerian Opinion* (February–March and April–June) (Ibadan).

Adeboye, T. O. (1978) 'Public sector participation in manufacturing', paper delivered to 1978 annual conference of the Nigeria Economic Society, Lagos.

Akeredolu-Ale, E. O. (1976) 'Private foreign investment and the under-development of indigenous entrepreneurship', in G. Williams (ed.), *Nigeria: Economy and Society* (London: Rex Collings).

Central Bank of Nigeria, *Annual Reports*.

Carlsen, J. (1978) 'Industrial co-operation in the Lomé Convention – the case of Nigeria', Centre for Development Research, Copenhagen.

Collins, P. (1977) 'Public policy and the development of indigenous capitalism: the Nigerian experience', *Journal of Commonwealth and Comparative Politics*, 15, 2.

Daily Times, Lagos.

Eastern Nigeria (1964) 'Report of the fourth conference of leading person-alities of Eastern Nigerian origin', Enugu.

Fajemirokun, H. (1978) 'The role of private enterprise in Africa', in *Europe and Africa: Trends and Relationships* (London: Royal African Society).

Falegan, S. B. (1978) 'Trends in Nigeria's balance of payments and policy measures needed for self-reliance', *Economic and Financial Review*, 16, 2 (Central Bank of Nigeria).

Financial Times, London.

Forrest, T. G. (1980) 'Agricultural policies in Nigeria, 1900–1978', in J. Heyer, P. Roberts and G. Williams (eds), *Rural Development in Tropical Africa* (London: Macmillan).

Forrest, T. G. and Odama, J. S. (forthcoming) 'Nigerian budget policy in the 70s', *Nigerian Journal of Public Affairs*.

Hoogvelt, A. (1980) 'Indigenization and foreign capital: industrialization in Nigeria', *Review of African Political economy*, 14.

IBRD (1974) *Nigeria – Options for Long Term Development* (Baltimore, Md: Johns Hopkins University Press).

IBRD (1978) 'An analysis of industrial incentives and location in Nigeria', unpublished report submitted to the Federal Ministry of Industries.

IBRD (1979), *World Development Report*.

Iteke, K. (1978) 'First steps to autonomy in process technology. FSFC's experience in phosphate fertilizer technology', paper delivered to a symposium of the Nigerian Society of Chemical Engineers, Kaduna.

Leys, C. (1978) 'Capital accumulation, class formation and dependency – the significance of the Kenyan case', *Socialist Register* (London: Merlin Press); see also Chapter 8 in this volume.

Ministry of Economic Development (1975) 'A directory of establishments in the private sector having five or more workers east central state' Enugu.

Nigerian Economic Society (1975), *Nigeria's Indigenization Policy*, proceed-ings of the Nigerian Economic Society symposium, 1974 (Ibadan).

Northern Nigeria (1966) White Paper on the military government policy for the reorganization of the Northern Nigeria Development Corporation, Ka-duna.

Olakanpo, O. (1968) *Indigenous Enterprises in Distributive Trades in Nigeria, a Preliminary Report* (Ibadan: Nigerian Institute for Social and Economic Studies).

Pearson, S. R. (1970) *Petroleum in The Nigerian Economy* (Stanford, Calif.: Stanford University Press).

Sanusi, J. O. (1979) 'Reflections on the indigenization exercise' (mimeo.), Lagos.

Teriba, O. (1966) Development strategy, investment decisions and expenditure patterns of a public development institution, the case of the Western Nigeria Development Corporation, 1949–1962', *Nigerian Journal of Economic and Social Studies*, 8, 2 (Ibadan).

Turner, T. (1976) 'The transfer of oil technology and the Nigerian state', *Development and Change*, 7, 4.

Turner, T. (1977) *The Cement Racket* (London: Africa Guide).

Williams, G. (1974) 'Political consciousness among the Ibadan poor', in E. de Kadt and G. Williams (eds), *Sociology and Development* (London: Tavistock).

17 The Volta Dam: Energy for Industry?

HAROLD DICKINSON

The building of the Akosombo Dam, the central feature of the Volta River Project in Ghana, is frequently instanced as the archetypal development scheme in which the hydraulic power of a great river is harnessed. The various alternative schemes put forward to utilize the electricity ranged from the establishing of an aluminium industry in British West Africa to the industrialization of independent Ghana. In its final form the Volta River Project was the dream of two men: Kwame Nkrumah, the first President of Ghana, and Robert Jackson, the Special Commissioner of the Preparatory Commission concerned with the project.

Antecedents[1]

The first proposal for the building of a dam on the Volta River was made in 1915 by Sir Albert Kitson, the then director of the London-based Gold Coast Geological Survey, following his discovery of bauxite in the territory the year before. The idea became public knowledge at the first World Power Conference which was held in London in 1924.

Nothing further happened until 1938 when a South African engineer, Duncan Rose, formed a syndicate which proposed a Volta River dam, 40 metres high, at a cost of about £3 million. A year later C. St John Bird carried out a survey for Rose and suggested a 75 metres high dam estimated to cost £6·5 million. Rose maintained his interest in an aluminium industry in the Gold Coast. He became, in 1945, the founder and managing director of West African Aluminium Ltd (WAFAL) but passed financial control to the United Africa Company, a subsidiary of Unilever Ltd, in the following year. By 1949 St John Bird had made a further estimate of £11 million as the current cost of a power-producing dam. In the same year the Canadian (ALCAN) and British (BACO) aluminium interests acquired a 25% interest in WAFAL.

The wartime need for aluminium had stirred the UK government's interest in the bauxite reserves of its West African colonies. The importation of bauxite to the UK was started in 1941 and has continued, at around 200,000 tonnes, to the present. It was in the immediate postwar period that the UK and Gold Coast governments began to take cognizance of the proposals of WAFAL and to consider producing aluminium metal in West Africa. Following disturbances in the Gold Coast the Watson Commission of Inquiry, reporting in 1948, mentioned the Volta River Project in the following terms:

> Such a scheme apart from creating a new industry, capable so far as yet seen of very great expansion, might well enable large tracts to become fertile by irrigation. At the same time the surplus electrical energy set free could be utilized to great advantage . . .[2]

Subsequently the Gold Coast government invited Sir William Halcrow and Partners to consider schemes for the economic use of the Volta River. In their final report, in 1951, a dam and power station costing some £40 million were proposed. This was followed by a UK government White Paper, on the Volta River Aluminium Scheme, which again was narrowly concerned with a source of aluminium for the United Kingdom. The dominance of the electricity demands of the proposed smelter may be seen in the proposal that over 90% of the 560 MW power output would be destined for use in the aluminium smelting process.

The Preparatory Commission headed by Robert Jackson now took over the development of a dam scheme adequate to the needs of a substantial smelter. At the same time Nkrumah consulted the United States government which, in turn, arranged for a firm of consulting engineers, Kaiser Engineers, to make a reappraisal of the project. The estimates of the Preparatory Commission and Kaiser Engineers for a scheme which included a 120,000 tonne per annum smelter were substantially similar for the power component (around £65 million) and the bauxite mines and smelter (£57 million). By the almost total exclusion of public works and social costs the commission's total costs of £185 million were reduced, by Kaiser, to £130 million.[3]

Despite criticism within Ghana, especially in the university, and by economists elsewhere, the Volta River Project was accepted by the government of the Gold Coast in the euphoric period of transition to an independent Ghana. At the same time external aluminium interests coalesced to form the Volta Aluminium Company which soon became concentrated in the hands of the Kaiser Corporation, the parent of Kaiser Engineers, and the Reynolds Metal Corporation, their holdings being 90% and 10% respectively.

The financial provisions of the scheme were settled in 1962. The government of Ghana became responsible for one-half of the costs of the dam and the power station with the remainder being covered by loans totalling £G30 million from the International Bank for Reconstruction and Development (48%), the Development Loan Fund (24%), the UK government (17%) and the Export-Import Bank (12%).[4] The smelter was financed by US interests, the Export-Import Bank (75%) and VALCO (25%) and underwritten by the US government.

In the process the idea of an aluminium industry in Ghana was lost. To get the unit cost of electricity down to an acceptable level the government of Ghana had to accept the following: abolish social and public works expenditures not directly related to power production; permit the import of alumina from Kaiser interests in the Caribbean; export unprocessed, ingot, aluminum; give a tax holiday on alumina and aluminium movements until 1980 and refrain from imposing company tax until 1978.

Akosombo Electricity

The dam as first constructed had four generating units in operation by 1965 and with a further two put into operation in 1972 the total installed capacity amounted to 912 MW. However, the firm capacity, available when one machine is shut down for repair, is 760 MW. In 1976 the demand reached about 600 MW with two-thirds being the base load demand of the smelter (base load = near-uniform load continuing over the full twenty-four hours). This surplus is being reduced by demand growth and is unlikely to meet load projections beyond 1981.[5]

The price of electricity for the smelter is a contrived figure as all the indirect costs to Ghana were reduced or estimated from the original capitalization. It was set at 0·2625 US cents per kWh when the smelter went into operation and this was to be maintained unchanged for thirty years. However, following an agreed examination of financial performance it was subsequently raised to 0·275 cents and a further rise to 0·3125 cents has been negotiated. Even at this rate is is likely that unit production costs exceed the charges paid by VALCO for the power taken by the smelter. The effect of such low pricing is reflected in the charges made by the Electricity Corporation of Ghana which buys and sells the power not taken by the smelter. In 1973 the Corporation supplied power at the equivalent of 1·3 US cents per kWh to their industrial consumers, at 2·2 cents for domestic use and 8·3 cents for commercial lighting.[6] The corresponding 1973 figures for England and Wales were 1·8 cents, 2·3 cents and 2·6 cents respectively.[7] Similar figures held for other industrialized countries.

The significance of the different rates charged to the smelter and other consumers of Volta-generated power is clear with regard to Ghana's foreign exchange position but much less so in relation to the price of power being a factor in industrialization.

The loans made available to Ghana for the Volta River Project were adequate for the project. Some adjustment was made as some cheaper capital came on offer and since some tied loans limited the competitive procurement of materials. However, the expected revenue from power sales was not achieved and payment of interest placed demands on the foreign exchange earnings from Ghana's principal export, cocoa. Capital repayments were not achieved on schedule and by 1974 the outstanding loans remained at $US82 million rather than the projected $US60 to 65 million. It appears likely that when the loan is finally repaid it will have taken some fifty years rather than the twenty-five to thirty years which was the basis of the original agreement. If the fifty-year period becomes a reality the total interest and capital repayments will be some two and a half times the original loan. In addition the production of aluminium involves the import of substantial quantities of alumina and other materials which cost further foreign exchange.

These costs would be of less importance to Ghana if the electricity provided to other industries had brought about rapid growth in these industries. Examination of trade figures show that this is not the case. The Bank of Ghana's published reports show that aluminium amounts to no more than 7% of the total exports. If aluminium is excluded, over 90% of other export earnings is from the traditional products cocoa, timber, diamonds, gold and manganese – much the same as in the pre-smelter era. With regard to employment some 2,300 jobs have been created in the smelter and others in the electricity supply industry. This is what may be expected in a highly capital-intensive industry such as aluminium smelting but it has made little impact on Ghana's unemployed and underemployed.

Industrial Growth

The rapid growth of other industries in Ghana has not come about as a consequence of the availability of the Volta power distributed by the Electricity Corporation of Ghana. As we have seen the charges made by the corporation to their industrial consumers cannot be called cheap. Even recognizing the position of the smelter as a base load consumer it receives its power at a fraction of the full industrial price. Can the failure of industry to expand in response to the increased availability of electricity be attributed to its relatively high price? This is only likely to be true if, in fact, the hypothesis that cheap power is a major stimulus to growth can be supported by evidence from Ghana or elsewhere.

What then is the relationship between industrial development and the cost of electricity? If it is of key importance then industry will be attracted to the points of power availability. The whole basis of the aluminium industry rests on such a premise as does the determination of smelter operators to drive a hard bargain when seeking power supplies. The Volta River Project and the VALCO smelter bear this out. However, aluminium smelting is, as we have seen, a capital-intensive industry and one of the few variables which can keep up production in a particular plant, in an industry which has up to now been characterised by the existence of surplus capacity, is the unit cost of electricity. However the aluminium industry is one of the few in which energy costs may exceed 10% of the total.[8] Few other industries show such cost dependence on fuel or power. In Rhodesia industry has not been attracted to the Kariba Dam and when promoting industry, in the 1950s, the overall cost of electricity to industry, amounted to no more than 1·25% of total costs.[9] In 1961 Kenya had an overall fuel cost of 3·2% of total running costs with electricity amounting to no more than 1·5%.[10] In 1969 it could be said that in East Africa the percentage of electricity costs in total industrial running costs was low and that 1% of total costs would be a reasonable figure. Further, electricity had not stimulated industry in Kenya or Tanzania.[11] The situation in West Africa was much the same and, in 1961, Hance was able to say that 'there are no examples of strictly power-oriented industries in West Africa'.[12]

It is thus unlikely that cheaper electrical power would have made much impact on the general industrialization of Ghana. Indeed, part of the power supplied from the Volta River Project was taken in by gold mines which shut down their own generators which had supplied power at a unit cost greater than that charged by the Electricity Corporation of Ghana.

Direct Effects of the Project

There is no doubt that Ghana has been irreversibly affected by the Volta River Project. For better, or worse, the economy of Ghana is linked to the world aluminium industry and will continue to be for another generation. In the future it may be able to achieve full control of the aluminium smelter and to integrate it into a complete aluminium industry. At present there is no plant in Ghana able to convert bauxite, the ore, to alumina, the intermediate product; nor is there a plant able to roll the ingot and billet aluminium which are the exportable outputs of the smelter. The user of sheet aluminium in Ghana must seek imported material so that it may be formed or pressed into useful shapes and utensils. This also applies to the principal producer, Ghana Aluminium Products Ltd, which is operated by the government of Ghana in association with ALCAN.

At the time of its inauguration the Volta River Project was one of many projects being undertaken by the new rulers of independent Ghana. The overextending of the economy at that time has been a continuing feature of post-independence Ghana. It has continued to play a part in preventing the growth of a stable economy and the accumulation of capital, and must be one of the internal factors which have led to the political instability of the country.

Indirect Effects of the Project

We have noted earlier that social costs were excluded from the costs attributable to the Volta River Project. This exclusion may have produced a unit price for electricity acceptable to VALCO but it did not relieve the government of Ghana of its responsibilities and the costs that these entailed.

Some 80,000 people lived in the area flooded by the waters held back by the Akosombo Dam. Over the period 1964–6 about 68,000 were settled through government intervention whilst 12,000 fended for themselves. The major problem of the new settlements was the complete absence of familiar elements of the old socioeconomic structure. Communities were divided, new skills were demanded for food production and fishing, leadership was found not to be transferable, and essential features of the old life, such as markets and bus services, were not organized. In the face of such insecurity it is not surprising that over 45,000 people drifted away over the following decade. Food production proved impossible as only about 7,000 hectares of cleared land was provided to replace the 50,000 hectares which had been flooded. As a consequence food supplies had to be obtained from the World Food Programme to avert starvation. The housing provided was limited to a single core room on to which a family had to build the extra rooms it required. There was no incentive to do this when insufficient food was available and when funds for materials were inadequate. The management of resettlement was also a failure as it was an unexpected burden placed on the Volta River Authority which had neither funds nor adequately qualified staff for the task.

Sanitation and hygiene in the new settlements also proved less than adequate. Water supplies failed when pumps broke down and sewage disposal became impossible as a result. Accordingly many of the settlements succumbed to the spread of waterborne disease. Other public health hazards were to arise due to intervention in the flow of the river. Shistosomiasis (bilharzia) followed the spread of aquatic weeds and intermediate-host snails around the margins of the lake. Incidence rates of 80% to 100% were reported from settlements of people in whom the pre-lake incidence was no more than 5%.[12]

On the other hand the incidence of onchocerciasis, river blindness, was reduced. The vector for this disease, a blackfly, lives in rapidly flowing water. The rising waters behind the dam flooded many sections of the various rivers where the flow had been rapid, thus eliminating river blindness only to replace it with bilharzia. Below the dam there was some increase in rapidly flowing sections and this increased the numbers of blackfly. Fast streams entering the lake continue to house this vector of onchocerciasis.[14]

Fisheries and Navigation

With the building of the dam and the creation of the Volta Lake some forms of fisheries on the seaward side of the dam were destroyed. However the lake itself has become a rich source of fish as the stock of introduced lake species has prospered. Settlements of fisherman around the margins of the lake now catch some 38,000 tonnes per annum, which is twice that envisaged by the Preparatory Commission. However, insufficient capital has been put into the distribution side of the fishing industry and as a consequence much of it is marketed in an imperfect state and revenues from sales are less than could be reasonably expected.

One feature of the saving in initial costs may be seen by the most casual observer on the shore of the lake. The tree cover of the Volta River valley was not felled in advance of the rising waters. This places restraints on the navigational use of the lake. In particular, the ferries are unable to make the shortest passage across the lake. They are constrained to follow the route of the old road so as to avoid substantial trees which, though dead, still stand and present a hazard to shipping. In addition the expected cargoes to be carried to and from lakeside wharves have not yet materialized in the quantities anticipated by the planners.

An Assessment

As we have seen, the main participants in the Volta River Project were the government of Ghana, the Kaiser Corporation and the government of the United States. To what extent have the benefits of the scheme been shared by the three parties?

From the Ghanaian point of view the Volta River Project has not been a success. It did not generate new industry, provide cheap electricity, or give Ghana any stake or influence in the world aluminum industry. It continues to burden the Ghanaian economy and has tied up capital which might well have been better used in modest schemes more specifically directed to overcoming obstacles to industrialization.

The benefits to the Kaiser Corporation are clear. As a large corporation with worldwide interests the cheap power from Akosombo has played a role in preserving its stake in world aluminum. We have seen that the interests of the company were best served by importing alumina from the Caribbean and exporting VALCO billet to be rolled elsewhere. That such benefits should accrue to the Kaiser organization is not surprising as it came on the scene at an early stage, had US government backing and was able to negotiate the rate structure directly with the much less experienced Ghanaian authorities. The latter cannot impose a high price for electricity as surplus smelting capacity is available in other countries to which the alumina could be shipped.

The benefits to the United States were less tangible but real. Ghana, by receiving aid and by borrowing US funds guaranteed by the US government, was likely to remain non-aligned in world affairs. It also gave the United States a place in a major African development which could be seen to compensate for an earlier failure to be involved in the Aswan High Dam in Egypt. In the long run tangible benefits have occurred to the United States as Ghana has had to import inputs from the United States for the Volta scheme. Accordingly the United States enjoys better trading relationships with Ghana than existed previously.

The Future

Ghana still needs to industrialize. The power from the Volta River Project is now fully utilized, first by enlargement of the smelter and latterly by the modest rate of growth of the electrical power demand of Ghanaian industry.

The way ahead in Ghana is still seen to be based on harnessing the Volta River. A new dam is to be built at Kpong some 50 kilometres below Akosombo. At least 140 MW of power will become available in the early 1980s to support industrial demand but much greater emphasis will be placed on use of the retained waters for irrigation of the Accra plains. In this way the project will also further food production and diversify the cropping pattern away from a high dependence on cocoa. Again Ghana will become dependent on a further influx of external loans amounting to some $US180 million with the Volta River Authority finding a further $US65 million.[15]

Even with the Kpong scheme Ghana will not have an aluminium industry.

No plant for the conversion of bauxite to alumina and no rolling mill for aluminium are planned. Cheap electricity for Ghanaians remains an illusion and even if it were provided there is no evidence to indicate that it would generate a leap forward in industrialization.

Notes

In the preparation of this paper I had the advantage of discussions with Dr David Hart, of the Imperial College, University of London, who has spent many years studying and reflecting on the Volta River Project.

1 Much of the material in this section is to be found *in extenso* in James Moxon, *Volta: Man's Greatest Lake* (London: Deutsch, 1969); and David Hart, *The Volta River Project: a Case Study in Politics and Technology* (Edinburgh: Edinburgh University Press, 1980).

2 Watson Commission, *Report on the Commission of Enquiry into Disturbances in the Gold Coast* (London: Colonial Office, 1948), para. 314.

3 See Hart, op. cit., p. 26, and R. G. A. Jackson, 'The Volta River Project', *Progress* (Unilever), (1964), pp. 146-61.

4 Hart, op. cit., p. 31.

5 Volta River Authority annual reports (various dates).

6 Electricity Corporation of Ghana, *Annual Report*, 1973.

7 Electricity Council, *Handbook of Electricity Supply Statistics* (London: Electricity Council, 1975).

8 A report by Gordian Associates in 1974 gave a figure of 9·8% as being the proportion of primary energy costs in the selling price of primary aluminium. Figures of 10·8% and 18·3% were given for primary steel and portland cement respectively. See Gordian Associates, *The Potential for Energy Conservation in Nine Selected Industries – the Data Base* (Washington D. C.: National Technical Information Service, 1974). Recent unofficial figures suggest that escalating energy costs will put the 1980 figure for primary aluminium into the range of 20%–25%.

9 D. S. Pearson, *Industrial Development in East Africa* (Nairobi: Oxford University Press, 1969), p. 87.

10 See, for example, *Census of Manufacturing*, Nairobi, 1961.

11 Hans Amann, *Energy Supply and Economic Development in East Africa* (Munich: Weltforum-Verlag, 1969), pp. 90, 142.

12 William A. Hance, 'West African industry: an analysis of locational orientation', *Journal of International Affairs*, XV, 1 (1961).

13 L. K. A. Derban, 'Some environmental health problems associated with industrial development in Ghana,' *Health and Industrial Growth* (Elsevier Excerpta Medico, North Holland: Ciba Foundation Symposium 32, 1975), pp. 49-66.

14 ibid.

15 Ghana's Kpong Power, *West Africa*, (London: West African Publishing Co: 14 November 1977), pp. 2308-9.

PART FIVE
SMALL-SCALE INDUSTRY

18 Alternative Approaches to Small Industry Promotion

IAN LIVINGSTONE

Throughout the 1970s governments in Africa and the developing countries as a whole and international agencies such as UNIDO and the ILO, particularly, have shown an increasing interest in small industry development. Within the category of small industry increasing attention has fallen specifically on rural industry. Reasons for the interest include:

(1) a desire for localization and local control of industry;
(2) the increasing emphasis on rural development;
(3) a search for more labour-intensive appropriate technology, and concern regarding the slow growth of employment opportunities associated with import substituting formal sector industrial development;
(4) the objective of dispersal of industry.

Tanzania and Kenya were among the first countries into the field in Africa, and their programmes offer some interesting similarities and contrasts. These programmes are therefore examined first, before their relevance to efforts in the same direction in Botswana is assessed.

The Tanzanian Approach: Workshop Clusters

In Tanzania the National Small Industry Corporation was established in 1965 as a subsidiary of the National Development Corporation, with an authorized equity capital of £80,000, 80% of which, was held by the NDC and 20% by the Workers' Development Corporation (WDC). Its aim was to promote small-scale industry, cottage industry, to 'improve the working conditions of artisans'.[1] Subsequently this structure was reorganized and the institution renamed the Small Industry Development Organization (SIDO). This recognized the fact that, contrary to original intention, NSIC had come to be concerned with craft industry rather than the whole range of small industry.

This has tended to be the case with many of the small industry development programmes in Africa. To see why, we need to start with some definitions relating to small industry.

The size of the firm may be measured by the amount of capital used, by the numbers employed, the value of output (value added), or the form of energy used. Information on the value of physical and financial assets is generally not available, but for other reasons also the most convenient measure may be the average number of employees per establishment. This gives a good visual impression of the kind of establishment under discussion. Thus if an industry is characterized by firms employing less than ten employees it is likely to be either a handicraft industry producing, for example, furniture or leatherwork, or a workshop of some kind employing some skilled labour, such as a tailoring establishment. If a firm employs anywhere between, say, ten to a hundred employees it is likely to be a small factory using 'production-line' methods on more or less modern lines. Establishments with more than a hundred employees can be considered medium- or large-scale factories.

There is likely to be a further difference between the three categories on the basis of business and financial organization. Handicraft industries may be carried out in a family's home, perhaps largely with family labour. Small factories will hire more labour, but are quite likely to be *owned* as family businesses or as partnerships and private companies. Large-scale factories may well be owned by jointstock companies issuing shares. Thus we may make a division between:

(1) craft or household industry employing, say, under ten employees or family workers in a typical establishment;
(2) modern small-scale industry employing ten to ninety-nine employees in a typical firm;
(3) medium- and large-scale industry employing a hundred or more people per establishment.

This was the division made by Staley and Morse (1965) in their classic text emphasizing the prospects for *modern* small industry development, meaning small factory production. The NSIC–RIDO programme in Tanzania, intentionally or otherwise focused on (1), covering artisan-based enterprise, rather than (2). Even in Kenya, where manufacturing is more developed than in neighbouring countries, a quick glance at the statistics for manufacturing industry shows that a large proportion of 'modern' industrial establishments are in the range of ten to ninety-nine employees with a concentration, in fact, at the lower end.[2] Thus in East Africa a factory employing ninety or a hundred people would appear a relatively large concern, and it is not surprising that such an enterprise would, in Tanzania, be the concern of the NDC rather than NSIC or SIDO.

Initial promotional efforts in Tanzania centred upon an industrial estate for craft industrialists (artisans) located in Dar es Salaam at Kisarawe Street, with a smaller version at Singida. The workshops in Dar es Salaam consisted of very rudimentary prefabricated buildings housing a collection of 140 'cubicles' which could be rented by artisans carrying out their own independent work with the help of minimal supporting facilities provided by management, particularly sawing facilities for woodworking. This scheme was very much a prototype, and the 1969–74 Development Plan made provision for some 250 industrial workshops and ten additional common facility centres of this type spread throughout Tanzania.

A survey of artisans at the workshop may be briefly summarized (for more detail see Livingstone, 1972) to bring out the most interesting aspects. Of the ninety-eight 'enterprises' occupying the simple workshop spaces, fifty-nine were woodworkers or carpenters making furniture and thirty-nine were metalworkers, making small metal products such as charcoal stoves, buckets, or implements. Recruits from the locality had been obtained out of large numbers applying to a simple advertisement, numbers sufficient to fill the workshops several times over.

The median earnings of partners in woodworking were 323s per month and in metalworking 193s, comparing favourably at the time with a minimum wage applying in the *formal* sector in Dar es Salaam of 150s. It was possible to earn much higher sums in woodworking and some 12% of woodworkers earned over 500s a month. These figures are probably subject to some *under*declaration and this particularly at the upper end of the scale, among the more successful woodworkers. This data indicate the possibilities for earning useful incomes within the informal sector, first, and also that there is need to see this sector as a diversified one with a variety of different income opportunities, some substantially better than others.[3] This is evidenced also at the lower end of the scale where 53% of metalworkers earned less than 200s monthly, compared to only 21% in the case of woodworkers.

A second feature was the very wide dispersion in the value of tools and equipment owned: for instance, in woodworking 29% had equipment worth less than 200s while 17% owned a value over 600s. Undercapitalization was much greater in metalworking, 54% owning less than 100s' worth of equipment (equal at the time to UK£5). A similar pattern was revealed in the value of materials used. Value of equipment and materials used were also shown to have a clear correlation with gross revenue obtained. In the case of the metalworking units the supply of materials (sheetmetal) by the NSIC management was crucial to the artisans: NSIC did not organize the supply of wood to the furniture makers.

The variable endowment of tools and equipment among the artisans, and the effect of this on profitability, were reflected in the statement by 86% of the units that they would like credit. However, the allocation of the simple premises themselves represented an important increase in capitalization of these entrepreneurs. Beyond the provision of these the corporation had not done a great deal to improve the businesses, in terms of training, product development, marketing, or the like. But in contrast to the sorry tale told by so many development schemes, only 17% of artisans contemplated leaving the scheme at the time of the survey, and these probably because of a need to expand. About half the woodwork enterprises wanted either a second unit or a bigger workshop (only 15% in the case of metal), this also showing the scope which exists for the development and upgrading of craft enterprises.

In addition, tenants were asked to indicate which of the following advantages they considered most important: selling, supplies of materials, space, common facilities and learning of skills. The most important, in four cases out of five, was space, including perhaps lockability, despite the simple and economical nature of the premises. Tenants were also asked what difficulties they would have if they were forced to leave: again, 80% said this would be finding a workshop, easily the greatest perceived problem.

Two other advantages of the estate emerged which one might not have anticipated. First, there appeared to be a quite marked demonstration effect on the supply of effort by the tenants, from working in close proximity. The tenant system of independent businesses did, of course, permit the free operation of incentives, but this would have applied anywhere. Here about 60% of the units put in sixty-five hours or more per week[4] – something of a contrast to the often alleged backward-sloping supply curve of African labour.

The second most important advantage of location at the estate mentioned by tenants was selling: 53% of tenants gave this as an advantage of the estate, while 34% listed it as one of the major problems which would arise from leaving the estate. However, the NSIC itself gave little assistance in marketing products. The fact that the majority of woodworking units sold a large part of their output at the estate itself indicates that traders were attracted by the concentration of production in the estate to bid for the products on the spot, and even to offer contract jobs.[5]

Training was not provided by management on a significant scale, although clearly the concentration of partners and more junior 'helpers' at the estate would have provided the ideal vehicle for upgrading skills. Even without this, some such development did take place, some tenants, particularly those of many years' experience, operating relatively systematic apprenticeship training for young assistants. There was an observed tendency (limited by the availability of units) for apprentices and helpers to split away from the parent to set up in pairs in other units. As will be seen later, this is significant from the point of view of the problem in Botswana of assisting brigade movement trainees to establish themselves in business after 'graduation'.

In summary, the estate arrangement for organizing artisans in Tanzania can be seen as a means of facilitating the injection of capital into craft industry, offsetting the undercapitalization of the African artisan.

A second general advantage is the divisibility of the managerial element involved and the possibility of progressively increasing the managerial contribution. Starting with simple workshops and a common facility centre, training and hire purchase programmes, and marketing and bulk purchase functions can be expanded. Initially, however, relatively small managerial and capital inputs are possible, with correspondingly small risks of financial loss.

Finally it may be observed that the ninety-eight workshop enterprises on the estate employed some 350 persons, equivalent to a medium-sized factory: a significant contribution compared to most manufacturing concerns in Tanzania. It should be stressed, of course, that this is not a *net* increase in employment, as many of the artisans would already have been engaged in businesses elsewhere. Nevertheless twenty such units could engage some 7,000 persons.

Kenya: The Extension Approach

There have been three elements in the promotion of small industry in Kenya.

(1)   Modern small industry is included among the 'larger' businesses which may be given loans through the Industrial and Commercial Development Corporation (ICDC).

(2)   A programme of industrial estates exists under the KIE (Kenya Industrial Estates Ltd), which is itself a subsidiary of ICDC. This programme was established as long ago as 1966. In 1974 estates existed only at Nairobi and Nakuru, but others at Kisumu, Mombasa and Eldoret were to be set up over the period of the 1974–8 Development Plan, with five others subsequently.

The existing estates were criticized by the ILO mission in 1972 (ILO, 1972) for 'featherbedding' inefficient producers. The mission recommended instead an emphasis on rural industrialization, including agricultural processing, a recommendation which makes our discussion of Kenyan experience with rural industry promotion more relevant.

(3)   The Rural Industrial Development Programme (RIDP) is under the aegis of KIE but operates independently outside the main towns. Launched about the end of 1971, it has been operational since January 1973. The programme benefited principally from Danish technical and financial assistance under an agreement between the Danish and Kenyan governments for the period 1972–7. It is this programme, which parallels closely efforts in Tanzania and Botswana, which will be considered here.

The strategy of the RIDP was to establish Rural Industrial Development Centres (RIDCs) in the smaller townships located in the centre of agricultural areas, comprising central workshops, offices and classrooms, to serve as bases for extension efforts to scattered local artisans. In 1975 there were four such centres, at Machakos (40 miles east of Nairobi), Embu, (north-east of Nairobi), Nyeri (due north) and Kakamega in West Kenya.

Mention may also be made of a largely separate experimental programme for the promotion of rural business run by an American organization, Partners for Productivity (PFP) as part of the Special Rural Development Programme at that time in the Vihiga–Hamisi divisions of Kakamega District. PFP currently has a programme in Botswana.

The 1974–8 Kenya Development Plan proposed the establishment of twenty-three RIDCs in all by 1978, involving a total expenditure on the programme by the end of 1977–8 of K£2 million, a very substantial commitment.

The RIDCs service 'clients', some of whom may be based at the centres themselves and a larger proportion through business 'extension services' in their own locations. The data of Table 18.1 show them to have been concerned largely with 'craft' industry, as NSIC was in Tanzania, rather than modern small industry as defined earlier. The chief activities were furniture making and metalworking (as at the NSIC estate in Dar es Salaam), together with motor repair: perhaps accounting for as many as 80% of the clients. Taking data from three of the RIDCs reporting in 1973, only 17½% of enterprises serviced employed ten or more persons and 66% employed less than six (Kristensen and Kongstad, 1973). The most common size of unit embraced three to five persons.

In order to assess the effectiveness of the centres a detailed investigation was carried out of their activities over a period of twelve to fourteen months (Livingstone, 1976). This was possible because job cards are made in respect of all equipment used at the centres. A count of job cards carried out at three of the four centres, together with examination of client record cards, permitted a fairly accurate picture of the activities of the centres to be built up. We consider first the use of centre facilities, then success in reducing the undercapitalization of craft industrialists, and finally the effectiveness of extension services away from the centres.

Table 18.1   *Distribution of clients at RIDCs by industrial activity, Kenya, 1973*

Activity	Clients	
	No.	%
Furniture	146	30
Sheetmetal work	53	11
Other metalworking	22	5
Auto/bicycle repair	81	17
Tools and machines	5	1
Sawmilling	41	8
Posho milling	28	6
Other and unknown	109	22
TOTAL	485	100

Source: Kristensen, 1974.

Use of Centre Facilities

The workshops were generally equipped with some very expensive machinery, provided through donor assistance, which proved to have been barely utilized. Thus at Embu four machines which had cost shs41,800 (approximately UK£2,600 historically, now perhaps costing £5,000) had been used twelve times in ten months. In contrast a simple electric welder accounted for 91 out of 153 machine jobs in the same period. Other jobs mostly involved simple power tools, whilst the expensive machinery lay idle.

This would seem to have resulted from a failure to appreciate the true nature of the (craft) enterprises that would be catered for, and the type of machinery which their requirements could sustain. Most industry in the rural areas of Kenya is at present of a very simple type. A rough survey of local small industry carried out by Embu RIDC soon after its establishment, summarized in Table 18.2, gives a realistic picture of the current rural manufacturing and repair activities which it was the task of the RIDCs to develop. To emphasize this simplicity we may list the kind of products made by twenty-nine of the sheetmetal workers: these were water tanks and containers (by 23 workers),

Table 18.2 *Local manufacturing and repair activities in the Embu area, 1973*
(number of establishments)

	Embu Town	Shauriyako (near town)	Manyatta	Runyenjes	Other	Total
Sawmilling	3	0	1	0	1	5
Woodworking	21	2	3	8	15	49
Sheetmetal working	10	11	2	3	8	34
Bicycle repair	2	0	1	4	2	9
Panel beating	1	0	0	1	0	2
Garages	11	0	1	2	1	15
Leather work (shoes and bags)	6	0	4	2	4	16
Posho mills	0	0	1	2	6	9
Tailoring	1	0	0	1	0	2
Dry Cleaning	1	0	0	1	0	2
Mattress Making	1	0	0	0	0	1
Masonry	0	0	0	0	2	2
Concrete blocks	1	0	0	0	0	1
TOTAL	58	13	13	24	39	147

charcoal braziers (21 workers), wash basins (12), buckets (11), bicycle repair (9), steel windows (9), watering cans (2), dustbins (2), water heaters (1), panel beating (1), brooders (1), ox-carts (1), pipe chairs (1) and gates (1).

A second feature of the use of centre facilities was the concentration of jobs among relatively few clients. Thus at the Nyeri Centre just three clients accounted for 179 out of 222 jobs in a twenty-two-month period, 80% of the total. These were in effect resident clients. The position at other centres was similar. RIDP administrators strongly resisted any increase in numbers of such semi-residential clients, favouring an extension approach aimed at reaching much larger numbers. But the fact that the heavy equipment and static facilities were not very relevant to the mobile approach meant that those few clients who were accepted as semi-residential enjoyed lavish facilities at subsidized rates. There is a marked contrast between the intensity of capital utilization in the 'appropriately' designed Dar es Salaam craft industry estate and that here. With a total cost per centre of over a million shillings ($160,000), the cost per job 'created' (taking into account clients served by extension), in an activity noted for its labour intensiveness, was estimated at 7,450s in 1973. At that time sixty-one RIDP employees (including two at the Head Office) served 205 clients (Kristensen, 1974). The programme in effect fell between two stools, the heavy equipment not being particularly relevant to the mobile extension approach and the number of resident clients being kept to a minimum to avoid the development of anything like an industrial estate.

The Provision of Capital

Evidence regarding the undercapitalization of craft industrialists in East Africa has already been given in respect of Tanzania. A scrutiny of clients' files in Machakos indicated strongly that their main interest was in financial assistance (as opposed to business advice, etc.). Files at the Machakos Centre also gave details of the nature of the 'premises' owned or used by clients served by the extension service. These showed that a considerable proportion of artisans lacked proper premises and were working under 'shades' as protection against sun and rain. This is likely to be typical of the rural informal sector in Kenya. Not surprisingly access to power, related to the problem of premises and lack of capital, was also a crucial constraint.

In the situation as just described, the non-provision of capital in the form of basic working premises implied by the absence of residential clients is a major disadvantage of the Kenyan approach. Further evidence is given by an inquiry into clients' problems at the RIDCs in 1973, summarized in Table 18.3.

Table 18.3   *Clients distributed by recorded problems, all centres, 1973*

Problems	% of clients mentioning
Plots and premises	13
Raw materials	15
Production methods	10
Lack of skilled manpower	3
Lack of tools and machinery	32
Lack of electricity	6
Bookkeeping	5
Marketing and sales	5
Unknown problems	12
TOTAL (882 problems mentioned)	100

Source: Kristensen and Kongstad, 1973.

If lack of power is considered to be associated with lack of capital, the latter could be taken to account for at least two-thirds of the problems mentioned.

Very little credit was extended to clients via the RIDCs. More important was the supply of materials under bulk purchase. The main material stocked was wood, a stock of which was maintained by the centres and financed by a small revolving fund. This was particularly heavily utilized at Machakos, due no doubt to the availability of short-term credit at this centre for this purpose: reflecting again the shortage of even minimum working capital among artisans.

The Extension Approach

As already indicated, there was a deliberate attempt in the Kenya RIDP to pursue a different approach from that of industrial estates, by emphasizing extension. Underlying this was the hope that a larger number of entrepreneurs would be reached, spreading the benefits of the programme more widely and equitably. An especially great effort in this direction was made at Machakos: here in 1975 sixteen out of thirty-three clients were located more than 40 kilometres away from Machakos and three were more than 140 kilometres away.

This approach turned out to be extremely expensive, as shown by the costings of Per Kongstad (1975). He estimated (p. 44) direct costs to average 7,000s per client given field (extension) assistance under the programme, a vast sum in comparison with the annual income of the average craft enterprise. Kongstad's data also showed free field assistance (FFA) to be very expensive as compared to free assistance at the centre (FCA). Details are given in Table 18.4. This shows the direct cost of field assistance excluding overheads to have been 60 shillings an hour.

Table 18.4   *Direct costs of free field and centre assistance in the Kenya RIDP, 1974*

| | | Average, all centres | | | Mackakos RIDC (yearly basis) | | |
	Hours	Direct costs	Cost per hour	Hours	Direct costs	Cost per hour
FFA	642	38,661	60·2	1,283	77,262	60·2
FCA	2,243	63,905	28·5	1,833	52,222	28·5
TOTAL	2,885	102,564	15·6	3,126	129,484	41·4

Source: Kongstad, 1975.

Three problems of the extension approach may be distinguished. A major one is that of transport cost. First of all, this requires organization, which here appears to have been poor: the 1973 RIDC evaluation report (Kristensen and Kongstad, 1973) stated that 'a really systematic planning of the extension services has not been possible due to lack of transport facilities, especially transport of small machines, tools and materials'. As regards costs, it is significant that over 40% of field assistance hours were actually spent travelling to the client's workplace. Costs of advice thus vary directly with distance of the client from the centre, as shown in Table 18.5.

This factor affected one of the main objects of the extension approach, that of reaching a large number of clients. RIDP clients are divided for extension purposes into 'intensive' and 'extensive' categories, the former being eligible for more contact hours and much closer support. The number of intensive clients per centre was in 1974 no more than twenty-five to thirty, while progress with extensive clients had in general not gone far beyond their registration.

The second set of problems relates to the amount of benefit obtained to offset these costs. A 1974 RIDP evaluation (Kristensen, 1974) judged that 131 out of 205 clients in February 1974, had not made progress as a result of

Table 18.5   *Cost of a visit depending on distance to client*

Distance to client (km)	Travelling time (hrs)	Time spent with client (hrs)	Total time spent (hrs)	Cost of visit (K.shs)	Cost per hour spent with client (K.shs)
0– 9	0	3	3	180	60
10–24	1	3	4	240	80
25–49	2	3	5	300	100
50–74	3	3	6	360	120
75 and under 100	4	3	7	420	140

Source: Kongstad, 1975.

extension. This might be due to unresponsive clients or lack of concrete advantages offered. As regards the first of these a separate evaluation of results at Machakos (Edebe and Geels, 1974) concluded that

> it must be considered a reality that RIDP is not able to raise the general level of the entrepreneurs and their employees . . . It is difficult to measure any improvement of the employment situation etc. over a relatively short period when work is done with already established entrepreneurs . . . They are satisfied with their present situation, are too old to be receptive, etc. . . . Any advanced (established) client considers the presence of the technician as a disturbance.

It is interesting to compare this with the programme in Botswana which is centred upon school leavers of between 16 and 20 years of age.

As regards concrete advantages, it is clear that considerable uncertainty existed as to what extension advice was appropriate to craft industrialists in rural areas and townships. An important aspect of the extension approach at Machakos was the attempt to introduce clients to profitable new product lines. This was done as a matter of routine, using a 'standard working plan' (SWP) under which at least two new products were to be introduced to all 'intensive' clients. This, together with bookkeeping advice, was the main element of extension at Machakos. Not a great deal of success was achieved in product development in the period 1974–5, however. The two main products advocated were a maize sheller and a wheelbarrow, which clients were prepared to accept only with some reluctance. Given that, apart from a few samples purchased by the RIDC itself, the records showed only three successful sales, of one wheelbarrow, a folding chair and a folding table, this was not surprising. Other experiments with new products, particularly low-cost small-scale production of standard tools at Embu, appeared more promising. A major obstacle here associated with the preference for the extension approach, directed to scattered rural enterprises, over the residential estate, was the lack of a 'production line' at the centre to guarantee production if interest in the product was obtained.

A second ingredient was bookkeeping and management advice, a common element in small industry promotional programmes all over the world. Of about a hundred clients at Machakos about twelve received fairly intensive assistance in bookkeeping and price calculation during 1974, amounting to some twenty or thirty hours. These efforts were clearly unsuccessful in five cases, and no results were reported in another three: partial results appear to have been obtained in no more than three of four cases. It may well be the case that management advice in the form of extension assistance is simply not appropriate to craft industry, as opposed to somewhat larger enterprises. The offering of advice on layout of the workshop, for instance, appears more appropriate to factory layouts and plant design than to rural artisan establishments employing three or four people, an example of misplaced transference from 'modern small industry' to craft industries. Other technical and economic advice which the RIDCs were in a position to dispense was probably quite limited, given the heterogeneous nature of the craft enterprises.

The third problem of the extension approach was that it failed to recognize the artisan's greatest need, which was capital rather than advice. This is apparent from the discussion above. This would have been alleviated if working capital in the form of materials could have been provided, but in general centres lacked the capacity to deliver materials to enterprises located away from the townships. As already stated, this is a major potential advantage of workshop estates.

The term 'extension approach' is based on an analogy with the agricultural extension service, an analogy which is superficially attractive but not necessarily appropriate. It assumes that the problem is to make the small-scale 'industrialist' – who is generally no more than a skilled artisan – into a better 'entrepreneur' by teaching him bookkeeping or providing him with ideas for more rewarding products, rather than giving him access to a minimum amount of capital. Unlike the agricultural case (or to a greater extent) it exaggerates the technical or economic advice which the service is likely to be able to dispense, given the nature of craft industry and the limited expertise likely to be available in practice.

Trusts Brigades and Technical Training in Botswana

It is not surprising that there is comparatively little small or medium-scale industry in Botswana, given the small national market in terms of population (some 750,000 people only) and cash income, given its locational disadvantages as a landlocked country, and given intense competition from a relatively efficient, established South African manufacturing sector. Nevertheless Botswana is almost unique among African countries for its extreme paucity of informal sector activities and village craft industries. This is compounded by the underdeveloped state of the commercial system which penetrates only very weakly the rural areas. Many village artisans find it difficult to obtain materials, parts and other supplies and in any case lack the finance to purchase them. The relative weakness of the informal sector in Botswana in respect of productive activities, trade, transport and other services undoubtedly reduces the standard of living for the mass of the population in the rural areas particularly, and especially those lacking wealth or income from livestock. It also sets special problems for craft and small industry development.

This weakness is almost an immediate impression in Botswana, but has not been systematically measured. One or two village surveys give some indication of it, however, as for instance a survey of five villages in the Southern District carried out in October 1978 by the Extension Service of the Rural Industries Innovation Centre. The five villages, Mabutsane and Samane in the west, Manyana in the northeast, Goodhope in the south-east and Ralekgetho in the central lands area, represent different geographical areas within the district. There is no reason to think that other districts would be better endowed and many would most likely be in a worse position. The survey revealed sixty-two craft enterprises in all. However this included fifteen tanners (an activity to be expected in a livestock economy) and sixteen knitters. Beyond these there were just six carpenters, four tailors, three mechanics, three bicycle repairmen, two shoemakers, and one builder, miller (not functioning), basketmaker, and painter: not a large number in relation to population.

In addition, a serious employment problem is emerging in Botswana (Lipton, 1978). The low labour intensity of both the country's main economic activities, mining (which is capital-intensive) and livestock (which is land-intensive), has produced growth but comparatively little employment. At the same time productivity in arable farming is low and production both risky and arduous, rendering self-employment in the main employing sector unattractive, and encouraging rural – urban migration.

The absence of an established artisan sector, together with the need to create employment opportunities for increasing numbers of primary school leavers, underlies the distinct feature of Botswana policy towards rural/small industry, which is the emphasis on training and orientation towards the training of school leavers in particular, articulated through the Brigade movement.

This movement, which aims to provide primary school leavers with vocational training in a variety of trades, was initiated in 1965 by Patrick Van Rensburg, a liberal South African refugee, when the Swaneng Hill Secondary School was constructed on a self-help basis by students forming the Serowe Builders Brigade. The movement has expanded rapidly since that time and in addition to individual brigades has a number of 'brigade centres' which involve bringing together a cluster of brigades centred on different activities. At the end of 1978 there were said to be over forty brigades and fifteen brigade centres (Chilisa, 1979).[6]

Great enthusiam and idealism surrounds the brigade movement not only on the part of those directly involved in management and of the government of Botswana, but also of donors, who have given it substantial financial support. The movement certainly has some attractive features, and has introduced a number of useful-looking ventures. Yet this enthusiasm has been somewhat uncritical, not to the best advantage of sound long-run development.

For example, a widely quoted success is the Kweneng Rural Development Association (KRDA), a community organization which first came together in 1969 as an informal discussion and pressure group. It has certainly shown an impressive rate of development since that time, diversifying its activities into training programmes for handicrafts and textiles, builders, mechanics and (recently) woodworkers; the manufacture of school uniforms; the supply of building materials and general hardware; a vehicle maintenance and repair centre; a forestry unit; small-scale market gardening; a bee-keeping pilot project; and a hotel. Further ideas exist for the future.

If these activities are viewed more critically, however, one might say that the training activities at the KRDA fall between the two stools of training artisans in a genuine work situation (the environment at KRDA is of a training centre, not a realistic village situation where artisans work independently) and training artisans in sufficient numbers, as might be done in a technical college. Moreover, the KRDA has not concerned itself with the situation of artisans away from the enterprise itself, or with the subsequent careers of its own 'graduates'.

To consider specific enterprises, the production of school uniforms is entirely dependent upon a government-guaranteed market and has yet to break into the 'free' market. The vehicle maintenance and repair unit is a highly capitalistic enterprise, useful, perhaps, in the small township of Molepolole, but divorced from the objective of producing large numbers of effective 'bush mechanics'. The forestry unit represents a valuable initiative, but afforestation and the provision of wood-lots might be considered a more appropriate function for a Ministry of Natural Resources. The small hotel may pay its way in the absence of effective competition, but is based on expatriate management and access to capital. While current revenue is stated almost to cover costs, a main source of revenue stems from the supply of building materials (the success of which again depends in part on the provision of capital and expatriate direction). Finally, the allocation of common costs to different activities is not clear, particularly the costing of external assistance. More generally a strong top-down element is involved in KRDA, rendering the replicability of the enterprise and its relevance to genuine village industry uncertain.

Brigades as a whole are not such large organizations as the KRDA but have many of the same features. We can distinguish the following:

(1) The policy-making body of a brigade is a board of trustees comprising elected and nominated members, including the brigade manager, all of whom have voting rights.
(2) An important function of the manager is to secure donor assistance, on which brigades are highly dependent. Much of the manager's time is said to be spent on preparing project memoranda for securing such aid.
(3) Training at the brigades takes the form of one day a week in the classroom and four days practical training in the course of production. The normal academic subjects, mathematics, science, english and development studies, are taught, on the basis of an agreed curriculum. Brigade centre staff and facilities may also be involved in adult education activities and community service projects such as nutrition and libraries.

A disadvantage of the dominance of the training function is that it increases reliance on aid and subsidy and may obscure the business and production objective. According to Lloyd Addison[7] this policy has brought many difficulties through people being unaware of their roles and responsibilities, and has resulted in large financial losses. All brigades have financial or cash-flow problems of varying severity, and have difficulty in finding surplus-generating projects (Addison, 1979). Once obtained, rather than permit capital accumulation within the enterprise, they are likely to be used to fund service projects such as a literacy programme, say, which might have been left as the responsibility of a well-endowed government. At the same time moral attitudes have affected the debate – perhaps because of the role played by volunteers – as to how far brigades should stress the revenue-earning as compared to the training or service objectives (Addison, 1979).

(4) The umbrella type of organization, embracing a variety of activities and projects, which is typical of the brigades, makes for complicated administration. The Serowe Brigade, for example, keeps twenty-seven separate bank accounts.

(5) The management structure, with manager and board of trustees, taken in conjunction with the age of most trainees, between 16 and 20 years, produces a tendency to paternalism. All brigades employ expatriate volunteers as business advisers to provide marketing, bookkeeping and other commercial skills, including the entrepreneurial role of initiating new activities. These are often on short contracts and do not always have the most relevant business or industrial background. While they may do excellent jobs, there is an obvious problem of continuity in management.[8]

(6) As in the case of KRDA the most serious problem is that brigade finishers are given very little, if any, assistance in job-limiting or setting themselves up in business. This itself, together with the training emphasis, may contribute to an insufficient focus on activities in which artisans have the greatest chance of establishing their own productive enterprise. There is no guarantee that the skills produced are those in demand, or that the quantity produced of different types of skilled worker will be proportional to the quantity required.

As regards needed assistance to 'finishers', the evidence provided earlier from Kenya and Tanzania suggests that the chief handicap affecting informal sector (rural and urban) artisans is undercapitalization, extending to premises, minimum tools and equipment, and basic materials. The situation in Botswana is clearly similar or more severe, and is compounded by a shortage of skilled and experienced artisans themselves. The Botswana Village Survey cited earlier showed the average amount invested to be P87 (£51) among thirty-three producers, out of which twenty had invested no more than 1 pula each (60p) and twenty-seven had invested an average of P3 (£1·85).[9] Asked what the main problems they were facing were, 30% of village producers referred to lack of capital and access to credit. The full list of problem areas cited is given in Table 18.6.

In addition to the acquisition of fixed capital, problems in paying for or securing raw material as working capital are shown to be very great, confirming direct impressions quickly obtained.

While trainees are not helped to establish themselves as village producers, existing artisans in the villages fall outside the ambit of the brigade movement. Twenty-nine village producers in the survey responded to a question on how they had acquired their skills. Answers included family or friends (41%), clubs (10%), village producers (13%, presumably through some form of apprenticeship or low wage employment), South Africa (13%), government work (11½%), and advisers, schools and hospital (11½%). Again without putting too strong an interpretation on this small sample, this suggests that the skills of actual village producers have been picked up informally, in the village, or indirectly,

Table 18.6 *Problems faced by village producers in the Southern District of Botswana*

Problem area	No. of recipients facing problems
Access to credit or investment capital	18
Inability to purchase raw materials in bulk	14
Inability to acquire basic raw materials required for production	32
Access to transport facilities for either supply of raw materials or distribution of finished goods	26
Access to further technical training	8
Problems relating to the marketing of goods	17
Pressure associated with competition from other village producers	27
Problems related to licensing	3
TOTAL number of respondents	56

Note: The numbers in this table should be considered as no more than indicative. The question as asked leaves its interpretation and the possible response much too open.
Source: Survey of Village Production Activities, op. cit.

through other jobs, with little contribution from formal training. The paucity of village skills does give support to the strong training element in the brigade movement, but at the same time raises the question of neglect in the upgrading of existing village artisans.[10]

All these considerations do suggest that there would be considerable advantage in the Botswana context of a modified approach based on some form of craft industry estate on Tanzanian lines. Advantages would include:

(1)   action in respect of the severe capital constraint affecting informal sector artisans;
(2)   emergence of a clearer network or framework of activities under which the deficiencies of the existing distribution system in making available supplies of inputs and distributing locally made products could be circumvented through, for instance, bulk purchase arrangements;
(3)   a stronger link between training and current or subsequent productive activity;
(4)   greater urgency in identifying and concentrating on the most profitable lines of activity.

This would differ from the conventional programmes which already exist in Botswana alongside the brigade movement: a system of industrial estates for small entrepreneurs sponsored by the Botswana Enterprises Development Unit (BEDU), and a Factory Shells Programme for Rural Industrialization. The former programme is probably even more open to the criticisms of feather-bedding made in respect of industrial estates in Kenya. According to Lipton (1978, p. 98), 'few BEDU entrepreneurs have left the estate – with its expatriate expertise – and prospered'.

One element in this feather-bedding is the award of government contracts. The Directory for BEDU Assisted Entrepreneurs (BEDU, 1979) contains thirteen establishments in the 'garment sector', seven in leatherwork, ten in metalwork, seven in woodworking, fourteen in building and construction, seven in jewellery and pottery and three in allied sectors: sixty-one establishments altogether. Seven of the garment establishments produce school uniforms as one product while nine of the metalwork and woodwork enterprises produce school furniture. These most obviously offer scope for favoured treatment, though this could apply also to builders and contractors, for instance, or printing services (in the allied sector).

The Factory Shell Programme under the Ministry of Commerce and Industry is for the construction of a limited number of single and double factory shells over the second half of 1979 at six industrial estates, located at Pilane, Mogoditshane, Palapye, Ramotswa, Mahalapye and Maun. These were identified in 1978 among twelve secondary growth poles for rural industrialization[11] supplementing the primary growth poles of Gaborone, Francistown, Lobatse and Selebi-Phikwe.

The sites mentioned are all very small rural townships and it would seem unlikely that 'modern small industrialists' who are already scarce in the major townships would emerge. For local artisans as in the Kenya case, these appear inappropriate. The sheds, of standard design, are to be 140 m² (1,500 sq. ft) single, and 280 m² (3,000 sq. ft) double. The rent for a single shell would be P55 per month (£32) or P660 p.a. (£385), with P165 (£96) payable quarterly in advance. If the rent charged covers the capital cost of the building depreciated over five years, the capital investment involved would be P275, to be seen alongside the investment of P1 made by twenty village producers in the survey of village production cited earlier. Though the industries which might occupy the factory shell remains unspecified, there is at least a suspicion of the tendency already mentioned with respect to Kenya and Tanzania of a failure to distinguish clearly between craft industry and modern small industry.

Conclusion

Household and craft industry (0–9 employees) is only the tail of the whole range (0–99 employees) of what constitutes 'small industry' according to the standard definition.

The scarcity of larger-scale, indigenous entrepreneurs to promote, perhaps, has nevertheless led small industry promotional programmes in Africa in many cases to focus on this sector.

The lack of explicit recognition that such programmes will be dealing with craft industrialists and other informal sector activities has, however, frequently produced elements of inappropriateness in the design of such programmes, and in particular neglect of the problem of undercapitalization of craft enterprises.

Approaches which deal with this problem, such as the workshop estate approach of Tanzania, offer more hope than those which offer extension advice and education in bookkeeping.

Programmes which focus largely on training, understandable in the context of Botswana, without direct concern for the establishment of effective independent craft enterprises, have the same disadvatage, with the risk also of needing permanent subsidy and dependence on external management and direction.

A workshop estate approach would need to concentrate on appropriate standards and technologies and avoid the generally recognized disadvantages of ordinary industrial estates, but could be used to upgrade informal sector artisan enterprise in both rural and urban areas.

Notes

The section on Botswana has benefited from discussions with Lloyd Addison of the School of Development Studies, University of East Anglia.

1 See Livingstone, 1972, for a fuller account of activities of NSIC over the period 1965–72.

2 See Livingstone, 1980, figure 23.1.

3 This corroborates the findings of Bienefeld, 1975, for the informal sectors of Dar es Salaam and other Tanzanian towns.

4 In one workshop, two workers with full-time jobs elsewhere put in some 40 – 45 hours here.

5 In contrast the majority of metalworkers had to spend considerable time away from the estate hawking their wares.

6 17 by end-1979.

7 Personal communication.

8 For example, the Tshwaragano Brigade was established at Gabane during 1976 as a craft centre for post-primary school girls by Helen Young, a lecturer at the university who however had to leave at the end of her contract in 1977. Administrative problems followed inevitably upon her departure.

9 The high overall mean was due to a few entrepreneurs having made more substantial investments, a mechanic with an investment of P1,000, two knitting machinists with investments of P700 and P320 respectively, and a miller with a mill costing P560 (but no longer functioning).

10 According to Lipton, 'NCVT (National Centre for Vocational Training), NDB (National Development Bank), BEDU (Botswana Enterprises Development Unit) and the Brigade movement have done almost nothing to upgrade the techniques or business skills of the village carpenter' (Lipton, 1978, Vol. 1, p. xii).

11 Except for Mogoditshane which is not mentioned. The others are Kanye, Molepolole, Serowe, Serule, Orapa, Kasane and Ghanzi.

References

Addison, L. (1979) *Report for Tshwaragano Brigade Trust on Gabane and South East Kweneng*, Gabane (September).

BEDU (1979) *Directory for Bedu Assisted Entrepreneurs, Who They Are, Where They Are, What They Produce* (Gaborone: Botswana Enterprises Development Unit),

Bienefeld, M. A. (1975). 'The informal sector and peripheral capitalism: the case of Tanzania', *IDS Bulletin*.

Edebe, D. A. and Geels, K. (1974) *On Extension Service at RIDC Machakos*, Machakos (April) (mimeo.).

Extension Service of the Rural Industries Innovation Centre, (1978), *Survey of Village Production Activities (October/November)*.

ILO (1972) Employment, Incomes and Equality, a Strategy for Increasing Productive Employment in Kenya (Geneva: ILO).

Kongstad, P. (1975) *Rural Industrial Development Programme extension services to rural industries: a partial assessment of RIDP*, IDR Project Paper D. 75.1 (Copenhagen: Institute for Development Research).

Kristensen, H. (1974) *Report for the Programme Conference, Kisumu, 24-26/4-73*, IDR Paper A. 74.7 (Copenhagen: Institute for Development Research).

Kristensen, H. and Konstad, P. (1973) *Assistance Problems, Policy Planning and Administration*, Report of the Programme Conference Nyeri, 5-6/9173, IDR Paper A. 73.7, (Copenhagen: Institute for Development Research).

Lipton, M. (1978) *Employment and Labour Use in Botswana, Final Report, Vol. 1., Footnotes and Appendices, Vol. 11* (Gaborone: Government Printer).

Livingstone, Ian (1972) 'The promotion of craft and rural industry in Tanzania', *Viertel Jahres Berichte* (March).

Livingstone, Ian (1977) 'Rural industries for developing countries: an evaluation of Kenya's Rural Industrial Development Programme', *Journal of Modern African Studies*, XV, 2 (June). 1977.

Livingstone, Ian (1980) *Economics for Eastern Africa* (London: Heinemann Educational Books).

Staley, E. F. and Morse, R. (1965) *Modern Small Industry for Developing Countries* (New York: McGraw Hill).

19 Lomé's Informal Industrial Sector

ERIK DEMOL, G. NIHAN & C. JONDOH

I Industrialization and Employment in Togo

Togo is one of the smaller West African countries, with a population of roughly 2·5 million inhabitants on 56,000 km². The capital city, Lomé (approximately 280,000 inhabitants), is at the same time the main port, with a hinterland reaching Upper Volta and Niger, and a busy trading centre on the coast road, which provides the main links with Ghana, Ivory Coast, Benin and Nigeria. The per capita GDP is in the 200–300 range.[1] Gross domestic product, at constant prices, rose between 1960 and 1966 at an average annual rate of 10%.[2] During the First Five-Year Plan (1966–70) this rate was approximately 7% against only 4·5% for the Second Five-Year Plan (1971–5), despite the 7·7% target. The balance of trade has been moderately negative for a considerable number of years, and has suffered from price difficulties for phosphates, and major production shortcomings for Togo's two main export products: coffee and cocoa. Imports have risen constantly, with major growth rates for both investment and intermediate goods.

The sectoral contribution to GDP shows relatively important movements between 1970 and 1975; these, however, are largely due to primary sector problems, where agriculture has suffered from both drought and structural recession. On the whole, 30% of GDP is attributable to the primary sector, 20% to the secondary and approximately 50% to the tertiary sector. Between 1965 and 1975 an annual growth rate of 36% has taken place in manufacturing, which accounts now for approximately one-third of the secondary sector's present contribution; however, two breweries and soft drinks producers, the cement factory and one cotton mill alone represent roughly 70% of manufacturing GDP. The relative and increasing importance of the tertiary sector is due mainly to the considerable development of the commercial sector as a result of the trading tradition along the West African coast and the preferential agreements which exist with the other members of the franc zone.

The Third Five-Year Plan (1976–80) relies less on infrastructural projects than the two former plans, and its main objective seems to be the strengthening of the present economic structure in preparation for an 'economic take-off in 1985'.[3] This would roughly coincide with the widened perspectives which ECOWAS – the West African common market – will bring, in terms of both a broader market and communal industrial projects. Accordingly, a major emphasis in industrial development lies in the integration of different existing import substitution oriented production units and new agro-industrial projects into an interrelated economy.

Notwithstanding the broadening of the market which ECOWAS will ultimately provide for the Togolese economy, the present industrialization strategy stresses the importance of small- and medium-scale enterprises. Bearing in mind the narrowness of the present domestic market, both in terms of numbers and of purchasing power, and the fact that – except in the case of phosphate, which accounts for three-quarters of Togolese exports – mineral resource exploitation is considered unprofitable (given present world prices), the Third Development Plan clearly states that 'the future of Togolese industry lies in the development of small and medium-scale industry, harmoniously spread over the whole national territory and utilizing as far as possible local resources'.[4] In addition, 'the first objective of existing [production] units is the improvement of the product, in accordance with the local consumers' taste; the main emphasis will be on the production of essential commodities'.[5] Government policy aims at promoting an industrial structure where 'modern enterprises with advanced technology constitute the framework supplemented by smaller units with more labour-intensive technologies'.[6] These labour-intensive units are much needed in view of the country's factor endowments (in terms of labour and capital), and more specifically the problems that arise from the excess supply of labour – including those with school qualifications. The plan forecasts for the 1976–80 period a total of 175,000 school leavers without professional qualifications; of these only 16,000 will find employment in the modern formal sector.[7] Despite the present efforts to channel larger proportions of them into the agricultural sector, the excess supply of unskilled labour, especially in urban centres, remains a problem, which the 1985 universal primary education programme is unlikely to alleviate.

It is within this context that the Togolese Ministry of Planning and Industrial Development requested the ILO to carry out a study of the modern informal sector in Lomé as part of its Research Programme on Skill Acquisition and Self-Employment in the Urban Informal Sector of Francophone Africa.[8] The aims of the programme – which also covered the capital cities of Cameroon, Mali, Mauritania and Rwanda – were first, to obtain a clear picture of how the sector functions; and second, to provide government with concrete recommendations regarding the development of production, employment and training potential in the informal sector.

II The Survey of the Informal Industrial Sector[9]

Following the procedure adopted in the earlier surveys, our study on Lomé began with an exhaustive census of the informal sector conducted in October and November 1977. In order to obtain a comprehensive picture of this sector all categories of activity were covered, including commerce. The sample survey of the categories thought to be the most dynamic was carried out in April and May 1978. The activities selected in this case were woodworking, metalworking, building and mechanical and electrical repairs (further data are given in the appendix to this chapter). These activities make up what we call the 'modern' informal sector,[10] because it produces goods and services similar to those of the modern formal sector for which consumer demand may be expected to expand if appropriate steps are taken to improve the undertakings' productivity and quality standards.

The census[11] enumerated a total of 23,824 informal economic units in Lomé. If wage-earners and apprentices are also taken into account,[12] it can be estimated that at least one-fifth of the economically active population is engaged in informal sector activities.

An initial analysis of the results of the survey[13] enabled us to identify in some detail the part played by the modern informal sector in Lomé with regard to both employment and apprentice training as well as the incomes derived from this type of activity. We found that the sector is expanding with respect to both employment and capital investment. However, the rate of expansion is slow, partly no doubt because of limited room to manoeuvre but also because the technical and financial management of the undertakings is still at a rudimentary stage – even in those that have invested heavily in equipment – with the result that growing capital intensity leads to serious productivity problems. These problems could become even worse if the apparent satisfaction of the more capital-intensive entrepreneurs with their present – often considerable – profits were to destroy their will to introduce more advanced production methods. Such attitudes could in the long run jeopardize the survival of a sector which is in danger of missing its chance to develop into a 'national' small- or medium-scale sector capable of competing with the large-scale firms in the rapidly expanding modern sector.

In the short term, however, the diagnosis that emerges is far from negative: this sector, without obstructing the modern formal sector, performs an important training and income-generating function for the vast majority of those engaged in it. It also represents an intermediate stage which, if skillfully handled, could become an important component of development policy, as acknowledged by the Third Plan.

The survey revealed that there were 3,586 apprentices in the modern informal sector.[14] It should be noted, however, that they make up 88% of the employed workforce in these undertakings, which raises the possibility of their being used as a source of cheap labour. The conclusion to which our analysis leads, while not underestimating that danger, is that there is also much to be said in favour of this type of apprenticeship. For example, it was found that as many as 84% of the apprentices covered by our investigation were trained under conditions that may be described as satisfactory. This positive assessment is confirmed by the fact that entrepreneurs who served an apprenticeship in this sector – i.e. 96% of them – run their businesses just as productively as entrepreneurs who were trained in a vocational centre or in the formal sector.[15] We have here, then, a traditional and inexpensive training process which performs an important function as a preparation for self-employment and at the same time acts as a springboard to employment in the modern formal sector since one-third of former informal sector apprentices were able to find jobs in the formal sector at some stage of their working lives.[16]

The informal 'industrial' sector provides employment at the present time for 1,863 craftsmen and entrepreneurs and 87 partners actually working in the undertakings. The average life of the undertakings is 5·9 years and 57·5% of them have been in operation for at least four years. In addition to the 1,950 jobs thus created there are also 483 wage-earning employees, 450 of whom are skilled workers, which brings the total 'permanent' labour force (i.e. excluding apprentices) up to 2,433. If we compare this figure with the 12,000 or so jobs in manufacturing, services and building in Togo, it can be seen that the modern informal sector in Lomé provides employment for the equivalent of 20% of the workforce in the formal sector throughout the country, without the benefit of the capital resources invested in large-scale industry. If the number of apprentices is added, the proportion rises to the equivalent of 50% of employment in the formal sector.[17] Assuming a stable market, the number of jobs in the modern informal sector will continue to rise, if slowly, at a rate of about 2·5% a year, with skilled employment tending to increase more rapidly since its weighted average rate of growth is greater than that of the apprentices (9·5 and 3·4 per cent respectively). Nevertheless, this 9·5 per cent rate only applies to a numerically small group, so the informal sector cannot be expected to resolve the whole problem of youth unemployment. Nor can the observed growth in this sector as measured by the establishment of new undertakings be expected to produce any radical change in the situation: its annual rate of growth was estimated at approximately 5% on the basis of the census and survey findings.[18] Assuming that these trends continue, one can expect an annual increase in the modern informal sector of approximately 270 apprenticeships and 160 productive jobs in the short run.[19] These figures are merely indicative, but they show clearly enough that the sector's contribution to the solution of the employment problem is important without, however, being sufficient in itself.

Participation in the modern informal sector is far from being a form of disguised unemployment: taking into account their levels of skill, 72·9% of the entrepreneurs probably make a better living than they would if they worked in the modern formal sector, which makes it easier to understand why 64% of those who previously had a job in the formal sector moved from modern sector wage-earning employment to artisanal activity: 82·5% earn incomes equal to or greater than the guaranteed inter-occupational minimum wage (SMIG) and the same applies to 68·6% of the wage-earners. The wages of apprentices – on average 17·8% of the SMIG – should not be analyzed in the same context since their status is quite different.[20]

The social contribution made by the modern informal sector is important for the city. Its undertakings cater mainly to the needs of the low-income groups, artisans and petty traders, with whom the volume of business amounts to 56·1% of their turnover, while sales to public employees and workers in the modern sector make up another 40%. Its contribution to the economic activity of the country as a whole is no less striking. Confining ourselves to activities for which data are available in the formal sector, the value added in woodworking in the informal sector of Lomé, for example, is 28·5% of that produced by modern sector woodworking throughout the country, the corresponding figure for repair services provided for households being 10·6%; taking Lomé on its own, the ratio rises to more than 350% for woodworking and is still 28% for the building trades. And yet these results are achieved on the whole with a relatively low level of capital investment: half the undertakings possess capital assets with a current value estimated at less than 62,000 francs CFA,[21] with the overall average approaching 200,000 francs CFA only because one group of undertakings (those comprising the top decile of the survey distribution) own equipment valued at over 500,000 francs CFA. This investment, which originates within the sector itself (normally personal savings for starting capital and self-financing for subsequent development), has produced a weighted average rate of increase in fixed assets of 5·7% a year and 8·4% in the case of the top decile. The self-financing capacity is considerable, since after outlays for housekeeping and assistance to the extended family are deducted,[22] 80% of the entrepreneurs still have a balance of at least 50,000 francs CFA a year for further investment and 50% are left with 157,000 francs CFA or more, which goes to show that there is a disparity between many entrepreneurs' capacity to invest and their willingness to do so.[23]

These figures confirm the special place occuped by the modern informal sector in the Togolese economy, where it has carved out a market of its own and enjoys a relative independence of commercial and industrial capital. Most of its undertakings seem to be operating in a fairly satisfactory manner; the fact, however, that there does not seem to be any clear indication of its prospects in the medium and long term suggests that it has not adopted the forward-looking approach to development found in large modern undertakings.

Generally speaking, the findings show clearly that the main problem facing the informal sector arises out of its very rough and ready methods of enterprise management and price fixing.[24] The standards of technical management and bookkeeping are poor whatever the level of capital investment. Out of the 280 entrepreneurs covered by the survey, only 15 (5·4%) state that they devote any time to bookkeeping (an average of 3·3 hours a week). Moreover, only 20·7% keep a record of receipts and expenditure and 2·5% maintain more sophisticated accounts; and although 52·5% state that they calculate their production costs, only 1·1% can break them down correctly – mainly because only 2% of all entrepreneurs take depreciation into account.

An improvement in economic behaviour can be observed to take place as the undertaking's level of capital investment rises. The effects are particularly noticeable in the best-equipped group: 60% of entrepreneurs in the top decile keep a record of receipts and expenditure and 18% keep more elaborate accounts. There is thus a certain awareness of the need to organize the undertaking along more sophisticated lines as its capital assets increase. This conclusion, however, is placed in better perspective when one adds that only

20% of this group state that they devote time to bookkeeping (2·6 hours a week on average), while none of them has an employee to assist with this work. It is scarcely to be wondered at, then, that even in this group only 8% are able to identify with precision the components of their production costs and only 13% allow for depreciation. Nor, it should be noted, are these entrepreneurs any different from their less capital-intensive colleagues in the field of work organization.

Technical management seems to require just as much improvement: labour productivity in the modern informal sector is low in all the various sizes of undertakings compared with the modern formal sector. Depending on the category of activity, it ranges between 14% and 55% of that of the corresponding large undertakings in Lomé. Moreover, greater investment in machinery and equipment seems to be accompanied by a disproportionate *decline* in the productivity of capital considering the meagre improvement in labour productivity resulting from the increase in capital intensity. Furthermore, the fact that the entrepreneurs' willingness to invest is lower than their self-financing capacity could cause problems in the long run for these undertakings since competition from the large modern firms seems bound to increase, thus reducing the small entrepreneurs' room to manoeuvre in a market which 66% of them already describe as irregular and providing an insufficient volume of sales.

Although so far the majority of the undertakings operate satisfactorily – only 13·6% report frequent selling at a loss – this can mainly be put down to the fact that the formal sector is not well developed in the corresponding production fields. The corollary to this is that the market still has room for the small undertaking if the latter can improve the quality of its products. However, as the survey showed, this possibility is seriously compromised by an underlying weakness that is characteristic of the informal sector's difficulties in adjusting to a changing market. Quite apart from the constraints arising out of behaviour patterns, which are conditioned by a sociocultural environment which is not always receptive to modern ideas,[25] there is no denying that the sector's low standards of technical and financial management and bookkeeping are due to inadequate education and training: 25% of the entrepreneurs are illiterate, 18·6% have at most three years of primary schooling and only 5% have attended secondary school, which means that the majority of them would be incapable of applying advanced management methods unless they received specially designed training. Future prospects are equally disturbing since 36·2% of present apprentices are illiterate.

To sum up, the informal sector in Lomé provides opportunities for the absorption of a considerable number of unemployed young people; it gives productive employment to a sizeable body of workers who would be looked upon as unskilled in the formal sector; it stimulates the development not only of economic activity but also of skills and the use of labour-intensive technology; and it assists the redistribution of income. It is essential that these unique characteristics be preserved, but this must not imply stagnation; on the contrary, it is important to promote the dynamism of the informal sector and its gradual metamorphosis into a national modern sector still firmly anchored in the country's distinctive social, economic and cultural fabric.

III Future Policy

The following paragraphs discuss some of the considerations which should be taken into account in devising a programme of action to strengthen the economic potential of the informal sector and its capacity to provide employment and training. It should be kept in mind that the proposals made here only concern the modern informal sector in Lomé since it is by no means certain that they would be appropriate, or even desirable, for activities not covered by the survey such as tailoring and various types of commerce, or, more particularly, traditional handicrafts. On the other hand, they are probably adaptable in most cases to artisanal production, services and construction in the country's secondary urban centres.

Traditionally, assistance for the development of the informal sector has been provided through the establishment of special (usually state-run) agencies. By their very nature, these institutions are ill-adapted to the dynamics of the informal sector since the reasoning behind their creation is to a large extent alien to the very principles on which this sector functions. It is not surprising therefore, that 59% of the entrepreneurs prefer the state not to intervene in any assistance to be given.[26] And indeed, when these entrepreneurs are in difficulty, they seldom use the official channels of assistance open to them; they rely entirely on themselves or on their relatives. Aid through 'co-operatives' meets the same mistrust; the sole type of assistance whose acceptability was general – 90% of the responses – was the creation of a mutual aid association by the entrepreneurs themselves.

The results of the analysis showed clearly that a systematic recourse to the oft-recommended solution of capital injection and broadening of credit facilities, which are supposed to promote rapid business expansion, should be avoided. The principal reason for this is that the modern informal sector operates in a 'free enterprise' environment, diametrically opposed to interventions of this kind; moreover, the self-financing capacity of the sector exceeds the willingness to invest. Second, any sudden injection of capital would probably encourage the accelerated development of a few privileged enterprises, penalizing small undertakings whose share of the market might be considerably reduced. At the same time, it would thereby disturb the natural process of training and selection of entrepreneurs who are capable of entering the modern small and medium-scale sector, jeopardizing the modern informal sector's unique contribution to national development.

The additional skills required in the informal sector are far from being sophisticated and complex; assistance in this area should therefore focus on supportive and innovative help in the solution of day-to-day problems (in terms of production, management and techniques, etc.), adapted to the needs and the environment in which the sector functions. In this sense, any formal and institutionalized approach to those who have not acquired or retained the necessary technical skills and literacy is likely to fail, alien as it is to the *ad hoc* basis of the sector's functioning. Similarly, training and advice by management and marketing 'experts' would be vitiated by their sheer technicality and their bias towards a certain specialization in the various management functions, which are contrary to the pragmatic approach of the informal entrepreneurs. Moreover, this would upset the internal organization of the undertakings and hence their versatility, which determines their strength and comparative advantage compared to larger production units.

On the technological side, there would appear to be an important discontinuity in the available range of equipment between basic tools and the more sophisticated machinery;[27] the latter, if available in the undertaking, therefore tends to be under-utilized under present conditions. The considerable drop in capital productivity with increasing capital investment is indicative of the entrepreneur's present inability to optimize his production function.[28] Although little work has been done in the field of alternative production techniques (especially in the urban sector in Africa), there is scope for an investigation into the subject of more appropriate means of production. This should take into account the existing technical environment and the local capacity to develop, build and use this equipment.

To be successful, assistance to the informal sector must be organized within the framework in which the undertakings operate. Such an approach should regard these as self-contained production units, where the artisan's full control of the production process ensures the versatility of the enterprise, both in production and in transmitting skills to the apprentices. It should, therefore, utilize the human, material and technical resources available within the sector, combining them if appropriate with those available generally. Nevertheless, whatever assistance is provided, it must necessarily be selective and temporary, aimed at promoting a system which has stood the test of time but which, given the scale of the problems that developing countries face, will be called upon to increase its contribution and which needs accordingly to be strengthened.

IV   Conclusions

A number of facts emerge from our diagnosis of the informal industrial sector in Lomé. The modern informal sector appears to offer an employment and training potential that national policy-makers cannot afford to ignore. Nevertheless, the way the undertakings operate raises some doubt as to their capacity to adapt in the face of a modern sector whose share of the market is still small at the moment but which will probably rise rapidly in the future. The situation therefore requires that assistance be given to these undertakings but the actual details of such assistance are complicated. The optimism currently displayed by the 'evolutionist' school of thought is supported by very few, if any, examples of successful programmes in this field.[29] That is why the recommendations made to the Togolese government stressed the constraints discussed in the preceding section and suggested the setting-up of an experimental unit with the initial task of carrying out a detailed feasibility study. The main object of this operation would be to verify by a combination of research and action the possibility of involving the entrepreneurs in the gradual development of mutual aid bodies which they would eventually be able to run themselves.

Appendix:

Table 19A.1 *Estimation of certain characteristics extrapolated to the parent population[a] of the modern informal sector in Lomé*

Type of activity	Apprentices (1)	Regular employees[b] (2)	Entre- preneurs[c] (3)	Partners working in the undertaking (4)	Total of cols 1 to 4 (5)	Weighted average annual rate of employment growth (%)[d] (6)	Capital assets[e] (7)
Production	*1,324*	*383*	*747*	*56*	*2,510*	*1·8*	*200·4*
Woodworking	816	334	575	56	1,781	0·7	163·5
Metalworking	508	49	172	—	729	4·7	36·9
Services	*1,835*	*84*	*827*	*26*	*2,772*	*3·9*	*130·2*
Vehicle repairs	1,435	84	552	26	2,097	5·1	107·1
Electrical repairs	359	—	158	—	517	2·4	20·1
Small-scale engineering	41	—	117	—	158	−0·8	3·0
Building	*427*	*16*	*289*	*5*	*737*	*1·9*	*21·1*
Building trades	233	16	130	5	384	3·6	16·2
Subcontractors	194	—	159	—	353	−1·1	4·9
TOTAL	**3,586**	**483**	**1,863**	**87**	**6,019**	**2·6**	**351·7**

Type of activity	Weighted average annual rate of growth of capital assets[f] (8)	Turnover[g] per annum (9)	Raw materials used[g] (10)	Wage bill[g] (11)	Net trading results[g] (12)	Gross value added[g] (13)	Self- financing capacity[g] (14)
Production	*5·3*	*1,221·0*	*721·2*	*83·2*	*346·8*	*445·7*	*219·7*
Woodworking	5·9	957·0	559·5	67·5	280·0	360·2	172·6
Metalworking	2·5	264·0	161·7	15·7	66·8	85·5	47·1
Services	*6·5*	*1,155·1*	*700·8*	*39·2*	*316·8*	*366·1*	*224·8*
Vehicle repairs	7·3	742·7	436·5	32·8	209·0	249·6	141·0
Electrical repairs	7·3	354·1	236·0	5·4	83·6	90·6	63·9
Small-scale engineering	−1·7	58·0	28·3	1·0	24·2	25·9	19·9
Building	*6·8*	*514·2*	*380·7*	*9·4*	*112·5*	*123·7*	*93·9*
Building trades	8·4	231·5	158·8	5·8	59·7	67·0	55·1
Subcontractors	0·2	282·7	221·9	3·6	52·8	56·7	38·8
TOTAL	**5·7**	**2,890·3**	**1,802·7**	**131·8**	**776·1**	**935·5**	**538·4**

Notes:

[a]Figures calculated from the survey data as analysed in G. Nihan, E. Demol, D. Dviry and C. Jondoh,[6] 'Le Secteur non structuré 'moderne' de Lomé, République togolaise, Rapport d'enquête et analyse des résultats' (mimeo.), ILO, Geneva, 1978; World Employment Programme research working paper, restricted.

[b]Manual workers skilled or not, plus seven junior employees. In Lomé there were no family helpers or day-labourers in the undertakings surveyed.

[c]Figures equivalent to the number of undertakings.

[d]The average annual rate of growth for each undertaking was calculated using the following formula:

$$\delta_i = \sqrt[y_i]{\frac{N_{it_n}}{N_{it_0}}} - 1.$$

where N_i is the number of workers in each undertaking, t_n the year in question, t_0 the year in which the undertaking was set up and $y_i = t_n - t_0$. (It was possible, by means of the survey, to determine the number of workers employed by the undertaking at its launching and at the date of survey.) The average rate of growth for each type of activity was weighted by the number of workers in the undertaking, calculated at its median point of growth, and by the number of years the undertaking had been operating, using the following formula:

$$\delta_I = \sum_{i=1}^{n} \delta_i \cdot a_i \div \sum_{i=1}^{n} \cdot a_i$$

where $a_i = N_{it_0}(1+\delta_i)y_i/2 \cdot y_i$.

[e]In millions of francs CFA. The capital assets were calculated from the estimates made by the entrepreneurs of the real resale value at current prices of their tools, materials, furniture, machines, vechicle(s), land and workshop; the calculation therefore takes into account the depreciation of the equipment since its purchase. Separate estimations were made for each of these headings.

[f]Rate of growth calculated by using a formula similar to the one used for employment. The value of the starting capital assets was estimated from the resale value at current prices, without taking into account depreciation since the purchase of the equipment owned by the undertaking at its launching.

[g]In millions of francs CFA. It was possible to calculated these variables with a fair amount of accuracy, thanks to the wording used in the questionnaire, for normal, good and bad weeks, reduced to the average week on the basis of the distribution of these weeks over the year and finally estimated for the year by multiplying by the number of weeks during which the undertaking operated. The following variables were taken into account: turnover and raw materials estimated for the three types of week, the wage bill (payment in cash and in kind for each worker per average week over the year), working expenses (electricity, water and other overheads per average week), rent plus charges for depreciation and taxes. No loan charges were included since not applicable (see technical document cited above, especially pp. 25, 62, 65, 109 and 110).

Notes

This is an adapted version of G. Nihan, E. Demol and C. Jondoh 'The modern informal sector in Lomé' in *International Labour Review*, September–October 1979, pp 631–44 (Copyright International Labour Organization, 1979).

1   Aggregate economic data, when available, are mainly based on the formal sector activities, and often include only rough estimates for the traditional and informal sectors, if at all.

2   *Marchés Nouveaux: Le Togo* (Paris: J. A. Group, 1977).

3   Ministère du Plan, du développement industriel et de la réforme administrative, *Plan de développement économique et social 1976–80* (Lomé, 1976), p. 43 (hereafter referred to as *Plan*).

4   '*Plan*', p. 35.

5   '*Plan*', p. 289.

6   '*Plan*', p. 290.

7   See G. Nihan, M. Carton, E. Demol and C. Jondoh, 'Le secteur non structuré 'moderne' de Lomé', République togolaise, Esquisse des résultats de l' enquête et programme d'action' (mimeo.), Geneva, ILO 1978; World Employment Programme research working paper, restricted; annexe.

8   This research programme was financed with the assistance of the Swiss Technical Co-operation Agency and the Belgian Technical Co-operation Agency and received a major contribution from the participating African states, which agreed to supply the census-takers, technical assistants and material resources needed for the field research. It also draws on the work done by the research group of the Institute of Development Studies, Geneva University, which in association with the ILO has been carrying out investigations in the area of non-formal training.

9   Informal 'industrial' sector as used here is equivalent to 'modern' informal sector 'industrial' is taken in the broad sense, covering also part of the service sector). However, other types of activities such as tailoring or stamp making were not included in the survey.

10   See note 9.

11   For the technical details see E. Demol, 'Analyse des résultats du recensement du secteur non structuré de Lomé, République togolaise' Geneva (mimeo.) ILO, 1978; World Employment Programme research working paper, restricted.

12   There are no figures available on wage-earning employment and apprenticeship for the categories of activity not covered by the survey. However, they are unlikely to change the overall picture much since the number of wage-earners and apprentices in commerce, which represents 86·4% of the activities not covered by the survey, is very small. The labour force participation rate is around 42% according to Ministry of Planning estimates for 1975.

13   For the technical details see G. Nihan, E. Demol, D. Dviry and C. Jondoh, 'Le Secteur non structuré 'moderne' de Lomé, République togolaise, Rapport d'enquête et analyse des résultats Geneva (mimeo.) ILO, 1978; World Employment Programme research working paper, restricted. The survey covered 280 undertakings, chosen at random. These were divided into three 'strata' corresponding to the production, services and construction sectors, and two independent random samples were drawn from each of the production and services sectors. A variance test did not invalidate the representativeness of the samples and they were combined for subsequent data treatment.

14   We use, unless otherwise specified, figures arrived at by extrapolating the parameters of the survey to the parent population, i.e. all the small-scale undertakings in the census of the corresponding categories, since, as already mentioned, there are no particular reasons for doubting the representativeness of the sample.

15   The indicators used to arrive at this conclusion are the entrepreneurs' net profit, gross value added, and the productivity of labour and capital. The results were similar for the other cities studied.

16   The value of such training is confirmed, moreover, by ILO studies on employment

in the modern sector which find, *inter alia*, that educated young people do not bother to report to the Manpower Service of the Ministry of Labour to find a job in this sector as long as they have not acquired specific additional training through a 'traditional' apprenticeship.

17 This comparison may seem highly biased, given the relative weight of apprentices in the percentage thus calculated. Apart from the fact that the modern sector uses apprentices as well, the question arises here of the relative importance of training and production in an apprenticeship post. It is clear that all apprentices participate in a very real sense in the undertaking's work, but this does not mean that they are simply an exploited workforce, as some authors would have it. An implicit training cost is incurred by the heads of undertakings, and paid back by the apprentices who accept a wage that falls below their productivity. The situation is equivocal, therefore, but it is characteristic of any human resources training programme which necessarily entails a trade-off between present and anticipated future benefits.

18 This rate takes into account the 'entries' into the modern informal structure (undertakings which have been operating for one year at most, i.e. 15·8%, and the 'departures' from it (undertakings which had been enumerated in the census but had gone out of business by the time of the survey, six months later). Extrapolated to a full year, the result thus obtained enables us to estimate a 'departure' rate of 10·8%. As regards the weighted average rate of growth, the formula used can be found in the appendix.

19 For 1979, for example, the projected figure based on the findings of the survey is 429, broken down into 122 apprenticeship posts and 46 skilled workers due to the natural growth of the undertakings, plus 149 apprenticeship posts, 19 skilled workers and 93 self-employed resulting from the launching of new enterprises. In calculating the last group of figures we extrapolated the average numbers of apprentices and workers that were estimated on the basis of the workforce employed by the undertakings in the survey at the time they were launched.

20 Contrary to what might be thought at first glance, there is no contradiction between the lower productivity of labour in the informal sector (a characteristic we shall consider in a moment) and wages that are competitive with those in the formal sector. Productivity in the formal sector is 'biased upwards' by the high wages paid to expatriate staff and probably by profits as well, while in the informal sector it is 'biased downwards' by the number of apprentices, which is generally greater than that found in the large enterprises, as well as by the type of equipment used.

21 At the time of the survey the rate of exchange was 100 francs CFA = US$0·432.

22 Household expenditure includes rent, food, health care, clothing, transport, children's education and sundries. The average for the survey is 3,135 francs CFA per week (standard deviation: 2,351), with 50% of the entrepreneurs spending more than 2,535 francs CFA per week. In addition, 25·4% of them give assistance to the extended family amounting on average to 824 francs CFA per week. The average weekly household expenditure per person amounts to 475 francs CFA, which is close to the figure recorded in Bamako (1,055 Mali francs). These figures are not invalidated by the results of a family budgets survey conducted in Togo by the *Societé d'études pour le développement économique et social*.

23 Interestingly, the '*Plan*' recognizes similar problems in the Togolese economy as a whole where the main reasons for the present insufficiency of the modern small- and medium-sized enterprises is found to be (1) a preference for speculative investment in real estate, instead of the improvement of productive capacity; (2) the lack of entrepreneural 'esprit', encouraged by socio-cultural values which do not accept the emergence and progress of the individual; and (3) the imperfections of the present credit system (though the plan stresses the grave problems of credit policies in developing economies which are too liberal and where the distinction between turnover and profit is rather vague). See '*Plan*' pp. 35–6.

24 This point had already been noted by J. K. Hadzi, *L'Artisanat dans le développement togolais* (Paris: Ecole pratique des hautes études, 1968), p. 66, who states: 'In any event, however, the simple rules of enterprise management still baffle (the small entrepreneur). Not only does he fail to appreciate the concepts of forecasting,

co-ordination and planning (since he attaches no importance to economic time) but he also ignores the most elementary rules of management. Studies carried out by experts give grounds for thinking that these difficulties could be overcome; it must, however, be admitted that these notions do not have the same meaning to a *homo economicus* and to an artisan for whom economics is a direct function of social relationships.'

25   Which no doubt explains why the notion of profit maximization plays only a marginal role in determining the attitude of the more capital-intensive entrepreneurs towards productivity. The survey showed that their profits rose less rapidly than their fixed assets.

26   Almost 70% want direct help without having to go through some type of official co-operative body, and more than 35% prefer no assistance to state interference.

27   Currently, in Lomé, informal sector undertakings sometimes use the services of a timber merchant or another small entrepreneur who owns a combine. Nevertheless, this entails loss of control over the production equipment and hence of the comparative advantage provided by operational flexibility and rapid adjustment to the needs of the market; these are important elements in the versatility of small undertakings, which gives the informal sector another advantage over the modern enterprise. In addition, the possible recurrence of this loss of control over the production apparatus at different levels could lead to the 'proletarianization' of the entrepreneur. A solution would be to set up mutual aid associations, which apparently do not have the negative effects noted in the cases where equipment is hired. Nevertheless, the sophistication of this type of equipment generally raises technical management and accounting problems so that it is the best-trained entrepreneur who gradually assumes responsibility for it; the other joint owners are thereby relegated to a sort of bureaucratic dependence.

28   This is observed in all the cities covered by the research programme.

29   It is interesting to read the commentaries on this point in the special issue of *World Development* (Oxford) edited by R. Bromley on the theme 'The urban informal sector: critical perspectives' (September–October 1978). One should also remember the scepticism expressed by Hadzi, op. cit., regarding the possibilities of intervention in a sector in which 'economics is a direct function of social relationships', as mentioned in note 24 above.

PART SIX

INDUSTRY IN AFRICA:
A STATISTICAL DESCRIPTION

20 Recent Industrial Development in Africa

UNITED NATIONS INDUSTRIAL DEVELOPMENT ORGANIZATION

Explanatory Note

References to dollars ($) are to United States dollars. In tables three dots (. . .) indicate that data are not available. Because of rounding totals may not add precisely. For the purpose of this chapter all references to Africa should be taken to mean developing Africa, that is, excluding the Republic of South Africa and its dependent territories. The non-availability of statistics is the reason why all countries are not always mentioned in the tables. The term industry is used to refer to division 3 of the International Standard Industrial Classification (ISIC), that is, manufacturing activities.

Introduction

This chapter is intended to provide a statistical review of industrial development in Africa during the period 1970–6. The present level and structure and recent growth of industry in Africa varies widely from country to country, even more so than in most regions of the world, so that data aggregated at the regional level, and generalizations derived therefrom, are not very meaningful. To avoid this problem most of the data presented here, though not in all cases complete, are at the country level. The statistical appendix in particular may be useful for reference purposes in that it brings together for the first time a large body of data by country, much of it previously unpublished, on both general economic indicators and industrial statistics broken down by subsector.

I General Economic Indicators

On average, African gross domestic product (GDP) per capita grew at an annual rate of 1·7% during the period 1970–6 to reach $194 in 1976 as expressed in constant 1970 values.[1] GDP increased at a rate of 4·4% but population grew at 2·7% annually, so that by 1976 the population of forty-nine developing African countries reached 381 million.[2] Gross fixed capital formation grew by 11·3% per annum and accounted for 24·3% of GDP in 1976. Imports grew at a rate of 10·3%, considerably more than exports, which grew at a rate of only 2·3%, so that by 1976 imports exceeded exports by 39%. The labour force increased at a rate of 2·1%, less than overall population growth, and in 1976 38% of population was included in the labour force. Manufacturing value added (MVA) grew at a rate of 5·3%, less than 1% more than GDP, and by 1976 MVA accounted for 11·4% of GDP.

These overall regional data conceal wide variations among the African countries in their progress towards economic development and industrialization. Table 20.1 groups the countries of Africa according to three key economic indicators, their shares in regional GDP as of 1976, their levels of GDP per capita in 1976 and their rates of growth in GDP per capita, 1970–6. Five countries – Nigeria, Egypt, Algeria, Libya and Morocco – accounted together for about 52% of regional GDP, whereas twenty-seven others accounted for less than 1% of regional GDP each.

Many of the countries of Africa are among the world's poorest and least developed. Thirteen countries had per capita incomes in 1976 of less than $100, as expressed in constant 1970 values, and twenty-three others had per capita incomes of between $100 and $250.[3] Two countries; Libya and Gabon, both oil exporters, had per capita incomes considerably above the average ($2,480 and $1,540 respectively).

Not only are most African countries poor, a significant number grew poorer during the period 1970–6 as a result of internal factors such as war and drought and external factors such as higher oil prices and the generally unfavourable world economic situation. The spread in gains and losses among African countries was remarkably large. Twenty African countries had negative rates of growth in per capita GDP ranging to minus 12·8%.

On the other hand, fourteen countries, including all the oil exporting countries, achieved relatively high rates of growth in per capita GDP, ranging from 3·4% to 17·7%.

Table 20.2 groups African countries according to their shares in regional MVA as of 1976, the proportion of their GDP accounted for by industry as of 1976 and the rate of industrial growth, 1970–6. Four countries – Egypt, Nigeria, Algeria and Morocco – accounted for about 53% of African industrial production. Twenty-three countries had a share in regional MVA of less than 1% each.

The most industrialized countries of the region, measured according to the proportion of GDP accounted for by MVA, were Egypt, Swaziland, Mauritius, Ivory Coast, Kenya and Rhodesia, all with MVA shares in GDP of over 15%. Nineteen other countries had shares of MVA in GDP of less than 8%, ranging to as low as 1·4%.

Table 20.1   *49 African countries grouped by share in regional GDP, level of GDP per capita and rate of growth in GDP per capita*

Share in regional GDP, 1976*		
(less than 1%)	Sudan	Egypt
	Tanzania	Equatorial Guinea
Benin	Tunisia	Gambia
Botswana	Uganda	Ghana
Burundi	Zaire	Guinea-Bissau
Cape Verde	Zambia	Kenya
Central African	TOTAL:	Lesotho
Empire	17 countries	Madagascar
Chad		Mauritania
Comoros		Mozambique
Congo	**(more than 3·5%)**	Niger
Equatorial Guinea		Nigeria
Gambia	Algeria (9·0)	Senegal
Guinea	Egypt (11·3)	Seychelles
Guinea-Bissau	Libyan Arab	Sierra Leone
Lesotho	Republic (8·4)	Somalia
Liberia	Morocco (6·4)	Sudan
Malawi	Nigeria (16·9)	Tanzania
Mali	TOTAL:	Togo
Mauritania	5 countries	Uganda
Mauritius		TOTAL:
Niger		23 countries
Rwanda	Level of GDP per	
São Tomé and	capita, 1976	
Principe		
Seychelles	**(less than $100)**	**($250–500)**
Sierra Leone		
Somalia	Benin	Algeria
Swaziland	Burundi	Botswana
Togo	Cape Verde	Congo
Upper Volta	Chad	Ivory Coast
TOTAL:	Comoros	Liberia
27 countries	Ethiopia	Mauritius
	Guinea	Morocco
	Malawi	Rhodesia
(1–3·5%)	Mali	Swaziland
	Rwanda	Tunisia
Angola	São Tomé and	Zambia
Cameroon	Principe	TOTAL:
Ethiopia	Upper Volta	11 countries
Gabon	Zaire	
Ghana	TOTAL:	
Ivory Coast	13 countries	
Kenya		**(more than $500)**
Madagascar		
Mozambique	**($100–250)**	Gabon ($500)
Senegal		Libyan Arab Republic
Rhodesia	Angola	($2,480)
	Cameroon	TOTAL:
	Central African	2 countries
	Empire	

Note: *Based on values expressed in constant 1970 dollars. Countries listed alphabetically within groups.
Sources: Appendix Tables 20A.1, 20A.2, 20A.3.

Table 20.1 (cont.)

Rate of growth in GDP per capita, 1970–76		
(less than 0%)	(0–2·5%)	(more than 2·5%)
Angola	Benin	Algeria (4·0)
Burundi	Cameroon	Botswana (12·9)
Cape Verde	Chad	Congo (4·5)
Central African Empire	Guinea-Bissau	Gabon (17·7)
Comoros	Kenya	Gambia (4·1)
Egypt	Mali	Ivory Coast (4·7)
Equatorial Guinea	Mauritania	Lesotho (6·9)
Ethiopia	Morocco	Libyan Arab Republic (6·5)
Ghana	Rhodesia	Malawi (3·4)
Guinea	Rwanda	Mauritius (9·4)
Liberia	Senegal	Nigeria (4·7)
Madagascar	Seychelles	Somalia (4·6)
Mozambique	Tanzania	Swaziland (8·7)
Niger	Zaire	Tunisia (6·6)
São Tomé and Principe	Zambia	TOTAL: 14 countries
Sierra Leone	TOTAL: 15 countries	
Sudan		
Togo		
Uganda		
Upper Volta		
TOTAL: 20 countries		

Table 20.2 *43 African countries grouped by share in regional MVA, proportion of GDF accounted for by MVA and rate of growth in MVA*

Share in regional MVA, 1976*		
(less than 1%)	(1–4·5%)	(more than 4·5%)
Angola	Cameroon	Algeria (11·2)
Benin	Ethiopia	Egypt (20·6)
Botswana	Ghana	Morocco (6·8)
Burundi	Ivory Coast	Nigeria (14·1)
Central African Empire	Kenya	TOTAL: 4 countries
Chad	Libyan Arab Republic	
Congo	Madagascar	
Equatorial Guinea	Mozambique	
Gabon	Senegal	
Gambia	Rhodesia	
Guinea	Sudan	
Liberia	Tanzania	
Malawi	Tunisia	
Mali	Uganda	
Mauritania	Zaire	
Mauritius	Zambia	
Niger	TOTAL: 16 countries	
Rwanda		
Sierra Leone		
Somalia		
Swaziland		
Togo		
Upper Volta		
TOTAL: 23 countries		

Table 20.2 (cont.)

Proportion of GDP accounted for by MVA, 1976*		
(less than 8%	Central African Empire	Guinea
	Congo	Madagascar
	Madagascar	Malawi
Angola	Morocco	Mali
Benin	Senegal	Niger
Botswana	Sierra Leone	Senegal
Chad	Upper Volta	Sudan
Equatorial Guinea	TOTAL:	Tanzania
Gabon	8 countries	Upper Volta
Gambia		Zaire
Ghana		Zambia
Guinea		TOTAL:
Liberia	**(more than 15%)**	14 countries
Libyan Arab Republic		
Malawi	Egypt (21·2)	
Mauritania	Ivory Coast (16·1)	**(5–10%)**
Mozambique	Kenya (15·5)	
Niger	Mauritius (18·3)	Benin
Rwanda	Rhodesia (15·1)	Burundi
Somalia	Swaziland (18·9)	Ivory Coast
Togo	TOTAL:	Kenya
Uganda	6 countries	Liberia
TOTAL:		Morocco
19 countries		Rwanda
	Rate of growth in MVA, 1970–6*	Sierra Leone
		Somalia
8–12%	**(less than 0%)**	TOTAL:
		9 countries
	Angola	
Burundi	Central African Empire	**(more than 10%)**
Cameroon	Chad	
Ethiopia	Equatorial Guinea	Algeria (11·1)
Mali	Gambia	Botswana (11·9)
Nigeria	Ghana	Congo (15·2)
Sudan	Mozambique	Gabon (28·6)
Tanzania	Rhodesia	Libyan Arab Republic (21·2)
Tunisia	Togo	Mauritania (11·0)
Zaire	Uganda	Mauritius (14·4)
Zambia	TOTAL:	Nigeria (15·8)
TOTAL:	10 countries	Swaziland (19·6)
10 countries		Tunisia (12·7)
		TOTAL:
	(0–5%)	10 countries
(12–15%)	Cameroon	
	Egypt	
Algeria	Ethiopia	

Note: *Based on values expressed in constant 1970 dollars. Countries listed alphabetically within groups. Cape Verde, Comoros, Guinea-Bissau, Lesotho, São Tomé and Principe and Seychelles not included because of lack of data.

Sources: Appendix Tables 20A.1, 20A.2, 20A.3.

Table 20.3 *Major industrial sectors in 22 African countries, 1970, with shares in total MVA (%)*[a]

Country	Major sectors (with shares in MVA)
Burundi[b]	Beverages (46), clothing (16), metal products except machinery (15), food (14)
Cameroon[b]	Food (30), non-ferrous basic metals (17), beverages (12)
Congo	Beverages and tobacco (20), petroleum refining and products (18), food (16)
Egypt	Textiles (32), food (10)
Ethiopia	Textiles (28), food (27), beverages (16)
Ghana	Petroleum refining (15), textiles (11), food (11), non-ferrous basic metals (11), beverages (10)
Kenya	Food (19), transport equipment (11)
Libyan Arab Republic	Tobacco products (44), food (14), other chemical products (11)
Madagascar	Food (29), textiles (20)
Malawi	Food (22), beverages (17), tobacco products (12), textiles (11)
Mauritius	Food (61)
Mozambique	Food (36), textiles (11)
Nigeria	Textiles (24), beverages (15), food (12)
Rwanda	Food and beverages (89)
Somalia	Food (89)
Rhodesia	Food (12)
Sudan	Textiles and clothing (27), food (21), beverages (14)
Swaziland	Wood, wood products and furniture (57), food and beverages (37)
Tanzania	Textiles (22), food (21)
Togo	Textiles (37), beverages (33), food (20)
Tunisia	Food (19), industrial and other chemical products (13)
Zambia	Beverages and tobacco products (41), food (14)

Notes:
[a] Major sectors defined as accounting for at least 10% of total MVA (1970).
[b] Refers to shares of output.
Source: UNIDO figures.

Like growth in GDP per capita, MVA grew during 1970–6 at widely varying rates from country to country. Ten countries had negative rates of MVA growth, ranging to as low as minus 10·8%. Very high rates of MVA growth, over 10% to as high as 28·6% were achieved by Gabon, Libya, Swaziland, Nigeria, Congo, Mauritius, Tunisia, Botswana, Algeria and Mauritania.

II Structure of Industrial Production

For most African countries the structure of industrial production is relatively undiversified, consisting largely of food, beverages and textile manufactures (Table 20.3). As of 1970 food products accounted for more than 10% of MVA in each of twenty-two countries for which data were available and for ten of these countries food products were the largest component of MVA, ranging up to 89% of the total.[4] Beverages accounted for more than 10% of MVA in twelve of the twenty-two countries, while textiles accounted for at least 10%

Table 20.4   Growth rates of MVA, grouped by major ISIC division, in seventeen African countries, 1970–75 or latest available year^a (average annual growth, %)

Country	Food, beverages and tobacco products (ISIC 31)	Textiles, wearing apparel and leather industries (ISIC 32)	Wood and wood products (ISIC 33)	Paper and paper products, printing, and publishing (ISIC 34)	Chemical, petroleum, coal, rubber and plastic products (ISIC 35)	Non-metallic mineral products, except of petroleum and coal (ISIC 36)	Basic metal industries (ISIC 37)	Fabricated metal products, machinery and equipment (ISIC 38)	Other manufacturers (ISIC 39)
Burundi^b	24–34	16	-2		3			-1	
Congo	7–16	-4				-10	13	-27–0	
Ethiopia	6–10	7–19	2–7	-20–17	-9–41	-29–3	1	3–8	
Kenya	27	13–22	17–18	4–30	56	17		-16–13	
Libya Arab Republic	25–26	13	16–52	8	24–33	36		8–22	39
Madagascar	1–27	-4–25	6	0–19	3–9	-3–56		4–24	33
Malawi	-11–11	0–12	31–57		-5–7	0		13–35	
Mauritius	29–32	27	22	29	15			6–80	
Mozambique	-3–7	7–47	1–6	12–18	-35–33	4–13	11	2–45	8
Nigeria	8–21	-22–40	13–25	21–24	-64–29	-7–47	118	15–110	-1
Rwanda	17		17		84			13	63
Somalia	-17–4	43–67	36	34	205	41		81	61
Southern Rhodesia	9–18	14–25	4–14	13–14	14–24	12	4–27	7–19	-2
Swaziland	24		-50						
Tanzania	3–18	12–44	-20–16	31–86	90–113	6–15	69	2–47	58
Tunisia	9–17	15–25	15–17	11–16	-1–28		-1–19	19–35	6
Zambia	4–13	6–58	3–7	18–26	30–121		-2	17–46	30

Notes: ^a Within each two-digit ISIC division, the range of growth rates at the four-digit level is given. Terminal year is 1974 for Burundi, Madagascar, Nigeria, Rwanda, Somalia and Tanzania and 1973 for Congo, Malawi, Mozambique, Swaziland and Zambia.
^b Refers to output growth rates.
Source: UNIDO figures.

of MVA in ten countries. Tobacco products and clothing were important sectors for several countries.

Somewhat surprisingly, given Africa's resource endowment, manufacture of wood, wood products and furniture was important in only one country, Swaziland. Chemicals and petroleum refining were of importance in four countries, non-ferrous basic metals in two countries and in one country each (Burundi and Kenya respectively) metal products except machinery and transport equipment accounted for more than 10% of MVA.

Thus as of 1970 the structure of industrial production in Africa consisted largely of a limited range of traditional manufactures reflecting internal demand requirements and simple technologies with (probably) relatively high labour intensities. Some countries were producing more technologically

Table 20.5 *African gross fixed capital formation, wage bill and employment in industry, 1970 sectoral shares in total manufacturing, unweighted averages based on country samples*[a]

ISIC sector	1970 sectoral shares in total manufacturing, % (with number of countries in sample)		
	Gross fixed capital formation	Wage bill	Employment
3110	19 (13)	22 (22)	25 (21)
3130	11 (10)	9 (20)	6 (19)
3140	3 (8)	6 (16)	7 (17)
3210	16 (11)	15 (19)	19 (17)
3220	2 (8)	4 (15)	6 (16)
3230	1 (4)	1 (12)	1 (12)
3240	2 (5)	2 (13)	2 (14)
3310	2 (8)	4 (14)	7 (15)
3320	1 (8)	2 (17)	3 (17)
3410	6 (7)	2 (14)	2 (15)
3420	2 (9)	5 (17)	4 (18)
3510	15 (4)	2 (10)	1 (11)
3520	6 (6)	5 (13)	4 (14)
3530	3 (5)	2 (13)	0 (14)
3540	1 (6)	1 (14)	0 (14)
3550	1 (6)	2 (15)	1 (16)
3560	1 (5)	1 (11)	1 (12)
3610	0 (6)	0 (13)	0 (12)
3620	0 (5)	1 (13)	1 (13)
3690	13 (7)	5 (14)	5 (14)
3710	2 (7)	2 (14)	2 (15)
3720	1 (8)	1 (15)	1 (15)
3810	4 (10)	7 (18)	8 (17)
3820	1 (6)	2 (14)	1 (15)
3830	3 (8)	2 (16)	1 (17)
3840	3 (9)	5 (17)	4 (17)
3850	0 (8)	0 (16)	0 (15)
3900	2 (9)	1 (16)	1 (17)

Note:[a] Data shown are unweighted averages. The data should be considered as rough indicators only, since many countries and data for combined sectors are not included and proportional weighting has not been undertaken. Due to rounding shares may not equal 100 in total.

sophisticated goods such as machinery, but such products generally accounted for a small proportion of MVA (see Table 20A.4).

The picture is changing, however, as Table 20.4 shows. From 1970 to 1975 (or in some cases to 1973 or 1974) rates of growth in seventeen countries varied widely from sector to sector, ranging from -64% to 205%, and from country to country, but in general growth rates tended to be high. Moreover, for these countries rapid growth was not confined to any particular sector; both traditional manufactures and more technologically advanced manufactures grew at high rates in many cases. Such high growth rates may be somewhat misleading in terms of the average growth of manufacturing, for very high rates occurred only for types of manufactures starting from a low production base. Nevertheless, the table indicates increased diversification and the growing importance of non-traditional manufactures.

Particular importance is often attached in economic analysis to the role of manufactures such as fabricated metal products, machinery and electrical goods (ISIC 38) in the development process. It is argued that these have high growth potential, extensive linkages with other industries and help develop labour skills through 'learning by doing'. In most of the seventeen countries included in Table 20.4 growth rates in this sector tended to be high.

The size and growth of individual manufacturing sectors depends in part on the amount of investment in those sectors. Table 20.5 shows the sectoral composition of gross fixed capital formation in 1970. Together, food products, beverages, textiles, industrial chemicals and other non-metallic mineral products accounted for three-quarters of GFCF in 1970. The food and textile industries are also major contributors to wages and employment, accounting together for 37% of wages and 44% of employment in industries in 1970. Of the more technologically advanced industries fabricated metal products, except machinery and equipment, was the most important provider of wages (7% of total) and employment (8% of total).

III Trade in Manufactures

African trade in manufactures is characterized by a large and increasing imbalance of imports over exports. Table 20.6 shows that Africa's share in world exports of manufactures declined from 1·12% during 1970–1 to 0·60% during 1975–6. In comparison the share of developing Asia excluding the Middle East and centrally planned economies rose from 3·07% to 4·90%, the share of Middle Eastern countries rose from 0·25% to 0·46% and the shares of other groups of developing countries rose slightly.

These changes in export performance are analysed in Tables 20.7 and 20.8. Table 20.7 shows that from 1970–1 to 1975–6 exports of manufactures increased in all groups of developing countries outside the African region, which suffered a decline in exports of $2,842 million. In contrast *Asia excluding centrally planned and Middle Eastern countries, gained $10,063 million. Most of Africa's loss was due to a decline in exports of non-ferrous metals amounting to $2,180 million.

In Table 20.8 this decline in Africa's export performance is broken down into three effects: change in commodity composition, in market composition

Table 20.6   *Share in world exports of manufactures, by developing region and country group, 1970–1 and 1975–6 (%)*

Exporting area	Average share, 1970–1	Average share, 1975–6
Africa	1·12	0·60
Latin America	1·51	1·59
Asia Middle East	0·25	0·46
Other Asia[a]	3·07	4·90
OPEC countries	0·20	0·23
Centrally planned economies of Asia	0·57	0·62

Note:
[a] Including Oceania.

Source: UNIDO, based on *Monthly Bulletin of Statistics*, XXXII, 6 (June 1978); XXXI, 5 (May 1977); and XXX, 8 (August 1976) (United Nations publications).

and in competitiveness (a residual reflecting the difference between total change in exports and the commodity and market composition effects). The table shows that almost all of Africa's decline in export performance was due to decreasing competitiveness (especially in non-ferrous metals and other manufactures) and losses due to the composition of exports (declining demand for non-ferrous metals).

Table 20.9 breaks down exports of Africa and other developing regions into six stages of processing. For several food products – fish, cereals, sugar and coffee, tea and cocoa – the level of processing is higher on the whole for Africa than for the rest of the developing world, and is roughly equivalent for some others. Excluding food products, however, it appears that the level of processing of African exports is significantly less than that of other developing regions, especially for pulp and paper, leather and furs, wood and cork, textiles, non-metallic mineral products, chemicals and other goods. This indicates a potential for increasing the value of African exports through increased processing of those products now exported as raw materials or as semi-processed products.

In Table 20.10 value added, imports and exports of seven African countries are divided into four components: consumer non-durables, industrial supplies and intermediate goods, capital goods and consumer durables and other manufactures. Value added is largely composed of other manufactures and industrial supplies and intermediates. The composition of exports is rather similar to value added, but the largest component of imports is capital goods and consumer durables, thus indicating the foreign exchange effect of a lack of capital goods industries in Africa, while industrial supplies and intermediates and other manufactures are second and third, respectively, in importance.

Various trade indicators are given in Table 20A.4 by SITC group and country. Perhaps the most important indicator is the trade ratio, which can range from +1 in the case of complete export dominance (no imports) to −1 in the case of complete import dominance (no exports). It can be seen that, for manufactures trade as a whole, the ratio is negative for all thirty-six countries covered and close to -1 for many countries with the exceptions of Zambia (1970 only) and Zaire. Furthermore, all but two of the positive trade

Table 20.7 *Change in export performance in developing regions/country groups, 1970–1 to 1973–6 (million current US% f.o.b.)*

Developing region/country group	Textile yarns and fabrics	Clothing	Chemicals	Non-ferrous metals	Iron and steel	Metal products	Machinery and transport equipment	Other manufacturers	TOTAL
Africa	−127·0	—	−43·6	−2,179·6	—	—	−31·1	−460·4	−2,841·7
Latin America	212·0	201·1	532·2	−1,366·8	−75·0	—	715·1	249·4	468·0
Asian Middle East	16·7	—	417·1	—	—	—	358·9	380·0	1,172·7
Asia other than Middle East	372·8	2,576·6	297·8	18·0	288·6	237·9	3,461·9	2,809·1	10,062·7
OPEC countries	−76·9	—	439·6	—	—	—	−152·5	−15·8	194·4
Centrally planned Asia	129·5	243·8	21·5	48·0	−12·7	12·3	−2·2	−172·0	268·2

Source: UNIDO, based on United Nations, *Monthly Bulletin of Statistics*, XXX, 8 (August 1976); XXXI, 5 (May 1977); and XXXII, 6 (June 1978).

Table 20.8 *Factors affecting change in export performance in Africa, 1970–1 to 1975–6 (million current US% f.o.b.)*

	Textile yarns and fabrics	Clothing	Chemicals	Non-ferrous metals	Iron and steel	Metal products	Machinery and transport equipment	Other manu-facturers	TOTAL
Commodity composition effect	−84·5	—	33·0	−1,227·8	—	—	9·4	−45·4	−1,315·3
Market-composition effect	35·6	—	8·1	−172·0	—	—	35·4	117·2	24·3
Competitiveness effect	−78·1	—	−84·7	−779·8	—	—	−75·9	−532·2	−1,550·7
Change in performance (sum of effects)	−127·0	—	−43·6	−2,179·6	—	—	−31·1	−460·4	−2,811·7

Source: UNIDO, based on United Nations, *Monthly Bulletin of Statistics*, XXX, 8 (August 1976); XXXI, 5 (May 1977); and XXXII, 6 (June 1978).

Table 20.9 Proportions of exports of African countries (and other developing countries) in six stages of processing, 1975 (%)

Category	Processing stage[a]					
	1	2	3	4	5	6
Live animals	100·00 (100·00)	0·00 (0·00)	0·00 (0·00)	0·00 (0·00)	0·00 (0·00)	0·00 (0·00)
Meat	46·96 (69·24)	2·19 (0·84)	0·00 (0·00)	0·00 (0·00)	5·42 (3·15)	45·43 (26·77)
Dairy products	20·23 (11·16)	0·00 (0·00)	0·00 (0·00)	79·77 (88·84)	0·00 (0·00)	0·00 (0·00)
Fish	45·62 (89·22)	5·52 (2·61)	0·00 (0·00)	0·00 (0·00)	48·85 (8·17)	0·00 (0·00)
Cereals	38·06 (67·35)	56·45 (26·19)	0·00 (0·00)	3·64 (3·32)	0·04 (0·92)	1·81 (2·23)
Fruits and vegetables	78·52 (76·53)	1·04 (1·55)	0·00 (0·00)	9·81 (11·32)	0·00 (0·00)	10·64 (10·60)
Sugar	0·17 (1·13)	0·00 (0·00)	45·69 (75·91)	52·02 (20·97)	0·81 (1·05)	1·31 (0·95)
Coffee, tea, cocoa	90·59 (93·74)	0·00 (0·00)	0·06 (0·20)	8·71 (2·39)	0·44 (2·52)	0·20 (1·15)
Pulp and paper	0·01 (0·02)	29·36 (9·53)	0·00 (0·00)	11·23 (15·91)	59·40 (74·55)	0·00 (0·00)
Tobacco	89·90 (88·68)	0·24 (0·15)	0·00 (0·00)	0·35 (2·51)	9·85 (8·81)	0·00 (0·00)
Animal and vegetable oils and fat	41·65 (29·68)	17·01 (42·18)	9·44 (23·00)	0·62 (1·32)	47·40 (43·73)	0·64 (2·12)
Leather and furs	71·67 (12·60)	6·53 (0·01)	0·03 (0·05)	0·00 (0·00)	2·95 (3·55)	8·34 (41·62)
Rubber	86·06 (90·34)	22·62 (26·92)	0·00 (0·20)	1·37 (0·88)	0·32 (1·55)	5·68 (7·02)
Wood and cork	65·51 (44·23)	2·66 (5·50)	7·21 (21·93)	1·81 (3·29)	0·84 (3·63)	0·00 (0·00)
Glass	0·00 (0·00)	0·26 (0·07)	7·41 (16·64)	32·41 (12·83)	35·35 (40·19)	22·17 (24·84)
Textiles	62·55 (20·97)	0·00 (0·00)	11·51 (8·42)	8·51 (17·87)	3·32 (7·08)	13·83 (45·59)
Non-metallic minerals	59·83 (43·27)	67·34 (27·10)	32·69 (36·35)	6·25 (10·58)	0·37 (5·07)	0·87 (4·74)
Metals	29·14 (45·74)	2·05 (7·39)	0·02 (1·19)	0·76 (4·55)	1·12 (8·50)	1·61 (12·92)
Chemicals	81·16 (13·32)	0·00 (0·00)	3·48 (24·00)	8·13 (14·79)	3·37 (9·60)	1·81 (30·91)
Other goods	59·66 (19·51)	0·00 (0·00)	0·00 (0·00)	2·30 (9·15)	30·83 (24·43)	7·21 (46·91)
Machinery	0·00 (0·00)	0·00 (0·00)	0·00 (0·00)	0·00 (0·00)	0·00 (0·00)	100·00 (100·00)

Note: [a] Figures in parenthesis are for other developing countries.
Source: UNIDO figures.

Table 20.10 *Manufacturing value added, imports and exports by and use in selected African countries, 1975 (as % of total production or trade flow)*

Country	Consumer non-durables			Industrial supplies and intermediates			Capital goods and consumer durables			Other manufactures		
	Value added	Imports	Exports	Value added	Imports	Exports	Value added	Imports	Exports	Value added	Imports	Exports
Egypt	22	3	18	35	39	52	22	34	23	21	24	28
Ghana[a]	8	6	1	31	34	19	7	39	1	54	21	79
Ivory Coast[b]	11	8	2	32	27	34	11	44	10	46	21	54
Kenya[a]	19	7	4	25	34	27	22	37	3	34	22	66
Libyan Arab Republic[c]	20	12	—	25	21	—	9	15	—	46	22	100
Nigeria[a]	6	8	7	48	25	8	8	44	—	38	23	85
Tunisia[a]	18	7	20	31	24	43	8	48	4	43	21	33

Notes:
[a] Value added refers to 1971 instead of 1975.
[b] Value added refers to 1973 and imports and exports to 1974 instead of 1975.
[c] Imports and exports refer to 1971 instead of 1975.

Sources: UNIDO, based on *Yearbook of Industrial Statistics*, Vol. I, various issues; *Yearbook of International Trade Statistics*, Vol. I, various issues.

ratios for one-digit SITC groups are in group 6, manufactures classified chiefly by material, indicating exports based on local natural resources, rather than on the manufacturing process as such. Moreover it may be seen that the degree of import dominance increased from 1970 to the mid-1970s for most countries.

IV Conclusion: Africa's Contribution to Achieving the Lima Target

The rate of real industrial growth in Africa during the period 1970–6, about 5% per annum, must be judged as inadequate in terms of the development goals implied by the Lima target. This rate of growth allowed Africa to maintain its share in world industrial production at about 0·7% (Table 20.11), mainly because industrial growth in the developed market economy countries, which account for the bulk of world industry, was relatively low during the period, but meanwhile the non-African developing countries were able to increase their share from 6·6% to 8·0%, so that while these countries made progress toward achieving the Lima target, Africa did not.[5]

If Africa is to achieve its regional target of a 2% share in world industrial production by the year 2000 and thus meet its declared contribution to the Lima 25% target for the developing countries as a whole, it will need to maintain its share of Third World industrial production at a minimum of 8%. Table 20.11 indicates that from 1970 to 1976 Africa's share in Third World industrial production dropped from 9·4% to 8·2%.

To halt this trend Africa will need substantially to increase its rate of industrial growth in the future. Roughly a doubling of the current rate to about 10% annually will probably be required.

If such a growth rate is to be achieved, changes in the framework of policies affecting industrial development will be necessary in many African countries. In particular these changes will need to encourage greater saving and industrial investment, export of manufactures, foreign participation in industry, local processing of natural resources, improvements in technology, infrastructure, managerial skills and marketing arrangements and the restructuring of the

Table 20.11 *Shares of Africa, other developing countries and all developing countries in world manufacturing value added, 1970–6 (%)*

Year	Africa	Other developing countries	All developing countries
1970	0·69	6·64	7·33
1971	0·70	6·60	7·65
1972	0·70	7·10	7·80
1973	0·71	7·21	7·90
1974	0·72	7·54	8·26
1975	0·74	7·96	8·70
1976	0·71	7·96	8·67

Source: UNIDO, compiled from UNSO data. Based on prices in 1970 US $.

industrial product mix to achieve greater economic efficiency in the use of resources. Furthermore, the countries of Africa will need to co-ordinate closely policy changes with the aim of achieving greater regional co-operation in industrial development, especially with regard to assisting the least developed countries of the region.

Notes

1   All data given in this section are taken from appendix tables 20A.1, 20A.2 and 20A.3.
2   Excluding Djibouti and Reunion because of lack of data.
3   Constant 1970 dollars are used to facilitate comparisons among countries and over time. It should be noted, however, that this standard suffers from several technical difficulties, especially as the period covered was one of high inflation and widely fluctuating exchange rates. A more satisfactory, but more complex, method of comparison is being developed by the United Nations International Comparison Project. First results show per capita incomes of developing countries relative to developed countries to be considerably higher than those indicated by existing method of comparison.
4   In all but a few countries the share of food products in total manufacturing output was even larger than the share in MVA.
5   Based on 1970 prices. If based on 1975 prices, Africa's share in 1976 is 0·84% (0.86% in 1977) and the share of other developing countries equals 8·74% (8.84% in 1977).

Statistical Appendix

Table 20A.1 *General economic indicators, by country, 1976[a]*

Country	Population	Labour force	GDP	Manufacturing value added	Gross fixed capital formation	Exports of goods and services	Imports of goods and services
	(millions)			(constant 1970 US $m)			
Algeria	17·3	3·7	6,671·4	943·1	2,582·9	908·6	1,978·2
Angola	6·4	1·7	923·3	40·6	169·7	358·8	400·8
Benin	3·2	1·5	256·6	16·3	38·8	62·5	73·4
Botswana	0·7	0·3	226·9	14·7	50·0	80·7	139·0
Burundi	3·8	1·9	249·4	27·9	36·4	22·7	28·1
Cameroon	6·5	3·1	1,363·7	157·9	187·1	376·6	341·9
Cape Verde Island	0·3	0·1	24·8	–	–	–	–
Central African Empire	1·8	0·9	184·8	23·0	38·5	21·7	50·5
Chad	4·1	1·5	323·7	22·7	42·0	105·6	162·0
Comoro Islands	0·3	0·1	29·6	–	–	–	–
Congo	1·4	0·5	382·1	55·4	48·7	56·5	146·0
Egypt	38·0	10·5	8,206·9	1,740·3	1,303·0	2,005·3	2,483·2
Equatorial Guinea	0·3	0·1	58·5	2·8	10·2	35·1	33·2
Ethiopia	28·7	11·9	2,016·1	182·1	121·9	278·2	250·7
Gabon	0·5	0·3	769·1	58·2	549·4	220·8	456·1
Gambia	0·5	0·3	64·1	0·9	6·4	44·4	52·9
Ghana	10·3	3·7	2,309·2	167·0	451·7	762·9	608·1
Guinea	4·5	2·0	368·9	22·9	32·8	95·2	107·3
Guinea-Bissau	0·5	0·2	107·9	–	–	–	–
Ivory Coast	5·0	2·5	2,334·8	375·7	502·2	850·9	695·1
Kenya	13·8	5·2	2,120·3	327·6	350·4	539·2	425·3
Lesotho	1·1	0·6	113·6	–	11·8	13·4	109·1
Liberia	1·7	0·7	461·4	23·4	120·1	212·0	201·8
Libyan Arab Republic	2·5	0·6	6,206·2	185·7	1,233·6	1,186·6	3,218·8
Madagascar	8·3	4·0	889·9	121·1	113·3	165·2	129·1
Malawi	5·2	2·2	473·9	35·0	135·7	113·8	134·5
Mali	5·9	3·1	333·4	33·7	43·5	86·6	98·7
Mauritania	1·4	0·4	239·8	10·6	61·8	122·1	138·2
Mauritius	0·9	0·3	346·6	63·3	93·1	321·7	261·0
Morocco	17·8	4·6	4,674·6	573·1	1,242·5	719·8	1,447·2
Mozambique	9·4	3·6	1,470·6	113·5	129·0	260·1	194·1
Niger	4·7	1·4	476·8	26·1	42·6	91·4	122·5
Nigeria	64·8	24·7	12,289·0	1,192·8	5,005·4	2,287·7	5,409·5
Rhodesia	6·5	2·1	1,985·4	299·1	314·1	325·0	350·2
Rwanda	4·3	2·3	283·4	11·3	46·0	37·7	57·4
São Tomé and Principe	0·1	–	8·5	–	–	–	–

Table 20A.1   *General economic indicators, by country, 1976[a] (cont.)*

Country	Population	Labour force	GDP	Manufacturing value added	Gross fixed capital formation	Exports of goods and services	Imports of goods and services
	(millions)			(constant 1970 US $m)			
Senegal	5·1	1·9	1,085·9	151·5	119·4	384·9	468·1
Seychelles	0·1	–	18·3	–	–	–	–
Sierra Leone	3·1	1·2	433·5	53·6	46·9	96·0	104·6
Somalia	3·3	1·2	331·7	23·2	71·1	48·8	109·8
Sudan	16·1	5·8	2,261·8	240·7	307·5	526·7	551·0
Swaziland	0·5	0·2	215·5	40·8	51·3	141·5	123·3
Tanzania	15·6	6·5	1,659·6	173·4	308·3	403·6	323·1
Togo	2·3	1·0	270·9	18·7	67·5	55·7	111·3
Tunisia	5·7	1·4	2,486·2	291·1	629·7	516·6	754·6
Uganda	11·9	4·8	1329·9	94·7	78·9	170·8	209·9
Upper Volta	6·1	3·3	359·6	50·4	36·3	38·7	85·6
Zaire	25·6	10·7	2,218·0	196·1	638·4	1,316·6	1,058·4
Zambia	5·1	1·9	2,213·2	243·7	456·1	1,073·6	383·1
TOTAL AFRICA	381·0	142·9	73,826·4	8,445·7	17,914·2	17,528·9	24,477·0

Note: [a] 1975 for labour force data.
Source: UNIDO, compiled from UNSO and ILO data.

Table 20A.2   *General economic indicators, growth rates, by country, 1970–6[a]*

Country	Population	Labour force	GDP	Manufacturing value added	Gross fixed capital formation	Exports of goods and services	Imports of goods and services
	trend average annual growth rates (%)						
Algeria	3·22	2·84	7·22	11·09	11·13	–1·50	9·86
Angola	2·21	2·02	–8·95	–11·06	–5·64	–3·96	0·99
Benin	2·75	2·04	3·14	7·90	1·32	–4·74	–4·03
Botswana	3·34	2·09	16·23	11·94	10·14	14·05	11·86
Burundi	2·28	1·70	1·62	5·64	12·03	–0·50	2·30
Cameroon	1·85	1·37	4·30	3·66	5·90	9·58	4·11
Cape Verde Island	2·80	2·44	–4·35	–	–	–	–
Central African Empire	2·14	1·79	–1·42	–3·02	4·20	–9·91	0·53
Chad	2·08	1·48	3·32	–2·16	5·08	5·55	5·56
Comoro Islands	2·21	1·81	–0·05	–	–	–	–
Congo	2·56	2·04	7·07	15·20	–3·85	–6·74	3·40
Egypt	2·21	2·45	1·55	1·94	9·34	10·24	11·54

Table 20A.2   *General economic indicators, growth rates, by country, 1970–6[a]*
(cont.)

Country	Population	Labour force	GDP	Manu-facturing value added	Gross fixed capital formation	Exports of goods and services	Imports of goods and services
			trend average annual growth rates (%)				
Equatorial Guinea	1·64	1·52	–3·45	–0·11	–5·33	–0·33	3·58
Ethiopia	2·47	1·95	2·11	2·08	–7·78	5·29	4·47
Gabon	1·01	0·36	18·72	28·65	41·14	5·28	26·91
Gambia	2·57	1·25	6·63	–0·23	4·21	16·53	14·54
Ghana	2·93	2·06	0·95	–5·11	7·19	5·95	3·26
Guinea	2·43	1·73	2·39	1·20	7·13	5·65	4·39
Guinea-Bissau	1·54	1·02	3·02	–	–	–	–
Ivory Coast	2·58	1·86	7·33	9·66	8·63	6·61	5·59
Kenya	3·53	2·60	4·68	8·89	–0·62	1·80	–3·45
Lesotho	2·25	1·40	9·19	–	9·48	25·07	21·67
Liberia	2·30	1·54	1·64	7·55	6·26	–2·50	1·64
Libyan Arab Republic	4·04	2·41	10·58	21·22	11·01	–12·76	23·07
Madagascar	2·98	2·26	–0·19	2·29	–2·45	2·46	–5·34
Malawi	2·49	1·91	5·90	0·25	12·70	7·47	3·89
Mali	2·66	1·96	2·75	1·98	0·80	7·34	10·14
Mauritania	2·63	1·80	3·88	10·95	10·89	5·12	10·22
Mauritius	1·31	3·26	10·71	14·41	24·48	24·09	18·23
Morocco	3·00	2·78	5·31	5·80	16·91	–0·54	10·71
Mozambique	2·42	1·53	–3·67	–10·50	–12·19	4·84	–10·13
Niger	2·86	2·51	1·94	1·27	8·67	4·82	7·16
Nigeria	2·73	2·06	7·48	15·78	25·85	6·35	26·53
Rhodesia	3·52	2·67	4·94	–1·03	6·65	–6·88	–3·84
Rwanda	2·61	2·54	4·08	5·26	20·75	5·53	7·84
São Tomé and Principe	1·97	–	–10·84	–	–	–	–
Senegal	2·80	1·69	3·31	3·34	4·62	17·35	19·33
Seychelles	2·33	–	3·26	–	–	–	–
Sierra Leone	1·53	1·81	1·20	6·40	–1·70	–5·59	–5·16
Somalia	2·59	2·73	7·15	7·57	14·24	3·43	13·79
Sudan	2·44	2·74	–1·31	2·82	9·11	7·32	8·38
Swaziland	2·96	2·18	11·68	19·56	15·48	12·30	9·52
Tanzania	2·83	2·38	4·21	4·44	1·76	1·35	–2·85
Togo	2·49	2·10	0·17	–4·13	11·10	–8·56	0·03
Tunisia	2·43	2·30	9·07	12·74	13·20	7·08	11·86
Uganda	3·35	2·40	–0·10	–4·55	–12·69	–7·90	–3·85
Upper Volta	2·19	1·78	1·47	3·31	6·63	15·20	11·22
Zaire	2·77	1·87	2·78	3·10	6·15	7·28	2·56
Zambia	3·57	2·44	4·18	4·92	–0·90	1·96	–7·00
TOTAL AFRICA	2·69	2·14	4·39	5·34	11·36	2·31	10·33

Note: [a] 1970–75 for labour force data.
Source: UNIDO, compiled from UNSO and ILO data.

Table 20A.3 *General economic indicators, derived relationships, by country, 1976*

Country	GDP per capita (constant 1970 $)	Labour force/ population	MVA/ GDP	Gross fixed capital formation/ GDP %	Exports/ GDP	Imports/ GDP
Algeria	386	21·6	14·6	38·7	13·6	29·7
Angola	144	27·0	4·4	18·4	38·9	43·4
Benin	80	45·5	6·4	15·1	24·4	28·6
Botswana	324	47·1	6·5	22·0	35·6	61·3
Burundi	66	49·1	11·2	14·6	9·1	11·3
Cameroon	210	47·5	11·6	13·7	27·6	25·1
Cape Verde Island	83	29·0	–	–	–	–
Central African Empire	103	54·6	12·4	20·8	11·7	27·3
Chad	79	37·2	7·0	13·0	32·6	50·0
Comoro Islands	99	38·0	–	–	–	–
Congo	273	33·8	14·5	12·7	14·8	38·2
Egypt	216	27·7	21·2	15·9	24·4	30·3
Equatorial Guinea	195	31·3	4·8	17·4	60·0	56·8
Ethiopia	70	41·5	9·0	6·0	13·8	12·4
Gabon	1,538	51·0	7·6	71·4	28·7	59·3
Gambia	128	51·2	1·4	10·0	69·3	82·5
Ghana	224	36·0	7·2	19·6	33·0	26·3
Guinea	82	45·3	6·2	8·9	25·8	29·1
Guinea-Bissau	216	33·2	–	–	–	–
Ivory Coast	467	50·5	16·1	21·5	36·4	29·8
Kenya	154	37·7	15·5	16·5	25·4	20·1
Lesotho	103	56·6	–	10·4	11·8	96·0
Liberia	271	38·5	5·1	26·0	45·9	43·7
Libyan Arab Republic	2,482	23·4	3·0	19·9	19·1	51·9
Madagascar	107	48·8	13·6	12·7	18·6	14·5
Malawi	91	43·3	7·4	28·6	24·0	28·4
Mali	57	53·2	10·1	13·0	26·0	29·6
Mauritania	171	28·4	4·4	25·8	50·9	57·6
Mauritius	385	33·3	18·3	26·9	92·8	75·3
Morocco	263	25·7	12·3	26·6	15·4	31·0
Mozambique	156	38·8	7·7	8·8	17·7	13·2
Niger	101	30·8	5·5	8·9	19·2	25·7
Nigeria	190	38·1	9·7	40·7	18·6	44·0
Rhodesia	305	32·9	15·1	15·8	16·4	17·6
Rwanda	66	52·4	4·0	16·2	13·3	20·3
São Tomé and Principe	85	–	–	–	–	–
Senegal	213	37·1	14·0	11·0	35·4	43·1
Seychelles	183	–	–	–	–	–
Sierra Leone	140	37·2	12·4	10·8	22·1	24·1

Table 20A.3   *General economic indicators, derived relationships, by country,*
1976 (cont.)

Country	GDP per capita (constant 1970 $)	Labour force/ population	MVA/ GDP	Gross fixed capital formation/ GDP %	Exports/ GDP	Imports/ GDP
Somalia	101	37·6	7·0	21·4	14·7	33·1
Sudan	140	35·8	10·6	13·6	23·3	24·4
Swaziland	431	44·2	18·9	23·8	65·7	57·2
Tanzania	106	41·6	10·4	18·6	24·3	19·5
Togo	118	41·4	6·9	24·9	20·6	41·1
Tunisia	436	23·9	11·7	25·3	20·8	30·3
Uganda	112	40·3	7·1	5·9	12·8	15·8
Upper Volta	59	53·7	14·0	10·1	10·8	23·8
Zaire	87	41·7	8·8	28·8	59·4	47·7
Zambia	434	36·9	11·0	20·6	48·5	17·3
TOTAL AFRICA	194	37·5	11·4	24·3	23·7	33·2

Source: UNIDO, compiled from UNSO and ILO data.

Table 20A.4 Manufacturing trade statistics, by SITC group and by country, 1970 to mid-1970s

| Country (with period covered) and SITC group[a] | 1970 (and mid-1970s) shares (%) of SITC group in total manufacturers trade (SITC 5–8) and 1970 values of total manufacturers trade (in $000) | | Adjusted average annual trade growth rates, 1970 to mid-1970s (%)[b] | | 1970 (and mid-1970s) trade ratio $((x-m)/(x+m))$ — varies from +1 complete export dominance to −1 (complete import dominance) |
	Exports	Imports	Exports	Imports	
Algeria 1970 and 1976					
5	5·8 (20·8)	10·2 (6·8)	9·8	9·7	−0·930 (−0·930)
6	68·3 (75·2)	38·8 (31·5)	−9·8	13·6	−0·798 (−0·945)
7	25·9 (4·0)	46·0 (58·1)	−34·8	22·2	−0·931 (−0·998)
8	— (—)	4·9 (3·6)	—	11·8	−1·000 (−1·000)
5–8	53,435	995,403	−11·2	17·6	−0·880 (−9·977)
Angola 1970 and 1974					
5	— (—)	13·6 (18·4)	—	12·3	−1·000 (−1·000)
6	95·7 (93·0)	27·5 (31·2)	−3·4	7·5	+0·042 (−0·170)
7	2·5 (6·6)	45·4 (43·8)	24·2	3·2	−0·996 (−0·930)
8	1·8 (0·3)	13·4 (6·7)	−36·9	−12·9	−0·921 (−0·978)
5–8	90,162	288,179	−2·7	4·2	−0·523 (−0·616)
Benin 1970 and 1974					
5	8·1 (1·4)	11·7 (12·6)	−29·0	15·9	−0·905 (−0·993)
6	59·0 (60·0)	50·1 (39·9)	10·1	7·5	−0·845 (−0·830)
7	25·8 (30·9)	27·4 (36·7)	14·6	22·3	−0·874 (−0·901)
8	7·0 (7·6)	10·8 (10·7)	11·8	13·6	−0·911 (−0·916)
5–8	3,488	48,256	9·3	13·7	−0·865 (−0·884)
Cameroon 1970 and 1976					
5	2·6 (5·0)	14·0 (15·9)	16·3	9·5	−0·927 (−0·896)
6	67·4 (72·9)	36·6 (30·0)	5·2	3·8	−0·444 (−0·410)
7	15·9 (9·2)	39·2 (45·4)	−5·2	9·9	−0·843 (−0·932)
8	14·1 (12·8)	10·2 (8·7)	2·3	4·4	−0·555 (−0·593)
5–8	41,071	196,620	3·9	5·2	−0·654 (−0·706)

Table 20A.4 *Manufacturing trade statistics, by SITC group and by country, 1970 to mid-1970s (cont.)*

Country (with period covered) and SITC group[a]	1970 (and mid-1970s) shares (%) of SITC group in total manufacturers trade (SITC 5–8) and 1970 values of total manufacturers trade (in $000)		Adjusted average annual trade growth rates, 1970 to mid-1970s (%)[b]		1970 (and mid-1970s) trade ratio $(x-m)/(x+m)$ — varies from +1 complete export dominance to −1 (complete import dominance)
	Exports	Imports	Exports	Imports	
Central African Empire 1970 and 1976					
5	4·2 (1·3)	12·0 (12·8)	−26·3	1·8	−0·685 (−0·948)
6	93·9 (98·7)	32·2 (34·1)	−10·2	1·7	+0·219 (−0·148)
7	1·4 (—)	44·8 (42·2)	—	−0·3	−0·968 (−1·000)
8	0·5 (—)	11·0 (10·8)	—	0·4	−0·950 (−1·000)
5–8	13,544	25,315	−10·9	0·7	−0·303 (−0·592)
Chad 1970 and 1974					
5	— (24·9)	14·6 (17·7)	32·6	6·5	−1·000 (−0·942)
6	24·1 (47·8)	33·4 (31·5)	−8·0	−0·0	−0·979 (−0·937)
7	59·1 (27·2)	39·3 (41·1)	—	2·6	−0·957 (−0·972)
8	16·8 (—)	12·7 (9·7)	—	−5·1	−0·962 (−1·000)
5–8	477	32,948	11·7	1·5	−0·971 (−0·958)
Congo 1970 and 1976					
5	31·9 (72·4)	11·4 (9·7)	24·9	7·3	−0·277 (+0·169)
6	63·5 (11·1)	33·5 (32·5)	−18·6	11·3	−0·447 (−0·880)
7	4·6 (16·5)	43·0 (45·6)	10·2	34·7	−0·958 (−0·873)
8	— (—)	12·2 (12·2)	—	10·2	−1·000 (−1·000)
5–8	8,882	44,031	8·9	10·2	−0·664 (−0·684)
Egypt 1970 and 1977					
5	7·3 (12·0)	22·8 (15·7)	13·4	17·3	−0·743 (−0·792)
6	74·0 (69·0)	27·5 (27·3)	4·5	23·7	+0·110 (−0·445)
7	2·9 (0·8)	46·7 (51·8)	−11·8	25·6	−0·944 (−0·995)
8	15·8 (18·1)	3·0 (5·2)	7·7	34·1	+0·422 (−0·307)
5–8	206,951	447,049	5·6	23·8	−0·367 (−0·736)

Table 20A.4 Manufacturing trade statistics, by SITC group and by country, 1970 to mid-1970s (cont.)

| Country (with period covered) and SITC group[a] | 1970 (and mid-1970s) shares (%) of SITC group in total manufacturers trade (SITC 5–8) and 1970 values of total manufacturers trade (in $000) | | Adjusted average annual trade growth rates, 1970 to mid-1970s (%)[b] | | 1970 (and mid-1970s) trade ratio ($(x-m)/(x+m)$) — varies from +1 complete export dominance to −1 (complete import dominance) |
	Exports	Imports	Exports	Imports	
Ethiopia 1970 and 1976					
5	40·4 (4·0)	8·6 (19·9)	−23·6	18·8	−0·897 (−0·992)
6	59·6 (24·4)	31·7 (26·1)	−3·4	0·0	−0·958 (−0·965)
7	– (60·6)	43·4 (44·0)	–	3·5	−1·000 (−0·949)
8	– (10·9)	10·5 (9·9)	–	2·3	−1·000 (−0·902)
5–8	1,599	138,530	12·2	3·3	−0·977 (−0·963)
Gabon 1970 and 1976					
5	– (–)	8·5 (8·1)	–	25·9	−1·000 (−1·000)
6	91·6 (100.0)	34·3 (39·9)	−4·4	30·1	−0·392 (−0·871)
7	8·4 (–)	47·1 (43·1)	–	25·0	−0·943 (−1·000)
8	– (–)	10·1 (8·9)	–	24·2	−1·000 (−1·000)
5–8	10,776	65,792	−5·8	26·9	−0·719 (−0·946)
Gambia 1970 and 1975					
5	–	10·5 (14·7)	–	18·6	−1·000 (−1·000)
6	–	54·8 (48·6)	–	8·3	−1·000 (−1·000)
7	–	22·5 (21·4)	–	9·8	−1·000 (−1·000)
8	–	12·2 (15·3)	–	16·0	−1·000 (−1·000)
5–8	–	13,409	–	10·9	−1·000 (−1·000)
Ghana 1970 and 1975					
5	– (–)	22·8 (21·7)	–	4·7	−1·000 (−1·000)
6	96·9 (96·5)	34·5 (36·5)	−3·3	6·9	−0·504 (−0·667)
7	3·1 (3·5)	37·0 (36·7)	−0·5	5·5	−0·981 (−0·986)
8	– (–)	5·6 (5·1)	–	3·7	−1·000 (−1·000)
5–8	33,590	286,163	−3·2	5·7	−0·790 (−0·859)

Table 20A.4 *Manufacturing trade statistics, by SITC group and by country, 1970 to mid-1970s (cont.)*

Country (with period covered) and SITC group[a]	1970 (and mid-1970s) shares (%) of SITC group in total manufacturers trade (SITC 5–8) and 1970 values of total manufacturers trade (in $000)		Adjusted average annual trade growth rates, 1970 to mid-1970s (%)[b]		1970 (and mid-1970s) trade ratio $((x-m)/(x+m))$ — varies from +1 complete export dominance to −1 (complete import dominance)
	Exports	Imports	Exports	Imports	
Ivory Coast 1970 and 1977					
5	10·1 (13·7)	9·7 (10·5)	24·0	16·4	−0·813 (−0·723)
6	66·3 (54·3)	38·1 (31·2)	15·3	12·0	−0·806 (−0·648)
7	16·7 (21·6)	42·3 (50·2)	23·1	18·0	−0·924 (−0·900)
8	7·0 (10·5)	9·8 (8·1)	25·7	12·0	−0·868 (−0·725)
5–8	30,062	300,662	18·7	15·2	−0·818 (−0·781)
Kenya 1970 and 1977					
5	39·5 (29·7)	13·3 (17·4)	12·4	13·0	−0·616 (−0·627)
6	47·6 (55·6)	32·9 (26·3)	19·7	5·3	−0·793 (−0·558)
7	2·0 (5·8)	43·7 (48·0)	36·1	10·2	−0·993 (−0·968)
8	10·9 (8·9)	10·1 (8·3)	13·9	5·7	−0·842 (−0·748)
5–8	24,953	312,404	17·1	8·7	−0·852 (−0·763)
Liberia 1970 and 1975					
5	27·3 (51·4)	8·8 (9·8)	7·2	11·2	−0·781 (−0·814)
6	24·2 (8·5)	34·3 (31·9)	−23·5	7·2	−0·946 (−0·990)
7	32·4 (36·7)	45·4 (48·3)	−3·2	10·1	−0·945 (−0·971)
8	16·2 (3·5)	11·5 (10·0)	−30·4	5·8	−0·895 (−0·986)
5–8	4,344	110,105	−5·5	8·8	−0·924 (−0·962)
Libyan Arab Republic 1970 and 1976					
5	— (—)	8·0 (4·8)	—	16·6	−1·000 (−1·000)
6	— (—)	29·5 (35·1)	—	30·3	−1·000 (−1·000)
7	— (—)	40·9 (42·3)	—	27·3	−1·000 (−1·000)
8	— (—)	21·6 (17·7)	—	22·5	−1·000 (−1·000)
5–8	—	401,655	—	26·6	−1·000 (−1·000)

Table 20A.4 Manufacturing trade statistics, by SITC group and by country, 1970 to mid-1970s (cont.)

Country (with period covered) and SITC group[a]	1970 (and mid-1970s) shares (%) of SITC group in total manufacturers trade (SITC 5–8) and 1970 values of total manufacturers trade (in $000)		Adjusted average annual trade growth rates, 1970 to mid-1970s (%)[b]		1970 (and mid-1970s) trade ratio ($(x-m)/(x+m)$)— varies from +1 complete export dominance to −1 (complete import dominance)
	Exports	Imports	Exports	Imports	
Madagascar **1970 and 1975**					
5	31·1 (16·8)	16·4 (20·4)	−14·2	9·8	−0·732 (−0·914)
6	29·1 (71·1)	34·3 (35·2)	16·0	5·6	−0·871 (−0·801)
7	28·4 (6·6)	38·5 (36·8)	−27·4	4·2	−0·887 (−0·980)
8	11·4 (5·5)	10·8 (7·6)	−16·1	−2·1	−0·841 (−0·923)
5–8	10,852	133,052	−2·9	5·1	−0·849 (−0·896)
Malawi **1970 and 1976**					
5	4·7 (16·8)	11·6 (15·5)	13·1	13·2	−0·927 (−0·927)
6	17·6 (35·2)	35·7 (35·6)	2·8	7·7	−0·912 (−0·933)
7	62·4 (10·0)	41·7 (41·0)	−32·5	7·5	−0·756 (−0·983)
8	15·2 (38·1)	10·9 (7·9)	6·7	2·2	−0·771 (−0·712)
5–8	5,739	61,672	−8·4	7·8	−0·830 (−0·932)
Mali **1970 and 1976**					
5	4·0 (1·2)	16·2 (18·6)	−36·4	19·0	−0·935 (−0·998)
6	79·5 (54·8)	36·2 (29·1)	−26·8	12·1	−0·537 (−0·955)
7	1·5 (35·6)	37·8 (45·0)	31·7	19·7	−0·989 (−0·981)
8	15·0 (8·4)	9·8 (7·3)	−29·3	10·7	−0·653 (−0·972)
5–8	3,420	24,936	−22·2	16·3	−0·759 (−0·976)
Mauritania **1970 and 1975**					
5	– (–)	9·5 (6·2)	–	3·6	−1·000 (−1·000)
6	57·4 (87·1)	27·9 (27·0)	22·3	12·4	−0·923 (−0·884)
7	42·6 (2·6)	55·9 (57·8)	−35·6	13·8	−0·971 (−0·998)
8	– (10·3)	6·7 (9·0)	–	19·9	−1·000 (−0·957)
5–8	739	37,878	12·5	13·0	−0·962 (−0·963)

Table 20A.4 Manufacturing trade statistics, by SITC group and by country, 1970 to mid-1970s (cont.)

Country (with period covered) and SITC group[a]	1970 (and mid-1970s) shares (%) of SITC group in total manufacturers trade (SITC 5–8) and 1970 values of total manufacturers trade (in $000)		Adjusted average annual trade growth rates, 1970 to mid-1970s (%)[b]		1970 (and mid-1970s) trade ratio ($(x-m)/(x+m)$) — varies from +1 complete export dominance to −1 complete import dominance)
	Exports	Imports	Exports	Imports	
Mauritius 1970 and 1975					
5	– (–)	20·8 (14·6)	–	17·3	−1·000 (−1·000)
6	55·6 (8·0)	41·6 (39·7)	15·1	24·6	−0·886 (−0·922)
7	21·5 (29·8)	24·3 (34·9)	81·2	35·2	−0·923 (−0·705)
8	22·9 (62·2)	13·3 (10·8)	107·4	20·5	−0·856 (+0·080)
5–8	1,868	41,236	69·7	25·8	−0·913 (−0·663)
Morocco 1970 and 1976					
5	20·6 (17·7)	13·0 (11·5)	15·1	12·6	−0·692 (−0·655)
6	55·1 (42·0)	33·8 (29·1)	12·8	12·0	−0·684 (−0·672)
7	4·7 (1·5)	48·4 (54·9)	−2·6	17·2	−0·978 (−0·993)
8	19·6 (38·9)	4·8 (4·5)	32·3	13·6	−0·360 (+0·079)
5–8	51,427	446,749	18·0	14·8	−0·794 (−0·761)
Niger 1970 and 1975					
5	– (–)	9·4 (8·2)	–	−4·5	−1·000 (−1·000)
6	43·8 (34·3)	49·0 (37·0)	38·4	−7·3	−0·965 (−0·769)
7	50·7 (59·1)	35·6 (48·5)	49·8	4·3	−0·945 (−0·707)
8	5·5 (6·6)	6·0 (6·3)	50·8	−1·1	−0·965 (−0·742)
5–8	854	43,350	45·3	−2·0	−0·961 (−0·753)
Nigeria 1970 and 1976					
5	– (–)	13·9 (9·1)	–	21·6	−1·000 (−1·000)
6	100·0 (100·0)	35·5 (27·2)	−10·3	24·8	−0·704 (−0·953)
7	– (–)	44·4 (54·7)	–	35·1	−1·000 (−1·000)
8	– (–)	6·2 (8·9)	–	38·6	−1·000 (−1·000)
5–8	54,684	891,324	−10·3	30·5	−0·884 (−0·987)

Table 20A.4 Manufacturing trade statistics, by SITC group and by country, 1970 to mid-1970s (cont.)

Country (with period covered) and SITC group[a]	1970 (and mid-1970s) shares (%) of SITC group in total manufacturers trade (SITC 5–8) and 1970 values of total manufacturers trade (in $000)		Adjusted average annual trade growth rates, 1970 to mid-1970s (%)[b]		1970 (and mid-1970s) trade ratio ($(x-m)/(x+m)$) — varies from +1 complete export dominance to −1 (complete import dominance)
	Exports	Imports	Exports	Imports	
Rwanda 1970 and 1976					
5	—	11·1 (6·8)	—	3·7	−1·000 (−1·000)
6	—	51·8 (44·8)	—	10·0	−1·000 (−1·000)
7	—	26·3 (38·5)	—	20·1	−1·000 (−1·000)
8	—	10·7 (9·9)	—	11·2	−1·000 (−1·000)
5–8	—	19,443	—	12·7	−1·000 (−1·000)
Senegal 1970 and 1975					
5	11·8 (15·0)	13·5 (17·0)	34·6	29·7	−0·628 (−0·568)
6	50·1 (37·5)	37·5 (37·6)	21·1	23·8	−0·484 (−0·525)
7	21·5 (32·7)	39·9 (37·1)	39·6	22·0	−0·754 (−0·569)
8	16·6 (14·8)	9·1 (8·2)	25·6	21·4	−0·356 (−0·279)
5–8	31,069	119,308	28·4	23·8	−0·587 (−0·524)
Sierra Leone 1970 and 1974					
5	—	9·3 (10·2)	—	6·5	−1·000 (−1·000)
6	100·0 (100·0)	39·5 (41·2)	−3·6	5·2	+0·324 (+0·158)
7	—	37·9 (34·2)	—	1·5	−1·000 (−1·000)
8	—	13·3 (14·4)	—	6·2	−1·000 (−1·000)
5–8	61,148	79,098	−3·6	4·1	−0·128 (−0·277)
Somalia 1970 and 1975					
5	—	12·5 (10·9)	—	20·9	−1·000 (−1·000)
6	2·8 (1·3)	43·9 (34·6)	−11·0	18·4	−0·992 (−0·998)
7	83·0 (86·2)	30·7 (47·8)	4·9	35·7	−0·707 (−0·910)
8	14·2 (12·6)	12·9 (6·7)	1·5	9·0	−0·869 (−0·906)
5–8	1,544	24,284	4·1	24·2	−0·880 (−0·949)

Table 20A.4 Manufacturing trade statistics, by SITC group and by country, 1970 to mid-1970s (cont.)

Country (with period covered) and SITC group[a]	1970 (and mid-1970s) shares (%) of SITC group in total manufacturers trade (SITC 5–8) and 1970 values of total manufacturers trade (in $000)		Adjusted average annual trade growth rates, 1970 to mid-1970s (%)[b]		1970 (and mid-1970s) trade ratio ($(x-m)/(x+m)$) – varies from +1 complete export dominance to –1 (complete import dominance)
	Exports	Imports	Exports	Imports	
Sudan 1970 and 1975					
5	–	15·7 (16·7)	–	22·2	–1·000 (–1·000)
6	– (–)	39·0 (39·9)	–	21·3	–1·000 (–1·000)
7	100·0 (100·0)	39·6 (40·0)	23·6	21·0	–0·978 (–0·975)
8	– (–)	5·7 (3·4)	–	9·1	–1·000 (–1·000)
5–8	935	208,668	23·6	20·7	–0·991 (–0·990)
Tanzania, United Republic of 1970 and 1976					
5	5·9 (11·7)	10·9 (14·6)	9·3	6·5	–0·867 (–0·847)
6	94·1 (88·3)	32·6 (31·0)	–3·6	0·7	–0·477 (–0·546)
7	– (–)	48·8 (50·0)	–	1·9	–1·000 (–1·000)
8	– (–)	7·8 (4·4)	–	–7·8	–1·000 (–1·000)
5–8	29,632	224,419	–2·6	1·5	–0·767 (–0·783)
Togo 1970 and 1975					
5	10·3 (6·4)	9·8 (12·2)	1·8	21·8	–0·864 (–0·942)
6	51·8 (74·3)	49·7 (44·1)	20·6	13·8	–0·865 (–0·824)
7	36·1 (11·2)	32·1 (35·1)	–11·2	18·6	–0·856 (–0·964)
8	1·8 (8·1)	8·4 (8·6)	51·8	17·2	–0·971 (–0·898)
5–8	3,091	44,669	12·2	16·6	–0·871 (–0·892)

Table 20A.4 *Manufacturing trade statistics, by SITC group and by country, 1970 to mid-1970s (cont.)*

Country (with period covered) and SITC group[a]	1970 (and mid-1970s) shares (%) of SITC group in total manufacturers trade (SITC 5–8) and 1970 values of total manufacturers trade (in $000)		Adjusted average annual trade growth rates, 1970 to mid-1970s (%)[b]		1970 (and mid-1970s) trade ratio $(x-m)/(x+m)$ — varies from +1 complete export dominance to –1 (complete import dominance)
	Exports	Imports	Exports	Imports	
Uganda 1970 and 1976					
5	– (–)	13·9 (15·2)	–	–12·8	–1·000 (–1·000)
6	100·0 (100·0)	34·8 (27·4)	–20·7	–17·4	–0·265 (–0·375)
7	– (–)	39·7 (49·1)	–	–10·9	–1·000 (–1·000)
8	– (–)	11·6 (8·3)	–	–18·7	–1·000 (–1·000)
5–8	21,183	104,918	–20·7	–14·0	–0·664 (–0·779)
Upper Volta 1970 and 1975					
5	– (–)	11·8 (19·2)	–	32·1	–1·000 (–1·000)
6	61·5 (68·1)	38·6 (34·5)	22·9	17·2	–0·918 (–0·898)
7	26·7 (16·9)	42·0 (38·1)	9·8	17·5	–0·967 (–0·976)
8	11·9 (15·0)	7·7 (8·2)	26·3	21·4	–0·920 (–0·904)
5–8	810	30,285	20·4	19·8	–0·948 (–0·947)
Zaire 1970 and 1975					
5	– (–)	11·3 (14·9)	–	9·6	–1·000 (–1·000)
6	100·0 (99·1)	33·5 (32·2)	–5·2	2·9	+0·633 (+0·494)
7	– (–)	45·4 (44·2)	–	3·2	–1·000 (–0·963)
8	– (0·9)	9·8 (8·7)	–	1·4	–1·000 (–1·000)
5–8	599,369	402,044	–5·1	3·7	+0·197 (–0·022)
Zambia 1970 and 1975					
5	– (–)	9·9 (17·2)	–	19·6	–1·000 (–1·000)
6	100·0 (100·0)	28·4 (32·2)	–9·6	9·8	+0·807 (+0·560)
7	– (–)	50·1 (44·2)	–	4·5	–1·000 (–1·000)
8	– (–)	11·6 (6·4)	–	–4·8	–1·000 (–1·000)
5–8	982,467	368,285	–9·6	7·1	+0·455 (+0·065)

Notes: [a] SITC 5: chemicals; 6: manufactures classified chiefly by material; 7: machinery and transport equipment; 8: miscellaneous manufactures; 5–8: total manufactures.
[b] Based on mid-1970s current values corrected to 1970 values using a world trade inflation index (source: *Monthly Bulletin of Statistics*, June 1978). Deflators used were: SITC, 5: 1·49 (1974), 1·34 (1975), 1·58 (1976–7); SITC 6: 1·42 (1974); 1·31 (1975), 1·51 (1976–7); SITC 7: 1·44 (1974), 1·43 (1975), 1·62 (1976–7).
Source: UN Yearbook of International Trade Statistics, 1972–3, 1974, 1975 and 1976; *Monthly Bulletin of Statistics,* June 1978.

A Select Bibliography

ROBIN FINCHAM

The criterion for inclusion of items pertains primarily to manufacturing and related activities within industrialization. Other areas have been excluded, such as class formation, industrial relations and government planning (development plans, surveys of industry, etc.). Additionally, some topics which may contain information on industry, such as multinational corporations, investment, the informal sector and studies in economics and economic history, have been covered only partially. All items have appeared since 1960. With the exception of Zambia, items deal only with those countries represented in articles in this book, which means that most of the countries in Africa south of the Sahara with significant industrial sectors have been included.

Africa

Agodo, O., 'The determinants of US private manufacturing investment in Africa', PhD, Northwestern University, 1976
Agodo, O., 'Determinants of US private manufacturing investments in Africa', *Journal International Business Studies*, 9, 3 (1978), 95-107
Andriamananjara, R., 'Relating industrialization in Africa to people's needs', *International Labour Review*, 117, 6 (1978), 757–60
Bailey, R., *Africa's Industrial Future* (Boulder, Co: Westview, 1978)
Battian, N., 'Le développement récent de l'industrie textiles dans les pays africains et malgache de la zone franc', *Cah. d'Outre-Mer*, 25, 98 (1972), 121–41
Benner, R. F., 'International subcontracting and industrial development in Africa', PhD, University of Kentucky, 1972
Bhagavan, M. R., 'Choice of scale in basic materials industries for African countries', Scandinavian Institute of African Studies, Uppsala, 1978
Cadribo, A. R., 'The problem of organizational control: parastatals', *Taamuli*, 5, 2 (1977), 49–61
Dinwiddy, B., *Promoting African Enterprise* (London: ODI, 1974)
Ewing, A. F., 'Industrialization and the UN Economic Commission for Africa', *Journal of Modern African Studies*, 2, 3 (1964), 351–63
Ewing, A. F., *Industry in Africa* (London: Oxford University Press, 1968)
Fieldhouse, D. K., *Unilever Overseas* (London: Croom Helm, 1978)
Garmany, J. W., 'Enterprise management and organisation in Africa: a plea for research', *Journal of Modern African Studies*, 9, 4 (1971), 634–9

International Labour Office, *Symposium on Small Enterprise Development Schemes in Africa – Abidjan, 1977* (Geneva: ILO, 1977)

Kamarck, A. M., *The Economics of African Development* (London: Pall Mall, 1967), esp. ch. 7: 'Industrialization'

Kaplinsky, R., 'Control and transfer of technology agreements', *IDS Bull.*, 6, 4 (1975), 53–64

Kobrin, S. J., 'Multinational corporations, sociocultural dependence, and industrialization: need satisfaction or want creation?', *Journal Developing Areas*, 13, 2 (1979), 109–25

Langdon, S., 'Technology transfer by MNCs in Africa', *African Development*, 2, 2 (1977), 95–114

Luney, P. R., 'Development of an iron-based and steel-based metallurgical industry in sub-Sahara Africa', *Review Black Political Economy*, 5, 4 (1975), 404–22

Marcus, E. and M., *Investment and Development Possibilities in Tropical Africa* (New York: Bookman, 1960), esp. Ch. 6: 'Industrial development'

Marris, P., 'The social barriers to African entrepreneurship', *Journal Development Studies*, 5, 1 (1968), 29–38

Marris, P. and Somerset, A., *African Businessmen* (Nairobi: East African Publishing House, 1971)

Mosley, P., review of *Industrial Decentralisation in South Africa* (Bell), *Industries in Southern African Periphery* (Selwyn), *Industrial Diversification in Zambia* (Young) and *Underdevelopment and Industrialisation in Tanzania* (Rweyemamu), *Journal of Modern African Studies*, 14, 3 (1976), 543–6

Pearson, D. S., 'African advancement in commerce and industry', *Journal of Modern African Studies*, 3, 2 (1965), 231–47

Pickett, J., 'The choice of industrial technology in African economies', *Economic Bulletin for Africa* (UN), 10, 2 (1974), 1–24

Rood, L. L., 'Foreign investment in African manufacturing', *Journal of Modern African Studies*, 13, 2 (1975), 19–34

Schamp, E. W., *Industrialisierung in Äquatorialafrica* (Munich: Weltforum, 1978)

Seers, D., 'The lessons for Africa of Latin American industrialization politics', Conference on Strategies for Economic Development: Africa and Latin America, IDEP, Dakar, September 1972

Thomas, C. Y., 'Industrialization and the transformation of Africa: an alternative strategy to MNCs', in Widstrand, C. (ed.), *Multinational Firms in Africa* (Uppsala: Scandinavian Institute of African Studies, 1975)

Toure, M. A. F., 'Perspectives de l'industrialization et marchés africaines', *Présence Africaine*, 86 (1973), 68–85

United Nations, *Industrial Growth in Africa, a Survey and Outlook* (New York: UN Economic Commission for Africa, 1962)

United Nations, *Industrial Growth in Africa* (New York: UN Economic Commission for Africa, 1963)

United Nations, 'Industrialization and economic planning', *Economic Bulletin for Africa* (UN), 3 (1963), 55–65)

United Nations, 'Analysis of future production possibilities of selected African industries', *Economic Bulletin for Africa* (UN), 3 (1963) 66–83

United Nations, 'Iron and steel industry in Africa', (New York: UN Economic Commission for Africa, 1964)

United Nations, *Economic Bulletin for Africa* (UN), 7, 1/2 (1968), special volume on industrialization; articles included on: general development, finance, building materials industry, chemicals and textiles

United Nations, 'Exports of primary commodities and semi-manufactured and manufactured products', *Economic Bulletin for Africa* (UN), 9, 1 (1969), 31–60

United Nations, 'Industrial growth in developing Africa from 1950 to 1968 and prospects for 1980', *Economic Bulletin for Africa* (UN), 10, 1 (1970), 1–13

Nigeria

Aboyade, O., 'The economy of Nigeria' in Robson, P. and Lury, D. A. (eds), *The Economies of Africa* (London: Allen & Unwin, 1969)

Aboyade, O., 'Approaches to industrialization: the cases of Mexico and Nigeria', Conference on Strategies for Economic Development: Africa and Latin America, IDEP, Dakar, September 1972

Adeboye, T. O., 'Public sector participation in manufacturing', paper read at annual conference of Nigeria Economic Society, Lagos, 1978

Adeyoju, S. K., 'The economic importance of Nigerian wood-based industries', *Nigerian Journal of Economic and Social Studies*, 11, 3 (1969), 309–26

Afonja, S., 'The participation of Nigerian women in industry', *Ife African Studies*, 1, 1 (1974), 39–41

Akeredolu-Ale, E. O., 'Nigerian enterpreneurs in the Lagos state', PhD thesis, University of London, 1970–1

Akeredolu-Ale, E. O., 'The "competitive threshold" hypothesis and Nigeria's industrialization process: a review article', *Nigerian Journal of Economic and Social Studies*, 14, 1 (1972), 93–108

Akeredolu-Ale, E. O., 'Environmental, organizational and group factors in the evolution of private indigenous entrepreneurship in Nigeria', *Nigerian Journal of Economic and Social Studies*, 14, 2 (1972), 237–56

Akeredolu-Ale, E. O., *The Underdevelopment of Indigenous Entrepreneurship in Nigeria* (Ibadan: Ibadan University Press, 1975)

Akeredolu-Ale, E. O., 'Private foreign investment and the underdevelopment of indigenous entrepreneurship in Nigeria', in Williams, G. (ed.), *Nigeria: Economy and Society* (London: Rex Collings, 1976)

Akinola, R. A., 'Factors affecting the location of a textile industry – example of Ikeja Textile Mill', *Nigerian Journal of Economic and Social Studies*, 7, 3 (1965), 245–56

Akintola, J. O., 'The pattern of growth in manufacturing in south-western Nigeria, 1956–1971 and the role of direct public policy in that growth', PhD thesis, University of Boston, 1975

Anschel, K. R., 'Problems and prospects of the Nigerian rubber industry', *Nigerian Journal of Economic and Social Studies*, 9, 2 (1967), 145–59

Awojinrin, J. E., 'British direct investment and economic development in Nigeria 1955–72', PhD thesis, University of Keele, 1974–5

Balogun, M. J. et al., *Managerial Efficiency in the Public Sector: Patterns and Problems in Nigeria* (Ife: University of Ife Press, 1979)

Bauer, P. Y. and Yamey, B. S., 'Industrialization and development – Nigeria experience', *Economic History Review*, 25, 4 (1972), 674–89

Berger, M., *Industrialization Policies in Nigeria* (Munich and Ibadan: IFO Institute für Wirtschaftsforschung München Abteilung Entwicklungsländer/ Afrikastudienstelle and Nigerian Institute for Social and Economic Research, 1975)

Callaway, A., 'From traditional crafts to small scale industry', *Odu*, 2, 1 (1965), 28–51

Callaway, A., 'Nigerian enterprise and the employment of youth', Nigerian Institute for Social and Economic Research, Ibadan, 1973

Camara, C., 'Industrialization in open economy – Nigeria, 1945–1966', *Annales de Geographie*, 81, 448 (1972), 774–6

Carlsen, J., 'Industrial cooperation in the Lomé Convention: the case of Nigeria', Project Paper D78.5, Centre for Development Research, Copenhagen, 1978

Collins, D. O., 'The role of government in the development of an indigenous private sector: the case of the Nigerian Enterprises Promotion Decree', University of East Africa Social Science Conference, 1973, Vol. I, 393–435

Collins, D. O., 'The Nigerian Enterprises Promotion Decree', *African Review*, 4, 4 (1974), 491–508

Collins, P., 'Public policy and the development of indigenous capitalism: the Nigerian experience', *Journal of Commonwealth and Comparative Politics*, 15 (1977)

Diaku, I., 'Non-corporate sector finance and financing of small industries in developing countries: the Nigerian experience', *Annals of Public and Co-operative Economy*, 48, 2 (1977), 207–26

Egwim, C. N., 'Import substitution in Nigeria', PhD thesis, University of Georgia, 1974

Ekuerhare, B., 'The economic appraisal of import-substituting industrialization with special reference to the Nigerian textile industry, PhD thesis, University of Manchester, 1978

Ekundare, R. O., 'The political economy of private investment in Nigeria', *Journal of Modern African Studies*, 10, 1 (1972), 37–56

Emmanuel, T., 'A comparative management study of industrial enterprises in Nigeria', PhD thesis, University of Missouri, 1978

Equere, I. U. and Longe, A. A., 'Rate of return on capital in Nigerian industries', *Economic and Financial Review* (Bank of Nigeria, Lagos), 13, 2 (1975)

Fabayo, J. A., 'An economic analysis of capacity utilization in selected Nigerian manufacturing industries, 1974–75', PhD thesis, University of Purdue, 1978

Fajana, O., 'Import licensing in Nigeria', *Development and Change*, 8, 4 (1977), 509–22

Faust, G., 'Small industries credit scheme in northern Nigeria', *Nigerian Journal of Economic and Social Studies*, 11, 2 (1969), 205–27

Frank, C. R., Jnr, 'Industrialization and employment generation in Nigeria', *Journal of Modern African Studies*, 9, 3 (1967), 277–97

Hakam, A. N., 'The motivation to invest and the location pattern of foreign private industrial investment in Nigeria', *Nigerian Journal of Economic and Social Studies*, 8, 1 (1966), 49–65

Hakam, A. N., 'Foreign industrial investments in Nigeria 1946–66', PhD thesis, New School for Social Research, New York, 1974

Harris, J. R., 'Industrial entrepreneurship in Nigeria', PhD thesis, Northwestern University, 1967

Hilton, A. C. E., 'Foreign investment in Nigeria: perceptions and reality', PhD thesis, University of Pennsylvania, 1973

Hoogvelt, A., 'Indigenisation and foreign capital: industrialization in Nigeria', *Review African Political Economy*, 14 (1979), 56–68

Idemudia, T. D. A., 'The performance of Nigerian indigenous entrepreneurs', PhD thesis SUNY-Buffalo, 1978

Iyanda, O., 'Impact of foreign direct investment in manufacturing on the Nigerian economy, PhD thesis, New York University, 1975

Iyaniwura, J. O., 'Production functions in Nigerian manufacturing industry', PhD thesis, University of Exeter, 1973–4

Kalu, G. K. I., 'Effective rates of protection and patterns of industrial growth in Nigeria, 1950–1970, PhD thesis, University of Wisconsin, 1972

Kilby, P., *African Enterprise: The Nigerian Bread Industry* (Stanford, Calif.: Hoover Institution Studies No. 8, 1965)

Kilby, P., 'Industrialization in Nigeria', D. Phil. thesis, Oxford, 1966–7

Kilby, P., *Industrialization in an Open Economy: Nigeria 1945–1960* (Cambridge: Cambridge University Press, 1969)

Langley, K. M., 'Production functions for Eastern Nigerian industry; a note', *Nigerian Journal of Economic and Social Studies*, 9, 3 (1967), 387–90

Lewis, A. O., 'A study of small enterprises in the printing industry in Nigeria's Lagos State', *Quarterly Journal Administration* (Ife), 8, 2 (1974)

Lewis, A. O., 'The development of small scale industries in Nigeria's North East State: prospects, problems and policies', *Savanna*, 3, 2 (1974), 185–95

Lewis, A. O., 'Indigenous entrepreneurship in Yaba industrial estate', *Odu*, 9 (1974), 45–63

Lewis, A. O., 'Small scale industries in Nigeria's former Western State', *Quarterly Journal Administration* (Ife), 12, 1 (1977), 29–43

Liedholm, C. E., 'Production functions for Eastern Nigerian industry', *Nigerian Journal of Economic and Social Studies*, 8, 3 (1966), 427–39

Lubeck, P. M., 'Early industrialization and social class formation among factory workers in Kano', PhD thesis, Northwestern University, 1975

Mabawonku, A. F., 'Incomes and factor productivity in Western Nigeria small-scale industries', *Development Economies*, 16, 3 (1978), 269–82

May, R. S., 'Direct overseas investment in Nigeria 1953–63', *Scottish Journal Political Economy*, 12, 3 (1965), 243–66

Nafziger, E. W., 'Nigerian entrepreneurship: a study of indigenous businessmen in the footwear industry', PhD thesis, University of Illinois, 1967

Nafziger, E. W., 'Inter-regional economic relations in the Nigerian footwear industry', *Journal of Modern African Studies*, 6, 4 (1968), 531–42

Nafziger, E. W., 'The relationship between education and entrepreneurship in Nigeria', *Journal Developing Areas*, 4, 3 (1970), 349–59

Nafziger, E. W., *African Capitalism: A Case Study in Nigerian Entrepreneurship* (Stanford, Calif.: Hoover Institute Press, 1977)

Nigerian Economic Society, *Nigeria's Indigenisation Policy* (Ibadan: Proceedings of Society's Symposium, 1975)

Ntamere, C. C., 'The feasibility of an integrated iron and steel industry in Nigeria and Biafra', PhD thesis, University of Notre Dame, 1970

Odufalu, J. O., 'Indigenous enterprise in Nigerian manufacture', *Journal of Modern African Studies*, 9, 4 (1971), 593–607

Ogbonna, M. N., 'Nigerian industrial strategy', *Asian Economic Review*, 17, 1/3 (1975), 25–34

Ogunpola, A., 'The Nigerian Enterprises Promotion Decree', *Ghana Social Science Journal*, 4, 1 (1977), 40–53

Ojo, E. F., 'Training for industrial development in Nigeria', *Manpower and Unemployment Research in Africa*, 7, 1 (1974), 69–82

Olaloye, A. O., 'Technology transfer and employment in Nigerian manufacturing industries', *Quarterly Journal Administration* (Ife), 12, 2 (1978), 167–76

Olayemi, J. K. and Abaelu, J. N., 'Estimates of the cost of protecting Nigeria's sugar manufacturing industry', *Nigerian Journal of Economic and Social Studies*, 16, 2 (1974), 203–16

Omopariola, O., 'The financing of manufacturing industry in Nigeria', PhD thesis, University of Bradford, 1978

Osagie, E. and Oyelabi, J. A., 'Net foreign exchange costs of manufacturing industries in Nigeria', *Economic Bulletin of Ghana*, 4, 2 (1974), 36–45

Osoba, S., 'The deepening crisis of the Nigerian national bourgeoisie', *Review African Political Economy*, 13 (1979), 63–77

Oyaide, W. J., 'The role of direct private foreign investment in Nigeria 1963–73', PhD thesis, Temple University, 1977

Oyejide, T. A., 'Tariff structure and industrialization in Nigeria, 1957–1967', PhD thesis, Princeton University, 1971

Oyejide, T. A., *Tariff Policy and Industrialization in Nigeria* (Ibadan: Ibadan University Press, 1975)

Oyelabi, J. A., 'Production functions and costs in Nigerian manufacturing industries', PhD thesis, Columbia University, 1970

Oyelabi, J. A., 'Tariffs, domestic prices and industrial growth in Nigeria', *Nigerian Journal of Economic and Social Studies*, 14, 2 (1972), 275–99

Peace, A., *Choice, Class and Conflict: A Study of Southern Nigerian Factory Workers* (Brighton: Harvester Press, 1979)

Quarterly Journal Of Administration (IFE), issue on indigenization, 9 (1975)

Ransom, B. H. A., 'Northern Nigerian managers: an African commercial elite', *Journal Administration Overseas*, 11, 1 (1972), 28–37

Rowe, M. P., 'Indigenous industrial entrepreneurship in Lagos, Nigeria', PhD thesis, Columbia University, 1971

Schatz, S. P., 'Economics, politics and administration in government lending', Regional Loans Board of Nigeria, Ibadan, 1970

Schatz, S. P., *Nigerian Capitalism* (Berkeley, Calif.: University of California Press, 1978)

Schatzl, L., *Industrialization in Nigeria: A Spatial Analysis* (Munich: 1973)

Simmons, E. B., 'The small scale rural food processing industry in N. Nigeria', *Food Research Institute Studies*, 14, 2 (1975), 147–62

Sokolski, A., 'The establishment of modern manufacturing industry in the Federation of Nigeria', PhD thesis, Columbia University, 1962

Sokolski, A., *The Establishment of Manufacturing in Nigeria* (New York: Praeger, 1965)

Teriba, O., 'Development strategy, investment decisions and expenditure patterns of a public development institution: the case of the Western Nigeria Development Corporation, 1949-62', *Nigerian Journal of Economic and Social Studies*, 8, 2 (1966), 235–58

Teriba, O., Edozien, E. C., and Kayode, M. O., *The Structure of Manufacturing Industry in Nigeria* (Ibadan: Ibadan University Press, forthcoming)

Teriba, O. and Kayode, M. O. (eds), *Industrial Development in Nigeria* (Ibadan: Ibadan University Press, 1977). An important collection of articles, mostly reprinted from the *Nigerial Journal of Economic and Social Studies*. The articles are not cited separately in this bibliography

Thomas, D. B., 'Technology transfer and capital accumulation in Nigerian manufacturing industries', PhD thesis, University of Indiana, 1973

Thomas, D. B., *Capital Accumulation and Technology Transfer: A Comparative Analysis of Nigerian Manufacturing Industries* (New York: Praeger Special Studies in International Economics and Development, 1975)

Traore, D.-M., 'Industrial growth and foreign trade in four West African Countries: Ghana, Nigeria, the Ivory Coast and Senegal', PhD thesis, University of Pittsburgh, 1969

Turner, T., 'The cement racket', *Africa Guide* (London), 1977

Turner, T., *Two Refineries: A Comparative Study of Technology Transfer* (The Hague: Institute of Social Studies, Occasional Paper 62, 1977)

Turner, T., 'Two refineries: comparative study of technology transfer to Nigerian refining industry', *World Development*, 5, 3 (1977), 235–56

Turner, T., 'Commercial capitalism in the 1975 coup', in Panter-Brick, K. (ed.), *Soldiers and Oil* (London: Cass, 1978)

Vielrose, E., 'Import and export substitution in Nigeria', *Nigerian Journal of Economic and Social Studies*, 10, 2 (1968), 183–90

Vielrose, E., 'Manufacturing industries in Nigeria: notes on profits, growth and capital utilization', *Nigerian Journal of Economic and Social Studies*, 12, 1 (1970), 141–51

Wells, F. A. and Warmington, W. A., *Studies in Industrialization: Nigeria and the Cameroons* (London: Oxford University Press for the Nigerian Institute of Social and Economic Research, 1962)

Williams, G., 'Colonialism and capitalism: the Nigerian case', African Studies Association (UK), conference, Liverpool, 1974

Williams, G., 'Nigeria: a political economy', in Williams, G. (ed.), *Nigeria: Economy and Society* (London: Rex Collings, 1976)

Williams, S., 'Start-up of a textile industry', *Nigerian Journal of Economic and Social Studies*, 4, 3 (1962), 247–56

Winston, G. C., 'Increasing manufacturing employment through fuller utilization of capacity in Nigeria', Geneva, ILO–WEP working paper

Wolgin, J. M., 'Manufacturing industry in Nigeria's third development plan', *Journal Modern African Studies*, 16, 4 (1978), 687–93

World Bank, *Nigeria: Options for Long-Term Development* (Baltimore, Md: Johns Hopkins University Press, 1974)

World Bank, 'An analysis of industrial incentives and location in Nigeria', Washington, DC 1978 (unpublished report, submitted to Federal Ministry of Industries, Lagos)

Wrigley, C. C., 'The development of state capitalism in late colonial and post-colonial Nigeria', African Studies Association (UK), conference, Liverpool, 1974

East Africa

Frank, C. R., Jnr, 'The production and distribution of sugar in East Africa', *East African Economic Review*, 10, 2 (1963), 96–110

Frank, C. R., Jnr, *The Sugar Industry in East Africa* (Nairobi: East African Studies No. 20 for Makerere Institute of Social Research, 1965)

Ghai, Y. P., 'East African industrial licensing system – device for regional allocation of industry', *Journal Common Market Studies*, 12, 3 (1974), 265–95

Grundmann, H. E., 'Industrial development in East Africa: an appraisal', Universities of East Africa Social Science Conference, Makerere, December 1971

Henning, P. H. and House, W. J., 'Slow employment growth in the manufacturing sector', *Journal Eastern African Research and Development*, 2 (1975)

Herman, B. M., 'Strategies of foreign manufacturing investment in poor countries: a general theory and an application to oil refining in East Africa', PhD thesis, University of Michigan, 1974

Kristensen, H. and Inukai, I., 'The rural industrial development programme: a case study', Universities of East Africa Social Science Conference, 1973, Vol. I, 301–24

Maitra, P., *Import-substitution potential in East Africa*, East African Institute of Social Research Occasional Paper 2 (Nairobi: Oxford University Press, 1967)

Massell, B. F., 'Industrialization and economic union in Greater East Africa', *East African Economic Review*, 9, 2 (1962), 108–22

Nixson, F. I., 'Industrial location in East Africa, with special reference to its determination by and its effect on the East African Common Market', PhD thesis, University of Leeds, 1969–70

Ord, H. W., 'East African companies', *East African Economic Review*, 7, 1 (1960), 35–48

Pearson, D. S., *Industrial Development in East Africa*, Studies in African Economics, No. 2 (Nairobi: Oxford University Press, 1969)

Seidman, A., 'Comparative industrial strategies in East Africa', Dar es Salaam, University of Dar es Salaam, ERB Paper 69.21, 1969

Seidman, A., 'Industrial strategies of East Africa', *East Africa Journal*, July 1970

Seidman, A., *Comparative Development Strategies in East Africa* (Nairobi: East African Publishing House, 1972)

United Nations, 'The textile industries in the East African sub-region', UN Economic Commission for Africa, E/CN. 14/INR/86

United Nations, *Industrial Co-ordination in East Africa*, report of the ECA Industrial Co-ordination Mission to East Africa (New York: UN Economic Commission for Africa, 1964)

United Nations, 'Investigation on fertilizer and chemical industries in East Africa'(New York: UN Economic Commission for Africa, 1965)

United Nations, Conference on the Harmonization of Industrial Development Programmes in East Africa, Lusaka, 1965 (papers summarized in 'Some aspects of public finance and industrial development in the East African sub-region', *Economic Bulletin etc for Africa* (UN), 7, 1/2, 1965)

van Arkadie, B., 'Import-substitution and export promotion as aids to industrialization in East Africa', *East African Economic Review*, 1, 1 (1964), 40–56

van Arkadie, B. and Ghai, D., 'The East African economies', in Robson, P. and Lury, D. A. (eds) *The Economies of Africa* (London: Allen & Unwin, 1969)

Wionczek, M. S., 'Economic integration and regional distribution of industrial activities: a comparative study, Part II: East Africa', *East African Economic Review*, 3, 1 (1967), 31–43

Kenya

Amsden, A. H., *International Firms and Labour in Kenya, 1945–1970* (London: Cass, 1971)

Bailey, M. A., 'Capital utilization in Kenya manufacturing industry', PhD. thesis, Massachusetts Institute of Technology, 1973

Child, F. C., 'Employment, technology and growth: the role of the intermediate sector in Kenya', Nairobi, University of Nairobi, IDS Occasional Paper 19, 1976

Child, F. C., 'Small scale rural industry in Kenya', UCLA African Studies Center, Occasional Paper 17, 1977

Cooper, C. and Kaplinsky, R., *Second-Hand Equipment in a Developing Country: A Study of Jute-Processing in Kenya* (Geneva: ILO (WEP Study on Technology and Employment), 1974)

Greaves, M. J., 'The social and educational backgrounds and career paths of African business managers in Kenya', PhD thesis, Edinburgh University, 1978

House, W. J., 'Market structure and industry performance: the case of Kenya', *Oxford Economic Papers*, 25 (1973), 405–19

House, W. J., 'Market structure and industry performance: the case of Kenya revisited', *Journal Economic Studies*, 3, 2 (1976), 117–32

House, W. J. and Rempel, H., 'Determinants of and changes in the structure of wages and employment in the manufacturing sector of the Kenyan economy', *Journal of Development Economics*, 3, 1 (1976)

House, W. J. and Rempel, H., 'The impact of unionization on negotiated wages in the manufacturing sector in Kenya', *Oxford Bulletin Economics & Statistics*, 38 (1976), 111–23

International Labour Office, *Employment, Incomes and Equality in Kenya* (Geneva: ILO, 1972)

Kaplinsky, R. (ed.), *Readings on the Multinational Corporation in Kenya* (Nairobi: Oxford University Press, 1978)

Kim, K. S., 'An inter-industry comparison of the employment and balance of payments effects of import-substitution in Kenya', *Eastern African Economic Review*, 6, 1 (1974), 70–80

King, K. J., 'Kenya's informal machine makers', *World Development*, 2, 4/5 (1974), 9–28

King, K. J., 'Productive labour and the school system: contradictions in the training of artisans in Kenya', *Comprehensive Education*, 10, 3 (1974), 181–92

King, K. J., 'Industrial training in Kenya: the British model and African practice', African Studies Association (UK), conference, Liverpool, 1974

King, K. J., *The African Artisan* (London: Heinemann Educational Books, 1977)

Kongstad, P., 'Rural industries in Kenya: problems of analysis', Copenhagen: Centre for Development Research, Project Paper D76.1, 1976

Langdon, S., 'Multinational corporations, taste transfer and underdevelopment', *Review of African Political Economy*, 2 (1975), 12–35

Langdon, S., 'Multinational corporations in the political economy of Kenya', PhD thesis, University of Sussex, 1976

Langdon, S., 'Multinational firms and the state in Kenya', *IDS Bull.*, 9, 1 (1977), 36–41

Leys, C., 'Limitations to African capitalism: the function of the monopolistic petty bourgeoisie in Kenya', in *Developmental Trends in Kenya*, proceedings of a seminar, Edinburgh, Centre of African Studies, 1972

Leys, C., 'Foreign investment in Kenya', paper presented at conference on Neocolonialism, Capital Accumulation and Political Change, Sussex, July 1972

Leys, C., *Underdevelopment in Kenya* (London: Heinemann Educational Books, 1975)

Leys, C. and Borges, J., 'State capitalism in Kenya', paper presented to Canadian Political Science Association, annual meeting, Saskatoon, May/June 1979 (to be published in *Canadian Journal of African Studies*)

Livingstone, I., 'An evaluation of Kenya's rural industrial development programme', *Journal of Modern African Studies*, 15, 3 (1977), 295–304

Maitha, J. K., 'Industrial production in Kenya', *Journal East African Research and Development*, 2, 1 (1972), 79–84

Maitha, J. K., 'Capital-labour substitution in manufacturing in a developing economy: the case of Kenya', *East African Economic Review*, 5, 2 (1973), 43–52

Miller, J. W., 'Industrial protection in the Republic of Kenya', PhD thesis, University of California, Berkeley, 1970

Mureithi, L. P., 'Employment, Technology and Industrialization in Kenya', PhD thesis, University of Claremont, 1974

National Christian Council Of Kenya, *Who Controls Industry in Kenya?* (Nairobi: East African Publishing House, 1968)

Ndegwa, J., 'Printing and publishing in Kenya', MA thesis, University of London, 1970–1

Nixson, F. I. and Stoutjesdijk, A. J., 'Industrial development in the Kenya and Uganda Development Plans', *East African Economic Review*, 2, 2 (1966), 65–77

Ogendo, R. B., 'The location and structure of Kenya's agricultural processing industries', PhD thesis, University of London, 1966–7

Pack, H., 'Employment and productivity in Kenyan manufacturing', *East African Economic Review*, 4, 2 (1972), 29–51

Pack, H., 'The substitution of labour for capital in Kenyan manufacturing', *Economic Journal*, 86 (1976), 45–58

Phelps, M., 'The operation of protection of industry in Kenya', in *Developmental Trends in Kenya*, proceedings of a seminar, Edinburgh, Centre of African Studies, 1972

Porter, R. C., 'Kenya's future as an exporter of manufactures', *Eastern African Economic Review*, 6, 1 (1974), 44–69

Power, J. H., 'The role of protection in industrialization policy with particular reference to Kenya', *Eastern African Economic Review*, 4, 1 (1972), 1–20

Senga, W. M., 'Wages, market imperfections and labour absorption in Kenya's manufacturing industries', *Eastern African Economic Review*, 5, 1 (1973), 55–72

Snowden, P. N., 'Company finance in Kenya's manufacturing sector 1963–70', PhD thesis, University of Leeds, 1973–4

Snowden, P. N., 'Company savings in Kenya's manufacturing sector', in Newlyn, W. T. (ed.), *The Financing of Economic Development* (London: Oxford University Press, 1977)

Swainson, N., 'The history of investment in Kenya before 1945', Nairobi, University of Nairobi, IDS Working Paper 242, 1975

Swainson, N., 'Company formation in Kenya before 1945', Nairobi, University of Nairobi, IDS Working Paper 267, 1976

Swainson, N., 'Foreign corporations and economic growth in Kenya', PhD thesis, University of London, 1977

Swainson, N., 'The rise of a national bourgeoisie in Kenya', *Review African Political Economy*, 8 (1977), 39–55

Swainson, N., *The Development of Corporate Capitalism in Kenya 1918–77* (London: Heinemann Educational Books, 1980)

Zarwan, J. I., 'Indian businessmen in Kenya during the twentieth century', PhD thesis, Yale University, 1977

Tanzania

Arthur D. Little, Inc., *Tanganyika Industrial Development* (Dar es Salaam and Boston: 1961)

Barker, C., Bhagavan, M. R., von Mitschke-Collande, P. M. M. and Wield, D., 'Industrial production and transfer of technology in Tanzania: the political economy of Tanzanian industrial enterprises', Dar es Salaam, University of Dar es Salaam, Institute of Development Studies, 1976

Bienefeld, M. A., 'The informal sector and peripheral capitalism: the case of Tanzania', *IDS Bulletin*, 6, 3 (1975), 53–73

Coulson, A., 'Blood-sucking contracts', Dar es Salaam, University of Dar es Salaam, Department of Economics, 1974

Coulson, A., 'Tanzania's fertilizer factory', *Journal Modern African Studies*, 15, 1 (1977), 119–25

Coulson, A., 'The automated bread factory', in Coulson, A. (ed.), *African Socialism in Practice: the Tanzanian Experience* (Nottingham: Spokesman, 1979)

Dobraska, Z., 'Criteria for public investment in manufacturing: five Tanzanian case studies', Dar es Salaam: University of Dar es Salaam, ERB paper 68.28, 1968

El-Namaki, M., 'Business planning in Tanzanian state enterprises', *Long Range Planning*, 10, 5 (1977), 52–63

Green, R. H., 'Relevance, efficiency, romanticism and confusion in Tanzanian planning and management', *African Review*, 5, 1 (1975), 209–34

Hagg, I., *Some State-Controlled Industrial Companies in Tanzania* (Uppsala: Scandinavian Institute of African Studies, Research Report 8, 1971)

Hyden, G., 'Public policy-making and public enterprises in Tanzania', *African Review*, 5, 1 (1975), 141–65

International Labour Office, *Towards Self-Reliance: Development, Employment and Equity Issues in Tanzania* (Geneva: ILO, 1978)

Kessel, D. M., 'The effective protection of industry in Tanzania', *East African Economic Review*, 4, 1 (1968), 1–18

Kessel, D. M., 'Effective Protection Rates and Industrialization Strategies in Tanzania', PhD thesis, Cornell University, 1969

Khamis, I. A., 'Industrial development in Zanzibar', Dar es Salaam, University of Dar es Salaam, ERB Paper 75.6, 1975

Kim, K. S., 'The linkage effects of basic industry in Tanzania: some policy issues and suggestions', Dar es Salaam, University of Dar es Salaam, ERB Paper 76.11, 1976

Kim, K. S., 'Industrialization strategies in a developing socialist economy – evaluation of the Tanzanian case', *Developing Economies*, 16, 3 (1978), 254–68

Kim. K. S., Mabele, R. B. and Schultheis, M. J., *Papers on the Political Economy of Tanzania* (London: Heinemann Educational Books, 1979)

Kuuya, P. M., 'Import substitution: cement', Dar es Salaam, University of Dar es Salaam, ERB Paper 76.10, 1976

Livingstone, I., 'The promotion of craft and rural industry in Tanzania', *Viertel Jahres Berichte*, March 1972

Loxley, J. and Saul, J. S., 'Multinationals, workers and the parastatals in Tanzania', *Review of African Political Economy*, 2 (1975), 54–88

Loxley, J. and Saul, J. S., 'The political economy of the parastatals', in Mapolu, H. (ed.), *Workers and Management* (Dar es Salaam: Tanzania Publishing House, 1976)

Mtei, E., 'The financial situation and prospects for industrial development', *Economic Bulletin* (Bank of Tanzania), 5, 2 (1973), 21–30

Muller, J., 'Regional planning for small industries in Tanzania', Copenhagen, Centre for Development Research, Paper A76.2, 1976

Muller, J., 'Decentralized industries and inadequate infrastructure', Copenhagen, Centre for Development Research, Paper A76.5, 1976

Mulokozi, A. M., *Industrialization Efforts and Expectations – Tanzanian Experience.* Abstracts of Papers of the American Chemical Society, September 1979

Mwapachi, H. B., 'The restructuring of public enterprises for improved performance', *Mbioni*, 8, 1 (1976)

Phillips, D., 'Industrialization in Tanzania: the case of small scale production', in Kim, K. S., Mabele, R. B. and Schultheis, M. J. (eds), *Papers on the Political Economy of Tanzania* (Nairobi: Heinemann Educational Books, 1979); also ERB Paper 76.5, 1976

Roe, A. R., 'The future of the company in Tanzanian development', *Journal of Modern African Studies*, 7, 1 (1969), 47–67

Roemer, M., Tidrick, G. M. and Williams, D., 'The range of strategic choice in Tanzanian industry', Cambridge, Massachusetts, Harvard University, Institute for International Development 1975; also *Journal Development Economics*, 3, 3 (1976), 257–276; also *Ekistics*, 43, 259 (1977), 346–50

Rweyemamu, J. F., 'Industrial strategy for Tanzania', PhD thesis, Harvard University, 1971

Rweyemamu, J. F., 'The structure of Tanzanian industry', Dar es Salaam, University of Dar es Salaam, ERB Paper 71.2, 1971

Rweyemamu, J. F., 'Planning, socialism and industrialization: the economic challenge', *Development & Change*, 3, 3 (1972), 26–42

Rweyemamu, J. F., *Underdevelopment and industrialization in Tanzania: A Study of Perverse Capitalist Industrial Development* (London and Nairobi: Oxford University Press, 1973)

Rweyemamu, J. F., 'The historical and institutional setting of Tanzanian industry', in Kim, K. S., Mabele, R. B. and Schultheis, M. J. (eds), *Papers on the Political Economy of Tanzania* (Nairobi: Heinemann Educational Books, 1979); also ERB paper 71.6, 1971

Segal, M., 'Business and industries after ten years', *Tanzania Notes and Records*, 76 (1975), 133–40

Seidman, A., 'Tanzania's industrial strategy', in Cliffe, L. and Saul, J. (eds), *Socialism in Tanzania*, Vol. 2 (Dar es Salaam: East African Publishing House, 1973)

Schadler, K., *Manufacturing and Processing Industries in Tanzania* (Munich: IFO Institute, 1969)

Shivji, I., *Class Struggles in Tanzania* (London: Heinemann Educational Books, 1976)

Shivji, I., *The Silent Class Struggle* (Dar es Salaam: Tanzania Publishing House, 1974)

Shivji, I., 'Capitalism unlimited: public corporations in partnership with multinational corporations', *African Review.*, 3, 3 (1973), 359–84; also in Mapolu, H. (ed.), *Workers and Management* (Dar es Salaam: Tanzania Publishing House, 1976)

Silver, M. S., 'Labour productivity trends in Tanzania: manufacturing sector 1965-72', Birmingham, University of Aston Management Centre, Working Paper 91, 1978

Silver, M. S., 'A regional analysis of industrial production and labour productivity trends in Tanzania, 1965–72', Birmingham, University of Aston Management Centre, Working Paper 113, 1978

Singh, A. and Bienefeld, M. A., 'Industry and urban economy in Tanzania', background paper for the ILO–JASPA Employment Advisory Mission to Tanzania, 1977

Svendsen, K. E., 'Decision-making in the National Development Corporation', in Cliffe, L. and Saul, J. (eds), *Socialism in Tanzania*, Vol. 2 (Dar es Salaam: East African Publishing House, 1973)

von Freyhold, M., 'Notes on Tanzanian industrial workers', *Tanzania Notes and Records*, 81/82 (1977), 15–21

Wangwe, S. M., 'Factors influencing capacity utilization in Tanzanian manufacturing', *International Labour Review*, 115, 1 (1977), 65–78

Wangwe, S. M., 'Excess capacity in manufacturing industry', in Kim, K. S., Mabele, R. B. and Schultheis, M. J. (eds), *Papers on the Political Economy of Tanzania* (Nairobi: Heinemann Educational Books, 1979); also ERB paper 76.2, 1976

Williams, D., 'National planning and the choice of technology', in Kim, K. S. *et al.* (eds), ibid,; also ERB paper 75.2, 1975

Williams, D., 'Choice of technology and national planning', PhD thesis, Harvard University, 1976

Zambia

Baylies, C., 'The state and class formation in Zambia', PhD thesis, University of Wisconsin, 1978

Beveridge, A. A., 'Varieties of African businessmen in the emerging Zambian stratification system', Syracuse, African Studies Association Conference, 1973

Beveridge, A. A., '*Converts to capitalism: the emergence of African entrepreneurs in Lusaka*', PhD thesis, Yale University, 1973

Beveridge, A. A., 'Economic independence, indigenization and the African business-man', *African Studies Review*, 17, 3 (1974), 477–90

Beveridge, A. A. and Oberschall, A. R., *African Businessmen and Development in Zambia* (Princeton, NJ: Princeton University Press, 1979)

Bhagavan, M. R., 'Zambia: state, industry and class struggle', Uppsala, Nordic Seminar on the State in the Third World, 1976

Bhagavan, M. R., *Zambia: Impact of Industrial Strategy on Regional Imbalance and Social Inequality* (Uppsala: Scandinavian Institute of African Studies, Research Report 44, 1978)

Bull. For Int. Fiscal Documentation, 'Zambia – Industrial Development Act 1977', *Bull. for International Fiscal Documentation*, 32, 3 (1978), 127–8

Chaput, M. J., 'The Zambian state enterprises', PhD thesis, Syracuse University, 1971

Curry, R. L., 'Global market forces and the nationalization of foreign-based export companies', *Journal Modern African Studies*, 14, 1 (1976), 137–43

Curry, R., *Nationalizing Export Companies: Lessons from Zambia's Experience* (Gaborone: Institute for Development Management, 1978)

Dore, M. H. I., 'Planning industrial development in Zambia: with special reference to iron and steel', PhD thesis, Oxford, 1975

Elliott, C. (ed.), *Constraints on the Economic Development of Zambia* (Nairobi: Oxford University Press, 1971)

Enterprise, Journal of the Industrial Development Corporation of Zambia (INDECO Ltd), 1969; various articles on manufacturing industries in Zambia

Fincham, R., 'Economic dependence and the development of industry in Zambia', *Journal Modern African Studies*, 18, 2 (1980) 297–313

Fortman, B. de G. (ed.), *After Mulungushi: the Economics of Zambian Humanism* (Nairobi: East African Publishing House, 1969)

Fry, J., 'Manufacturing industry in Zambia', *African Development*, October 1972

Harkema, R. C., 'Zambia's cotton production and textile industry', *Geography*, 57, 257 (1972), 345–8

Harvey, C., 'The structure of Zambian development', in Damachi, U. G. *et al.* (eds), *Development Paths in Africa and China* (London: Macmillan, 1976)

Hodges, G., 'Zambia: opening the gates and tightening the belts', *Review African Political Economy*, 12 (1979), 87–98

International Labour Office, *Narrowing the Gaps: Planning for Basic Needs and Productive Employment in Zambia* (Addis Ababa: ILO, 1977), esp. ch. 5, manufacturing sector

Johns, S., 'Parastatal bodies in Zambia: problems and prospects', in Simonis, H. and U. (eds), *Socio-economic Development in Dual Economies: the Example of Zambia* (Munich: Weltforum Verlag, 1971)

Mutukwa, K. S., 'Political control of parastatal organizations', *Zango*, 1 (1976)

Seidman, A., 'The distorted growth of import-substitution industrialization: the Zambian case', *Journal Modern of African Studies*, 12, 4 (1974), 601–31

Seidman, A.,'The need for an industrial strategy in Zambia', in Seidman, A. (ed.), *Natural Resources and National Welfare: the Case of Copper* (New York: Praeger, 1975)

Semonin, P., 'Nationalizations and management in Zambia', *Majimaji*, 1, January 1971

Simwinga, G. K. 'Corporate autonomy and government control in the Zambian public sector', PhD thesis, University of Pittsburgh, 1977

Turok, B., 'The penalties of Zambia's mixed economy', in Turok, B. (ed.), *Development in Zambia* (London: Zed Press: 1979)

Turok, B., 'Control in the parastatals in Zambia', School of Humanities and Social Sciences seminar, UNZA, April 1980

United Nations, *Final Report of the Zambia Managerial, Manpower and Training Needs Survey of the Private and Parastatal Sectors* (Lusaka: UNDP–ILO, Management Development Unit, Zambia, 1977)

Williams, M., 'State participation in the Zambian economy', *World Development*, 1, 10 (1974), 43–54

Young, A., 'Patterns of development in Zambian manufacturing industry since independence', *Eastern Africa Economic Review*, 1, 2 (1969), 29–38

Young, A., 'Industrial diversification in Zambia', PhD thesis, University of Reading, 1973

Young, A., *Industrial Diversification in Zambia* (New York: Praeger, 1973)

Zimbabwe

Clarke, D. G., 'Economic development in Rhodesia: a selected bibliography', *Rhodesia Journal Economics*, 4, 4 (1970), 46–59

Clarke, D. G., 'Economic development in Rhodesia: a revision of a selected bibliography', *Rhodesia Journal Economics*, 5, 4 (1971), 37–42

Dickenson, N. J. 'Performance and prospects in Rhodesian manufacturing industry', *Rhodesia Journal Economics*, 5, 4 (1971), 9–16

Disler, L., 'The effects of the rand devaluation on Rhodesia with particular reference to manufacturing industry', *Rhodesia Journal Economics*, 6, 1 (1972), 20–3

Faber, M., *Economic Structuralism and its Relevance to Southern Rhodesia's Future* (Manchester: Rhodes Livingstone Paper No.36, University Press, Manchester 1965)

Graylin, J. C., 'Industrial development in Rhodesia', *Rhodesia Journal Economics*, 3, 4 (1969), 38–43

Krogh, D. C., 'Industrial development and foreign trade with particular reference to South Africa', *Rhodesia Journal Economics*, 7, 4 (1973), 175–88

Marais, G., 'Is industrialization possible in a small market without inflation?', *Rhodesia Journal Economics*, 5, 3 (1971), 1–6

Pearson, D. S., 'Industrial development in Rhodesia', *Rhodesia Journal Economics*, 2, 1 (1968), 5–27

Ramsay, D., 'Productivity and capital in Rhodesian manufacturing, 1955–72', *Rhodesia Journal Economics*, 8, 2 (1974), 67–82

Ramsay, D., 'Value added at constant prices: estimates for Rhodesian manufacturing industries and some observations', *Rhodesia Journal Economics*, 8, 4 (1974), 191–214

Rhodesian Journal Of Economics, special issues, industry in Rhodesia, 3, 2/3 (1969)

Stoneman, C., 'Foreign capital and the prospects for Zimbabwe', *World Development*, (1976), 25–58

Stoneman, C., 'Foreign capital and the reconstruction of Zimbabwe', *Review African Political Economy*, 11 (1978), 62–83

Stoneman, C., 'Zimbabwe's prospects as an industrial power', *J. Commonwealth and Comparative Politics*, forthcoming

Stringer, B., 'Closer economic co-operation in Southern Africa: trade and industry', *Rhodesia Journal Economics*, 4, 2 (1970), 23–8

Sutcliffe, R. B., 'Stagnation and inequality in Rhodesia, 1946–68', *Oxford Bulletin Economics & Statistics*, 33, 1 (1971)

Taylor, W. L., 'Problems of economic development of the Federation of Rhodesia and Nyasaland', in Robinson, E. A. G. (ed.), *Economic Development for Africa South of the Sahara* (London: Macmillan, 1964)

Taylor, W. L., 'The economy of Central Africa', in Robson, P. and Lury, D. A. (eds), *The Economies of Africa* (London: Allen & Unwin, 1969)

Tow, L., 'The manufacturing economy of Southern Rhodesia: problems and prospects', PhD thesis, Columbia University, 1960

Whyte, P., 'Export prospects of manufacturing industry', *Rhodesia Journal Economics*, 6, 4 (1972), 64–71

Wield, D., 'Technology and Zimbabwean Industry', report prepared for the *UNCTAD Economic and Social Survey of Zimbabwe*

Southern Africa, Lesotho, Swaziland

International Labour Office, Small enterprises development in Swaziland, Technical Report No.1 (Geneva: ILO, 1977)

Seidman, A. and Seidman, N., US Multinationals in Southern Africa (Dar es Salaam: Tanzania Publishing House, 1977)

Selwyn, P., Industries in the Southern African Periphery (London: Croom Helm for Institute of Development Studies, Sussex, 1975)

Tandon, Y., 'The role of transnational corporations and future trends in Southern Africa', Journal Southern African Affairs, 2, 4 (1977), 391–402

United States, US Business Involvement in Southern Africa (Washington, DC: Government Printing Office), Congressional Hearings, 2 vols

World Bank, An Appraisal of the Lesotho National Development Corporation and its Subsidiary Basotho Enterprises Development Corporation, Report No.1332a (Washington, DC: World Bank, 1977)

South Africa

Barker, H. A. F., 'A comment on textile development in South Africa', South African Journal of Economics, 31, 4 (1963), 285–303

Beacham, A., 'Some thoughts on industrial decentralization in South Africa', South African Journal of Economics, 42, 3 (1974), 325–30

Bell, R. T., Industrial Decentralization in South Africa (London and Cape Town: Oxford University Press, 1973); review articles: Ratcliffe, A. E., South African Journal of Economics, 42 2 (1974), 157–76; Hawkins, A. M. Rhodesian Journal of Economics, 7, 4 (1973), 217–24

Bell, R. T., 'Some aspects of industrial decentralization in South Africa', South African of Journal Economics, 41, 4 (1973), 401–31; comment 1: Brand, S. S., ibid., 432–4; comment 2: Lange, J. H., ibid., 435–7

Bell, R. T., 'Capital intensity and employment in South African manufacturing industries', University of Colorado, Department of Economics, Discussion Paper 120, 1978

Bell, R. T., 'Capital intensity and employment in South African industry', South African Journal of Economics, 46, 1 (1978), 48–61

Bergman, L. F., 'Technological change in South African manufacturing industry, 1955–1964', South African Journal of Economics, 36, 1 (1968), 3–12; comment: Fransman, M., South African Journal of Economics, 37, (1969), 161–3

Botha, D. J. J., 'On tariff policy – the formative years', South African Journal of Economics, 41, 4 (1973), 321–55

Bozzoli, B., 'Origins, development and ideology of local manufacturing in South Africa', Journal of Southern African Studies, 1, 2 (1975), 194–214

Bozzoli, B., 'Ideology and the manufacturing class in South Africa 1907–26', in The Societies of Southern Africa in the 19th and 20th Centuries, Vol. 5 (London: Institute of Commonwealth Studies, 1974)

Christian Concern For Southern Africa, Britain's Economic Links with South Africa: A Study of Existing Ties and a Preliminary Assessment of the Impact of Disengagement (London: Christian Concern for Southern Africa, 1979)

Christie, R., 'South African industrialization 1915–1925', in The Societies of Southern Africa in the 19th and 20th Centuries Vol. 8 (London: Institute of Commonwealth Studies, 1978)

Cipolat, D., Industrial Concentration in South Africa (Master of Business Administration, University of the Witwatersrand, 1978)

Clark, D., US Corporate Interests in South Africa (US Senate, Committee on Foreign Relations, 1977)

Davies, R. H., Capital, State and White Labour in South Africa (Brighton: Harvester Press, 1979)

Dickman, A. B., 'The financing of industrial development in South Africa', South

African Journal of Economics, 41, 4 (1973), 373–95; comment 1: Kantor, B., ibid., 395–8; comment 2: Knox, J., ibid., 398–400

du Plessis, P. G., 'Concentration of economic power in South African manufacturing industry', *South African Journal of Economics*, 46, 3 (1978), 257–70

du Plessis, S. P. J., 'Effective tariff protection in South Africa', *South African Journal of Economics*, 44, 2 (1976), 158–70

Ehrensaft, P., 'Polarised accumulation and the theory of economic dependence: the implications for a South African semi-industrial capitalism', in Gutkind, P. C. W. and Wallerstein, I. (eds), *The Political Economy of Contemporary Africa* (Beverly Hills, Calif.: Sage, 1976)

First, R., Steele, J., and Gurney, C., *The South African Connection* (London: Temple Smith, 1972)

Gaebe, W., 'Industrial decentralization in South Africa – conflict between strategic political and social spatial planning', *Geographische Zeitschrift*, 66, 2 (1978), 124–55

Gervasi, S., *Industrialization, Foreign Capital and Forced Labour in South Africa* (New York: U.N. Unit on Apartheid, 1970)

Gottschalk, K., 'Industrial decentralization, jobs and wages', *South Africa Labour Bulletin*, 3, 5 (1977), 50–8

Holden, M. G. and Holden, P., 'An intertemporal calculation of effective rates of protection for South Africa', *South Africa Journal Economics*, 43, 3 (1975), 370–9

Houghton, D. H., *Source Material on the South African Economy* 3 vols (Cape Town: Oxford University Press, 1973), esp. Vol. 3, pts V and VI, 'Industrial breakthrough 1933–45' and 'Industrial Expansion'

Houghton, D. H., *The South African Economy* (Cape Town: Oxford University Press, 1967), esp. ch. 5, manufacturing

Kaplan, D. E., 'Politics of industrial protection in South Africa, 1910–39', *Journal of Southern African Studies*, 3, 1 (1976), 70–91

Kaplan, D. E., 'Class conflict, capital accumulation and the state: an historical analysis of the state in twentieth century South Africa', D. Phil. thesis, University of Sussex, 1977

Kleu, S. J., 'Import substitution in the South African automobile industry', PhD thesis, Harvard University, 1967

Kooy, M. and Robertson, H. M., 'The South African Board of Trade and Industries: the South African customs tariff and the development of South African industries', *South African Journal of Economics*, 34, 3 (1966), 205–24

Kroch, D. C., 'Industrial development and foreign trade', *Rhodesian Journal Economics*, 7, 4 (1973), 175–88

Lachmann, D., 'Import restrictions and exchange rates', *South African Journal of Economics*, 42, 1 (1974), 25–42

Legassick, M., 'Ideology, legislation and economy in post-1948 South Africa' *Journal of Southern African Studies*, 1, 1 (1974)

Legassick, M., 'South Africa: capital accumulation and violence', *Economy and Society*, 3, 3 (1974), 253–91

Legassick, M., 'South Africa: forced labour, industrialization and racial differentiation', in Harris, R. (ed.), *The Political Economy of Africa* (New York: Wiley, 1975)

Legassick, M., 'Race, industrialization and social change in South Africa: the case of R. F. A. Hoernle', *African Affairs*, 75, 299 (1976), 224–39

Legassick, M., 'Gold, agriculture and secondary industry in South Africa, 1855–1970', in Palmer, R. and Parsons, N., *The Roots of Rural Poverty in Central and Southern Africa* (London: Heinemann Educational Books, 1977)

Legassick, M. and Innes, D., 'Capital restructuring and apartheid: a critique of engagement', *African Affairs*, 76, 305 (1977), 437–82

Lipton, M., 'Race, industrialization and social change in South Africa – a comment', *African Affairs*, 76, 302 (1977), 105–7

Levine, F. S., 'The Financial Response to Price Control in the South African Cement

Industry' Master of Business Administration, University of the Witwatersrand, 1978

Lewis, J. M., 'Industrialization and industrial unions in South Africa 1925–1930', *South Africa Labour Bulletin*, 3, 5 (1977), 25–49

Lumby, A. B., 'Tariffs and printing industry in South Africa, 1906–1939', *South African Journal of Economics*, 45, 2 (1977), 129–46

Meyer, N., 'The development of the footwear industry in South Africa, 1947–1961', *South African Journal of Economics*, 31, 3 (1963), 220–40

Nieuwenhuysen, J. P., 'Iron and steel: future industry for border areas?', *South African Journal of Economics*, 30, 3 (1962), 221–34

Nieuwenhuysen, J. P., 'The industrialization of the Tugela Basin', *South African Journal of Economics*, 31, 1 (1963), 26–37

Reynders, H. J. J., 'Black industrial entrepreneurship', *South African Journal of Economics*, 45, 2 (1977), 229–42

Rogerson, C. N., 'Industrialization of the Bantu homelands', *Geography*, 59, 264 (1974), 260–63

Savage, M., 'Interlocking directorships in South Africa', in Meer, F. (ed.), *Sociology in South Africa* (Durban: ASSA 1973)

South Africa, *Investigation into Manufacturing Industries in the Union of South Africa: First Interim Report*, Board of Trade and Industries, Report No. 282, 1945

South Africa, *Report of Commission of Enquiry into the Policy Relating to the Protection of Industries in South Africa* (Viljoen Commission), U.G. 36/1958, 1958

South Africa, *Report of the Commission of Enquiry into the Import Trade of the Republic of South Africa* (Reynders Commission), R.P. 69/72, 1972

Steenkamp, W. F. J., 'Pharmaceutical industry in South Africa', *South African Journal of Economics*, 47, 1 (1979), 75–89

Stokes, R. G., 'The Afrikaner industrial entrepreneur and Afrikaner nationalism', *Economic Development and Cultural Change*, 22, 4 (1974), 557–79

Suckling, J. Weiss, R. and Innes, D., *The Economic Factor* (London: Africa Publication Trust/Study Project on External Investment in South Africa, 1975)

Thornton, R. D., 'A survey of the South African ceramics industry', M. Phil. thesis, University of Leeds, 1973–4

Trapido, S., 'South Africa in a comparative study of industrialization', *Journal Development Studies*, 7, 3 (1971), 309–20

United Nations, 'Involvement of foreign economic interests in South Africa's industrial development projects', Geneva, UN Unit of Apartheid, *Notes and Documents*, 3S/75, 1975

van Coller, D. L., 'State direction of funds in industry in South Africa since 1948', B. Litt. thesis, Oxford, 1963–4

van der Merwe, E. J. and du Plessis, D. P., 'A regional classification of South Africa's balance of payments', *South Africa Reserve Bank Quarterly Bulletin*, September 1973

Various, 'Industrialization in South Africa', *South African Journal of Economics*, special issue, 41, 4 (1973)

Wolpe, H., 'Capitalism and cheap labour power in South Africa', *Economy and Society*, 1, 4 (1972)

Yudelman, D., 'Industrialization, race relations and change in South Africa', *African Affairs*, 74, 294 (1975), 82–96

Zarenda, H., 'The Policy of state intervention in the establishment and development of manufacturing industry in South Africa', MA thesis, University of the Witwatersrand, 1977

Index